H46:18

136.7354
155.5

DYNAMICS OF

ADOLESCENT

ADJUSTMENT

Photo by A. Devaney, Inc., N.Y.

These are adolescents—interesting, complex, but understandable, and needing the help of adults in growing up easily and wholesomely.

DYNAMICS OF

ADOLESCENT

ADJUSTMENT

Thomas F. Staton

Professor of Psychology

HUNTINGDON COLLEGE

THE MACMILLAN COMPANY, NEW YORK

COLLIER-MACMILLAN LIMITED, LONDON

First Printing

Library of Congress catalog card number: 63–7379

The Macmillan Company, New York
Collier-Macmillan Canada Ltd., Toronto, Ontario
Divisions of The Crowell-Collier Publishing Company

Printed in the United States of America

Dedicated to
My first and most revered
Teacher
of child and adolescent psychology
Hassie MacMillan Staton

PREFACE

THIS book is designed to help people better understand adolescents—what is happening to them, how they think and feel, why they act as they do, how to recognize when they need help, and how to help them. It is planned as a text for people preparing to be junior or senior high school teachers or counselors, and as a reference manual for parents, youth workers, teachers, and counselors already at work in their professions.

The study of human behavior and adjustment can hardly, at present, be called an exact science. It becomes less and less an exact science as one moves from the controlled conditions of the psychological laboratory or the carefully designed experiment into the complex interrelations of motives, emotions, self concept, biological inheritance, social pressures, cultural influences, past experiences, and personal values. Yet, despite many varying views held by different members of the profession, psychologists have formulated concepts and theories which go far toward affording an understanding of what makes people act like human beings and, equally important, why they sometimes fail to do so. Clinical psychologists and psychiatrists have, in the past few decades, achieved much insight into the dynamic forces activating and directing human behavior. This insight makes possible increasingly greater understanding, guidance, and, where necessary, correction of behavior.

The author taught in junior high school for six years, took a doctorate in clinical psychology, and has worked in adult education and private practice as a clinical psychologist for fifteen years. He is fundamentally a clinician, devoted to helping individuals with problems of adjustment more than to laboratory-type experimentation and theory formation. Throughout this book, therefore, the emphasis is principally on theories and concepts which his clinical experience has proved to be of practical value in work with real boys and girls and their real personal problems.

References have been cited to acknowledge the origins of points of specific fact or inspiration of ideas. Orientation of the text has been greatly influenced by the various analytical schools of psychology, and recourse to such general professional knowledge has not been identified point by specific point. *In all instances, the decision as to whether to present for the reader's guidance a particular theory, concept, interpretation, or application has been based on the extent to which that factor has proved true and useful in the author's own clinical experience.* In short, the material in this text has, in the author's opinion, demonstrated its reliability and usefulness on the testing ground of actual work with boys and girls in normal life situations.

THOMAS F. STATON

TABLE OF CONTENTS

CONTENTS

PART THREE SPECIAL PROBLEMS OF
ADOLESCENCE AND GUIDELINES
IN COUNSELING

DYNAMICS OF

ADOLESCENT

ADJUSTMENT

CHAPTER 1

A FRAME OF REFERENCE

FOR STUDYING ADOLESCENTS

PREVIEW

Approaches to the Study of Adolescents

APPROACH	CHARACTERISTICS
Descriptive	Describes the adolescent as to various attributes. Emphasizes statistical surveys of adolescents.
Topical	Detailed examination of many aspects (often highly specific and technical) of adolescence.
Longitudinal	Portrays the differences of adolescents of different ages in various respects.
Crucial Areas	Presents and interprets the significance of factors influencing adolescents and characteristics of adolescents.
Case Study	Analyzes case histories of adolescents to identify and interpret significant features.
Dynamics	Seeks the causes of and reasons for adolescent attitudes, thoughts, and behavior.

The Present Text

Approach: Dynamic, utilizing descriptive material, case digests, and clinical concepts and theories.

Content: Expository material furnishing background for analysis of and recommendations regarding cases described.

Study Plan: Designed for the student to spend equal time studying the expository material and applying it in analyzing the cases and formulating answers to the questions about them.

ADOLESCENTS are human beings in a particular phase of development. Roughly speaking, they are human beings in their teens. Their phase of development leads to many conditions, problems, and adjustments either

1

not required of people at any other stage of life or more intense during this phase than at any other period. All of us are familiar with jokes and parents' laments about the peculiarities and the difficulties of living with adolescents. "Are you in favor of clubs for high-school boys and girls?" asked one parent, to which the other replied, "Only when less drastic disciplinary measures have failed." One sixteen-year-old girl had long begged for her own private telephone line and was finally given one, largely so that the remainder of the family would not be shut off from communication with the outside world. Two days later her mother found her sprawled on the living-room sofa talking on the family line— sandwich in hand, bottled drink on the floor beside her, transistor radio beside the telephone going full blast—obviously settled down for the remainder of the afternoon. Upon her mother's asking why she was not using her own telephone, she condescendingly explained, "Somebody might want to call me on it while I'm talking." It is this sort of egocentricity which makes the attitude of the second parent in the first story all too reasonable to so many workers with adolescents.

APPROACHES TO
THE STUDY OF ADOLESCENTS

In 1904 Dr. G. Stanley Hall, one of the great pioneers in psychology, published a two-volume work entitled *Adolescence,* containing more than a thousand pages.[1] In the decades since the publication of that book, there have been thousands of research studies conducted on the subject of adolescence and adolescents. Additional hundreds of books have been written about this age period, setting forth research findings, clinical data, theories, opinions, and points of view. A text attempting even approximate coverage of what is known, proved, or for sound reasons believed about the psychology of adolescents would wind up with the dimensions of an encyclopedia. So, for instructional purposes, it is customary either to adopt one approach to the study of adolescents or to concentrate on one aspect of adolescent development. Then, from the selected point of view, or within the selected frame of reference, the student may obtain a concept of adolescence as a period of life, or the nature of adolescent boys and girls, or perhaps both. Keeping the text to usable size inevitably requires omission of many aspects of adolescent

[1] G. S. Hall, *Adolescence.* Appleton-Century-Crofts, Inc., New York, 1904.

psychology which each author feels are important and which he omits not through choice but through necessity.

The Descriptive Approach

Some psychologists, in their texts on adolescent psychology, choose to present facts and data that give a cross-sectional picture of what adolescents are like. They use tables to show the distribution of boys or girls on a specific characteristic—opinion on a given topic, age of first shaving, proportions smoking at various ages, attitudes regarding religion, or the relationship between automobile ownership and academic grades. Such texts rely heavily on individual statistical studies, citing one or more such studies as the basis for factual statements made by the author. One widely used text in adolescent psychology contains references to more than 1,500 studies as sources for the facts presented, most of them studies of the proportions of adolescents demonstrating this or that characteristic to this or that degree.[2] Such a book is an invaluable source of data from which a mental picture of the typical adolescent can be obtained and by which the degree of variation from the norm of a given sample of behavior, attitude, or physical characteristic can be estimated.

The Topical Approach

This term seems to the author an appropriate one to apply to the text that selects a large number of specific and rather minute aspects of adolescent nature and development and examines each one in detail. Texts composed of short articles or monographs by different authors, usually referred to as "Readings in . . . ," constitute common examples of this approach. The approach has the advantage of making accessible to the student the best thought available (in the opinion of the text's editor) on each of many facets of adolescent psychology. As many as seventy to a hundred monographs by as many different authors may be included in a text composed from this approach. Sometimes it is difficult to synthesize the views of so many people on a multitude of special topics into a cohesive, coherent concept of the adolescent. It may become a case of the trees obscuring the forest.

The Longitudinal Approach

Some authors prefer to examine the characteristics of the pre-adolescent period and pre-adolescents; then early adolescence; then middle

---

[2] E. B. Hurlock, *Adolescent Development*. McGraw-Hill Book Company, Inc., New York, 1955.

and late adolescence. This approach has the merit of setting forth vividly the changes that take place in different psychological areas—mental, emotional, social, and others—as boys and girls pass through various stages of maturation within the adolescent period. Seldom is one of the approaches described here used exclusively without the employment of other methods to assist it. Thus, the text *featuring* the longitudinal approach may use the descriptive approach, or some other, to present data relating to each of the stages discussed.

The Crucial Areas, or Elements, Approach

This is similar to the topical approach, but the areas treated are likely to be broader and less technical than those of the topical approach, and one author or a small group working as a team will usually produce this type of text. "The religious development of adolescents," "the gang," and "sources of emotional conflict" are representative areas commonly encountered in this approach. In essence, the author identifies the most significant factors (to him) in adolescent development and nature and examines each one in some detail, at the same time fitting them together so they represent intertwined aspects of a boy or a girl and not technical entities within themselves. Such texts not only are interesting to read, but also leave the student with the feeling that he knows something of the adolescent as an integrated human being.

The Case Study Approach

In this method detailed case histories of adolescents are presented, with or without expository or theoretical material. Through analysis of the information given about a boy or girl, the student gains an understanding of why the boy or girl was this or that way, and he derives principles and concepts as to wholesome development. In advanced courses this technique is often used, exactly as in advanced literature courses a story or essay is studied in minute detail to ascertain the distinctive elements which produced the over-all impression of the article. The case-study approach is also used, on occasion, in introductory courses, but in such instances much explanation or exposition of principles involved is usually necessary to compensate for the students' limited knowledge in the subject. Case studies are often presented under the title "Case History." The amount of information given may range from two or three pages to hundreds of pages on a single case. Cases even shorter than two and three pages are sometimes used. They are, in reality, case digests or illustrative anecdotes rather than true case studies or case histories, but for many purposes they are more appropriate than longer, more complicated presentations of case data.

The Dynamics Approach

This title appeals to the author as a description of an approach which places primary emphasis on what makes adolescents develop, think, and act as they do. What makes adolescents seem to their parents to be rebellious? Why do adolescent boys seem so clumsy? What is the probable effect on an adolescent of making an embarrassing mistake in class, and why will it affect one so differently from the way it affects another? The "why's," the *reasons* underlying all the phenomena of adolescence are the concern of the text written from the standpoint of the dynamics of adolescence. People who actually have to work with adolescents, teach, counsel, or supervise them, often find this approach helpful since it explores the fundamental psychological forces that make adolescents what they are, and with which the worker has to cope to work effectively with the individual boys and girls.

Clinical study—intensive study of individual people, their problems, mechanisms of adjustment, and personality structure—is the fundamental research technique of the dynamics approach. Individual case studies are made as a part of the clinical examination, but the subjects of clinical study are the actual flesh-and-blood people involved, and not the digested or interpreted material included in the recorded case history. In fact, case studies generally are simply the records of clinical study, and this text uses digests of such records of clinical study as cases for examination and interpretation.

THE ORIENTATION OF THIS TEXT

As implied by its title, this text is concerned with the dynamics of adjustment, with such questions as: "What makes adolescents as they are?" "How can a boy or girl be changed in this particular aspect?" "What are the basic forces which critically influence the temperament of a boy or girl?" or, to use a slang expression, "What makes adolescents tick?"

The secondary (sometimes primary) purpose of every worker with adolescents is to help boys and girls develop into adults who will be assets to society and who will live their lives in such a way as to be happy themselves. Being in harmony with one's environment and with one's own inner self—one's conscience and feelings—is called being adjusted to life. By integrating the concepts of dynamics, the nature of adjustment, and the need of workers with adolescents for understanding these factors, we have the purpose of this text: to enable workers with adolescent boys and girls to understand what makes them as they are, and, through a knowledge of what molds their personalities and natures, to be able to help them make the best possible adjustment to life.

The dynamics approach involves factual data about adolescents. In fact, the more the factual data known about adolescents, other things being equal, the better the job an adult can do in understanding the adolescent. Therefore, a considerable amount of descriptive data will be found in this text. Some descriptive data is, of course, much more significant than others, and only that data most crucial in understanding the dynamics of adolescent development and adjustment will be included here. As an example, information might be presented on clinical judgment as to why adolescents drink, but not on what proportion of them drink. The former type of data is essential in understanding the actions of the adolescent who drinks and in helping him; the latter type is interesting and educational, but not necessary in order to be able to help the adolescent drinker. The student will find this book concerned principally with psychological and physical facts, concepts, and clinical theories relating to the dynamics of behavior rather than to descriptions of adolescents or their behavior. (The author was tempted to use the term "clinical approach" to describe the orientation of this text, but decided against it because of a personal preference for reserving the term "clinical" for work with actual patients. Nevertheless, this text is written from the clinical point of view, in that it stresses the understanding of dynamics, diagnosis of conditions, identification of causal factors, and design of remedial measures as applied to the lives, adjustments, and problems of adolescents.)

A person will never become a competent artist through reading alone, no matter how thoroughly he masters the principles and philosophy of art; on the other hand, he is extremely unlikely to become a competent artist through practice alone, without an acquaintance with the principles and philosophy of art. Thus it is in dealing with adolescents. One never becomes competent solely through reading theory and principles. On the other hand, trying to fathom the complexities of the behavior of boys and girls and to cope with it effectively without a sound background in knowledge of the dynamics of behavior and adjustment is almost equally impossible. This text is intended to teach adolescent psychology as an applied art or science. It aims to develop in the student an improved capacity to understand the feelings, behavior, and thinking of adolescent boys and girls, to fathom the cause of those feelings, thoughts, and actions, and to help the boys and girls adjust their feelings, thoughts, and actions to the demands of life and their own happiness. Doing this requires both background knowledge of the fact and theory of human behavior (especially of adolescent humans) and skill in analyzing and correctly interpreting information about a specific boy or girl.

To develop that background knowledge and that skill, the author has arranged this text into two parts, although the parts are intertwined with each other from beginning to end. (These parts are not to be confused with the part division seen in the Table of Contents.) There is the text proper: the expository presentation of the fact and theory of the dynamics of adolescent adjustment, and then, scattered through the book are numerous case digests or illustrative anecdotes. Each case is followed by a number of questions. (Occasionally throughout a chapter will be presented additional information or questions about a case digest begun earlier.) To profit most from this text, approximately equal amounts of time should be spent on each of the two parts: the expository portion and the case material. This is true even though the cases comprise only a small portion of the pages of the book. They give the student opportunity to practice the use of the concepts presented in the expository material. By such practice the concepts will become much more meaningful to the student than if he merely read and tried to remember them. Concepts of the dynamics of adolescent adjustment are useful only to the extent that one can apply them to the lives and problems of individual boys and girls, and one learns to apply them only through practicing such application. Spending much time in comprehensive analysis of the illustrative cases included in this text, in formulating the best and most complete answers to the questions following each case, is the means by which the student can achieve not only an understanding of the principles and theory of adolescent adjustment, but also a very real skill in using this knowledge to understand and help the boys and girls with whom he will work.

As a matter of fact, the expository portion of the book was held to a certain brevity so that all study time would not be required to read the textual material. It was made short, at the expense of omitting much material the author believes might well have been included, in order that the student might, after studying the expository material, devote substantial time to studying the cases and formulating answers to the questions regarding them.

All except two of the cases (Fred and Mike, see pp. 132, 185) are from the author's own files, with details changed to prevent identification. Most are cases he encountered as a high-school teacher and counselor, although some represent fragments of clinical cases from his files. In all instances, the data actually collected on a case vastly exceed that included in this text, even in the case of Vincent Vogel (see p. 510). Brief digests are presented here, with only the basic pertinent factors for consideration being included. Fred and Mike never, to the knowledge of the author, sought counseling on problems of adjustment. They are, however, real-life characters, friends' sons whom the author has known, observed, and talked with often over the years.

READINGS

Crow, L. D., and Crow, A., *Adolescent Development and Adjustment*. New York: McGraw-Hill Book Company, Inc., 1956, Chapt. 3.

———, *Readings in Child and Adolescent Psychology*. New York: Longmans, Green and Co., Inc., 1961, Chapt. 1 (representative of the topical approach).

Dalton, R. H., *Personality and Social Interaction*. Boston: D. C. Heath and Company, 1961 (representative of the case-study approach).

Hurlock, E. B., *Adolescent Development*. New York: McGraw-Hill Book Company, Inc., 1955 (representative of the descriptive approach).

Jersild, A. T., *The Psychology of Adolescence*. New York: The Macmillan Company, 1957 (representative of the crucial-areas approach).

Mead, M., *Coming of Age in Samoa*. New York: William Morrow and Co., Inc., 1928.

———, *Sex and Temperament in Three Primitive Societies*. New York: William Morrow and Co., Inc., 1935.

Seidman, J. M., *The Adolescent*. New York: Holt, Rinehart and Winston, Inc., 1960 (representative of the topical approach).

Strang, Ruth, *An Introduction to Child Study*. New York: The Macmillan Company, 1959 (representative of the longitudinal approach).

Thompson, L., and Joseph, A., *The Hopi Way*. Chicago: University of Chicago Press, 1944, pages 55-64.

Wattenberg, W. W., *The Adolescent Years*. New York: Harcourt, Brace and Company, 1955 (representative of the crucial-areas approach).

Zachery, C., *Emotions and Conduct in Adolescence*. New York: Appleton-Century-Crofts, Inc., 1940 (representative of the dynamics approach).

PART ONE

DYNAMICS OF BEHAVIOR

PREVIEW OF PART ONE

An adolescent is not a static, relatively unchanging object, like a lump of granite, which can be thoroughly understood by examining it in its present form alone. An adolescent is a dynamic, *evolving* organism at a particular stage of development. When you, as a teacher, parent, or youth worker, are dealing with Bernice, age twelve, or Ronnie, age fifteen, you are dealing with a personality and a physical body which has spent thirteen or sixteen years becoming what it is. From the time a sperm fertilized an ovum and began the person you now know as Bernice or Ronnie, many forces have been at work to produce that adolescent. Those forces have created a unique organism, not exactly like any who has ever lived before.

To determine how you can best help Bernice and Ronnie make a good adjustment to the present and achieve a successful future, it is as necessary that you know *how* they got to be as they are now as it is to know *what* they are like now. This is obvious when you think about it, for although two adolescents may show much the same traits, if one developed the traits from one cause and the other from another, you might need to handle one in one fashion and the other in quite another way to bring the best results to each. Therefore, to study the *dynamics* of adolescence, the vital forces which mold personality and direct behavior, we must begin not with the adolescent as he stands before us, but with the things bred into his original make-up and the major factors which molded a sperm and an ovum into the unique person who is now Bernice or Ronnie.

Some of Bernice's and Ronnie's characteristics were predestined from the instant the sperm and ovum that created them united, because each individual sperm and ovum carries within it determinants of certain characteristics that normally stay throughout life with the creature the sperm and ovum create. Color of eyes, tendency toward heavy or fragile bone structure, and pigmentation of the skin are examples of such inborn or "hereditary" characteristics. Certain fairly well-understood principles govern the process by which Bernice and Ronnie inherited such inborn characteristics. But whether or not they also inherited character traits, emotional patterns, or other psychological factors is less well understood. Is Ronnie's sunny disposition or Bernice's serious application to her schoolwork an inherited tendency, or the product of forces subsequent to conception—"environmental" forces? We are not sure just how big a relative part heredity or environment plays in such psychological areas.

We do know, however, that environmental forces have played a big part in making Ronnie and Bernice what they are at ages fifteen and twelve. We suspect the environmental forces had more to do with their present psychological characteristics than did heredity, just as we believe that heredity normally has more influence than environment on their physical characteristics.

Chapter 2 discusses the part heredity plays in making the adolescent what he later becomes, and then moves on to a study of the environmental forces most influential in shaping him into that pattern. The part which maturation, the mechanical process of growing older and bigger, plays in producing a Bernice and Ronnie is also discussed.

All humans (some psychologists believe all flesh-and-blood organisms) have certain "motives," inborn tendencies to want or do certain things. For instance, all seem to want food and to become tired and try to rest. As a result of environment (and perhaps some inborn tendencies) most seem to want to belong, to achieve a place among, and be accepted by, others of their kind. These motives, some of which are sometimes called "drives" and others "psychological needs," profoundly influence the way a person feels, acts, thinks, and responds to the environment around him. Environmental forces may create some of these motives; certainly the environment influences all of them and the way they develop and manifest themselves. At the same time the motives are being produced or influenced by environmental factors, these motives (really the mainsprings of human behavior, the things that make people tick) are themselves exercising an influence. They are busily urging Bernice and Ronnie to act, think, and develop along certain lines and in certain fashions.

Sometimes hereditary or environmental factors block motives which other hereditary or environmental factors have produced—frustrate them—and a person has to work out an adjustment to the "stress" that results. Ronnie wants to go to the party the gang is throwing, a psychological need to be with the crowd and have a pleasant experience. However, his parents say that he must study for tomorrow's test; or perhaps within Ronnie himself the motivation for success on the test is more powerful than the need of being with the group. In either case, one of Ronnie's psychological needs is frustrated. This frustration is likely to produce in Ronnie a condition of stress or tension. It makes him angry, resentful, or irritable; in other words, it produces an "emotion" in Ronnie. The emotion, in turn, becomes still another force pushing Ronnie to think this, feel that, and do so-and-so. Sometimes emotions last a long time and exert a strong influence on the way a person thinks, feels, and acts.

It is quite evident, therefore, that Bernice and Ronnie are not simple, uncomplicated objects as they stand before you at ages twelve and fifteen. In addition to highly complex bodies, each one has acquired an almost infinitely complex psychological make-up from hundreds of hereditary factors, thousands of environmental influences, and many innate or acquired drives and psychological needs. Finally, to tie the whole conglomeration into one package, Bernice and Ronnie have each developed a "self concept," a characteristic feeling about oneself and the world as it affects him. It could be called a philosophy of life, a mental picture of oneself, an evaluation of what the world is, and an attitude of how to deal with the world, all rolled into one. Thus, Ronnie may have had a heredity and environment generally similar to that of his fraternal twin Roddie, but may be completely different from him in nature and disposition because he used his hereditary endowments, perceived, evaluated, and fit together his environmental experiences, and managed his drives and emotions in a different way from Roddie. This self concept is of dominant importance to the person teaching, guiding, or helping Ronnie, Roddie, or Bernice because it will powerfully influence the way each reacts to a stimulus, a word of praise, a reproof, a suggestion, or an assignment.

Part One of this book outlines the way major hereditary, environmental, emotional, and motivational forces cooperate and conflict to produce the unique person which is Bernice or Ronnie. Knowing how they got to be the way they are will help one decide how best to influence them in a desirable way for the future. Knowledge of the dynamics of human development will enable one to perceive more accurately just what sort of person Bernice is, where to look to find the explanation of why she is this way, and what is the best way for the teacher, parent, or counselor to help her.

CHAPTER 2

THE BEGINNING OF LIFE

TO ADOLESCENCE

PREVIEW

(To understand adolescents, and particularly to help them, we must understand the crucial influences of their earlier lives.)

Formative Influences in Human Development

FACTOR	OPERATION
Heredity	Predominant determinant of physical characteristics and intelligence.
Environment	Predominant determinant of psychological characteristics other than intelligence. Changes produced by environment are not transmitted to progeny.
Self Concept	An attitude, point of view, or predisposition produced by the interaction of a person with his environment and affecting the nature of subsequent interactions and attitudes.

Developmental Stages

SENSE TO BE DEVELOPED	CRUCIAL TIME FOR DEVELOPMENT
Trust and security	Early infancy
Autonomy	Later infancy
Initiative	Early childhood
Accomplishment and duty	Later childhood
Socialization	All of life. Infancy, childhood, and adolescence probably most crucial.

THE teacher, parent, or counselor who wants to teach, guide, or counsel an adolescent has to understand the adolescent before he can do an

15

intelligent job. Understanding the adolescent involves not only knowing what the adolescent is like right now, but also how he came to be like that. Clark and Dick are both inclined to be talkative and noisy in class. However, Clark became so only a few weeks ago, about the time his parents were divorced, while Dick has been so all of this year (his second in the seventh grade). Sue and Pattie are both reduced to tears if they make less than 90 on a test; but Sue cries because she wants to make the highest grade in the class, while Pattie cries because her parents punish her if she falls below their "A" standard.

If a teacher tries to use the same methods in controlling Dick and Clark, he is unlikely to succeed in at least one instance, because their present behavior results from very different causes. It might be appropriate to try to persuade Sue to be content with an occasional grade below 90. To use the same approach with Pattie might easily make her problem worse, because while Sue is striving to achieve the goals she had set for herself, Pattie is trying to please or satisfy others to avoid punishment. Intelligent guidance must consider not merely an individual's nature and behavior, but how he came to be what he is, for different causes of the same behavior require different methods of treatment if the treatment is to be effective.

How far back, then, should one delve into an adolescent's life to determine how best to guide or assist him in a current situation? Strictly speaking, the farther back the better. But in actual practice, how far back one can go must be influenced greatly by how important the situation is and how practical it is to obtain a detailed case history.

How far back, and into how much detail, one goes in studying adolescents must be determined by one's professional judgment as to the requirements of each case. Whether the amount of information gathered is large or small, however, it must be interpreted accurately for it to be of help to a counselor or parent working with a child. "With all thy getting, get understanding" is certainly a key here. To interpret information accurately, to understand its significance, will require a knowledge of certain principles of child development. Why does one girl apply herself, while another irresponsibly fritters away her time? What caused each one to become the way she is? Are these behavior patterns hereditary, and if so, does this mean they cannot be changed? Or are they acquired? If so, what environmental forces or drives within the girl produced such behavior, and what should be done about it now that she is fourteen years old? The remainder of this chapter will begin to answer such questions.

THE INFLUENCES
AND LIMITATIONS OF HEREDITY

Some of the forces that produced the adolescent with whom the teacher, the parent, or the counselor must deal existed in the one-celled sperm and ovum which united to form the living organism that became, in turn, an embryo, fetus, baby, child, and now an adolescent. Structures called "genes" within every sperm and ovum are believed to carry certain *fundamental* hereditary characteristics within them. Thus, every human sperm and ovum will (barring some freakish mischance) produce a human being, not a four-legged creature or one covered with fur. The offspring will also always possess (again, barring the unexplainable exception) specific *subcharacteristics* of the parents, for example, racial characteristics such as slanting or level eyes, yellow, black, or white skin, straight or kinky hair, and the like.

But there are also areas of vast genetic variation, where a given maternal or paternal characteristic may or may not appear in the make-up of the child. Two red-haired parents may produce two red-haired offspring, two light-haired ones, and a black-haired one—unusual, but possible within normal hereditary variation. So it becomes apparent that every sperm or ovum produced by a person does not contain the same pattern of hereditary determinants. In fact, it is unlikely that a woman, during her entire period of fertility, will ever produce two ova carrying precisely the same hereditary determinants.[1] Even a man might seldom do so, and he produces an estimated seventy-five to a hundred million sperm a day. Remembering that only one sperm normally unites with one ovum to produce a human life and that every ovum and most sperm carry within themselves a different pattern of hereditary characteristics, it is easy to see why siblings differ as they do.

If we knew everything about a child's ancestors, we could, by applying the Mendelian principle of hereditary influences, estimate the *probability* of a child's possessing certain physical characteristics. However,

[1] A. Q. Sartain, A. J. North, J. R. Strange, and H. M. Chapman, *Psychology: Understanding Human Behavior.* McGraw-Hill Book Company, Inc., New York, 1958.

with millions of theoretical combinations of characteristics that *could* result from the chance selection of one of all those sperm to fertilize a specific ovum, the impossibility of precision in determining the characteristics of one particular child is obvious.

Generally, however, we are safe in assuming that most of the adolescent's *basic* physical characteristics were predestined from the moment his father's sperm fertilized his mother's ovum. At this instant, at least under normal circumstances, it was determined whether, as an adolescent and in adulthood, he would be tall or short, dark or light, big-boned or delicate in frame, have a receding or prognathous chin, and so on.

When it comes to the individual's psychological characteristics, however, the evidence is less clear as to how much is inherited and how much is the result of environmental forces. (It should be kept in mind that when the sperm and ovum unite, hereditary processes have been completed. Whatever happens to the fertilized egg, the embryo, or the fetus is the result of environment. If the fetus is malformed because of prenatal position, the abnormality is environmental, not hereditary. Likewise, if the mother's malnutrition, ill health, or injury affects the unborn child, it is an environmental, not a hereditary, factor.) There is considerable reason to believe that the upper limits of a person's intelligence may be set by heredity.[2, 3] Beyond this, in areas such as character, disposition, industry, temperament, emotional stability, and the like, the present weight of evidence indicates that environmental influences, not heredity, are the overwhelmingly powerful determinants.[4] Apparent differences between races in intelligence, sense of rhythm, and disposition are attributed by many psychologists to environmental rather than hereditary forces.

The evidence is not conclusive, but seems to the author sufficiently strong to require at least the tentative assumption that most of the psychological characteristics of an adolescent with whom one is dealing today came about as a result of things that have happened to him and of the way he has reacted to those things. From a purely practical viewpoint, as well as a scientific one, this is a reasonable assumption to pro-

[2] J. Conway, "The Measurement of Intelligence and Its Social Implications," *British Journal of Statistical Psychology*, 1958, *11*:171–190.

[3] K. U. Smith and W. M. Smith, *The Behavior of Man—Introduction to Psychology*. Holt, Rinehart & Winston, Inc., New York, 1958.

[4] P. H. Mussen and J. J. Conger, *Child Development and Personality*. Harper & Brothers, Publishers, New York, 1956.

ceed upon, because if the way an adolescent now acts is the result of environmental influences and his reaction to them, there is hope that new influences may produce new reactions. Hereditary influences we are powerless to change. Thus, according to this theory, which present evidence supports, if we (1) know what the adolescent is now, psychologically, and (2) know the environmental and personal forces that made him this way, we can, by (3) giving him new understandings, insights, experiences, and environmental influences, (4) develop in him new attitudes, perceptions, and characteristics, and thus (5) help him to develop in an optimum fashion and direction.

With these five possibilities in mind, let us explore some of the potentialities and limitations of environment in influencing both physical and psychological development, the mechanisms by which such influences are exerted, and the practical significance of these possibilities and limitations for workers with adolescents.

HEREDITARY AND ENVIRONMENTAL INFLUENCES ON PHYSICAL DEVELOPMENT AND THEIR SIGNIFICANCE

Within certain limits set by the hereditary genes, environment is capable of producing marked physical differences in a person. A naturally fair-skinned person may acquire a much darker skin through exposure to the rays of the sun. The greater number of years he undergoes daily exposure to the sun, the darker his skin will become and the more nearly permanent will be some degree of darkening. His skin will never become "black," however, but merely a darker shade of blond, and if the blond's exposure to the sun ceases, his skin will gradually fade toward its original complexion. It may never regain its original light tone, but it will regress toward that original shade.

Severe malnutrition may prevent the full skeletal and muscular growth of a person. He may, because of insufficient food, wind up as a five-foot-eight-inch-tall adult instead of the six-footer his genes would have produced had they been given the material with which to work. Obviously, it would require pretty severe malnutrition over a prolonged period of years to produce such a result, but such stunting is possible.

On the other hand, no matter how much he may stuff himself with wholesome foods, he will not grow to be seven feet tall instead of six, for hereditary factors have established an upper limit on his height. Weight is much more influenced by environment than is height. The multi-million-dollar, low-calorie, diet-food and reducing-pill businesses attest to our acceptance of the fact that environmental influences can greatly alter our "natural" weight.

Intensive practice can never make a champion basketball player of a person whose genetic structure geared him exclusively for slow physical reaction. However, neither will a person ever become a first-rate basketball player without long, assiduous practice, no matter how fine a set of reflexes, muscles, and coordination potentialities nature originally gave him.

The champion ping-pong player was born with the visual and muscular capacity to make fast, precise, well-coordinated movements, but he had to cultivate his potentialities (the environmental influence) or he would have had only the *potential* of being a champion ping-pong player instead of having become a real champion. As a matter of fact, if he practiced only a little, the potential champion probably could have been beaten by the average person who *did* practice assiduously, honing his mediocre talents to their finest possible edge.

It has been accurately said, "Heredity deals the cards, but environment plays them." Heredity sets the limits one can achieve, while environment determines how fully one achieves what he is capable of. Heredity gives the person the original raw material which will be fashioned into an adult shape, thus setting limits on what he will or can become. Environment determines whether he will fully fill out that shape, reach those limits, or fall short of them, and to what extent he will fail to reach his hereditary potential. Heredity gives one person the potential, the necessary physical equipment, to become a great athlete. Environment determines whether he will become a great athlete or only a potentially great athlete who never cultivated his possibilities.

Quality of eyesight, muscular coordination, pitch of voice, auditory discrimination—most of our physical senses—are basically determined by our heredity, but can be at least temporarily altered or expanded to some degree by cultivation and practice. Witness the blind person: he does not actually hear more acutely than the sighted person, but merely cultivates the habit of greater attention to sounds and more extensive and intensive interpretation of their significance than seeing persons normally find it necessary or profitable to do. The cultivation of his potential produces the impression of extraordinary hereditary capabilities, whereas, in reality, they are usually ordinary capabilities capitalized on to a high degree.

So we see that while physical characteristics may be in large measure limited by one's heredity, they may also in most cases be expanded, increased, or considerably altered in their expression by the environmental influences brought to play on them. Appreciation of this fact and understanding of its significance is of more importance to workers with adolescents than is a knowledge of the precise degree to which physiological structure can be altered by environmental influence. The fact that the accomplishments of people may vary much more than their physiological endowment means that almost every adolescent has the possibility of doing better than the average, even of excelling, at *something,* if only he will work hard enough at it. Effort, motivation, determination (none hereditary factors) can do much to overcome handicaps of hereditary endowment. Demosthenes became the great orator of his age despite a "naturally" weak voice and severe stammer. Theodore Roosevelt deliberately cultivated a physique predisposed to weakness into a model of strength and endurance. Many of history's most sought-after women, many of the great actresses through the years, many of the most popular girls and boys you have known possessed little actual physical attractiveness. It was not what they had but what they made out of what they had that did it.

Heredity establishes physiological limits, but few people even approximate their theoretical physiological limit in any area whatsoever. If you can encourage a boy or girl to really work at it, he or she can probably achieve ego-gratifying success in some area of physical development. From the standpoint of the dynamics of adolescent growth and adjustment, the gap between most people's physiological limit and their actual accomplishment in athletics, physical attractiveness, weight control, or other physical areas is of tremendous importance. By pushing to his or her hereditarily set limit of possible modification of a physical trait or ability, an adolescent can usually equal or surpass in some prestige-giving area many people of higher natural endowment. Such successes in the field of physical endeavor can be immensely valuable in building the confidence of the adolescent and in helping him develop a favorable concept of himself and his potentialities.

Thus, even though heredity does set the limits on physical traits and abilities, these limits are to some extent elastic. They define the shape or characteristic a person will assume under normal conditions. Hereditary factors also unquestionably set the upper limits of skill, attractiveness, and size that one can attain, regardless of environmental conditions designed to carry the person further. But *maximum improvement* of hereditarily limited physical characteristics and traits goes so far beyond the improvement the average person achieves that, in reality, one's "physiological limit" becomes a goal to strive for, not a limit beyond which one cannot progress. A moment's common-sense reflection will reveal the truth of this statement. How many people do you know who have actually cultivated even one physical trait or characteristic to their maximum capability—skill at golf, physical attractiveness, driving skill, posture or carriage, strength, speed of movement, or anything else? In dealing with adolescents, treat inborn physical factors as bases to work from, not as handicaps making success impossible.

Case of Arthur

Arthur is fourteen years old, slightly small for his age, with a skin marred by pimples. His I.Q. on a group intelligence test is 90, and his schoolwork is on the borderline of failing, although he always seems to squeeze by somehow with a pass. He is not shunned by other pupils, but has no close associations. He is "the little man who isn't there." He takes a moderate but unenthusiastic part in class athletics. His family is below the socio-economic mean of his class and never participates in PTA or other school activities. Arthur reads a great deal, but mostly comic books and lurid magazines which he swaps with other boys. He never gives trouble in the classroom, although he will join into any minor mischief that goes on. He is passively friendly, but does not actively seek friends or associates.

1. How might a teacher or counselor go about finding ways to help Arthur?

2. What are some ways in which it might be possible for a generally slightly below-average boy like Arthur to develop greater self-confidence and aggressiveness, achieve better social acceptance, and improve himself in any area?

Adolescents sometimes will profit from counseling concerning what physical characteristics they may have inherited from their parents (and thus, like the color of their eyes, be unchangeable) and which of their own characteristics they may pass on to their children. Their knowledge on the subject is often surprisingly limited, as in the instance of the young mother who feared her unborn child would have the same malformed skull the father had as a result of an automobile wreck. The Mendelian principles of heredity have already been mentioned, but, in addition, it is worthwhile to note that acquired physical characteristics are *not* inheritable, because the process of acquiring a characteristic (except in rare "mutations" from radiation exposure or similar extraordinary circumstances) does not alter the structure of the genes, and only the structure of the genes determines heredity.

Two young people may bake their naturally fair skins to the color of a schoolgirl's blush or the darkness of saddle leather, but this will not change one iota the complexion of the child they conceive, because suntanning does not alter the structure of genes. Adults who never reached their normal expectancy in size because they grew up in famine-stricken areas may safely expect to produce children who, given normal food and exercise, will become average-size members of their race. Malnutrition stunts a person's growth, but does not change the structure of his genes.

In summary, it can be said that within specific limits for some physical characteristics, such as color of eyes and height, and within general limits for characteristics such as weight and motor coordination, heredity is the basic determining factor. However, in many areas the limits set by heredity are so far beyond what people normally achieve that, for practical purposes, they become goals rather than limitations. This latter fact should inspire both adolescents and those who work with them to look for ways to maximize achievement, whether hereditary endowment is high or low.

HEREDITARY AND ENVIRONMENTAL INFLUENCES ON PSYCHOLOGICAL DEVELOPMENT AND THEIR SIGNIFICANCE

The weight of presently available evidence indicates that heredity plays only a minor part in determining the psychological development of the adolescent in areas other than intelligence. Most psychological characteristics are now believed to be acquired and, therefore, as noted earlier in this chapter, are not capable of being transmitted by heredity. Bravery, honesty, cheerfulness, shyness, patience, industry, laziness—all the thousand-and-one psychological qualities observed in people—seem to be not innate, but to result from the interaction of the person with his environment.

When we speak of "intelligence," we usually mean intelligence *as we can observe or measure it,* and this, as Stagner[5] points out, is really innate capacity *plus* what has already been learned. We cannot yet measure "pure" intelligence. It appears, however, that limits of intellectual capabilities are set by heredity, just as are limits of physical development.

Intelligence remains relatively constant throughout life under normal circumstances. The six-year-old child who is mentally retarded or advanced will (unless some environmental factors have undergone cataclysmic changes) show about the same proportion of retardation or advancement at fourteen or forty. [6, 7] However, it has been demonstrated beyond doubt that scores on all intelligence tests can be influenced markedly by environmental influences. Children who show normal intelligence at the age of six, when measured by the best available tests, usually will appear conspicuously retarded if deprived of schooling and cultural advantages and tested again when twelve years old. Children brought from extremely poor environmental conditions, taken from the care of neglectful, unloving, and ignorant parents, and placed in foster homes where they are given every advantage customarily show a notable increase in measurable intelligence.[8, 9]

Children who spend the first thirty or forty months of their lives in orphanages or similar institutions seem to possess much less than average measurable intelligence even after a later ten years of loving care in a foster home.[10] This fact may be of profound significance, suggesting as it does that early postnatal environmental influences, as well as hereditary factors, may establish limitations on the level of psychological development a person can ultimately attain.

[5] R. Stagner, *Psychology of Personality*. McGraw-Hill Book Company, Inc., New York, 1961.

[6] Z. I. Hirt, "Another Study of Retests with the 1916 Stanford-Binet Scale," *Journal of Genetic Psychology*, 1945, *66*:83–105.

[7] L. M. Terman, "Psychological Approaches to the Biography of Genius," *Science*, 1940, *92*:293–301.

[8] E. S. Lee, "Negro Intelligence and Selective Migration: A Philadelphia Test of the Klineberg Hypotheses," *American Sociological Review*, 1951, *16*:227–233.

[9] M. Skodak and H. M. Skeels, "A Follow-up Study of Children in Adoptive Homes," *Journal of Genetic Psychology*, 1945, *66*:21–58.

[10] W. Goldfarb, "The Effects of Early Institutional Care on Adolescent Personality," *Journal of Experimental Education*, 1943, *12*:106–129.

\ DEVELOPING THE SELF CONCEPT

A child is born with certain biological needs or "drives," such as the need for food, the drive to avoid or escape from pain, and the drive to move freely. From the moment of birth he reacts to his environment to satisfy those drives, although his attempts are vague and ineffectual at first, as in the aimless reachings and restless movements of a hungry baby. As he reacts to the stimulus affecting him (i.e., the hunger drive), still other things happen: crying, wiggling his arms, or moving his lips result in either his being fed or his not being fed.

As he grows older (or perhaps even from birth—there is not complete agreement on this point), many social or psychological needs or drives appear. A small bright object attracts him (this is a psychological stimulus), and he strives to get his hands on it, to hold it and manipulate it; his efforts are either frustrated and he undergoes the disappointment of not achieving his goal, or they are successful and he grabs the object. When he grabs the object, still other things happen; it causes him pain, it tries to get away, it feels nice and soft, it makes a noise, or it is disappointingly cold and unrewarding.

The infant soon begins to want attention, not because he is hungry or wet, but simply because he wants people to pay attention to him. He tries to get attention. He finds that some actions produce the desired attention. Others produce an unpleasant sort of attention. Still others produce no attention at all. Or he wants freedom, freedom to roam the room instead of staying in his crib, to explore the neighborhood instead of staying in his own back yard. Things happen when he attempts to satisfy all these drives and needs.

Indeed, things happen to him all the time, whether he seems himself to be making them happen or not. People appear before him. Sometimes he is picked up and sometimes not. Sometimes he is comfortable and sometimes he is too hot or wet; and if wet, sometimes his condition is immediately alleviated and sometimes it is not.

All the things that happen to the child are obviously environmental factors. Some of the things he does are expressions of innate biological drives which he does without having learned. Very quickly he begins to learn not only to do things but also to want things, such things as attention, rocking, or being crooned to.

As a result of this interplay between himself and his environment, the infant quickly begins to develop a "personality," by which non-psychologists usually mean a unique impression he makes on people, an impression a little different from the impression any other infant makes on them. (Psychological concepts of "personality" will be discussed in Chapter 5.) It is easy to observe the emergence of the distinctive personality of an infant as we watch him day after day. But meanwhile, inside his own little head, mind, soul, or what have you, unlike what most people speak of as personality (in that it is hidden from the view of others), he is simultaneously developing a "self concept." [12] His personality is the way he affects others, how they perceive him as part of their environment. His self concept is how he perceives himself and how he perceives his environment in relation to himself.

This self concept becomes a third stream of forces joining heredity and environment.[13] Together, as a triple-force team, they will make of the infant whatever he eventually becomes.

(It is only fair to point out that some psychologists hotly dispute the idea of a self concept. They say that such ideas as the self concept, the concept of a soul or "mind" as something apart from cellular matter, are holdovers from mystical, witch-doctor superstition. They maintain that only genetic influences and environmental influences determine the manner of development of the individual. They say that if one certain experience is undergone by an infant of certain genetic structure, only one response, learning, or result upon the infant is possible. There is no room for choice as choice is commonly thought of; this stimulus acting on the organism with that heredity and past "conditioning" means that the organism must respond in a certain way. On the other hand, many clinical psychologists, dealing with human beings in their complex adjustment to themselves and their environment rather than with laboratory situations, find the self concept a more realistic explanation of human variation in behavior than the concept of entirely materialistic determination of behavior. Therefore, the self concept and its role in determining human behavior and development will be treated in this book as a fact, recognizing some dissidents.)

The self concept, paradoxically, begins with the child's perception not of himself but of factors in his environment. He perceives the significance of his mother's face and reacts to it before his own face has any

12 D. Snygg and A. W. Combs, *Individual Behavior*. Harper & Brothers, Publishers, New York, 1949.

13 R. M. Brandt, "Self: Missing Link for Understanding Behavior," *Mental Hygiene*, January, 1957, pp. 24–33.

meaning to him. He perceives and reacts purposefully to temperature extremes before he knows that there is any difference between his feet and the things he sees on his feet when he looks in their direction. By the time his cognitive processes have matured to the point of forming the abstract images or ideas we call concepts, he has been affected by and has reacted to literally thousands of environmental stimuli. These stimuli have made impressions on him, producing in him the unthinking feeling that the world is a cruel, uncomfortable place over which he has no control, that people are kind and benevolent forces on whom he can depend for comfort and help, that he can in some manner manipulate himself and his environment so as to achieve what he wants, or the converse of all these impressions.

Therefore, by the time the infant begins to form meaningful, thoughtful concepts and his impression of things begins to include himself instead of his environment only, he has already achieved a nucleus of his self concept by the conscious or unconscious impression he has formed as to the nature of the world, how he fits into it, how it treats him, and what he can do about it. Day by day and year by year, as he matures, he will react to his environment not as a puppet involuntarily jerked by the unstretchable, irresistible cords of heredity and situations, but as a sentient creature who reacts according to the unique interpretation he applies to the experiences he undergoes. The results he achieves when reacting according to his interpretation, whether he is disappointed or gratified, successful or unsuccessful, quick to achieve a result or slow, will in turn alter microscopically or more profoundly his self concept. This modification of the self concept will in turn cause him to act, in the future, slightly (or considerably) differently from the way he acted last, and so the circle continues in ever widening horizons of the child's self concept.

Many psychologists regard the self concept as an important, if not decisive, factor in an individual's ability to adjust wholesomely to life, to maintain mental health, and to successfully assume and carry out the responsibilities of adult life.[14, 15, 16, 17] If a person has a "strong, well-

14 L. B. Ames, "The Sense of Self of Nursery School Children as Manifested by Their Verbal Behavior," *Journal of Genetic Psychology*, 1952, *81*:193–232.

15 R. M. Brandt, "Self: Missing Link for Understanding Behavior," *Mental Hygiene*, January, 1957, pp. 24–33.

16 J. J. Brownfain, "Stability of Self-Conception as a Dimension of Personality," *Journal of Abnormal and Social Psychology*, 1952, *47*:597–606.

17 G. S. Hall, "Some Aspects of the Early Sense of Self," *American Journal of Psychology*, 1897, *9*:351–395.

integrated self concept," he has gained it through successfully coping with the situations he has encountered during life. His successes have inspired self-confidence as he has repeatedly resolved in a wholesome manner the problems he has encountered in adjusting to his own feelings and aspirations as well as to his environment. A person who has a "weak, inadequate self concept" may not have grown up emotionally, and may still be reacting to life situations within the frame of reference normal for a younger child but not for a person of his chronological age. He may have met with many frustrations and failures which caused him to form a concept of himself as an inferior, inadequate, or helpless person. He may suffer from conflicting wishes or conflicts between his desires and his conscience, and quite literally may not have a clear concept of the sort of person he is and what he really wants to be and do.

From all that has been said, the question may logically arise as to whether the self concept is a psychic image of oneself gradually developed by, at the same time that it controls the perception of and reaction to, hereditary and environment forces. Or is it a "mind" or force, analogous perhaps to the concept of a soul, having an existence completely independent of all other aspects of a person's life? Probably the former. [18, 19] The self concept is probably an integrative system which develops in the life of every normal person, but it probably grows out of the particular experiences the individual undergoes and the hereditary endowments with which he meets those experiences. However, and this is most important, probably from a few hours after birth an infant begins to be impressed by experiences he undergoes not only in terms of the individual experience but also in terms of what has happened to him previously, just as, on a more advanced level, an older child will evaluate a cat placed before him not merely in terms of its appearance, but in terms of whether previous cats he has encountered have scratched him or been his soft, cuddly playthings. Thus, although the self concept is molded by a child's experiences, as the self concept develops it becomes a concrete force which simultaneously influences the significance an experience has for a child.

Often the term "ego" is used as a synonym for "self concept." "Ego" is a term used by Dr. Sigmund Freud to denote the conscious portion of

18 J. C. Coleman, *Personality Dynamics and Effective Behavior*. Scott, Foresman and Co., Chicago, 1960.

19 C. S. Hall and G. Lindzey, *Theories of Personality*. John Wiley & Sons, Inc., New York, 1957.

our feelings and mind which serves as a mediator between our unconscious and reality. The term has achieved wide psychological usage, however, as meaning a person's feelings about or opinion of himself. From time to time the term "ego" will be used in our discussions as somewhat analogous to the self concept.

Case of Arthur

(Review case digest on Arthur, page 22.)

When Arthur's teacher began to strike up conversations with him, finding out what he was like and attempting to strike a spark of interest in him, he talked readily and freely, but seemed mildly disturbed. At first he seemed to think that he was doing something wrong, and the teacher was trying to "get at" it. Was he failing? Upon being reassured that he was not, he was relieved, but a little surprised and puzzled that the teacher should seem interested in him. He was passing his schoolwork, so what else was there to do? Friends? He shrugged. He got along O.K. Yeah, he'd like to take a bigger part in things, but didn't know how to go about it. He didn't bother people and they didn't bother him. Games? He wasn't very good at sports. He liked them O.K., but usually couldn't get on a team, so why beat his brains out?

The teacher continued to talk with Arthur informally at irregular intervals—before the homeroom period in the morning; while waiting for the class's time to go to lunch once in a while; when they would meet in the hallway, neither in a hurry. Arthur seemed to enjoy the light, casual conversation, and it seemed to the teacher that he began to show a little more animation in his general approach to life.

3. Suppose Arthur were articulate enough to formulate his self concept in words. What would it be like?

4. Assuming the teacher is correct, that Arthur is showing more animation toward life, what could account for it? Why?

5. What further possibilities for self-improvement are emerging from the conversations described above?

DEVELOPMENTAL STAGES OF
INFANCY AND CHILDHOOD

Recent psychological and sociological study has evolved the interesting theory that there are certain developmental tasks or areas of the self concept which it is overwhelmingly important for a person to learn at each of several ages, or "developmental stages." [20, 21, 22, 23] Present evidence strongly suggests not only that there is an age when the sense of trust, for instance, can be developed more readily than at any other time, but also that if the sense of trust is *not* developed at that particular age, the child will in most cases never develop a fully normal sense of trust during his life. Similarly for a sense of initiative; the adult's tendency to be overcautious and repressed, or enterprising and venturesome, is believed to be determined, in most instances, by the extent to which his sense of initiative is developed during a certain era of childhood.

Of course, this does not mean that every child, for a given period of months, is developing solely one trait or quality and, having developed it, ceases forever to change in that respect. It means that there is a tendency for psychological development to be predominant in one area during a certain era of life, another area during a succeeding one, and so on. Probably *all* psychological areas are being developed *all* the time, but each area appears to hold the center of the stage at a different time in the life of the child.

Many maladjustments in adolescence and adult life, many personality defects, most of the inadequate self concepts which weaken the psychological constitution of maladjusted people are thought to be the result of failure of a child to develop in an appropriate area at the time uniquely important to development in that area. Once the crucial time has passed, many child psychologists feel, the best opportunity for maturation of the attitude or concept uniquely related to that period has also passed. Under

[20] E. H. Erikson, *Childhood and Society*. W. W. Norton & Company, Inc., New York, 1950.

[21] R. J. Havighurst, *Developmental Tasks and Education*. Longmans, Green and Co., New York, 1952.

[22] Midcentury White House Conference on Children and Youth, *A Healthy Personality for Every Child—Fact Finding Report: A Digest*. Health Publications Institute, Inc., Raleigh, N. C., 1951.

[23] C. Stendler, "Critical Periods in Socialization and Overdependency," *Child Development*, 1952, *23*:3–12.

normal circumstances of life there is no turning back and catching up the lost opportunity. Other developmental tasks are then occupying the center of the stage. Furthermore, the child's self concept in the neglected area has crystallized and is much more resistant to being molded into another form than it was during its own period of plasticity and development. Without doubt, people *do* change their concepts in certain respects, certain aspects of their self concept, throughout life.[24, 25] But whereas in the crucial period for a developmental task a pattern was easily acquired, in later life violent forces are required to alter it.[26]

If this idea seems farfetched to you, consider the period of adolescence as you observe it in boys and girls you know. Does it not seem that these years are crucial ones for development of easy, normal relations with the opposite sex? Do you think that an eight-year-old child could be given a concept of heterosexual relations which would be adequate to enable him to withstand the social pressures of adolescent development without further growth in the area of heterosexual adjustment? Or, on the other hand, do you believe that a boy or girl who reached the age of twenty without ever having learned to associate easily and normally with members of the opposite sex has much chance of ever acquiring that quality? Don't you think that good heterosexual adjustment is somewhat unlikely for such a person, even though it may have been deficient opportunity rather than innate social incompetence that prevented his acquiring it when most boys and girls do? Of course, physical development and glandular changes enter into the picture of developing wholesome heterosexual adjustment. But it appears that there are other periods of life (when no such physical complications are present) as crucial in developing other personality characteristics as the adolescent period is in developing normal adult adjustment to heterosexual relations.

It is important for workers with adolescents to know these crucial areas of personality development and the chronological periods in which they most uniquely develop, because many of the problems encountered in adolescents will be found to have their roots in a failure to achieve maturity in an area of the self concept which is particularly identified with a specific period of time. An understanding of the dynamics of

24 C. R. Rogers and R. F. Dymond, *Psychotherapy and Personality Change*. University of Chicago Press, Chicago, 1954.

25 D. M. Taylor, "Changes in the Self-Concept Without Psychotherapy," *Journal of Abnormal and Social Psychology*, 1955, *19*:205–209.

26 P. Lecky, *Self-Consistence: A Theory of Personality*. Island Press, New York, 1951.

individual development in various psychological areas is required to give one a reasonable chance of dealing successfully with such immaturities or maladjustments, and a knowledge of the normal chronological order of developmental stages will help the worker locate the cause of a puzzling problem of attitude or behavior presented by an adolescent.

The remainder of this chapter will briefly explore the developmental tasks, the aspects of the self concept which the adolescent should have mastered at earlier stages of his life. We will examine the normal process of development in each of these areas, the types of maldevelopment or nondevelopment commonly leaving their mark on the attitudes and behavior of the adolescent, and the maladjustments and personality disturbances which may result from imperfect learning in these critical periods.

Early Infancy—the Sense of Trust or Security

The newborn infant is more helpless than the newborn of most species. At the age of six months he is even more helpless, as compared with six-month-olds of other species, than he was at birth. This means that the human infant is more dependent on others for his early care than are the young of other species. Probably the first subjective impression of the world, the first "feeling" or psychological reaction of the human infant, is one of being loved, cherished, and cared for, or being rejected, shut out, or neglected. During the first few weeks of life the baby begins to form his basic evaluation of the world as a friendly place in which he is well treated and can depend on being looked after and not disappointed.[27] He has developed a feeling that the world is predominantly a friendly, accommodating place, filled with figures who want to be nice and kind rather than unpleasant, but that unpleasant situations do occur and can be expected to occur from time to time. Or the converse, which, of course, is the less common case; he has developed the concept of himself as an unwanted intruder, liable to discomforts and neglect, surrounded by an indifferent or hostile world in which he can anticipate little help or consolation.

This attitude which the infant develops, the self concept which evolves (which includes, you remember, one's evaluation of his place in the world as well as his evaluation of himself), as it relates to trust and security, seems to depend predominantly upon the way he is treated dur-

27 R. Strang, *An Introduction to Child Study*. The Macmillan Company, New York, 1959.

ing this crucial first year. Evidence is lacking that the infant "inherits" either a suspicious nature or a trusting acceptance of the world. Bountiful evidence indicates that in the first few months of his life he develops the attitude toward the world, based on his evaluation of what it is like and how it will treat him.[28, 29] This is understandable. Think back to things you learned in childhood, important things of deep emotional significance to you, such as whether your parents yelled at each other and the children, or were always cheerful, loving, and affectionate. As you examine your present feelings about parenthood, you can trace the influence of your own early impressions of parents on your present-day attitudes. More than that, you will probably find, if you examine yourself closely, that you feel that the conditions under which you were reared were "normal" conditions. (At least, this is true unless your early home conditions were conspicuously abnormal, and even in this event you tend to evaluate them as *less* abnormal than would people who had never lived under them.) If your parents never showed anger toward each other or the children, you will tend to have a feeling now, even though your mind and observation tell you differently, that showing anger in the family is abnormal. If, in your family, you all yelled at each other right regularly, you will have a deep-down feeling (even though you intellectually question the accuracy of your feeling) that a good healthy burst of anger clears away the air and prevents feelings from festering under cover and grudges from developing.

The impressions gained in childhood are more likely to persist even in the face of contradictory evidence than are adult impressions, because *childhood beliefs are accepted so wholeheartedly and unreservedly.* They are accepted wholeheartedly and unreservedly because the child has no "reality check," no basis for comparing his impression with other situations and seeing whether there is some, none, or absolute grounds for his belief. So he believes without reservation or evaluation. Take, for instance, the charming myth of Santa Claus. Remember how hard your belief died? This was not due entirely to your reluctance to give up the myth, although reluctance undoubtedly had something to do with it. It was due considerably to the fact that you wholeheartedly believed in Santa Claus and seemed to find reinforcement of your belief

28 F. H. Allen, "Special Problems of Infancy and Childhood," *Annals of the American Academy of Political and Social Science,* CCLXXXVI, March, 1953.

29 E. Fromm, *Man for Himself: An Inquiry Into the Psychology of Ethics.* Holt, Rinehart & Winston, Inc., New York, 1947.

every Christmas morning. When someone springs a new idea on you now, such as, for instance, the idea that the adult's basic attitude of trust and security was determined by his infant experiences, you do not immediately accept the idea. You say, "Hmmm . . . now let me think. What caused me to feel as I do about the world? Did I always feel this way? How easily do my feelings change? Which of my feelings *have* changed, and why?" As an infant and small child you accepted and believed; now you reason and decide. So when evidence arises later that conflicts with a feeling gained in infancy, if the world actually becomes a friendly place for you although it was hostile and uncomfortable to you as an infant, you do not easily change your opinion about the world. Your conception of normality of conditions was *built into* the warp and woof of your feelings, far deeper than the level of intellectual realization.[30] So although you *think* the world seems friendly, you *feel* that maybe you are just being overly optimistic.

Clinical psychologists customarily pay less attention to experiments with lower animals than do many psychologists. Nevertheless, there sometimes pops up an animal experiment which suggests to them profound evidence perhaps transferable to human reactions. One such experiment had to do with two groups of rats.[31] One group was raised normally, fed regularly and amply. When they reached adulthood, they were for three days put on scanty rations, kept hungry and chronically in need of food. Then they were given again an abundance of food. They ate it eagerly and hoarded some, but hoarding was not extreme. Having plenty of food was "normal." It just happened that for a few days they had been short-rationed. Why worry? No reason to think that it would happen again.

A second group was deprived of food in infancy. For fifteen days they were fed irregularly, always hungry, never given as much as they wanted or even needed to eat. The remainder of their growing-up time they were fed adequately. Then they, too, were put on scanty rations for three days, then again fed normally. But these rats, deprived in infancy, did not accept as "normal" a plentiful food supply. For several days following their adult period of food shortage they hoarded food. They hid bits

[30] J. C. Coleman, *Personality Dynamics and Effective Behavior*. Scott, Foresman and Company, Chicago, 1960.

[31] J. McV. Hunt, H. Schlosberg, R. L. Soloman, and E. Stellar, "Studies of the Effects of Infantile Experience on Adult Behavior in Rats: I. Effects of Infantile Feeding Frustration on Adult Hoarding," *Journal of Comparative Physiological Psychology*, 1947, *40*:291–304.

of it away. Their actions suggested neurotic anxiety that the scarcity of food which they had experienced in infancy would return. The fact that they were given plenty of food for many times the number of weeks that they had suffered deprivation had not completely undone their attitudes, not completely erased their anxiety. In infancy they had formed an evaluation of the world as a place in which one is not well fed, where food is something to be hoarded and jealously prized. Changed situations of life never completely changed this appraisal to a more normal perception.

Such experimental evidence as this, combined with the results of extensive clinical experience, convince many psychologists that suspiciousness, distrust, and fears of inadequacy in adolescents and adults can often, if not always, be traced back to the care they received as infants. Did Mother believe that picking up a crying baby would spoil it, teach it to cry, and did she, therefore, let little Felix cry himself to sleep when he was hungry and wet? Why shouldn't Felix gain the impression that in this old world one has to look out for himself, that no one else would look out for him? Did little Alice's mother take her everywhere she went, making her comfortable on the sofa at her bridge parties, in her lap at church, settling her in the cart with nose and eyes inquisitively exploring the new environment of the grocery store? Why shouldn't Alice form the opinion that she was an essential and well-loved member of her family and that the world wanted nothing more than to take care of and be nice to her?

The parental philosophies under which both Felix and Alice were reared may produce maladjustment in adolescence. The maladjustive behavior of Alice and Felix in adolescence may even be similar. Alice may be demanding, self-centered, selfish, and oblivious to the rights and welfare of others. Felix may display substantially the same attitudes and behavior, but obviously the two cannot be treated in the same manner with hope of success in both cases. The teacher or counselor of Felix and Alice must be able to look behind their apparent attitudes and behavior and detect the dynamics producing the behavior and apparent attitudes. A physician would be considered incompetent who, week after week, prescribed for a patient medicines to cure a stomach-ache due to drinking milk, medicines to cure a stomach-ache due to eating apples, medicine to cure a stomach-ache due to eating sandwiches, but did nothing to determine why everything this child ate seemed to give him a stomach-ache. The worker with adolescents must undertake the even more delicate and difficult task of diagnosing the psychological difficulties underlying undesirable behavior or attitudes. Dynamic forces, not symptoms, must be treated.

Alice needs to alter the self concept which produces the attitude that her pleasure is the only thing in the world which must be considered, ignoring the idea that others have an equal right to their convenience and satisfaction. This is difficult at adolescence, because the first year of life is the crucial time for developing it, but, like the physician, the worker with adolescents must deal with them as they are, not as they ought to be. Alice's sense of trust and security developed so far that she fails to perceive that the role of everyone she meets is *not* merely to cater to and serve her. Being kind and sympathetic but persistent and firm in pointing out this fact, and helping Alice learn from experience that serving others and making them happy increases rather than decreases the feeling of warmth and security she expects from the world, will eventually help Alice. Harshness may easily turn her from a "spoiled" child into a disciplinary problem who fights the authority that would alter her self concept from an egocentric one to one in which she is not the all-important element in every single situation she encounters.

Felix also is demanding and aggressive, self-centered and callous to the rights and wishes of others. But will he be helped by being shown that others must be considered as well as himself? Obviously not. The reason he is self-centered and callous to others is because he knows so well that others must be considered also; in fact, he feels as he does because throughout his life he has had the impression that people have considered themselves and others rather than considering him. His aggressiveness and demands are based on his impression (probably unconscious, but possibly conscious) that the only way he gets anything in this world is by demanding it. If Felix is given special consideration, attention, and help when he does *not* demand it, if he is treated as someone whose happiness and desires should be considered as a natural course, he will probably, eventually, develop a more socially acceptable attitude.[32]

Notice the word "eventually." It applies both to Felix and Alice. Neither of them will readily give up lifelong attitudes and reaction patterns on the basis of a few days' experience that goes against the evaluations they have held of people and situations since infancy. Felix will be slow and suspicious in responding to freely given attention and consideration.

[32] C. R. Rogers and R. F. Dymond, *Psychotherapy and Personality Change*. University of Chicago Press, Chicago, 1954.

"There must be a catch to it; watch out!" his deep-seated feelings whisper to him. Neither does Alice readily and willingly give up her expectations of being the center of the universe. Without consciously reasoning it out, she *feels* that if she persists in her demands long enough, all opposition will fade and she will get what she wants. She always has, hasn't she? Why should this time be different? If she will just persist in her demands long enough. . . .

Human motivations, deep-seated reaction patterns, can seldom be diagnosed by routine formulae. Another child with the loved and cared-for background of Alice or the underprivileged background of Felix may not become aggressive and demanding when faced with normal life situations. Alice-type backgrounds may produce a timid child so accustomed to having everything done for her that she is helplessly ineffectual when cast upon her own resources and reacts to being shoved off the center of the stage with hopeless surrender to oblivion. Felix-type backgrounds may not produce a ruthlessly self-assertive, selfishly demanding child, but a child who feels from experience that life holds nothing for him except neglect. That is his evaluation of the normal state of things, and in adolescence we find him meekly accepting whatever the world wants to give him, never thinking of really expecting anything good. The case of Arthur illustrates such a reaction.

Both the aggressive, selfish child and the timid, withdrawing child, then, may be produced by either parental oversolicitude or undersolicitude in infancy. Now that Felix or Alice has reached adolescence, how is the teacher or counselor (much less the parent, who certainly did not consciously do anything wrong in rearing Alice or Felix, and probably can scarcely accept the fact that he did do anything to cause this present difficulty) going to know what produced his or her problem?

The answer is: By patiently putting together all the bits and pieces of information an alert and professionally knowledgeable person can collect through prolonged association with a boy or girl. Is a certain problem adolescent overly shy and distrustful? It may be a withdrawal reaction to infantile failure to develop a sense of trust and security. Does his conversation suggest parents busy with their own affairs and giving him little attention? Perhaps he is experiencing a continuation of the infantile neglect. Does he show up at school after an absence without the required note of explanation from parents? Is it difficult to get the parents to come to school to discuss their child's adjustment? All are bits of evidence, pieces of a jigsaw puzzle building up a picture of the home environment that produced Alice or Felix. Perhaps the most valuable principle the teacher or counselor has to work with is that *indications* of the influences which produced the maladjusted adolescent are usually present in his current home environment. Not always—parents divorce, remarry, and change their attitudes—but in most cases. Where maladjustive influences which could be expected to produce the adolescent's problem are not observable in the present home situation, a more extensive history of the boy or girl's early life is necessary as background for understanding him.

Case of Arthur

When a popular, good-natured boy in the class (prompted by a suggestion from the teacher) began to address remarks to Arthur and casually ask his opinion when the boys were talking about something, Arthur did not at once respond. He answered questions or replied to remarks, but made no effort to keep the part in the conversation which his participation opened for him. He did, however, begin to "hang around" with the group where the boy who spoke to him happened to be, and occasionally he would speak up or initiate some minor activity.

By this time the teacher had found that Arthur's mother and father both worked. Arthur had a brother two years older than he. He and his brother did not get along very well. The teacher learned that a few weeks after Arthur's birth his mother had returned to work, putting him in the care of a woman who kept infants and small children for working mothers during the day. On weekends the mother had the accumulated housework of the week to do, and the father was in and out of the house. Arthur didn't know just why. This year, for the first time, Arthur is expected to go home and study after school rather than stay under the supervision of some adult in the neighborhood.

6. Describe the "sense of trust" portion of Arthur's self concept.

7. How do you arrive at those conclusions concerning his sense of trust?

8. What environmental factors caused Arthur's sense of trust to take the particular form it did? Describe the treatment he may have received in the nursery during the first few years of life.

9. What other type of sense of trust might a person have devel-

oped under the conditions Arthur probably encountered in the nursery?

Later Infancy—the Sense of Autonomy

Have you seen an adolescent or adult who seems merely a shadow of a parent, a ditto mark having no identity or meaning except as a reflection of the personality of another person? We say such a person lacks autonomy, lacks the strong self concept which makes one an independent person. He or she lives a life wrapped around a stronger person, even in middle age perhaps known as "Mrs. Q.'s son" or "Old Man Z.'s girl." We remark that such a person has no mind of his own.

Failure to achieve a sense of autonomy seldom occurs as a result of experiences in adulthood. Usually the seeds of inadequate development can be detected in childhood, and show forth clearly in adolescence. Note the three-year-old whose mother prompts, "Tell Miss Brown you are glad to have met her," who mechanically parrots, "I am glad to have met you." Note the six-year-old who still automatically glances at Mother before taking the apple offered him, hesitating until she nods and smiles, and the adolescent who seldom or never voices an independent opinion, but to the best of his ability cites what someone else said when he is called on for comment. These are the embryo misfits who promise to become the pale ghosts of people under whose suzerainty they live. These are boys and girls who are not achieving autonomy, not learning to think, feel, and react as distinctive personalities but as extensions of the egos and minds of someone else, usually a parent.

The *way* love is given to a child can be the decisive element in whether or not he develops a strong sense of autonomy. If he is loved freely, for himself alone and not as a reward for good behavior, he acquires a strong self concept with himself in the role of an independent, autonomous individual. If love is given or withheld as a reward or punishment for good or bad behavior, the child is likely to develop a self concept of himself as someone who must anticipate his parents' wishes and convert himself into as faithful a carbon copy of them as possible, or suffer the crushing effects of being cast out of the family circle.[33]

The time period encompassing the second and third years is believed to be the crucial time of life for developing a feeling of individuality in

[33] A. T. Jersild, *The Psychology of Adolescence.* The Macmillan Company, New York, 1957.

one's own right, acquiring a feeling of identity and developing a personality of one's own. Your own observation can substantiate the theory of the criticalness of this era in a child's development. Observe the difference in outlook on life of the child who is permitted or encouraged to depend on himself and his own decisions as much as possible and one who is not. Observe the one who is not kept in a playpen or crib, nor yet required to stay always within Mother's sight. With due allowance for supervision necessary to hold within reasonable limits the danger of his hurting himself, he is permitted to go his own way, determine his own pattern of reactions. Typically, he will display much more self-confidence, independence, and "positive personality" than will the one kept more closely confined.

Holding and carrying the child too much can produce a feeling of dependence on the parent at a time when the child should be learning to navigate on his own legs independently of other people. Baby talk, which subtly prolongs the child's reactions as a helpless infant, stunts his psychological emergence into a distinctive individual.

A moment's reflection will reveal how easily and naturally a stultifying environment that interferes with the development of the sense of autonomy can follow overattentiveness which, during the first year of life, carried the development of a sense of trust and security to the extreme of overdependence. Anticipating and meeting Baby's every need without regard for any other consideration, if continued into later infancy, tends to produce the child who looks to the parent for everything instead of seeking to help himself.

Early Childhood—the Sense of Initiative

This stage of development is so closely related to the last one, the development of the sense of autonomy, that some psychologists prefer to treat them as substantially the same stage, the distinction being primarily one of relative emphasis. Initiative and autonomy seem to these psychologists as intertwined threads of the same era of life, with highly similar if not identical dynamics. They will be so treated here, the brief exposition of the sense of autonomy presented in the previous section being elaborated by the illustrations and explanation of dynamics of the present step.

The essential element of becoming an individual in one's own right is *doing things,* doing things as a result of one's own inclinations and ideas rather than in response to the expressed or implied wishes of another. The sense of autonomy, literally "having a mind of one's own," is the first step along the road to being an enterprising person of great initiative. The child who reaches the age of six without having acquired the attitude that having one's own ideas is good, that things in the world exist for the purpose of being examined and manipulated, that life is an adventure to be lived imaginatively and actively, has been deprived of a part of his rightful, normal psychological development. He is on the way to becoming the adolescent and the adult who only follows others, never leads or advances original ideas, never thinks.

While mastering the skills of walking and talking, an infant has to go somewhere, say something. If he learns to walk and talk through doing and saying things which occur to *him,* going places *he* sees as interesting and challenging, he is learning to act on his own initiative. If he learns these skills only within the patterns set for him by parents or others, he is acquiring the physical skills of maturity without acquiring corresponding psychological maturity. It is more difficult for the average conscientious parent to encourage the child's development of a wholesome sense of initiative than most other characteristics. Parents' very love and protectiveness come to be obstacles in the way of their children's health and welfare. How hard it is for Mother, seeing Annie bravely attempting to climb up into a chair, not to help her, thus safely getting her into the chair, but robbing Annie of the confidence-building experience of one day accomplishing what she had never before been able to accomplish. Even harder, perhaps, is letting her try (and consequently develop) her gymnastic skill in maneuvering herself about the arms and back of the chair like a squirrel—up, over, under, and around. Mother knows that chairs are made to be sat in and that Annie could get a nasty bump if she slipped. The problem is magnified when little Eddie wants to test his new-found arm and leg skills by climbing high up into every tree, ladder, or anything else he can find that goes up.

Which is worse, teaching the child that he is never supposed to do things without obtaining parental approval and thus safeguarding him against possible injury but stifling his initiative, or letting him try things and find out for himself that some activities get him hurt? Besides, there are social considerations: not only is it potentially dangerous for little Eddie and Annie to blithely grab anything and everything that catches their eye and to start pulling at it or banging with it, but hostesses frown on such actions on the part of small guests! And how can Eddie and Annie be taught that it is all right to do such things at home in Mother's kitchen (where dangerous and breakable objects have been painstakingly put out of reach), but not all right when away from home in Mrs. Jones's parlor? Every situation obviously has to be handled on its own merits. Are the dangers of permitting free exercise of initiative so great (as in the case of playing in the busy street) as to require curbing the child's activities even at the cost of stifling some of his initiative? Or does the importance of wholesome personality development outweigh the dangers involved (as in the case of his wanting to putter around the flowers where bees and other stinging insects swarm)?

Decisions on such important points as these are made by parents long before the teacher or counselor encounters the adolescent, and the results of their decisions are reflected in the attitudes of the adolescent toward the people and things in his environment. It is a safe assumption that the girl who readily volunteers to try out the new recipe in "home-ec" class and the boy who has never tried to write a poem but will gladly make a stab at it if it might please the girl who currently holds his heart in her hands have been given sufficient freedom and encouragement in developing initiative to have acquired self-confidence through experience in many situations. It is also a safe assumption that each has been unobtrusively guided away from experiences which would have exposed him or her to repeated or crushing frustrations, guided away so subtly that they were not given the impression that it was dangerous to try new things.[34]

What can be done for the child who, at the ripe old age of adolescence, obviously is lacking in self-confidence in a manner suggesting failure to develop a sense of initiative—the unimaginative, play-it-safe child who never risks being wrong or making a mistake; the adolescent equivalent of the Biblical servant who buried his one coin to make sure he never lost it, rather than venturing it to obtain an increase?

The principle involved will be discussed at length in later chapters, but it is basically simple: give—or better yet, encourage the adolescent to assume—tasks new to him but ones he can reasonably be expected to perform satisfactorily. Let him succeed in new tasks, preferably ones he was encouraged to design for himself. Every successful experience will contribute to his late-developing sense of initiative, will give him a firmer, stronger base from which to venture out next time. It is very im-

[34] L. J. Stone and J. Church, *Childhood and Adolescence*. Random House, New York, 1957.

portant for the worker with adolescents to be alerted to signs that a boy or girl lacks the desired degree of initiative, and to understand the developmental forces which probably resulted in stultified development in this area.

It is natural for infants, children, adolescents, and adults to be curious, to want to think of and try new things. When an adolescent is not curious about his environment, when he makes no attempt to try new experiments with it, it means that a desirable, natural tendency necessary for his fullest and happiest development has been somehow squelched. Adolescents being what they are, their initiative frequently leads to activities of which adults who work with them do not approve. They devise ingenious methods of avoiding duties and assignments, which may or may not work out successfully from their standpoint. They hit upon novel ways of attracting attention—or equally novel ways of avoiding it. If a boy gets an automobile with lots of chrome, he wants to de-chrome it. If he gets one without chrome, he spends his allowance buying chrome ornaments with which to adorn it. A common thread runs through these apparently contradictory practices: all are attempts to express one's own individuality in a manner devised through one's own initiative or the initiative of the group of which one is an integral part.

Only through the development of initiative can a meaningful concept of right and wrong be acquired. Children can be taught a list of right things to do and wrong things to avoid. But what happens when a situation not covered in the list confronts them? Through thousands of experiences conceived or managed by one's own initiative, there gradually emerges one's philosophy of what is good and what is not. This philosophy is not a memorized set of principles dictated by adults. It is a set of values meaningful to the adolescent because they developed in his own mind as he tried things and found that some brought him approval and a feeling of pride, others disapproval and a sense of unworthiness which outweighed the temporary pleasure of the behavior. Of such ingredients is built the person's moral and ethical sense.

The degree to which a child develops a sense of autonomy and initiative has a great, almost a dominant, effect on his self concept. The child who has learned independence and the self-confidence which goes with successfully acting on his own initiative inevitably views himself as one who succeeds. He is willing to venture, to try new experiences and act upon his own ideas because he views the world as an environment with which he can successfully cope. He is able to function easily and naturally in interpersonal relations, because he takes it for granted that he can achieve acceptance and group approval. Therefore, he does not feel forced to thrust himself upon people, but reacts to them with normal warmth.

The adolescent who views new experiences as threatening and social situations as stressful, who feels the need to attach himself to someone more aggressive or popular than he and bask in reflected glory, may see his environment this way because of inadequate development of a sense of autonomy or initiative. It is worse than useless to thrust such people willy-nilly into situations with which they are not psychologically prepared to cope. In fact, faced with a situation with which he feels unable to cope, the adolescent lacking in self-confidence and autonomy may be demoralized and unable to manage himself even as well as he ordinarily would.

It often requires considerable perceptiveness of an adult to recognize lack of self-identify and initiative in an adolescent. Adolescents naturally strive to conceal such a dimly felt weakness. Sometimes they resort to bizarre, pointless actions or manner of dress to simulate individuality or adventurous imagination. More frequently they simply are overlooked; they make themselves inconspicuous in the unconscious hope that if they are unobtrusive nothing will be expected of them and they will not be hurt, will not be exposed to failure, will not lose status from making a *faux pas*, or will not risk rejection by the group, because they will escape notice. One of the marks of the highly competent worker with adolescents is the ability to identify such boys and girls and gently "lead them out" by managing to involve them in activities in which they experience success and thus acquire the confidence to venture further on their own.

Questions re Case of Arthur

The sense of autonomy and sense of initiative were said to be closely related in the development of most children.

10. Does Arthur show equal signs of autonomy and initiative? In what way?

11. How can any apparent difference in Arthur's development of autonomy and initiative be accounted for?

12. In what respects does Arthur differ from most adolescents in his manifestations of initiative and autonomy?

Later Childhood—the Sense of Accomplishment and Duty*

The period from about the time the child starts to school until the onset of adolescence is believed to be the critical one in which he acquires his attitudes toward doing what he ought to do and toward coping with difficult things expected of him. Before starting to school he may have had duties in the home—he certainly should have—such as picking up his toys and clothes and the newspapers from the living-room floor, carrying silver from the dining table to the sink, and the like. However, of necessity these tasks were sporadic, and his failure to perform them often was overlooked. Upon beginning school he is faced with the obligation to perform certain tasks consuming much of his waking time, often in direct opposition to what he wishes to do and with strict demands to perform up to a certain standard, whether this standard seems to him justified or not. At home, too, now that he is "a big boy in school," what is expected of him is increased, rather than diminished in view of his new responsibilities at school.

All this is as it should be for the healthy and wholesome development of a child into a competent, successful, happy adult. Just as the environment in which the newborn infant lives indelibly colors his sense of trust and security, the environment in which the child newly born into a world of responsibilities finds himself appears to indelibly color his future attitudes toward performance of his responsibilities and toward meeting the standards set for him.

If the primary and upper elementary-school child is consistently given responsibilities to work constructively with others, to subordinate himself to the group at times, to prepare assignments given him, and to work to his reasonable maximum level of accomplishment, he will emerge into adolescence with minimal feelings of oppression from what is expected of him, because he has learned to fulfill these expectations as a natural, normal way of life. Doing the increased work expected of him in later grades and as an older member of the home group will not tax his patience, because the increase in what is expected of him is no greater than his increase in ability to live up to responsibilities.

* The report by the Midcentury White House Conference on Children and Youth, 1951, whose philosophy and theoretical system is being followed closely in this section, does not specifically include duty as a part of this developmental task. However, the author's clinical experience convinces him that duty is an essential developmental area for this period, and it is therefore included here.

It is not enough, however, to provide plenty of responsibilities for the child and see that he does them to the best of his ability. If they are to help him grow rather than to fix him in infantile reactions, the tasks and responsibilities must be of sufficient complexity to challenge him, and yet simple enough that he is able to succeed in his attempts to cope with them. TASKS + SUCCESS = GROWTH. Tasks repeatedly beyond the child's ability to accomplish teach acceptance of failure and encourage him to remain on an infantile level where little is expected of him.

As the child meets new demands successfully, his self concept is strengthened. Increasingly he views the world as his oyster, his success as limited only by his willingness to strive. Every achievement lends him new strength and the ability later to meet frustration without being demoralized, because the frustration will be viewed as a transient accident, nothing more than a departure from the routine of successful accomplishment.

Failure to master the developmental tasks of one period appreciably injures the child's chance of succeeding in the tasks of subsequent ages.[35] The child without the firm foundation of security and trust will feel less able to venture, less assured in asserting his own individuality, than will the child who acquired that foundation in the first year of life. The child who is afraid to venture, to try his own legs and mind, is likely to approach duties imposed upon him at this age with a timidity and uncertainty that carry within themselves the seeds of failure. After all, everyone fails sometimes; the child with a strong self concept in the areas of trust and security, autonomy, and initiative can encounter such failures and come through with little damage and only passing frustration. The child without such a solid base of successful development of self cannot accept even minor failures without feeling terribly threatened.

Refusal to meet responsibilities in a mature fashion, failure to perform work which he should perform, lack of self-discipline in the adolescent period are natural results of failure to successfully complete the developmental task of duty and accomplishment appropriate to the primary and elementary school years. Defeatist attitudes, disgust with schoolwork, resentment of being expected to do things are natural results of years of failure to achieve as much or as highly as he should have. When you encounter an adolescent who shirks responsibilities, it

35 J. C. Coleman, *Personality Dynamics and Effective Behavior*. Scott, Foresman and Company, Chicago, 1960.

is important to determine *why* he does so. If it is because he has never acquired a sense of duty, your task may be difficult. It may involve designing ingenious situations in which carrying out his responsbilities is the only way the adolescent can maintain his position in the group's good graces, situations in which the group will fail if this one member is a slacker. Many months may be required to develop even a belated hint of mature acceptance of duty and responsibility.

If the trouble is due to discouragement or disgust from repeated failures, the solution is obvious: give your problem boy (or girl) tasks he can perform successfully and from which he can acquire the self-confidence that comes from triumphant achievement. One or a dozen such tasks will not wipe out the self concept of failure in the adolescent's mind, but eventually, over the months, reasonably consistent success can produce a cooperative and constructive person in place of a frustrated and disgusted one. Again, *eventual* desirable change is your time schedule.

Socialization*

Socialization, the process of progressing from the egocentric infant to the socially adjusted and proficient adult,[36, 37] is a developmental task, which, unlike the others just mentioned, does not seem to be basically identifiable with a specific age. It begins when the infant becomes able to make conscious responses to anyone approaching him, and continues until senility or death. It blankets all the other developmental tasks in its time span and is a fundamental factor in human adjustment.[38]

The first stages of socialization involve an infant's responses and adjustment to adults. This is, of course, inevitable since adults, and not other infants, are the humans with whom a baby is in closest and most influential contact. The adult actions which determine the development of

* Socialization is regarded by some psychologists as not a developmental task, because it is not identifiable with one specific age period and also because the term is often used to refer to the process of learning how to live in a specific cultural pattern. The term is used here because it seems to the author that developing skill in interpersonal relations *is* a genuine developmental task, and "socialization" seems a good descriptive term for the process.

36 I. L. Child, "Socialization," *Handbook of Social Psychology*, G. Lindzey (ed.). Addison-Wesley, Cambridge, Mass., 1954.

37 R. I. Watson, *Psychology of the Child.* John Wiley & Sons, Inc., New York, 1960.

38 L. J. Cronbach, *Educational Psychology.* Harcourt, Brace and Company, New York, 1954.

the infant's sense of trust also determine the degree and nature of the socialization the infant achieves. The more the infant is attended by a parent or nurse, of course, the more opportunity he has to gain impressions of another human and make responses to those impressions. This, in substance, is what socialization is: gaining impressions of other humans and making responses to them. The impressions may be mental, emotional, or physical, and the responses may also be any of these types; all are involved in socialization. Socialization is achieved as an infinite number of such impressions and responses gradually develop within a person a pattern of relationships with other people, a personality, and a self concept.

Impressions and responses which develop the infant's sense of trust are a good foundation for the next stage of socialization: establishing relations with other children. Patterns of reaction produced in infancy by well-balanced attention and affection from adults, or patterns produced by neglect or overindulgence, will affect the way the child responds to other children, what he expects of them and how he feels about them. Infant care which has produced in the child a reasonable pattern of expectations in what he can look for as his due from others and what is expected of him produces a child well equipped to respond appropriately to other children and to establish gratifying relations with them.

During early infancy, children react only to adults or older children; infants their own age seldom approach them and, if placed beside them, are ignored. By the time a child is about two years of age he becomes conscious of others his own age to the extent of noticing them and resenting it if they ignore him. Even more, he resents being ignored by adults. He actively seeks relations with people, and his original social responses of smiling and gurgling when being petted have become elaborated by crawling into laps, talking, attempting to perform little services, and trying to do things to please or attract the attention of others. With other children he does not want to be ignored, but his play will customarily be *parallel to* the play of his age-mates, not *with* them. That is, two or three two-year-olds may play in a sandpile, but each will usually attend to his own business rather than cooperate in activities.[39, 40]

By the age of four or five, children play together, instead of merely

[39] A. T. Jersild, *Child Psychology*. Prentice-Hall, Inc., Englewood Cliffs, N. J., 1960.
[40] M. B. Parten, "Social Participation Among Preschool Children," *Journal of Abnormal and Social Psychology*, 1932, 27:243–269.

in the presence of one another.[41] Here the self concepts they have formed and the patterns of attitudes and responses they have acquired from their close contact with adults begin strongly to affect their socialization, their social adjustment, the way they react to their playmates. If their early impressions of people have been warm, pleasant, and promoting of security, they will react to other children in the same way.

If the child in his early relations with adults has learned a pattern of well-balanced give and take, wholesome affection, ability to take frustrations as well as gratifications in stride, if he has recognized the importance of pleasing others and has learned well-conceived, wholesome ways of pleasing others, he simply transfers this pattern of responses to his age peers and seldom has much trouble in his social adjustment. He will have problems, true, because people his age do not react exactly as adults do. But he is well equipped to cope with the problems; he reacts to them in ways that will solve or circumvent them, not by neurotic defense mechanisms.

If, on the other hand, children's self concepts have formed in an egocentric fashion, recognizing no limits to the gratification of their own desires and perceiving others merely as objects whose function it is to cater to their wishes, they will react to other children accordingly and be frustrated. Many of the bases for future personality problems, as well as for immediate problems of misbehavior (temper tantrums, withdrawal, bullying, and many other adjustment problems that children display), have their foundation in this situation. During the most intensely formative years of his life the child was led to accept without doubt (without even recognizing that there *was* any other possible condition!) the world and human relations to be of a certain form. Suddenly, upon being cast into association with other children instead of with adults, from whom he has gained this early feeling, he finds the world, the only world he has ever known, seeming no longer to exist. He is confused or frightened or resentful or, usually, all three. If his self concept is a strong, aggressive, confident one, he will customarily bull ahead, trying to make this strange situation fit his accustomed picture of things by sheer energy and determination. If his concept of himself and his relations with his environment emphasize his need of assistance and protection, he will withdraw, becoming shy and fearful of this big, cold world.

41 E. H. Green, "Group Play and Quarreling Among Preschool Children," *Child Development*, 1933, 4:302–307.

George Peabody College for Teachers.

Figure 2. "The elementary school years are predominantly years of making an adjustment to a second world."

The elementary school years are predominantly years of making an adjustment to a second world, supplementing the home world of the preschool child. It is a new world in the sense that it is a world of play, work, and study, instead of entirely a world of play. It is a world of one adult and many children, instead of a world where the child received more individual attention from adults. Along with learning academic skills and acquiring a formal education, the schoolchild is literally living in a laboratory for the development of human-relations skills, a socialization laboratory. He learns what he must do if he is to have the attention and approval of his peers, and also the things that bring unpleasant results to him. He learns that there are ways of saying things that get him what he wants from teachers as well as from other boys and girls, and other ways of saying the same thing which do not accomplish what he wants. Through trial and error, imitation, and through deliberate thought and reasoning he develops ways of perceiving and responding to other people. He learns what to do in this situation and that —when he wants a book someone else is reading, when he is angered by what someone does or says, when he wants to have a particular role in a game, when he wants to get people to do a certain thing, and when he wants to win someone's favor or approval.

By the time a boy or girl stands before you as an adolescent, he or she has had hundreds of thousands of these experiences in socialization. Every one has left its mark on his attitude, on what he thinks of people and of himself, on his idea as to the best way to respond to others who do this or that, on what he expects from the people with whom he comes in contact. Much of his present pattern of social response is due to the self concept which these experiences have helped to form, and part of our evaluation of him rests on the type and effectiveness of his responses. If his socialization mechanisms are childishly awkward, we say he is immature; if they are notably inappropriate, we say he is maladjusted. (Actually, in this context the two words are often interchangeable.) If they are unusually effective, we think of him as a leader or a "personality kid." If he gets along pretty well with us and his age-mates —some fusses, some notable blunders, some unreasonableness, but by and large a liking of others and an acceptance by them—we think of him as "normal." He has achieved the degree of socialization normal for people his age.

Sometimes faulty socialization is a symptom of a deeper problem, not a simple failure to have mastered some human-relations techniques. It may be due to a failure to have matured, to having never dropped infantile responses. It may be a sense of inferiority which prevents active efforts to mix with others, defeatism from numerous unhappy experiences in trying to establish relations with others, or other more or less severe psychological deficiencies. There is no clear-cut criterion for determining whether poor socialization on the part of an adolescent is an uncomplicated lack of social skills, to be remedied by giving him more opportunity to be with his peers under favorable, undemanding conditions, or whether he needs psychological treatment. Even in this eventuality, however, simply through pleasant experiences with his age-mates over an extended period of time the seriously maladjusted person often will improve markedly or achieve a satisfactory relationship with others which substantially compensates for his basic defect.

Unwillingness on the part of an adolescent even to *try* to achieve good socialization with his age-mates generally signals past failures and frustrations of serious frequency and magnitude, a sense of insecurity derived from imperfect mastery of one of the other developmental tasks, or reasons connected with the basic psychological needs (discussed in Chapter 3). In either case, gentle encouragement to participate in activities with other adolescents (who sometimes may be privately asked to show some consideration for your problem boy or girl) is usually the best treatment you can give. Supplement it by being an understanding person to whom the nonsocializer can retreat for sanctuary and encouragement if he encounters difficulty, and you will succeed in gradually improving the socialization of most of your adolescents who have not achieved the appropriate level of maturity in this respect. (You will be able to identify many boys and girls who can and will help gladly and efficiently in encouraging the reticent person. Most of your adolescents who are above average in ability, achievement, and popularity will respond readily to such an opportunity, and many others in whom you can recognize a warm, friendly attitude will do so also.)

The boy or girl who is distinctly above average in popularity and leadership qualities (in health, intelligence, and ambition, too, it may be noted) is often neglected in mid-century America, presumably on the pseudemocratic theory that assistance should be given in proportion to need, rather than by a more equitable distribution. The adolescent of unusual accomplishments in the area of socialization and intelligence is the potential leader of tomorrow. It is indeed shortsighted sentimentality to fail to notice these boys and girls and give them all possible encouragement in increasing their superiority in their areas of greatest promise. Appoint such people chairmen of committees, and perhaps suggest to them that they try to draw out a bit the reticent person whom you also put on the committee. Encourage them to enter into school politics and community youth activities. They have an unusual capacity for profiting from help and attention, which will double the results of your efforts.

Questions re Case of Arthur

13. How would you evaluate Arthur's sense of duty and sense of accomplishment? What accounts for their being as they are?

14. Obviously, Arthur's socialization is poor. What probably

caused it to be so? How may his relations with his brother have affected his socialization?

15. Probably most of the children in Arthur's nursery failed to develop the behavior patterns he developed. How could his particular pattern of development be accounted for?

16. To what extent should a teacher try to remake Arthur? To what extent is he justified in digging into his background and feelings? To what extent justified in talking with or advising his parents?

*   *   *

The child who has successfully mastered the developmental tasks discussed in this chapter has a background favorable for becoming a happy, well-adjusted, and successful adolescent. Most of your boys and girls will be of this sort—normal adolescents who have their troubles, but work them out; who have some conflicts with authority, but are not chronic rebels; who are by turns self-conscious and brash, but do no great harm by either extreme. They will succeed most of the time, and may or may not be concerned when they fail, but will take both success and failure in stride.

When an adolescent departs radically from what your common sense tells you is "normal," you want to do something about it. Many times the basis of his maladjustment will be found in the expanding world of adolescence to which he is adjusting. Many times it will be found in his development through infancy and childhood. In this chapter we have surveyed the hereditary and environmental forces which produced the adolescent who stands before you now. The remainder of this book will be devoted to increasing your understanding of the forces working on the adolescent at the time you are dealing with him, and to helping you understand how to cope with the forces of both his past and present so as to produce the most favorable future for him.

READINGS

Breckenridge, M. E., and Vincent, E. L., *Child Development*. Philadelphia: Saunders, 1960, Chapt. 4.

Jersild, A. T., *Child Psychology*. Englewood Cliffs, N. J.: Prentice-Hall, Inc., 1960, Chapt. 9.

Jourard, S. M., *Personal Adjustment*. New York: The Macmillan Company, 1958, Chapt. 9.

Midcentury White House Conference on Children and Youth, *A Healthy Personality for Every Child—Fact Finding Report: A Digest*. Raleigh, N. C.: Health Publications Institute, 1951.

Newcomb, T. M., *Social Psychology*. New York: Holt, Rinehart & Winston, Inc., 1950, Chapt. 1.

Sartain, A. Q., North, A. J., Strange, J. R., and Chapman, H. M., *Psychology: Understanding Human Behavior*. New York: McGraw-Hill Book Company, Inc., 1958, Chapt. 2.

Smith, H. C., *Personality Adjustment*. New York: McGraw-Hill Book Company, Inc., 1961, Chapt. 7.

Smith, K. U., and Smith, W. M., *The Behavior of Man—Introduction to Psychology*. New York: Holt, Rinehart & Winston, Inc., 1958, Chapts. 4, 5.

Strang, R., *Introduction to Child Study*. New York: The Macmillan Company, 1959.

CHAPTER 3

MAINSPRINGS OF HUMAN
ACTIVITY

PREVIEW

(*All deliberate behavior is caused by some motive or combination of motives.*)

MOTIVE	CHARACTERISTICS
Pain avoidance	Biological drive. Strong influence, but often less dominant than some psychological needs.
Sex	Biologically based drive with prominent acquired psychological overtones. Typically will give way to other strong motives.
Sleep and rest	Drives often frustrated by overactivity of adolescents with potentially harmful physical and psychological effects.
Hunger, etc.	Extremely powerful drives, but in U. S. culture seldom the basis of severe problems.
Belongingness	Psychological need, "gregarious instinct." Causes adolescents to identify with age-mates rather than with adults.
New experiences	Psychological need for breadth of thought and action, variety, escape from stultifying monotony.
Curiosity	A need closely related to new experiences. The desire to understand one's environment and the forces which affect one. Can be profitably exploited as a motivating force for students.
Achievement	The need for ego gratification through doing things, experiencing success. Full satisfaction requires that achievement be recognized by others and also fulfill one's own standards.
Security	The most fundamental of all needs. Involves protection against deprivation of satisfaction of all other motives.

MOTIVES AND THEIR FUNCTIONS

WHAT makes people do things? Why do we move about? What makes us work, eat, sleep? Become lonely or frightened? Fall in love? In short, why do we do what we do? Why do we think what we think?

All humans have internal forces which nudge us into activity and tend to keep us moving in directions appropriate to the nature of the force. Some of these forces are biological conditions which require activity on our part to prevent our becoming uncomfortable or even unwell. Thirst is one such force; it is a biological condition which makes us uncomfortable if not attended to. To satisfy thirst demands activity; water or some substitute must be obtained, lifted to the mouth, and swallowed. If thirst were the only internal force requiring activity to satisfy, we could at least theoretically keep activity to a low level by staying always close to a bubbling stream. But there is also the internal force of hunger, and satisfying this force usually requires more effort than does thirst, for food ordinarily requires more effort to obtain than does water.

Such biological forces as these which impel us to activity are called "drives"—which is reasonable, because they literally drive us to activity. They produce conditions in our bodies which cause us to do things to relieve or satisfy them, even though the things we must do may be more or less unpleasant, as in the case of the hungry primitive man who may have to scratch his limbs and body painfully in climbing a tree in order to obtain the food he needs to satisfy his hunger. And the civilized man must get out of a warm bed on a cold morning and go out into the sleet to earn money to trade for food and for clothing and medical care for his family.

There are forces other than biological cravings which goad us into activity, however. A man set down alone on a desert island with ample food, shelter, clothing, and water for a lifetime would seldom be content to remain there, eating, drinking, and sleeping for the remainder of his life. He would want companionship and would be willing to engage in considerable, rather onerous and dangerous activity to transport himself to some place where he could have companionship. Even if there were a hundred companions of both sexes on the island, in most instances all of the hundred would be interested in getting away from there, because people want new scenery, they desire new experiences and the opportunity to do things other than eat, sleep, and reproduce. None of the former goads to activity are based on organic needs, but on psychological cravings which drive us to activity as effectively as do many biological cravings.

All these mainsprings of activity are called "motives," "drives," or "needs." Some psychologists use either of these terms to designate all mainsprings of activity. Other psychologists attempt to differentiate between organically based forces and those which have no known organic basis. Some use the term "motives" to refer to all such forces, and subdivide them into two classes: drives, which are biological in nature, having their origin in organic conditions within the body or physical conditions acting upon the body (such as heat and cold), and needs, which are psychological motives and may either be inborn, may develop as we mature, or may be produced by our experiences and our self concept.

Obviously, one thing that all drives and needs have in common is that they impel people (of course, dogs and other animals have motives, too) to activity. But we can go a bit further than this. Not only do they impel people to activity; to some extent they dictate the type of activity in which the person engages by establishing a goal which the person is trying to attain.[1] Thus, a biological drive of fatigue will establish for a person a goal of rest, which will impel him to find or make a place in which he can relax. Curiosity (which appears to be an almost universal motive not only in humans but in most animals and birds) sets a goal of seeing, investigating, or understanding, which a person becomes active to achieve.

It is widely believed that *all deliberate activity* comes as a result of some drive or need, biological or psychological. Since every drive and need has a goal, it follows that all deliberate activity is *in pursuit of some goal;* none is purposeless. There is a reason for everything one does or thinks. Some simple physiological reflexes may be exceptions to this rule, but as far as deliberate activity (which, of course, includes thinking) goes, it seems safe to generalize that every action has a purpose, is made for a reason, is for the purpose of advancing the person toward some goal.[2]

Certainly, many of the goals are minor, trivial, so casual that one does

[1] C. T. Morgan, *Introduction to Psychology*. McGraw-Hill Book Company, Inc., New York, 1961.

[2] F. L. Ruch, *Psychology and Life*. Scott, Foresman and Company, Chicago, 1958.

not consciously recognize that they are there, but they probably are. The student who idly turns a page, dispiritedly noticing the picture on it while the voice of the professor beats ceaselessly on his helpless ears—is this behavior motivated, purposeful, goal-seeking? It certainly is, as we see in a moment if we examine the situation. This student is bored and disinterested. The situation he is in has no attraction for him. His mind is mildly seeking something, any experience, to give it satisfaction, and his hand is cooperating by turning over the page to let the mind browse around in what, hopefully, may be a greener pasture. Shifting your position in the chair may be either to relieve a biological drive of discomfort or the symptom of a psychological need, the desire to do something other than sit there.

The fact that all deliberate activity is motivated and goal-seeking is not an abstract principle of no practical value. On the contrary, it is fundamental to the understanding of human behavior. From the universal truth of this fact you can safely assume that when an adolescent does something, no matter how unreasonable it seems, he does it for some purpose. He did not do it for no reason at all. Phyllis does not speak impertinently to her teacher for no reason at all; she does so to assert her independence, excite the admiration of her classmates, or for some other reason. Often Phyllis, herself, will not know her real reason for speaking impertinently, but the reason is there, somewhere. This means that if you can reconstruct Phyllis' motive, determine what drive or need she was trying to satisfy and why that drive or need directed her in that particular way, you usually can understand her behavior. Understanding it, you are in an infinitely better position to guide it or deal with it effectively than you are if you have no idea what was behind the overt actions. Sometimes a psychological need will be obscure or perverse (drives are usually simple, obvious, and straightforward), but it will be there. The challenge to the adult is to untangle the combination of the adolescent's feelings, actions, and consequences, and ascertain what motive and goal guided his actions and what reasoning made this action seem to him to be the best way of achieving the goal.

As the title of the chapter implies, motives are the fundamental determinants of behavior, the mainsprings of human behavior. They not only impel people to action, they also establish the goals people have and thus channel their actions along certain lines. It is hardly an exaggeration to say that the foundation for understanding human behavior is an understanding of motives, of drives and needs, what they are, how they come into being, and how they operate. Upon this foundation is then built the elaborate structure of perception, thinking, defense mechanisms, and all the other paraphernalia of psychology. The remainder of this chapter will be devoted to an exploration of the principal biological drives and some of the more common or important psychological needs. Not only their nature will be considered, but their origin and (perhaps most important of all to the worker with adolescents) their customary effects upon behavior and some of their mixed-up, noncustomary effects in the behavior of a particular boy or girl.

Case of Betsy

Betsy M. is fifteen years old, living with her mother who works as a secretary to supplement her alimony payments. Mrs. M. has been divorced about a year. Money is not an urgent problem, so Mrs. M. was baffled as well as shocked when she was called to the school as a result of Betsy's having been apprehended for taking a five-dollar bill from a teacher's purse. However, she reported that Betsy had been a problem to her for some time. She was irritable and sullen, untidy both in her room and her personal appearance, and rebellious.

"She was as sweet a child as you could find up until she was thirteen," Mrs. M. said. "Then she began to snap and fuss. She resented everything I said to her. Her father took up for her, which made it worse. Since her father left, she has steadily got worse. She won't come home in the evenings when she is supposed to. I have to work until five, and it is five forty-five by the time I can get home. Half the time she won't be there, and may not come in until eight or nine. She's too big for me to whip any longer, and when I order her to her room she simply won't go. Then she sits up until all hours reading, watching TV, or listening to records. I have a fight every morning to get her off to school. On weekends I want her to go with me to Mother's, but often she won't, so I have to come back Saturday night because I can't leave her alone. I've wanted so much to find some way of handling her, but didn't know what to do. And now this! Maybe you can tell me what I ought to do with her."

Betsy's teachers were as surprised as her mother at the unexplained theft. Betsy had, they agreed, been a good, conscientious, steady pupil, although not exceptional. She showed average intelligence based on group intelligence tests, and made B's and C's on her subjects. She got along all right with the other boys and girls, although her closest friends were in the ninth grade, one behind Betsy. She showed no interest in boys, took a normal part in class activities, and seemed devoted to her homeroom teacher, Mr. Roberts, whose assistant she was. He thought she was a pleasant, dependable girl and was dumfounded to learn of her theft and the problem she posed at home.

Betsy said, "Mother always gripes every time I ask her for money. As a matter of fact, she gripes all the time anyway. I don't blame Daddy for leaving her. I will, too, as soon as I can. She wants me to sit around the house with her all the time or go visit those dull clods she enjoys hanging around with. She says I'm no good—just like my father. Every time I try to do anything around the apartment she finds fault with it. All the other girls have those new jackets. I was going to get me one with the five dollars. It's no wonder nobody wants to have anything to do with me, the way she tries to keep me looking!"

Physically Betsy was in good health, although a trifle overweight from constant "nibbling," which she admitted. Menstruation began when she was thirteen, and was rather trying for about a year. Her physical appearance was average; her somewhat pudgy figure was accompanied by a pleasant face. She was often sleepy in her last class of the day, English, and was doing her poorest work in it.

All these facts were elicited by the school counselor to whom the problem was referred as soon as Betsy's teacher indicated that she did not want to press charges of any kind against the girl for the theft. The counselor recognized that while Betsy's problem at home might superficially be merely a clash between personalities, there was evidence in Betsy's life of maladjustments much more fundamental than just a personality clash.

As you read this chapter, watch for thwartings, frustrations, or lacks in Betsy's life which might account for some of her various troubles.

BIOLOGICAL DRIVES

Biological drives are sometimes referred to as homeostatic mechanisms.[3] Homeostasis is the process of maintaining the balance, the

---

[3] A. Q. Sartain, A. J. North, J. R. Strange, and H. M. Chapman, *Psychology: Understanding Human Behavior*. McGraw-Hill Book Company, Inc., New York, 1958.

equilibrium, of internal and external forces affecting the body so that the body's physical welfare will be maintained and its personality needs met. Thirst is a homeostatic mechanism in that it impels an animal to become active to replenish the body's fluid supply when that fluid supply becomes so low that the body's chemical balance is upset. Without this homeostatic device, if we did not experience thirst as our body lost moisture, we could become dehydrated and die, without its occurring to us to replenish the fluid supply of our body.

Many of our drives are satisfied automatically, with no voluntary effort on our part. Bodily temperature of warm-blooded animals such as humans will maintain a good approximation of normality under any, except extreme, conditions of heat and cold through the operation of built-in thermostatic devices which operate with no conscious effort on our part. Maintaining the chemical balance of the bloodstream is another example. Other homeostatic drives may require voluntary activity, but operate without being at all understood. Years ago most people were puzzled and disgusted by the fact that certain individuals, families, or communities of people ate clay. "Dirt-eaters" they were called. Modern science has discovered that certain dietary deficiencies can be alleviated through ingesting certain types of clay, and it is now realized that the action of clay-eating was a homeostatic activity meeting an unrecognized bodily need.

Biological drives, then, not only initiate behavior, set goals, and influence behavior; they also, through these processes, maintain the bodily conditions required for health and physical welfare. What are the drives most significant to workers with adolescents?

Pain Avoidance

To avoid pain is a drive inherent in the biological organism. It is not learned; it comes naturally. Some ways to avoid pain are "born into" the organism; no one has to teach an infant to draw back a hand that has touched a hot object. This pain-avoidance response is called a "reflex," a simple, automatic, involuntary, unlearned response to pain. It is a homeostatic mechanism which activates the body to avoid a destructive influence. Other ways of avoiding pain must be learned. Avoiding sunburn, for instance, is a learned response, whereas drawing back from a hot object is not. Avoiding pain is a major drive in humans. It is the basis for the multimillion-dollar commerce in headache remedies, arch supports, and a host of pain deadeners of all sorts.

The desire to avoid pain is the basis for most of the primitive systems of punishment, the systems of child discipline employed by many parents, and the systems of keeping order and promoting learning of most past and some present schools. Imprisonment, without or instead of the infliction of pain, is a relatively recent concept of mankind. Reasoning with a child, instead of whipping him to keep him from repeating an offense or to cause him to do something he is unwilling to do, is much more prevalent now than it was a century ago, and the same applies to controlling and motivating him in school.

On the face of it, it seems that such a powerful drive as we easily perceive pain avoidance to be would constitute an ideal, failure-proof mechanism for controlling human behavior. A person wishes to avoid pain; if he offends or fails to obey, pain will be inflicted on him; ergo, he will avoid offending and will obey to avoid pain.

Actually, it does not work out this simply, for several reasons. You will recall that all behavior is motivated—is in response to some drive or need. So, avoiding pain may not be the only motive working on a person when he faces a situation from which he may incur punishment; he wants to avoid pain, but he also wants to do this thing which, if he is caught, would cause him to suffer. So he is torn between two conflicting motives. Physical pain is unpleasant, but unless it reaches the point of sheer torture (and most civilized people are repelled by the idea of inflicting unbearable pain), it is often the lesser of conflicting motives, more easily endured than whatever other motives would be frustrated if one escaped the pain. We do not have to seek our examples of this conflict in the crime-and-punishment area. We all know the woman who will suffer the agony of shoes several sizes too small in order to gratify her drive to be attractive. Whether a smaller foot really does contribute to the achievement of this goal is beside the point; she *thinks* it does, and hence is willing to endure fairly extreme discomfort to gratify her stronger motive of being attractive. Similarly, a child will choose the pain of a spanking rather than frustrate his motive of being "one of the gang" and engaging in their forbidden activities. The schoolboy's motive of socialization, which would be partially blocked by his studying a prescribed two or three hours a day, very often is stronger than the drive to avoid a minute or two's moderately severe pain plus fifteen minutes of decreasing discomfort when grade cards are received. In short, the stronger drive or need wins. Frustration of the pain-avoidance drive may be chosen in preference to frustration of some other competing motive.

In the life of an adolescent, the pain resulting from his failure to perform the required act is seldom as unpleasant as the frustration resulting from his not doing the act he desires.

Avoidance of pain tends to control behavior only so long as the pain is made to *accompany* the misbehavior. Whipping Joey may possibly make him study as long as he is whipped every day that he brings home a bad grade, but what about the time when he is too big, too old, off at college, and too far away to whip? There is considerable evidence that the infliction of pain in connection with poor schoolwork often does not achieve in Joey a drive to do good schoolwork, but creates a drive to avoid, to shun schoolwork of all types, a drive that Joey gratifies to the fullest the moment he is out from under the threat of punishment! [4, 5] So, dependence on the power of the drive to avoid pain wins the battle but loses the war, as concerns the wish to cause Joey to obtain an education!

Finally, the drive to avoid pain is of dubious value as a basis for controlling a boy's or girl's behavior, because usually the pain is a threat lying in the future.[6] It may not take place for some time; in fact, with intelligence and cleverness it may be avoided altogether by one's feigned sickness or atoning behavior. The conflicting drive (hunger for the piece of cake) or need (desire to stay out late with the crowd) is present right now—and wins!

Questions re Case of Betsy
    1. What suggests that Mrs. M. may have tried to use pain avoidance as a drive through which Betsy's behavior could be controlled?
    2. Evaluate the probable success of this means of control. Why do you suppose it worked that way?

Sex

Sex is a biological drive with powerful psychological needs as strengthening and complicating factors. Unlike most drives, it can be thwarted indefinitely or permanently without perceptible ill effects to the body. You will die if your rest and sleep drives are completely

---

[4] J. P. Seward, "Learning Theory and Identification: The Role of Punishment," *Journal of Genetic Psychology*, 1954, *84:*201–210.

[5] B. F. Skinner, *Science and Human Behavior*. The Macmillan Company, New York, 1953.

[6] D. D. Wickens and D. R. Meyer, *Psychology*. Holt, Rinehart and Winston, New York, 1961.

frustrated for three weeks, possibly much less. Your sex drive can be thwarted forever without necessarily injuring your health.

Most other drives and some needs will normally take precedence over the sex drive.[7] Humans or animals threatened with danger, a frustration of the need for security, usually lose all interest in sex temporarily, no matter how strong the sex drive was at the moment the threat to security was perceived. When the hunger drive is frustrated, or even partially frustrated, over a long period of time, as in some prisoner-of-war camps and severely famine-stricken areas, the sex drive among the people involved weakens or completely disappears, as far as the people involved can perceive.[8]

In spite of all this, the sex drive is a much more significant drive for people preparing to work with adolescents than are most, or even all, of the more powerful drives, and for a simple reason: most drives under normal circumstances are routinely gratified about as fast as they arise, and their gratification produces no social or psychological complications. The sex drive in adolescents is customarily thwarted, or gratified at the cost of great social or psychological complications, and besides all that, by its very nature and existence produces one of the greatest problems of social adjustment the adolescent has to face. The social and psychological aspects of the sex drive and sexual motivation will be discussed at length in a later chapter. Here we will consider primarily the drive's biological basis and its physical concomitants.

In subhuman females the sex drive is essentially related to the menstrual cycle.[9] The female is receptive to the male only around the time when ovulation is taking place, the few hours or days when conception is possible. Subhuman males display perfunctory or no sexual interest in the female except at this period known as "estrus" or "heat." The sexual drive in subhuman animals seems primarily or totally controlled by chemical factors of the body, notably the sex hormones secreted by the sex organs, although secretions of the pituitary and certain other glands also exercise some influence. In the lowest forms of animal life sexual activity may be totally controlled by the sex hormones, but

[7] C. J. Warden, *Animal Motivation Studies*. Columbia University Press, New York, 1931.

[8] A. Keys, J. Brozek, A. Herschel, O. Mickelson, and H. L. Taylor, *The Biology of Human Starvation*. University of Minnesota Press, Minneapolis, 1950.

[9] F. Beach, "Neural and Chemical Regulation of Behavior," in H. Harlow and C. Woolsey (eds.) *Biological and Biochemical Bases of Behavior*. University of Wisconsin Press, Madison, Wisconsin, 1958.

the higher subhuman forms display evidence of some reaction to sexual stimuli apart from chemical conditions in the body. Humans, of course, react to a wide range of sexual stimuli. In fact, a castrated adult human male normally will retain considerable sexual drive and the ability to perform the sexual act for years, although, naturally, the biological conditions necessary to make reproduction possible are entirely lacking.[10]

In lower animals the sex drive, like any other drive, produces direct goal-seeking behavior and is satisfied as easily and naturally. Among humans, and particularly among adolescents in our culture, who reach the state of sexual maturity long before they typically reach the condition of permitting free gratification of the drive, the sex drive is consistently frustrated.[11] Being frustrated in its natural expression, the drive may seek expression in numbers of other ways. Every worker with adolescents is familiar with the half-afraid, brash-because-they-are-selfconscious, socially awkward adolescents. When any drive is active and frustrated, a condition known as "stress" or "tension" is produced. Tension leads to heightened activity in seeking a way to relieve the stress, preferably by finding a way to avoid the frustration and gratify the desire. Nature prepares adolescents to react to the sex drive by sexual activity. Blocked in this reaction by religious and social standards, they have internal tensions which seek other outlets. Athletics may constitute a partial outlet. Girls may find some relief in maternal-type activities, such as looking after small children. Adolescent "crushes" or infatuations with movie stars or older, married, and unavailable members of the opposite sex are manifestations of outlets of these physical tensions. Probably the choice of an unavailable object for the attachment is an unconscious protective device by which the sexual tension can be permitted expression to some extent without the dangers which would arise from direct sexual advances toward a boy or girl of the same age.

Nature has provided an involuntary relief measure, or safety valve, for the sexual tensions of the male in the form of "wet dreams," in which a sexual orgasm and biological relief of the sex drive is experienced during sleep. Thus, the chemical and neural tensions are not built up indefinitely, but reach a peak, are relieved, and begin to build up again.

[10] K. V. Smith and W. M. Smith, *The Behavior of Man—Introduction to Psychology.* Holt, Rinehart & Winston, Inc., New York, 1958.

[11] K. Davis, "Adolescence and Social Structure," in *Annals of The American Academy of Political and Social Science,* 1944, 236:8–16.

The female has no such relief mechanism, but neither does she have the intensity of biological urge for sexual gratification that the male has. At the time of ovulation, about halfway between the beginnings of menstrual periods, she is likely to become more physically active and to experience a general feeling of well-being, happiness, and even elation. Again, toward the time of menstruation, a period of increased activity is likely to ensue, but this time accompanied by tension and irritability. With the beginning of menstruation a general relaxing, a letting down, with somewhat more than usual susceptibility to fatigue, is likely.[12] Keeping in mind these facts regarding physical effects of the sexual drives on adolescents will help the parent, teacher, or counselor to understand better some of their apparently reasonless attitudes and actions.

Question re case of Betsy

   3. In what ways may sex have had a direct or indirect influence on Betsy's adjustment, problems, and behavior at home? In school?

Sleep and Rest

There is reason to suspect that people might die more quickly from complete deprivation of sleep than from complete deprivation of food. Lack of sleep produces marked psychological, as well as physiological, effects. College students who submitted to a test involving their going one hundred hours without sleep displayed not only considerable physical debilitation but also irritability, lack of sociability, hallucinations, difficulty in concentration, and marked deterioration of reading speed and comprehension.[13]

Fatigue, particularly fatigue carried past the point where rest would ordinarily have taken place, produces much the same psychological manifestations as loss of sleep. The chemical or neural factors involved in rest and sleep, the mechanics of physiological processes of resting and sleeping, are not well understood. Sleep, particularly, is the subject of several theories, none of which seems completely satisfactory.

Adolescents often have an abundance of energy which carries them far beyond prudent and wise limits of fatigue and wakefulness. Often chronic irritability, poor schoolwork and concentration, poor social

12 M. Altmann, E. Knowles, and H. D. Bull, "A Psychosomatic Study of the Sex Cycle in Women," *Psychosomatic Medicine,* 1941, *3*:199–225.

13 A. S. Edwards, "Effects of the Loss of One Hundred Hours Sleep," *American Journal of Psychology,* 1941, *54*:80–91.

adjustment, and physical complaints, such as headaches, can be traced to insufficient rest and sleep. Continued frustration of these drives always exacts a physical and a psychological toll. The importance of permitting these drives to fulfill their homeostatic functions of restoring the body to a normal state of nonfatigue should be recognized by all workers with adolescents. It is a good idea to encourage the boy or girl who is on the go too fast for too many hours a day to rest and sleep more; often an adolescent's baffling attitudes and behavior can be understood and dealt with more effectively if the adult is conscious of the effect of the sleep-and-rest drive and its frustration on the entire adjustment of the adolescent.

Other Drives

From the standpoint of health and survival, some of these drives are even more important than some of those discussed at greater length. However, in American society their effects on the adjustment of boys and girls are generally much less than the effects of the sex drive, less prominent in the theories of controlling boys and girls than has been the pain-avoidance drive, and usually less prominent in the psychological well-being of the adolescent than the drives for sleep and rest.

Hunger. Irritability, lack of sociability, dejection and depression, loss of sexual interest, and loss of interest in personal appearance accompany severe deprivation of food. "Semistarvation neurosis" was a term coined to describe the condition of experimental subjects who underwent severe food deprivation for a number of weeks.[14] The hunger drive increases in intensity for several hours after it begins and then gradually diminishes, unless the subject is fed, which causes the drive to return in full or intensified force as the effects of that feeding wear off. Important to survival as it is, the hunger drive is of relatively little significance in dealing with adolescents in this country.

Thirst. This drive is even more intense than the hunger drive and, if not gratified, increases until an agonizing death ensues. Life without food is measured in weeks, without water in days (in hot, dry climates, in hours). The thirst drive is seldom significant in work with adolescents.

Maternal Drive. In humans this drive, like sex, is heavily overlaid with psychological factors, although there is some reason to believe that

14 A. Keys, J. Brozek, A. Herschel, O. Mickelson, and H. L. Taylor, *The Biology of Human Starvation.* University of Minnesota Press, Minneapolis, 1950.

it may have its origin in the biological mechanisms.[15] Workers with adolescent girls can sometimes capitalize on this drive by interesting girls in constructive work with small children in community nurseries, volunteer work on children's wards of hospitals, and similar activities that will provide an outlet for otherwise frustrated energies, give them an area in which to experience success and acceptance, and, at the least, fill their time, keeping them from less wholesome activities.

Questions re Case of Betsy

4. What biological drives besides pain avoidance and sex seem likely to be involved in Betsy's emotional and behavior patterns, based on the information we have and the inferences that can be drawn from it?

5. What suggests the influence of each of those drives?

6. Explain the dynamics of how each exerts its influence.

PSYCHOLOGICAL NEEDS

Psychologists, biologists, and physiologists generally agree that humans have biological drives which initiate and direct activity. Whether or not there are a few fundamental psychological needs whose fulfillment is essential to mental and emotional health, as the gratification of some biological drives is to physical health, is hotly disputed. All psychologists agree that there are psychological needs which are found in most, possibly all, humans. But whether such needs are reducible to a few basic factors which constitute an essential psychological framework for personality development is a matter of widespread, and sometimes acrimonious, disagreement. Many clinical psychologists believe that such a pattern of basic psychological needs does literally exist; others feel that even if its existence is problematical, the treating of it as a working concept by which motives, attitudes, thought patterns, and behavior can be more easily understood and dealt with is still justifiable and profitable.

Considering the diversity of opinion as to whether such a group of basic psychological needs actually exists, one would logically expect that there would be differences of opinion on what psychological needs comprised the group—and one would not be disappointed. Practically as many lists will be found as there are psychologists who believe in the

---

15 O. Riddle, R. W. Bates, and E. L. Lahr, "Maternal Behavior in Rats Produced by Prolactin," *Proceedings in Social Experimental Biology,* 1935, 32.

existence of such a group. But careful reading will reveal that differences between the many groups is more apparent than real, more a difference in grouping of similar ideas than a difference in the ideas themselves. The list used here is one which the author has found useful both as a basis for clinical diagnosis and psychotherapy and as a schema for teaching the understanding and counseling of normal adolescents.

Whereas biological drives are innate and spring from organic bases, psychological needs are predominantly, if not wholly, social and cultural in origin. There is not a single one of these psychological needs that some group of people, somewhere in the world, does not appear to be almost or totally without. This argues strongly that the needs are culturally produced and not really basic. The argument is not conclusive, however. Motives cannot be directly observed. They can only be *inferred* from observation of behavior and reference to known biological conditions. They are logical constructs. A motive may be present in a person but have its expression repressed; it may be universal, organic, in occurrence and nature, but its expression be inhibited by cultural forces. Some cultures have produced men who, after early childhood, never showed a sign of pain, but it would be fatuous to argue that, therefore, since there have been people in some cultures who did not evidence signs of pain, pain is a culturally produced phenomenon. Some psychologists believe that in some cultures the manifestation of certain basic psychological needs has been artificially repressed.

There appears to be much more variation in the intensity and relative importance or force of psychological needs among people than there is variation in the nature and intensity of the biological drives. Thirst is a more intense and pre-emptive drive than hunger among all peoples of the world; but among one people of one culture one psychological need will take precedence over another which is dominant in the people of a different culture. Such variations are evidence that, regardless of whether or not any organic basis for psychological needs exists, environmental influences, the experiences a person undergoes, and the form and strength of his self concept are decisive in determining the precise nature and strength of the psychological needs in every person. A real or fancied slight, which a person with a strong self concept would disregard, may cause a person of immature self concept to overreact to the extent of exaggerating his status need until it overshadows all other aspects of his life. In another person maternal oversolicitude about health may give the security drive overwhelming importance. It is the *differences* between the relative importance attached to the psychological needs and the different evaluations of how these needs can be fulfilled best which account for much of the variation in the way different people react to the same situation.

Questions re Case of Betsy

   7. Describe Betsy's probable self concept. In what ways is it good? Bad?

   8. Account, on the basis of the case material and inferences to be drawn from it, for each factor of the self concept you ascribed to Betsy as to (1) its cause and (2) its manifestation.

The Need to Belong

This has been called the "gregarious" drive or instinct. There seems to be a well-nigh universal feeling among people of a need to be with others. Solitary confinement is the most severe form of noncapital punishment used in most civilized countries. Simply removing a person from contact with other people—no one to talk to, no one to see, no one to drive away a feeling of aloneness—is a terribly demoralizing thing. It is a rare personality that can stand such treatment for long without serious ill effects. Some recent evidence suggests that considerable contact with one's kind is essential to good psychological development. For example, puppies raised in isolation proved to be incapable even of avoiding pain, repeatedly sniffing at lighted matches, for instance, instead of learning from the first experience to avoid them, as "normal" dogs do, and showing in other ways a remarkable inability to learn and adjust.[16, 17]

Some few people simply prefer to be alone, and become the hermits or prospectors who show up at a village on rare occasions to obtain food, then leave at once for their preferred solitude. But to most people the most luxurious of homes and the most sumptuous of food, lived in and eaten alone with never a sight of another human being, would gladly be swapped for a life of work amid less opulent surroundings, but with people.

Actually, the need to belong goes much deeper than merely demanding the physical presence of others. We want to be not merely *with* the

[16] R. Melzack, "Genesis of Emotional Behavior: An Experimental Study of the Dog," *Journal of Comparative and Physiological Psychology*, 1954, 47:166–168.

[17] R. Melzack and W. R. Thompson, "Early Environment," *Scientific American*, January, 1956, pp. 38–42.

group but a *part* of the group. The person who is given a job and then ignored by everyone else working around him is not likely to do his job well or stay with it long. He is *with* the group but not *of* it, and will generally be unhappy. You may have had the experience of joining a club or church in which your presence was politely acknowledged, but in which you were given no real part in the functioning of the organization and were not admitted into the close circle of fellowship which existed among other members. Didn't you feel left out, alone, frustrated, and discontented?

As was seen in Chapter 2, an important part of the child's growth and development is socialization, developing the attitudes and social skills which make it possible for him to associate pleasantly with other people. In its fullest sense, however, the need for belonging is deeper than the simple necessity of getting along with people. It means feeling that you are a part of some human group larger than yourself, drawing strength from association with others like yourself who assist and support each other, share the same values and ideals, and are interested in each other, not just each one in himself alone.

The history of American soldiers held in Communist prisoner-of-war camps during and after the Korean war revealed two important things about the psychological importance of belonging. First, isolating men from their companions physically or by fostering distrust among them, and isolating them from home contacts by withholding mail and telling them stories of being forgotten by their government and families, did more to break their will to resist Communist indoctrination than did physical torture. Second, men who maintained their military organization within the POW camps, keeping their squad or platoon intact as a tight, cooperative body, not only resisted. brainwashing better than did other prisoners, but actually held their death rate to a fraction of what it was among less well-organized groups in the same camp.[18, 19]

Either inherently or as a result of becoming accustomed to it, then, the human mind and personality have an overpowering need to be accepted by and amalgamated with other people. By the time the adolescent reaches you, he has spent a number of years seeking, achieving, losing, and re-achieving belongingness in many groups. Driven by this

[18] R. E. Chambers, "Discussion of Survival Factors," *American Journal of Psychiatry,* 1952, *109*:247–248.

[19] H. A. Segal, "Initial Psychiatric Findings of Recently Repatriated Prisoners of War," *American Journal of Psychiatry,* 1954, *111*:358–363.

powerful need to be a part of groups of his own age, the child and adolescent has devised many ways of either achieving this belongingness or compensating for failure to achieve it. Mary achieves it by slavish and inconspicuous conformance to the dress and customs of a group of girls with whom she goes but who do not quite accept her as a full-fledged, full-privileged member. By being pleasant, useful, undemanding, and playing up to an influential member of the group, Mary has learned to achieve some measure of the acceptance she desires. This manner of achieving acceptance both is influenced by and influences her self concept, and will color her attitudes and behavior in getting along with other people, meeting adults, adjusting to her teachers, and all her human relations.

Billy has a knack for being liked and accepted wherever he goes. If his family moves, he is quickly absorbed into the boys' society in his new school. This gives Billy a different self concept and causes him to approach people with a different attitude and behavior from Mary. If Billy should join a group and, for his popularity, be resented by one or more of the other members, who, therefore, display veiled or open resentment toward him, this will affect him. Both in that group and subsequent groups his desire to belong will manifest itself in a slightly different form as a result of the experience of partial rejection. Similarly, if Mary approaches another group which welcomes her warmly and admits her fully, this will influence her subsequent approaches to other people.

Marilyn resorts to lavishing her liberal allowance on refreshments for her friends as a means of being accepted under some terms, in preference to being totally rejected. Eric dresses and acts in a loud, blustery manner, trying to impress people so that he will be held in respect or awe, if he cannot gain acceptance. Each is trying, in the most effective way he or she knows, to achieve belongingness in a group important to an adolescent or to compensate for failure to achieve such belongingness. Experience entering into the construction of his or her self concept has caused each of these adolescents to make his effort in a different way. And every different way, to say nothing of the attitudes and concepts which produce that way, poses a different situation with which the worker with adolescents must deal.

The infant wants to be accepted only by his parents and perhaps a few other adults. The schoolchild is usually more interested in being accepted and held in esteem by other boys and girls than by adults. The adolescent typically is trying to grow into the pattern of adulthood, but still owes primary allegiance to the world and society of those his own age, and so is more concerned with pleasing them than with pleasing adults. This fact is the cause of much of the friction which may develop between parents and their children. The attributes and actions which make for high acceptance and belongingness in the group of the boy's or girl's age are not the attributes and actions which parents and teachers are likely to regard most highly. Some adolescents are able to make skillful adjustments between these two forces (their peers and adults) and keep in the good graces of both groups. Others, less adept, become social outcasts as regards their contemporaries, or experience constant friction with parents, teachers, and other adults.

Whatever an adolescent's attitude and behavior toward adults, toward authority, he has learned them. He was not "born that way." Often he has learned these attitudes and behaviors in the process of trying out various ways of achieving belongingness. Often his attitude and behavior are influenced by his present sense of belongingness, rejection, social uncertainty, or aspiration. Attitudes and behavior growing out of an adolescent's attempts to satisfy the need for belongingness have a long history—as long as his life. Thousands of experiences have combined to produce the exact manifestation of the need for belongingness encountered in the case of an individual boy or girl. In his behavior and attitudes the counselor must look for cues to his adjustment in this important area. Could his actions be a device for displaying resentment of rejection? Could her anxiety to please, her nervous tension, be a result of a feeling of not being completely accepted by her group? If so, look for ways of helping them gain some acceptance—if not by their peers, at least by you.

The need to belong, to be accepted by the group, is one of the great mainsprings of human behavior. It is relatively easy to study the effects of this drive and deduce its place in the behavior and attitudinal pattern of a boy or girl, because the effects of the drive are open and obvious every time the person is approached by or reacting to another human. Observe the boys and girls with whom you work. See how they act toward other boys and girls and observe the treatment they receive at the hands of these boys and girls. Give those who are partially rejected the moral support of *your* acceptance of them. Tactfully direct their attention to ways they can strengthen themselves in the group. The need for belongingness produces behavior which speaks volumes to the parent, teacher, or counselor who will but notice.

Questions re Case of Betsy

9. In what ways does Betsy's need for belongingness show lack of fulfillment?

10. In what ways may her need for belongingness have influenced her attitudes and behavior?

11. Given the relatively unchangeable family circumstances, such as the divorce and her subsequent living with her mother, how might Betsy's need for belongingness have still been filled better than it apparently has been?

The Need for New Experiences

This need is responsible for much of the progress mankind has made. Subsumed under the general title New Experiences are such related but nonidentical needs as the need for opportunity to do new and better things, the curiosity motive (which makes the scientist spend years studying a subject for no monetary return or material gain, but finally producing a major advance in science), the desire to exercise initiative and assume responsibility, rather than forever follow the beaten path of "Standing Operating Procedure" which others have followed for years. The need for new experiences is the basis of the whole vacation business, which today is a big business indeed. It produces the pioneers, the men who open new doors of science and widen the horizons of man's economic, philosophical, and social thought. It produces the need to *create* new things as well as the desire to enjoy new experiences which other people have designed for us.

Observation of their activities suggests that the need for new experiences is much greater in children and adolescents than in older people, especially people of middle age or older. Wonderful and productive of human betterment and progress as this need is, it is a source of endless problems to every worker with young people. The very fact that an experience is new and different seems to make it fascinating to adolescents, and they want their new experiences so fast! They want their new experiences so much that they are willing to take rather great chances to get them—try out the new skates in spite of the ice being thin, risk the chance of pregnancy "to see what it's like," perhaps fail a semester of math because the gang has a big, new project planned for the night before the exam, or join in a new "cause" which appeals to their imagination.

Disciplinary problems in the classroom and everywhere else can often be attributed to the desire for new experiences. Young people tend to become bored with a thing quickly, to want something else, anything, so long as it is new. The phonograph record listened to with ecstatic adoration today is discarded, literally next week, as of no possible interest: a new one is out that has negligible differences, but is *new*. This being the case, it is hardly surprising that spending hour after hour, day after day, at desks studying things they never found *very* interesting in the first place is a disciplinary effort many children and adolescents simply refuse to put forth. If required to remain physically in the classroom (as, of course, they are), they do their best to compensate for this frustration of their desire for constantly new experiences by seeking the new experiences in their minds—inattentiveness and daydreaming result —or in their actions: to obtain the greatest novelty possible in their restricted classroom environment, they think of and put into effect the million and one things boys and girls do in dull classrooms or meetings. They whisper. They manufacture strange devices from articles they have about them. They devise novel means of attracting the attention of, communicating with, or annoying other people. Anything, everything, to have something new and novel to occupy their attention.

"If you can't lick 'em, join 'em." You can't lick this drive. Probably the progress of the world would stop if you did. The desire for new experiences is a mainspring of motivation which thousands of alert teachers, parents, and counselors have used successfully to elicit more and better work from boys and girls than less resourceful adults ever thought possible. If you can show a boy or girl how he can gain a new idea, perceive something he has never encountered before, do something he could never do before or something nobody in his crowd ever thought of doing before, through a bit of assigned study you have lifted that assignment out of the boring, tiresome (to him) routine of again living through a dreary academic preparation and given him a new experience.

When growing up you had, if you were fortunate, some teacher or adult advisor who had a talent for "making things seem interesting." If you will analyze, in retrospect, what they did, you will probably find that a key part of their procedure lay merely in making what they wanted you to do seem new and different from what you had done before, a new adventure, a new challenge. Few boys and girls have absorbing interests, conceived and nurtured by themselves, in things adults want them to spend hours on. You can get their constructive cooperation if you will design your activities in such a way as to be novel and challenging to them. Make a real effort to capitalize on this interest in things that are new.

Part of the desire for new experiences is the desire to do things as one wants to, rather than the way they have been done in the past. Boys and girls want to exercise their imagination and initiative. Hundreds of elementary- and high-school courses have achieved greater knowledge increase than average in pupils because the students were given the opportunity to determine how they were going to go about achieving the results expected of them in the course. The imperfections of their methods, their time-wasting milling around, was more than compensated for by the increased energy with which they attacked the work and responded to the experience of trying things in new ways instead of the old conventional methods they had, by direction of others, used so long.[20]

Even though the sameness and dullness of their activity is temporarily frustrating their need for new experiences, many boys and girls will dutifully do what is expected of them, do what they are "supposed" to do, faithfully and obediently. Usually this is fine, meaning simply that these boys and girls have acquired a rather mature sense of responsibility and either good self-discipline or good adjustment to external discipline. Some psychologists and educators intimate that such dutifulness is somehow unhealthy, a sign that the child lacks spontaneity, a "mind of his own," or that his spirit has been crushed under the iron heel of adult discipline. It is conceivable that this is the explanation of what some people deprecatingly refer to as "adult-approved behavior" in some instances, but such instances are rare. Usually such children have merely learned, earlier than others, mature, responsible attitudes toward their work. Doing assigned work well and faithfully in no way interferes with broad, free exercise of initiative in the adolescent's life generally. It merely suggests good development of the sense of accomplishment and duty.

Even those boys and girls who work well and faithfully, whether the experiences they are having are new and exciting or dull and boring to them, will do *more* and *better* work if their desire for new experiences is appealed to. They have this desire just as strongly as other people, and will respond just as enthusiastically to opportunities to gratify it. The fact that you, their adult leader, are not *forced* to appeal to the power of this mainspring of activity is no reason why you should not do

20 L. J. Cronbach, *Educational Psychology*. Harcourt, Brace and Company, New York, 1954.

George Peabody College for Teachers.

Figure 3. "The need for new experiences is much greater in children and adolescents than in older people."

so in working with them. The extra effort required on your part to devise ways of making their work more novel and challenging will be amply repaid, not only in the better work they do, but also in the better reputation you will earn as an adult able to work well with adolescents and elicit from them superior work.

Individual differences in the form or strength of this drive in different persons arise from basically the same factors that produce individual differences in the strength and manifestations of other drives: nature of previous experiences, maturity, degree of self-discipline, trial-and-error results, and self concepts which supply or do not supply the self-confidence to make venturing into new experiences a challenging, rather than a fearsome, thing. Health is also a factor; the child who is vigorous and bursting with life and energy will be less willing to curtail his desire for new experiences than will a less robust and energetic child.

The chief value which the need for new experiences can supply in the work of anyone dealing with boys and girls is as a mainspring which, if properly utilized, can inspire practically unlimited effort and work. A secondary function is making possible the understanding of restlessness, anti-social behavior, and inattentiveness which appear purposeless but, like all other patterns of behavior, are not.

Curiosity.   Curiosity is considered by some psychologists a basic motive. Some think of it as a part of the need for new experiences. Certainly it is almost, if not completely, universal in its occurrence among normal humans and among many subhuman species. Monkeys will spend hours investigating articles and trying to solve puzzles with no apparent motive except the drive of innate curiosity.[21] Birds, notably jays and crows, display what appears to be curiosity with no purpose except satisfaction of the drive. Children manifest their curiosity by asking innumerable questions, as well as by their well-known tendency to "get into everything."

If schoolwork can be presented in such a way that it becomes a challenge to curiosity instead of a bunch of facts to be monotonously and meaninglessly shoved into and filed in one's mind, a teacher's job becomes both easier and more successful. If a scoutmaster can devise programs and projects in which scouts feel that they discover things, facts, or concepts, the troop will be popular. The books on educational psychology base much of their preference for this or that method on the degree to which it capitalizes on or presents challenges to pupils' sense of curiosity.

Curiosity seems to be a natural, unlearned trait and its satisfaction a basic motive in life.[22] Unfortunately, adults often discourage this valuable quality in children because curiosity does lead to activity, often unpredictable activity. When you encounter an adolescent who seems to have no interest in things (such as Arthur in Chapter 2, for instance), whose curiosity about things cannot be aroused, you have a boy or girl who needs help and understanding. He has lost some of his birthright, whether through ill health, unfortunate treatment by adults, repeated experiences of failure which have quenched his spirit of adventure, or perhaps stultification by repressive educational methods. It is worth

[21] H. F. Harlow, "Motivation as a Factor in New Responses," *Current Theory and Research in Motivation.* University of Nebraska Press, Lincoln, Nebraska, 1953.

[22] D. E. Berlyne, *Conflict Arousal and Curiosity.* McGraw-Hill Book Company, Inc., New York, 1960.

considerable effort on your part to find an approach that will rekindle the fire of curiosity in a boy or girl who has lost it, because without curiosity a person will lose much of the potential of life.

Questions re Case of Betsy

12. What, in our case digest, suggests that Betsy may feel an ungratified need for new experiences?

13. What are some of the "new experiences" a fifteen-year-old girl may normally want, expect, or receive? Wherein does Betsy's range of new experiences fall short of the optimum?

14. What "new experiences" might a fifteen-year-old boy want which would differ from those of a fifteen-year-old girl?

15. Given her present conditions of life, how might Betsy's need for new experiences better be satisfied (1) at school and (2) at home?

The Need to Achieve

This need has at least two aspects, but their dynamics are so similar that they can most conveniently be considered together. People, from infancy to senility, want to achieve status and recognition (as well as the simpler achievement of belonging). People also want to *achieve,* to do things, to accomplish things, for the sheer sake of having done something. Why will a child spend hours building an elaborate sand-house village and then never look at it once it is built? Why will a millionaire, with more money than he can ever spend, strenuously object to retiring and "enjoying life," and instead take as keen a pleasure in making his tenth million as he did his first? To pass on to his heirs is not an adequate explanation, inheritance taxes being what they are. Careful psychological study of motivational patterns of children and adults indicates strongly that normal people have a powerful urge to do things just because they want to accomplish something. A famous mountain climber, asked why he wanted to scale a difficult and dangerous peak, replied, "Because it's there."

The need to achieve, like the desire for new experiences, is a powerful mainspring of activity. It causes people to move, act, think, even though often no tangible results are achieved except the sheer satisfaction of moving, acting, and thinking.[23] It is often sufficiently powerful to

---

[23] D. C. McClelland, J. W. Atkinson, R. A. Clark, and E. L. Lowell, *The Achievement Motive.* Appleton-Century-Crofts, Inc., New York, 1953.

outweigh fairly intense biological drives, as witness the hungry but aspiring young artist working in a cold apartment.

There is some evidence that sheer desire to move, to do things physically and mentally, the desire to avoid inactivity may be a basic psychological need or, conceivably, a biological drive. A group of presumably normal young men were hired to participate in an experiment in which each lay on a comfortable bed in a comfortable, isolated, soundproofed room twenty-four hours a day, except for brief periods for toilet needs and eating. Their arms and hands were covered with cardboard containers to minimize tactual sensations, and they wore opaque goggles. Physically they were completely comfortable, and they were paid twenty dollars a day. During the first day they were enthusiastic about their new job. However, one by one they resigned and refused to continue their "soft snap" jobs after two or three days. Upon quitting the experiment, they reported severe-seeming phenomena of feeling detached from the world, from their own bodies, as if there were two of a person instead of one, and vivid hallucinations. Their mental processes were confused, and they showed a marked decline in ability to perform mental tasks of all types after even a few hours of being partially isolated from normal sensations and activities. Although isolation from the normal range of sensations was also present, dissatisfaction with a state of complete inactivity seemed to have been a notable factor in the discontent of the experimental subjects. It is possible that the sheer need to be moving, doing something, is an important motive in the adolescents whose twisting and "pointless" movements annoy adults so much.[24]

The self concept and one's outlook on life are profoundly influenced by the experiences one has in striving to satisfy the need to do, to achieve. In infancy the baby tries to do things—reach this, manipulate that, attract attention, move his body for no apparent reason except to have asserted himself. Every month of life brings new opportunities to try to do things, and every opportunity carries with it the chance of success, failure, or part success and part failure. The degree to which this need is gratified in childhood will go far toward determining whether the child matures with a confident, optimistic, success-oriented approach to life, or becomes an uncertain, hesitating person lacking in self-confidence and constantly fearing failure. The relation of this drive to the successful mastery of the developmental tasks discussed in Chapter

24 W. H. Bexton, W. Heron, and T. H. Scott, "Effects of Decreased Variation in the Sensory Environment," *Canadian Journal of Psychology*, 1954, *8*:70–76.

2, particularly the acquiring of the sense of autonomy, initiative, and accomplishment, is obvious. Achievement, successful trying and doing of things, is not the only ingredient of any one of these tasks, but it is certainly an essential ingredient of every one of them.

It seems more than probable that many tiny, apparently insignificant things exercise tremendous control over how a child feels about and expresses this desire for accomplishment. There is evidence that the mother who solicitously lends a hand to put the finishing touches on the doll dress little Ellen thought she herself had already finished beautifully, the father who shows young Ollie how his fine kick could have been even finer if only he had turned sideways a little, may, by their oversolicitude, give Ellen and Ollie the unconscious feeling that they cannot do things well. Their excessive "helpfulness" may cause the boy and girl unconsciously to lower their opinions of themselves and their abilities, and settle for lower aspirations and successes in life than they otherwise would have achieved. Certainly, the child who grows up disappointedly trying but always failing to live up to the standards set for him by parents or other adults will almost certainly have this desire to achieve thwarted within him and develop a defeatist attitude toward life, although he may try to conceal it beneath a compensatory cover of overconfidence.

The ideal background for an adolescent to have had, so as to satisfy and perpetuate the need to accomplish, is one in which he was given, throughout his whole developmental period, a constant series of opportunities to do things which he could successfully do, but which were difficult enough to challenge him.[25] The challenge will keep him interested, prevent the things he does from seeming to be beneath his ability. If he fails in an occasional one, no harm at all is done so long as *most* of them are of a level which challenge him, yet which he can successfully accomplish. Such experiences develop the child's self-confidence, produce the self concept of a capable person who can cope with whatever situation may arise to confront him, do what is necessary to succeed.

The well-known "inferiority complex" is the result of frustration of the need for achievement, with consequent self-devaluation. Boys and girls suffering from too much frustration of this need may present either of two pictures, in varying degrees. If the adolescent is unsure, hesitant, gives up easily, is afraid to attempt new tasks, expresses doubt that he

25 I. M. Josselyn, *The Happy Child*. Random House, New York, 1955.

can do what is expected of him, in all likelihood he has had an inadequate opportunity for successful achievement in the years past. If, on the other hand, he is boastful, recklessly tries things far beyond his ability, professes to see nothing wrong with obviously poor work or inglorious failures, he may be overcompensating for an inferiority complex.

There is no precise formula for a discriminative diagnosis between overcompensation and normal, but mistaken, overconfidence due to lack of perception of one's limitations. As with most other problems, you must study the adolescent's whole pattern of attitudes and behavior. In most cases a note of anxiety and/or defensiveness will be evident in the attitude of the overcompensating boy or girl, and absent in the case of the one who blithely tackles anything or everything without reservation. The overconfident adolescent, too, can accept failure cheerfully or, at most, with a transient emotional outburst. The overcompensating one is harder hit by failure and often exhibits marked anxiety and anger.

It is vital for the worker with adolescents to distinguish between the overconfident and the overcompensating. The one has to be led to look more realistically at his abilities, and his venturesomeness must be gently curbed. The adolescent who either shies away from new tasks or overcompensates by indiscriminate tackling of everything that comes along needs to be given tasks within his limits, in an attempt to build a solid self-confidence so that his defensive behavior is less satisfying to him than the real accomplishments he can achieve in normal patterns of activity.

Part of gratifying achievement, especially in a culture where social approval is highly valued, as it is in ours, is for a quality or achievement to be recognized and to bring status to the achiever. We want the ego gratification of being admired for our skill or accomplishment. You know how quickly you will lose interest in doing your best on a job if you find that no one ever notices or knows how well or poorly you do anyhow, and if no recognition or increase in status is forthcoming to distinguish you from the slacker beside you. Sometimes apathy, "do-lessness," discouragement on the part of the adolescent is due not to his lack of success, but to lack of success in his being recognized.[26] In a way, this lack of recognition becomes a lack of success.

In fact (and this is a useful thing to keep in mind when determining how to help a retarded or handicapped boy or girl), sometimes some-

26 I. M. Josselyn, *The Happy Child*. Random House, New York, 1955.

thing less than literal success can, by a sensitive adult, be made a source of great gratification to the adolescent. By your noticing what *was* achieved and remarking on it in a manner appropriate to what it represents of his ability, a boy or girl whose work represents little *objective* achievement but good achievement *for him* can magnificently satisfy his need for achievement and recognition of achievement.

To correct a popular but erroneous impression, it should be noted that praising achievement (even mediocre achievement, except in rare instances) *does not* result in a person's feeling, "I can get by with this, so why try to do better?" The desires for achievement and recognition of achievement seem to *increase,* rather than decrease, as they achieve gratification. A moment's personal reflection will reveal the truth of this statement. If you received praise from your parents for making an over-all B average last semester, would it lessen your desire to make B's this semester as well? You will probably want B's even more than you would if you had made C's last semester. Your self concept identifies you as a better-than-C student, and you must live up to it or suffer self-devaluation.

Sugar catches more flies than vinegar. Praise produces more effort than criticism (not a universal truth, but a sound generalization!).

Questions re Case of Betsy

16. In what areas does Betsy seem to have achieved fulfillment of the need for achievement?

17. What frustrations of the need for achievement has she encountered?

18. How might her need for achievement be more fully met? What could Betsy do to better satisfy her need for achievement, if neither the school nor her mother helped her? How might they help her?

The Need for Security

Security is the most fundamental of all psychological needs. In situations where a person is subjected to a serious threat, the need for security is likely to take temporary precedence even over most of the biological drives, such as hunger and fatigue. There are many kinds of security, and much of mankind's effort is expended in trying to satisfy the need for all kinds. There is the need for security against hunger and want, which causes people to work to satisfy not only present needs but also the anticipated or dreaded conditions of the future. This need is the basic support of the whole insurance business, as a moment's reflection will confirm. Insurance is merely a device for protection against financial loss that could be injurious—i.e., cause loss of security either for oneself, one's dependents, or others. There is the need for security against the loss of loved ones or one's own life or health. The medical professions, hospitals, and multimillion-dollar medical-research projects are direct outgrowths of the need of this type of security.

Less spectacular, but equally influential in the lives and efforts of people, is the need for security in more subtle and abstract areas: the feeling of need for security after death; the need for security in the love and affection of one's family, a need which, as we have seen, if left unsatisfied in the young child, may later produce serious developmental and adjustment problems; the need for security in the possession or companionship of a loved one, a security threatened by his illness or defection, or frustrated by his death; the need for security in one's position in the community or among one's associates, which makes one willing to do things of some trouble, but expected of us by our friends or group; and most subtle, yet potentially most demoralizing of all if frustrated, the need to appear good, competent, and successful in our own eyes. It is the all-important self concept or "ego drive" of psychoanalytic theory which is threatened by frustration in this area. The two types of security discussed in this chapter were chosen because of the frequency with which they are found to affect profoundly the development and adjustment of adolescent boys and girls.

Security in the love and affection of one's family bears a close relation to the sense of trust discussed in Chapter 2. A child making an adjustment to the world faces a task which would terrify the normal adult. So many things to learn, people to meet, adjustments to make. Fortunately, the child is too lacking in knowledge and experience to be afraid. A sense of trust, acquired from proper care and affection received in infancy, gives the child the confidence to begin his contacts with others and helps him through the inevitable disappointments which arise.

The sense of trust is not enough, however; there will be many experiences which will shake the child's trust in humanity. Then the need for security in the family becomes all-important in the child's adjustment. With such a sanctuary to retreat to for comfort and recovery from the occasionally bruising contacts with the world, the child can try his wings of independence, socialization, new experiences, and the achievement of ambitious goals. If he is rebuffed, if he fails, he knows where he can obtain bountiful love, comfort, and acceptance. Not because of what he accomplishes or how well he can do something, but just because *he is he*. Enveloped in a much-needed feeling of security, he regains confidence and is soon ready to venture forth again for another try at doing things, maturing and developing his skill at dealing with people and the world. In brief, security gives him high frustration tolerance.[27]

The child who does not have such a completely secure place, as he perceives it, in the home of which he is a part, who feels rejected, left out, or feels he must merit the love and earn the security he needs, is at a great disadvantage in growing up and adjusting to life. When the world is temporarily too much for him, where can he go for complete protection and unstinted acceptance and encouragement, to recuperate for another try? Not home; it is another threatening arena of competition. Too frequently he gradually withdraws more and more from the struggle to adjust to the world, and constantly hugs the minimal security he has in his home—not enough to strengthen him to resume his attack on life, but more than he finds elsewhere, more than he is willing to run the risk of losing by getting out and trying things at which he might fail, and thus losing *all* the acceptance he needs.

Perhaps a younger sibling now holds the attention of the parents who once lavished it all on him. Perhaps he is unfavorably compared with an older sibling and feels incapable of deserving love and acceptance, which he vaguely feels must be earned. Perhaps bickering between the parents fills him with a vague, indefinable dread that his home may somehow disappear and that he will not have a Daddy and Mamma to make a home for him. Or even overpraise for good behavior may impress him that if he *doesn't* continue to be such a good boy, Mamma and Daddy won't love him any more.

An infinite number of circumstances may shake the child's feeling of security in his home and in the affection of his parents. Fortunately, natural mother love and father love are usually so strong and so warmly displayed that the potential ill effects of occasional feelings of insecurity produced by various combinations of circumstances are completely dissipated. Love freely bestowed and openly displayed from birth to maturity is the best insurance against the adolescent's having feelings of insecurity.

But if you do have an adolescent who seems insecure, distrustful,

[27] R. Stagner, *Psychology of Personality*. McGraw-Hill Book Company, Inc., New York, 1961.

afraid to venture new experiences socially and every other way, it may be a result of generalized insecurity developing from his home situation. Probably his parents are quite unaware of his unsupplied need for security, and will eagerly rush to do anything possible to make him feel more secure in their love if they recognize the nature of his lack. Sometimes, particularly in the case of a boy or girl without parents, a sympathetic teacher who will show him warm acceptance will be enough moral support to enable him to achieve at least a minimal feeling of security. Try to help the insecure adolescent; his wholesome adjustment to life may be at stake.

The feeling of security, or lack of it, in one's own competence, likelihood of success, personal worth and morality, is usually a determining factor in the formation of the self concept. As the infant begins to do things, engage in activity instead of merely being the recipient of attention and care, he experiences success, failure, mixtures of the two, praise, and reproof. These elements, involved in developing the sense of autonomy and sense of initiative discussed in Chapter 2, are sources of security or insecurity in the child's own evaluation of himself.

The majority of adults developing neuroses, emotional maladjustments, and personality disturbances *do not* do so in response to overwhelming troubles or threats from their environment, from reality. More frequently they develop these troubles as a result of feelings of insecurity originating in a devalued perception of themselves and their ability to cope with the problems of life.[28] Whether, technically, the weak self concept causes the insecurity or the insecurity causes the weak self concept, whether they are different aspects of the same condition or precisely the same factor called by differing names, is a theoretical matter of little practical significance in helping the adolescent. The one whose environment has given him experiences of success, with a sanctuary filled with love and affection into which to retreat to recover from his inevitable bruises, trials, and defeats, will usually have a strong self concept and a gratification of his need for security which will enable him to cope successfully with life's problems. The one whose self concept is weak, inadequate, who has little feeling of security in his ability to achieve, is overwhelmed by quite ordinary problems and only moderately threatening circumstances. He becomes a psychological casualty.

28 J. C. Coleman, *Abnormal Psychology and Modern Life.* Scott, Foresman and Company, Chicago, 1956.

An insidious factor appearing frequently in the insecure person is guilt feelings—anxiety about things he should not have done, should have done but did not do, feelings of unworthiness because of real or fancied defects, and undue concern over minor accidents of socially disapproved behavior for which he blames himself morbidly. Thus we have the insecure person who suffers severe guilt feelings over a normal history of childhood callousness toward a parent, or who feels guilty because one of his children wants a cultural advantage he is financially unable to supply. The circumstances alone are insufficient to produce appreciable feelings of guilt in the normally secure person, but to the insecure person they represent grave threats.

Secure or insecure, people are motivated by their psychological need for security. In the life of the normally secure person, the need for security serves as a mainspring of activity and accomplishment. Because of it he industriously works, cares for his family, cultivates the good graces of his neighbors and associates, and generally exerts himself to perpetuate and strengthen his state of security. The insecure person typically tries even harder, but seldom succeeds in achieving even a vestige of the internal security he needs, although he may achieve a plethora of external security in the form of wealth or social position.

The insecure person fails to achieve internal security because his efforts are misdirected, concentrated on factors which are not the real cause of his insecurity, or because he adopts essentially unwholesome ways of achieving security. In the first instance, he may seek security through improving his material resources and social position, but he gains no feeling of security because his insecurity was not based on the lack of achievement in his adult life in the first place, but on a devalued self concept developed in childhood. This devalued self concept will not be changed by external successes, because it is basically unrelated to present life conditions. In the second instance, he may seek security through withdrawing from active competition, hiding in the shadow of a protective boss, or projecting blame for his lack of greater success onto his boss, his wife who will not help him, or jealous co-workers who knife him in the back.

Questions re Case of Betsy

19. What are evidences of Betsy's lack of a feeling of security?

20. What factors in her environment caused and contributed to her insecurity?

21. Evaluate Betsy's probable feelings of personal worth and competence, and explain the dynamics of her arrival at those feelings.

* * *

Whenever you find it necessary to decipher the reason for a boy or girl's attitudes, actions, or personality pattern, remember the basic drives and needs which are the mainsprings of such a large portion of human behavior. Remember that all deliberate behavior has a cause; none is purposeless. Both the cause and the purpose, if not obvious, merely lie in a more complex pattern or more camouflaged form somewhere in the mind and feelings of the individual. Usually the explanation can be found, if you can learn the details of his past experiences and his relations with parents and other influential figures in his life.

Drives are usually simple and, even though they may be urgent in their motivation, direct in their means of satisfaction. They seldom cause deep-seated problems of adjustment that will not clear up if the immediate physiological need is cared for. Psychological needs are not so. They are complex. They are insatiable, because the need for affection, achievement, and other psychological "food" is never fully gratified, but merely assuaged for the moment. If the psychological needs of the adolescent with whom you are dealing have remained unsatisfied for a long time, his frustrations may cause him to engage in many sorts of maladjustive behavior seeking some gratification of his needs. This makes him a "problem boy" or her a "problem girl." To untangle actions and attitudes having their roots in psychological needs requires professional knowledge and skill, patience, and knowledge of your specific case's history and present circumstances.

When a drive or need is active, a person is in a state of stress. There is within him an unsatisfied condition, a condition of imbalance or tension which urges him into activity, which renders it uncomfortable for him to remain idle and make no effort to satisfy the need or drive. Therefore, normal people usually try to satisfy their drives and needs in order to make themselves physically and psychologically comfortable. Restoring the physiological balance and achieving psychological adjustment is a simple and straightforward matter when the drive or need can be satisfied. When such satisfaction cannot be achieved, however, the tension becomes greater, and the person then seeks means of adjusting to the continued stressful situation. Inability to satisfy drives and needs and to relieve the tension they generate is known as frustration. What happens when drives and needs are frustrated will be discussed in Chapter 4.

READINGS

Baller, W. R., and Charles, D. C., *The Psychology of Human Growth and Development*. New York: Holt, Rinehart and Winston, 1961, Chapt. 6.

Cronbach, L. J., *Educational Psychology*. New York: Harcourt, Brace and Company, 1954, Chapt. 15.

Heyns, R. W., *The Psychology of Personal Adjustment*. New York: Holt, Rinehart & Winston, Inc., 1958, Chapt. 4.

Hilgard, E. R., *Introduction to Psychology*. New York: Harcourt, Brace and Company, 1958, Chapts. 5 and 6.

Lindesmith, A. R., and Strauss, A. L., *Social Psychology*. New York: Holt, Rinehart & Winston, Inc., 1956, Chapts. 9 and 10.

Lindgren, H. C., *Educational Psychology in the Classroom*. New York: John Wiley & Sons, Inc., 1956, Chapt. 11.

Stagner, R., *Psychology of Personality*. New York: McGraw-Hill Book Company, Inc., 1961, Chapt. 15.

Wickens, D. D., and Meyer, D. R., *Psychology*. New York: Holt, Rinehart and Winston, 1961, Chapt. 5.

CHAPTER 4

STRESS AND REACTIONS

TO STRESS

PREVIEW

(The motives which generate human activity are sometimes frustrated, producing tension or stress. The stress of frustration often produces emotions which profoundly affect thought and action. Reaction to stress can be adjustive or neurotic.)

Frustrations

SOURCE	OPERATION
Environment	Circumstances prevent gratification of our motives.
Human relations	The motives of other people direct their actions, often contrary to the gratification of our own motives.
Personal limitations	We are unable to accomplish what is needful to gratify our motives.
Conflicting motives	Sometimes we want two things, and choosing one necessarily frustrates achieving the other.

Emotions

THEY ARE	EFFECTS
Physiological states	Body goes on "war emergency" basis, all resources concentrated for activities required for physical survival.
Mental states	A stirring-up of feelings, which colors one's thinking, reasoning, and reactions.
Motives	Once aroused, emotions themselves become powerful generators and guides of activity, and complicate adjustment to frustrations.

gage in all the activities of human life. From the desire for new experiences come plans for a weekend pleasure trip. From the desire for recognition comes the new car that furnishes no better transportation than the old one, but is a symbol of success and status. More money must be made to buy the car and pay for the trips in it, so the amount of work to be done increases. Opportunity to belong to an exclusive organization comes along. It offers recognition and status, and helps to satisfy the desire for belongingness, but membership costs money and imposes obligations of service and attendance at meetings. And so *more* activities are generated. All come from motives, the goals the motives set, and the activities produced by activities themselves, similar to the necessity for investment of surplus money after it is earned.

Motives impel people to activity because they produce *stress*, a state of imbalance or tension in the physical or psychological constitution. For example, emptiness in the stomach produces an uncomfortable feeling, a type of stress, and the person normally becomes active in an effort to relieve the tension produced by the imbalance. In the psychological realm, when the security of one we love is threatened by serious illness, or their financial security by economic reverses, we experience stress analogous to the feeling we would have if we, ourselves, were the person concerned. And we are impelled by our tensional state of anxiety to try to do something to rectify the situation. *Unsatisfied motives produce stress,* and to relieve the resultant tensions and restore a state of comfortable adjustment within the physiological or psychological constitution requires activity.[1]

FRUSTRATIONS

A major cause of stress in normal day-to-day living is frustration—being blocked in one's attempt to achieve the goal of a motive, and being left in the tensional state of experiencing an urgent drive or need that cannot be satisfied. Necessity to prepare for an important test may prevent the boy or girl from resting to relieve the drive of fatigue or from going with the crowd and fostering the sense of belonging and the desire to be with people. Or one falls in love with someone who does not return the love, and the desire for acceptance is thwarted. Or one wants to go to a movie, but is short of money. Life is full of instances in which we

[1] E. B. Hurlock, *Adolescent Development.* McGraw-Hill Book Company, Inc., New York, 1955.

do not get what we want, in which our desires and strivings are frustrated.

Such frustrations increase the stress aroused by the original motive, because now not only is the unfulfilled motive exerting more pressure as its gratification is denied (the thirsty person gets thirstier, and the prolonged monotony of a hard routine generates increasing desire for something new), but also our egos are involved. We are trying to achieve the goal set by the motive, and failure injures our self concept, making us more tense and further out of adjustment than we were before.

A part of wholesome adjustment to life is the learning of skills and acquiring of habits which lead to achievement of the goals set by our motives. Education's purpose is to enable a child to earn a better living in the future and to enjoy life more fully by reason of the understandings and appreciations, as well as the social and vocational skills, which he has acquired. Despite the most perfect preparation for life, however, frustrations are going to be encountered, and a part of wholesome adjustment is learning to cope with the stress produced by frustrations, either by overcoming the frustrations or adjusting to the stresses which they produce.

Adolescents are in a period of development in which frustrations come with particular frequency, and the resulting stresses are likely to be severely felt because the adolescent has so little background of experience to give him perspective on the frustrations. Not being able to go to the lake with the crowd one Saturday afternoon is, in reality, a trivial thing, but to an adolescent it seems a major catastrophe. However, the frustrations of adolescence *are generally much less far-reaching* in their effects on a boy or girl than were the earlier stresses of infancy and childhood which affected his development of the senses of trust, autonomy, and initiative. Adolescents need help in evaluating their motives and goals and in devising suitable ways of adjusting to their drives and needs either by effectively satisfying them or learning to live more or less comfortably with them without having them satisfied. The girl who longs for greater popularity needs help in satisfying her longing or in devising ways of adjusting happily to the lower level of popularity she may have to accept.

A wise man devised a prayer thus: "Oh, Lord, give me the strength to change those things which I can change, the patience to adjust to those things which I cannot change, and the wisdom to distinguish between the two." It would be difficult to devise a better statement of human needs in dealing with the problems of life: The ability to overcome frustrating factors in our lives, the ability to adjust wholesomely to stresses we cannot overcome, and the wisdom to ascertain whether we should expend our energy in trying to beat down obstacles or to adjust to things as they are.

Sources of Frustration

Frustrations come from several broad areas. *Environment* is a frequent source of frustration, with resulting physiological and psychological stress. The infant cannot reach a bright object because the table is too high. The covers in his crib are uncomfortably warm, but are pinned down so he cannot get away from them. The child wants to be outdoors playing ball, but he must remain in the classroom. The adolescent bursts forth with a crop of pimples just when he or she wishes to appear most attractive. We become sleepy in a college classroom, where it is extremely unwise to satisfy this drive. Rain prevents our going on the picnic. Jammed traffic impedes our progress. A clap of thunder or a barking dog frightens us, disturbing our sense of security. Or the car refuses to start at a crucial moment. Learning to overcome or adjust to such frustrations is a part of life, particularly of growing up. Nevertheless, they are stressful.

Human relations, sometimes called social environment, are another major source of frustration and stress. In infancy and early childhood such frustration usually comes from relations with the parents, who compose most of the social environment of most infants. The baby wants attention, to be petted, but Daddy and Mother are busy getting ready to go to Grandmother's, and until they pick him up to go out to the car he is frustrated in his desire for attention. As he grows older and becomes aware of siblings, he wants from them the same consideration he receives from adults, and is frustrated when it is not forthcoming. The child's ability to adjust adequately to frustration is sometimes shattered, with lasting scars, upon the arrival of a new baby. The stress of this situation may be more than he can adjust to, and he reverts to outgrown, babyish ways of demanding gratification of his desires (a mechanism of adjustment which will be discussed at some length later in the chapter). The child's frustrations range from the trivial—not getting to sit in the chair he wanted to sit in—to the shattering—feeling that a newcomer in the family has displaced him in his parents' love.

As the boy or girl grows older, frustrations of psychological needs by contacts with parents become broader and more numerous, because the boy or girl is seeking to achieve autonomy and identity as a separate personality, and in the process of doing so he wants to go places, do things, and have things of which the parents disapprove. It is important to understand that these intense frustrations emanating from relations with parents may be *noticed* more than the stresses of earlier childhood and infancy, and yet be much less profound in their effect on the boy or girl. The small child has not learned effective ways of compensating for or adjusting to stress, and has little experience against which to evaluate whether a frustration is important or not. Therefore, things which happen to him may leave a deep imprint on his self concept, while an older boy or girl would make ten times the fuss about such a frustration as would the infant or younger child, but, underneath all the noise, would be only slightly and temporarily affected by it. Every year a boy or girl lives has a tendency to produce greater noise but fewer ill effects as a result of frustrations.

From the time the child starts to school, he encounters new elements in the social environment which may frustrate him in the fulfillment of his motives. Instead of only his parents and siblings, there are now in his life dozens of people who really do not care whether or not he is happy or gratified by what goes on. In the past, if he wanted to be "It," Daddy or Mamma was usually willing. His schoolmates are not, and it is sometimes a bitter pill for him to swallow to find that his preferences count for so little. He wants the recognition and praise he has been accustomed to and finds that his playmates give or withhold these favors on the basis of *their* desires, not his. Even Teacher, the important adult in his life now, looks on him as just one more little boy or girl, not as the center of the whole universe!

The broader the child's environment and the more extensive his relations with other children, the more he encounters frustrations based upon his *personal limitations*. He simply cannot draw as well as Allen, run as fast as Johnny, or make people laugh the way Joan can. He tries as hard as anybody, but he simply cannot achieve as much as they can. If his intelligence is below a certain level, he probably will be blissfully unaware of this fact and suffer no frustration. If he has been conditioned by parental attitudes to be indifferent to accomplishments, so long as he is warm and well fed he may be unconcerned over them. "Paw says you get about as much on relief as you do working, so why worry about earning a living?" is an attitude encountered with disturbing frequency in fact, if not in open statement. But children of moderate or above-average intelligence who have a wholesomely competitive attitude toward life often find it most frustrating to be unable to achieve to the comparative level of their age-mates what they set as their goal.[2]

Frustrating personal limitations may come from a combination of personal-environmental conditions. Frances cannot get the part she wants in the school play because she cannot dance, and her family is unable to afford private dancing lessons for her. Or the costume would cost more than her parents could afford or are willing to spend. William makes the basketball squad and knows he could make All-Conference, with a college scholarship in prospect, if only he could practice more, but he cannot—either because he has to work part time, because he has to study harder than the others to keep from being dropped from the team for academic reasons, or for some other unalterable reason.

Going a step further along the same road of William's economic-academic-athletic conflict and frustration, we arrive at what is potentially the most demoralizing of all the sources of stress frustration: *conflicting motives.* Adolescents frequently have contradictory desires.[3] Edgar wants to go to camp for a week, but it would mean leaving his ill and widowed mother alone. He is torn between love and normal juvenile desires; either decision will cause a severe frustration, producing feelings of guilt on the one hand and resentment on the other. Norma wants to go with the crowd to the corner drugstore every afternoon to eat potato chips and a chocolate malt—and this is what "everybody" orders—but the first thing the doctor told her was, "No chocolate or greasy foods when you have skin trouble, young lady!" She wants to eat like the crowd and wants a clear complexion too, but she cannot have both. Sol wishes to assert himself by defying his boss, yet fears the loss of his job. All these are conflicts within the person, between two wishes he has which are mutually incompatible.

One of our most common and powerful sources of internal conflict, of conflicting wishes which inevitably frustrate us in one area or the other, is conflict between our desires and our conscience. Sex, which is both a biological drive and a psychological need, is rigidly repressed in our culture by social pressure and religious principles. From adolescence

2 H. C. Schumacher, "Mental and Emotional Disturbance in Adolescence," *Journal of Child Psychiatry,* 1948, *1:*113–120.

3 O. Fenichel, *The Psychoanalytic Theory of Neurosis.* W. W. Norton & Company, Inc., New York, 1945.

onward, both boys and girls, men and women, frequently find themselves in situations where the sex drive is intense, highly aroused, but gratification is inhibited by conscience. So the drive is frustrated. Or gratification is sought regardless of conscience, and one's self concept is injured as the sacrifice of principle and moral integrity results in self-devaluation.

Internal conflicts have been classified under three headings: (1) approach-approach conflicts, occurring when one wants to do two things but must sacrifice one to achieve the other, such as go to a ball game or prepare for an exam; (2) avoidance-avoidance conflicts, where two alternatives would each be avoided but one must be accepted, such as arising for an eight-o'clock class after a late dance and breakfast on the way home, or taking the cut which will jeapordize credit for the course; and (3) approach-avoidance conflicts, where one wants to do one thing and avoid another when this is impossible, such as wanting to ask someone a favor, yet being unwilling to be placed under obligation to him. All types may produce more or less grave frustrations.

Case of Carolyn

The social worker left the J.'s house mentally shaking her head. Mrs. J. had called saying that her family badly needed help. Mr. J. had had a serious heart attack several months before and would not be able to work again for several more months. Mrs. J. was working in a department store as a clerk while her semi-invalid husband looked after their two small children, but her earnings were insufficient to support the family. As the worker left the house, she was met by Carolyn J., sixteen, who obviously had been waiting for her.

"Maybe you can help me, Mrs. Hughes," said Carolyn. "Somebody's got to or I'm just going to *die!* There's this dance our class is having Saturday night, and there's this cute new boy all the girls are simply *wild* about, and he's asked me, and I haven't got a thing to wear. Mother just won't listen. There's this darling strapless dress down at the store where she works, and you can get it for just a dollar down, but she just can't *see* how I've simply *got* to have it. I've tried to tell her I'd do *anything*—I'd cut out my allowance, look after the children, *anything!* But she still says I can't have it. I'll eat less, I'll do anything! Can't you talk to her and get her to realize how I just *can't* go unless . . . I've *got* to go . . . it means more than anything on earth to me . . . and I just *can't* wear . . ." Here Carolyn burst into tears.

The social worker overcame her first impulse to give her a bawling-out as a selfish brat, adding to her mother's already heavy load instead of helping her carry it.

1. Why was Carolyn so intent on her own pleasure and oblivious to the grave problems her family, and particularly her mother, labored under?

2. How did environment, human relations, and personal limitations each contribute to Carolyn's frustrations?

3. What is the possibility that Carolyn is also suffering from an internal conflict of motives? How might her actions reflect such a conflict?

4. How might the social worker help Carolyn?

EMOTIONS

Emotions are subjective experiences, hard to define and explain in scientifically approved language. There is no general agreement among psychologists as to the precise mechanism by which stimulation of the optic nerve by one approaching figure produces the reaction of running away, and by another the reaction of opening the arms for an embrace. Yet for practical purposes, it is desirable to have a substantially accurate concept of what emotions are, what causes them, and the effect they have on an individual.

Leuba[4] writes, "An excited state is especially likely to occur when obstacles and threats give rise to intense muscular tensions, producing an extreme degree of kinesthetic stimulation, and there are few ready outlets in the individual's repertoire of habits for the nerve impulses thus created." This concept is a valuable one in working with boys and girls. We might add that anticipation or experience of pleasurable conditions likewise has the capability of giving rise to intense kinesthetic stimulation.

Teachers, counselors, and parents will find it practical to consider that emotions are closely related to motives, that frustration or gratification of motives tends to produce emotions. For this hypothesis to be workable, we must think of motives not as a few conspicuous impulses, but, as discussed in Chapter 3, the mainsprings of all human activity. Considered thus, the death of a companion constitutes frustration of the

[4] C. L. Leuba, *Man: A General Psychology*. Holt, Rinehart & Winston, New York, 1961.

Robert E. Lee High School, Montgomery, Alabama.

Figure 5. What emotions are shown here? What could account for the different reactions of the people in the picture?

desire for companionship, a deprivation of the gravest sort, and the emotion of grief results. A scratch on the fender of a new car causes stress or tension in the owner because his investment (of pride as well as money) deteriorates as a result of it, a different but very real sort of deprivation. Threat of losing one's job forebodes frustration of the desire for security and produces anxiety. Excitement over the prospects of going to a ball game, on the other hand, is the result of anticipated gratification of the desire for new experiences, a desire to escape from loneliness or routine, or perhaps gratification of the desire for social acceptance or approval if going as one of a group. Most, if not all, emotions which you will find complicating the lives of boys and girls you work with can be traced to frustration or gratification of their motives, or the prospect of such frustration or gratification. These frustrations or gratifications produce tension or stress within the boy or girl—Leuba's ". . . extreme degree of kinesthetic stimulation . . ." for which "there are few ready outlets in the individual's repertoire of habits. . . ." [5]

Although not all-inclusive, the crude equation, MOTIVE + GRATIFICATION OR FRUSTRATION (*or perhaps some other factor?*) → A STATE OF STRESS → AN EMOTION, constitutes an effective framework for understanding and helping adolescents with their adjustment to life.

Emotions, then, may be considered, for practical purposes, as the stressful feelings produced by the gratification or frustration of motives. We often overlook the fact that satisfaction of motives often produces emotions, as witness the joy (an emotion) of a girl whose wish to go to a dance with a certain boy is gratified by his asking her to do so. Observe the triumph of the boy who gets the car motor started after others have failed, or his excitement in a pleasantly tense moment of a movie. But gratification-induced emotions are not as significant in dealing with adolescents as are frustration-induced emotions, because the former usually leave the person well adjusted and satisfied, while effort and wisdom are required to cope effectively with the latter. Therefore, although gratification of motives can produce emotions, only cursory reference will be made to them, the "pleasant" emotions. The unpleasant ones are the ones which cause most of the problems of adjustment, so we will concentrate on them.

A full discussion of the nature and physical concomitants of emotions can be found in any textbook of general psychology. Such a discussion is unnecessary here, but at the same time a brief examination of certain aspects of emotions is necessary as a background for understanding human behavior, adolescent or other. This is because emotions are not merely

[5] C. L. Leuba, *Man: A General Psychology.* Holt, Rinehart & Winston, New York, 1961.

states of feelings which are pleasant or unpleasant to a person. Emotions are aroused by all sorts of situations and conditions—loss, deprivation, thwarting, inabilities, the whole range—but once aroused, emotions become powerful forces in and of themselves.[6] Sometimes they actually come to overshadow in importance the very situation that produced them. Thus we have the child who wants a pretty pencil which, for some reason, is not given him. Frustration arouses emotion: he becomes angry. He rages. At last the parent gives in and offers him the pencil, which the child strikes from the offering hand in a paroxysm of rage. Or we have the tennis player who becomes so angry at flubbing several shots (thus losing points) that he deliberately knocks an easy ball completely over the backstop, thus losing still another point, but securing, it is hoped, some easement of his emotions. In both of these instances emotion has become, for the moment, a more powerful determinant of behavior than was the wish whose frustration produced the emotion. In addition to these situations, it is also important to understand that when an emotion is aroused in a person, certain bodily and mental changes take place, and these changes alter the person's subsequent thoughts and actions.

To understand human behavior, therefore, it is necessary to know some of the dynamics of emotions. We have seen, briefly, how they are a particular type of tensional state often growing out of stress, out of frustrations, or sometimes out of gratifications. Three important aspects of emotions govern their influence on thoughts and actions. We will consider these aspects as a background for understanding adolescents' thinking and actions which take place when frustrations have aroused emotions. Boys' and girls' thinking and behavior often cannot be fathomed without an understanding of the emotions which control them.

Bodily Changes in Emotion

The autonomic nervous system is a part of the nervous system and consists of nerves connecting the brain and various internal organs of the body, including blood vessels which serve various muscles of the body.[7] There are two parts to the autonomic nervous system, and these two parts tend to oppose rather than assist each other. One part is called the "parasympathetic" system. This system is in control of the functioning of our organs and circulatory system most of the time. It is the "house-

6 K. F. Muenzinger, *Psychology*. Harper & Brothers, Publishers, New York, 1942.

7 W. B. Cannon, *Bodily Changes in Pain, Hunger, Fear and Rage*. Appleton-Century-Crofts, Inc., New York, 1929.

keeping" or "business as usual" system of control of the organs and functions of the body. Under its direction the stomach manufactures and secretes digestive juices and carries on the normal digestive processes. The kidneys, liver, heart, lungs, sweat glands, all function at the rate and in the manner most desirable to get their normal jobs done and to keep us feeling good.

When an emotion arises, the functioning of the parasympathetic system tends to diminish, and the other portion of the autonomic nervous system, called the "sympathetic" system, springs into action and takes over predominant control of our bodily functions. The sympathetic system is the "emergency" or "war control board" of the body and produces changes in the functioning of bodily organs designed to prepare the body to cope with the tension-producing situation which threw the sympathetic system into action. In exciting emotions, such as anger (as contrasted to depressive emotions, such as grief), the adrenal glands of the body are stimulated to secrete a substance called adrenaline into the blood. The presence of adrenaline in the blood going to various organs produces many of the bodily changes accompanying emotions. The liver releases stored sugar into the bloodstream to provide energy to cope with the exciting situation, and the lungs enlarge to supply oxygen to the body in a hurry in order to support increased activity. The chemical composition of the blood is changed so it will clot more quickly, and another substance simultaneously fed into the blood, called noradrenaline, causes the blood vessels near the surface of the body to constrict. Thus nature tries to protect us against loss of blood (which, you realize, is a logical concomitant of anger among animals or primitive humans) by having less blood in the portions of the body most exposed to injury and having that blood coagulate faster if bleeding starts. It has even been found that tears shed as the result of an emotion have a different chemical composition from those shed in peeling an onion! [8]

The nature of the "waves" habitually produced by the brain changes in emotional states, and in some states of emotion the amount of blood received by the brain is decreased. Thus, the brain may literally be on "starvation rations" during a strong emotion and physiologically incapable of its normal functioning. This was reasonable in the eons of man's history when emotions most frequently meant the perception of danger, and muscular action, not brainwork, had the best chance of insuring his

[8] R. Brunish, cited in *Saturday Review of Literature*, 1957, 40:41.

survival. Unfortunately, the same physiological reaction has carried over into the present, when brainwork is more frequently needed than muscles to cope with an emotion-arousing situation. Thus we experience the unhappily common phenomenon of doing and saying things under the influence of emotions which we would never do or say if our brains were working properly. Threats to beat up people, proposals of marriage, and promises obviously impractical to keep are examples of the by-products of things that often happen under the influence of a strong emotion, which would not have happened if the person involved had been thinking instead of feeling.

Although considerable physiological differences have been found to exist in different emotional states, attempts to identify emotions on the basis of physiological changes accompanying them have been unsuccessful.[9] All emotions involve some degree of upset of the homeostatic condition of the body and are, therefore, tensional states. There are many physiological accompaniments of emotion besides those mentioned here, but these will serve to establish the important point that a person under the stress of an emotion *is chemically and physiologically a different person,* with different mental and physical capabilities than he usually possesses, and his behavior must, therefore, be evaluated on a different basis from that used when he is in his normal condition.

Emotion as a Mental State

This is the aspect of emotion most familiar to us. It is "feeling" a certain way—excited, happy, afraid, sorry, depressed, anxious, or other states described by a thousand other words. These states of emotion are often referred to as "affective states" or "affective reactions," and our popular use of this concept is reflected in such expressions as "The experience affected him deeply." It has been already pointed out that although emotion is in part a mental state, it is often a mental state of lowered thought quality in which a person is more influenced by nonintellectual feelings than by intellectual considerations. A boy or girl wildly in love, a parent seeing a child drowning, a person insulted in public, none are likely to act in a manner reflecting their normal best judgment. Under all these conditions the mind may be overactive, filled with whirling, chaotic thoughts, and although sometimes brilliant flashes of inspiration emerge from such mental activity, usually irrationality

[9] C. T. Morgan, *Introduction to Psychology.* McGraw-Hill Book Company, Inc., New York, 1961.

rather than sensibility characterizes the thought processes under such circumstances.

Mild emotional states sometimes develop and endure for long periods of time. Worry, a mild fear reaction anticipating a future situation or condition which may or may not materialize, is an example. Annoyance, a mild form of anger, usually is of short duration. When emotional states persist for more than a few moments they usually are called moods.

Often a person feels an emotion but does not show it openly or admittedly. This is of extreme practical importance to the person dealing with the education and guidance of adolescents. A boy or girl may resent very much certain treatment, a casual reprimand, a condition, or someone's personality, and not show it by facial expression or his words, but signal it loudly in his subsequent behavior. Therefore, while it is important to recognize the physical and cognitive effects of emotion, it is equally important to be alert to behavior which may signal an emotional state not perceptible in any other form.

You have perhaps encountered people who seemed to have a gift for sensing the worry, anger, or fear of others and responding to a person's *feeling* rather than to the picture he presents to the casual observer. This ability is called empathy, meaning the ability to perceive, understand, and to some extent share the feelings of another. Empathy is one of the greatest professional skills the worker with adolescents can possess. A high degree of empathy enables a parent, teacher, or counselor to see beneath the surface indications of feelings and behavior and respond to an emotional state which the boy or girl may, through self-consciousness or insecurity, conceal, but which dominates his reaction for the time being, even though he presents an outward picture of calmness. Probably some people are born with the potential of achieving higher empathy than others, but like other skills or sensitivities, empathy can be developed greatly by conscious practice. To work most effectively with adolescents, one should practice careful attention to their words and facial expressions and, perhaps above all, mentally check back for possible explanations of the behavior the adolescent is presently engaging in to try to ascertain if there is anything causing it besides what appears on the surface.

Empathy is not a "sixth sense"; it is a highly developed use of our ordinary five senses, plus skill at deducing the motivation or stimulus behind what a person is doing or saying. It is required even when the emotional state of the person with whom you are concerned is obvious, because it enables you to better understand why he feels as he does and, therefore, more intelligently respond to him. It is even more necessary when an emotional state exists but is being concealed, because such an emotional state is likely to be extremely critical in the situation being handled. (If it were not critical, there probably would be no reason for the boy or girl to conceal it.) Often, too, empathy enables the adult to perceive the influence of an emotional state in an adolescent when the adolescent is not himself aware that his feelings, rather than his logic, are dictating his actions. Often a girl who arrives at school in a state of irritation actually does not realize that she *is* irritated. To admit she is irritated would mean admitting that she *minds* that Hank didn't pick her up on the way, and, she tells herself, of *course* she doesn't mind! Not one bit! In such a situation the adult must avoid reacting to the surface appearance of feelings and behavior. He must also allow for the fact that often the reasons for the attitude or behavior exhibited are not even perceived by the adolescent himself.

Emotion as a Motive

Emotions may arise when a motive achieves gratification, or when such gratification is blocked. In turn, an emotion itself may become a motive, which also may be gratified or blocked, thus constituting a spiral of experience, reaction, new experience, new reaction. We have seen that emotion is a tensional state, a state in which the homeostatic condition of the body and mind has been altered. One explanation of the effect of emotions on thinking and behavior is that emotions cause tension, and as tension develops, *the relief of the tension becomes a motive.*[10]

Examples of this phenomenon are extremely common among small children and often encountered in adolescents and even adults. The child wants to go outside and play, and his desire is frustrated by Mother's concern about the weather. Not only is little Ray's desire frustrated; his developing ego, his sense of autonomy, is also outraged. You can watch the tension rapidly building up, the reddening face, the clenched fists, the tenseness coming into his voice. He becomes angrier and angrier. He seems literally to "puff up." But his demands have no effect. He tries the door in order to go out anyway, and it is locked. He throws himself on the floor, kicks his feet against the floor, pounds it with his fists, and perhaps even his head. We call it a temper tantrum. It may be persisted in if it gains him attention, but whether it gains attention or not, it ex-

[10] G. Murphy, *Personality*. Harper & Brothers, Publishers, New York, 1947.

pends some of the tension generated by the frustration and resulting anger. That such temper tantrums are not wholly attention-getting devices, but may even be totally tension-relief mechanisms is evidenced by the man who reads in the paper something that angers him, crushes the newspaper, hurls it violently into the trash can, and walks on at a furiously fast pace, clenching his fists and pumping his arms vigorously. Abraham Lincoln recommended chopping wood as an excellent device for relieving the tension developed by anger whose natural manifestation (fighting, perhaps) was blocked.

Paroxysms of grief are frequently accompanied by extreme muscular activity (called hysterics), which serves to relieve some of the excess tension generated in the body by the activity of the sympathetic nervous system. Violent weeping, the whole body shaking with sobs, relieves tension, as can be seen in the weak, exhausted state which commonly follows such violent discharge of emotional energy. Joy similarly produces an excess of energy, tension "all built up and no place to go." Common appreciation of this fact is shown in such expressions as "leap for joy" and "bursting with happiness." Emotions, therefore, often constitute a powerful urge to activity, either to further gratification, remove frustration, or merely to release the unbearable internal tension (stress) which the emotion has produced.

We have already seen that emotions are not conducive to logical thought and reasonable reactions. So it is, therefore, not surprising that when emotional tension builds up to a certain point, *relief of the tension,* regardless of the consequences, may become the overwhelming motive of the individual. Some naturalists say that a wasp knows it will kill itself if it stings a person, but when sufficiently enraged, it will vent its anger regardless of the consequences to itself. Whether this is true or not, we do know that a man sufficiently angry may hit a much bigger man, despite the obvious fact that he will not really injure his Goliath, but will receive a beating for his attempt.

This circumstance, the power of an emotion to provoke activity for the sheer purpose of relieving unbearable tension, regardless of its futility as a means of genuinely coping with the emotion-producing situation, is of tremendous importance in dealing with people. The younger the person, the more important it generally is, because young people customarily will engage in relieving the tension, rather than in coping with the situation intelligently, more readily than will adults. It accounts for the pupil who fails a test and becomes furiously angry, but then goes to play ball instead of studying to do better next time, and the man who, anxious over threatened failure of his business, goes on a week-long drunk just when his best efforts are needed most to salvage his business. Both are examples of tension-relief activity being substituted for action intelligently designed to handle the emotion-producing situation.

Case of Dick

Dick T. is fourteen years old and in the tenth grade, where he is barely passing despite an I.Q. of 120. At his parents' insistence, he had been permitted to skip the sixth grade because of his high I.Q. and exceptionally good work in the fifth grade, although school authorities had agreed somewhat reluctantly. Surprisingly, Dick did fairly well in the seventh grade, although not as well as his parents demanded that he do. In the eighth and ninth grades his marks steadily slid down, despite growing parental disapproval and pressure.

This year Dick has suffered from stomach trouble, with frequent vomiting. Often he does not seem well enough to prepare his homework, and he sometimes leaves school because of nausea. He complains of constant tiredness and seems depressed. Worry over his physical health has superseded anxiety about his grades in the minds of his parents.

At times Dick shows a wild, ungovernable temper; he stamps, yells, and voices wild threats toward both himself and others. A low grade, a reprimand, or refusal of an apparently trivial request can bring on the tantrum.

Finally, the parents have sought the help of the school counselor, saying that Dick needs help on how to study. You are the counselor.

1. Which of Dick's problem areas may have their roots in emotional reactions?

2. How could each one be emotionally oriented?

3. Why may Dick's problems have "come to a head" just now?

ADJUSTMENT TO STRESS

Emotions are typically reactions to stress produced by frustration or other factors. But emotions, though they may be reactions to stress, hardly constitute effective ways of adjusting to the stresses. In fact, as previously noted, they are more likely to increase the stress produced by a frustration than to cope effectively with the situation producing it.

And so people devise many procedures, often called mechanisms, for coping with stress. An understanding of some of these mechanisms will often enable a parent, teacher, or counselor to perceive the motivation behind things adolescents say and do, thus enabling the adult to deal with causes of adolescent behavior rather than with the mere superficial symptoms.

In most instances, a person encountering the frustration of a motive either devises a way of achieving gratification and thereby avoiding the frustration, experiences an emotion for a time and adjusts to the frustration as the emotion wears off, or just philosophically accepts the frustration with minimal concern, "without letting it bother him," as the popular expression goes. These are generally wholesome, even if sometimes unwise, ways of handling a frustration: overcome it, get it out of your system, or adjust to it, i.e., do not let it bother you.

Many more subtle and indirect devices than these straightforward ones also are employed to achieve one sort of adjustment or another to stress. Any of these devices may be perfectly normal if employed in moderation, but they tend to become maladjustive or "neurotic" devices if carried to an extreme. Thus, it is normal, when faced with a frustration, to try to beat it down and achieve gratification, as does a boy with a weak tennis volley by intensively practicing volleying against a practice wall. It becomes a maladjustive rather than an effective adjustive pattern of re-action when one is unable to do anything else because all his resources are being futilely expended on persisting in an obviously lost cause of trying to gain a certain end. A 120-pounder losing match after match through insisting on trying to out-volley bigger, stronger opponents would be an example. We say such a person has an obsession on that point.

In general, adjustive mechanisms are wholesome when they enable one to make a constructive adjustment to a stressful problem or situation, and unwholesome, maladjustive, or neurotic when they merely constitute a screen behind which the person can avoid making a genuine adjustment. Generally, avoiding an argument, refusing to become involved in a fuss, is a constructive way for an adolescent to adjust to a situation in which emotions are running high. It becomes maladjustive behavior when "keeping peace" or "restraining my temper" is used as an excuse for failure to stand up for important principles. Being agreeable to the wishes of the group ordinarily suggests good social adjustment; it does not when it causes one to go along with the group into delinquent behavior. When a boy is unable to buy something he wants, it is healthy for him to think of ways he can get along satisfactorily without it. It is maladjustive for him to form the habit of saying to himself every time he cannot get something he wants, "Aw, it's no good. I don't want it anyhow."

Often adjustive mechanisms are used quite unconsciously. This is especially true of maladjustive mechanisms, whose injuriousness lies in their causing or permitting us to see a situation in one way, when actually it is quite another way. The girl who blames a low grade on the teacher's dislike for her instead of trying to find what was wrong with her preparation is a good example of such distortion of thinking. Do not expect an adolescent immediately to agree with you when you point out to him that he is blaming someone else for something that is his own fault; often he *genuinely believes* what he is saying, because his explanation defends his ego, his self concept, more effectively than would a clear perception of the facts. Therefore, he is genuinely unable to see the real facts without patient, sympathetic help in arriving at a better understanding of his motives and frustrations. His desires also blind him to logic. The boy who wants to use his sturdy, serviceable sedan as down payment on a small, high-performance sports car may emphasize to his father the economy resulting from the small car's high gasoline mileage. If the father attempts to change his son's mind by demonstrating how the gasoline savings will never offset the greater cost of the new car, he is doomed to failure, because economy had nothing to do with the boy's real reason for wanting the sports car.

It is well to understand a few of the common methods of dealing with stress and to perceive differences *in degree* which make them normal adjustive mechanisms or abnormal neurotic defenses. It is well to understand them, because adolescents as well as adults often employ these devices when faced with stress-producing situations. If the parent, teacher, or counselor does not understand the dynamics involved, he may be thrown off the track and try to react to the adolescent's behavior on the basis of meeting apparent logic with logic, whereas the apparent logic may not be at all the adolescent's real reason for thinking or acting as he does. The real reason, underneath the camouflage of assumed logic, may be his having adopted a completely irrational mechanism for coping with stress. Obviously, if he is to be genuinely helped, the *real dynamics* of his behavior and attitude must be considered rather than the camouflage he has drawn over them (often unconsciously).

Case of Ernest

(*Read this brief picture of Ernest F. and his life, and as you study this section on adjustment to stress, watch for descriptions of ways Ernest has adjusted to life. At the end of the section there will be questions to help you clarify your thinking about Ernest and the mechanisms of adjustment.*)

Ernest F. sought help from the college counselor for "difficulty in concentrating." He is nineteen years old, a sophomore in college, of average size and build, reasonably good-looking and healthy. He estimates that he is "about average" in popularity and social adjustment. His major professor guesses that he is barely average in intelligence as compared to the population of the college he attends, but by virtue of hard work he maintains a B average. He participates in all intramural athletics and is substitute second-baseman on the varsity baseball team.

His father is the sole owner of a fair-size machine shop, a four-letter man at the college Ernest is attending, and obviously anxious that his son be successful, a leader. Ernest's mother is a pleasant woman, active in civic affairs in her town, where Ernest's siblings, two older sisters, have married and are living.

Ernest described his childhood as a happy one, his family moderately prosperous and enjoying life and each other. "We were always doing something," he said. "Dad would take me hunting every weekend during the fall from the time I was big enough to stagger along with a twenty-gauge shotgun. I could never shoot as well as he could, but I could spot squirrels or handle a bird dog better, so I kept right up with him. I got along fine with everybody except my basketball coach; he tried to boss every move I made on the court, and I would kick over the traces every once in a while. I was the smallest man on the varsity, and got put out of a lot of games for personal fouls or blowing up at some big jake who tried to step on me."

Ernest just missed being valedictorian in his high-school class. "The girl who got it wasn't practicing basketball all afternoon for four months of the term," he explained. He started going with girls when he was fifteen and "could get a date any time I wanted to, but sometimes I'd stay home from something because I couldn't get the girl I wanted to go with."

Ernest says he is happy, likes his courses and professors, and is having a good time in college. But he feels on edge and irritable and thinks this may in some way be connected with his difficulty in concentrating.

Aggressive Reactions

Attack. This is the simplest and most natural way of dealing with a stressful situation when you are confident, when the situation does not appear so big, threatening, or inevitable that attack seems hopeless or even suicidal. Unless a child has suffered acute emotional deprivation in infancy or early childhood, he will ordinarily respond to a frustration, for example, with an attack upon it.[11] Another child has a toy he wants and cannot otherwise get, and he will aggressively attempt to remove the frustration by physically taking the toy from the other child. A manufacturer threatened by the loss of a big contract will undertake to do something to stop the undesired from happening; he will try to persuade his customer, find other facilities to supplement his own which have broken down, halt the strike which has closed down his production, or by other direct action remove the threat.

A long succession of defeats or emotional conditioning which leaves one with the feeling of helplessness, the idea that he cannot overcome obstacles or threats, may make attack seem impractical to him. The child whose older sibling successfully annoyed him and always succeeded in making him feel inferior may have developed a defeatist attitude which makes him chronically hesitant to commit himself to attack as a way of getting what he wants. The child who was overprotected, not allowed to cross the street alone until he was eight years of age, or who was always "helped" to do things because "he's such a little fellow and we can do it so easily," or whose parents, kindly or unkindly, but *persistently,* added just a bit more to what the child had done "to fix it exactly right"—all are prime prospects for reluctance to meet difficult situations head on and try to overcome them. Such a child grows up into the adolescent whose deficient sense of initiative, autonomy, and achievement prevent his making a wholesomely aggressive attack on circumstances which threaten or frustrate him.

Overemphasis on "never leave a thing until you have mastered it" may produce a boy or girl neurotically inclined to attacking frustrations, not necessarily as reasoned attempts to overcome them (which char-

---

11 R. Stagner, *Psychology of Personality.* McGraw-Hill Book Company, Inc., New York, 1961.

acterize, of course, a desirable adjustive mechanism), but because he is emotionally unable to concentrate on new subjects while the frustrating condition continues to exist and he does not know a more effective means of coping with it than blind persistence in attack. The tennis player who was losing match after match because of his insistence on volleying is an example.

Displacement. If circumstances render it impractical or unsatisfactory to react aggressively toward a source of stress, the hostility aroused by the stress and the aggressive behavior we would ordinarily direct toward the unpleasant stimulus may be "displaced" onto something we can attack or resent with less threat to our well-being.[12, 13] The boy who, as a child, was strictly trained that he *must* love his mother may become very angry at her, but conceal it from everyone and even from himself by displacing his resentment of her prohibition or punishment onto a girl friend with the violent statement that "Doggone gurrls got no sense, anyway!" Thus, he finds some release from his tension, but does not run the risk of greater stress through direct attack on the object disturbing him. A similar principle operates in the case of the boy who, out with his girl, accepts a dressing-down from a traffic policeman and then snarls at a service-station attendant who is (or, more probably, is just thought to be) slow. This is sometimes known as the "kick the cat" mechanism of adjusting to stress. It is "normal" in that all of us do it to some extent. It is an essentially unwholesome mechanism of adjustment, however (except in such mild forms as railing against the obstinacy of other drivers because it is unsafe to lambaste a friend who has irritated us in some way), because it tends to conceal real causes of stress and thus blocks effective coping with them.

Projection. Projection involves ascribing to others feelings or motives we ourselves have, thus serving the double purpose of absolving ourselves of blame for a tensional state and acquiring an object against which to exhaust the feeling disturbing us. A common example is the irritable girl who angrily accuses her parents of being bad-tempered, citing as evidence the fact that they irritate *her,* who, goodness knows, is as smooth-tempered a person as you can find! The boy who slights a

---

12 R. R. Bush and J. W. M. Whiting, "On the Theory of Psychoanalytic Displacement," *Journal of Abnormal and Social Psychology,* 1953, *48:*261–272.

13 N. E. Miller, "Theory and Experiment Relating Psychoanalytic Displacement to Stimulus-Response Generalization," *Journal of Abnormal and Social Psychology,* 1948, *43:*155–178.

friend and defends himself in his own mind by accusing the friend of indifference is another example. This mechanism is particularly useful in providing an alibi for failure to do, or justification for doing, something we want to do. If we have a passing twinge of guilt about keeping someone talking until he is late for class, we easily pass it off by saying, "Oh, he was enjoying it as much as I was." Or if we dislike someone, we interpret anything he does or says as evidence of his dislike for us. One of the most transparent examples of projection is the fielder who muffs a ball and unbelievingly scrutinizes his innocent glove for the hole through which the thing *must* have passed. As with displacement, projection is a basically unwholesome mechanism of adjustment in that it removes from ourselves responsibility for making the needed adjustment.

Identification. "If you can't lick 'em, join 'em" represents a common way of dealing with situations which are a little too much for us. Prisoners of the Nazis in World War II sometimes identified with their captors, adopting their values and even imitating their uniforms.[14] The fat and lazy boy loses some of his feelings of frustration over his inactivity by knowing every detail of the athletic performance of an outstanding baseball player. Adolescent girls strongly identify with movie stars, thus vicariously sharing some of the glamour they possess instead of being limited so closely by gawky bodies and pimply faces they possess and are unhappy with. Small boys gain prestige in their own eyes by the ideal they carry of their father as a brave, strong, skillful man.

In most instances, identification is a relatively helpful and wholesome way of easing ourselves through frustrations.[15] Parents achieve through successful children more sense of achievement than they were able to attain themselves, and usually no harm done. People *usually* pick more or less admirable persons to identify with, from the neighborhood policeman in the case of the four-year-old boy, to the athletic hero of the adolescent and the successful businessman of the adult. Obviously, it becomes unwholesome if the identification proceeds to the point that one tries to live his life through the other person. The overpossessive parent who lives like an incubus on the life of a son or daughter is an example of identification carried to a neurotic degree, harmful not only to the iden-

14 B. Bettelheim, "Individual and Mass Behavior in Extreme Situations," *Journal of Abnormal and Social Psychology,* 1943, *38:*417–451.

15 R. R. Blake and J. S. Mouton, "Personality," in P. R. Farnsworth and Q. McNemar (eds.) *Annual Review of Psychology.* Annual Reviews, Inc., Palo Alto, California, 1959.

tifier in that it stultifies his life, but to the person identified with, who is thereby denied his rightful life of independence.

Withdrawal Reactions

Simple Withdrawal.   The girl who feels she cannot compete success-fully with her age-mates for social status and popularity may drop out of social activities rather than continue to encounter frustration in her at-tempts to achieve the desired status. The boy whose suggestions in class are regularly met with disapproval may shut up and cease participation in discussions. These are examples of escaping stress-producing situations by avoiding the situations in which frustrations are likely to occur, by withdrawing from those aspects of life whose activities may cause stress.

As in the case of virtually all adjustive mechanisms, within reason this device is good. As was noted earlier, it is maladjustive to continue striving in areas where frustration is inevitable. The danger of withdrawal as an adjusting mechanism is that it may make the person gradually less and less willing to encounter the hard knocks which inevitably ac-company grappling with life and living it to the full. It is so easy just to cut out an activity with which you are having trouble, and thereby not run the chance of failing and encountering frustration.

As people give in to fear of failure and avoid challenging situations, their self concept is weakened; they begin to conceive of themselves as people who *must* avoid, because they cannot overcome, difficulties. This devalued self concept lessens their competence to meet the problems of life, and thus makes them encounter frustrations ever more frequently. As more and more activities become taboo to the boy and girl because of the frustrations they might encounter, their pattern of living becomes more and more restricted, until much of the best of life is denied them because they are afraid to try to reach out and take it. In its extreme form such withdrawal may eventuate in schizophrenia, in which the in-dividual may completely lose touch with reality and live a mere vegeta-tive existence.

Denial of Reality.   Most of us avoid unpleasant things when we reasonably can. We look away from a bloody accident. We do not get around to doing an unpleasant job until we are forced to. We develop a headache or vague stomach upset when the time approaches to go to a class or a meeting we would like to avoid. Loving relatives quite often refuse to admit the actuality of serious mental deficiency on the part of children, citing their verbatim memory of frequently heard TV advertisements as clear evidence of intelligence. Sometimes the denial of reality involves "escape *into* reality," in which one becomes so busy doing inconsequential things that he never has time to get around to the really important problem or task he needs to face. Thus, the girl who does not wish to prepare the book report due tomorrow suddenly *must* clean up her room, as Mother has been insisting for a week that she ought to, and by the time this chore is done it is bedtime, and there was simply no time to prepare the report.

Ignoring things which are unpleasant permits us to avoid many stressful situations. Unfortunately, it may also cause us to ignore things which need to be faced. Many people have died of cancer because they feared to face the possible revelation of a physical examination.

Fantasy. Daydreaming, fleeing from the unpleasant world in which we live to an imaginary world in which we can make things happen just as we wish, is one of the most popular forms of withdrawal from frustrating or otherwise stressful situations. Some boys use detective stories, and girls romantic novels, as the magic carpets to carry them into the land of make-believe, some use the changing screen of the TV set, and some construct their own imaginary scenarios. Daydreaming is a pleasant and harmless way to entertain ourselves and temporarily escape from a situation that we are not enjoying. It becomes harmful if it begins to take the place of constructive adjustment to life, if the boy or girl constructs imaginary worlds to live in rather than making the real world a good one for him or her. Carried to an extreme, such fantasy is called autistic thinking, in which the dreamworld may gradually become more real to the dreamer than the real-life world around him. Teachers and parents can aid adolescents to keep within healthy limits by helping them find ways of achieving real-life successes or satisfactions.[16]

Repression. This mechanism involves refusing to recognize stressful thoughts or feelings. The adolescent may have a strong hostility toward a parent, but his emotional conditioning makes him feel that this is wrong, so he simply refuses to admit that the feeling of enmity is there. It is buried even deeper than in the mechanism of displacement, where it finds relief in a slightly disguised form. The girl forces her mind to the thought of how much she should love her mother, how good she is to her and how much she *does* love her, whenever the horrifying thoughts

16 H. C. Smith, *Personality Adjustment*. McGraw-Hill Book Company, Inc., New York, 1961.

of hostility arise. This is one of the less wholesome adjustive mechanisms, because it prevents a person from facing his thoughts and feelings and intelligently trying to do something about them. It provides a convenient rug under which odorous scraps can be swept for concealment, but, thus sheltered, the "forgotten" unpleasant objects eventually make their presence known in a variety of ways, all unpleasant.

Regression. When a younger sibling is born, a four-year-old may revert to crawling and bed-wetting, reassuming the time when he was the undisputed center of family attention.[17] Adolescents often change from swaggering, independent teenagers to frightened children wanting to be held in parents' arms when they become sick, get in trouble with the law, or are crushed by an unhappy love affair. These retreats from stress involving adoption of behavioral or emotional characteristics of an earlier age are known as regression. Usually they are temporary, disappearing as soon as the individual becomes adjusted to his new situation and gains some confidence in his ability to cope with it. When continued over a period of time, this is, of course, a definitely undesirable reaction.

Compromise Reactions

Compensation. Compensation is emphasizing one's strength or ability in one trait as a means of concealing a weakness in another. The girl who is rather low in physical attractiveness, but who cultivates an unusually pleasant manner and a flattering air of attentiveness to her male companion, is a good example. Sometimes the compensation is undertaken within the very area of weakness. Gene Tunney and Theodore Roosevelt, both of whom deliberately set out to overcome frail physiques, are outstanding examples. They carried their compensatory adjustments to the extent that one became a boxing champion and the other a hunter of legendary endurance. This degree of making up for a deficiency is referred to as "overcompensation." The bully is a common example of compensation, capitalizing on his physical strength to atone for an inner feeling of inferiority. Generally compensation is a wholesome defense mechanism, but, like all others, it can be neurotically distorted, as it indeed is in the case of the bully. Lonely people frequently eat too much, satiating a bodily hunger to compensate for a psychological one. Insecure people may try to deny their insecurity by brashness or flamboyant display. Thus we have the lonely adolescent girl who eats for consolation

[17] G. F. J. Lehner and E. Kube, *The Dynamics of Personal Adjustment.* Prentice-Hall, Inc., Englewood Cliffs, N. J., 1955.

and the boy who fails a course and becomes a behavior problem. Defying authority is a trait frequently earning the admiration of adolescent boys.[18] A boy who is physically underdeveloped or lacking in social skill will sometimes use delinquency as a means of impressing his fellows.

Compensation is sometimes carried to the extreme of developing the opposite attitude or behavior from the one which originally caused the feeling of inferiority or guilt. An individual with sexual inclinations which disturb him, and which he feels he must frustrate for moral or social reasons, may quite unconsciously develop a puritanical attitude and become the loudest, most vociferous opponent of real or alleged sexual misbehavior, lewd literature, or suggestive movies. "Methinks the lady doth protest too much," says Shakespeare, showing a precocious awareness of the psychologically confirmed tendency of people to conceal a feeling by a conscious display of the opposite one. This mechanism is known as "reaction formation."

Sublimation. Sublimation is escape from threatening wishes or inclinations through finding a more socially approved way of expressing the feelings. As Freud [19] originally conceived the term, it referred to substituting innocent activities as an outlet for sexual urges; dancing as a socially acceptable means of satisfying a desire for close bodily contact with a partner is often cited as an example of sublimation. The term "sublimation" is also often used in the broader sense implied in the first sentence, and the example previously cited of Lincoln working off his fury against a stick of wood instead of a human being is a good one.

Technically speaking, it is doubtful whether a drive or need can be satisfied by a substitute activity. Dancing may actually arouse instead of exhaust sexual drives, and one's desire to hurt someone will hardly be removed by chopping wood. There is, however, little room for doubt that sublimation is at least a partially effective means of adjustment, because, as we have seen, almost any sort of activity which serves as an outlet for the tension accompanying a strong feeling at least lessens the psychological and physiological stress, making some return to homeostasis possible.[20]

Rationalization. This would certainly rank as one of the most commonly used means of evading a frustration. It consists in doing whatever

18 C. M. Tryon, "Evaluations of Adolescent Personality by Adolescents," *Monographs of the Society for Research in Child Development*, 1939, *4*, No. 4.

19 S. Freud, *Three Contributions to the Theory of Sex*. Random House, New York, 1938 (English translation).

20 I. M. Josselyn, *The Happy Child*. Random House, New York, 1955.

one has decided to do and then constructing a plausible justification for having done it, so one does not feel guilty or evasive of duty. It is substituting a fake reason for a real one, usually where the real one would not justify what one is going to do. This is a dangerous device, because by it we train ourselves to think faultily and accept specious nonsense as sound logic. A classic example of rationalization is the defense of a Sunday-morning golfer whose companion remarked to him that they really should be at church instead of on the golf course. The golfer explained, "But I couldn't have gone to church this morning even if I hadn't played golf—my wife is sick, and I would have had to stay home with her."

Questions re Case of Ernest

1. What are possible frustrations in Ernest's life, and from what do they spring?

2. What mechanisms can be identified or inferred as means he has employed to cope with the frustrations?

3. Have his adjustments been healthy, or unwholesome? How?

4. How might Ernest's difficulty in concentration be accounted for?

THE DEVELOPMENT
OF NEUROTIC REACTIONS

It is normal for a person to overcome, avoid, or adjust to frustrations and the stress they produce. If, through inability to do any of these things, the person is left with a feeling of stress that he cannot bear, he may resort to one of the self-deceptive or artificial evasive mechanisms just discussed. If used in moderation, those mechanisms may enable the person to achieve fairly adequate and comfortable adjustment to life situations which otherwise would be unbearable to him. A boy may live fairly comfortably, if not happily, with the fact that a girl chose another boy in preference to him if he can maintain the self-deception that it was because his rival had a newer car, not because of his own jealous disposition. True, this is not a procedure which argues well for his future development, because it focuses his attention on false issues and conceals from him his own deficiencies and need for improvement, but it keeps him from devaluating his self concept to an injurious extent.

Sometimes, however, stress builds up to such a degree that adjustive mechanisms such as sublimation or fantasy cannot bring even minimal essential comfort to the individual. The sharpness of the feelings of frustration he experiences penetrates the attempts to lay the blame on others, follows him into the world of fantasy, turning his dreams to ashes, and vitiates his attempts at rationalization. He erects more and more elaborate defenses, but they, too, crumble as stress grows greater.[21] Their very crumbling frustrates him still more; now he cannot even explain away his failures or hide from situations which seem to threaten him; he has failed even at explaining and hiding.

When this happens, when the person becomes unable to cope with life either through direct adjustment or the normal use of defense mechanisms, he is said to be neurotic. Just as a person whose body has been unable to cope with its physical environment may be incapacitated by malaria, frostbite, or hepatitis, this person is partially or wholly incapacitated psychologically. Such a person is mentally ill, although psychotherapists usually try to avoid use of this term in talking with him because it is so upsetting. Few adolescents reach this stage of incapacitation; with rare exceptions, adolescent self concepts are strong enough, their use of defense mechanisms skillful enough, to avoid neurosis. Even though progressive deterioration of psychological mechanisms of adjustment and increasingly overpowering stresses may eventually bring on a neurosis, such a development will usually be held off until past the adolescent years. However, it is well for the worker with adolescents to recognize signs of incipient neuroses, not for purposes of diagnosis or treatment, because this requires the skill of the clinical psychologist or psychiatrist, but in order to recognize boys and girls who need to be referred for examination and possible treatment.

The expression is often heard, "Everyone is neurotic to some extent." This statement is worthy both of criticism as a rationalization which may conceal from recognition a maladjusted condition which should be treated, and of praise as a common-sense warning not to interpret all out-of-the-ordinary behavior as evidence of neurotic tendencies.[22] Is not everyone physically sick to some extent—i.e., would not a comprehensive physical examination reveal something less than perfect in everyone? In the same way, anyone will at times display some of the symptoms of

21 R. S. Lazarus, *Adjustment and Personality*. McGraw-Hill Book Company, Inc., New York, 1961.

22 S. W. Ginsburg, "The Neuroses," *Annals of the American Academy of Political and Social Science*, 1953, *286*:55–64.

neurosis, especially adolescents who are subject to numerous stresses and who have not yet acquired adequate skills in adjusting to them. Such symptoms are normal unless they are more than transient symptoms—here for a few weeks, then replaced by others—and unless they reach the point of serious interference with one's adjustment to life. So be sensibly alert to evidence of serious maladjustment (often referred to as "personality disturbances") in the boys and girls with whom you work, but do not see a neurosis in every instance of a girl displaying anxiety because she may not be asked to join a sorority, or a boy complaining that everyone has it in for him.

Contrary to popular opinion, a person who enters adolescence with a well-developed self concept, having achieved normal maturation in the developmental tasks set forth in Chapter 2, seldom becomes neurotic. Certainly, such people sometimes do, but seldom. The person who makes a normal adjustment to life during adolescence and a wholesome transition from adolescence to adulthood even more rarely develops later neurotic reactions. In short, in the overwhelming proportion of instances, the seeds of neurosis are sown in the personality development of infancy and childhood, and most of the remainder in adolescence.[23] Lack of wholesome development in infancy and childhood prepared the ground and sowed the seed of later neurosis.

Coleman[24] outlines the typical dynamics of the development of neurotic reactions as follows:

(1) An inadequate personality, insecure from early deprivation of affection, immature because of failure to have developed a strong sense of autonomy, accustomed to distortion of thought and feelings as defense mechanisms, or having other structural weaknesses,

(2) is exposed to ordinary stresses of life, and because of weakness and inadequacy perceives these stresses as terribly threatening and dangerous.

(3) Perception of such threat and danger, along with low ability to cope with stresses, due to faulty personality development, causes

(4) retreat to neurotic use of defense mechanisms, including, but not limited to the ones mentioned earlier.

23 H. C. Smith, *Personality Adjustment*. McGraw-Hill Book Company, Inc., New York, 1961.

24 J. C. Coleman, *Abnormal Psychology and Modern Life*. Scott, Foresman and Company, Chicago, 1956.

(5) Resorting to these neurotic defenses, instead of constructively coping with the stresses, devaluates the self concept and deprives the person of the development of competence in dealing with stress situations, and thus doubly weakens the individual in his ability to deal with future stresses and completes a vicious circle.

Anxiety, beyond that which people normally experience, over ego-threatening or self-threatening stresses, anxiety carried to the point of *paralyzing* effective coping with the stress, is the most frequent trademark of the neurotic reaction. Symptoms and manifestations of neuroses cover such a wide range that anything approaching an enumeration is impractical; almost any emotional response, and many mental ones, under certain conditions can be a neurotic indicator. However, here are some of the most common symptoms of neurotic conditions. It will be seen that most of them grow out of faulty personality development and devalued self concepts.

Anxiety

This is the most common of neurotic symptoms, as well as an actual result of the breakdown of adjustmental mechanisms,[25] although in advanced cases it may have been replaced, at least on the conscious level, by other symptoms which more effectively conceal from the neurotic his basic inadequacy in adjusting to life situations. Neurotic anxiety is often "free-floating"—that is, it is an emotional state that will attach itself to any situation or circumstance. The neurotic girl will worry about whether a letter she wrote hit exactly the right note or whether she put the stamp on it, whether she will fit into the group at the party next Saturday night, whether the telephone call she missed was terribly important, whether she really deserved the A she received in English, or if the teacher just gave it to her because she felt sorry for her, and on and on. The anxiety is generally a camouflage for a deeper source of anxiety unrecognized by the sufferer. Therefore, it will flit from one thing to another, because none of the multitude of things about which the person is anxious is the real thing bothering him; they are merely convenient objects for the anxiety generated by an unconscious condition to fix on.

25 H. Basowitz, H. Persky, S. J. Korchin, and R. R. Grinker, *Anxiety and Stress.* McGraw-Hill Book Company, Inc., New York, 1955.

Phobias

Phobias are fears which persist in the absence of objective bases for fear. An example is the boy who has a persistent fear of contracting typhoid fever, a completely unfounded fear because his activities do not expose him to such a danger. Just as anxieties usually are disguises, the phobia is usually a cover-up for a fear of something the individual *has* done or experienced, but represses facing and learning to live with. Sometimes, however, the fear is a direct result of a specific experience, as in the case of a child who, frightened by a vicious dog, retains a lifelong fear of all dogs, even small or gentle ones.

Tenseness

This is a natural concomitant of anxiety. Psychological and bodily resources are held in an intense state of readiness to react to whatever threat or stress may arise. Such a state of hypertension tends to result in overreaction to stimuli of all kinds. Praise or criticism may produce more pleasure or deeper resentment than normal because the person is already in a state of some emotional mobilization, and merely triggering off, not arousing, the emotion is all that is necessary to produce the reaction. Similarly, success or failure may produce elation or depression completely out of proportion to the objectively considered circumstances.

Poor Insight

Most people can pretty shrewdly recognize their tendencies to exaggerate, to worry more than is normal, and occasionally to respond by self-deceptive devices instead of facing situations squarely. The neurotic is typically less able to do this. The neurotic boy will insist that Bill and Jane and Okie get along with people because they are just naturally well liked, that if people naturally resented and disliked them as they do *him*, they would feel exactly as he does. Such a rigid, dogmatic pattern, excluding logical analysis, is necessary to the neurotic because he is afraid to face an examination of his real self. Blindness to real conditions is his defense against the danger of being confronted with personal defects, thoughts, or motives too terrifying to face.

Chronic Fatigue or Somatic Complaints

Habitual fatigue is a common symptom of the neurotic, attributable to two circumstances (besides actual physical debility of some sort):

(1) chronic hypertension, which maintains a constant drain of energy, producing fatigue when most people would develop none; and (2) the means of escape it furnishes. An exhausted person is an object of sympathy; people understand why he does so little or is irritable, and they want to help him. Equally important, he himself actually feels fatigued and, therefore, is able to face his lack of accomplishment or maladjustive behavior with less injury to his ego. Oh, he would be such a ball of fire if only he were like other people and not absolutely worn out all the time!

Fatigue is often accompanied or replaced by somatic complaints, usually rather vague and prone to change in nature from day to day, but sometimes specific and persistent. This reflection of psychological trouble through physical complaints is called hysteria or conversion reaction.[26] Of course, if an organic basis exists for the physical complaint, the person is not considered neurotic. If none is found, and headaches, strange sensations in the stomach, oppressive feelings around the heart, back pains, and other complaints succeed each other, a neurotic condition is indicated. It should be understood that these pains or sensations are *real;* they are actually *there,* and the person cannot turn them off simply by *wanting* to do so—and they hurt just as much as if they were organically caused.[27] Neurotics are often the victims of utter cruelty and inhuman treatment because ignorant people do not, or cannot, grasp the fact that a neurotic headache is absolutely as painful and uncontrollable by the sufferer as one caused by a brain tumor.

Guilt Feelings

As a result of his general inadequacy and inability to appraise circumstances realistically, a neurotic person may develop severe guilt feelings over things he has done, has not done, has thought, has not thought, or has felt or not felt. Typically, the guilt feelings will be attached to some trivial matter, because they will be merely a camouflage through which the neurotic inflicts self-punishment for a real or fancied guilt so horrendous or threatening to his ego that he cannot admit its existence. Thus, the adolescent boy may display tremendous concern over his envy of a classmate who won a coveted honor, castigating himself without

26 J. C. Coleman, *Personality Dynamics and Effective Behavior.* Scott, Foresman and Company, Chicago, 1960.

27 R. S. Lazarus, *Adjustment and Personality.* McGraw-Hill Book Company, Inc., New York, 1961.

mercy for his improper attitude. In so doing, he may be easing his conscience, by undergoing punishment for his sin, of the burden of an unconscious hostility toward a sibling or parent. The latter hostility might be too severe to admit into consciousness, but the tension produced by its existence in the unconscious could be at least partially dissipated by self-punishment for a similar, *but more acceptable,* offense.

Feelings of Inadequacy

This is one neurotic symptom of which the neurotic is commonly aware, although this is by no means always the case. He simply feels incapable of meeting the demands of life. Sometimes he overcompensates for these feelings of inadequacy by exaggerated independence, brash overconfidence, and refusal to accept advice or assistance. In other cases he will seek the support of a stronger or more aggressive person, often content to live in his shadow, under his protection, even at the cost of never achieving the potential which his ability would otherwise enable him to. Thus, a girl with strong feelings of inadequacy may insist on refusing even normal assistance in doing things expected of her. Or she may attach herself to a confident, dominant person, tacitly claiming protection in return for faithful vassalage. Such personalities are understandably unwilling to enter into competitive situations and, if through overcompensatory efforts they do so, will attach abnormally great importance to defeat or success.

Egocentricity

In the presence of all the foregoing conditions accompanying neurosis (and most neurotics will display several of them to a strong degree), it is not surprising that the thoughts, feelings, and behavior of the neurotic are conspicuously self-centered. The boy who feels inadequate, fears failure, is chronically and desperately tired, tense, and anxious, can hardly be expected to think of and consider others rather than himself.

Social Maladjustment

Being egocentric, inadequate, and extremely defensive and hypersensitive, the neurotic typically finds it difficult to get along with people. It is hard for him to form a successful close personal relationship with anyone. Even the neurotic relationship inspired by overdependence is likely to be transient, as the more normal person is alienated by the neurotic's attempts at possessiveness, his anxious jealousy, his essentially negative outlook on life, and his oversensitivity to imagined slights.[28] Warm, natural relations with people in general become increasingly difficult as the rigid, unrealistic, hypersensitive nature of the neurotic promises his acquaintances little inspiration, pleasure, or congeniality. Lack of social success furthers the feelings of inadequacy, and adds another round to the vicious circle.

Chronic Unhappiness

Under the conditions described above, could you be happy? In this respect the neurotic might be said to react normally. He is not happy either. Unfortunately, he does not know how to break out of the vicious circle, because the defenses he is using are the best he knows. And if he is uneasy and inadequate *with* them, he unconsciously says, "What on earth would I do *without* them?"

Neurotics are often difficult to help, because they developed their neurotic defenses in the first place to avoid facing unpleasant facts or conditions, or to escape from unacceptable thoughts or feelings. Stripping away the defenses by which the unconscious guilts, fears, or other factors are kept repressed below the level of awareness would reveal the very things which produced the psychological necessity for the defense mechanisms. Therefore, neurotics may pathetically cling to their symptoms (in reality, their defenses) with pitiful tenacity.

To adjust happily and successfully to life, people must learn to live with their motives and unavoidable frustrations and emotions they encounter in life. Failure to do so results in the neurotic conditions just described. Successful integration of motives, adjustments, handling of frustrations and emotions, and the developmental factors discussed in Chapter 2 produces a wholesome personality in a manner which will be described in the next chapter. Some of the "personality types" produced by the maladjustive reactions we have just considered also will be further described in Chapter 5.

Case of Dick

(*Review case digest on Dick on p. 110.*)

The counselor, in an attempt to help Dick, began to gather more background material from him and his parents. Dick has twin sisters,

---

[28] R. Stagner, *Psychology of Personality.* McGraw-Hill Book Company, Inc., New York, 1961.

now nine years old, of whom he seems quite fond. Parents report that he has "mothered" them since he was about ten, although prior to that time he resented them, and when they were about a year old, he was found making them cry by bumping their heads together.

Dick was born when his parents were both twenty years old. Birth and infancy were apparently normal. He was breast-fed for a month and then bottle-fed because of illness of the mother. When Dick was eight months old, further illness on the part of his mother necessitated her hospitalization for several months. During this time he was cared for by his father's younger, unmarried sister, who kept the apartment for her brother while Mrs. T. was in the hospital. Dick was slow to adjust to his aunt and almost equally slow to re-establish confidence in his mother when she returned from the hospital. The father was absorbed in anxiety about his wife during this period. Mrs. T. did not fully regain her health until Dick was about two years old.

During the years when Dick was from two to five, his mother "tried to make up for all the time I couldn't look after him properly." She worked hard to teach him nice manners and "keep him looking nice." He required very little punishment; abundant praise for good behavior and withdrawal of affection for bad was sufficient. When he was six, Dick had a brief recurrence of bed-wetting, which soon ceased when the parents followed the pediatrician's advice to "just ignore it." When he was nine, he stuttered for a few months, but this, too, disappeared without special treatment.

Dick's father says he was always an obedient child, eager to please and crushed by a reproof, "and still is, except when he's in one of his rages." The parents think these began "three or four years ago."

Recently Dick has manifested some desire to increase his associations with girls. He has made awkward attention-getting efforts in the presence of some of his sisters' older friends, but has never had any real heterosexual associations.

4. Describe Dick's probable self concept.

5. What have been the principal stresses in Dick's life?

6. What neurotic behaviors are revealed in Dick's history and present circumstances?

7. What factors in his life would tend to make Dick susceptible to neurotic maladjustments?

8. What would be involved in helping Dick?

READINGS

Coleman, J. C., *Abnormal Psychology and Modern Life*. Chicago: Scott, Foresman and Company, 1956, Chapt. 3.

Johnson, D. M., *Psychology, A Problem-Solving Approach*. New York: Harper & Brothers, Publishers, 1961, Chapts. 2, 9.

Leeper, R. W., and Madison, P., *Toward Understanding Human Personalities*. New York: Appleton-Century-Crofts, Inc., 1959, Chapt. 8.

Morgan, C. T., *Introduction to Psychology*. New York: McGraw-Hill Book Company, Inc., 1961, Chapts. 3, 4, 5, 6.

Ruch, F. L., *Psychology and Life*. Chicago: Scott, Foresman and Company, 1958, Chapts. 5, 6, 7.

Smith, H. C., *Personality Adjustment*. New York: McGraw-Hill Book Company, Inc., 1961, Chapts. 5, 11, 13.

Steckle, L. C., *Problems of Human Adjustment*. New York: Harper & Brothers, Publishers, 1957, Chapt. 3.

Wickens, D. D., and Meyer, D. R., *Psychology*. New York: Holt, Rinehart & Winston, 1961, Chapt. 7.

CHAPTER 5

PERSONALITY FORMATION

PREVIEW

("Personality" is all aspects of the individual which influence his inter-relations with his environment—a broad definition.)

The Development of Personality

MAJOR COMPONENTS	OPERATION
Intelligence	Influences the interpretation of and ability to devise effective reactions to the environment.
Attitudes	Emotional predispositions to interpret and respond to experiences in certain ways.
Interests	The motive of curiosity, new experience, or achievement focused on specific areas.
Reality testing	Discriminating between one's desires, feelings, thoughts, and beliefs and reality. Promotes rational reactions to life and experiences.

The Healthy Personality

CRITERIA

Toleration of external threat
Dealing with guilt feelings
Capacity for effective repression
Balance of rigidity and flexibility
Planning and control
Self-esteem

Common Distortions of Adolescent Personality

Anxiety states	Feelings of inferiority	Rebelliousness
Immaturity	Bullying	
Lack of self-discipline	Withdrawal	

Case of Fred

Fred G. is nineteen years old and a sophomore in college, where he makes average or slightly below-average grades. He is a member of a fraternity and is popular both within it and among the student body generally. He is a stocky, husky youth, average in appearance, active socially, and well liked by girls. He is an avid supporter of all his college's teams, but does not participate in any sports except interfraternity leagues where he conscientiously does his best for his fraternity in any way possible. He has a liberal allowance which he spends freely, without regard to whether or not his liberality will be reciprocated. He is known as an unusually unselfish person who likes every-

Robert E. Lee High School, Montgomery, Alabama.

Figure 6. "Personality includes the impression one makes on others, but also includes the ego image, the self concept, he holds."

body, knows everybody, and is known and liked by everybody. According to his scores on entrance examinations, he could be making considerably higher grades; he admits he does not study as much as the average student and ought to do better, but also adds that there are so many more interesting things to do than study that he will probably do no more than just pass his courses for a degree in business administration. He has no clear vocational plans.

Fred's father is traffic manager for a brewing company and has always provided well for his family. He is a huge, bluff man who conceals a violent temper under a genuinely friendly nature. The men who work under him like him, although they consider him a driver. His softer side shows at home, where he has always been indulgent to his wife and children. Even in his not infrequent rages he only roars and complains, never striking or threatening members of his family. He works hard, is on the governing board of his church, and a member of several social and fraternal organizations. He drinks moderately and holds to higher-than-average moral standards. He is, perhaps, somewhat partial to Fred and has always indulged him freely. He seldom made the boy do much of anything he did not want to, and was inclined to laugh off Fred's juvenile misdemeanors. Relations between the two have always been sufficiently good that Fred genuinely has tried to do what his father wanted in most instances and, considering the liberty he was given and the permissive atmosphere of his home, really did or failed to do very little which would call for reprimand or punishment.

Mrs. G. is a small woman, interested in people, but a little shy. She looks after her men and looks forward to her daughter being able to help her do so soon. She entertains well and frequently, mostly business acquaintances of her husband's. She and her husband talk over family problems and "don't bother the children with those things." She wants her children to enjoy life fully, but to adhere to high moral principles in so doing.

Fred always got along well with his brother (fourteen) and sister (twelve), probably somewhat better than the usual boy. He was given a car when he was sixteen, and used it extensively for dating and to ferry his many friends around. He let them buy gasoline for the car, although he never asked them to do so, and from the time he was sixteen he worked vacations and some weekends at a grocery warehouse to earn money to supplement his rather generous allowance.

Parents agree that Fred worked hard and conscientiously. He was treasurer of his high-school senior class, and attended as many social events during high school, it is safe to estimate, as any other person in the school! He received no formal sex education from his parents, but picked up a wide assortment of sex lore from his many friends. He has had sexual relations with several girls, although he does not attempt to become intimate with all his dates as a matter of course. He says that he has some guilt feelings about this conduct, of which he knows both his parents would disapprove, but with an engaging grin says that he will never overpersuade a girl nor "do her wrong." He has never gone steady, and was one of the few boys socially active in his high school who did not do so.

Mr. and Mrs. G. take their children to church with them, and Fred has always been active in his church's young people's activities. Since going to college, he says, he is "not quite as regular" in church attendance, but holds a minor office in his Sunday-school class.

Questioned about his hopes and plans for the future, Fred is vague. He'll get a job. Some day, no doubt, he'll marry. In the meantime he'll sort of take things as they come. Maybe he'll take a little part next year in campus politics; he has met a few times with a student group vaguely "liberal" in their convictions who have a desire to make their college more "progressive." Fred doubts that he will affiliate himself with that group; he says they are "against" various things about the college, but do not seem to have any constructive ideas. He regards himself as an "extrovert" and says he probably does not take life as seriously as he ought, "but I'll settle down when I get started in a career."

(As you read the sections entitled "The Nature of Personality" and "The Development of Personality," try to identify the principal forces which made Fred into the person he is at the age of nineteen, as described in the case digest. Specific questions will follow these two sections.)

THE NATURE OF PERSONALITY

Allport[1] defines personality as "the dynamic organization within the individual of those psychophysical systems that determine his unique

[1] G. W. Allport, *Personality: A Psychological Interpretation.* Holt, Rinehart & Winston, Inc., New York, 1937.

adjustments to his environment." This is a serviceable concept of adequate accuracy for the understanding of and effective work with adolescents. It merits close analysis, because the implications resident in words and relations of words in the definition carry a fuller portrayal of the entire concept of personality than casual reading of the sentence conveys.

Personality is "dynamic." It is not static, either in form or effect. Personality changes as experiences change, habits change, and thought patterns change. Personality, in turn, changes our effectiveness in coping with various situations and the views others have of us, and these altered influences exert pressures which change the personality. Personality not only can be changed, as bodily weight can be changed by attention to diet; it also changes in the natural course of living, without our conscious effort, as weight fluctuates if one eats just what comes naturally without a thought of gaining or losing.

Personality is an "organization of psychophysical systems." This organization can well be thought of as a dynamic balance of forces, as when a half-dozen puppies are pulling their mightiest in a half-dozen different directions on an old coat, with the result that it is moving and changing shape at all times, and shifts in one direction or another as the balance of forces playing on it changes force, nature, or direction.[2] An infinite number of environmental forces affect the formation of personality. Whether an adolescent's skin is clear or covered with pimples affects the physical appearance he presents to others. It also affects the feelings he has about being with others, and what he thinks they think about him, and these feelings are reflected in his manner toward them, which, in turn, affects the response they make to him. Whether an adolescent's life has been one of security and comfort or strife and frustration will not only have affected his personality, but the personality thus influenced will affect the future nature of that life. Such seemingly diverse forces as job success, social acceptance, climate, clothes splashed by a passing automobile, an attractive store window, suggest the wide range of environmental forces which produce lesser or greater, more or less permanent, alterations in personality.

Hereditary forces certainly have an indirect effect on personality. Physical beauty, which strongly influences the course of personality development, is largely a matter of heredity, even though art has found

2 M. M. Shirley, *The First Two Years*, Vol. II. University of Minnesota Press, Minneapolis, 1933.

many ways to improve upon nature. Improper glandular functioning or optimum glandular balance is almost certainly influenced to some degree by heredity, and may incline an adolescent to be lethargic or vivacious, calm or excitable, with corresponding influence on the personality.

The self concept, discussed in Chapter 2, is formed by and simultaneously interprets and alters the effects of both heredity and environment. The influence of this force produces different results in the lives of different individuals, even though they may have very similar hereditary backgrounds, and be reared with only slightly differing environmental influences.

Personality is "within the individual"; it is not merely the superficial impression the individual makes on people. (Here you will note the difference in the concept of personality held by the psychologist and the one held by most laymen.)[3] Personality is the self concept, plus other things as well. It includes the impression one makes on others, but also includes the ego image, or self concept, he holds. The impression made on people is the outward manifestation of the personality, but not the core of it.

Personality "determines . . . adjustments to . . . environment." This implies that it determines whether the two-hundred-pounder decides to go out for the football squad, quit college altogether and take up professional boxing, or become a psychologist. It determines whether the physically unattractive girl retreats from life or determinedly makes herself attractive through developing such a pleasing manner that people scarcely notice what she looks like. It determines whether the boy responds pleasantly to praise and with hostility to criticism, ignores both, or tries by charm to win praise and prevent future criticism. Personality determines whether Wally runs or fights back when assaulted, and whether he cries or grits his teeth when hurt. It even determines whether Martha will try consciously to alter her personality or live with what seemed to come to her naturally.

Careful analyses of the foregoing paragraphs will reveal why many textbooks in psychology do not include a specific chapter on personality formation. Personality formation is in a sense the sum total of everything the science of psychology considers; it is the title of the book, not of a chapter in it. But this book is a study of the dynamics of adjustment of adolescent boys and girls, not general psychology. In this chapter, with

3 D. W. MacKinnon, "The Structure of Personality," in J. M. Hunt, *Personality and the Behavior Disorders,* Vol. I. The Ronald Press Company, New York, 1944.

the concept of personality just analyzed as our frame of reference, we shall briefly recapitulate some of the elements in personality formation already mentioned and a number of elements not previously discussed, exploring how they are integrated into an adolescent's personality. In other words, after having studied the parts, we shall examine ways in which they combine to produce a whole, a personality which is not a conglomeration of traits and characteristics tossed together but an integrated, synchronized organism which functions as one unit. We shall also examine some examples of boys' and girls' personalities in which successful integration of all necessary components of personality has not been achieved.

Questions re Case of Fred

    1. In what ways does Fred's history substantiate the idea that the personality is dynamic?

    2. Does Fred's pattern of development suggest a conflict between his heredity and environment, or their mutual reinforcement of each other? In what way?

    3. How has Fred's personality influenced his adjustment to his environment?

THE DEVELOPMENT OF PERSONALITY

Obvious personality development begins with the baby's ability to be aware of things and respond to them, although technically it might be said to go back even further to whether the infant was a boy or girl, whether it was the sex the parents desired, and whether or not it was healthy.[4] All these factors will subtly affect the atmosphere the infant perceives in his environment long before he is conscious of their significance. Then he becomes able to make responses, and the outward manifestations of his personality are easily observable. He passively accepts his environment or reacts actively to it. When a stranger approaches him, he coos invitingly or is indifferent or shows fear or resentment, and the responses he receives from *his* responses affect his future perception and responses. By this time the beginnings of a unique personality are obvious. He likes a toy of one color better than a similar one of different color. He watches the cat more attentively than the dog, or vice versa.

    [4] N. L. Munn, *The Evolution and Growth of Human Behavior.* Houghton-Mifflin Company, Boston, 1955.

So we can safely infer that he has already acquired the beginnings of preferences, interests, and attitudes. A number of such factors exert a powerful, if not dominant, influence on the personality structure and development.

The development of certain factors of personality such as trust and security were discussed in Chapter 2. Now let us examine some other crucial elements influencing personality development.

Intelligence

Somewhere in these early months intelligence undoubtedly begins to play a significant role in the infant's development. The child who learns faster, who "picks up cues" from his environment more alertly and accurately than another, is thereby not only making a different impression on those with whom he comes in contact, but is actually becoming a different sort of person in fundamental make-up from the one who fails to note things happening around him or responds less effectively to them. One infant may perceive, for instance, a basis for trust or for distrust, where another may not.

How early can a child's memory be impressed by complex material, as contrasted to merely being impressed by pain and comfort? It is not known. However, trying to find out, one father read his fifteen-month-old son selections in Greek daily for three months. Without having heard these selections again, the boy at the age of eight memorized them in 30 per cent less time than he took to memorize selections of Greek which he had never heard before.[5] This is significant support for psychologists who believe that babies are conscious of and affected by much more of what goes on around them than most people believe. Thus, it is reasonable to assume that the child's innate intelligence, his ability to remember and probably to reason in an elementary way, probably begins to play a major role in his acquisition of attitudes, reaction patterns, and perceptions at an extremely early age.

Of course, intelligence is only one of the hereditary influences affecting the early development of factors which, in their totality, constitute personality. Glandular predisposition to activity or passivity, wakefulness or fretfulness, influence parents in the amount of cuddling and petting they give the infant. The amount of cuddling and mothering makes a different impression on the child depending not only on his receptivity

5 H. Burt, "An Experimental Study of Early Childhood Memory: A Final Report," *Journal of Genetic Psychiatry*, 1941, *58*:435–439.

to it but also on the intelligence he applies to his perception and interpretation of the petting. Furthermore, each such experience colors the
way he will feel and, therefore, the way he will act the next time he is
picked up.

Awareness of himself as a distinct individual is probably a great mile-
stone in the personality formation of the child.[6] The self concept has
probably been developing for months before the infant becomes aware
that he is actually an independent element of the universe. Many simpler concepts of what Mamma and Daddy are—simpler because they
can be perceived in terms of behavior of which he is conscious—seem to
precede baby's awareness of what *he* is. What is the difference between
the thing on the end of me (shoe) that comes off sometimes and the
thing on the end of me (foot) that does not? Why does it not feel good for
the thing to get hot while it is on the end of me, but doesn't hurt at all
if it is off? What is the difference between a bottle in my mouth and in
the mouth of that baby over there? From such primitive perceptions
gradually emerges the concepts of I and me.

We have noted how intelligence influences personality development
through the different responses produced by different degrees of intelligence. Intelligence may produce even greater effects on personality development through the habits of using it which children acquire, and
their methods of using it. Janie uses her superior intelligence to attract a
playmate whom she likes by thinking up an attractive activity. Joan uses
hers to plan a good substitute activity when her friend does not respond to an invitation to come over and play. Enough such experiences
and Janie grows up into a person unusually good at socializing and unusually popular. Joan matures as a pleasant person of considerable reserve, self-sufficient and proud of it. Sol is of average intelligence, and
early conditioning has made him desirous of pleasing his parents. To do
this he tries to adapt to the study program laid out for him and make
good marks in school. Olin's relations with his parents are not such as to
make their approval or disapproval highly important to him. His intelligence is turned to finding ways to avoid the things he does not
want to do. Thus, the intelligence which Sol and Olin apply to their
problems accentuates divergent personality development, the conformist
versus the person primarily bent on pleasing himself regardless of others.

6 R. Strang, *An Introduction to Child Study*. The Macmillan Company, New York,
1959.

Attitudes

Of course, it was attitudes which caused Janie, Joan, Sol, and Olin to use their intelligence in different ways to cope with similar situations, and attitudes are obviously a part of the personality. How do they get into the picture of personality formation? Where do they come from? Probably no area of psychology is more complex than the complicated interrelationship of experiences and attitudes. We have seen how an attitude of trust or security is developed from affection and care in infancy, and how self-confidence or lack of it may result from the degree of independence and new experience permitted the young child. A child's relations with his parents are the chief determinant of the degree of love he bears them, or the degree of fear he has of them, or the respect he has for them.[7] His love, fear, or respect is crucial in the attitudes he will develop, because parents are for years dominant, and for more years crucial, forces in the life of the child. If Reba loves her mother, she will tend to adopt the attitudes her mother has about whether children should be quiet or noisy, how important cleanliness and neatness are, whether boys are nice playmates, how you should respond when a stranger, a friend in your home, or the clerk in the store speaks to you or offers you candy. These attitudes become a part of her personality. They influence the reaction she presents, the adjustment she makes to portions of her environment, and the way people regard her.

If Dorothy fears her mother, she is less likely to adopt her attitudes, but she may, for the sake of prudence, *pretend* to accept them. Thus, she is learning a completely different set of values and practicing a completely different set of skills from Reba. Reba is practicing exactly what her mother's attitudes are; Dorothy is practicing putting on an act, engaging in behavior inappropriate to her feelings, and concealing the feelings. If Dorothy strongly resents her mother, or even if she merely is indifferent to her but does not fear her, she may actively turn against the attitudes her mother displays. Mother doesn't care for candy or TV Westerns, but Dorothy loves them. Mother thinks school grades are important, so Dorothy does not. It is seldom as obvious as these examples, but these dynamics of attitude formation apply in the cases of most children.

As children begin to mix with people besides their parents, attitude

[7] R. D. Dewey and W. J. Humber, *The Development of Human Behavior*. The Macmillan Company, New York, 1951.

formation becomes more complicated. Parents' attitudes often conflict with those of the children's age-mates, or even with the teacher's. Now the child must choose between the loyalties of infancy and his emerging identity as a person among people of all kinds. Daddy has taught Hubert that things will turn out all right if you are just nice and polite— attitudes of optimism and politeness. But now Hubert finds that day after day an impolite, rude child gets his way in the playground games. What will be the effect on Hubert's attitudes? We cannot tell from this amount of data, except to suspect that they will change to some degree, and the direction and nature of the change will influence Hubert's personality and make it somewhat different in the future.

Interests

There used to be a parlor game in which a "characterologist" would collect from each person participating a slip of paper containing the answers to such questions as, "If you could be reincarnated as anything other than a person, what would you prefer?" and "What part of the newspaper do you read first?" and "If you had a million dollars, what would you do with it?" From the answers he would deduce the probable personality structure of the individual, who would then be identified and his perceived personality compared with the inferred one. The prominence of interests in determining one's personality is well recognized; interests (or "values," if you prefer) influence whether a person thinks and reacts in terms of the profit motive, the social motive, the pleasure motive, or what have you.

The origin of interests is unclear, which is a pity when their importance in personality development is considered. Children's interests, even those of young children, do not appear to reflect the influence of parents as much as do attitudes. Part of this is probably due to the fact that to develop interests commonly requires some degree of knowledge and experience in "doing," and young children are incapable of the sophistication which makes possible parents' interest in a given area. It is appealing to say that interests come from successful accomplishment, that we become interested in the things we do well. A moment's reflection, however, will reveal that this is a specious conclusion. Many boys and girls make good marks in school and yet are not at all interested in schoolwork. Another child who, by greatest effort, scarcely produces passing work may actually be highly interested in his work. The person with a flair for art will tend to be interested in art, but by no means is this always the case. Fishing and hunting are often appealing, interesting, even to the poor hunter or fisherman.

Probably interests arise through a complex interrelationship of attitudes, skills, knowledge, and liberal dashes of X, an unknown quantity. Garrison[8] equates them closely to the person's need at a given time and the nature of his experiences. Perhaps romanticized concepts connected with the activity or area come into it—the boy interested in medicine because of glamorized presentations of the work of the physician, or the girl in music because of some emotionalized association. Whatever their origin, interests afford one of the most usable avenues in winning the confidence and cooperation of adolescents. Find a boy's or girl's interests, show a sympathetic interest in them yourself, and you are in a good position to influence that adolescent. The nature of his interests will influence his behavior and the impression he makes on others, thus affecting both his personality development and structure.

Reality Testing

This is an integrative process of checking all the impressions, attitudes, and reactions which build a personality against the criterion of "Does it fit in with the other things I know or feel, and does it correspond to fact as I see it around me?" The process of reality testing may enable the overindulged child to begin to acquire a more realistic evaluation of life when he leaves the parental nest. It can do so and improve his adjustment to life, unless he persists in the previously noted tendency to regard his earliest experiences as "normality," and refuses to accept the evidence of reality as he later encounters it. If there is such a thing as a cornerstone of sound personality formation, this is it: testing of reality. Do my reactions to people produce the results I want? If not, how should I change my thinking and acting? Are my feelings about work, people, myself, about "ships and shoes and sealing wax, cabbages and kings," justified by objective fact or based on erroneous perceptions? When something happens, do I view it with reason or do I react blindly? Do I distinguish between fact and my feelings and beliefs? Do I check my beliefs and feelings against facts and evidence, and make appropriate changes when they do not coincide?

These processes are typical of what is involved in reality testing. The neurotic finds it difficult or impossible to effectively test his feelings

8 K. C. Garrison, *Growth and Development*. Longmans, Green and Co., New York, 1959.

against reality; his inability to do so is usually one cause (and sign) of his neurosis. The well-adjusted adolescent makes a mistake in judgment, but correctly interprets the situation and avoids that mistake in the future. The person who does not periodically test his behavior or thought patterns against reality—check up on what his beliefs or attitudes are, the practical result of them, and the reason things turn out for him as they do—is less likely to achieve a well-integrated personality, a personality with no weak or ineffective spots of adjustment.[9]

Questions re Case of Fred

4. How is Fred's probably superior intelligence manifested in his life?

5. What interests of Fred's parents have had apparent strong effect on his pattern of personality development?

6. Summarize Fred's probable self concept. Account for the presence of factors of his self concept.

7. What is Fred's greatest single shortcoming in his process of maturation thus far?

THE HEALTHY PERSONALITY

So the child grows, and from his original endowment his personality forms, experience by experience, attitude by attitude, reaction by reaction, result by result, interpretation by interpretation, and by the soundness with which each one is tested and interpreted against facts and evidence. As it is done well and soundly, good adjustments are made, self-confidence is developed, frustrations are met and coped with, realistic attitudes are formed, successful reaction patterns are adopted, and a "mature personality," a "stable personality," a "well-integrated personality" is formed.

Symonds[10] presents a list of six criteria of "ego strength," which Stagner[11] terms "indicators of the relative strength of the ego (or self) or the efficiency of the personality in dealing with internal and external disturbances of equilibrium." In other words, these are criteria for evaluating

---

9 C. R. Rogers, *Client-Centered Therapy*. Houghton-Mifflin Company, Boston, 1951.

10 P. M. Symonds, *The Ego and the Self*. Appleton-Century-Crofts, Inc., New York, 1951.

11 R. Stagner, *Psychology of Personality*. McGraw-Hill Book Company, Inc., New York, 1961, p. 200.

the capability of the personality to adjust to both internal stresses and the external environment. Boys or girls approaching adolescence with their development in one or more of these areas notably below the norm for their age are likely to display signs of maladjustment or "emotional immaturity" (which, of course, is a form of maladjustment). Many things can cause deficiencies in each of these areas, just as many experiences are involved in high attainment of them, and weaknesses in any area may manifest themselves in many ways. The causes of strong development, causes of weakness, and symptoms of weaknesses discussed are, therefore, illustrative only, not exhaustive or comprehensive.

Toleration of External Threat

The healthy personality is capable of enduring extreme physical discomfort, repeated and severe disappointments and frustrations, and objectively founded fears and psychological stresses without becoming neurotic or deteriorating in its organization and reality-testing capacity. Dr. Edith Bone, a Hungarian physician, was kept in solitary confinement by the Communists for seven years, subjected to brutal physical deprivation and ruthless interrogation and threats. She emerged from her ordeal emotionally stable and healthy, intellectually alert and competent, and without perceptible personality deterioration.[12] Contrast Dr. Bone with the person whose minor business reverses or normal frustrations in human relations produce in him an excess of self-pity, egocentricity, and defeatism. Of course, *enough* stress can cause the disintegration of the strongest personality and the development of neurotic tendencies. But the case of Dr. Bone re-emphasizes the fact pointed out in previous pages that neurotic manifestations seldom develop as a result of external threat in the case of people who were initially psychologically healthy.

Inability to tolerate external threat—in its rawest physical form called cowardice and in more abstract forms, low frustration tolerance—may result from overprotection which denies the child the opportunity to grow in skill and endurance in handling pain, disappointments, and fear-producing situations. It may equally result from repeated subjection to situations beyond his ability to handle or endure. A high level of security in the self concept seems to be accompanied by a high frustration tolerance.[13]

12 *Newsweek,* December 10, 1956, *48:*116–117.
13 R. Stagner, *Psychology of Personality.* McGraw-Hill Book Company, Inc., New York, 1961.

Case of Grant

Grant was a well-developed, intelligent, and popular boy of fourteen. But he became anxious, fearful, and resorted to some extreme form of withdrawal mechanism in the face of an unusually trying situation. If a contest became intense, he gave up, permitting his opponent an easy victory. His pleasantness in getting along with people minimized the occasions when he faced the threat of physical violence, but when he did have to face it, he immediately took refuge in flight. In his reactions to external stress Grant was so far below the normal tolerance of fourteen-year-olds as to justify his being regarded as inadequate in this area of personality development.

Talks with Grant and his parents, who were called in because the counselor felt his condition merited remedial treatment of some kind, suggested possible explanations of his behavior. His father was a wealthy, self-made contractor. From the time Grant was three, the father had tried to fashion him into his own ideal of an aggressive, two-fisted boy. As one of a thousand instances, he had placed the screaming and protesting toddler atop a horse, thinking to start him early on the road to self-confidence and virile accomplishment. Unfortunately for the father's hopes, Grant fell off and was further terrified, although unhurt.

Grant's mother was a different person. An artistically inclined woman who reverenced culture and gracious living and clearly thought her husband crude and primitive for his interests, she wanted Grant to be a sensitive boy with an interest in "the finer things of life." Whenever possible, she would protect him from his father's overambitious projects and explain to Grant how and why she was doing it. He was too young and small, too delicate, might get hurt. Such things were dangerous. Why subject oneself to such unpleasant experiences? Together they would find that Grant had "the sniffles" and was unable to go out when Daddy wanted to show him how to tackle and block this afternoon. And when Grant was put over the hurdles by his father, Mother was right there to commiserate with him over his bruises, both bodily and spiritual, when the ordeal was over.

1. What environmental influences in Grant's life would tend to produce his lack of tolerance of stress?

2. What parental policies of cooperation would give Grant a good environment in which to learn to cope with problems?

Dealing with Guilt Feelings

All of us do things of which we are not proud, have thoughts which we feel are wrong or unworthy of us, experience feelings and desires which we regard as "evil." Unless we are abnormally blunted in our sensitivity, principles, and conscience, we experience some feelings of guilt about such acts, thoughts, and desires. Normal adolescents, as well as adults, also have feelings of guilt about things they should have done but did not do—the help they did not give when a friend really needed it; the school service they could have, but did not, perform; the windows they promised Mother they would wash but didn't, and when they got home she had washed them, but had stumbled and fallen off the stepstool. . . .

Normal adolescents have such guilt feelings, but normal boys and girls add up the credit and debit sides of their ledger of life and decide they measure up pretty well, or they decide they do not measure up as well as their self concept requires and so proceed to do something about it in the future. If they have wronged or neglected someone, they try to atone for it; if the wronged or neglected party is no longer available, they atone through service to someone else, thus evening their score toward humanity.

The person whose personality is weak or inadequate may be unable to take effective positive steps to get from under his burden of guilt. His time and energies are consumed in futile self-accusations and depression over his unworthiness, leaving none for designing an improved pattern of thought and behavior in the future. As mentioned in Chapter 4, his feelings of guilt are often irrational, attached onto some inconsequential incident not objectively worthy of such feelings. Often, as in the case of anxieties, the conscious guilt feelings are not attached to the real cause, but to a factor less disturbing to the person than would be the recognition of the real basis of guilt, thereby enabling him to hide from his real problem. Thus, the boy with severe guilt feelings over hostility toward his father may be quite unconscious of those feelings, rationalizing them out of conscious existence in various ways, but have severe guilt feelings over failing to follow the vocational choice made by his father for him, or a cruel or unkind remark he made to a classmate. Or he may, in fact, feel oppressive guilt over his feelings toward his father, but make little or no effort to change his behavior toward him.

Case of Hilary

Hilary was the daughter of rigidly moral, religious parents, who reared her strictly and under extremely close control. They taught her to regard sex as something nasty, evil, which nice girls never even thought of, much less desired. Hilary, however, developed into a healthy adolescent girl with normal thoughts, curiosity, and cravings. As she took on the physical form of sexual maturity, parental admonitions increased in frequency, intensity, and emphasis on the evil of sex. But Hilary *did* think about sex, more and more, with greater and greater feelings of attraction, and greater and greater feelings of guilt. She was in many respects an emotionally immature girl, overprotected, lacking initiative and self-confidence.

Finally Hilary built an elaborate fantasy experience for herself. She fancied herself seduced by the young, handsome, and popular music director of her church, whom she knew her parents greatly admired. Her fancied seducer then brutally discarded her, saying she was not a girl of decent moral character.

Intellectually Hilary knew that the seduction did not happen, but she was able, through wishful thinking, to *feel* that it had happened and therefore to feel guilt over it.

Now Hilary felt guilty about her sexual thoughts no longer, at least not consciously. She felt guilty about having been a "bad girl," certainly—so guilty that she had to tell several people how guilty she felt, and why. But she told no one who would try to investigate and take appropriate steps about the matter. Over a period of weeks she came to think of herself as no longer a virgin, and began planning how she would explain the situation to whomever she someday might marry. Hilary was not at all psychotic, not "crazy," not even suffering from a delusion, because she knew none of this ever happened.

Finally Hilary confided in her school counselor, who proceeded to talk with her at length about her feelings and thought patterns, and the whole story came out. Re-education of Hilary on the basis of sensible morality and a realistic perspective on matters pertaining to sex eventually absolved her of her guilt feelings. It undoubtedly contributed somewhat to her over-all personality development as well, but Hilary still has a long way to go in developing a mature, healthy personality.

1. What probably causes Hilary to be so extremely susceptible to guilt feelings?

2. Why would fancying actual sexual delinquency, as Hilary did, cause her to have less severe guilt feelings than she had from merely thinking about sex?

3. What is the possible significance of her selection of the church music director as her seducer?

Capacity for Effective Repression

Repression, as used in this sense, means a curbing of impulses—by implication, impulses which are antisocial or whose expression would produce undesirable results. Children have little capacity for curbing impulses, from the impulses connected with elimination to impulses to throw food they do not want or like. Some adolescents continue to display behavior inadequately censored by social responsbility and the dictates of good judgment. In this category falls the boy or girl who gives way to excesses of temper or does things on impulse without adequate consideration of their effects. Effective repression also includes exercising reasonable control over one's thoughts. While no one can completely control his thoughts, preventing one from coming into his mind or making his thoughts take a certain form, the psychologically healthy person can discipline them to an appreciable extent. He is not the helpless prey of obsessive thoughts, and his thoughts do not wander to the extent that he cannot hold them on a subject with some degree of concentration. Furthermore, he can cope with most anxieties, guilt feelings, and resentments by logical examination and dismissal, rather than having his mind dominated by them.

In children, lack of effective repression is usually dismissed as immaturity and lack of proper training. Normal children grow in their ability to exercise control over their thoughts, feelings, and behavior just as they do in physical respects. As in the physical area, exercise is essential to proper growth, and children require encouragement by suggestion, explanation, and precept to help them achieve the capacity for effective repression appropriate to their age.

When an adolescent or adult fails to inhibit antisocial impulses to the extent required for group living, or when he is unable to exercise normal control over his thoughts or feelings, simple immaturity is an insufficient explanation. *Why* did he not mature sufficiently?

Case of Ida

Ida was twelve years old, in the sixth grade, and a problem to teachers and classmates alike. If things did not suit her, she became angry, and when she became angry, she lashed out verbally or physically at anyone who crossed her, or she had a screaming tantrum. She thus presented the common pattern of low frustration tolerance and ineffective self-control when the limit of tolerance was reached. A check with other teachers revealed that Ida had always shown these tendencies, but they were less noticeable when she was among children whose ages normally might produce such behavior occasionally. Also, she appeared to have become worse during the past months.

When asked by telephone to come to the school to discuss Ida's problem, her mother stated that she was unable to come. Her head was swimming, she did not drive, and the father was working and unable to bring her to the school, and besides, she did not know what she would do with the baby. Talk with Ida brought forth the information that her mother was sick a lot, "especially when Daddy has to go out of town," and cried a great deal. The teacher discreetly avoided direct questioning on family conditions, but, having an interested audience, Ida talked enthusiastically about a chaotic home, a complaining mother who took refuge in tears and illness whenever she was unhappy, and treated Ida with a mixture of fatuous indulgence "to make up for Daddy being away so much" and a violent temper when, for reasons often unclear to Ida, the mother was displeased by what Ida did.

The teacher's being invariably kind, firm, and calm with Ida and guiding her classmates in a pattern of completely ignoring and isolating Ida whenever she might misbehave improved her behavior to the point that she was tolerable in the classroom and on the playground, but extensive psychotherapy would be necessary to re-educate Ida into a wholesome personality.

1. What environmental influences might account for Ida's lack of effective repression?

2. What neurotic mechanisms does Ida's mother display?

3. If a complete case history were available, what other defects in personality development and adjustment would you expect to find in Ida?

Balance of Rigidity and Flexibility

In recent years much has been said about the "rigid personality" which is unable to adapt to circumstances, maintaining its habitual pattern of attitudes, thought, and behavior whether or not they are appropriate to the situations encountered. Popular expressions describing such people are "narrow-minded," "intolerant," "not open to conviction," "stereotyped behavior," and "iron pants." Less criticism is heard of the person as adaptable as the chameleon, who changes his spots to blend perfectly with the prevailing coloration of thought, opinion, and action.

George Peabody College for Teachers.

Figure 7. What individual differences could be noticed at a dance such as this?

This is natural, because when we see a person reacting to a situation in a manner closely resembling our own (which is the tendency of the over-flexible or adaptable person; he changes to suit the climate of the moment), we do not accuse him of being wishy-washy, but mentally compliment his intelligence. On the other hand, we are prone to deplore the neurotic rigidity of the person who fails to see that his pattern of thought and action (which, of course, differs from ours) is inappropriate to a situation.

(The above should not be regarded as a facetious remark. Perusal of editorials, articles, and columns will reveal dozens of instances of the tendency to blandly characterize the attitudes of anyone whose conservatism keeps him from sharing the writer's "advanced" views as rigid and reacting on the basis of out-of-date concepts.)

Actually, as mature reflection reveals, either inability to make appropriate adaptation to new circumstances or adoption of new modes of thought and behavior on unrealistic or capricious grounds is a symptom of the same personality defect: imperfect adaptation. The formative influences on each of these extreme types of personality are likely to be similar in one respect: both have probably been characterized by emotionally dictated attitudes and ethics rather than intellectually dictated ones. If the prevailing emotional climate in which the child developed was one of steadfast adherence to authoritarian principles, he is more likely to develop a rigid, nonadaptive personality[14, 15] (although in some cases, as the child matures, he will go to the opposite extreme in secret, if not open, revolt against what he conceives to have been oppressive upbringing).[16] The child reared in an atmosphere reeking with the latest songs, the latest books, and the "best contemporary thought" develops with an unconscious tendency to view newness and correctness as related. Since no sane person consciously or admittedly equates newness with right, each person advocating a new, "nonrigid" approach or ideology must contend that the new *is* the better in this case. Therefore, the unduly "flexible" person must rationalize inconsistency and premature or unrealistic opinions.

Examples of both of these personality defects, including lack of ego adequacy, abound in pre-adolescents and adolescents. The overflexibles tend to outnumber the overrigids during adolescence, as boys and girls eagerly seek what is new, especially if it enables them to assume intellectual emancipation from their parents. The extremists are known in different generations and cultures as bohemians, beatniks, angry young men, and idealists.

The school is society's specially designed instrument for teaching the reasoned, intellectual approach to meeting the problems of life, as

14 F. McKinney, *Psychology of Personal Adjustment*. John Wiley & Sons, Inc., New York, 1960.

15 G. B. Watson, "Some Personality Differences in Children Related to Strict or Permissive Parental Discipline," *Journal of Psychology*, 1957, *44*:227–249.

16 E. Frenkel-Brunswik, "A Study of Prejudice in Children," *Human Relations*, 1948, *1*:295–306.

opposed to the emotionally dominated approach. Educational methods which either stress rigidly authoritarian dogma, or encourage capricious following of whims as a distortion of reasonable consideration of pupil interest, encourage the adoption of these nonintellectual bases of attitude formation. The teacher who emphasizes full and unprejudiced consideration of all available evidence and interpretation of that evidence in the least tortuous and most realistic manner possible will be exerting a wholesome influence on the personality formation of his students.

Planning and Control

The strong ego, the healthy personality, is able to make definite plans for the future and steadfastly carry them out, despite normal interferences and shifts of interest. It is obvious that this capacity is closely related to the rigidity-flexibility factor just discussed. Obsessive adherence to a predetermined plan, or even discomfort in living without a preplanned schedule anticipating every activity or eventuality, is obviously evidence of an insecure or overrigid personality structure. However, more than the previous factor, lack of consideration of the necessity for planning and control emphasizes the defectiveness of a too-flexible approach to life. Preparation for almost any vocation, for marriage, provision for economic security—the whole ability to anticipate and prepare for future eventualities, which so sharply differentiates man from most subhuman species—rests squarely on the effective planning and control of activities of which the healthy ego is capable. This planning and control involves what is known as the "reality principle" (different from reality testing).[17] The reality principle stresses seeking long-term values and satisfactions, as contrasted with immediate pleasure or gratification sought under the pleasure principle. In the course of normal, healthy maturation people increasingly renounce the pleasure principle in favor of the reality principle.

Adolescent boys and girls deficient in this important aspect of ego strength and personality development are numerous. Causes of deficiency in this area, as may be deduced from the previous section, cluster around parental or educational overemphasis on the gratification of immediate impulses (usually rationalized as "capitalizing on interests" or "encouraging initiative"), failure to require reasonable self-discipline in persevering in plans and tasks, and failure to habituate the child to looking

[17] S. Freud, *Beyond the Pleasure Principle*. International Psychoanalytic Press, London, 1922.

to the future and making intelligent anticipation of its demands. Jack is an example of typical deficiency in this area.

Case of Jack

Enthusiastic and energetic, fourteen-year-old Jack is a leading spirit in every project conceived in his class. In his rush to get started, he typically skips the first stage of the task—planning—and enters into the next operation of collecting data, making a field trip, or some other activity, preferably physical. In a short time, due to lack of planning, Jack begins to reach dead ends, or his efforts produce chaotic, conglomerate results. Frustrated and impatient, his interest lags, and he is ripe for another, newer, "better" activity. Homework and preparation show the same irresolute pattern. Time is badly allocated, to capitalize on some immediate opportunity or interest at the expense of a systematic program.

1. What can reasonably be predicted for the next ten or fifteen years of Jack's life if his capacity for planning and control does not improve?

This important aspect of ego-personality strength can accurately be classed as the rudder of life, a stabilizing factor which enables an individual to hold a true course despite the vagaries of breeze and current, changing course only when cogent circumstances dictate a change. Boys and girls leaving childhood with serious deficiencies in their ability to plan and control are exceedingly difficult to help on any long-term-improvement basis. Following whims is much easier and productive of more immediate pleasure than is building for the future in a steadfast, continuing manner, and when an individual has been emotionally conditioned through childhood to regard immediate gratification of desires as tremendously and rightfully important, it is difficult to replace this personality structure with a more responsible one. The same principles applicable to re-education for a balance between flexibility and rigidity apply here, but the re-educative process must usually be accompanied by extensive psychotherapy to achieve desired alteration in personality structure.

Self-Esteem

This factor most closely corresponds to the popular conception of ego strength, a strong personality, or strong self concept, although in reality is is only one facet of healthy psychological adjustment. It *is* an essential element.[18] The person who lacks the self-esteem appropriate to normal personality will be insecure, because he fails to perceive in himself those qualities which are necessary to cope with the exigencies of the world. He will be afraid to seek new experiences because of doubt as to his capabilities of coping with them, afraid of being rejected as inferior, and will even deprecate and falsely evaluate his own achievements because they surpass his self image.

Self-esteem involves an optimistic evaluation of one's character, abilities, and personal dignity. "Optimistic" is the appropriate adjective, because ideally self-esteem should be geared to a person's reasonable maximum of virtue, ability, and achievement. People seldom surpass in actual achievement their self image, but often exploit their native abilities to an above-average extent to substantiate their self-evaluation. Self-esteem high in proportion to actual ability, then, is a promoter of maximum self-realization.

Case of Kathy

Kathy is an example of a girl with healthy self-esteem. She has never been indulged or allowed to "do just as she pleased," but has always been treated by her parents with respect as a being of intelligence, who should be dealt with on the basis of reason rather than arbitrary authority or blind emotion. Admonitions from early childhood not to do things were accompanied by explanations of why the action was undesirable. While not being permitted to dominate family conversations (impractical, since she was the second of four children), her opinions were permitted expression and given courteous attention, even when not accepted. She was, as much as possible, punished in private, and although her parents used corporal punishment freely, it was administered in a brisk, impersonal manner and did not involve Kathy's subjugating herself to others or treatment which would injure her pride. It was discontinued before Kathy began to achieve a sense of the privacy of her body. Kathy's clothes were not always the newest or the most expensive (sometimes they were her older sister's outgrown things), but the parental attitude was never apologetic or suggestive of either defending or "explaining" her clothes. They were nice clothes, their attitudes said, appropriate for school, party, or whatever Kathy was doing. Her intelli-

18 K. Horney, *Our Inner Conflicts*. W. W. Norton & Company, Inc., New York, 1945.

gence was average. She was taught that she should perform her schoolwork as thoroughly as she reasonably could, and that the grades under those conditions would be her proper grades.

Kathy is now in college, a slightly below-average student who works hard and accepts her C's and occasional D's cheerfully and without any feeling that her grades degrade her.

1. How would explanations of why things she was to do were desirable, or things she was not to do were undesirable, help Kathy develop a sense of self-esteem?

2. Why is the way Kathy's parents handled punishment considered good?

3. What do Kathy's parents' attitudes toward her grades and her wearing her older sister's clothes have in common?

4. Why is Kathy's self concept not injured when she works hard and yet receives only a D in a college course?

From the experience of succeeding, of trying new things and getting along successfully at them, of being paid attention to and heeded, of being treated as a respected person, self-esteem is created. Of course, the opposites of these experiences, the opposites of the way Kathy was reared, may logically be expected to produce a person with an unfavorable self image, a poor self concept, a weak ego, low self-esteem, all common terms used to describe similar conditions. In addition, neurotic tendencies such as guilt feelings unsuccessfully resolved, severe anxieties, and low frustration tolerance may injure the development of normal ego strength in this area through producing low self-confidence even in the absence of objective reason for a depreciated self-evaluation.[19]

A boy or girl lacking optimum self-esteem because of simple environmental deprivation is less likely to show other symptoms of maladjustment and deficiencies in other areas of personality formation than is the child whose inadequate self-esteem is due to a generalized neurotic pattern of personality formation. The simple deprivation case can be helped greatly by experiences in school of success and by being treated with perhaps a little more than routine courtesy and attention. Where a more extensive distortion of the personality pattern is involved, treatment of the problem of inadequate self-esteem becomes one part of the process of psychotherapy.

[19] J. C. Coleman, *Personality Dynamics and Effective Behavior*. Scott, Foresman and Company, Chicago, 1960.

COMMON DISTORTIONS
OF ADOLESCENT PERSONALITY

In the foregoing discussion of criteria of ego strength or maturity of personality, the illustrative cases identify several deviate personality patterns commonly encountered by teachers, counselors, and parents. Personality problems considered in the case digests included those of the immature adolescent, the anxious one, the adolescent lacking in self-control or self-discipline, and the one with feelings of inferiority. Some other common personality distortions are worthy of consideration for the assistance which an understanding of them will give in handling certain adolescents. Of course, such problems seldom occur singly or in "pure" form. The boy or girl conspicuously displaying one of the lacks of a healthy personality will probably display others as well.

The Bully

This is the most commonly noticed of personality distortions affecting boys' and girls' dealings with their peers. The bully is so objectionable that he demands notice. Often his overbearing and hectoring manner is an overcompensation for feelings of inferiority. This can easily be verified by noticing the relative frequency with which boys over-age in grade because of academic deficiency, and conscious of their deficiency, resort to bullying behavior. They are asserting their equal or superior achievement in the only area open to them, the area of physical dominance. Less frequently, examples of bullying behavior are observable in girls. By the time girls reach adolescence, their bullying will usually take the form of ruthlessly trying to dominate the activities of their groups, imposing their will arbitrarily and hectoring girls who try to oppose them.

Sometimes bullying behavior is a direct imitation of the behavior the child has observed in the home situation. A father who dominates his household on the basis of superior raw strength is likely to condition a boy in his formative years to an unquestioned acceptance of the principle that might makes right and that the exercise of his pleasure on weaker beings is the normal procedure for a physically superior being.[20] Sometimes parental dominance or brutality will produce a bully not because of

20 W. W. Wattenberg, *The Adolescent Years.* Harcourt, Brace and Company, New York, 1955.

an acceptance of bullying as normal, but because of a resentment of society which the child expresses in the same manner that it was produced in him.

Because of physical limitations and social pressures, adolescent girls are less likely to exhibit bullying behavior of a physical sort than are adolescent boys. However, like boys, they may, through observation of parental behavior, acquire attitudes productive of bullying in a nonphysical way. A daughter may observe her mother dominate the family through verbal bullying—using threats, abusive language, tirades, and diatribes against any who do not submit to her demands and dominance. Subsequently the girl may attempt to dominate her fellows by similar tactics. If she is of an aggressive disposition, she may, without parental example, develop a behavior pattern such as that just described to cope with a domineering or physically brutal father.

Whatever the dynamics of a specific bullying personality, the general principles of effective handling by parents, teachers, and counselors are similar. First, protect other boys or girls from the bully's harassment by the least drastic, but still effective, measures—from reasoning to social ostracism and corporal restraint or punishment. Sometimes the adult becomes so concerned with the misfortunes the bully underwent in making him what he is that the adult sentimentally allows the bully's whims to take precedence over the welfare of his hapless victims. This is pseudohumanitarianism of the worst sort. Second, seek opportunities for him (or her) whereby he can achieve some success and status in socially approved ways. This does not mean necessarily letting him be boss of something. Let him participate successfully in academic activities of some sort, or give him a normal role in athletic or social activities. Give him assignments, academic, social, or athletic, which he can perform successfully, and encourage students to notice his successful performance. Try to avoid rejection of him as a person, both on your part and on that of the group. It is more pleasant to be liked and respected than to be disliked and thereby gain notoriety. Try to remove the bully's feeling of inferiority or resentment toward the world.

The Withdrawn Adolescent

Parental dominance which produces the bully in one boy or girl will produce the withdrawn adolescent in another instance, depending on the self concept acquired by him in infancy and perhaps influenced by his constitutional make-up. Withdrawal may also be because of lack of

social experience which produces doubt of his ability to relate successfully to others, frequent or traumatic failures in attempts to relate to
others, or feelings of self-consciousness over real or imagined defects
which might expose him to ridicule or rejection.

Effective handling of the withdrawn adolescent requires fairly accurate understanding of background factors. Treating such a boy or girl
with kindness and extra attention can hardly fail to be helpful, but ones
who are withdrawn because of lack of social experience, unsuccessful experience, or self-consciousness require a bigger proportion of emphasis
on successful social experience mixed with kindness than does the one
who is simply afraid to do anything that will cause him to be noticed.
Getting the adolescent to talk about why he does not converse and mingle more with others in his age group will usually *eventually* provide
the needed information to determine the basis of his withdrawal. Such
information is less likely to come as a direct response to a direct question than as a gradual emergence, as when the boy or girl is kept talking
about how he feels toward others and why. A picture of causal factors
will usually emerge if the adolescent can be kept talking about his
thoughts and feelings. Such conversations will also serve to call attention
to possible serious personality disturbances of which withdrawal was
merely a symptom.

The Rebellious or Uncooperative Adolescent

This boy or girl (speaking frankly and avoiding euphemistic platitudes) is the bane of teachers' and counselors' existence. His (or her)
symptoms take a variety of forms, all frustrating to the adult attempting to help him mature into successful, well-adjusted adulthood. He may
be noisy, eternally engaging in bothersome activities, rude, defiant, unwilling to work, and a bully. He may be indifferent, bothering no one but
simply living through, existing during, the activities in which he is supposed to participate, inaccessible to any appeal the adult knows how to
make to get him to put forth an effort. Usually there is a mixture of the
two. The pupil not participating in the activity of the group finds
things of his own to engage in, and these things usually upset the work of
the group.

Lack of effort may be due to physical causes which leave the boy or
girl deficient in energy. More frequently the roots are psychological.
Without getting into the question of the relative depth of personality
distortions involving rebellion or noncooperation, and others, it can be

said that these symptoms are usually hard to deal with. Adolescents who are withdrawn or anxious, for instance, usually want help and welcome attention. It is likely that the rebellious or noncooperative adolescent went through a phase of desiring help, too, back there sometime. But often the boy or girl who constitutes a severe behavior problem simply does not want what adults consider to be help. He has worked out a pattern of living which is at least minimally satisfactory to him, and he distrusts the efficacy of the patterns that adults would lead him into. Reading case histories of such adolescents, one is struck by the number of instances in which, under the kind and understanding leadership of a sympathetic teacher, foster parents, or other adult, a behavior-problem boy or girl will apparently be making a fine readjustment to life; then, without perceptible reason, his antisocial tendencies will burst out in what appears to be pointless misbehavior.

The keynote of handling all types of personality distortions or deviations from normal personality formation is patience and understanding, but the behavior-problem boy or girl requires more patience and more understanding on the part of adults assisting him than do most adolescents. Unfortunately, the personality and attitude of a rebellious or uncooperative boy or girl make it more difficult to attain and maintain this relationship with him than with other problem types. Punishment is usually worse than futile in dealing with him, except as a part of a process of understanding and re-education.[21] We sometimes have to remind ourselves that human nature does not naturally predispose one to be unpleasant and exasperating. What the behavior-problem adolescent is, he has been made, usually being kept unhappy and resentful in the process. So remember that, exasperating as he may be, he is that way as a result of years of frustration, mishandling, and maladjustment. Without getting into the knotty question of free will, it can safely be assumed that boys and girls do not become antisocial and misbehavior problems premeditatedly, and probably not even intentionally. Self concept and environment shape them into such behavior patterns.

READINGS

Baller, W. R., and Charles, D. C., *The Psychology of Human Growth and Development*. New York: Holt, Rinehart & Winston, 1961, Chapt. 14.

21 C. B. Zachry, *Emotion and Conduct in Adolescence*. Appleton-Century-Crofts, Inc., New York, 1940.

Dewey, R., and Humber, W. J., *The Development of Human Behavior*. New York: The Macmillan Company, 1951, Chapt. 8.

Garrett, H. E., *General Psychology*. New York: American Book Company, 1961, Chapt. 15.

Gorlow, L., and Katkovsky, W., *Readings in the Psychology of Adjustment*. New York: McGraw-Hill Book Company, Inc., 1959, Chapt. 3.

Lazarus, R. S., *Adjustment and Personality*. New York: McGraw-Hill Book Company, Inc., 1961, Chapt. 2.

Leeper, R. W., and Madison, P., *Toward Understanding Human Personalities*. New York: Appleton-Century-Crofts, Inc., 1959, Chapts. 1, 2.

Leuba, C., *Man: A General Psychology*. New York: Holt, Rinehart & Winston, 1961, Chapts. 18, 19, 20, 21.

McKinney, F., *Psychology of Personal Adjustment*. New York: John Wiley & Sons, Inc., 1959, Chapt. 4.

Stagner, R., *Psychology of Personality*. New York: McGraw-Hill Book Company, Inc., 1961, Chapt. 9.

Tussing, L., *Psychology for Better Living*. New York: John Wiley & Sons, Inc., 1959, Chapts. 7, 8.

SUMMARY OF PART ONE

Thus far we have considered how life begins, the forces which mold the child, the essential developmental tasks which he must master for normal maturation, the problems of frustration and adjustment he faces, and the way all these forces combine to produce what we call a personality. We have outlined criteria for evaluating the maturity and strength of a personality, with illustrative cases of good and poor maturation and adjustment.

This gives us a picture of the human beings the worker with adolescents faces, what they are like and what made them that way. In Part Two we will go into the nature of the lifespan called adolescence, studying what it is, the purpose it serves, and some of the unique adjustments it requires.

PART TWO

MATURATION AND ADJUSTMENT IN ADOLESCENCE

PREVIEW OF PART TWO

The forces discussed in Part One and the principles governing their operation function throughout human life, from the prenatal period in the case of hereditary factors, and childhood in the case of some culturally developed motives, until senility or death. Their relative significance varies at different times of life and under different circumstances, and their manner of operation differs in response to environmental changes and changes in the self concept.

People change all their lives. Never is a person the same at one birthday as he was at the last. His body has changed. His amount and type of knowledge has changed. We are certain that his personality will have changed, too, although often the change will not be readily identifiable. The child at five is different from the child at four. The woman at thirty-six is different from the woman at thirty-five. Adolescence, however, is a period of time, roughly the period of the teens, when changes are unusually dramatic and far-reaching in their effect. Some psychologists have evaluated the changes of adolescence as so profound as to justify calling adolescence "a second birth," referring to the emergence of the adult body and personality in place of the childish ones. While this term may, in its implication, exaggerate the degree of change the boy or girl undergoes in adolescence, it is generally agreed that the changes of this period are profound and present certain problems unique to this era of life.

If not an era of rebirth, adolescence is indisputably an era of growing up. The boy or girl enters adolescence as a child and emerges as a man or woman, expected to be ready to assume an adult's place in the world. This growing up involves much more than merely living through the teen years and increasing in size. During adolescence the boy or girl is expected to *mature,* to change from childish ways of thinking, feeling, adjusting, and acting to the ways of an adult. Maturation in at least four areas must take place during adolescence for the boy or girl to become a "normal" or "well-adjusted" adult.

Intellectual Maturation

Adults not only think "better" than children; they think differently from children in many respects because of the different goals, values, and language habits they have developed. Part of the difference between the thinking of a mature adult and that of a child is that the former is more realistic and disciplined. Mature adults tend to think in terms of realities and necessities, as contrasted with thinking in terms of wishes and imaginary conditions as do children. Achieving adult modes of thought usually requires practice and ever improving self-control on the part of the adolescent. Assistance from an understanding adult can help an adolescent grow into adult modes of thought more easily and thoroughly than he is likely to do by his own unaided efforts.

Emotional Maturation

People's feelings, their reactions to things which please, displease, bore, frighten, or attract them, are expected to "grow up" as their bodies do. Society does not expect a hostess whose guest says or does something displeasing to her to react as does a child whose playmate displeases her. In addition to changes in emotions which existed in childhood, however, maturation also seems to bring into being other emotions which literally did not exist in childhood. The capacity for romantic love is an example. Maternal or paternal love may be another. In the area of emotional maturation (as in intellectual), self-discipline, the habit of making oneself do what is necessary, proper, or right, is a vital element. Adolescents need assistance, too, in achieving emotional maturity without the emotional and social injuries they are likely to suffer if left to their own devices.

Physical Maturation

Physical maturation takes place just as a result of living. Nevertheless, the physical changes taking place in adolescence pose problems which, in one fashion or another, tax the adjustmental capabilities of most boys and girls. Not only is the difference between the sexes intensified in the physical maturation which takes place during adolescence; the bodily changes which occur are often difficult for boys and girls to adjust to emotionally. They cause self-consciousness and sometimes serious feelings of inferiority, and boys and girls need sympathetic guidance and understanding help in adjusting to them.

Social Maturation

Simultaneously the adolescent is faced with adjustment to several differing aspects of relations with other people. He or she is learning to play a different role in relation to the opposite sex. At the same time, different relations with parents are evolving. Simultaneously, although involving different mechanisms, the adolescent is assuming a differing role and relationship as regards other people. In many respects, social maturation places the adolescent under more stress and demands more extensive adjustment and psychological change than does any other maturational area. Adjusting to maturity in this area often precipitates severe emotional conflicts and environmental stresses. The adolescent's need of assistance in achieving social maturation is correspondingly great.

All the factors discussed in Part One exercise their influence on adjustment in each of the four areas we have identified. Heredity not only influences physical development and intellectual capacity, but also the physical form one achieves exercises profound effect on one's emotional and social development, and one's intellect will also influence greatly the course of one's emotional and social development. The potential influence of environment on emotional, social, and intellectual, as well as physical, development has already been discussed at length. The influence of the self concept on an adolescent's confidence, or lack of it, in establishing social relations with the opposite sex is obvious. It is correspondingly influential in determining how he will go about achieving emancipation from parents or adjusting to the emancipation once it is achieved. Will he be a confident, self-reliant, aggressive adult or an insecure person hesitant to plunge into life as an independent agent? The self concept often determines the answer.

All motives characterizing humans, how the boy or girl seeks to satisfy them, the relative values ascribed to them, the relative intensity of each in a given instance, influence the day-by-day thought, feelings, and actions of adolescents in every area of maturation. A strong drive to distinguish himself in athletics will cause Henry to maximize the development of his naturally mediocre physique and physical capabilities. A strong desire for parental approval causes Debra to spend more time studying and less in social activities than the average girl.

In Part Two we shall discuss in some detail what adolescence really is and the process and dynamics of maturing in each of the areas already identified. We shall consider the influence of the factors discussed in Part One on the process, dynamics, and results of maturation in these areas. Also, to bring all the concepts and principles down to the level of their effect on the life and development of a particular adolescent, we shall present cases illustrating the mechanisms we discuss. From study of this mixture of theory and its practical application, the parent, teacher, or counselor will grow in his ability to help adolescents solve their problems of adjustment and achieve better-adjusted adulthood.

CHAPTER 6

WHAT ADOLESCENCE IS

PREVIEW

(Adolescence is an era of growth from childhood into adulthood. It is, roughly, the teen years.)

Pre-adolescence

. . . when the things of childhood begin to be put away, and the biological, social, and psychological paraphernalia of adolescence are being readied for their appearance.

Views of Adolescence

VIEW	TASKS INVOLVED
As psychological maturation	Achieving an adult self concept.
	Formulating a philosophy of life.
	Achieving adult self-direction.
	Acquiring an adult perception of the world.
	Developing a sense of intimacy.
As physical maturation	Achieving the capacity for reproduction.
	Skeletal maturation.
	Achieving adult glandular homeostasis.
	Developing secondary sex characteristics.
	Developing adult bodily proportions.
As achieving integration	Synchronizing a multitude of new physiological and psychological characteristics into a harmonious personality.

ADOLESCENCE can be thought of most accurately as an era, not a point in time. It has no precisely identifiable point of beginning or ending, emerging gradually as it does from childhood—first one aspect, then another—and merging imperceptibly into adulthood as one after another adult pattern of thought, action, and feeling develops and replaces the less mature personality characteristics of childhood and adolescence. A functional definition of adolescence is "that span of years during which boys and girls move from childhood to adulthood, mentally, emotionally, socially, and physically." [1] Its onset in the majority of boys and girls is between the ages of eleven and fourteen, and its completion between the ages of eighteen and twenty-one.

This movement toward adulthood requires further development of the boy or girl, the mastery of new developmental tasks to supplement the ones of childhood discussed in Chapter 2. The transition from childhood to adulthood involves much more than physically growing up, much more than the passing of years and the acquisition of more practice in the social and personal skills of childhood. The adult is not merely a child grown big, any more than the child is merely a miniature adult (as was thought a hundred years ago). Adults have fundamentally different philosophies, self concepts, and modes of adjustment from those of children. In this chapter we shall explore the process of entering into adolescence, a few of the major developmental tasks of adolescence, and some of the specific changes in boys and girls which result from their maturation and mastery of developmental tasks.

PRE-ADOLESCENCE

The onset of adolescence is prepared for by a phase of development identifiable as pre-adolescence. Usually beginning at around age ten to twelve,[2] this period marks the gradual abandonment of the attitudes, thought processes, and behavior of childhood. During the pre-adolescent years boys and girls begin to abandon the games of childhood—marbles, dolls, crude imitations of adulthood involving dressing up in mother's clothes or playing house, hide-and-seek, and games emphasizing violent person-versus-person activity of a disorganized sort. In their place emerge systematized and group-oriented activities.

Pre-adolescence is the time when the boys begin to form gangs, to establish their own society in a form which shows the beginning of a sort of

[1] A. T. Jersild, *The Psychology of Adolescence*. The Macmillan Company, New York, 1957.

[2] E. C. Britton and J. M. Winans, *Growing from Infancy to Adolescence*. Appleton-Century-Crofts, Inc., New York, 1958.

social organization.[3] The gang will typically have identifiable membership
—some boys belong, some are on the fringe, not really members, and
some quite excluded—but there are seldom the formal admission procedures found in the more tightly organized gangs of adolescence. The
gang will engage in strenuous physical activity, loosely organized athletics, and just talk, talk in which the precursory attitudes of masculinity
are developed, talk of what they are going to be, what they will do,
what is wrong with people, and talk of sex. Their gang society begins to
give a sense of security outside the home, a security in human relations
thus far satisfied only by parents. Thus, the gang promotes an ever
stronger independence of adults and a drawing of group strength and
security from one's own peers instead of from the family.

Atlanta, Georgia, Public Schools.

Figure 8. Pre-adolescent boys and girls generally do not mix well.

Much less can be found in psychological and sociological literature
about pre-adolescent girls' gangs than boys'. Observation suggests that

[3] P. H. Furfey, *The Gang Age*. The Macmillan Company, New York, 1928.

this comparative dearth of information is less a reflection of the less prominent place of groups in the lives of pre-adolescent girls than of the nature of girls' groups. Their activities do not take them away from the homes of members to the extent common in boys' groups, and their amusements do not stress team action or other such highly structured activities. In the girls' groups, members begin to assume mentally the roles society will expect them to fill in the future; they will discuss and make games of dressing, social affairs, and religious and school activities. They will not play house or school anymore, but will explore, through discussion and exchange of ideas, the worlds of their older sisters. And they, too, will explore in conversation the new area—sex.

During pre-adolescence the sexes divide sharply and display distinct avoidance of each other.[4] It is as if boys and girls prematurely perceived that they would in a subtle form always represent divergent or conflicting interests and points of view, perceived the socially and biologically fated competition in which they would be later engaged, before they acquired the biological urges which would make them attractive to each other, as if the basis of conflict between the sexes dawned on their consciousness before the dawning of the basis of attraction. Seldom will a pre-adolescent boy or girl permit himself or herself to be identified with the opposite sex in interest, activity, or association. Can you imagine the Cub Scouts admitting a few *girls* to the troop?

Different theories of personality development ascribe different bases for the sharp sexual differentiation of pre-adolescents, from the esoteric foreshadowing of later-life roles, to the mechanistic explanation that they prefer different kinds of games and activities. Whatever the reason, the pre-adolescent period, with its intense sexual segregation, provides a period in which boys and girls begin to identify firmly with their own sex. They may not clearly perceive *why* boys and girls are different, but they are working in the laboratory at molding themselves into the sexually distinct roles which society and nature will later require them to enact.

Sex interests of pre-adolescents are usually vague because of lack of knowledge necessary for detailed interests. The interests usually are confined to talk and speculation because of the relative segregation of the sexes when not in adult-directed activities. The strictly anatomical aspects of sex are not ordinarily the subject of major speculation; living with siblings of the opposite sex, especially younger siblings for whose

4 E. H. Campbell, "The Social-Sex Development of Children," *Genetic Psychology Monographs*, 1939, 21:461–552.

care the pre-adolescent may be partially responsible, gives most children the minimal acquaintance with the bodies and genitalia of the opposite sex necessary to satisfy that curiosity. But stories repeated by older boys and girls and the noticeable reserve of adults on this point awaken curiosity as to the personal-social aspects of sex which are stimulated by, rather than removed by, knowledge of anatomical differences. This is not to say that interest, and even experimentation, regarding sexual anatomy is absent at this time. There *is* discussion of sexual anatomy, and sexual experimentation, both homosexual and heterosexual, is not uncommon.[5, 6, 7] But sexual processes, the social aspect of sex, is of growing interest in pre-adolescence.

Boys of pre-adolescent years engage in extensive sexual fantasies, both in solitary daydreaming and gang discussions. These fantasies, especially solitary daydreams, do not as frequently involve imagining actual intercourse as imagining other physical contacts with, and fantasied domination, humiliation, or subordination of girls. Psychoanalysts often explain such fantasies as the natural outcome of the resolution of the Oedipus complex (in which the son is theorized to have romantic love, incestuous desires, for the mother). As the childish idealization of the mother wanes and she is gradually being rejected as an authority figure, the boy's fantasies reflect his intense reaction against female domination by the female's being dominated and possessed.

Girls seem to engage less in erotic fantasies and more in general speculation on sexual roles and experiences. This is doubtless in part because of the less sexually aggressive nature of the female and (a very real likelihood) the usually greater familiarity of the girl with the masculine sex than vice versa, because of her frequent "mothering" role of younger children. This role, also, gives social acceptance to the girl's curiosity about children of the opposite sex which usually is lacking in the boy's case.

Compared with adolescents, children are relatively tractable and manageable creatures. Although conspicuous exceptions occur, and although all children at times seem hopelessly defiant and unmanageable, in general they want to please adults (with the possible exception of the

5 A. Alpert, "The Latency Period," *American Journal of Orthopsychiatry*, 1941, *11*:126–132.

6 A. C. Kinsey, W. B. Pomeroy, and C. E. Martin, *Sexual Behavior in the Human Male*. Saunders, Philadelphia, 1948.

7 A. C. Kinsey, W. B. Pomeroy, C. E. Martin, and P. H. Gebhard, *Sexual Behavior in the Human Female*. Saunders, Philadelphia, 1953.

two-to-four age, sometimes called the "negativistic age"). They lack the self-confidence to risk serious parental disapproval: "What would I do if my parents turned against me?" they feel. They are physically so inferior to the parents that they feel unable to risk conflict, if the parents exercise reasonable judgment in discipline. With the coming of pre-adolescence, however, children begin to assert themselves as more independent creatures. Group identification with their peers is an important factor in this process; the group furnishes the feeling of belongingness formerly only satisfied by the family. With wider social experience and intellectual exploration the pre-adolescent more and more develops ideas of his own, independent of the ideas and attitudes of parents and often in conflict with them. Much of the growing disagreement between parent and pre-adolescent is a simple matter of mathematics; the number of activities and interests of the pre-adolescent is larger than that of the younger child, and these interests and activities cover a much broader range. Therefore, the potential points of conflict are multiplied.

Pre-adolescents are subject to the restlessness (the desire for activity) of the child, and are so much bigger and demand so many more ways than children do of satisfying their drive to activity that restlessness is magnified as a problem presented by pre-adolescents. Strange postures and squirmings, not wanting to remain at home, generalized violence of activity, all are more obvious as boys or girls grow older and larger. And yet they have only the inhibitions of children in these areas. They want independence, yet they act like children. Here, more than anywhere else, perhaps, the pre-adolescent foreshadows the adolescent!

The pre-adolescent is by nature, without premeditation, the *enfant terrible,* the person who, under the protective guise of childishness, says and does things quite unchildish. He makes shocking remarks, which he dimly perceives to be indelicate, but how could *a child* be expected to know that they are indelicate? [8]

"Daddy and Mamma had a fight last night and are both mad today."

"Come in, Reverend Smith. It's a good thing you didn't get here before we got the living room straightened up from Daddy's party last night—beer bottles and ash trays and cards all over the place!"

"Daddy, why don't you say funny things at home the way you did yesterday with Miss Drake?"

In a multitude of ways they show the ambivalence of their feelings,

[8] M. S. Mahler, "Les Enfants Terribles," Paper read at the Meeting of the New York Psychoanalytic Society, December 9, 1947.

childish innocence and unexpected sophistication, the desire for independence—"I don't see why I can't go with them if *they* think I'm old enough!"—and for the security of parental protection—"It's too far; I'm scared to walk home by myself!"

All this is natural, because the pre-adolescent is feeling his way along. He is driven not only by a desire for independence, but also by endocrine changes which begin to emphasize the child's masculinity or femininity of feelings years before the onset of puberty. As early as ten years of age in girls and eleven in boys, there typically begins a strong secretion of sex hormones, the male androgen and the female estrogen.[9] These secretions prepare the boy and girl for the physical roles they will increasingly assume,[10] and may also influence their developing emotional, mental, and social characteristics. They are breaking away from childhood, sporadically, and with many half-frightened retreats into its security. In its own way, pre-adolescence may mean as great a change in the boy's and girl's life as the adolescence for which it prepares them.

Case of Linda

Eleven-year-old Linda has become an enigma to her parents, her younger sister, and, to a considerable extent, herself. Always a quiet, affectionate, and confiding child who tended her younger sister "like a little mother," she has recently become a regular grasshopper, running here and there, "never still a minute." Her mother grieves that she does not confide in her as she used to; instead, she is eternally on the telephone talking to girls, some of whom Mother does not even know, and either visiting with them or having them into her room for interminable chattering which ceases abruptly when Mother enters. Little Sister is hurt that Linda no longer wants her to go along when she goes to the drug store or movies with her friends. Her father is puzzled over how one day Linda is demanding high-heeled shoes, and the next is insisting on running around barefoot. She fusses about having to go to bed at 9:30 and tries by every stratagem to avoid her chore of helping with the dishes in the evening. Her mother and the mother next door have resignedly accepted the fact that their daughter and son, respectively, detest each other, despite

9 I. T. Nathanson, L. Towne, and J. C. Aub, "Urinary Sex Hormone Studies," in R. N. Sanford, *Physique, Personality and Scholarship*, Monographs of the Society for Research in Child Development, *8*:70–81.

10 F. L. Ruch, *Psychology and Life*. Scott, Foresman and Company, Chicago, 1958.

the families' friendship, although, amazingly enough, that twelve-year-old boy recently took a sound beating from an older boy whom he attacked for teasing Linda. He walked her home, bloody nose and all, and later that afternoon they were insulting each other. Linda's mother is relieved that her daughter has shown no interest in sexual matters, but is uneasy about the conversations between Linda and her little clique which suddenly terminate when she enters the room.

1. List as many manifestations of pre-adolescence shown by Linda as you can.

2. What is the developmental significance of each of these phenomena?

3. Are there any indications of abnormality in Linda's attitudes and behavior?

ADOLESCENCE AS PSYCHOLOGICAL MATURATION

Achieving an Adult Self Concept (The Sense of Identity)

The child must, because of his size and dependence, primarily regard himself as one who moves within an environment created by others. Others determine where he lives, what he wears, whether he goes to school, to a great extent what he does, what happens when he becomes ill, how he gets where he is going, and a thousand other things. Most of these things the adult not only determines for himself, but regards himself as the final judge of whether or not they are wise. In American culture today a person legally of age can manage or mismanage his life, commit disastrous blunders of poor judgment, mis-raise children, and, short of proven criminality or mental illness, no one can do anything about it. It is a tremendous jump from the child whose every action is subject to veto by the adult, who by sheer virtue of age is independent of all restraint short of legal action, which never touches most portions of his life.

Adolescence is a period in which the boy or girl begins to think of himself or herself as an independent agent.[11] The self concept he has already acquired of mastery or submission, competence or incompetence, sociability or nonsociability, is not necessarily altered, but all the ele-

---

[11] K. C. Garrison, *Psychology of Adolescence*. Prentice-Hall, Inc., Englewood Cliffs, N.J., 1951.

ments of childhood self concepts must be reinterpreted in light of greater personal responsibility for one's fate. The conflicts faced by the adolescent in adjusting to growing independence, vigorously and aggressively fought for and yet bringing with it situations in which guidance and protection are sought, are a continuation of similar feelings in pre-adolescence, but with a difference: by the end of this stage of development there is not, within the boundaries of normality, a sanctuary or way of turning back. The child can easily surrender, temporarily, independence for immunity or protection if a situation becomes too rough for him; it is harder to do so as adolescence progresses, and when the age of eighteen or twenty-one is reached, it becomes impossible in many areas and impractical in others. Thousands of young adults have thought, with a twinge of unbelief, "Can this be *me,* signing this paper that makes me pay for *a house?* How on earth can I know this is the right thing to do? What if I've made a mistake? There won't be any way I can get out of it now." Even more poignant are the frequent misgivings, "What am I doing with a baby? I don't even know how to hold one! What will I do to make him stop crying, and what will I do if he doesn't?" In fact, it can safely be ventured that every sensible, responsible person has similar feelings to some extent; those who do not simply do not know what they should be anxious about. Only the completely ignorant are completely blissful! Doubts assail even the best-adjusted, most mature person of good intelligence, and continue to do so to some extent throughout life.

A growing breadth of experience, self-confidence based upon past experience and successes, realistic appreciation of one's own limitations as opposed to the brash overconfidence of ignorance, the gradual assumption of greater and greater areas of self-determination, learning to live with ever greater penalties attached to poor judgment, are some of the raw materials from which the adult self concept is formed. As in the case of younger children, the adolescent who is overprotected, provided immunity from normal ill results of his misbehavior or poor judgment, is being carefully prepared for future trouble or tragedy. He is being taught to adjust to a world which does not exist except in the never-never land of parental oversolicitude and misguided love. When the normal course of events forces him to assume a place in the world as an independent agent, he is insecure, as he has a right to be.

Adolescence, then, requires the experience of accepting both growing adult opportunities for self-determination and the responsibility for the results of the use of those opportunities. Thus boys and girls learn to identify themselves, as the years pass, as competent men or women, and be justified in such self concepts.

Formulating a Philosophy of Life

This adult self concept or sense of identity may be thought of as the answer to the question, "Who and what am I?" and a philosophy of life as the answer to, "What are my values and goals in life?" [12], [13] Do I want to raise a family, put roots down in one community, become one of its pillars, and die with the respect of lifelong friends as my enduring monument? Do I want to go where there is a certain type of work or activity, making the world my home and letting the future take care of itself? Do I want to build a business empire or a fortune more than I want the games of golf or the evenings with my family that I think I would have to sacrifice to build the empire? Am I most interested in doing what I believe will help humanity, or do I feel that in the long run humanity will be helped most by my doing whatever will help me achieve most? Does personal gain come as a natural by-product of genuine contribution to the long-run welfare of society?

There are philosophies of life which promote good adjustment and happiness in life, and those which do not. The "beatnik" has a definite philosophy of life, but a shallow and defeatist one which will inevitably lead to neurosis or criminality if persisted in; a bad philosophy of life is *not* better than no philosophy! But at the same time, a clear philosophy provides a rudder for the child embarking on the sea of independence. Religion attempts to provide such a philosophy, along with other things. But religion is typically silent on nonmoral, but highly important, personal questions such as the ones in the preceding paragraph. "Beauty is Truth, Truth Beauty; That is all ye know, and all ye need to know" may be a succinct statement of the life values of a dedicated scientist and may be a wholesome philosophy. Most of us, however, have questions, such as "What do I believe about capitalism as opposed to socialism?" "How important is friendship?" and a thousand others, whose answers will determine the course of our lives at critical points.

The quest of adolescents for guiding principles of life frequently can be detected in their questions. "Ought a mother to work when she has

---

[12] H. Cantril, *The "Why" of Man's Experience.* The Macmillan Company, New York, 1950.

[13] J. C. Coleman, *Personality Dynamics and Effective Behavior.* Scott, Foresman Company, Chicago, 1960.

small children?" seeks a concept balancing superior provision for material needs against a closer parent-child relationship. "Ought a person to do what he thinks is right, even if it makes him unpopular?" usually is asked in relation to a specific situation, but illustrates the seeking for a principle which goes beyond opportunism. "Ought a person to quit work in order to live a few years longer, or accomplish all he can before he dies?" "Is it better to have a job that pays good money or one that offers security, if you can't have both?" "I am interested in a lot of things. How can I tell what sort of work it will be best for me to go into?"

Many educators and psychologists believe that to best prepare boys and girls for happy, successful lives, at least as much time should be devoted to helping them think through the answers to questions such as these, *as applied to their individual personalities and lives,* as is given to more conventional subjects of school and college.[14] Certainly, the person who leaves school or college with a clear plan of what he wants from life and what he regards as the most rewarding way of living has a very real asset as he begins his post-education adjustment.

Observation reveals that some adolescents in their early teens seem naturally to begin planning their lives far into the future, planning in general terms of life goals, if not specific vocations or procedures. Others live for the pleasure of the moment. To that extent these latter boys and girls are failing to mature psychologically in keeping with the passage of years. The former have a better chance of avoiding delinquency and maladjustment, because they are developing a mature concept of life before they are thrust willy-nilly into it. Such a concept of life is one of the psychological structures adolescents need to build as an essential part of their development into adulthood.[15]

Achieving Adult Self-direction

We have recognized the fact that the adult must identify himself as a person who accepts ultimate responsibility for his actions and their results. A corollary of that condition is that the adult needs to school himself to do the things that need to be done whether or not he wants to do them, and refrain from doing the things not in his or others' best interest even if he wants to do them.

14 L. J. Cronbach, *Educational Psychology.* Harcourt, Brace and Company, New York, 1954.

15 R. J. Havighurst and H. Taba, *Adolescent Character and Personality.* John Wiley & Sons, Inc., New York, 1949.

Adult self-direction involves two qualities: the self-discipline to act on the basis of discretion rather than preference, and the perceptiveness to recognize what action discretion dictates. Neither of them is inborn, or comes as a result of maturation, or springs into being of its own accord. Each of them is both an attitude and a skill, to be developed by experience, accompanied by guided study and analysis of their roles in a multitude of situations. During adolescence, boys and girls need to begin the self-determination they will have to exercise as adults, but not haphazardly; they need to begin and execute instances of it as a studied program of increasing their sensitivity to and perception of the implications of situations.[16]

Lennie wants to buy a swimsuit and beach coat for the Senior Day outing. She cannot, because of family finances, do this and also get the new formal she wants for the graduation dance. If left alone, she will probably buy the beach attire, because Senior Day is this week. Should she be permitted to, or told not to, or told that she must make her choice? All leave something to be desired. How can this situation be managed so that Lennie will handle future situations better because of having dealt wisely with this one? How about asking her about the relative advantages of the beach outfit and the formal in terms of the outing and the dance, but also in terms of this fall when she will be going away to college or to work? Which would satisfy the most acute need between now and four months hence, when the family budget might reasonably be stretched to buy the other? By making such an analysis, Lennie not only buys an article of apparel more carefully; she also acquires experience in evaluating alternatives and in basing her decision on mature consideration rather than on impulse. By hundreds of such decisions successfully made, Lennie acquires the capacity for wise adult self-direction.

Self-direction can be made too heavy a load for the adolescent to carry, defeating its own purpose by taxing him with responsibilities beyond his maturity of character. Seventeen-year-old Jake wants to go to the coast during the spring holidays, as many of his classmates do each year. His parents know there are frequently wild drinking parties, dangerous driving, and serious trouble with police on this traditional spree. A seventeen-year-old boy can hardly, by his unaided judgment, be expected to weigh all these factors wisely. How can his parents cause Jake

[16] A. Gesell, F. L. Ilg, and L. B. Ames, *Youth, the Years from Ten to Sixteen.* Harper & Brothers, Publishers, New York, 1956.

to make a mature, responsible decision about the advisability of his going, and how he shall act if he does go? How can teachers help?

Self-direction at this level is properly postponed until very late adolescence, almost until the time Jake will be able to do what he wants to regardless of what his parents wish. It involves the most intense desires on one side and a multitude of quite imponderable factors on the other. Self-direction here should probably be granted adolescents only when they have displayed a consistent pattern, over years past, of self-direction in matters of less magnitude intelligently made and successfully carried out. Whose car? Where staying? With whom? Such factors can be anticipated and weighed. Whom will you meet? What will they be doing? What will be your alternative if you do not join them? These questions and dozens of others cannot be answered, and yet they are the key issues involved in the self-direction which will be required.

When is the proper time to be in at night? Encouraging responsible decisions based on good judgment of individual situations, perhaps with preliminary discussion of "What about if . . . ?" promotes better maturation into adult self-direction than adherence to a specific hour. Yet, if the boy or girl proves incapable of exercising such judgment and discretion, learning self-direction on a lower level of complexity is indicated.

Self-discipline plus intelligent evaluation of situations equals adult self-direction. Such skills and attitudes are best learned by guided experience. Children act on impulses, because that is the way to follow the course of least resistance—"doing what comes naturally." Adults act on impulses sometimes too, but the adults who make the best adjustment to life do so less frequently than children do. In fact, one of the descriptions of a person who acts on the basis of feeling rather than thought, impulse rather than judgment, is "immature"; this implies acting in a childish, rather than an adult, fashion.

Adolescence, particularly middle and later adolescence, brings a multitude of impulses with which the child did not have to contend. The powerful impulse of the sex drive, the adolescent boy's near mania to drive (and preferably fast), to drive whether he has legitimate access to a car or not, and the adolescent girl's typical craving for popularity which often demands satisfaction regardless of the cost in other areas, are all examples of new and unusually intense impulses with which the adolescent must cope to avoid delinquency and achieve well-adjusted maturity. All emphasize the importance of systematic training in how to exercise intelligent self-direction and training in exercising this self-direction on the basis of personal judgment. Practice in self-direction is better than repression and parental domination, which prevent both mistakes and the opportunity of learning!

Left to themselves, like Topsy who "just growed," boys and girls will usually achieve reasonably intelligent self-direction. Many will not, and will wind up as delinquents or general misfits in life, and many who do achieve adequate adult self-direction will bear the scars of unnecessary trials and tribulations experienced through finding out how to evaluate and cope with situations through blind trial and error. Teaching, counseling, and parental control which help adolescents develop a considering, evaluating, thinking-through of issues as an *habitual* way of selecting a course of action is probably as good insurance as can be given them against making disasterous mistakes in adulthood.

Acquiring an Adult Perception of the World

Did you ever think how very different the physical world must look to a child as compared with how it looks to you? The author once knew an extremely successful kindergarten teacher who spent most of her working day either sitting on the floor or on a tiny, child-size stool, because only then, she said, could she perceive the world as it looked to her children. The table may be something you can look over, with difficulty, but cannot reach things on. A doorknob must be grasped in both hands, and the door opened by backing up—difficult unless it works well. The people with whom the child is most closely associated tower over him, as not even the tallest man towers over the most petite woman. Money is something that comes out of a purse or pocket, and its only perceptible use is to exchange it for ice cream or candy.

The nonphysical world is perceived by the child just as differently from the way the adult perceives it. Work is a task that takes you five minutes or fifteen minutes or an hour. Responsibility is something you are supposed to do that your parents will make you do (maybe) if you don't. If you do not and they do not, nothing bad happens. Christmas is a time in the dim future, so far off as to be unreal. You go to the dentist because Mamma says you have to, which is mean of her because it is not fun to go to the dentist; the tooth *felt* all right, so why all that fuss about it?

The adolescent is slowly and gradually gathering deeper concepts than those above, but he has a long way to go. He wants to be a lawyer because to him a lawyer is somebody who becomes famous by making brilliant deductions and speeches in court. Security is something he is maladjusted without, but as far as he consciously perceives, it means having a home, parents, friends, and something to eat. He is yelled at by a brickmason whose materials he disturbed, and feels that brickmasons are grumpy people. She honestly cannot see any reason for her to wash her face when she is going to put powder on it anyway, or perceive any difference between the way mascara, high heels, and low-cut dresses look on her at fourteen and the way they look on her favorite movie star. Why does Daddy want to stay at that old office so long every day that there isn't time to go swimming afterward? What is the use of having money if you don't spend it? Why spend your time doing things you don't want to do; you only live once, don't you? Cops want to cause people trouble.

All of the above are representative of the perception the adolescent is likely to have of the world. It is the perception of a person who reacts to the surface appearance of things, who has yet to understand the principles on which a social order operates, who does not comprehend the demands made on one by life and circumstances. Predominantly they are perceptions which are badly distorted by desires and emotions, but which the boy or girl thinks actually reflect reality.

Erroneous perceptions die hard, particularly when they are based on feelings rather than on a thoughtful but mistaken evaluation of reality. A constant plaint of parents and teachers dealing with an adolescent is, "Can't she *see* that it will hurt her all the rest of her life if . . . ?" and "I can't get him to realize that he simply *has* to. . . ." The adolescent has an extremely limited perception of the relation of the future to the present; even intellectually it looks to him as if so many things could happen that it is hardly worthwhile to do so-and-so because it will help you *later on,* instead of thus-and-such which will be so very pleasant *now.* When the distorting effect of emotions on reasoning is brought into the picture, clear perception is even more difficult.

As in other areas, experience holds the answer to growing into adult perceptions of the world, experience accompanied by sympathetic help in looking backward and piecing together the answer to *why* things turned out this way, and how unhappy results could have been avoided. Hindsight is easier and much more certain than foresight. By a teacher's or parent's helping him to examine what he did and what happened as a result, the adolescent becomes better able to grasp, emotionally as well as intellectually, what he needs to do now or in the future to achieve goals he desires and an adjustment to the world as it actually exists. Thus, gradually, as water erodes a stone, childish conceptions of how things operate in the world are worn away, and in their place develops an adult picture of life as it really is.

Developing a Sense of Intimacy

It has already been noted that children are egocentric. First they notice people who do things for them. Then they play *beside* other children (parallel play) but not *with* them. Later they engage in group activities and show concern for the feelings and happiness of others. Before the end of childhood they are capable of great love for parents or friends. They are also confiding, and tell parents and each other things with minimal reserve. They develop friendships, but the friendships are typically based on mutual interests and activities, geographic proximity, or transitory affections.

Adult relationships are "close," not primarily on the level of interests and activities, but in a sense of fellowship and sharing, of finding in others qualities that supplement their own, making them more whole, more complete, as a result of their association. The adult's need for association with a member of the opposite sex to complete his or her sense of identity, to achieve full self-realization, is an expression of the mature achievement of a sense of intimacy. In a less conspicuous manner, adult friends of the same sex are selected less on the basis of sterling qualities they may possess than on the basis of the responses each elicits from the other.[17]

It is a subtle thing, this ability to open oneself so that another becomes not merely a cooperative partner but, particularly in the case of happily married people, a part of one's own ego. One becomes happy for no reason at all except that the other is happy, is sad only because the other is sad, and, when the other succeeds, achieves vicarious triumph almost indistinguishable from that coming from one's own achievement. Thus, the devoted wife feels she is succeeding when her husband does, and the good husband feels he is a member of the community through his wife's activities. The phenomenon is also observed when men who work closely together are genuinely indifferent as to

17 N. Reader and H. B. English, "Personality Factors in Adolescent Female Friendships," *Journal of Consulting Psychology*, 1947, *11*:212–220.

which receives a mark of esteem because of intimate ego identification with each other.

Such a sense of intimacy is seldom possible in the absence of a strong self concept, a feeling of security which makes it possible for the individual to place some of his sense of identity in trust with another without a feeling of loss or apprehension. People who marry without having achieved the mature personality able to let part of itself be taken by another, and in turn embody a part of another within itself, are unusually likely to separate from their partners, finding the marriage state incompatible with their personality structure.

Experiencing a multitude of relations with others, superimposed upon the mastery of the preceding developmental tasks which produce a healthy, mature personality, is the course through which the sense of intimacy is achieved.[18] Through many associations, some close, some casual, the adolescent gradually begins to acquire a basis for evaluating people with whom he comes in contact. As he acquires an adult self concept, he seeks a more complete relationship with some of those he meets whom he inarticulately perceives as people with whom a sharing of some aspect of life will make his own life more complete. In some of his choices he will find himself mistaken, find that his personality and that of the other person do not each become stronger and more complete as a result of their interaction. On such occasions it is important that he recognize his evaluation as faulty and continue his quest, instead of concluding that "people are no D—— good!" and fixating at an immature level of personality development. This is one of the dangers of too early and too intense adolescent love affairs or attachments to one of the same sex; the almost inevitable breakup of such an attachment may inhibit the adolescent's willingness to expose himself to another such disappointment or frustration, and thus seriously interfere with his eventual adult adjustment to persons of both the same and the opposite sex. ". . . all men count with you, but none too much" is a sound policy for adolescents to follow, but on a declining scale, because having some people count with you very much indeed is one mark of the healthy maturation of personality.

Case of Mike

Mike's parents had heard and read so much about the "revolt" of

18 E. H. Erikson, "Identity Versus Self Diffusion," in M. J. Senn (ed.) *Symposium on the Healthy Personality*. Josiah Macy, Jr., Foundation, 1950, pp. 134–143.

adolescents and their unpleasant attitudes and behavior that they dreaded their son's entering a period in which he would be so different from the sweet, agreeable child he had always been. Mike is now sixteen. In many ways he has fulfilled the prophecies of the J.'s friends, who had older children, but in many ways, too, Mike has pleasantly surprised them. His process of growing up has not, by any means, been one solely of fighting with them, making himself obnoxious, and demonstrating insufferable ignorance and simultaneous conviction of his own omniscience. In many ways, living with Mike during his adolescence has been a rewarding experience for his parents.

Although the family was in good economic circumstances, Mike insisted on getting a job this summer. He was no longer a child, he said, although from the allowance his parents gave him you would think he was. He found a job ten miles from town on a truck farm. "It's not," he explained to his parents, "exactly what I'd rather do, but it pays better than anything else I can find."

His mother dreaded the idea of getting him up and fed in time to catch the truck a half-mile away at five o'clock each day for the ride to the farm. To her surprise, the first morning, going in to awaken Mike, she found his bed empty and found him finishing a plate of eggs in the kitchen. He looked at her in surprise. "Gee whiz, Mom, you can't get up at four every morning! Don't worry about me. After I get paid, if I want to, I'll eat something down at the diner on my way to catch the truck."

The end of the first day Mike came home exhausted, somewhat worried but happy. "The boss said I wasn't hefty enough to 'work a row.' " he explained. "He's having me drive the tractor and the trailer down between the rows that the fellows gather from, and load the trailers. The way I drive makes a lot of difference in how hard they have to work. I don't want to make them mad, but I've got to keep up the speed the boss tells me to. Sometimes I don't know just what to do, but I have to do *something*. You can't just let the tractor sit while you make up your mind."

The end of the second day Mike was exhausted and grumbling. He had spent most of the day in the shed packing and had angry blisters to show for it. His mother was shocked at his weariness and the raw red splotches on his palms where the blisters had burst.

"Hadn't you better look for something else, Son?" she asked. "It looks to me as if that job is a little too heavy for you."

Mike was outraged. "You don't do that, Mom," he said. "The fellows all kidded me some about having a soft snap riding the tractor. If I quit, they'll think I wasn't willing to do my part. In a few days the blisters will turn to calluses and I'll harden up to it. Besides, the boss says that next week he'll need every hand he can possibly get. He's counting on me. After all, I asked for the job!"

As the summer wore on, Mike had to deal with the decision of answering some malcontents who wanted to take advantage of a crucial need for pickers on a perishable crop to demand higher wages. He had refused. "When I asked for a job, they didn't try to beat me down and get me for a little less because I was little," Mike told his father. "I'd look good trying to hold them up, wouldn't I? I'm going to do a job here that will help me get jobs in the future."

Mr. and Mrs. J. were surprised that only rarely did they have to urge Mike to get up and on his way in time. One morning he snarled at them to leave him alone, and they did. When he awakened at nine he was furious, and he dressed and hitchhiked to the farm. After that he was up on time. He was relieved of most of his chores around the house when he took the job, but did the others better than ever before. "They're simple compared to what I'm *used* to doing," he said with obvious pride.

As a result of his early rising, Mike's social life has been restricted this summer to early-evening dates. He seems to his parents, however, to be more self-confident and unself-conscious in his relations with the girls he sometimes brings by the house. Mr. and Mrs. J. fear that Mike's going to work signals the end of his being their obedient child, but do not know what they can do about it.

1. What part has Mike's job played in the changes that can be inferred to have taken place in him? What if he had not taken a job?

2. Construct hypothetical self concepts for Mike: his self concept when he started to work, and his self concept two months later.

3. How do you explain Mike's various attitudes and experiences regarding getting up in the morning to go to work? Why did he angrily drive his parents away and later be outraged because he had overslept?

4. Explain the implications of Mike's discussing his dilemma about how to drive the tractor. How would such a situation help him mature?

5. Was Mike's mother's reaction to his blistered hands a reasonable one? What about Mike's determination?

6. What fundamental issues confronted Mike regarding the proposal to demand higher wages?

7. Explain Mike's changing attitude regarding doing his chores.

8. How might Mike's work experience be affecting his sense of intimacy?

ADOLESCENCE
AS PHYSICAL MATURATION

For centuries it was believed that emotional and organic differentiation of the sexes began at the approximate time of the menarche (beginning of menstruation) for girls and the beginning of seminal emissions ("wet dreams") for boys. Recently it has been recognized that the outward evidences of sexual differentiation are the culmination of months or years of increasingly differential glandular activity.[19] Many criteria have been established to denote the approximate onset of adolescence, also referred to in slightly varying shades of meaning as "puberty" and "pubescence," as a point in the process of maturation. The point at which reproduction becomes possible is a widely accepted criterion.

Acceptance of capability of reproduction as the beginning of adolescence, however, merely transfers the difficulty of recognition from one process to another, because, contrary to popular belief, neither the menarche nor nocturnal emissions necessarily mark the onset of reproductive capability. Degree of ossification of bones, eruption of the "wisdom teeth," and enlargement of neck and pelvic region in boys and girls respectively have been suggested as more valid criteria of sexual maturity than any primary or other secondary sex characteristics.

Marked changes in bone structure take place during maturation, and, in the minds of many, the most dependable criterion of maturity is the boy's or girl's osseous development, the state of maturation displayed by

19 I. T. Nathanson, L. Towne, and J. C. Aub, "Urinary Sex Hormone Studies," in R. N. Sanford, *Physique, Personality and Scholarship.* Monographs of the Society for Research in Child Development, 1943, *8:*70–81.

the bones when X-rayed. Typically, the bones not only grow larger and heavier, but their ends, especially ends which form joints, change in shape and proximity as maturation progresses. Replacement of carti- lage by bone in the joints accompanies maturation. Sexual maturation has been found to relate highly to the occurrence of certain changes in joint structure. "Skeletal age" is a term sometimes used to indicate de- gree of maturity achieved in terms of bone growth and bodily structure.

It is desirable for the worker with adolescents to be aware of these biguities resident in such terms as "adolescence," "puberty," "pubes- e," and "sexual maturity," because they account for much of the rgence among the reports of investigators as to when these periods gin. If adolescence is given its common social connotation of a period evolving independence and heterosexual interests, the divergence be- mes even greater. Fortunately, as far as effective work with boys and rls is concerned, the precise onset of adolescence and its exact con- mitants are of only academic interest. What is vital is a sensitivity to e occurrence in adolescence of numerous bodily changes which accom- ny or produce far-reaching changes in the psychological lives of boys d girls.

These changes begin as early as nine years of age in girls and eleven boys. They may, on the other hand, delay their appearance until as as fifteen in girls and sixteen in boys, with individual adolescents aying even wider variations. The pre-adolescent production of sex nes will ordinarily have been accompanied by a growth spurt, e earlier onset of that function in girls means that from the age of ugh twelve girls are, on the average, somewhat taller and heavier ys. This phenomenon is easily observable in upper elementary ten in the first two junior high-school grades. During this period uperior social maturity of girls is also conspicuous. Production of sex s in the sex organs begins at an average age of fifteen years for girls d probably about sixteen years for boys.[20]

The most important single determining factor in age of maturation seems to be heredity. Early and late maturational patterns definitely "run in families." A temperate climate is also conducive to early matura- tion. Until a few years ago this fact was not realized, cultural patterns of early marriages in certain primitive societies having led to erroneous conclusions as to the age of maturation, especially of girls. Healthy, well-

[20] C. S. Ford and F. A. Beach, *Patterns of Sexual Behavior*. Harper & Brothers, Publishers, New York, 1951.

The Atlanta Journal-Constitution

Figure 9. "During this period the superior social maturity of girls is also conspicuous."

fed children tend to reach sexual maturity earlier than do less favored ones. Boys who mature early tend to have more feminine body build, broader hips, and more slender shoulders than later-maturing boys. Correspondingly, late-maturing girls tend toward the masculine pattern of weight distribution, with broader shoulders and narrower hips than their earlier-maturing friends.[21]

Various changes in bodily proportions accompany adolescence.[22] The child's head has achieved almost its adult size when adolescence is reached, and becomes smaller in proportion as other bodily parts continue to grow at an accelerated rate. The legs become longer in proportion to the length of the trunk as the infant matures into adulthood. A bigger proportion of total body weight becomes concentrated in the muscles during adolescence, especially in boys. A boy's physical strength is likely to double during the time in adolescence that his body weight is increasing by perhaps a fourth or a third.[23] This phenomenon can easily be noted by comparing the physical feats of the average boy in late adolescence with an overgrown boy of the same weight who is only entering adolescence.

Hardly a part of the body of a boy or a girl is not influenced by the physical changes accompanying adolescence. Arms and legs grow at a faster rate than do the trunk and the head during these years. The hips of girls and the shoulders of boys widen. Often both boys and girls develop a temporary "fat period," in which fatty tissue accumulates on boys much in the feminine pattern—on chest, abdomen, hips, and thighs. Girls are likely to be overdeveloped in these areas for a time. The fat period usually begins toward the end of pre-adolescence, at the beginning of the growth spurt, and lasts for about two years. All these and many other changes take place in addition to the development of the sexual and reproductive organs.

Present knowledge indicates that ultimate control of sexual maturation rests with the *endocrine* glands, ductless glands whose secretions are entirely within the body. Of these, the *pituitary* gland is the most influential in precipitating sexual maturation.[24] While the pituitary gland does not itself produce the hormones which cause sexual maturation, its secretions trigger into activity the glands which do produce such hormones.

[21] N. Bayley, "Skeletal Maturing in Adolescence as a Basis for Determining Percentage of Completed Growth," *Child Development,* 1943, *14*:1–46.

[22] M. S. Margolese, "Mental Disorders in Childhood Due to Endocrine Disorders," *The Nervous Child,* 1948, 7:55–77.

[23] H. E. Jones, *Motor Performance and Growth.* University of California Press, Berkeley, California, 1949.

[24] C. H. Li and H. M. Evans, "Chemistry of Anterior Pituitary Hormones," in G. Pincus and K. V. Thimam (eds.) *The Hormones: Physiology, Chemistry and Applications.* Academic Press, New York, 1948.

Pituitary overactivity of a certain sort can set off the glandular mechanisms of sexual maturation so early that some babies have been known to develop mature sexual characteristics. Failure of the pituitary gland to stimulate the glands directly responsible for sexual development, on the other hand, can delay indefinitely the individual's sexual maturation.

The *adrenal cortex* is also influential in controlling sexual development through the hormones called *adrenal androgens*. These hormones control the "secondary" sexual characteristics, such as the deepening of the voice which occurs in both sexes, the appearance of pubic hair on both sexes and beards in the case of boys, the pimples which plague so many adolescents, and certain sweat glands. Overactivity of the adrenal cortex in girls produces marked masculinity in appearance, known as *virilism*. The "bearded lady" of the circus usually owes her condition to overactivity of the adrenal cortex.

The *gonads* are the actual sex glands which directly control primary sexual functioning. Triggered by the pituitary gland, the gonads produce not only sex hormones which influence sexual development, drives, and behavior, but also the reproductive cells. It is the gonads which begin the secretion of sex hormones in pre-adolescence and set off the "adolescent growth spurt." The nonreproductive sex hormones produced by the gonads are called, in the male, *testicular androgens,* and in the female, *estrogens* and *progestin*.

The female gonads are called *ovaries*. Their nonreproductive hormones, called estrogens, are responsible for the typically feminine development of the body, the development of child-bearing organs, the breasts, the other bodily functions related to child-bearing and motherhood. It seems likely that estrogens also influence the development of attitudes of femininity much as the testicular androgens influence masculinity. The secretions called progestin produce changes in the womb (uterus) which enable it to support fetal life.

The menarche, the time of first menstruation, occurs in the girl at an average of about thirteen and a half years, and menstruation continues in a more or less regular twenty-eight-day cycle for some thirty or thirty-five years until the menopause (also called the climacteric and the involutional period). Usually the first periods of menstruation occur quite irregularly, the time between them varying from two to six weeks.[25] As adolescence advances and the newly developing glandular activities

[25] L. B. Arey, "The Degree of Normal Menstrual Irregularity," *American Journal of Obstetrics and Gynecology, 37,* Jan., 1939.

of the body achieve a degree of homeostasis, the periods tend to become regular, but notable irregularities may occur through the late teens. Occasional instances of irregularity, in fact, may occur at all ages and usually indicate nothing more than a temporary variation of ovarian functioning.

Male and female reproductive cells are collectively called *gametes*. The female reproductive cell is produced by the ovaries and is called the *ovum*. Its appearance usually follows the menarche by several months. Ordinarily each ovary produces and releases one ovum about every fifty-six days, and, there being two ovaries, this means that one ovum is released approximately every twenty-eight days. It is sucked into the Fallopian tube, leading from the ovary to the uterus, and proceeds into the uterus. If it has met and been fertilized by a sperm on the way, it attaches itself to the wall of the womb, and reproduction has begun. If it was not fertilized, it disintegrates and is voided in the menstrual flow, along with the progestin-stimulated materials which the womb had prepared to nourish the new life, if it had begun. Release of the ovum, called ovulation, occurs about midway between the beginning of the periods of menstrual flow, ordinarily twelve to sixteen days after the beginning of the preceding menstrual flow.

There is considerable variation in adolescent girls in the order of appearance of "secondary" sex characteristics, meaning those not directly related to the reproductive processes. In the most frequent pattern, the pre-adolescent secretion of sex hormones gives the first external signal of approaching puberty by a plumpness of the abdomen due to the growth of the uterus and other internal organs of reproduction. This growth usually begins prior to the skeletal enlargement that makes room for the enlargement of these organs. Then the pelvic bone grows, enlarging the abdominal cavity, and the characteristically plump abdomen of the pre-adolescent girl disappears as the pelvic cavity becomes large enough to accommodate the organs. In its place come the wider, rounder hips of the woman, due partly to the enlargement of the pelvis and partly to the increase in amount of subcutaneous fat around the hips. While these changes are taking place, the breasts usually begin their growth with the development of subcutaneous fat, and then in a few months begins the growth of pubic hair around the external genitalia. About this time, also, the growth of hair under the armpits becomes noticeable, and a light fuzz develops on the upper lip. It is at about this stage that the menarche usually occurs, during the period of growth of pubic and axillary hair. It may be either preceded or followed by the deepening of the voice, which, however, is seldom as noticeable as in the case of boys. All the secondary sex characteristics take some time to develop, and the process of physical maturation that began at age ten or thereabouts will not be completed until around age eighteen.

Testicular androgens influence the virile skeletal development of the boy, as contrasted with the more delicate bone structure of the girl. They also control sexual desire and are responsible for the greater sexual aggressiveness of boys as contrasted with girls. With sexual aggressiveness go the qualities popularly associated with masculinity—the capacity for romantic love, energy, and aggressive ambition. Loss of the *testes,* the male gonads, early in life prevents the development of masculine sex characteristics and the masculine psychological pattern. Men who have been without testes since boyhood constitute the popular conception of the eunuch. As was noted previously, however, the testes are not the only controlling factor in sexual appetite; males deprived of testes after physical maturation has taken place often retain both the appetite and the capability for sexual activity for years, although they are incapable of reproduction. The male reproductive cells are produced exclusively by the testes and are called sperm.

Growth of the external male reproductive organs, the penis and the testes, usually marks the approach of puberty in boys at about the age of twelve. The penis and the testes are small and inconspicuous in infants and small boys. About the beginning of the adolescent growth spurt of boys, the penis and testes begin rapid development, reaching approximately their ultimate size considerably before over-all physical growth is completed. Early in the growth spurt of the testes and penis, downy hair appears around and particularly above the penis, replaced by short, scant pubic hair. Development of body hair dominates the picture of the development of secondary sex characteristics in boys, appearing on the upper lip, the arms, legs, face, armpits, and perhaps around the nipples, in roughly that order. "Breaking" and deepening of the voice usually occurs around the age of fourteen and lasts for two to four years before his voice again becomes a boy's dependable tool.

Maturation of boys in primary sex characteristics, the ability to reproduce and mechanisms for it, does not parallel that of the girl in drama or extent of change accompanying it. The penis is capable of becoming erect and hard even in infancy, and thus no change in its habitual pattern is involved in sexual maturation. Production of sperm and, there-

fore, capability of reproduction may be considered the technical criterion of puberty in the male, but the time at which this maturation takes
place is often obscure. In the majority of instances the production of
sperm by the testes is followed in about a year by the beginning of nocturnal emissions, commonly called wet dreams, in which the body rids
itself of surplus sperm and the fluid, called semen, accompanying them.
Most men whose sexual activities do not expend their accumulations of
semen will have seminal emissions about every two to five weeks until
the male climacteric is reached, usually in the sixties. However, the time
of the beginning of seminal emissions seems to be even more variable
than the time of the origin of reproductive capability is thought to be.
They usually occur first, however, between the ages of twelve and sixteen, with the average probably about fifteen or slightly earlier.[26] Production of sperm is not accompanied by any other organic functions or
bodily changes in the male, although certain activity of the prostate
gland accompanies the activity of the testes.

These, then, are the physical changes of greatest psychological significance which take place in adolescence. The profound psychological
effects accompanying them and the problems of adjustment they produce
will be discussed in Chapters 10 and 11.

ADOLESCENCE
AS ACHIEVING INTEGRATION

The beginning driver will often, in his preoccupation with the shifting of gears, veer dangerously across the road, then suddenly, his attention recalled to steering, relax his foot from the gas, and so on. He has
not achieved a smooth synchronization of thought and movement in a
complex pattern of behavior. Forming a consistent, nonconflicting life
pattern from the several abilities, attitudes, and conditions discussed in
this chapter also involves a high degree of synchronization. Forming a
Gestalt, a systematized pattern or configuration, giving each element its
proper place and perspective, is fully as difficult as mastery of any one
of the adjustmental demands made by the different aspects of adolescence. This synchronization, like the smooth handling of an automobile,
comes from proper practice. Some of the vital factors influencing how

26 W. W. Greulich, *et al.*, *Somatic and Endocrine Studies of Pubertal and Adolescent Boys.* Monographs of the Society for Research in Child Development, 1942, 7,
No. 3.

well the adolescent is able to make all these adjustments, and the procedures he goes through and the problems he faces in making them, will now be considered.

READINGS

Britton, E. C., and Winans, J. M., *Growing From Infancy to Adulthood*. New York: Appleton-Century-Crofts, Inc., 1958, pp. 58-67.

Crow, L. D., and Crow, A., *Adolescent Development and Adjustment*. New York: McGraw-Hill Book Company, Inc., 1956, Chapt. 1.

Jersild, A. T., *Child Psychology*. Englewood Cliffs, N. J.: Prentice-Hall, Inc., 1960, Chapt. 10.

Jersild, A. T., *The Psychology of Adolescence*. New York: The Macmillan Company, 1957, Chapt. 1.

Jones, H. E., *The Family in a Democratic Society*. New York: Columbia University Press, 1949, pp. 70-82.

Stone, L. J., and Church, J., *Childhood and Adolescence*. New York: Random House, 1957, Chapt. 10.

Strang, R., *Introduction to Child Study*. New York: The Macmillan Company, 1959, Chapt. 16.

Watson, R. I., *Psychology of the Child*. New York: John Wiley & Sons, Inc., 1959, Chapts. 11, 12.

CHAPTER 7

ACHIEVING MENTAL

MATURATION

PREVIEW

(Cognitive changes in adolescence are quantitative rather than qualitative. "Mental abilities" is a more accurate expression than "mental ability," but here, as elsewhere in psychology, the holistic principle prevails and people's "general intelligence" factor is more dominant than their "special abilities.")

Factors Affecting Mental Growth

FACTOR	EFFECT
Innate ability	Sets a seldom reached upper limit on mental achievement.
Effort	Determines the degree to which innate ability is exploited.
Environmental facilities	Influence the opportunity to cultivate innate ability to its full potential.
Emotional adjustment	Provides the basic confidence and self concept needed for full mental maturation.

Features of Mental Maturation

GROWTH	
	Toward facility in manipulating abstractions.
	In the ability to analyze and synthesize.
	In the ability to make fine discriminations.
	In the ability to make accurate generalizations.
	Away from trial-and-error methods.
	Toward appreciation of remote goals.
	Away from two-valued orientation.
	Toward self-criticism and evaluation.
	Toward rational self-control.
	In knowledge.
	In logical reaching of decisions.

197

THE NATURE OF COGNITIVE CHANGES IN ADOLESCENCE

IT is unlikely that any new mental abilities make their appearance in adolescence. This is in contrast to the three other areas of the dynamics of adolescence which we shall discuss. Physical maturation brings about new conditions, conditions which did not exist in lesser degree earlier. These new physical conditions produce the capacity for emotions (romantic love, for instance) and heterosexual relations which did not exist before, and produce problems of social adjustment different in innate nature from those existing before maturation. But in the area of cognition, all elements have been present from childhood, if not from birth. Maturation during adolescence does not signal the emergence of the ability to apply divergent thinking to semantic concepts, for instance. It simply accentuates the productive capacity of the existing ability.

Adjustment to the changes in cognitive functioning is usually simpler than adjustment to the other changes, for several reasons. Not only do the cognitive changes produce no absolutely new problems with which the adolescent must cope, merely variations of old ones, but also emotions, ethical conflicts, and basic drives cause fewer problems in this area than in the other three. Rational, rather than affective, processes are principally involved.

A good picture of normally expected growth in mental abilities from the pre-adolescent to the late adolescent period can be gained from a comparison of the tasks to be performed by the ten-year-old and by the superior adult (representing a theoretical mental age of about seventeen years) on Form L of the Revised Stanford-Binet Scale.[1]

The ten-year-old is expected to know the meaning of eleven of the forty-five words in the vocabulary list, the upper limits of his vocabulary being such words as "muzzle," "haste," "lecture," and "Mars." The person with a mental age of seventeen is expected to know a minimum of twenty-three of the listed words, including such words as "tolerate," "stave," "lotus," and "bewail."

In the area of reasoning he should have progressed from being able to answer such questions as "Give two reasons why children should not be too noisy in school" to such sticklers as: "I planted a tree that was

[1] L. M. Terman and M. A. Merrill, *Measuring Intelligence.* Houghton-Mifflin Company, Boston, 1937.

8 inches tall. At the end of the first year it was 12 inches tall; at the end of the second year it was 18 inches tall; at the end of the third year it was 27 inches tall. How tall was it at the end of the fourth year?" This is to be solved without the use of pencil and paper.

At the age of ten the child is expected to be able to remember for immediate recall only six digits read to him one time. The adolescent with a seventeen-year mental age must remember eight. (Those extra two make a lot of difference; check and see by having a friend compose and read a six- and then an eight-digit series for you to try.)

Such expectations of mental growth—increased ability of the mind to cope with more complex, abstract, or uncommon symbols—are reflected in the curricula of our schools. Textbooks double in size and more than double in complexity of thought content and language from the elementary grades to senior high school. But in addition to growth in sheer mental power to comprehend more complex material and remember more, mental maturation involves growth in certain broader and complex areas, areas wherein growth is vital to successful adjustment to an adult state of life.

On the Army Alpha Intelligence Test the scores of examinees increased about 125 per cent between the ages of ten and eighteen. Examinees twenty-eight years old, on the other hand, made slightly lower rather than higher scores.[2] This indicates that during the adolescent years the rate of progress in mental activities is great indeed.

For the worker with adolescent boys and girls, the most significant facts relating to adolescent mental development are not revealed in graphs showing gains in the basic factors comprising the complex of intelligence. The most significant considerations lie in the complex application that the adolescent is learning to make of his growing mental powers to his life situation. Growth in memory span and spatial perception is paralleled by growth in decisiveness and ability to generalize accurately. His growth in "absolute strength" in different factors of intelligence, for instance, is multiplied by his skill and resourcefulness in applying this superior "strength."

This chapter will be devoted principally to an exploration of these most practically significant areas of mental growth during adolescence and the directions such growth takes. Specific ways in which growth

2 H. E. Jones and H. S. Conrad, "The Growth and Decline of Intelligence: A Study of a Homogeneous Group Between the Ages of 10 and 60," *Genetic Psychology Monographs,* 1933, *13,* No. 3.

occurs in various areas and directions will be included in the discussion of each type or dimension of growth, and the dynamics by which the growth is accomplished will be outlined. However, a few influences affecting growth of mental ability should be noted as a background for consideration of specific growth areas.

Any consideration of the rate and amount of growth in mental abilities during adolescence is complicated by the fact that mental abilities are just that—plural, not mental abili*ty*. Growth in different abilities proceeds at different rates during the adolescent years. However, despite the technical fact that "intelligence" is compounded of several different, less complex factors, a person's range of ability from the factor in which he is strongest (divergent thinking, cognition, memory, convergent thinking, and evaluation, to use one classification)[3] to the one in which he is weakest is typically relatively small—that is, the person distinctly superior in one of these factors will in most instances be superior, or at least above average, in most or all others.[4] Similarly, the person notably low in one factor will almost always be below average in most or all other factors. It is difference of interest and effort (or perhaps the teacher's strictness in grading) in different courses which account for most variations in a student's grades in his various courses, not a high intelligence for science, for instance, and a low one for history, or vice versa.[5]

A PRACTICAL CONCEPT OF INTELLIGENCE

A classic concept of the nature of intelligence held that intelligence was the capacity to carry on accurate, effective abstract thinking. The influence of that concept in the foregoing exploration of mental maturation is obvious. Recently there have been many attempts to identify abilities related to physiological senses which might be included as aspects of intelligence. "Mechanical reasoning," such as the ability to perceive functional relationships between a source of power and the direc-

[3] J. P. Guilford, "Three Faces of Intellect," *The American Psychologist*, 1959, *14*:469–479.

[4] L. J. Cronbach, *Educational Psychology*. Harcourt, Brace and Company, New York, 1954.

[5] J. B. Stroud, "The Intelligence Test in School Use: Some Persistent Issues," *The Journal of Educational Psychology*, Feb., 1957, pp. 77–85.

tion that force would be applied after passing through a set of gears and belts, is one example. Speed of perception is another.

By the use of factorial analysis, school grades, and reasoning, some educators and psychologists have arrived at the conclusion that there is no such thing as "intelligence." There are "intelligences." Of course, this is true to a certain extent, as was discussed in the preceding section. In various grades boys do sometimes show up above the class average in shopwork or reading and below the class average in arithmetic, and vice versa. Sometimes they rank notably higher on one type of intelligence subtest than on another. Such cases are rather exceptional, but spectacularly conspicuous when they do occur.

The concept that intelligence consists of several, perhaps many, different components, while not invalidating a conception of general, over-all "high" or "low" intelligence, does have a significant implication for people working with boys and girls. This implication has to do with a theory once strongly believed in, but for years past discarded as erroneous, and now once more appearing to be promising in light of the concept that many elements comprise intelligence. It is the theory of mental discipline in a more refined form, the theory that there are such entities as logical reasoning, imagination, and the like. Psychologists using the approach to mental abilities called factorial analysis appear to be successfully isolating separate mental abilities entering into the composition of an over-all "intelligence." Some leaders in the field are openly suggesting the possibility (believed in implicitly at the turn of the century, but considered an ignorant superstition for many later years) that education may actually develop certain mental abilities in a form which can be transferred and applied to all sorts of life situations.[6]

A most important concept for the teacher or counselor to keep in mind is that although for the sake of clarity different aspects of "intelligence" are identified and discussed as separate "factors," the holistic principle holds good here as elsewhere. Boys and girls react with "intelligence" as an integrated whole, not with this ability or that "type" of intelligence in isolation. Therefore, one should keep in mind that rates of growth and level achieved by a boy or girl in different aspects or factors of intelligence will vary. However, the variations are not usually great enough to be of practical significance, and for practical purposes it is seldom worth the teacher's or counselor's time to try to distinguish

6 J. P. Guilford, "Three Faces of Intellect," *The American Psychologist*, 1959, *14*:469–479.

between the adolescent's "intelligences" in the different areas. The observation of Burt[7] that the "general" factor of intelligence commonly accounts for about 50 per cent of the variance in cognitive ability, whereas each of the "special" factors accounts for 10 per cent or less, seems to imply accurately the significance of "general intelligence" to the teacher as contrasted with "special abilities." (A partial exception to this is the case of the boy or girl fairly adept at mechanical or other "concrete" types of work who is hopelessly lost at types requiring what most of us think of as intellectual ability. Such boys and girls can profitably be directed into areas where their sight, simple perception, and manual skills can partially compensate for their relatively lower ability in dealing with abstractions.)

Case of Mr. Neil's Homeroom

Mr. Neil is looking through the personal-record folders of his new homeroom class, to whom he will teach algebra as well. Bay High follows a policy of loose ability grouping. On the basis of a well-known group intelligence test, pupils are divided into three groups, those with I.Q.'s over 110, those with I.Q.'s between 90 and 110, and those with I.Q.'s below 90. Mr. Neil's class is one of those in the 90-to-110 range. He is pondering not only how well they will do in algebra, but also how well they will do in their other subjects, whether any are likely to fail a subject, and whether he can hope for any who display quite high ability in algebra and other subjects.

1. What range of achievement is Mr. Neil likely to find within his homeroom class in algebra? In other subjects? Why?

2. Will this range of achievement reflect accurately the range of ability within Mr. Neil's class? Why?

3. What implications does all this have for the policy of homogeneous grouping?

FACTORS AFFECTING MENTAL GROWTH

Innate Ability

This is the inherited capacity discussed in Chapter 2. It imposes a theoretical upper limit on the mental growth possible to the individual,

[7] C. Burt, "The Inheritance of Mental Ability," *The American Psychologist*, 1958, *13*:5.

but is less significant than many believe it to be because so few people achieve anything approaching the maximum mental growth of which they are capable. There is a limit on the extent to which effort can atone for limited ability, but few ever approach that limit. It is probable that in most areas of human endeavor the person with an I.Q. of 90 can, by working half again or twice as hard, achieve more and rise higher than will the average person with an I.Q. of 110 and conceivably even 120. Adolescents often do this in their schoolwork.[8] Of course, given equal opportunity and effort, the higher a person's innate ability, the greater heights his mental achievements will attain.

Effort

Even the greatest mental potential will produce lackluster results in the absence of effort to develop and exploit it, just as the potentially great bowler will never achieve excellence if he does not work at it. Part of the function of adults working with adolescents is to encourage them to capitalize as fully as possible on their inherent abilities through assiduous effort. (In all fairness it should be pointed out that some people disagree with this statement, which is, in actuality, a "value judgment." It is based on the assumption that to progress is good, and will probably in the long run bring greater life satisfaction to the individual than finding a safe, comfortable pace and jogging contentedly along at it. In defense of the concept that encouraging adolescents, or children, or adults, to their maximum potential of achievement is good, it may be noted that man's progress, from medical knowledge which saves the lives of mothers and babies to mechanization which makes it possible for the average worker to have his own automobile and power boat, is, by and large, the result of driving, persevering effort on someone's part. The "effortless" life of the more or less mythical, "unspoiled" South Sea islander sounds good, but his lifespan is short because of his lack of facilities which only intense and disciplined effort can design and provide.)

Environmental Facilities

A century ago it was possible for an Abraham Lincoln, with extremely limited facilities provided by the knowledge and efforts of others to help him, to achieve a position of pre-eminence. It probably still is. In fact, some of our important free-lance inventors and writers of today are

8 W. A. Bradley, "Correlates of Vocational Preferences," *Genetic Psychology Monographs,* 1943, 28:99–169.

largely self-educated. However, for every person who achieves eminence in the absence of such aids as schools, the encouragement of family standards, and some cultural elements in their community, there can be little doubt that many other potentially valuable human resources are lost. True genius may be self-starting, not requiring outside pushing, and even self-sustaining. But the simple facts are that the person who must figure everything out for himself instead of starting from the accomplishments of others and building on them has an almost impossibly big job. A high correlation seems to exist between a community's educational facilities and achievement of individuals in that community, just as the companies with the biggest research budgets make the greatest number of discoveries which advance man's health, safety, and comfort. Probably the greatest material gift a community can give its adolescents is the best facilities possible for promoting their mental growth. Mental ability does not wear out, but improves with use.

Emotional Adjustment

Failure to achieve the emotionally oriented developmental tasks of infancy, development of extreme anxiety, frustrations which discourage hope and initiative—such conditions inhibit people in their achievement of maximum mental growth. The discouraged person feels that effort will not bring him commensurate returns; the anxious person is afraid to venture, afraid to try, lest he encounter the crushing experience of failure or the disapproval of others.[9] The person who has not achieved a full sense of autonomy has not sufficiently freed himself from following the paths of others to even think of exercising his own initiative in an aggressive manner. The person with a strong self concept, accustomed to coping with situations from the "position of strength" provided by his good adjustment and emotional security, is psychologically able to strive.

Case of Ollie

Until he was ten years old, Ollie's school grades had been about evenly divided between A's and B's. He seemed to be a responsible youngster, showing good emotional and mental growth, alert, dependable, and conscientious in his home and school duties. The summer of Ollie's tenth year, his father became emotionally involved with a woman in another city, and home life was stormy. A year later

[9] M. Rokeach, *The Open and Closed Mind*. Basic Books, Inc., Publishers, New York, 1960.

the parents were divorced, and Ollie moved with his mother from the well-to-do, tightly knit suburban community where they had lived to the home of her parents in a downtown, economically below-average section of the city. Although the school he now attends is not reputed to have as high standards as the one he had previously attended, Ollie's grades have dropped considerably. Now, at thirteen, he neglects his chores around the house, does not prepare his homework unless closely supervised, shows no signs of the fine mental growth which had delighted his parents in the past.

1. What part did each of the four factors affecting mental growth (discussed in this section) probably have on the change in Ollie?

FEATURES OF MENTAL MATURATION

Mental growth involves much more than adding to one's storehouse of knowledge. It involves increasing mental efficiency in several types of intellectual activity and in several areas. Everyone knows that it involves an improved capacity to remember, as was indicated in the mention of memory for digits at different ages. But it also involves growth and increased skill in more complex operations than rote memory. Following are some of the skills and directions in which adolescents change as they mature mentally. It is probably not saying too much to say that an adolescent's mental maturation is determined by his achievements in these areas. Certainly his degree of maturation is largely *judged* by his status as regards these features, and much of education constitutes attempts to help boys and girls improve along these lines.

Note: Mental immaturity is seldom, if ever, found in the absence of other forms of immaturity. A girl, for instance, may be emotionally mature in her heterosexual interests, but if she is not mentally mature, she will still be emotionally immature from the standpoint of directing and regulating her emotional responses and her actions. The person who appears socially mature, who always knows just what to say and how to act, if not possessing mental maturity, will stumble into ridiculous-appearing situations as a result of poor judgment. Thus, any example of lack of mental maturity is practically certain to contain prominent symptoms of immaturity in other areas of development as well.

Case of Philip
   (As you read the section on features of mental maturation, keep

Philip's circumstances in mind. From time to time there will be questions involving interpretation of Philip's abilities and characteristics in light of facts presented regarding mental maturation.)

Philip S., seventeen, failed three of his four major courses in the tenth grade. He was already one grade retarded from having repeated the fifth. He works hard, spending an average of three hours per day on his studies and conscientiously prepares all assignments on time, although, being equally slow at reading and writing, this sometimes means that he stays up until one or two in the morning to finish an assignment. On a group intelligence test Philip's indicated I.Q. was 75, but on the Terman-Merrill individual intelligence test he achieved an I.Q. of 82. On an achievement test he scored an overall grade placement of 8.6, his highest score being a grade equivalent of 9.3 in mathematics, with history and science the lowest with a placement of 8.1 in each.

Beginning with his repetition of the fifth grade, Philip attended a private school through the eighth grade. He failed one course, history, in the ninth grade, but made it up during summer school and entered the tenth grade with no course deficiencies. He says that he studies until he thinks he knows his assignments, and indeed he does do fairly well in daily classes, but tests, especially final examinations, ruin him.

Physically Philip is somewhat undersize, weighing about 120 pounds. He has a sparse, bristly beard which he does not shave more than once a week. His voice breaks frequently and abruptly from deep bass to a high soprano, and vice versa. He dresses well and neatly. His father is part owner of a wholesale hardware company.

According to the parents (and substantiated by teachers and interviews with him), Philip is a well-behaved, conscientious, obedient, and good-natured boy. He has always been physically frail, and although he has no history of severe illness, he has always been underweight and never seemed to be in really good health. Thorough physical examinations have failed to reveal any definite deficiencies or organic pathology.

Mr. and Mrs. S. seem devoted to each other, to Philip, and to his older sister, Blanche, nineteen, who has now completed two years of college. Philip and Blanche have always seemed closer than the average brother and sister, and Philip sometimes wistfully remarks, without apparent jealousy, that he wishes he could learn like Blanche can. Altogether, the S.'s are a happier and more affectionate family in their relationships with each other than the average family group. The parents feel that Philip is doing the best he can, and consciously refrain from pressuring him for better academic achievement. They are distressed because Philip has several times said, "What's ever going to become of me if I can't even finish high school?" He thinks he would like to go to college, but also thinks that this is unlikely to be practical.

The immediate cause of Philip's referral to the psychologist by a physician was a persistent pattern of nausea and vomiting on school mornings, particularly on days when a test or examination was scheduled. Everyone, including Philip, recognizes that his nausea is probably due to his anxiety over the day's schoolwork, but this, of course, does not cure the nausea.

Philip's academic accomplishments and deficiencies follow this general pattern: He can solve simple arithmetic and algebraic problems pretty well. He has trouble with problems which he must "state" (i.e., put into equation form from verbal statements). His achievement in geometry has been exceedingly low. In English he learns his spelling words and the rules of grammar. He does pretty well on the sentences assigned as exercises in grammar. However, on compositions he makes many errors and receives low grades. Likewise, when asked facts about an author or characters in literature, he usually achieves at least minimally satisfactory answers. However, when asked to discuss some idea or interpret some happening, he falls down. On questions in which he is asked to make interpretations not previously covered in class he is particularly poor. He subsequently laments to his parents, "Some of those questions we hadn't taken up in class! How was I supposed to know them?" but with remarkably little bitterness, only despair.

Science and history follow much the same pattern. Daily or weekly tests which ask for factual information Philip passes, often with grades in the high 80's. When the questions involve his own reasoning, his application of facts to arrive at a conclusion, or examination of facts to determine their significance, he is lost. On final examinations he is likely to fail factual, as well as thought, portions of questions.

Socially Philip is inclined to be solitary. He occasionally takes a girl to a group function, occasionally mixes with boys to a degree.

Saturdays and vacations, despite his family's sound economic status, Philip wants to work and usually gets a job as a filling-station attendant. He bought an old car with his allowance and has got it in good mechanical shape, has done a custom job of upholstering it, and takes great pride in it. He has "souped up" the engine, but does not "drag" or race. He has got only one traffic ticket in almost two years of driving, for running a stop sign. He supplements his allowance (most of which is spent on his car) and his earnings by transporting neighborhood girls to school for the equivalent of bus fare. He has quite a stock of magazines on automotive subjects, and aside from working on his car, his favorite recreation is reading them.

Growth toward Facility in Manipulating Abstractions

Intelligence tests of youngest children consist exclusively of measuring their reactions to concrete objects, movements, or conditions.[10] A bright object is held out toward the child; the younger the age at which he will make coordinated movements toward grasping the object, the more mentally alert he is assumed to be. The first words he is expected to know, to tell the meaning of, are symbols representing concrete objects—"chair," "dog," and the like. Only as he becomes older are more abstract words supposed to be meaningful to him. "Play" is at least a semi-abstraction. Our own observation tells us that a child will usually be able to tell what a dog is before he is able to tell what play is. He will be able to tell what play is before he is able to tell what a more abstract symbol, such as "good," is.

By the time he reaches adolescence, his ability to deal with abstractions has developed beyond mere use of individual words and has begun to include abstract ideas.[11] At the beginning of adolescence he understands what "getting what you deserve," a primitive concept of justice, means. However, he is baffled by the more abstract conception of "social justice." By the time he completes the adolescent years, he should be able to handle several different abstractions simultaneously and construct a meaningful pattern from them in terms of their relation to each other and to a real or hypothetical situation. It is "bad" "sportsmanship" to "resent" the "victory" of an "opponent." Here five words, each representing an abstraction or abstract concept, are combined to produce an

10 A. Anastasi, *Psychological Testing.* The Macmillan Company, New York, 1961.
11 A. T. Jersild, *The Psychology of Adolescence.* The Macmillan Company, New York, 1957.

even greater abstraction, a "philosophy" or part of a "code of ethics."

Like juggling several balls at once, effective handling of abstractions requires practice, gradually increasing the number and degree of complexity of the abstractions. Thus we find the primary-grades pupil being told only of Columbus finding a New World. The abstractions "difficulty" and "navigation" are brought in at the upper elementary level. The concept of the Renaissance, the blossoming of man's spirit as it sought to break the bonds of dogmatic tradition, comes in high school or even college.

Experiences, in school or out, which encourage the boy and girl to exercise the ability to manipulate abstractions help them grow in this ability. This is an objection many serious-minded educators have to the

George Peabody College for Teachers.

Figure 10. "By the time he reaches adolescence, his ability has developed beyond the mere use of individual words and has begun to include abstract ideas."

extreme process of "adapting the curriculum to the child" to such an extent that it always remains well within his easy ability to handle. They question whether his ability to manipulate abstractions such as "city government," "legislative processes," and the like is strengthened as much by visiting the legislature in session as by constructing in his mind the *concept* of a legislature in session. Does it not merely add to his fund of facts and observations, rather than encourage him to produce and cope with a higher-level abstraction, they ask? Television is liberally criticized for the same reason. It is accused of representing ideas and situations so concretely that the boy or girl is not faced with the task of using imagination and abstract thought to attain an idea. Multiply these two situations several thousand times, say these educators, and you have robbed the adolescent of the practice necessary to mature in the handling of abstract concepts as surely and disastrously as you would rob him of physical exercise needed for growth by having him watch television baseball games instead of actually playing.

"Conceptualization" is the term used to refer to one aspect of handling abstractions.[12, 13] It refers to the process of forming a mental picture of something which can, or cannot, be pictured in concrete form. Thus, an engineer can form a concept, can conceptualize a mine shaft, form a literal "picture in his mind" of it, from an accurate written description of the mine as it actually exists. The skilled symphony conductor can, through conceptualization, "hear" a piece of music through looking at the orchestral score as realistically as you and I hear it when it is actually played. Indeed, some music lovers are said to read music they love as others of us read a novel, "living" the music as we "live" the actions of the characters of the novel. All these mental perceptions may be described as high abilities to manipulate abstract symbols so effectively that they become accurate substitutes for the literal timbers or sounds they represent.

Ability in the manipulation of abstractions is not necessary for academic pursuits alone. Nor is it limited to high-level executives who weigh "buying habits of the public" and "rate of increase of gross national product." The skilled sheet-metal worker is manipulating abstractions when he mentally evaluates the stress placed on a joint and the re-

12 G. M. Blair, R. S. Jones, and R. H. Simpson, *Educational Psychology*. The Macmillan Company, New York, 1954.

13 L. J. Cronbach, *Educational Psychology*. Harcourt, Brace and Company, New York, 1954.

inforcement of the joint. The worker less competent in manipulating abstractions does the joint as he has done other joints, depending on concrete experience. The more competent worker "abstracts" from "concepts" of the stress of a situation and the strength afforded by different constructions. Through manipulation of these abstractions (abstract because he constructed them in his mind through foresight, not by making and trying them in material form) he modifies the way he deals with the situation so as to best achieve the desired results.

The stenographer looks over several pieces of dictation given her and ascribes priority to this or that one; in doing so she has engaged in manipulation of abstractions, because she "weighed" the "likelihood" of this one's being "wanted" against the others, and "decided" that this one was most "urgent."

The skill the adolescent acquires in manipulating abstractions swiftly and accurately, finding the best answers or formulating sound opinions in the absence of concrete objects or situations from which to work, will have an important bearing on his future success. "Can't see something until he stumbles over it" is an expression commonly used to describe the person who cannot deal with a matter in the abstract, but must wait until confronted with it in concrete form and then handle it as best he can without the benefit of preplanning.

Question re Case of Philip
1. In what way does Philip show inability to manipulate abstractions?

Growth in the Ability to Analyze and Synthesize

To analyze is literally to take a thing, a situation, or an idea apart and see what it is composed of.[14] A primitive form of analysis is encouraged by curiosity; the small child, given a toy with a peculiar noise within it, is seldom content merely to listen to the noise. He wants to get inside and find out what makes it. On an abstract level and in the area of literary criticism, a part of the critic's work is to do the same thing. A drama is analyzed as to the characterization employed, the emotive factors utilized, the devices (dialogue or situations) which delineate the characters and produce the emotional tensions provoked both in the characters and in the audience.

When the teacher of a fifth-grade class says, "Why did Columbus have

[14] H. A. Larrabee, *Reliable Knowledge*. Houghton-Mifflin Company, Boston, 1945.

such a hard time with his sailors?" expecting such answers as, "They were scared," "They were made to go along and didn't want to in the first place," and "They didn't believe they would find anything," she is encouraging them to practice analysis. Having been told that those feelings existed among Columbus' sailors, but not told specifically that those reasons were back of their recalcitrance, the eleven-year-old child can usually recognize them as component elements in a situation on which he has not been previously coached. This is a simple level of analysis. Having been studying the Middle Ages in European history, a high-school student may be asked, "What were the forces active in Europe which produced the exploratory ardor which led to the colonization of America?" If he has not been taught this topic as a body of facts (how a topic is taught determines whether what is demanded of students regarding it is memory of facts or analysis), his answer will reflect his ability to examine a vast area of social, political, economic, and scientific conditions and pick out the elements crucial to the exploration and colonization of the New World.

The college student of economics may be given many facts relating to the economic structure of the United States in the late twenties, but not told specifically that those conditions produced the "crash." If asked on the final examination, "What was the cause of the collapse of the national economy in the late twenties and early thirties?" he would have to analyze what he had learned about economic conditions at that time to arrive at an answer.

Obviously such analysis represents a fairly advanced degree of growth in mental capabilities. This growth is usually accompanied by corresponding growth on the other side of the coin of analysis—synthesis. Synthesis is putting things together in their proper relation, the achievement of a unified picture from various component parts. Solving a jigsaw puzzle is a simple example of synthesis in concrete form. Looking over a mass of data and rearranging its component elements so that they form a coherent picture is a more complex example, and on the abstract level.

Although in a literal sense analysis and synthesis are precisely opposite activities, in actuality it is often difficult to distinguish between the two, and the same result may be obtained from the same mass of data using either of the two methods. If, in answering the hypothetical examination question as to the cause of the depression of the thirties, the student started with the component facts and put them together to achieve an answer, he would be synthesizing; if he starts with the situation and breaks it down to discover the component facts, he is analyzing. In actuality, both attacks are usually used on problems.[15] The boy or girl asked to explain how the American Revolution came about will run over in his or her mind all the causes of the American Revolution that can be remembered. If they seem sufficient, the question is answered by synthesis, putting together the known facts and arriving at the picture. If the student feels apprehensive about the adequacy of his answer, however, he may also resort to analysis: "Here is the situation in America and England at the time of the Revolution. Now let me break this situation down and see what in it may have promoted the Revolution." By this analysis he would hope to identify component facts which he did not recall from pure memory and to make his answer more complete through "working from both ends" to bring into play as nearly all appropriate elements as possible.

The small child engaging in analysis typically stops too soon; he finds one or a few explanations or critical elements and fails to follow through to a complete analysis. When he reads or hears that the colonists in America "wanted their independence," he is content. As far as he is concerned, he "knows" the cause of the Revolution. The adolescent learns to be more discriminating. Fine discriminations are, in fact, one sign of mental maturation and will be discussed later. *Why* did they want their independence? What made them dissatisfied? In the process of further analysis he learns that the concept of "independence" came along fairly late in the dynamic process which produced the Revolution. Before that, representation in the government of the mother country had been the goal sought by the colonists. Why was such representation wanted? Why did the English colonists demand it, whereas the colonists of other nations did not? As the adolescent grows more intellectually mature, his analytical ability can be developed to a level that makes possible a deeper and more thorough exploration of an abstraction, instead of stopping at a superficial level.

Synthesis is regarded by some psychologists and educators as a more demanding process than analysis. They reason that in analysis all parts of the final result of handling the abstraction or concrete object are present at the beginning. There is the "whole picture," and within it are all the parts; they merely have to be located. In synthesis, they say, only the parts are present; the whole is not there, and, at least in abstract

[15] D. M. Johnson, *Psychology: A Problem-Solving Approach.* Harper & Brothers, Publishers, New York, 1961.

situations (as, for instance, discussing the influence of Poe's personal life on his writings), the parts can be put together incompletely or in the wrong relation, thus producing an erroneous conclusion. They say that synthesis requires creativity, whereas analysis can be accomplished by technical ability without the creative aspect. Thus, the boy or girl might well concentrate on learning to analyze ideas, situations, and material before beginning to try to construct abstract concepts of his own.

We have seen that, in actuality, analysis and synthesis tend to supplement each other, with a person alternating between the two as he manipulates an abstraction in an attempt to arrive at the most thorough comprehension possible of what is involved in a situation. Taken together, proficiency in these two aspects of mental maturation gives the adolescent boy and girl the capability of judging ideas and situations with which they come into contact on deeper, more accurate levels than mere superficial appearances.

Faced with the decision of marrying or not marrying a boy who has proposed to her, the girl who, from lack of intelligence or lack of experience, is unable to marshal all facts which should bear on her decision is unable to analyze the probable marital situation to see what will be involved, and makes her choice on the basis of love and hope. Love and hope are wonderful things, but divorce-court records testify that they are utterly inadequate as sole criteria of suitability of a marriage.

The girl of higher intelligence and/or better education in the merits and processes of analysis and synthesis will ask herself, "What are the various considerations involved here? Certainly I love him. That is a 'yes' factor. Can he support us? Am I ready to settle down to being a wife and mother, through with dating, partying, going out with the crowd, for years to come? Do I want a higher education than I now have? Would I need it to support myself and possible children if anything should happen to Dick? And on the analysis side, what would our life together be like? Are there things about Dick that annoy me? What would be the effect of living with those attributes twenty-four hours a day? Would they weaken our marriage? What would life be like on the amount of money we would have?" Obviously the girl who, as an habitual way of life, approaches problems in this manner will avoid more potential unhappiness and be able to plan better for optimum adjustment than will one lacking the ability or never having been educated to the inclination of analysis and synthesis in making important decisions.[16]

[16] J. T. Landis and M. G. Landis, *Building a Successful Marriage*. Prentice-Hall, Inc., Englewood Cliffs, N. J., 1958.

"Would anyone get married if he or she went through such a process?" the sentimentalist, particularly the boy or girl madly in love, asks. Oh, yes. Millions analyze and synthesize marital possibilities before making the decision to marry or not to marry. The author suspects that these are the ones who account for most (not all, but the majority) of the happily married couples today. They account for the majority of the happily married couples not only because they analyzed and synthesized until they found a person they loved and also a situation in which a happy marriage would be possible, but also because their minds and methods of coping with life have achieved a maturity which qualifies them for the responsibilities and adjustments of marriage. The ones who have not achieved the maturity required for such evaluation of a situation not only get into impossible situations, but the deficiency of mental maturity which betrayed them into the situation also prevents their coping intelligently with the difficulties which arise.

This illustration of a practical application of analysis and synthesis to an important life situation is developed at some length because it not only illustrates the two procedures and their practical use; it also suggests to the counselor ways of helping adolescents plan their lives so as to give themselves maximum chance of happiness and minimum chance of tragedy in one great area of life.

Handling abstractions competently is obviously a prerequisite of analysis and synthesis of any matters except simple, concrete ones, such as whether this pole will reach from this wall to that.[17] The quality of analysis and synthesis of which the adolescent (or anyone else) is capable depends heavily on some refined aspects of dealing with abstractions, which will be discussed next.

Question re Case of Philip
    2. Evaluate Philip's probable ability to analyze and synthesize.

Capability of Finer Discriminations

Increasing proficiency in any field is typically signaled by the capability to make finer discriminations.[18] The beginning tennis player simply cannot discern the difference in the play of a five-dollar racket and one

---

[17] W. E. Vinacke, *The Psychology of Thinking*. McGraw-Hill Book Company, Inc., New York, 1952.

[18] G. G. Thompson, E. F. Gardner, and F. J. DiVesta, *Educational Psychology*. Appleton-Century-Crofts, Inc., New York, 1959.

costing five times that much. He cannot analyze the differences because he cannot perceive them, cannot recognize the significance of a certain type of stringing, etc. As he becomes more expert, he can make finer and finer discriminations of quality. Similarly, in the more abstract mental areas, the elementary-school child may be able to distinguish a phrase ᵢfrom a clause, but be unable to distinguish between an adjectival and adverbial phrase. In his study of history he may be able to distinguish between the political philosophies of Jefferson and Hamilton, but be unable to distinguish between those of more similar leaders such as Franklin D. Roosevelt and Harry S. Truman. By late adolescence a boy or girl might reasonably be expected to read a chapter describing the philosophies of each of the latter and distinguish their distinctive elements. At the college level such discrimination between the policies of Madison and Monroe might be within the capability of a student, but would require a fineness of perception quite beyond that of the elementary-school pupil.

Capability of making fine discriminations depends heavily on the ability to manipulate abstractions.[19] "Fiscal policy" is an abstraction, and so is "strict" or "loose" construction of Constitutional provisions. These and similar abstractions must be mastered to such an extent that conceptualization of them becomes automatic, requiring no conscious thought, leaving the full resources of the mind available to concentrate on even more esoteric concepts in the process of making fine discriminations in the field of political science. A multitude of facts and instances are gathered, analyzed, and interpreted as to the nature of Hamilton's and Jefferson's philosophies. The more precise and comprehensive the synthesis, the more similar the compared or contrasted forces can be and still permit differences in them to be perceived.

As in the case of the two previous areas of mental maturation, growth in the ability to make fine discriminations depends heavily on practice. General maturation of mental ability is, of course, required; no amount of practice will enable a person with a mental age of, say, ten years to make fine discriminations on highly abstract and complex subjects. But maturation alone is not enough. Being held responsible for increasingly fine discriminations in everyday work is the method by which such superior discrimination is developed. This is the great reason for the im-

19 J. Dewey, *Logic—The Theory of Inquiry*. Holt, Rinehart & Winston, Inc., New York, 1938.

portance of increasing standards of precision as the adolescent ages from year to year. Failure to use a comma properly may go unnoticed in the elementary grades. In high school it may justify a notation and slight mark-down in grade. In college the same error may demand a failing mark or redoing the paper, because discriminations of that degree of fineness are held to be essential for one to receive credit for a certain course.

Precision in making discriminations is partly an attitude, also. It is hard, demanding work; much harder than obtaining a general idea and calculating that two factors are "substantially the same." But success or failure is often determined by the accuracy of one's discriminations. The teacher who does not study his students carefully enough to identify the faint distinction between Bill's interest in science as science and Henry's interest in science as a promising area for a well-paid career will not meet Bill's and Henry's individualized needs as well as the one who does identify or perceive the difference. The broker who analyzes reports and spots a crucial element of difference in two stock situations which to most people appear identical will attract and hold a clientele of investors who seek his services, and one who is less thorough in making such a fine discrimination will not be as successful. The mother who can distinguish between a tired baby and a sick one will save herself untold anxiety and trouble, as well as rear a better-adjusted child. Unremitting attention to maintaining a high standard of accuracy of discrimination, until any lower standard is unsatisfying to him, is the need of the adolescent for mental maturation in this area.

Question re Case of Philip
   3. Why is Philip probably unable to make fine discriminations?

Growth in the Ability to Make Accurate Generalizations

In one sense, this is carrying the ability to synthesize one step further, to derive from the synthesis of abstractions (or concretes) a still greater abstraction—and to do it accurately. A small child sees a round ball. He throws it, it bounces, and he is delighted. He sees an egg, comparatively round to his imperfect discrimination, and he throws it. Maybe he still laughs, but not for the same reason. He generalized that one thing was round and bounced, so other round things should bounce also. His idea was good; at an early age he has begun to exercise his mind in a manner which may eventually produce a high ability to generalize. But his generalization was inaccurate. He had not synthesized all pertinent facts in deriving his generalization.

Faulty generalizations are rife among adults. I visit Chicago three times, and each time it is raining. The completely inept person might generalize, "It always rains in Chicago." A somewhat more knowledgeable, but slightly superstitious, person may say, "It always rains when *I* visit Chicago." Accurate generalization requires accurate perception of *all* pertinent facts regarding a situation and accurate identification of how they relate to the situation. One man generalized, "Stopping three feet from a car is enough safety margin," to which another replies, "Not when you skidded the last fifteen feet before stopping there!" One citizen generalizes, "There is always a depression when the Demublicans come into power." He may be right or wrong. Is it a depression when an unhealthy inflation is healthily readjusted? When unemployment rises 10 per cent; 5 per cent; 15 per cent? Does the depression (if any) result from fiscal policies pursued by the Demublicans' predecessors in power who were at last voted out because of their unsound policies? If ten persons at a dinner party partook of the broiled lobster and seven of them became ill, is it a sound generalization that the lobster caused their illness? If five? If nine? If all ten?

Children will generalize from a single instance; they have little concept of "probability," or the fact that one instance does not establish a rule. They are ignorant of the amount of data to be synthesized before a generalization is justified. Adults are prone to do this, as well as to commit other errors in generalization. A German or a Jew is guilty of some injury to someone, and the injured party generalizes, "You can't trust a German (or a Jew)." Much prejudice is the result of this type of misthinking. The action of one person is generalized into a description of a group.[20]

As part of the process of maturation, adolescents should learn the possibilities and limitations of generalization. They learn that not only are several mutually substantiating instances of a phenomenon required to provide the basis for a generalization, but that a logical relationship between the instances and the generalization must be present in order for the generalization to be justified.[21] Thus, the fact that five salesmen were given transfusions of type O blood and all died would not consti-

[20] A. R. Lindesmith and A. L. Strauss, *Social Psychology*. Holt, Rinehart & Winston, Inc., New York, 1956.

[21] E. A. Burtt, *Right Thinking*. Harper & Brothers, Publishers, New York, 1946.

tute reasonable basis for a generalization that type O blood was fatal to salesmen. On the other hand, if five men with type A blood were given transfusions of type O blood and all died, at least a tentative generalization that type O blood was fatal for people with type A blood would seem justified.

Accurate generalizing also requires the ability to identify the critical element of similarity in a number of instances, which is a type of analysis. From heeding a coach's instructions to take a chance in such and such a situation, the alert quarterback may arrive at the accurate generalization that when you are behind and the game is nearly over, you take chances you would not take if you had a narrow lead under the otherwise same circumstances. A student's experience may reveal that ten hours of study concentrated just before a monthly test gives him better results on the test than an hour a day for the ten days preceding the test, but that it later results in a lower grade on the part of the final examination devoted to that section of the course. From this the student may generalize that concentrated study gives better short-term recall but poorer long-term retention. Subsequent experimentation may prove whether in his particular case this is true. Which, in turn, brings up the question of another generalization: Does the fact that this principle of study holds true for James Jones mean that the generalization can safely be drawn that the principle holds good for most or all people? Probably not. Other people would have to try the experiment to ascertain the limits to which the generalization can be extended.

The diversity of elements which must be considered in making generalizations varies so much with the circumstances that a listing of them is impossible. Time, weather, sex, age, concomitant circumstances—the range is infinite. Thus, it is unrealistic to expect the adolescent to learn all the specific circumstances which render generalizations applicable or inapplicable. By literally thousands of trials, however, on questions such as, "What can we conclude from . . . ?" "To what extent does . . . ?" "What type of person is most likely to . . . ?" with guidance in perceiving why given answers are sound or questionable, he acquires a "feel" for accurate generalizations as opposed to spurious ones. A major weakness of school curricula which stress largely the memorization of facts (if there are such curricula) is that they give the student little guided experience to develop his skill and perception in generalization.

Acquiring the ability to generalize accurately bolsters the adolescent's self concept tremendously. It gives him confidence in his ability to cope with situations different from ones he has previously encountered, through use of generalized concepts acquired in specific situations but applicable to others. It is, indeed, a high thought process, carrying manipulation of abstractions to the nth degree. It is an outstanding characteristic of the mentally mature person.

Question re Case of Philip
    4. How would you evaluate Philip's ability to make accurate generalizations?

Growth away from Trial-and-Error Methods

All the foregoing areas of mental maturation produce increased ability to cope with situations through *mental* manipulation of pertinent factors, instead of the slower, more costly, and potentially disastrous method of physical trial and error. Thus, the girl who can, in abstract form, identify the elements which would be present in a particular marriage, analyze and synthesize all appropriate elements, exercising fine discrimination as to the effect this as opposed to that would have, can determine with considerable validity whether the contemplated marriage would prove satisfactory without actually trying it.[22] The advantage is obvious. It is also advantageous to be able to determine how thick a dam must be to withstand a specified pressure without building successive dams until one fails to break or building a dam four times as thick and expensive as needed. Determining whether one's budget will support a new car by analysis and synthesis is likewise preferable to finding out by trial and error.

Trial and error is the primitive "natural" way to find out. It is used exclusively by animals not having the power to engage in abstract thought. The monkey, trying to reach a banana, tries repeatedly and vainly to thrust a paw through a hole too small to accommodate it. The infant does the same. The older child tries it once or twice and stops. The adolescent does not try at all if the hole is obviously too small, but may analyze the situation in his mind: "The hole won't let my hand go through. It may be there just to fool me. On the other hand, it may have a real purpose that doesn't appear on the surface. Let me look over the whole puzzle situation and see if there is something there which

[22] E. A. Burtt, *Right Thinking*. Harper & Brothers, Publishers, New York, 1946.

will give me a clue. There is a stick. It would go through. Maybe I could reach the banana . . . no, it would not be long enough (he decides without even trying the stick). Let's see what tools I have to work with here and what I could do with them (synthesis). I could lasso it with this cord . . . but it wouldn't be long enough either. That other stick? Shorter still . . . but maybe tied together with the cord . . . would that makeshift rake the banana? Probably not. The coat hanging over there. Any help? No, not that I can think of . . . hanging there; it's on a hanger. Wire. Bent into a hook and tied to the stick with the string . . . O.K. I've as good as got that banana right now!" And so he has, in a few seconds of abstracting, analyzing, synthesizing, discarding certain possibilities through discrimination without even trying them, without ever touching a single one of the literal objects used in his thinking. Thus, manipulation of abstractions made quick and easy a job which on a trial-and-error basis could have been interminable.

The pre-adolescent will try to solve arithmetic problems on a trial-and-error basis. Do this and see if it gives the answer. If not, do something else. Eventually maybe something will. The younger adolescent will typically try to persevere in the same pattern. To write a term paper, he sits down and starts putting what he thinks of on paper. Eventually he finds that he overlooked something back yonder. Have to do it over. (Or, with a boy or girl with a different disposition, "Let it go; maybe the teacher won't notice it.") Then he can't think of anything else to say, and hasn't written enough to satisfy the requirement yet.

By middle adolescence it is to be hoped that the boy or girl has learned to substitute abstract planning for trial and error, learned to project a proposed course of action into the future and anticipate results without actually going through the motions of trying it out. Adolescents have to be encouraged to do this, especially boys. With a surplus of bodily energy and a dissatisfaction with sitting still, and sometimes with a marked reluctance to apply their minds to the taxing effort of formulating and projecting an abstraction (as difficult, mentally, as holding a weight at arm's length is physically!), the adolescent often prefers to try things at random rather than think them through. This is why teachers put great emphasis on method and reason for method and not just on answers in mathematics courses. Developing the habit of substituting thought for trial-and-error action is a valuable goal of education, for achieving this habit and capacity is an important aspect of mental maturation.

Question re Case of Philip

    5. To what extent does Philip probably depend upon trial-and-error methods for solving problems?

Growth toward Appreciation of Remote Goals

This aspect of mental maturation was discussed in a preceding chapter from the standpoint of developing adult values. Here we mention it as an ability, not as a desirable standard.[23] Appreciation of long-range goals, as we use the term here, implies both the emotional capacity to postpone immediate pleasure for the sake of later welfare and the mental capacity to project a plan into the future. In a sense, it is like building a bridge extending from one side of a ravine through and over empty space, aimed at a destination on the other side, but without tangible connection with the destination until it is actually reached. This calls for high facility in manipulation of abstractions, and manipulation systematically directed toward a specific goal. Involving, as it does, both emotional maturity and high facility in manipulating abstractions without a tangible point of reference at one end of the manipulations, formulation and pursuit of long-range goals might well be regarded as the outstanding criterion of mental maturation.[24]

Children have extremely limited ability to project their thoughts into the remote future on anything like a realistic basis. This is not surprising. Their ability in almost everything falls short of that of adolescents. We know that their ability to remember improves as they grow older. Just as the child's physical eyesight is poor by adult standards, he is also unable to "look ahead" figuratively, in the dimension of time. The average child at one year has a visual acuity of 20/200—that is, he can see at twenty feet what the average adult can see at two hundred. At three years of age he can only see at twenty feet what an adult can see at fifty feet (20/50).[25] Correspondingly, he is unable to exercise self-discipline to the extent that an adult can; not *unwilling* to, but *unable* to, just as he is unable to lift the weight an adult can. He is incapable of the degree of logical reasoning he will be capable of as an adult.

Ability to perceive cause-and-effect relationships and project these

23 L. Tussing, *Psychology for Better Living*. John Wiley & Sons, Inc., New York, 1959.

24 K. C. Garrison, *Growth and Development*. Longmans, Green and Co., New York, 1959.

25 B. H. Schwarting, "Testing Infants' Vision," *American Journal of Ophthalmology*, 1954, *38*:714–715.

relationships into the future is the basis of thinking and working in terms of long-range goals. People of low intelligence seldom acquire this ability to project their thoughts into the future and construct, by a logical extension of past experience, present experience, applicable principles, and anticipated conditions, a realistic picture of a future time. Consequently, not being able to construct the realistic picture, they are incapable of designing a rational course of action which will eventually achieve the reality of the picture constructed. Some people mature chronologically and in most mental abilities without ever achieving this ability to construct realistic remote goals and program their behavior in terms of them.

Question re Case of Philip
    6. Evaluate Philip's appreciation of remote goals.

Growth away from Two-Valued Orientation

A child sees things and thinks of things as right or wrong, big or little, this way or that—in short, black or white. A war was a good thing or a bad thing and was won or lost. This way of thinking is called two-valued orientation, as contrasted with thinking and values which recognize objects and conditions as possessing an infinite number of degrees of gradation from "allness" to "noneness." [26]

Such thinking is unrealistic because it is opposed to reality, in which things are seldom "all" or "none" but somewhere in between. Yet the pre-adolescent testifying as to a fight at school says, "It was his fault (pointing to one participant), not his (referring to the other)." Observation of the speech and behavior of small children gives strong evidence of what might be called man's search for absolutes. They are seldom contented with the explanation of a television character that "He was good in some ways and bad in others" or similar descriptions of a friend that "In some ways he is nice, but in other ways not so nice." The child persists, "But is he *good* or *bad?*" In deciding whose "fault" a fight was, children seldom seek a division of blame; they rule one party guilty and the other innocent.

Applied to life, such a two-valued orientation is ideal ground for frustration, maladjustment, and discontent, because it has the person attempting to adjust to a never-never land where all things are at one

26 S. I. Hayakawa, *Language in Action*. Harcourt, Brace and Company, New York, 1941.

extreme or the other.[27, 28] Is a marriage happy? Obviously most marriages are happy to some extent, unhappy to some extent. Ideally marriages should be "happy." Is mine "happy?" Well, there are some things about it which could be improved. With a two-valued orientation firmly entrenched as one's habitual pattern of evaluating life, this statement means that it is not happy; therefore, it must be unhappy. Every marriage counselor has had numerous cases where marital troubles sprang largely from a husband's or wife's looking for absolutes: a mate is "perfect" or he is "imperfect." If imperfect he (or she) should be changed. This ignores the fact of life that people are good or bad by *preponderance,* not by totality.

In evaluating Roosevelt's measures for combating the depression of the 1930's, the high-school student typically looks for "the answer." Were they good or bad? Were they effective or ineffective? Considerable effort and ingenuity on the part of the teacher is often necessary to lead the boy or girl to perceive questions as having mixed answers, neither all one way or another. The science experiment works or it doesn't work. The idea of partial success and partial failure, so familiar to you with your intellectual maturity, is really a difficult one for the adolescent to grasp.

It is especially difficult when his emotions are involved. A boy who loves a girl with adolescent fervor sees her not as a person with good and bad traits. He idealizes her. The one he dislikes he consigns to undesirability with the same totality. Thus, when by patient effort a teacher has developed in an adolescent the habit of thinking of a president or an author as having some capabilities and lacking some, the adolescent encounters a situation in which his feelings are involved and reverts to his more primitive evaluations, and thus subtly weakens the habit of recognizing all traits as falling on a continuum, not at opposite ends of a line. Parents, many adults, interfere with the adolescent's full comprehension of the significance of graded evaluations by oversimplification. Religion is good. (Some require human sacrifices; are *they* "good"?) The result of an election was bad. (Was the elected candidate all bad, the defeated one all good?) The company or the government "ought to" do this or that to rectify some situation. (Would that completely take care of the situation, without damaging side effects, as the opinion implies?)

[27] S. Chase, *The Tyranny of Words.* Harcourt, Brace and Company, New York, 1938.
[28] I. Lee, *Language Habits in Human Affairs.* Harper & Brothers, Publishers, New York, 1941.

The ability to make fine discriminations, the ability to analyze and synthesize, all the elements of abstract thinking, are obviously required to visualize and evaluate effectively along a continuum. Deliberately stressing the fact that things are seldom black or white but more frequently shades of gray, however, will increase the adolescent's appreciation of the fallacy of two-valued orientation and assist him toward more mature evaluation of situations or factors he encounters in life.

Question re Case of Philip

7. Evaluate the probable degree of Philip's "two-valued orientation."

Growth toward Self-Criticism and Evaluation

Ability to examine one's own thoughts, feelings, and performance, rendering an accurate and objective evaluation of them, is a sign of both emotional and mental maturity.[29, 30] This is an area in which a particularly large number of people never mature. They never achieve the capacity to render objective evaluations of their own processes. They underevaluate or overevaluate themselves (showing different self concepts, but equal lack of maturity). Some simply reject the idea that their thoughts or actions are subject to evaluation. They do or feel this way or that way, and that is all there is to it. It is the way they are, and it is good (they usually feel) because it is the best they can do, and they are certainly competent people!

This quality of self-acceptance without evaluation or question is conspicuous in the small child. He does what he feels like doing and regards it as good if it is pleasing to him. "Good" and "pleasing to me" are synonymous to him. He can perceive a missing element of a picture before he becomes dissatisfied with a picture he himself draws that is imperfect. Later, primitive criteria enter his system of values, and he evaluates in terms of them exclusively. He acquires, for example, the concept that the hand has on it five fingers. So, in drawing a man he draws arms terminated by five fingers. This, to him, is a "hand" because "fiveness" is associated with "handness" in his mind, and when this

29 G. W. Allport, *Personality—A Psychological Interpretation.* Holt, Rinehart & Winston, Inc., New York, 1937.

30 H. C. Smith, *Personality Adjustment.* McGraw-Hill Book Company, Inc., New York, 1961.

criterion of "hand" is met, he is uncritical of anything else about his drawing of the hand.

He gradually learns to become more critical and evaluative of his concrete productions—the picture that does not look right, the wagon that does not do like a wagon should, and the knot that is not tied just as he wants it. It is years later, however, that he becomes able to evaluate critically his abstractions or nonconcrete-product actions. He produces a poem which, to him, says something, and is oblivious of the fact that much of what it "says" was really pre-existent in his mind and not conveyed by the poem at all. He makes a decision that he has now studied "enough" and does not evaluate either his assignment or his performance to determine just what "enough" is and whether that is what he has achieved. In fact, he must learn that "enough" does not mean "pages read" but "ideas gathered." This perception does not come naturally. Many people go through college in some "by main strength and awkwardness" way without ever having acquired the ability to evaluate their performance in a given area accurately.

Contribution in this important area is one of the great assets of a well-administered program of "progressive" education. Traditional methods *can* do it as well, but in traditional courses the teacher typically carries the responsibility of determining how good the student's work is and tells the student, and may even be angry if the student attempts his own evaluation! In the finest examples of constructive "progressive" education, boys and girls are encouraged to evaluate their own work. Their evaluation is not necessarily accepted at its face value; this would deprive them of the educational value of critically examining their self-evaluation. Instead, under wise questioning by the teacher, they pursue their self-evaluations further along such lines as: Why do you conclude that your report is not good? What parts of it *are* good? In what ways are the other parts different from these good parts? How do you arrive at the conclusion that your citizenship is of B quality? What would justify a higher grade? A lower?

Few critics are as perceptive of the quality of a performance as is the genuinely competent person who gave it, be it singing, writing, diving, or the logical support of a position. Such judgment requires intelligence, the ability to manipulate abstractions and make very fine discriminations. It also requires a personality structure which is strong enough to endure the very real stress of self-analysis. Finally, it requires the *habit* of self-examination and objective self-appraisal to insure continuing performance at a level commensurate with one's reasonable maximum potential. One of the most valuable contributions an adult working with adolescents can give them is guided practice in evaluating themselves, their thoughts, feelings, and performances objectively.

Question re Case of Philip
    8. How will Philip probably attempt self-evaluation?

Growth toward Rational Self-Control

Here the elements of emotional maturation and mental maturation intermingle; maturity is the extent to which the boy's or girl's emotional life submits to direction by his or her intellect, rather than "doing what comes naturally." The condition of directing one's words, actions, and plans on the basis of intellectual considerations rather than on one's feelings is a characteristic of both emotional maturity and intellectual maturity. Infants and small children do what they "want" to do, what their feelings incline them to do, without regard to whether, from the viewpoint of logic, that is the most intelligent or reasonable thing to do.

There is no reason to assume that the feelings of adults, their desires and aversions, are less intense than those of children. Yet adults often voluntarily do things which they very much dislike doing and refrain from things which they very much wish to do. The extent to which the adult's mind has achieved primacy of control over his feelings, wishes, and emotions is an important indicator of the maturity of that mind, of the mental maturity of the individual. All the previously discussed areas of mental maturation combine with emotional maturation to contribute to the achievement of such maturity. Appreciation of remote goals causes the individual to attach less importance to immediate gratification than to more permanent satisfaction; other areas make their contribution according to their nature.[31] The result, if mental and emotional maturity is achieved in the various areas, is a person who feels deeply and sensitively, but is not a slave to his feelings; through mature cognitive processes and self-control, he directs his life not as the infant does, but in a manner which reason says is wise.

Some adolescents achieve rational self-control early. In fact, some boys and girls achieve in pre-adolescence amazingly mature patterns of rational self-direction. Such development is promoted by good mastery of

[31] L. J. Cronbach, *Educational Psychology*. Harcourt, Brace and Company, New York, 1954.

developmental tasks, particularly the development of the sense of accomplishment and duty. Some reach much older chronological age without having developed the cognitive controls needed to plan and direct a life wisely. It is this latter group who typically come into greatest conflict with society, school, family, law: fourteen-year-old Inez, who insists on associating with undesirable companions because they are "more fun," despite the obvious fact that their companionship encourages truancy, delinquency, and immoral behavior; fifteen-year-old Jeff, who is not eligible for a license, but who *wants* to drive a car and, therefore, insists on doing so despite the obvious unwisdom of a consistent pattern of law-breaking. These are examples of emotional rather than intellectual control of actions on the part of boys and girls. By contrast, Celeste wants to water-ski as badly as anyone, but knows that with her weak ankle it would be dangerous, even though she could probably go the entire summer without wrenching it too severely. So she does not water-ski, devising substitute activities from which she can obtain pleasure. And Bill stolidly spends an hour a day on English composition, which he cordially despises, because it is required for the degree in business administration, and his recognition of his need for professional education outweighs his dislike of studying English composition.

Boys and girls like Bill and Celeste are displaying the achievement of rational self-control which will enable them to make their lives successful ones. Inez and Jeff, unless they change, will skitter from one precarious adjustment to circumstances to another, without achieving a solid basis for life adjustment because opportunism, doing what gives promise of pleasure at the moment, rather than reason governs their lives.

Question re Case of Philip
　　9. Evaluate Philip's self-control.

Growth in Knowledge

Typically, growth in knowledge (as contrasted with mere growth in quantity of information possessed) involves disciplined thought and study.[32] Watching interesting pictures and listening to interesting talks on various subjects have the *potential of leading to* knowledge on the part of the viewer or listener, but their immediate product is hardly knowl-

---

[32] H. W. Bernard, *Toward Better Personal Adjustment.* McGraw-Hill Book Company, Inc., New York, 1957.

edge. It is a miscellany of facts which the individual must synthesize and integrate into a coherent and meaningful *systematized* body of material, and must then study and examine to ascertain its significance, implications, application, and meaning.[33] Have you ever wondered why universities do not immediately hire for their faculties men and women who readily recite on quiz shows an incredible number of obscure facts in response to difficult questions about art or history, questions such as "Who ran for vice president on the ticket with Tilden?" and "What was the highest price yet paid for a Van Gogh painting?" It is because these people, although walking encyclopedias of facts (and, make no mistake, an immense body of facts is the foundation of knowledge—but only the foundation, not knowledge itself), typically possess only an indifferent *knowledge* of their subjects. They seldom could answer intelligently such questions as "Evaluate the effect Van Gogh's use of color had on his contemporaries," unless they could recite what someone else had said on this subject. The quiz contestant in a special field will typically have an exhaustive knowledge of facts about his field, but not be so distinguished in his ability to evaluate the meaning and significance of those facts.

Children in school typically learn facts first of all, although in modern schools the attempt is made to introduce them at an early age to the interpretation and evaluation of those facts. Questions such as "How did the activities of men like Drake contribute to the development of the British Empire?" as contrasted with questions such as "Give the dates of Drake's principal voyages" represent attempts to emphasize knowledge as contrasted with mere information, meanings as contrasted with facts alone. The term "educated idiot" is sometimes applied to the person who has amassed a fund of information (sometimes, it is rumored, a college or advanced degree!) without having matured in knowledge, in appreciation of the implications of what he has "learned." Certainly the intellectually mature person is more assiduous in his pursuit of facts than is the less mature individual, but the truly mature person regards the acquisition of the facts as merely the starting point of his "learning" on a given subject. The real work follows: ascertaining the significance and implications of the facts learned and integrating them and this comprehension into one's prior body of knowledge of the subject.

From all this one can see that "knowledge" implies creativity, putting facts together and studying them so as to bring into being understandings

33 E. F. Von Fange, *Professional Creativity*. Prentice-Hall, Inc., Englewood Cliffs, N. J., 1959.

over and beyond the bare facts themselves. It implies competent use of the language to formulate and manipulate abstractions and engage in the other activities which eventuate in sound decision-reaching. It implies constructive use of one's imagination, not the day-dreaming type of imagination, but the type of imagination which reveals meanings and possibilities not apparent from mechanical listening to, or looking at, the material under consideration.

The relation of this evolution of knowledge to the desire for new experiences (discussed in Chapter 3) can be readily deduced—by a little synthesis and imagination. The quest for knowledge is a mental adventure, if properly presented to adolescents. Most adolescents like to figure things out for themselves, if the "things" are meaningful to them. Principles of etiquette as well as science can be learned, developed into knowledge, by guided reasoning. One of the great challenges to workers with adolescents is to devise ways of making the appreciation and pursuit of knowledge appealing to them.

Growth in Logical Decision-Reaching

This involves elements of both attitude and skill. Ask a child which is the "better" automobile, a Chevrolet or a Ford, or the "better" baseball team, the Dodgers or the Yankees, or the "best" popular singer. His answer, if forthcoming at all, will usually be forthcoming instantly. Seldom will he ponder, seldom will he qualify his answer by saying, "It depends on. . . ." He does not feel any need to do so, because he uses the two-valued orientation in stark simplicity, and because of his inability to make fine discriminations, analyze, and synthesize, he is incapable of logically arriving at a rational evaluation of factors involved. Furthermore, he *feels,* wants to believe, one way or the other. If he is persuaded to make a systematic comparison of the merits of two rivals, he typically starts out (or soon begins) to "prove" his preference, rather than to make an objective evaluation.

This pattern of childish behavior carries over into all areas of decision-reaching. Seldom does the child reason his way to a decision; his favorite exercise, after all, is jumping to conclusions. The adult who attempts to build his life on such a method of reaching decisions is inviting tragedy, in business, marriage, and every other sphere of his life. Adolescence is the time during which the objective, evaluative approach to decision-reaching should be developed both as an attitude, a behavior pattern, and a skill.

Figure 11. "Knowledge implies creativity, putting facts together so as to bring into being understanding beyond the bare facts themselves."

Logical decision-making involves all the skills and characteristics already discussed in this chapter, and certain others as well.

Awareness. Adolescents gradually begin to perceive things which simply made no impression on children. For instance, they become aware that different alternatives lead to different consequences; spending money in one way produces certain advantages and certain disadvantages, and another way leads to others. There were people who objected to George Washington's policies, as well as those who revered him. Looking at the sky may give a hint as to whether or not it is a good idea to start on a long walk. Bugs are attracted to an outside light bulb at night, and may drop into a bowl of punch set under one. With mental maturation, boys and girls increasingly take into consideration factors they simply never noticed before.

Reservation of Judgment. As boys and girls mature, they jump at conclusions less precipitately, require more complete evidence or survey of the situation before committing themselves. Many adults never reach full maturation in this respect, being always inclined to render "snap judgments" rather than find out pertinent facts and then decide. As boys and girls mature normally through the teens, they become less impetuous, less inclined to "go off half-cocked." This requires both emotional maturation, becoming willing to wait rather than act precipitately, and mental maturation in the ability to perceive the incompleteness of one's perception of a situation, recognizing that there are more facts which must be obtained and considered before enough is known to justify a decision.

Systematic Gathering of Pertinent Information. A seasoned businessman attempts to accumulate comprehensive information about a business before investing his money in it. A twelve-year-old boy invests his entire savings in a bicycle because he likes the color of it and it has a four-speed gear. During adolescence the boy (and his sister) will normally cultivate the habit of reserving judgment until he has found out more about whatever he must reach a decision on. When he is seventeen or eighteen and about to buy his first car, he will, if he is of normal maturity for his age, want to know not merely the make, year, model, and appearance of it, but its type of engine, horsepower, oil consumption, and relative repair costs. And the girl wants to know something of the reputation, social status, and character of her girl friends, rather than accept them at face value, as does the child.

Basing Decisions on Pertinent Facts. A man was complaining to his banker that an investment he had asked the banker to approve had not turned out well, and in the process revealed some compromising facts about the investment he had not previously given his advisor.

"Why didn't you tell me these things before?" the banker asked.

"I was afraid you'd tell me not to invest in it!" the man replied.

We laugh at the story partly because we recognize in the man our own tendencies to disregard facts which do not fit our preferences or preconceived ideas. "My mind is made up; don't confuse me with the facts!" is another example of humor based on this well-known tendency. However, we note that the anecdotes are humorous because the idea they represent is so ridiculous. Children are expected to disregard facts which displease them, but adults are not. During adolescence or young manhood or womanhood, people are expected to achieve a mature respect for facts as guides to decisions and conduct.

Questions re Case of Philip

10. Summarize the characteristics of mental immaturity which Philip shows.

11. Evaluate Philip's adjustment to life. How might it be improved?

READINGS

Guilford, J. P., "Three Faces of Intellect," *The American Psychologist,* 1959, *14:*469-479.

Kuhlen, R. G., *The Psychology of Adolescent Development.* New York: Harper & Brothers, Publishers, 1952, Chapt. 3.

Mitton, B. L., and Harris, D. B., "The Development of Responsibility in Children," *The Elementary School Journal,* Jan., 1954, pp. 268-277.

Pressey, S. L., and Kuhlen, R. G., *Psychological Maturation Through The Life Span.* New York: Harper & Brothers, Publishers, 1957, Chapt. 3.

Schneiders, A. A., *The Psychology of Adolescence.* Milwaukee: The Bruce Publishing Company, 1951, Chapts. 21, 22.

Stoddard, G. D., *The Meaning of Intelligence,* Parts I and III. New York: The Macmillan Company, 1943.

CHAPTER 8

ACHIEVING EMOTIONAL

MATURITY AND ADJUSTMENT

PREVIEW

(Emotions are powerful, primitive forces which the individual must temper to meet certain criteria in order to become a well-adjusted adult.)

The Need for Emotional Maturation

Dynamics of Achieving Emotional Maturity

GOAL	PROCESS INVOLVED
Objectification	Minimizing emotional distortion of perception, interpretation, and reaction to reality.
Perception of relative values	Discriminating truly between superficial and important factors in life and giving appropriate priority to all.
Dedication to long-range goals	Tolerating postponement of satisfactions in order to achieve important goals in the future.
Acceptance of responsibility	Strengthening the self concept and increasing personal competence through disciplined work at whatever one ought to do.
Tolerance of frustration	Withstanding failure and adverse circumstances and continuing constructive efforts toward a goal.
Empathy and/or compassion	True belongingness in our culture requires developing the capacity for sympathy and concern for the welfare of others.
Gradation of reaction	Holding one's intensity of feeling and behavior to that which is appropriate to each circumstance.
Socialization of responses	Patterning one's gradation of reaction to a form appropriate to existing social circumstances.

THE NEED
FOR EMOTIONAL MATURATION

ADULTS in twentieth-century America are creatures of logic and reason only to a limited extent. Fundamentally we are creatures of feelings, of emotions, of motives and reactions which lie far deeper than logic and reason; in fact, they often lie far deeper even than our conscious mind. If our ego protests our accepting the fact that our emotions often control us rather than we them, we need only contemplate the motorist who angrily disputes with a traffic policeman, when apology might well result in his receiving only a reprimand instead of the forthcoming ticket; or the golfer who smashes a club because he made a bad shot; or the father who persistently and sincerely regards his son, who is the ringleader of the local juvenile delinquency, as an innocent being led astray by his companions; or the mother who insists that her twenty-four-year-old divorced son is being cunningly seduced into marriage by a respectable eighteen-year-old girl whom he is pantingly pursuing.

Emotions are basic, primeval forces of great power and influence, designed by nature to enable the organism to cope with circumstances which demand the utmost effort for survival or success, or to "add color and spice to living." [1] The raging bellow of a moose signaling his readiness to defend his claim to a female against a rival until one is dead or disabled, the feelings of a mother bird which cause it to hurl itself against a huge marauder of its nest, the loyalty of a dog which binds it to its master in spite of cruelty and neglect, are all examples in nature of forces which emerge with little apparent alteration from the human psyche on appropriate (or inappropriate!) provocation. The unreasoning rage of the frustrated infant who holds his breath until parents are terrified, the blind infatuation of a teenage girl for a dissolute drunk flunking out of college and wasting his widowed mother's hard-earned money—any look at people around us reveals the occasional appearance in human beings of emotions apparently about as blinding in their power as are emotions in subhuman species.

Adolescents are more capable of effectively coping with their feelings than are children, but are likely to have frustrations sufficiently bigger and deeper than those of younger children which absorb this increased

[1] C. T. Morgan, *Introduction to Psychology*. McGraw-Hill Book Company, Inc., New York, 1961.

capability. Furthermore, because of their insistent, ever growing demand for independence, adolescents often have less desire, feel less obligation or need, to control their emotions (at least where parents and other authority figures are concerned) than does the more dependent child. Adolescents are less capable of appropriately coping with emotions than are adults, and generally arc less interested in trying to do so.

Psychologists have debated whether the emotional tribulations of adolescence justify this period's being classified as one of "storm and stress." Parents will generally affirm that it is, without debate. The reasons are several. A host of new drives and needs assails the boy and girl during the adolescent years; many of them they understand imperfectly and suffer inevitable frustration because they do not even know what they want so intensely, much less how to attain it.[2, 3] Many of the emerging drives and needs bring almost inevitable conflict with parental concepts of responsibility and propriety; the adolescent, on the other hand, driven by his dawning need for more complete autonomy, objects strongly to parental supervision of his actions, and more frustration and stress are produced.[4] In the area of sex, biological drive and psychological need both run head on into cultural prohibitions, and frustration or guilt is the equally unacceptable alternative.

Along with this multiplicity of areas of potential frustration is the sad fact that adolescents are not yet experienced in ways of avoiding or minimizing troubles which an older person could easily side-step. They blunder headfirst into emotionally undesirable situations which could have been avoided by exercise of more experience or wisdom, as witness the high-school girl who antagonizes her girl friends by coyly flirting with their boy friends. Their ego produces a demand for self-assertion before their judgment is capable of evaluating accurately the result of such self-assertion, and we have the boy who insists on purchasing an unsuitable suit of clothes and winds up inappropriately dressed for occasions important to him.

And, most provoking of all to the adults dealing with them and potentially most injurious to themselves, adolescents become partially capable of gratifying their drives and needs, in spite of obstacles placed in

2 I. M. Josselyn, *The Happy Child*. Random House, New York, 1955.

3 R. G. Kuhlen, *The Psychology of Adolescent Development*. Harper & Brothers, Publishers, New York, 1952.

4 R. S. Lane and R. F. L. Logan, "The Adolescent at Work," *Practitioner*, 1949, *162*:287–298.

their paths, long before they are able to appreciate the potential ill effects of such gratification. They acquire the ability to disregard sexual propriety, the desire to do so, and sufficient size and age to be held at least partially accountable for their actions before they acquire a comprehension of the importance of *not* disregarding social standards. They can outrage public opinion before they can comprehend the damage they, as well as others, will suffer if they do outrage it.

The adolescent does not see how neglect of disliked schoolwork which forfeits the respect of teachers will *really* injure him later on. A teenage girl does not perceive how going steady with a boy who is a ringleader in his crowd's drinking, reckless driving, or vandalism can *really* threaten her with tragic results. And often neither can truly comprehend why the opinion of the old fogies whom their parents stupidly sit around with could possibly be of real importance in his or her life.

In the adolescent, then, we have a person newly tempted or stimulated by a multitude of drives and desires, still possessing many of the ones he had in childhood, without the adult's experience or judgment or perspective in dealing with them, and fiercely resentful of adult supervision. No wonder these years are the despair of parents and, be it noted, times of "storm and stress" for the adolescent himself. Looking back on our own years of early adolescence, we are likely not to recognize in retrospect how stressful they were. The well-known psychological mechanism of forgetting the unpleasant more completely than the pleasant allows us to remember the wonderful graduation dance while forgetting the excruciating agony of wondering if we were going to have a date for it. We remember the last hours with classmates, but forget the agony of not knowing until the last minute whether Mother and Dad would insist that, like *babies,* we come home after the graduation ceremony instead of going on the traditional all-night trip to the mountains. But observe the adolescents around you, particularly heeding their talk of their problems with parents and other people, and the justification of thinking of adolescence as a time of storm and stress will be apparent.

We have identified adolescence as a time of change and maturation. In the area of emotional life this change involves primarily the process of maturing from a childish basis of emotional living to an adult one. Adolescence begins with a boy's or girl's thinking and feeling as a child as well as having the body of a child. When it is over, he or she has not only the body of a man or woman, but a man's or woman's emotional constitution as well; in fact, we regard as "immature" a person who has achieved an adult body, but who still reacts on the emotional level of a child.

The first paragraphs of this chapter illustrate the primitive nature and forces of emotions. Such forces must be brought under control before a person can function acceptably in adult society. They must be regulated and brought into perspective with other aspects of life, with the welfare of others, with the ultimate welfare of the individual as contrasted with his immediate impulse, with logic instead of in blind response to chemical-physiological conditions. Without the achievement of reasonable emotional regulation, the boy or girl can never adjust successfully to life. Achievement of this regulation is not a simple matter which comes automatically with growing older. It must be learned, and the adolescent can learn it much more easily and effectively with the guidance of adults who know how he needs to grow and how to promote such growth than he can if left to his own devices. So we will examine the process of commuting primitive emotional patterns into patterns which will help the adult adjust better to life.

Emotional maturation does not begin with adolescence any more than does physical maturation. It begins as soon as the baby begins to acquire differentiated responses to different stimuli. This differentiation, expressive of pleasure, anger, desire, or fear, as contrasted with original undifferentiated noises, represents a step along the way to emotional maturation.[5] The basis for good emotional maturation is laid in infancy and childhood with the successful completion of the developmental stages of achieving security, a sense of initiative, a sense of autonomy, and the others discussed in previous chapters.

With these successes, with these developmental challenges met and mastered, the boy or girl enters adolescence with a psychological constitution prepared to undergo certain modifications which will change it from a childish pattern to an adult one. Conversely, imperfect adjustment in the pre-adolescent developmental stages and, to a lesser extent, difficulty in accomplishing the major developmental tasks of adolescence weaken the ability of the psychological constitution to make the adaptations necessary for maturation. Just as the presence of too much sand in clay causes it to crumble instead of take on the shape desired of a finished vase, imperfect mastery of early developmental tasks produces a personality which "crumbles," which fails to respond properly, which

[5] K. M. B. Bridges, "Emotional Development in Early Infancy," *Child Development*, 1932, 3:324–341.

may indeed be *incapable* of responding properly to the maturing influences of adolescence. You as the teacher or counselor, however, must work with the material you receive in a boy or girl. If necessary background for emotional maturation is lacking, you must devise ways of belatedly providing it or ways of achieving the optimum development possible in its absence.

Emotional maturation, being a part of the whole psychobiological growth of the child, is holistic: it takes place as one all-pervasive part of the whole process of development. It does not proceed independently of intellectual growth; aspects of the intellect color the nature, extent, and direction of emotional maturation the while that emotional maturation is influencing the intellectual growth. Similarly, within the area of emotional maturation, the dynamic functions to be discussed next do not operate independently of each other. Neither are they steps, one completed before another is begun. Rather, they are a complex of intrinsically interrelated processes, each simultaneously affecting and being affected by progress in all others. The headings under which they are discussed emphasize important aspects of emotional maturation, each of which is, in turn, one aspect of the whole psychobiological process of maturation.

It should be particularly noted that the processes we are about to consider, which constitute the dynamics of emotional maturation, are not achieved by a boy's or girl's merely living and growing through a given number of years. Neither is their achievement accomplished by an adult, however well-informed and well-intentioned, who merely *tells* the adolescent that he or she should strive for thus and so. The conditions promoting emotional maturation are best achieved through boys and girls *consciously trying* to develop them, assisted by understanding adults who inspire and guide the adolescents in the experiences which can lead to emotional maturity.

Questions for You to Consider

1. From studying the foregoing pages, why would you expect that as children mature they become involved in fewer fights?

2. In Midcity there is one junior high school the student body of which is drawn exclusively from families in the middle and upper educational-economic brackets. Another draws its population exclusively from families very low in educational-economic status. In which school would more fights between students be likely to occur? Why?

3. Why is "just growing" or being told of the essentials of emotional maturation insufficient to produce emotional maturation in a boy or girl at the optimum rate?

THE DYNAMICS OF
ACHIEVING EMOTIONAL MATURITY

Objectification

A fundamental characteristic of the emotionally mature person is the recognition that his feelings, beliefs, even perceptions, are not necessarily reality; they are his impressions of, or reactions to, reality, and must be treated as such in making adjustments and evaluating circumstances. Furthermore, if he is to avoid maladjustive behavior, he must, insofar as possible, see things as they really are rather than in a distorted fashion.[6]

Neither of these tasks is easy, and the small child can do neither. He is incapable of distinguishing between "Mamma is mean to me" and "I want to do something and Mamma won't let me and I don't like it." To him the fear that there are bears in the bushes of the park means that there may actually *be* bears there. And when he tries to take his playmate's tricycle and is pushed over for his pains, he is quite honest and sincere in his complaint that "Tommy pushed me down," because to him only one interpretation of the situation exists—his own.

Objectification is the process of distinguishing between feeling and reality, between belief and actuality, between reasoning and wishful thinking, between opinion and evidence, or between needs and desires. To the emotionally immature girl the need for dental work may appear less urgent than the "need" for a new formal. The feeling that the wastrel referred to earlier is really a fine person, and that entrusting one's lot in life into his hands is the surest promise of happiness, is in direct contradiction to reality. But to the infatuated girl it *is* reality. The boys trying to persuade their scoutmaster that the weather is not too bad for the overnight hike point to a rift in the threatening clouds and argue that it is clearing up. Such distortion of reality to coincide with wishes or feelings is all too common among adolescents. Carried to its ultimate conclusion, lack of objectification is a symptom of psychosis; to the paranoid, the plot of the Knights of Columbus against him *is* real, and he is incapable of comprehending that it is not.

[6] L. J. Saul, *Emotional Maturity*. J. B. Lippincott Company, Philadelphia, 1960.

Objectification as an aspect of emotional maturation does not necessarily involve a lessening of affection for others, even for the drunken wastrel, but requires a realistic appraisal of traits or character as a basis for that affection and an affection based on what is there rather than on nonexistent qualities. Thus, the girl might continue to love the alcoholic young man, even want to marry him, but do so on the basis that she wanted a person whom others did not respect, who would constitute a challenge to her powers of reformation. Her judgment would be bad, but she would be making her decision on the basis of fact, however wrong the decision, rather than on emotionally produced distortions. It is expected that a mother will continue to love her son regardless of how undeserving he may be. If she does so in spite of recognizing his unworthiness, she is in better touch with reality than if her love continues on the fanciful grounds that fate and malicious misunderstanding make her son appear worthless when he is really a fine, upstanding man.

We do not expect the adolescent to love his father less by realizing that Daddy cannot actually "lick anybody in the whole world" and that he does not really have the final answer to every question that can be asked. The love should continue unabated, but on more realistic grounds, with a more objective picture of Dad's qualities which make him lovable or admirable.

Self-insight, a realistic evaluation of one's abilities, character, motives, and goals, is a highly significant aspect of objectification. The small child recognizes no limits upon his ability. He confidently sets out to walk around the world or "read all the books there are." The adolescent frequently is plagued by lack of self-insight in the other extreme; he has a feeling of self-consciousness or inferiority based on an emotionally dictated self concept which attaches too much importance to a defect and results in undue self-deprecation.

Many of the most excruciating anxieties of adolescents are the result of their failure to take objective stock of themselves, recognize their assets and liabilities and get them all in their proper perspective. Imaginary conspicuousness of a nose, a rebuff which humiliated him, a *faux pas* in some social situation are causes of adolescent concern or anxiety which are often based upon an unrealistic appraisal of the importance of factors.[7]

[7] W. W. Wattenberg, *The Adolescent Years*. Harcourt, Brace and Company, Inc., New York, 1955.

Discouragement over failure to achieve unrealistically high standards of popularity or academic or other success are examples of adolescent maladjustment resulting from imperfect objectification. Acceptance of lower than reasonable achievement because of self-deprecation is another.[8]

The home atmosphere and the thought habits of parents are crucial elements in objectification.[9] Boys and girls growing up in homes where parents habitually bring reason and logic to bear on questions or situations which arise tend to adopt objective appraisal as a natural way of looking at things. Was there a report that Mrs. Holmes was moving out of the neighborhood? Adults may react in their conversation (in the presence of children) by speculating as to why and arriving at an accepted version of why. Or they may adopt the attitude that it will be interesting to learn why, or may wish that they did know why. What they habitually do will influence their boy's or girl's objectivity of thought. Which predominates in your classroom conversations, expressions such as "Well, *I* believe that . . . ," or "From a news report yesterday it appears that . . ."? Repeated hundreds of times, the second alternative in each illustration tends to create a respect for accuracy rather than substitute feeling for facts. Was Aline not asked to the dance by the boy she had hoped would ask her? Parents can react either by encouraging Aline to look for face-saving ablibis—"It's so far out here; Jane lives just a few blocks from him"—or "sour grapes" attitudes—"He's not so much. You'll find someone better, wait and see." Or they can sympathetically help Aline figure out the most probable explanation of why Ted was not as impressed by her as she had wished. Not only will the latter course give Aline a better chance of impressing the next boy she wishes to, but it will also help her form the habit of evaluating herself and her life situations objectively, with carry-over into future situations which it will be to her advantage to interpret objectively.

Teachers and counselors may be responsible for great adolescent gains in objectivity by frequent and varied use of such questions as: "On what do you base your opinion?" "Is that a fact or someone's opinion? How can you tell?" "Why do you feel that way?" "What is the reasoning behind that conclusion?" In their own conversation they can meticulously avoid representing opinion as fact without labeling the substitu-

[8] G. G. Thompson, E. F. Gardner, and F. J. DiVesta, *Educational Psychology*. Appleton-Century-Crofts, Inc., New York, 1959.

[9] L. J. Saul, *Emotional Maturity*. J. B. Lippincott Company, Philadelphia, 1960.

tions. They can encourage objective reasoning when statements are heard about a person, a group, or a race by leading an analysis of known facts to see if they support the generalization.

Teachers and counselors who wish to do so can also help many boys and girls achieve a more objective perspective of themselves and their own lives. Without "preaching" or offensively moralizing, a teacher can say, "What do you imagine Liz thought was your purpose in calling Betty?" and recall a resentful boy from his fulminations to an appraisal of what a situation really involves. Or she can encourage a girl to consider how to make the most of her physical assets rather than spend her time lamenting her defects, thus developing a habit of analytical evaluation of herself rather than emotional reaction to a problem.

It appears axiomatic that, other things being equal, the person is best adjusted who adjusts to the world as it actually is instead of to a world that exists only in his distorted perception. Objectification is a process of freeing real-life circumstances from the distorting effects of emotions, conscious or unconscious. Many adults are considerably deficient in this quality, but careful examination of the most successful people of one's acquaintance will usually reveal them to be higher than average in this aspect of maturity. Reflection will also reveal that the person given to remarks that indicate feelings uninfluenced by facts— "Big business is strangling America"—or with a ridiculous lack of comprehension of things—"But do we *want* the U.S.S.R. to feel that the Woodlawn Garden Club favors their agricultural policy?"—are seldom held in respect as people on whose advice you would, for instance, invest your money!

Case of Quintella

Quintella's homeroom teacher is the only person in Columbus High whom she seems to like or trust. Since Mr. Roberts is sympathetic and will listen to his students, Quintella talks to him a great deal about her problems.

"Mrs. F. picks on me all the time," Quintella complains. "If two of us are talking, she makes me stay in and says nothing to the other person. And Mr. H. makes me write over a composition if I have two or three misspelled words in it, but he gives Bobby a grade on his, with more misspelled words in it than mine." About the girls in her class Quintella says, "They don't like me because I'll stand up for my rights. When someone snarls at me, I'll snarl right back."

1. Cite examples of what may be lack of objectification on Quintella's part.

2. Assuming that Quintella's teachers and fellow students do not have it in for her (which is a reasonable assumption), explain what may be the true situations which Quintella has distorted in her reports to Mr. Roberts.

Perception of Relative Values

Susan, seeing a black cloud the morning of a big football game, fervently breathes, "Oh, I *hope* it doesn't rain. It will simply spoil the game tonight!" while a few miles away emergency armies of fire fighters struggle to extinguish a drought-fed forest fire. Frequently such remarks are not merely unthought-out expressions; they represent an actual failure to comprehend relative values. Skimping on lunch to buy the newest record by a current idol, splurging on a lavish weekend trip instead of starting a savings account, preparing for a dance instead of for a final examination, weighing the inconvenience and trouble caused parents and others by delaying dinner against the importance of continuing a telephone conversation with Margie about whether Billie and Henry are *really* at outs—all these are examples of instances in which adolescents, basing their choice on an erroneous perception of the relative values of alternatives, frequently assign priority to an utterly inappropriate alternative rather than an important one.

As in objectification, accurate perception of relative values requires elimination of bias or the subjection of emotional values to intellectual or practical ones, as dictated by the circumstances of each individual situation. Giving up a summer trip to attend summer school may be severely against the feelings and preferences of the adolescent, but, if emotionally mature, he will consider doing so if it would save his spending an extra semester in high school. On the other hand, if the trip is a once-in-a-lifetime opportunity, and there is no significant reason for the boy or girl to finish school a semester earlier, making the trip might be a wise choice. Relative values, not feelings, will dictate the choice if the adolescent is maturing as he or she should.

Children are inclined to place paramount value on whatever they want, particularly whatever they want at that minute, regardless of other considerations. They characteristically obey the pleasure principle.[10, 11] Baseball practice takes precedence over homework. Winning a

10 S. Freud, *An Outline of Psychoanalysis.* W. W. Norton & Company, Inc., New York, 1949.

11 R. I. Watson, *Psychology of the Child.* John Wiley & Sons, Inc., New York, 1959.

pattern that honesty and hard work bring success. For every Horatio Alger-type success story in popular magazines (especially the cheaper sort often favored by adolescents), a baker's dozen of stories will be found in which the "dull, uninteresting office worker," no matter how high his income or social status, comes out second best against the gay, improvident, devil-may-care fellow who, by winsome personality and a stroke of genius, walks away with the girl and the fortune. It is simply not as appealing to our imaginations, or as soothing to our own tendencies toward self-indulgence, to glorify in fiction and drama the stable, self-disciplined man on the street who builds slowly by hard work and sound judgment as it is to glorify the erratic, brilliant, irresponsible, but irresistible, swashbuckler.

Magazines, novels, movies, and television programs are designed to cater to people's wants and to please them. Therefore, adolescents are subjected to a never ceasing barrage of appealing and dramatic presentations in which values important to successful life adjustment are subtly compared invidiously against essentially maladjustive value systems. This, along with the fact that superficial values are often more appealing than are vital ones, is a great obstacle to adolescents' developing a sound perception of relative values.

Perhaps the greatest assistance that can be given adolescents in forming sound value systems lies in two areas. The first involves adolescents receiving, from adults who are authority figures in their lives, precepts and examples which exemplify stable, sane value relations.

If a respected teacher, counselor, coach, or parent consistently puts first things first—"No thanks, I love chocolates but they put too much weight on me," "I surely do want to see that movie, but I'll have to catch it later at a neighborhood theater or drive-in, because the week that it's on downtown is the week before examinations, and I'll be making up tests"—if the adults whom he respects and is influenced by base their lives on fundamental values, the adolescent tends to do so too. The second area involves occasional discussion with the adolescent of relative values and especially of logical analysis of unwholesome value systems commonly encountered. Is there a well-advertised movie subtly glorifying romantic infidelity, "all well-lost for love," against a mother's or father's responsibility to children? See the show, and, in discussions with adolescents for whose guidance you are responsible, encourage an objective examination of what is involved in the relations portrayed. Which is more important, fulfillment of responsibilities you voluntarily assumed, or gratification of self, especially where innocent lives would suffer from your pleasure?

Some care must be taken to prevent these discussions from becoming mere adult moralizing; this can be prevented by encouraging the boys and girls to talk, instead of giving them explanations or exhortations. Most vital values are self-evident, if people are not permitted to ignore them by oversight. But since pleasure is often greater through ignoring them, in many instances adolescents (and adults also) fail to look below the surface of situations portraying the glorification of false values. Directing analytical attention to most situations will enable boys and girls to reach sound value judgments through their own mental efforts. This procedure has the advantage of causing them to see the relative values of the particular situation in their true light and also of giving them practice for making such appraisals independently in the future. Teachers have virtually unlimited opportunities to contribute to the emotional maturation of adolescents in this way.

No attempt will be made here to formulate a system of values which should be taught boys and girls. Representative examples of competing values in several areas have been presented. Religion, ethics, culture, social standards, and the hard realities of what it takes to build a successful life are all sources of fundamental values. As was intimated above, perception of relative values usually requires not a comprehensive list of what is good and bad, but merely objectification, appraisal of issues involved with one's best mental powers, instead of merely following the path of pleasure-seeking or the least resistance.

From this discussion it can be seen that objectification of thought and perception is fundamental to perception of relative values. Perception of relative values, in turn, facilitates another essential factor in the dynamics of emotional maturation.

Case of Roslyn

"Can you help us in some way about Roslyn's schoolwork, Mr. Nix?" Mrs. K. asked the counselor at Franklin High School. "We just can't get her to see how important it is. She wants to do everything in the world but study—take pictures for the school paper, go to the park to collect specimens for biology class, make fudge for her friends who drop by. She'll throw a tantrum if we won't let her go out for a hot dog with friends who come by, with her math problems not worked for tomorrow. Then in the morning she'll insist on reironing a dress I've already ironed for her, instead of doing them then. She'll call me from school and ask me to request that she be allowed to come home early for some reason, when all she wants is to get an early start to the lake and miss her last period, English, which she's barely making a D in. She's failing one subject and barely passing the rest. Her father and I have talked to her until we are blue in the face about the importance of her doing well in high school, and we can't get anywhere at all with her."

1. Examine Roslyn's perception of relative values. Why do you suppose she has these attitudes?

2. What are the probable reasons the parents have failed in their attempts to get Roslyn to perceive the importance of studying?

3. At this point, how can Roslyn be helped to achieve a more mature set of values than she apparently now possesses?

Dedication to Long-Range Goals

Children are typically incapable of sustained effort toward remote goals unless they achieve satisfactions, immediate pleasure, or short-range goals along the way. Some adults never mature to the point of being able to design and follow through on long-range plans, either being distracted along the way and winding up with a series of grandiloquent plans half-finished, or simply tiring of the work involved and abandoning the project. The emotionally mature person regulates much of his daily life in terms of ultimate goals whose realization may not be perceptibly brought nearer by present activity, and he works steadfastly toward those goals despite temptations to give up or capriciously change to more immediately appealing objectives.[13, 14]

Inability to regulate conduct in terms of long-range goals is one, but by no means the only, characteristic of a defective personality called variously a character disorder, antisocial reaction, psychopathic personality, constitutional inferior, constitutional psychopath, ne'er-do-well, drifter, and bum. The causes of such failure to grow up beyond the infantile level of behavior and emotional control are believed to be varied. An indulgent mother and hard-driving father often seem to produce a home enrivonment which does not produce children's emotional maturation

[13] A. T. Jersild, *The Psychology of Adolescence*. The Macmillan Company, New York, 1957.

[14] L. Tussing, *Psychology for Better Living*. John Wiley & Sons, Inc., New York, 1959.

in this area.[15] Preoccupation with external appearances of family relations to a greater extent than concern over the real relations existing within the family also seems to be a predisposing cause.[16] Inhibition of emotional maturation in this area also results from failure to achieve sound perceptions of relative values.

It is normal for boys and girls entering adolescence to have difficulty in making themselves persevere at tasks of which the rewards are remote or vague. This accounts for the almost universal tendency of adolescents to let schoolwork go undone if a daily check is not made on its accomplishment. Tests are far away, almost a week! As for a diploma, *that* is so far in the future as to be practically no goal at all, as far as immediate motivation to work is concerned. Even in college only exceptional students usually are permitted the option of course work under conditions which do not involve being held to some type of guarantee of daily work on the course. Even in popular activities such as sports only exceptional boys or girls willingly carry out monotonous and arduous, but necessary, nonplaying training activities without the immediate motivation of the coach standing nearby.

The opportunity (and responsibility) of the teacher in this area is not only to provide pupils with work through which they can learn habits of perseverance and responsibility, but also to show them the logic of such assignments. Thus students may gain both a habit of following orders and a comprehension of the significance of fulfilling requirements.

To be successful, a nation, corporation, family, or person must frequently, if not usually, subordinate short-term satisfactions to long-term goals. This is an aspect of maturity in which the "reality principle" is substituted for the "pleasure principle" mentioned earlier. The reality principle replaces seeking immediate pleasure with activity and goals which will result in greatest satisfaction *in the long run*.[17] Stockholders vote to forego dividends in order to plow them back into the company for future growth and expansion. People curtail their earning power from the ages of sixteen to twenty-two to achieve entrance upon a desired career. They often must accept a position paying less money than

15 D. M. Levy, "Psychopathic Behavior in Infants and Children: A Critical Survey of Existing Concepts," *American Journal of Orthopsychiatry*, 1951, *21*:250–254.

16 P. Greenacre, "Conscience in the Psychopath," *American Journal of Orthopsychiatry*, 1945, *15*:495–509.

17 R. Stagner, *Psychology of Personality*. McGraw-Hill Book Company, Inc., New York, 1961.

they need in order to acquire the position which offers the best opportunity for advancement and future rewards.

Boys and girls often need to regulate their immediate activities in terms of the results which will be realized a week, a month, a year, or ten years in the future. In most cases, by mid-adolescence or at least later adolescence, they intellectually perceive this need clearly. It is unusual for an adolescent to be unable to perceive the relative importance of a long-term goal, such as the high-school senior who insisted on quitting school in April, when he was passing all his subjects, to enter the Navy, and who would not believe that failure to graduate could be a matter of any later importance. Such instances are usually the result of severe breakdown in some other maturational area. Most boys and girls having difficulty in sustaining effort toward long-range goals will verbally recognize and even eloquently argue the necessity of such sustained effort. This area, more frequently than not, represents the situation of the adolescent whose intellectual comprehension of the desirability of a given course of conduct has developed faster than his emotional readiness to give that conduct sustained effort. Intellect has matured, but emotional control has not.

Helping the adolescent to acquire a dedication to long-range goals which will enable him to realize his maximum potential in life, therefore, seldom requires educating him to the necessity of such dedication; you seldom have to convince him. What he needs is practice in such dedication.

Paradoxically, the surest way to achieve his dedication to long-range goals may be to provide him with satisfying, rewarding short- and intermediate-range goals which will keep him actively working along the line that will eventually realize his long-range goal.[18] If Jean, who has ambitions to be a nurse but is failing her schoolwork, can come to think of preparation for nursing as beginning where she is right now, every course passed being one required step toward the coveted cap, she may be able to see her present schoolwork as a series of steps toward her goal, not as marking time until she can start toward it. Leading her to think of each test as one hurdle in the path ending at her R.N. designation will provide her with a series of immediate goals rather than with apparently meaningless and endless demands with no rewards.

Blake makes fine resolutions to keep right up with his work in the

18 L. J. Cronbach, *Educational Psychology*. Harcourt, Brace and Company, New York, 1954.

course, but quickly relapses into his old habit of procrastination. Perhaps a self-kept chart of work accomplished, which a favorite teacher checks and compliments him on each day, will constitute an effective immediate goal for him to work toward which is within the range of his vision.

Steady, consistent achievement of one immediate goal after another is an effective way of developing good habits of work which will make the achievement of long-range goals seem more realistic and possible. Not only does it train the boy or girl in systematic effort and the habit of work; it gives him practice in establishing or recognizing for himself goals which become satisfying symbols of accomplishment along the road to ultimate goals. This approach can carry over with important results into his future work toward long-range goals. And this is of great psychological importance, for achieving intermediate goals keeps him reminded that satisfactions and goals *are* achievable, that success *does* come to him, thus preventing development of an attitude of "It's no use trying; you never get anywhere anyway." This defeatist attitude has been found often to characterize adults of low socio-economic classes, constituting in their feelings justification for improvidence and lack of sustained effort and sacrifice for the future.

Questions re Case of Roslyn
  4. How might Roslyn be helped to develop an appreciation of the value of the long-range goal of education?
  5. What do you think Roslyn's present goals are?

Acceptance of Responsibility

This aspect of emotional maturation not only is an important dynamic factor in the developmental process, but exercises profound effect throughout the broad scope of adjustment. It is probably an essential element in acquiring and maintaining a sense of belongingness in the home on any level more mature than the egocentric demands of the infant.[19] There is considerable evidence to support the theory that as boys and girls grow older, from the age of four or five onward at least, they have a deep need to contribute to any unit of which they are a part. Without such contribution it is doubtful if they can achieve the fullest

---

[19] R. Benedict, "Continuities and Discontinuities in Cultural Conditioning," in Patrick Mullahy (ed.) *A Study of Interpersonal Relations*. Hermitage Press, Inc., New York, 1949.

sense of belonging to the unit and hence if they can find it possible to achieve a full sense of security in it.

The need for belongingness and security was discussed in Chapter 3, but the dynamic function of responsibility in promoting achievement of belongingness and security deserves exploration. It is a well-recognized fact that one typically becomes more emotionally tied to a person by helping that person than by being helped by him. The reason for this phenomenon, which may appear surprising at first glance, is not far to seek in the dynamics of emotions and the self concept. Helping someone gives us a subtle feeling of superiority, power, benevolence, self-righteousness, or all four. These are pleasing feelings, and we tend to feel kindly toward the person who, all unwittingly, was the cause of our having the pleasant feeling. We derive a feeling of importance from being able and willing to exercise our powers to help someone. The more we feel the person is dependent upon us, the closer we are likely to feel to him. Even a stray pup that we find on our doorstep and nurse back to health becomes an object of affection to us as we invest more and more of ourselves in his life and welfare. If we ourselves are helped by someone, we appreciate the help, unless we are ungrateful creatures, but the rich feeling of contributing or helping is denied us. Indeed, we are the objects, not the originators, of the benevolence.

We have all heard the saying "The best way to lose a friend is to do him a favor." This represents, of course, the reverse side of the coin. By our doing him a favor, the individual is tacitly forced to admit that by accepting the help, the favor, he is inferior to us, less powerful or able than we, the object of our sympathy or benevolence, less worthy than we. It is not emotionally wholesome for a child, an adolescent, to always be on this end of the stick.

A moment's reflective examination of our own lives will show us that the same principle applies to the boy or girl contributing to the family or school. Another small step of analysis discloses the fact that acceptance of responsibility in a group is a broad and direct form of making a contribution to that group. A responsibility is an obligation to do something. The "something" is typically desirable for the welfare of someone or some group. A boy's or girl's acceptance of responsibility in the school involves his making a contribution of some kind to the welfare of the school or some of its people, and making this contribution ties him more closely to the school by the same dynamics outlined in the illustration of helping an individual.

Ability to accept responsibilities, with the implication that accepting means fulfilling them, is clearly an acquired capacity. Infants are incapable of fulfilling responsibilities. Small children can do so only to a limited extent, partly because their power of constructive work is limited, but also partly because they possess neither the emotional maturity to comprehend the abstraction of "responsibility" nor the capacity of self-direction to fulfill its demands. They are accorded security and belongingness just through being. But as the child matures, his developing self concept and his biological drive to activity seem to make it necessary for him to render some contribution to the group of which he is a member in order to feel full belongingness and security in the group. Expressed in simplest terms, a parasite, taking all and giving nothing in return, seldom acquires a deep sense of belongingness and security. An ego cannot achieve healthy maturity under such conditions; normal pride begins, at an early age, to demand expression in service, in the acceptance and fulfilling of responsibilities. So the toddler begins to want to do things, to help Mamma, to help Daddy.

Fundamental as the need to accept and fulfill responsibilities is, however, adolescents frequently fail to satisfy it unless forced to do so. The need, although real and genuine, is often obscured by some immediate attractive activity, by the unpleasantness of tasks to be done, or by simple inertia. Thus, adolescents may bitterly protest having responsibilities laid upon them and seek with amazing persistence and resourcefulness to evade the responsibilities. This is completely natural, as natural as for them to dislike the study necessary for their future welfare, brushing their teeth, visiting the dentist, or eating the leafy vegetables needed for good health. The fact that they protest the responsibilities and honestly desire to evade them, however, does not remove their need of those responsibilities any more than their disliking to perform the previously mentioned necessities of living means that they do not need them. Even though they dislike fulfilling their responsibilities, they need to do so to achieve feelings of security and belongingness, as well as for emotional maturation.

The fact that children actually do things which contribute to the welfare of the family helps those children develop a closer, more secure relationship to the family. This is true regardless of whether they willingly perform the tasks or are required to do them. Obviously, being driven with a whip to wash the dishes every night or mow the lawn every Saturday will not necessarily bind a girl or boy closer to his or her

family. But within the bounds of reason, being held responsible for definite services to the family at large promotes the adolescent's general sense
of security and belongingness, and helps him develop skill in tasks he
must perform as an adult. Of course, the adolescent will achieve a
greater sense of security and belongingness, as well as profit more by the
mastery of desirable skills, if his cooperation is secured and he accepts
and fulfills his responsibilities as his proper share of the burden as a
member of the family team.

The same principle holds true in school. The boys and girls who do
their work conscientiously, support the program of the school, and,
through service, attitude, and work, promote the welfare of the school
and their class develop a feeling of belongingness. They identify more
closely with the school, and through their activities achieve emotional
maturation and adjustment far superior to the uncooperative student.

For greatest advantage to the adolescent, both in strengthening his
feeling of security and belongingness and in promoting his healthy emotional maturation and adjustment, his responsibilities around the home
and in school should be services to the family or to his class (or school)
at large, not merely to his own domain. Keeping his or her own room
and clothes up to the family standard should be taken for granted as a
responsibility of an adolescent boy or girl; service to the family only begins after those self maintenance activities are completed. Cleaning the
living room, washing the dishes or the family car, getting up the clothes
for the laundry, tending the garden, minding the baby, or going to the
grocery are tasks which can be done by either boys or girls as the family situation indicates is best. All constitute identifiable services to the
family, and their performance draws the boy or girl more firmly into the
family organization. Helping put the class over the top in some drive,
gathering and providing information needed by other class members,
contributing time to work on a school project, in addition to doing his
own course work, gives the adolescent a feeling of responsibility and subtly improves his whole relationship with his school.

Consistent performance of required duties helps a boy or girl achieve
the mature emotional pattern of matter-of-fact acceptance of work which
must be done or problems which must be met (as was seen in the case of
Mike, Chapter 6). The adolescent who learns from his daily relations
within the family or in school that unpleasant or unwanted situations
can be successfully run away from or avoided by displays of temper or
stubbornness is acquiring a distorted picture of how the world works. In

adult life, obligations are not evaded without payment of a severe price at some future time. Why allow the adolescent to grow up with an erroneous impression of the "facts of life"? By constant performance of obviously necessary tasks, getting homework done (on time!), studying for a test, or washing the dishes, a boy or girl acquires a gradual acceptance of the full reality of life; some of the things it brings are pleasant, some unpleasant; both kinds must be faced and handled with the same degree of conscientiousness, if not the same enjoyment. Teachers as well as parents share the responsibility of seeing to it that boys and girls achieve, through practice, emotional maturation in the area of accepting and fulfilling responsibilities.

Sheer habit helps the adolescent in carrying out his responsibilities. An invariable policy of turning from dressing to straightening up his room can gradually become such an integral part of a boy's morning routine that it is no longer an arbitrary task to be done, but a normal portion of getting ready for school. It becomes a matter of course, rather than a job to be done. When this state has been achieved, when boys or girls accept responsibilities as a normal part of life, to be adjusted to like the weather, and emotionally accept the fact that they cannot be avoided, but are an integral part of living, they are achieving part of the emotional maturation required for happy adjustment to life. It is the person who dreads, tries to avoid, and protests fulfilling his responsibilities in life who is unhappy, not the one who has learned to fulfill them briskly and effectively. Both evasion and procrastination are immature reactions, both maladjustive; full acceptance of responsibility is mature and adjustive.

For fullest emotional maturation, to be best adjusted to his role as an adult, the adolescent must not merely accept those responsibilities laid upon him by circumstances or people. He must develop a *sense* of responsibility which causes him to assume responsibility when circumstances render such assumption appropriate. The emotionally immature girl attempts to evade preparing her homework. The emotionally mature one prepares it. The girl of superior maturity goes further and reasons, "What am I supposed to get out of this work? It must be here for a reason; let me figure out what it is." The emotionally immature boy neglects the baby left in his care. The more mature one does not. The most mature one thinks, "This room is getting pretty cool, cooler than when Mother left. Maybe I'd better call her and find out if I should put something more over the baby." The last boy has not merely accepted responsibility laid upon him, he has developed a sense of responsibility. He perceives a responsibility which needs to be dealt with, and proceeds to deal with it himself when he seems the most appropriate person to do it.

Teachers, any workers with youth, who firmly require prompt and thorough carrying-out of responsibilities on the part of their boys and girls are helping those boys and girls in many ways. In acquiring the habit of preparing assignments on time, beginning work promptly and vigorously at the beginning of the period, and performing tasks to the best of their ability, adolescents are simultaneously acquiring good habits of work and achieving emotional maturity.

Thus, responsibility plays a role in developing security, belongingness, mature adjustment to the demands of life, and the superior sense of initiative and creativity which distinguish the exceptional person. Acceptance of responsibility may involve conscious self-discipline, following the habit of dealing with situations as they present themselves, or recognizing need for thought or action and taking the initiative of shouldering the job which someone has to do. Whether or not the latter level of maturity is ever reached depends to a great extent on whether the boy or girl is taught the acceptance of responsibility as a natural part of living, or is driven to it without an understanding of its importance. Responsibility, as a dynamic factor in emotional maturation and adjustment, is itself an attitude; but the attitude *toward* responsibility developed by a boy or girl will play a great part in determining the success of his or her adjustment to the demands of life. The best attitude toward responsibility comes as a result of boys and girls being given requirements of service to the family, their community, their church, their school, and their own future, and with love, explanations, and firmness held strictly to the fulfillment of those responsibilities. As the unwilling performance of a job slowly changes into a natural habit of everyday life and evolves from that into a sense of responsibility to perceive what needs to be done and doing it, the adolescent's psychological maturation is being forwarded in the area of emotional adjustment and in all other phases of personality development as well.

Case of Sam

Sam's parents are in a state of near despair. Sam will expend three times as much effort trying to escape doing something as it would take to do it. He never does his chores unless ordered and supervised in the performance of each individual one. His parents often wind up letting him get away with his evasive tactics rather than exercising the supervision necessary to make him fulfill his duties. He will try to disappear right after dessert and not return until the table has been cleared. He will go out to feed the dog and not come back. He will let his little brother wander off if left in his custody. He complains bitterly when he is required to run an errand. Told to straighten up his room, he will push the accumulated clutter into the corner behind the door, under the bed, or behind a cleverly arranged screen of chairs. His parents think that as a thirteen-year-old, Sam is too old to whip, and they frankly are baffled.

1. What can we infer as to why Sam will try so hard to avoid his duties?

2. How do his parents unintentionally encourage him in his activities?

3. Use your imagination to devise some ways of encouraging Sam to accept and fulfill his responsibilities more properly.

Tolerance of Frustration

(*You may wish to review the sections on stress and adjustive reactions to frustration in Chapter 4. In this section we will consider not the range of possible causes and reactions to frustration, but the contributors to wholesome reactions to frustration and the forms which the wholesome reactions may take. Chapter 4 discussed the dynamics of frustration. Here we shall discuss the dynamics of adjusting to frustration in the most wholesome ways possible, rather than through resort to defense mechanisms to a neurotic degree.*)

The ability to withstand disappointment, threat, failure, adverse circumstances, deprivation, or persistent difficulties and yet continue constructive efforts toward self-realization is a major factor in the dynamics of emotional maturation and adjustment.[20, 21] Life is inevitably beset by frustrations, by stresses and failures, by threats and difficulties which cause us to work for long periods without apparent gain or accomplishment. The farmer sees the work of a season destroyed in a few minutes of hail; the salesman invests days of work trying to get an order which goes to somebody else; the mother spends all day cleaning the house for her

---

[20] S. Rosenzweig, "An Outline of Frustration Theory," in J. McV. Hunt (ed.) *Personality and the Behavior Disorders,* Vol. I. The Ronald Press Company, New York, 1944.

[21] P. M. Symonds, *The Ego and the Self.* Appleton-Century-Crofts, Inc., New York, 1951.

family, and no one notices; the high-school girl tries hard to win acceptance by an exclusive group and is rejected; the boy is unable to achieve the popularity with girls he desires—all are frustrations with which people must live.

Hardly a day passes without some frustration, the small one of not finding a book or the car keys when you are in a hurry to start to school, or the larger one of studying hard for a test and then feeling completely blank when you see the questions. Reaction to the frustrations can be on any of three levels: (1) determined attempts to overcome or adjust to them, (2) neurotic attempts to evade them or adjust through extreme utilization of the mechanisms discussed in Chapter 4, or (3) "decompensation," disintegration of the personality or intellect to the level of mental illness.

Healthy personality development, healthy psychological maturation, involves ever increasing ability to endure frustration and continue to react on the level of attempts at overcoming or adjusting. Trying to cope with the stress of frustrations and succeeding also provides a background of strength which will benefit all aspects of one's personality. If the boy who fails to make the grade he desires has strong frustration tolerance, he will fall back momentarily to plan his next move, then return to the fray for another try. If the girl whose sense of security in the home is threatened by a younger sister who is excelling her in some way has developed healthy reactions to frustration, she will seek ways of making herself more admirable or successful rather than react by withdrawal, hostility, or rebellion.

At best, frustrations are stressful, destructive experiences. A strong self concept, one which maintains a realistic and optimistic picture of one's character, capabilities, and relations to the world, is the major bulwark against the confidence-destroying, deprecating influence of frustration. But tolerance of frustration is a prerequisite of a strong self concept, and the situation appears to be a job of lifting oneself by one's bootstraps. A strong self concept and a good frustration tolerance are each prerequisites of the other.

The answer to this dilemma is that neither produces the other so much as each is produced by healthful maturation and experience, and as the individual develops a good tolerance of frustration, he simultaneously develops a strong self concept. Then, in times of stress each dynamic factor lends reinforcing strength to the other, as two poles leaning against each other mutually support each other the while supporting a much greater load at their apex than either could support alone. As the infant experiences a frustration—inability to reach a toy he has thrown from his crib, for instance—if he resourcefully begins playing with something else instead of persevering in screaming, his tolerance of frustration is thereby infinitesimally strengthened. Also, his self concept as an autonomous unit not demoralized by the loss of something desired is strengthened. The adolescent who copes with the frustration of being confined to his room or the house for some misbehavior by constructively spending the time there in some pleasant activity or necessary job with a minimum of boredom, rather than abjectly begging pardon, futilely raging, or devising imaginary revenges, again infinitesimally develops a wholesome frustration tolerance and a concept of himself as one who is master of his destiny within whatever circumstances fate casts him. (Of course, in doing so he may frustrate his parents!) The boy or girl who studies the mistakes he made on prior tests or homework for the purpose of a better subsequent performance is likewise growing in both of these areas.

Tolerance of frustration, like most of the dynamic factors discussed in this chapter, is a product of experience.[22] Experience in coping with lesser frustrations through learning to endure them, or learning effective ways of removing them, enables one to handle the larger frustrations with the assurance born of past success in dealing with their smaller relatives.[23] Teachers are giving their pupils good exercise in meeting the situations they will encounter throughout life by not overprotecting them against a reasonable amount of failure, disappointment, and other forms of frustration.

Many experiments with subhuman species have confirmed the reasonable hypothesis that animals which have throughout life encountered situations that frustrated them in some way, but within limits which they were able to tolerate, developed a much higher degree of tolerance to more severe frustration than was possessed by animals who had never had the strengthening experience of successfully adjusting to frustrations as a normal pattern of life. Rats which have learned that sometimes they get what they want (usually a bit of food) through performing a certain task, but often do not get the reward, will diligently persevere in

[22] C. T. Morgan, *Introduction to Psychology.* McGraw-Hill Book Company, Inc., New York, 1961.

[23] B. R. McCandless, *Children and Adolescents—Behavior and Development.* Holt, Rinehart and Winston, New York, 1961.

attempts to obtain the reward in the face of repeated failures (frustrations) long after rats which had grown up invariably getting the reward whenever they performed the task had given up the struggle.[24, 25] It is almost certainly true that children, too, who grow up accustomed to the fact that their best efforts usually result in success, but that sometimes success is delayed or may not come, develop greater resistance to depression and discouragement in the face of frustration than do children who grew up accustomed to the idea that everything always must necessarily work out to their satisfaction.

It is seldom, if ever, necessary to devise situations which will frustrate the adolescent to provide this growth in frustration tolerance through experience. Life is so constructed that enough frustrations come in the natural course of things. In fact, far from maturing in a climate in which they invariably experience an insufficiency of normal frustrations, some adolescents will be found who have developed a low frustration tolerance through too much, rather than too little, experience with frustration. Their self concepts have deteriorated (or never assumed a healthy form) through repeated frustrations (disappointments or failures), and they lack the initiative, self-confidence, or simple hope to keep trying. They may present the exact superficial picture of the boys and girls who were "spoiled" by always being catered to, in that both, now, when faced with frustration, seem helpless, frightened, discouraged, unwilling or unable to react adjustively to the situation.

Refusal to perform assigned schoolwork often has its roots in too severe or too frequent frustration related to schoolwork in the past. If Joanie has encountered failure in schoolwork exceeding her frustration tolerance, she becomes unwilling to risk more frustrating failure and avoids it by not attempting to do the assigned work. Better reprimand or punishment without the ego-injuring effect of failure, than trying, failing, and being penalized both by a teacher and one's own injured self-esteem. Equal reluctance to tackle a new assignment may be shown by Jonathan, who has been accustomed to being led through his work and is unwilling to risk failure by venturing an attempt on his own.

It is important, therefore, to understand the intimate psychological background of the boy and girl with inadequate frustration tolerance,

24 F. W. Finger, "The Effect of Varying Conditions of Reinforcement upon a Simple Running Response," *Journal of Experimental Psychology*, 1942, *30*:53–68.

25 B. F. Skinner, *The Behavior of Organisms*. Appleton-Century-Crofts, Inc., New York, 1938.

because the approach in assisting them will vary drastically depending upon the causal factor in the deficiency. Both need to be given situations in which they can experience success—schoolwork or home tasks within their abilities—because at the present moment both are frustrated beyond their ability to make adjustment. However, in the case of the adolescent who is frustrated because he has been confronted with a stress situation such as he seldom had to cope with before, explanation should accompany the stress experience to the effect that frequent failures, deprivations, or other frustrations are encountered in life and must be accepted as a necessary part of living. In the case of the one who is apathetic or is developing neurotic defenses because of too long exposure to too severe frustrations (for instance, the child who has lived in the shadow of a preferred or more capable sibling), the explanation needed is that circumstances differ, frustrations are inevitable and may always be encountered in certain situations, but that efforts in other situations have the possibility of success. The element lacking in the frustration tolerance of the first boy or girl is psychological adjustment to the fact that some frustration is inevitable and must be tolerated. The element lacking in the latter boy or girl is the realization that frustration is not always inevitable, that areas exist in which endeavor may proceed with good hope of success rather than invariable expectations of failure.

From the foregoing discussion it can be perceived that tolerance of frustration does not mean a willingness to be frustrated, a resignation to being frustrated and the ability to exist in spite of it. Rather, as a dynamic of emotional maturation, tolerance of frustration refers to the ability to undergo frustrations and maintain the ego strength to continue indefatigably and resourcefully to look for ways of achieving one's goals despite the frustrating circumstances. Sometimes accepting lower goals will prove to be the mechanism for adjusting to frustrations; more frequently in the healthy personality the mechanism will involve more determined and imaginative efforts to achieve the same, or at least substantially equivalent, goals.

The process of developing frustration tolerance, an essential to prevent collapse in other personality areas when the inevitable frustrations are encountered, is essentially a twofold one. One part involves persistence and hope in the face of threat, stress, or discouraging factors. The other involves developing resourcefulness and a wide repertoire of methods, abilities, or skills in surmounting as many frustrations as possible. Such resourcefulness and wide repertoire are found in the "well-rounded personality" and the "resourceful," "inventive" person "full of initiative." Actually, most of what we call education is nothing more than an attempt to provide boys and girls, men and women, with the resources to cope with the problems and situations they encounter rather than to be overcome by them, to deal with them effectively rather than to be frustrated by them.

Case of Thelma and Toni

Thelma became confused on her first geometry test and was completely unable to solve one problem. Being persistent, and feeling that she could solve the problem eventually, she spent so much time on it that she was unable to complete the last problem either, and made 60 on the test instead of 85 to 95, which she was accustomed to making in her courses. Thelma was angry at herself, cried a bit, and settled down to work harder for the next test.

Toni's experience in trigonometry was much the same. However, she refused to study after she failed the test, insisted on dropping the course, and seemed to feel considerable resentment toward the instructor. Toni, too, usually made in the high 80's or the 90's on her courses. After the calamitous trigonometry test, she started looking for a program of study she could pursue in high school and college without taking any more mathematics courses.

1. Construct a hypothetical history of Thelma's experiences which would account for her reaction to failing the geometry test, and one for Toni's which would explain her reaction.

2. How should Toni's homeroom teacher or counselor advise her?

3. What would be the danger in insisting that Toni continue her study of mathematics, regardless?

Empathy and/or Compassion

Emotional maturity in this area is more properly conceived of as necessary for adjustment within the American culture than as necessary for the achievement or maintenance of psychological health. In the typical savage society, empathy or compassion is as likely, or more likely, to be destructive of good adjustment as promotive of it. Among the American Indians of the fifteenth century, for example, compassion was hardly a necessity for adjustment in the social order. Throughout the pages of recorded history, however, in retrospect those people who were motivated by concern for the welfare of others overshadow their famous but egocentric fellows in the esteem they inspire in Americans. The Grachii in martyrdom inspire our greater admiration than Peter the Great in his magnificence.

The cultural ethics prevalent in the United States today make the person who feels no concern over the want, suffering, or misfortune of others a deviate. He is regarded as lacking in an element of personality essential to full membership in the body of humanity within which he resides.

Empathy, the ability to imagine oneself in another's place and "feel for him" or "enter into kinship with him" or imagine his feelings, is probably the essential foundation of sympathy and compassion.[26] The extent to which one identifies himself with all mankind, and thus becomes uncomfortable at the thought of suffering or injustice anywhere, is regarded in our culture as a measure of the height of his moral development and emotional maturity.[27]

Since it is obvious that "adjustment" means adjustment to something, and "maturity" must mean mature according to the prevailing standards in which the person lives, empathy and compassion become social necessities for emotional maturity and adjustment in America, whereas they would not be in the Australian bushman's society. (On the other hand, tolerance of frustration and perception of relative values would be required for a healthy personality in bushman society as well as in our own.) Thus, this dynamic of emotional maturation may be thought of as a cultural, although not a developmental, essential. However, even from a strictly mental-hygiene point of view, and ignoring the moral and ethical principles involved, it is probable that a stronger, more stable and sustaining self concept can be developed by the person who draws strength through his close identification with mankind (sense of intimacy) than by the person whose personal aggrandizement is his only source of satisfaction.

Empathy and compassion are best inculcated in infancy through example and teaching. Parents who display kindness and affection not only toward their children but toward all beings with whom they come in contact, and who explain to their children that pain or want in other

26 A. T. Jersild, *When Teachers Face Themselves.* Bureau of Publications, Teachers College, Columbia University, New York, 1955.

27 A. T. Jersild, "Emotional Development," in L. Carmichael (ed.) *Manual of Child Psychology.* John Wiley & Sons, Inc., New York, 1954.

people and animals is a source of pain to thoughtful people, can hardly fail to produce adolescents with an active sense of empathy and compassion. Such boys and girls possess one of the dynamic forces necessary to produce personalities which draw the greatest richness from the experiences of life.

Emotional poverty in this area is usually, if not always, the result of materialism, opportunistic philosophy, egocentricity, and either coldness or egocentric affection on the part of parents. Unfortunately, many adolescents have developed under these conditions. Daily observations of disputes arising from attempts to "get more for less," and cynically settled in favor of the group with most votes or greatest ruthlessness in enforcing their demands, reinforce adolescent cynicism and contribute to a "What's in it for me?" and "Every man for himself" philosophy. Compassion must be used within the limits of justice to be constructive. Unscrupulous people sometimes attempt to use Americans' sense of compassion to foment a tolerance of Robin-Hood tactics of robbing Peter to pay Paul. As Freeman[28] cogently points out, the truly compassionate person will try to help the weak, but not at the expense of another group.

The adolescent will probably suffer little actual hurt if he never achieves optimum maturity in this area. The society in which he lives and those with whom he comes in contact will be hurt. He may be hurt if his callousness leads to criminal acts, gratifying his desires regardless of the effect of his actions upon others. In most cases his hurt will be of a negative sort, failure to achieve maximum richness of life rather than actual deprivation.

The opportunity of teachers to contribute in this area can hardly be exaggerated. By examples of patience, sympathy, and desire to help those who need it, they can encourage in their students acceptance of the principle of consideration and care for others. By encouraging boys and girls to assume responsibility for helping classmates of lower abilities than themselves, teachers can provide adolescents with practice in cultivating a sense of compassion. Getting boys or girls to make provisions for class members who are socially inept, academically deficient, or handicapped in physical participation in class and extracurricular activities will be easy in some cases, most difficult in others. However, if you *can* get them to do so, and do so not as a sacrifice, but as an opportunity to "thank humanity" for their own ability, you will have given them an attitude which will enrich their whole personal lives.

28 L. Freeman, *Fight Against Fears.* Crown, New York, 1951.

Best hope for helping adolescents deficient in this area lies in admirable examples of consideration and kindness on the part of adults dealing with them. Infinite patience is required in this; youth workers with juvenile gangs, who spend time on the street developing good relations with the boys and girls, can so testify. Altering attitudes of egocentricity and cultivating the ideal of one's responsibility for the welfare of others, against the background of a lifetime of conditioning toward selfishness and often in the face of cynical disregard for others which the adolescent encounters in other adults, is slow and difficult. It is also uncertain; one's own frustration tolerance must be high. The reward lies in the great benefits that not only the individual adolescent, but society as a whole, will derive from your success in inculcating the concept of empathy and compassion as a dynamic force in even one life from which it was previously absent.

Motion pictures portraying, in dramatic form, humanitarian concepts are powerful devices for cultivating adolescents' sensitivity to the feelings and needs of others. Some literature, especially biographical material on men such as Albert Schweitzer, can serve a similar purpose, particularly when a teacher uses it as a basis for discussion and analysis of motives, rewards, and moral considerations. Lecturing and moralizing on the subject of responsibility to others and the virtues of kindness have small effect, and even that small effect is usually most temporary. Some greater effect may be produced by getting boys and girls themselves to discuss issues or incidents, what constitutes compassion, and to what extent it is a moral obligation, and letting them draw their own conclusions based upon their own (probably their first) thoughtful evaluation of the question.

Much deeper clinical investigation of requirements for successful development of this formative force in human behavior would be of great benefit to society.

Case of Ute

Ute lives in the part of town graphically called Junktown. Several times he has appeared at school with visible bruises, which he explained succinctly and with some pride: "My ol' man came home drunk last night," or "My ol' man clobbered me for swiping his knife and losing it." His mother's one visit to the school was on the request of the principal after Ute had knocked a smaller boy down the stairs in a headlong rush for the playground.

Ute reasoned, "If he can't go faster than he was goin', he'd better stay out of the way."

His mother said, "Kids bump into each other all the time. Ute didn't mean to hurt him. You can't keep things like that from happening."

Ute has the reputation of running roughshod over anyone he is able to intimidate, bully, or beat. He does not seem to mind taking a beating if one of his intended victims proves unexpectedly capable as a rough-and-tumble fighter.

1. Account for Ute's ruthless attitude on the basis of what you know and can reasonably infer from the above description.

2. Why is he so little deterred by being beaten up himself?

Gradation of Reaction

As a dynamic of emotional maturation, gradation of reaction may be thought of as analogous to a gyroscopic stabilizer: it inhibits wild fluctuations in one direction or another. It does not prevent emotional responses, does not keep the individual from having or showing feelings; it merely subdues extreme reactions which might be set off by trivial stimuli, holding the reaction to an appropriate amount.

Children tend to react emotionally on an all-or-none basis. Stimuli of pleasure, anger, or fear produce emotional responses which appear to bear little appropriateness to the intensity of the stimuli. A frightened child is likely to become more frightened merely from the contemplation of his own fright, so to speak. The angry child becomes angry with an intensity frequently out of all proportion to the justification. The unreserved happiness of children over trivia, such as a new hair ribbon or pocketknife, as great as their happiness over important things is well known. One of the necessities for a well-balanced emotional life is achievement of an emotional perspective, a differentiation of response appropriate to the stimuli, rather than all-out emotional reaction to every emotion-producing stimulus. Without such a balanced pattern of emotional response, one is betrayed into inappropriate, maladjustive behavior and, incidentally, unnecessarily exhaustive behavior.[29]

Utter self-abandonment to emotional excesses is one of the trademarks of a certain type of neurotic personality. Numerous public figures, especially those in the entertainment or artistic world, have endowed

[29] L. Tussing, *Psychology for Better Living*. John Wiley & Sons, Inc., New York, 1959.

such maladjustive reactions with a certain glamour (or notoriety, depending upon your point of view). The prima-donna attitude and the "artistic temperament," characterized by low frustration tolerance and adult temper tantrums, are examples of the behavior of persons who have reached chronological maturity without having achieved the balancing effect exerted by healthy frustration tolerance and appropriate gradation of reaction to emotional stimuli. Imitations of this behavior can be frequently observed in the overdramatized reaction of the girl who treats a minor deprivation or disappointment—not getting a new dress for a dance, for instance—as a devastating catastrophe. At one time the caricature of the dynamic executive portrayed this type of immaturity, the man who raged and bellowed if a comma was misplaced in a letter. It is doubtful if such people often attained high status in the business world, but the reaction is still encountered in comic-strip burlesques. The boy who whips himself into a frantic rage when denied the use of the family car, however, is an all-too-common example of the adolescent who has matured chronologically, but has not achieved the emotional maturity to temper emotional response to the level of intensity appropriate for a given stimulus.

The degree to which gradation of emotional reaction is expected of an individual, and, therefore, the degree to which it is taught to children, varies widely with different racial and cultural groups. Among some groups, wailing during prayer with the intensity of one's emotion is considered appropriate behavior. In some cultures, frenzied rages manifested over relatively trivial incidents (especially where matters of the heart are concerned) or exhibitions of wild distress over some minor frustration are considered the mark of a fiery, magnificent spirit. In Anglo-Saxon cultures, by and large, such displays are regarded at best as immature, or at worst as denoting a psychological aberration.

Good health and mental hygiene are probably promoted by gradation of emotional responses to levels appropriate to the stimuli. On the one hand, rigid repression or inadequate discharge of emotional tension inhibits normal re-establishment of homeostasis in an organism undergoing the profound stress of a severe emotion. On the other hand, complete lack of effort to moderate the evolution of an emotion frequently results in the development of an emotional state potentially destructive to physical or mental well-being, whereas sensible efforts to inhibit the emotion would have held it to a minor upset which quickly would have passed away with little disturbance to the individual.

Gradation of emotional reaction to a level and form appropriate to the situation is, therefore, usually psychologically and physically wholesome as well as socially graceful.

Helping the adolescent achieve smooth operation of this dynamic factor, as may be deduced from the foregoing paragraphs, may involve assistance in either of two directions. It may involve motivating and assisting the boy or girl who exercises too little control over emotional responses to cultivate more appropriate control. On the other hand, it may involve helping the inhibited, overcontrolled child to develop the feeling of freedom necessary to permit expression of emotions to the extent normal for various situations.

The process of achieving adult socialization, adjusting to a world of people, acquiring adult values of behavior, will usually dampen the overreactions of the adolescent with too little emotional control. Boys and girls who do not temper their emotional reactions to the standards of good taste, who make themselves conspicuous by sulking over trifles, displaying excessive rage at frustrations, or even being given to fatiguing ecstasies of joy over minor or trivial things, are usually more or less ostracized by their peers. They do not "fit into" the group. Their excessive emotionalism quickly becomes annoying to other boys and girls, and the pressure of popular disapproval forces better adjustment of emotional reactions.

Sometimes group pressure is ineffective in regulating emotional response of a boy or girl. This may be due to one of three causes within the individual: (1) a neurotic condition may exist which renders it impossible for the boy or girl to exercise the desired self-control, (2) the personality structure may be such that surrender of the reactions which distinguish him or her are too threatening to the self concept, or (3) the person may simply not want to make the effort of self-control, preferring to indulge his feelings.

Neurotic lack of emotional control seldom occurs in the absence of a general neurotic personality structure. If the boy or girl seems otherwise stable, normal, and fairly wholesome in adjustment, the likelihood of the emotional intransigence being due to neurotic factors is small. When a weak self concept, unable to endure the stress of changing a well-established reaction pattern, is the basis for lack of gradation of emotional reaction, assistance in developing the general personality areas discussed as criteria of ego strength in Chapter 5, employing methods discussed there, is needed by the adolescent. It is reasonable to expect that more effective gradation of emotional reaction will accompany the adolescent's strengthening and maturation of personality.[30]

Extreme failure to exercise appropriate emotional control due to self-indulgence of feelings is usually a result of a history of parental spoiling, indulging, and "giving in" which subtly encourages the child or adolescent in such socially disapproved behavior. A teacher's having sympathetic, noncritical talks with the boy or girl involved, encouraging him to contrast his own behavior with that of the peer group, may promote greater self-consciousness of the deviate nature of his emotional overresponse. If you can get him to think and talk about what factors and conditions probably got him into the pattern of such reactions, and to evaluate the effect of his exaggerated emotional reactions on his social acceptance, you can probably lead him to gradually change his behavior.[31] This method of encouraging the adolescent (with leading but sympathetic questions) to analyze his own problem and express his own solution to it certainly will accomplish more in helping him acquire a suitable gradation of emotional reaction than will moralizing, attempting to shame him, or scolding him.

The overinhibited boy who represses his emotional expression to an abnormal extent ordinarily needs to learn to relax and "do what comes naturally" to a greater extent than he has been accustomed to do. Such an adolescent will usually show a general personality pattern of tenseness and rigidity of response in all areas. He has not acquired the confidence that he can be himself and yet get along nicely in his world. Sympathetic attention, encouraging some relaxation of the standards he holds for himself, getting him not to take so seriously the necessity for success or doing things exactly right, is the treatment most frequently indicated in such cases. As he experiences success and acceptance in tentative adventures at just being himself, his handling and expression of his emotional reactions will become more normal.

Case of Valarie

Sixteen-year-old Valarie and her "steady" have just broken up. Last night she was hysterical, threatening suicide to her distraught mother. Today she refused to come to school, lying in bed and weep-

[30] E. B. Hurlock, *Adolescent Development*. McGraw-Hill Book Company, Inc., New York, 1955.

[31] G. M. Worbois, "Effect of a Guidance Program on Emotional Development," *Journal of Applied Psychology*, 1947, *31*:169–181.

ing copiously. She says she will never return to her class, where "everybody knows what has happened."

1. How normal or abnormal is Valarie's reaction?

2. How normal or abnormal would it be if she were a junior in college?

Socialization of Responses

In the sense that emotional maturation and adjustment mean successfully fitting into the society in which one lives, socialization of emotional responses is the ultimate function of the dynamic process of achieving healthy emotional adulthood.[32] Socialization of responses involves adapting the expression of emotion, one's thoughts or feelings, of whatever type and level of intensity, to the exigencies of the social situation in which one finds himself. If a hermit alone at his cave in the deep woods encounters a frustration severe enough to justify the most violent of rages, there is no socially pressing reason why he should not hurl things at random and with his maximum strength, scream at the top of his voice, and engage in almost any other behavior which he feels would relieve some of the intensity of his feelings. This is exactly what the small child does, and if his emotion is sorrow rather than rage, he gives wild and uninhibited tongue to his lament against the heartlessness of fate.

Even when the appropriate gradation of emotion indicates the propriety of such a feeling in the adult, the *expression* of that feeling is expected to be "socialized," that is, attuned in form to the sensibilities of those around us. Society sympathizes with and fully condones the unrestrained, hysterical grief of a mother whose child has drowned, and some religious groups sanction the unrestrained ecstasy of a member who feels the Spirit of God is moving within him. With a very few exceptions, however, adults are expected to attune their emotional response in the last analysis to congruency with social usages rather than their own (even if appropriately graded) inclinations.[33] In ancient times an offensive remark was considered justification for a blow. For centuries the "socialized" response to an affront was a duel, if the two parties involved

32 R. S. Lazarus, *Adjustment and Personality*. McGraw-Hill Book Company, Inc., New York, 1961.

33 R. Stagner, *Psychology of Personality*. McGraw-Hill Book Company, Inc., New York, 1961.

were gentlemen. Now social convention requires, at most, an attempt at a withering counterremark.

Similarly with one's thoughts, convictions, or ideas. Society generally requires, as a part of the price of membership, that members exercise consideration and judgment in expressing themselves. The person who expresses his ideas or offers facts, sound though they may be, in inappropriate ways or situations is imperfectly socialized and runs the risk of exclusion from the group. It may be admirable objectivity for a boy or girl to recognize that the team has little chance of avoiding crushing defeat tomorrow; it is lack of social judgment to proclaim this fact at a pep rally. When a group is discussing some subject, an abrupt shift to another topic by an uninterested member may show lack of socialization of his behavior. Helping boys and girls learn to perceive when the expression of their thoughts is appropriate and when it is not is a potential contribution of class discussion to socialization of responses.

As in the case of gradation of reaction, social pressure in most cases effectively disciplines the adolescent into types of responses to emotion which are approved or condoned by the group. The crybaby or griper, the wet blanket or fearful, the obtrusive, uninhibited expressor of opinions or contributor of unwanted facts, even the overexuberant or the backslapper, is made to feel the inappropriateness of his responses. Too free displays of affection in public are generally disapproved of even by adolescents whose own behavior knows few bounds in privacy.

The expression "attuned in form to the sensibilities of those around us" has been used to describe a socialized response, and this is the key criterion of socialization. This fact places a considerable burden upon adolescents, because they actually move in two societies, adolescent and adult, in which the sensibilities of those composing the human environment differ radically. The adolescent boy or girl is acquiring a sense of the need to socialize his emotional responses; not to do so is "childish." At the same time, to socialize them to the extent of meeting the norm of adult society is both beyond his power and would set him apart from his peer group. In other words, a behavior pattern attuned to the sensibilities of adults would cause the adolescent's behavior to be inappropriate to his own age group. This is a major reason why adults so often regard adolescents' behavior—not only their emotional responses, but their handling of an infinity of other situations as well—as inappropriate. The behavior is attuned to the sensibilities of his peer group,

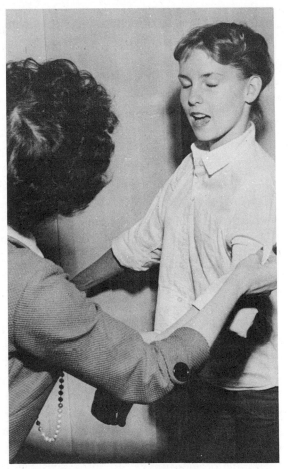

The Atlanta Journal-Constitution.

Figure 13. "To socialize the adolescent to the extent of meeting the norm of adult society both is beyond her power and would set her apart from her peer group."

which sensibilities are vastly different from those of his parents, teachers, or counselors.

"Toning down" of responses, being not quite so loud or uninhibited in expression of emotion (although adults generally would welcome such restraint), is not always the sort of socialization of response needed by the adolescent for emotional maturation and adjustment. It is not uncommon for adolescents who recognize their need to be less demonstrative of emotions, or who are making an inexperienced attempt at sophistication, to overcompensate and display a blasé attitude when a well-socialized response would call for more demonstration of feeling. Thus, one hapless adolescent may make a spectacle of himself or herself, embarrassing and alienating friends, by too profusely reacting to the loss of a ball game, while another equally inept incurs the resentment of the group for too casually accepting the tragedy!

Except in rare cases, socialization of responses will accompany general maturation and adjustment. It is a dynamic force in producing maturation and adjustment as well as a criterion of such development, because conscious patterning of responses to be appropriate to a social milieu subtly encourages the healthy functioning of the psychological process as a whole. Given the consistent end result of a reasoned, socially appropriate, overt manifestation of a thought or emotion, over a period of time the functioning of the entire psychological mechanism of the individual will tend to adapt itself to a pattern which will render this manifestation the logical and natural one.

This is an important concept in human adjustment generally, as well as in helping adolescents achieve emotional maturity and adjustment. Adjustive behavior will certainly not always produce mental and emotional adjustment where there is underlying psychopathy; however, maladjustive behavior usually intensifies rather than ameliorates the pathology, and, on the other hand, the adjustive behavior will often subtly reshape maladjustive mental and emotional functioning to fit the standards being adhered to by the overt behavior.

Where socialization of emotional responses does lag behind other aspects of personality maturation, the cause may be a neurotic condition rendering effective control impossible, or lack of self-discipline (both of which were discussed in reference to gradation of reaction), or simple ignorance or ineptness. Especially in instances where the boy or girl is from a home and neighborhood where there is little contact with other adolescents, or where parents are uneducated or versed in a culture markedly different from the prevalent one, the adolescent may not have acquired the social perceptiveness required to identify socially approved responses to emotion-arousing situations. Even adolescents who are generally socially adept are often baffled by how to respond to a specific emotionally charged situation. "What do you do in a case like that?" is a question frequently heard by adults in the confidence of adolescents.

Adolescents whose responses to emotions are injuring rather than promoting their social adjustment can be helped by reading one or more of several books for adolescents on how to get along with their fellows. Of course, a teacher or parent can help also, sometimes by recalling in a carefully inoffensive manner specific instances of inappropriate responses to emotionally charged situations which the boy or girl has displayed or which both have observed. Getting the boy or girl to engage in self-analysis and analysis of the probable feelings of others to infer the cause and effect of a particular response will accomplish more than the adult's suggesting how a situation might better have been handled. Often pointing out a boy or girl who is popular or who is unusually proficient at handling difficult situations to the satisfaction of all concerned, and suggesting that your counselee watch that person and try to determine the rationale of his method will prove helpful. (This must be done with caution, suggesting the other person not as a model but as a source of ideas, and suggesting not slavish imitation of his methods, but consideration of the underlying principles on which his responses seem to be based.)

Case of Wanda, Xerxes, and Yolande

Four-year-old Wanda is playing with her tricycle, and another child, by a combination of strength, ingenuity, and persistence, gets possession of it and rides off.

1. How will Wanda feel like responding to this situation?
2. How will she probably respond?

Thirteen-year-old Xerxes is pitcher for his gang's baseball team. Another boy moves into the neighborhood and in a couple of weeks, by popularity, skill, and ingenuity, wins the support of the team as pitcher.

1. How will Xerxes probably feel like responding to this situation?
2. How will he probably respond?

Eighteen-year-old Yolande has selected *the* formal for the senior prom. She hangs it on the end of the rack while she calls her mother for permission to buy it. When she returns, a saleslady is admiring it on another girl. Seeing Yolande's stricken look the saleslady says, "Oh, dear! Were you interested in this? When you hung it back up, I thought you were through with it, and now I've shown it to this other young lady."

"I'll take it," the other young lady says.

1. How will Yolande feel like responding to this situation?
2. How will she probably respond?

READINGS

Bayley, N., "The Emotions of Children: Their Development and Modification," *Childhood Education,* Dec., 1944, Vol. XXI, No. 4, p. 156-160.

Beres, D., and Obers, S. J., "The Effects of Extreme Deprivation in Infancy on Psychic Structure in Adolescence: A Study in Ego Development," in Eissler, R. S., *et al.* (eds.) *The Psychoanalytic Study of the Child,* Vol. V. New York: International Universities Press, 1950.

Bugelski, B. R., *An Introduction to the Principles of Psychology.* New York: Holt, Rinehart & Winston, Inc., 1960, Chapt. 12.

Coleman, J. C., *Abnormal Psychology and Modern Life.* Chicago: Scott, Foresman and Company, 1956, Chapt. 3.

Coleman, J. C., *Personality Dynamics and Effective Behavior.* Chicago: Scott, Foresman and Company, 1960, Chapt. 10.

Finesinger, J. E., "The Needs of Youth: The Physiological and Psychological Factors in Adolescent Behavior," *Psychiatry, 7,* 1, pp. 45-57.

Jersild, A. T., *The Psychology of Adolescence.* New York: The Macmillan Company, 1957, Chapts. 7, 8.

Symonds, P. M., *The Dynamics of Parent-Child Relationships.* New York: Teachers College, Columbia University, 1949.

CHAPTER 9

INHIBITING FACTORS IN

EMOTIONAL MATURATION

PREVIEW

Eight Inhibiting Factors, Their Dynamics and Effects

FACTOR	DYNAMICS AND EFFECT
Confusion of roles	The adolescent is part child, part adult in almost all personality areas. Ambiguity in his treatment by adults and his own self concept get in the way of maturation.
Early traumas	Repeated maladjustive experiences or, rarely, single incidents may arrest emotional maturation at the age level at which they occurred.
Early deprivation of affection	Produces an adolescent without the mastery of early developmental tasks needed for emotional maturation.
Biological defects	Organic defects may interfere with emotional maturation both through causing physical deficiencies and through psychological maladjustment to the defect.
Escapist use of defense mechanisms	Overreliance on evasive or compensatory mechanisms prevents experience in mature, adjustive processes.
Restricted experience	Prevents the breadth of experience in meeting and coping with life situations which is necessary for maturation.
Lack of training	Inhibits acquisition of skills necessary for success experience and strong self concept.
Unresolved internal conflicts	Conflicting emotions or desires inhibit the integrative function of the personality.

THROUGHOUT the discussions of the dynamic forces in emotional development we briefly touched on causal factors inhibiting the optimum progress toward emotional maturation and adjustment. These inhibiting factors are worthy of more systematic and complete examination, because they often contain the clue to understanding the problems of, and thus enable us to help, boys and girls with problems of emotional adjustment. Some inhibiting factors recur in different forms and manifestations in various areas of maturation and personality development. Some of them are the negative side of one of the developmental stages, the result if the task was not successfully accomplished.

In talking to boys and girls who demonstrate inadequate emotional maturation or adjustment, who are unable to objectify their perceptions, tolerate normal frustrations, or the like, it is a good idea to be alert for indications of any of these causal factors. Even one which is not a primary cause of an adjustmental or behavioral problem of some kind may be a complicating factor which should be taken into consideration in designing ways of helping the troubled adolescent.

EIGHT INHIBITING FACTORS, THEIR DYNAMICS AND EFFECTS

Confusion of Roles

Society, biology, and psychology unite to cast the adolescent in a variety of roles, with the frequent result that he lacks security because of imperfect self-identification. His self concept undergoes extensive and radical changes during this period, and the concepts others have of him do as well. The shifts in self concept and the concepts held of him by other people do not proceed in perfect synchronization or even steadily in their own course. The adolescent is literally looked on as one person one minute and another the next, and anxiously and uncertainly perceives himself in the same erratic pattern. Since stability and consistency are implicit requisites in most of the dynamic processes of emotional maturation and adjustment, this ambiguity of roles is sometimes a seriously upsetting factor.[1]

When thirteen-year-old Betty wants to accept an invitation to the junior-senior formal and wear a décolleté gown, she is "still just a child," according to the parents, and the father is particularly violent (masculine jealousy?) in insisting that she "act her age." However, when Betty shows up in tight short shorts and ditto halter, she is a "young lady, not a child, and dressing like that is plain indecent!" Again she is adjured to

[1] F. Gaul, "Criminals are Made, Not Born," *Teleclass Study Guide, Social Science 101*. Chicago Board of Education, Chicago, 1958.

"act her age," especially by Papa. Small wonder she ruefully muses over which she really is, a child or a young lady! Typically, Betty's actions reflect her wonderment, not only because parents' attitudes confuse her, but because she confuses herself, too. She longs for a boy to ask her to go to the movies with him, but when he does, she is terrified and often actually insists that her mother make some excuse as to why she cannot go. With complete self-assurance and without deigning to ask parental approval, she decides, with the help of a friend and a bottle from the ten-cent store, to become a dazzling blonde or a redhead. When results are not exactly what she anticipated, with childish naïveté she either fails to see the effect of blotchy, streaked locks, or else flies into her room, locks the door, flings herself onto the bed, and cries, in the apparent belief that she can stay there until her hair changes color again.

More subtle roles than simple maturation suggests are also involved in the emotional adjustment of adolescents. Are they little girls or boys who can wander in and out of the nice couple's house next door "like their own children," or old enough to use some discretion in their associations with adult friends and have respect for other people's privacy? What is it suitable to wear around the house with members of the family present? How about when adult friends of the family are there? Or boys or girls his own age? When should he try to be a leader and when a follower? When a pal and when a sweetheart, and what makes the difference, and how do you show it? Or know it? And legal provisions solemnly adjudge a boy old enough to carry a 5 A.M. paper route through rain, sleet, and snow, but not old enough to work in the warm stockroom of a wholesale dry-goods house.

Often a question, suggestion, or statement of fact to an adolescent who is not assuming a role appropriate to circumstances will set him thinking on the right track. But be gentle with this boy or girl, who is trying to find an appropriate way to act in a situation and making a miserable mess of it. He probably is being obnoxious so as to hide his utter frustration at not knowing the proper way to act.

Case of Zane

Sixteen-year-old Zane is indignant when denied the use of the family car for a Saturday-night date. After all, he's not a child! He is old enough to know what to do and how to do it! His maturity, however, undergoes a rapid decline when a teacher gets on him hard, and he looks to Mamma and Daddy to straighten things out for him.

But to even things up, Dad thinks Zane is not old enough to take a boat out on the lake alone, but old enough to understand that a football game, however long looked forward to, just has to be missed when something around the house breaks down unexpectedly.

Then, to little sister Zane is grown up, while to older brother he is just a kid. His teacher is aware of his propensity to throw paper wads and engage in a roughhouse if she steps out of the room for a minute, and of his furious rage if he is "treated like a kid" for engaging in such childish behavior.

1. What motives on the part of Zane and the various people in his life account for the confusion of roles which he faces or displays?

2. What dynamic forces will gradually cause Zane to adopt more consistently mature roles in his life?

Early Traumas

Sometimes puzzling maladjustments or failures to develop in some area in a normal fashion can be traced to an earlier experience which produced a psychic wound that over-sensitized the adolescent in that area.[2, 3] The boy who lost a key Little League game by muffing an easy fly ball and was made too conscious of his mistake *may* become an adolescent averse to accepting a responsibility in which failure would be noticeable. Amy forgot her "piece" on parents' night when she was in the first grade. She and everyone else has long forgotten the whole incident, but, now in the ninth grade, Amy becomes tongue-tied and incapable of expressing herself in any situation in which attention is strongly focused on her, and goes to great lengths to avoid the possibility of such situations arising. One college junior failed history, her only failure in her entire college program, because the slight, mild-mannered old professor reminded her of a great-uncle who had always seemed to her quite harsh and critical, and she could only shake her head dumbly whenever he asked her a question in class!

As a matter of actual fact, the role of a single instance of early psychic trauma in later maladjustment has been vastly overestimated in the popular mind. Relatively few adolescent or adult emotional problems are due to a single traumatic incident. But it produces much less guilt in

[2] J. C. Coleman, *Abnormal Psychology and Modern Life*. Scott, Foresman and Company, Chicago, 1956.

[3] L. J. Saul, *Emotional Maturity*. J. B. Lippincott Company, Philadelphia, 1960.

parents to ascribe Bennie's stuttering to his having been paralyzed with terror by a huge dog than to contemplate their overmeticulous demands for perfect speech which made him anxious and hesitant at trying to express himself. The adolescent finds it less damaging to his self concept to blame his uncontrolled hostility toward a teacher on an instance of alleged injustice experienced at the hands of an earlier teacher of similar characteristics than to face the fact that her insistence on properly completed homework is the real basis.

Early psychic traumas usually occur from repeated, habitual maladjustive treatment or reactions which produce their effect over a period of time, like water dripping on a stone, rather than as one shattering experience. Thus, moving to a new neighborhood and being rejected by the children there because of some difference, or alleged difference, or the existence of a tight clique, usually involves not merely one attempt to unite with the group and being shut out. Typically it involves repeated attempts to integrate over a period of time, which through repeated frustration produce a traumatic effect. It is difficult to draw a line and say exactly when a series of events ceases to be a simple unhappy environmental pattern and becomes a traumatic experience, and probably pointless to do so. The important fact to remember is that in trying to help adolescents with traumatically induced emotional patterns, you will usually need to look for their origin in *multiple experiences* which in combination constitute a traumatic experience, rather than finding one causal incident and feeling that you have got to the bottom of the trouble. This principle of multiple causation of emotional difficulties is one of the most significant concepts for workers with adolescents to remember. Understanding its implications will often prevent oversimplification or misinterpretation of a problem and forestall inadequate or misdirected assistance to the boy or girl.

Some common sources of early trauma are premature or undesirable sexual experiences (molestation, seeing parents having intercourse, harsh reprimands for sexual manipulation or curiosity, and the like), public embarrassment or humiliation, feeling of being displaced by a younger sibling, parental fights or severe discord, or severe frights from any cause.

The key element in the maladjustive effect of traumas is that traumas tend to produce *an emotionalized association with the traumatic episode,* and subsequent reactions to similar situations are in terms of *the emotion originally associated with the similar episode,* rather than in terms of realistic appraisal of the present situation.[4] Thus, the child who was frightened by many stories of the terrors of a forest near her home experiences apprehension in driving or walking through a forest today. And, of course, it *is* possible for a single traumatic incident to produce a permanent emotional disturbance. The author's own files include data regarding a grown woman who all her life had reacted with terror to any feathered creature and even to feathers. It was eventually brought to light that when she was an infant sleeping in her crib, a chicken had flown in through the open, unscreened door and into her crib, awakening and terrifying her with its fluttering, flapping, and squawking before the surprised parents came in and removed it. The woman herself had no conscious memory of the incident, even when her parents related it in her presence.

Obviously, such emotionally charged associations render objectification impossible. Depending upon their nature, they may inhibit development or adjustment in various areas, as already illustrated. If at all possible, the assistance of a clinical psychologist or a psychiatrist should be obtained for the treatment of emotional problems growing out of early traumas. Attempts by persons not professionally qualified in psychotherapy to ferret out the causes of the traumas and recondition the boy or girl to a better attitude are likely to worsen instead of better the situation. If such professional help is unavailable, it is usually not dangerous to encourage the boy or girl to talk about his problem of emotional adjustment, sympathetically listening to him, but refraining from asking probing questions or making interpretations. Seldom will an emotionally disturbed person penetrate the cause of his difficulty before he has the ego strength to face it when he discovers it. However, attempts by people who are not qualified in psychotherapy to help him reach the underlying cause of his difficulty may raise more demons than conscientious, well-meaning amateurs can exorcise.

Early Deprivation of Affection

An adolescent inevitably reflects back toward the world a reasonably accurate picture of the world as it has impressed him. If, as an infant, he perceived the world and the people around him as loving and responsive, offering him security and a warm feeling of acceptance, he accepts the

[4] O. H. Mower, *Learning Theory and Personality Dynamics*. The Ronald Press Company, New York, 1950.

world at that evaluation as he grows older.[5] He reflects this acceptance by being confident that he is a worthy and normal person and by responding readily to the opportunities to express himself and achieve self-realization. He is able and willing to give and accept love, because such mutual responses have been his accustomed way of life since birth. He has the confidence to accept responsibility and endure frustrations without being demoralized, because early experience produced in him the feeling that gratifications outnumber frustrations in the world. He is willing to venture because he neither fears failure nor is crushed by it. He readily feels empathy and compassion for others, because he has been conditioned to warm, affectionate relationships.

Deprivation of affection in infancy produces the reverse of all these conditions—an insecure and distrustful person, afraid to venture, unable to bear up under frustration, unsympathetic and unable either to give or accept love freely because love is not natural to him.[6] It retards the whole process of physical and psychological development.[7] Deprivation may, in fact, result in premature death of an infant or child. Human nature and our code of morality render it impossible to experiment on children and learn exactly the effect on them of deprivation of affection in various degrees. However, people were not always so tender-hearted. Frederick the Great, a patron of science as well as a statesman and military leader, became curious as to the language that infants would eventually speak if they heard no human voice. So he instructed a group of foster mothers each to care assiduously for her infant's physical needs, but to never speak to it. "But he labored in vain," records Salimbene, "because the children all died. For they could not live without the petting and joyful faces and loving words of their foster mothers." [8]

It is a fair statement that the love and affection parents normally give infants prepare a well-tilled and fertilized field, able to support the exploratory and self-actualizing activities which are the seed from which a strong self concept and personality structure grow. If the field is the

[5] C. B. Zachry, *Emotion and Conduct in Adolescence*. Appleton-Century-Crofts, Inc., New York, 1940.

[6] W. Goldfarb, "The Effects of Early Institutional Care on Adolescents," *Journal of Experimental Education*, 1943, Vol. XII, No. 2, pp. 106–129.

[7] E. R. Hilgard, *Introduction to Psychology*. Harcourt, Brace and Company, New York, 1958.

[8] J. B. Ross and M. M. McLaughlin (eds.) *A Portable Medieval Reader*. Viking Press, New York, 1946.

hard-baked ground of indifference, the stony field of neglect, or the arid desert of deprivation, it is simply unable to support and nourish a strong tree of ego development.[9, 10]

One of the great tragedies of handling wayward, rebellious and troublesome, or indifferent adolescents is that their attitudes often result from lack of normal love and affection, and those very attitudes in turn repel people and produce still more rejection and hostility. Unfortunately, too, a display of concern for and attention to the adolescent suffering the effects of early emotional neglect seldom brings results before the patience and good resolutions of the adult are completely exhausted. Months, sometimes years, are required for an adolescent to revise his image of the world and his self concept formed from the cradle until the teens. Why should he assume that things are different now? (He would not know, really, how to act if he did so assume; the inability of a hitherto rejected adolescent to respond appropriately to overtures of acceptance is an observation of all who have worked with such boys and girls.) In the past he encountered episodes of warm human relations, but they always faded, to be replaced by the "normal" pattern of inconsideration for him.

However, every worker with young people who tries with heart and head to supply the sympathy and consideration which an occasional boy or girl has lacked through prior life has had the experience of seeing a personality grow and blossom under his ministrations. To achieve such a success is worth much effort and even many failures.

Biological Defects

The role of heredity, of biological constitution in emotional maturation and adjustment (indeed, in the whole area of psychological development), is unclear and highly controversial. At one time or another nearly every element of personality and character has been attributed to, or suspected of being due to, inborn disposition, constitution, and heredity.[11] Every passing decade in the history of psychology, however, has seen the abandonment of some widely held theory postulating a relationship between organic constitution and psychological traits. Every decade has

[9] L. J. Saul, *Emotional Maturity*. J. B. Lippincott Company, Philadelphia, 1960.

[10] R. A. Spitz, "Hospitalism: An Inquiry into the Genesis of Psychiatric Conditions in Early Childhood," *Psychoanalytic Study of the Child*, 1945, *1*:53–74; "Hospitalism: A Follow-up Report," *Psychoanalytic Study of the Child*, 1946, *2*:113–117.

[11] F. A. Moss and T. H. Hunt, *Foundations of Abnormal Psychology*. Prentice-Hall, Inc., Englewood Cliffs, N. J., 1932.

thus far provided more evidence as to the dominant influence of environmental and developmental factors in determining the psychological pattern evolving within the growing individual.

However, some psychologists speculate that the self concept has an inherited and, therefore, presumably a biologically dictated "core" which accounts for the different effects produced by apparently similar stimuli on children. They cite as an example the fact that one child, denied adequate mothering in infancy, develops a withdrawn and hesitant adjustment to life, while another develops a ruthless aggressiveness, as if determined to seize that which fate did not spontaneously give him.

The evidence at present is convincing, if not conclusive, that the mental ability commonly and loosely referred to as intelligence is largely an innate, inherited, biological capacity. Even this belief has been tempered by studies of orphanage children who were not adopted until they had lived most of the first four years of their lives in the orphanage. As was noted in Chapter 2, in phenomenal proportions such children have been found to fall below the average in achievement on intelligence tests administered eight to ten years after their adoption. Thus, there is now serious theorizing that the emotional climate in which infancy is spent may account for much of the influence on intelligence usually ascribed to hereditary factors.

It can be safely postulated, however, that biological factors do exert considerable influence on the emotional development of children. A leg shorter than the other, discoloration of a portion of the skin of the face, and other gross defects will obviously affect the emotional pattern of the individual as one part of his whole self concept which will be influenced by such deformities.[12] On a more subtle, but perhaps quite as influential, level, a biological condition predisposing an infant to lassitude and apathy or to activity and eager response will inevitably influence parent-child relations and thus the whole pattern of personality development.

Glandular imbalances not sufficient to produce such conditions as mongolism or dwarfism may, without producing clearly identifiable symptoms of a physical nature, adversely influence a child's emotional balance and interfere with his maturation and adjustment.[13] For this reason it is wise, wherever at all possible, to obtain a thorough physical examination

12 H. R. Stolz and L. M. Stolz, "Adolescent Problems Related to Somatic Variations," *National Society for the Study of Education*, 43rd Yearbook, 1944, pp. 80–99.

13 K. C. Garrison, *Growth and Development*. Longmans, Green and Co., Inc., New York, 1959.

of a boy or girl who represents a problem of emotional adjustment. If circumstances permit, specific questions may well be directed to the examining physician as to the probable extent of influence on emotionality and "nerves" which any identified biological idiosyncrasy might have. Hyperthyroidism, for instance, rather than insecurity, may account for "nervousness" in a boy or girl. Sometimes medical treatment may ameliorate basic causes or aggravating accompaniments of emotional problems.

Psychologists and physicians almost universally agree that the emotional effect of such a gross physical abnormality as the defective limb mentioned above, unusual facial features, or peculiarities of motor coordination depend upon the attitude which the child develops toward and about his affliction, rather than the actual nature or severity of the defect.[14] Thus, one girl will withdraw from social activities because of self-consciousness about a nose only slightly larger than the average, while another with a sadly misshapen chin will be an energetic, happy, and accepted member of a social group. The teacher may, through encouraging the boy's or girl's participation in class activities and through counseling to help him objectify his self concept, greatly assist the adolescent suffering psychologically from a physical defect.

Obesity is a frequent-enough problem among adolescents to deserve special mention. It is a simple, but often ignored, fact that a boy or girl does not become fat if he ingests no more food than is required to support the energy he expends and a minute surplus for growth. Glandular imbalance can, indeed, render it difficult for a person to eat in a pattern which will support energy and health without putting on excess weight. Obesity is in the vast majority of instances, however, a psychological, usually an emotional, problem rather than a biological one.[15] Self-indulgence in eating, family habits as to type and quantity of food eaten, eating as an escape from boredom and frustration or as a compensation for pleasures being missed, account for the overwhelming proportion of overweight adolescents.[16] Physical examination can make possible the design of a diet, with medication if necessary, to reduce obesity. However, the attitude of the individual, often, but not always, centering around his ad-

14 B. M. Caldwell, "Factors Influencing Psychologic Reactions to Crippling Disorders," *Journal of the Missouri State Medical Association*, 1952, *49*:219–222.

15 S. C. Freed, "Psychic Factors in the Development and Treatment of Obesity," *Journal of the American Medical Association*, 1947, *133*:369.

16 S. Bayles and F. G. Ebaugh, "Emotional Factors in Eating and Obesity," *Journal of The American Dietetic Association*, 1950, *26*:430–434.

justment to his social environment, is usually the crucial element in whether diet or treatment of obesity will be successful.

Some people find obesity itself a refuge, in addition to the other complicating psychological factors already mentioned. It may provide them with an alibi for lack of social activity, inappropriate fatness being for them a less ego-injuring reason for the lack of effort than timidity, ineptness, or an unpleasant disposition. The adolescent who is overweight is in need of assistance, sometimes medical but always psychological, because medication alone is insufficient to cope with a condition with so many emotional ramifications.

In summary it can be said that biological defects may be influential factors in the emotional maturation and adjustment of adolescents. A few defects, such as glandular imbalance, can, because of their very nature, produce emotional problems. Whether or not most defects have undesirable psychological effects will depend upon the attitudes the boy or girl develops toward and about them. Some defects require medical attention to be remedied; virtually all require psychological treatment, with or without physical medication, to insure the boy's or girl's optimum emotional adjustment and general personality development.

Escapist Use of Defense Mechanisms

In Chapter 4 were discussed several mechanisms of adjustment which, used properly, can facilitate coping with frustrating or other stressful situations. But, if depended upon too heavily, these same, and other, mechanisms become neurotic escapes from facing the reality of a situation and inhibit emotional maturation and adjustment.[17, 18] Instead of making an adjustment to life, by escapist use of such devices as rationalization, identification, and withdrawal an individual may avoid coming to grips with life. Thus, instead of achieving the emotional maturity and adjustment which come as a result of successful experience, the individual uses the defense mechanisms as shields behind which his personality and self concept can hide and remain at an immature level of functioning.[19]

A few mechanisms already discussed should be noted because of their

[17] E. R. Hilgard, *Introduction to Psychology*. Harcourt, Brace and Company, New York, 1958.

[18] R. S. Lazarus, *Adjustment and Personality*. McGraw-Hill Book Company, Inc., New York, 1961.

[19] C. L. Leuba, *Man—A General Psychology*. Holt, Rinehart & Winston, New York, 1961.

frequent use as escapist devices. Denial of reality is a device by which boys and girls who have made themselves unacceptable to others of their age refuse to see the obvious. A boy may stubbornly continue to act as if everything is all right, shutting his eyes to his real social standing, and thereby avoid recognizing the need to improve his social relations. The mother who insists on planning a college program for her hard-working, but failing, high-school boy illustrates denial of reality. So does the erstwhile millionaire, now impoverished, who insists on buying the best clothes and patronizing the most expensive hotels as if his former fortunate state still prevailed. By preventing perception of the changing times or circumstances, denial of reality encourages a person to fixate on an immature level of emotional development, instead of maturing.

Projection involves transferring blame for our own shortcomings onto others or investing them with feelings which are really our own.[20] The girl who is late for class because she wanted to look at the store window says, "My little sister wanted to look at the Christmas scene on the way and held me up." The boy who fails an examination says, "Tim and Joe came by the house last night and didn't leave in time for me to study as much as I wanted to." It is the all-too-human tendency to blame others, dangerous because it relieves us of feelings of guilt and responsibility for our shortcomings without necessitating our rectifying them. By projection, adolescents continue in childish emotional patterns and reactions through excusing themselves in their own eyes for unwholesome attitudes and actions denoting immaturity. It is a way of avoiding responsibility, and, of course, it inhibits objectification.

Sympathism is an appeal for the sympathy of others as a substitute for genuine achievement or the self-discipline to earn approval of others on the basis of actual merit or accomplishment. The adolescent who attributes his automobile accident to bad luck, implying that he deserves sympathy rather than criticism or being required to improve his driving practices, is an extremely common example. The girl who becomes ill and thus unable to fulfill her responsibilities is often using the mechanism of sympathism. This escape mechanism functions by diverting the attention of people and often one's own attention (for sympathism is often unconsciously utilized) from one's unfulfilled responsibilities to sympathy. Thus the person is able to avoid both injury to his own self

[20] H. C. Smith, *Personality Adjustment.* McGraw-Hill Book Company, Inc., New York, 1961.

concept from unsatisfactory handling of situations and the disapproval of others for his irresponsibility or failure.

Fantasy is a particularly immature way of escaping from reality. Its dynamics have already been discussed. It is extremely common among adolescents and, as previously noted, is quite normal in most instances. The adolescent who uses fantasy as a substitute for actual achievement, however, is fixating his emotional life on an immature level.

Restricted Experience

The necessity for wide and continuous experience in all types of life situations has already been noted as an essential of normal maturation. Its importance was implied in the discussion of how tolerance of frustration is developed. Being overprotected denies the adolescent the opportunity of learning through trial and error, evaluation of results, and practice of the revised procedure.[21]

Sexual maturation, which looms so large in the lives of adolescents, affords a particularly good example of the need for experience. First of all, experience with both sexes in early childhood is needed to enable the boy or girl to acquire his or her identity as distinguished from that of the opposite sex. How can a boy or girl satisfactorily learn the differences in attitude, manner, preferences, and general psychology of the other sex as differentiated from his own other than through heterosexual experience? [22] From the base of knowledge thus established the boy or girl moves into the next psychosexual stage of firmly establishing his or her own sexual identity through intensified association with members of his or her own sex. Both of these types of experience, in turn, provide the necessary psychological development essential as a starting point for emotional adjustment to the highly charged tensions of heterosexual associations complicated by biological drives, cultural customs, and social taboos.

Lack of adequate experience in either the early heterosexual or subsequent homosexual activities constitutes a tremendous handicap to a boy or girl in assuming a normal role in adolescent heterosexual life. Of course, failure to achieve normal social experience in adolescence

[21] R. Dewey and W. J. Humber, *The Development of Human Behavior*. The Macmillan Company, New York, 1951.

[22] A. Ellis, "A Study of Human Love Relationships," *Journal of Genetic Psychology*, 1949, 75:61–71.

seriously handicaps the emotional development of the boy or girl, because so much of life centers around relations between the sexes. This relation is emotionally charged; it is governed by feelings and taboos more than by logic. Failure to achieve successful adolescent heterosexual adjustment, therefore, necessarily fixates emotional development at an immature level.

Lack of Training

Training facilitates success and broadens horizons. Success and broadened horizons promote diversity, breadth, and depth of experience. Diversified experience promotes emotional maturation. Those are the dynamics by which a child with well-designed training achieves an advantage in emotional maturation and adjustment over one who lacks such training. Training takes the form of developing proficiency in specific skills, the mastery of which strengthens the child's self concept and provides the ego strength needed by the adolescent as a base for achieving adult emotional development. The boy or girl with superior social, verbal, or even physical skills is more likely to show maturity in areas of emotional maturation and adjustment such as dedication to long-range goals, perception of relative values, and acceptance of responsibility than are less proficient adolescents.

Probably one reason for the emotional superiority so commonly encountered in adolescents of superior accomplishment in skill areas is the disciplined self-control learned through successful self-application to tasks until they are mastered. It is not surprising that a boy or girl who has undergone the conditioning of work necessary to achieve superiority in a skill tends to have acquired a more mature emotional pattern than one who has not. The constructive effect of such disciplined work on emotional maturation is augmented by the personality pattern which makes the discipline possible. Some adolescents are, because of faulty earlier environment, incapable of adjusting to the discipline necessary for successful achievement of demanding skills. Adjusting to life is in great measure a process of disciplining oneself to attitudes and patterns of behavior appropriate to a situation, regardless of the "natural" inclinations one might have about the situation. Failure to achieve such discipline results in an "immature" person, one who reacts to situations with a child's self-indulgent attitude rather than with the more disciplined reaction of the adult.

Unresolved Internal Conflicts

Some of the mechanisms discussed in Chapter 4 which are peculiarly potent in interfering with the normal emotional maturation of adolescents have to do with conflicts which are inevitable in the normal course of development. If the boy or girl has failed to reach a satisfactory resolution of these crucial problems, achievement of adult emotional adjustment will be difficult, if not impossible.

Unresolved parental attachments may constitute inhibitors of emotional maturation. Psychoanalytic study of children indicates that they typically go through a stage of love for the parent of the opposite sex which contains a definite component of jealousy of the parent of the same sex. This has been called the oedipal stage of erotic development, after the Greek character Oedipus who killed his father and married his mother.[23] In the normal course of emotional maturation the child passes through this stage and into a more mature stage of emotional identification with the parent of the same sex. This later identification provides a basis for realistic evaluation of one's subsequent role in life; fixation at the oedipal stage interferes with realistic emotional adjustment to life not only in the area of heterosexual development, but also in acceptance of adult emotional values generally. The boy who never completely outgrows his childish erotic attachment to his mother is likely to display an insecure, immature, self-indulgent, irresponsible attitude toward life situations generally.[24] The inhibiting effect of such a fixation on normal sexual adjustment is too obvious to require comment.

Hostilities toward parents frequently arise in growing boys and girls, either as a part of the Oedipus conflict (in the case of the parent *not* emotionally focused on) or as a part of the natural striving of the child and the adolescent for independence.[25] Sometimes these hostilities become so violent that they threaten to disrupt relations within the home. Even when they are at a much lower level of intensity, such hostilities may constitute a serious interference with emotional adjustment because of the guilt feelings commonly engendered by the hostilities. Fear may

[23] S. Freud, *An Outline of Psychoanalysis*. W. W. Norton & Company, Inc., New York, 1949.

[24] C. B. Zachry, *Emotion and Conduct in Adolescence*. Appleton-Century-Crofts, Inc., New York, 1940.

[25] O. S. English and G. H. J. Pearson, *Emotional Problems of Living*. W. W. Norton & Company, Inc., New York, 1955.

also be present as a result of apprehension of parental rejection repaying the hostility. Hostility, guilt, fear—all are attitudes promoting insecurity and consequent inability to make a free, confident approach to challenging or threatening situations. Failure to make such an approach, as has already been pointed out, renders impossible normal breadth of experience and, hence, normal emotional development.

Helping boys and girls whose conflicts revolve around their emotional relations with parents is a touchy business. The situation is most easily approached when hostility is open and recognized by the boy or girl. In such situations only assistance in re-evaluation of the relationships involved may be needed. Logic can be applied to the areas of conflict, choice of friends, grade expectations, and the like. Logic is not a guaranteed device for resolving such hostilities, but it often helps for the adolescent to take a reasoned look at the conflict situations and the different desires and points of view involved. Where the hostility is unconscious, not recognized by the adolescent, the job is one for a clinical psychologist or psychiatrist. As in the case of traumas, therapeutic attempts by those not clinically trained and experienced are likely to do harm rather than good. Sudden recognition of such hostilities, for example, is likely to precipitate an attack of extreme anxiety which taxes the resources of even the psychotherapist to handle without serious psychological injury resulting.

Conflicts between impulses and sense of responsibility or aspirations often cause the adolescent to regress to or fixate on immature levels of emotional adjustment where the demands of conscience are less severe. The boy unwilling to do the work he is expected to do around the house may retreat into the infantile pattern of petulance, sulkiness, or even temper tantrums as a denial of the maturity which would expose him to the obligations of such work. Use of such emotional reactions, of course, is going in the opposite direction from emotional maturity and adult adjustment.

Kay was thirteen years old when she found that she was adopted. Her unhappiness at discovering this was complicated by severe guilt feelings. She felt that it was wrong for her to have any different feelings toward her adopted parents, yet when they denied her something she wanted, she would find herself unintentionally blaming their attitude on the fact that she was not their "real" child. Along with a number of other maladjustive reactions Kay lost her budding interest in boys, began sucking her thumb from time to time, and displayed other behavior patterns that she had abandoned earlier in her life before she acquired the knowledge which led to her conflicting feelings.

Conflicts between moral and religious teachings on the one hand and desires and impulses on the other are common. As one adolescent put it, "Lying lips are an abomination to Jehovah, and an ever present help in time of trouble." Failure to reach a livable balance between such conflicts will inevitably inhibit the development of a mature and well-adjusted perspective of values and goals.

In summary, it can be said that unresolved internal conflicts tend to block the adolescent in his emotional maturation and adjustment whenever they fixate his development on a below-adult level or whenever they fail to provide a required base of security and achievement for subsequent growth.

Case of Albert Anderson

Albert Anderson was referred to the counseling clinic because of poor social adjustment and low achievement in school. At the time of his referral he was thirteen years and eight months, and in the sixth grade. Both test results and classroom performance indicate that Albert is performing at the fourth-grade level, although his I.Q. as measured by a widely used group intelligence test was 95. His low academic achievement is the chief concern of his parents, although each parent, when interviewed, also expressed some concern about his social development.

Albert's family consists of himself, his parents, and two siblings. They live in a middle-class residential neighborhood. Mr. Anderson is a lawyer, forty-five years old, a vigorous outdoorsman. He is extrovertive and a member of numerous civic, social, and professional organizations. The only member of the family to whom Mr. Anderson apparently feels very close is Albert's younger brother Dick, who is twelve. He feels that Dick is much like him, and enjoys his companionship. He indicates that his marriage has been something less than successful in filling his emotional-needs, although he makes no specific complaints about his wife except that she is extremely strong-willed and that he is unable to influence her once her mind is made up. He is proud of Constance, his eighteen-year-old daughter, but considers that she is "just like her mother," and therefore he feels little emotional closeness to her. As concerns Albert, he accepts that it is his duty as a father to do all possible to further his son's social adjustment and to help promote his intellectual growth, but indications are that he considers Albert another of his crosses to bear and feels no genuine affection for or interest in him. He expresses some concern about Albert's slowness, lack of self-confidence, and uncontrolled imagination, and verbalizes that his problem may be an emotional one.

Mrs. Anderson is forty-four, a meticulous housekeeper whose only interests seem to be her home, music (she has taught piano at home for the past fifteen years), and activities connected with the fundamentalist church of which she is a member. She is a quick, active, energetic woman, who appeared to the counselor to be rigid and lacking in insight, and who obviously has very fixed ideas about what is "right" and what is "wrong." She accepts her husband with indifference, much the same attitude she apparently has toward the younger boy, Dick. She is extraordinarily proud of and wrapped up in Constance, while Albert is a source of great frustration and humiliation to her. She is confident that she has the correct solution to the problem—Albert should be scolded for his poor academic achievement, punished for his use of profanity, and shamed by his failure to measure up to the achievement of his brother and sister—but these measures, she admits, have not been successful. She is greatly concerned about his swearing.

Constance is a senior in high school, colorless, well-mannered. She has a good academic record, is talented in music, moderately social, and fairly interested in the young people's program at the church. She early assumed a maternal role toward Albert, helped with his care when he was smaller, and now helps him with his studying.

Dick is also in the sixth grade (another section from Albert) at the same school. He is average in schoolwork and, like his father, is an athletic extrovert. Because of his greater physical development he early assumed a role of dominance toward Albert, but usually Albert was the one punished if they fought, since "he was older." Teachers report that Dick now picks on Albert at school, but the parents say this could not be true.

A sociometric study indicated that Albert is an isolate. Cumulative and anecdotal records substantiate his present teacher's statement that he does not participate in classroom discussion or group games, that he consistently chooses either girls or younger boys for his playmates. The teacher also reports that other children in the room tease

Albert because he will not defend himself in fights, and call him "Dumbbell" or "Stupid." All of his teachers have considered him a slow learner. He did not learn to read until the third grade, and subsequent private tutoring has not raised his reading level above fourth-grade norms.

Albert was a full-term, normal-size baby. His mother's health and pregnancy were normal, but although the birth was not instrumental, according to the parents there was "a head injury." He was breast-fed, but weaned early and abruptly so the mother could better resume her teaching. He cut teeth, walked, and talked at the normal time. Feeding, sleeping, and other habit training was carried out on a rigid time schedule. He was toilet-trained fairly early, but still occasionally wets his bed at night. He has always been pale, always underweight, and has had poor coordination. His appetite is good, however, almost excessive at times. He had the usual childhood diseases, was particularly susceptible to colds and earaches. Examinations made at the time just preceding referral to the psychological clinic showed no physical impairments of any kind.

In his preschool years Albert had little play with children other than his siblings. He was entered in kindergarten when he was five, but was retained at the end of the year because of his immaturity. He was overprotected in his early years because of his poor health, and he cried frequently during the first year in kindergarten, being fearful and timid. He has never accepted any responsibilities at home, although occasionally he has been willing to empty the garbage and the wastebaskets. However, his mother reports he is so slow and careless that usually she takes over the job herself. He is very fond of the family dog, but does not assume responsibility for feeding it. He spends most of his free time at home alone, playing with the dog, watching TV, looking at comic books, singing, or riding his bicycle. He goes to the movies every Saturday, preferring Westerns.

Albert's mother largely assumes the role of disciplinarian in the family, although both parents use corporal punishment when angered. At home Albert appears moody and unhappy and often reacts to correction with temper outbursts. He seems especially fearful of failure, and cried over the three F's on his last report card. His relationship with his mother and older sister is dependent, and he frequently seeks signs of affection from them. He has no real friends and is rejected by most of the children of his age group. Cumulative records show that he has never played well with other children at school. He attends Sunday school regularly now and was a Cub Scout for a year, but dropped out when his mother ceased being den mother.

Testing shows that Albert has "superior" musical aptitude, but he was very indifferent about practicing when his mother gave him piano lessons.

Interviews with Albert reveal that he is unhappy most of the time because of rejection by his brother and other age-mates, lack of affection from his parents, their scolding about his grades and behavior, and unfavorable comparisons with his brother and sister. He expresses acute discomfort that other children do not like him and taunt him. He says he is afraid to fight with boys his own size, and that it "makes him sick" for them to call him names. He says that his parents become easily angered and that they frighten him with their whipping and their temper. No sex knowledge, curiosity, or practices were admitted. (He had been punished for masturbation during his early childhood, and parents know of no sex practices since that time.) He has never evidenced any curiosity about sex and has received no information from parents regarding it.

Albert further indicates that he feels his parents' standards for his success in school are very high. He says that he would rather be younger than he is and that he wishes he were a girl. He rates his friends, especially girls, higher in his affection than his parents. He says he wishes he could do things other boys can do, but also states that he likes to be alone and imagine things. Both parents and teachers say his excessive daydreaming is obvious.

1. What signs of maladjustment and/or emotional immaturity does Albert present?

2. What environmental factors appear likely to have contributed to Albert's difficulties? How?

3. What are the possibilities of helping Albert?

READINGS

Barker, R. G., Wright, B. A., and Gonick, M. R., "Adjustment to Physical Handicaps and Illness: A Survey of the Social Psychology of Physique and Disability," *Social Science Research Council Bulletin,* No. 55, 1946.

Blos, Peter, *The Adolescent Personality.* New York: Appleton-Century-Crofts, Inc., 1941, Part 3.

Coleman, J. C., *Abnormal Psychology and Modern Life*. Chicago: Scott, Foresman and Company, 1956, Chapt. 4.

Dalton, R. H., *Personality and Social Interaction*. Boston: D. C. Heath and Company, 1961, Chapt. 11.

Ginsburg, S. W., "The Neuroses," *Annals of the American Academy of Political and Social Science*, 1953, *286*:55-64.

Jersild, A. T., *The Psychology of Adolescence*. New York: The Macmillan Company, 1957, Chapt. 9.

Pressey, S. L., Robinson, F. P., and Horrocks, J. E., *Psychology in Education*. New York: Harper & Brothers, Publishers, 1959, Chapt. 5.

Ruch, F. L., *Psychology and Life*. Chicago: Scott, Foresman and Company, 1958, Chapt. 7.

Steckle, L. C., *Problems of Human Adjustment*. New York: Harper & Brothers, Publishers, 1957.

CHAPTER 10

BODILY CHANGES IN

ADOLESCENCE AND THEIR

PSYCHOLOGICAL EFFECTS

PREVIEW

(Adolescents need understanding and help in adjusting to the physical and emotional changes of this period.)

CHANGES	SIGNIFICANCE
Pre-adolescent growth spurt	A period of rapid growth, starting earlier in girls than boys and during which girls are typically bigger than boys.
Glandular development	Vast glandular changes upset bodily and psychological homeostasis, predisposing various maladjustment. Skin blemishes are a common example.
Development of girls' sexual characteristics	Gradual dominance of estrogen over androgen secretions produces feminine physiological development—breasts, hair distribution, subcutaneous fat, and bodily proportions. Menstruation can be traumatic or easy depending on the girl's preparation for it.
Development of boys' sexual characteristics	Androgen dominance in boys promotes dominance of masculine characteristics. Maturational processes do not require as much psychological readjustment as do those of the girl.

In Chapter 6 we considered the far-reaching physical changes which take place in adolescence. These changes both produce and are accompanied by psychological changes of as great, or greater, magnitude than the physiological changes which underlie them. Literally from head to toe, from the boy's facial fuzz to the girl's often embarrassingly large feet, the bodies of adolescents are changing, and every change is accompanied by a corresponding necessity for psychological readjustment to the new bodily condition. As adults, we have come to take our bodies for granted; we are accustomed to their being as they are. Children become accustomed to rather inconspicuous growth in their bodies, too, and then, after about ten or twelve years of what they have come to think of as normal bodily development, new and unaccustomed things begin to happen. Even if they have been told beforehand that such new developments will take place, the changes come as something of a shock.

Suppose, for instance, that *you* were told that some time along you would begin to grow a tail. Do you suppose that the knowledge that other people had such tails concealed under their clothes would keep you from having considerable mental and emotional readjustment to do in order to live comfortably with your tail? Suppose, also, you found that having such a tail was accompanied by a tremendous urge to trip people with it, but tripping people was something not even mentioned in polite society, although it was rumored to be done secretly under certain conditions. For propriety's sake, even the existence of that overenergetic tail must be politely ignored. Can you imagine the mental and emotional problems you would encounter? Try to do so. It may give you a more realistic idea of one of many problems which hit the adolescent in rapid succession, another coming on before the first is successfully disposed of.

The adolescent faces a threefold psychological adjustment to the bodily changes brought on by physical maturation. From previous emphasis on the holistic development of physique and personality, the fact that people develop along many lines simultaneously—and development along every line both affects and is affected by development along every other line—it may be easily seen that psychological change is required to adjust to the sheer fact of bodily change. Two other sources of necessity for psychological change are attached to physiological change, in addition to the simple one of getting used to being different from what you have been in the past. You have to get used to other people noting the difference in you, too, and undoubtedly speculating on your bodily changes and their significance, even though propriety forbids their showing that they notice. It is a disconcerting thought that people are looking at you and mentally evaluating what is happening within and to you. Since adolescents do not have your background of social experience to give them poise, confidence, and perspective, think how disconcerting it must be to them. Then you can more easily understand the girl who refuses to go to school if her dress, which seems to her to be one of the few things she *can* dictate the form and function of, is not as she wants it to be.

Finally, in addition to adjusting himself to new bodily forms and functions and to the vividly imagined reactions of others to those forms and functions, the adolescent must adjust to powerful new psychological needs which he never experienced before and which social and religious teachings tell him he must keep rigidly repressed. No, not rigidly repressed; if he does not give them a certain type of outlet he is abnormal, immature. Some parts of the needs, however, must be repressed while other parts are being gratified and even cultivated to greater intensity. This is the psychological adjustment which the adolescent faces.

MATURATIONAL CHANGES

We considered in Chapter 6 the basic physiological and biological changes which cause or accompany adolescence. Here we shall consider some of the less fundamental, but often more conspicuous, changes which, because they are so noticeable, often require considerable psychological adjustment on the part of the adolescent. We also shall study more deeply the effects of some of the fundamental causes of and changes in adolescence.

Growth in Height and Weight

There is no "normal" pattern of growth for boys or girls, just as there is no "normal" age for the development of a beard. There are "typical" patterns of growth, patterns found in most boys and girls, but deviation from these patterns does not suggest abnormality or maldevelopment. It merely indicates that the individual is developing at a rate somewhat different from that of most boys and girls. But patterns of growth for all boys and girls tend to be similar, the chief difference being in the age at which the "growth spurt" is reached.

Infants increase in height at a faster rate than they will as children, adolescents, or adults. Every year of life usually produces slightly less growth in height than the preceding one, except for slightly accelerated growth near the beginning of adolescence. This adolescent growth spurt takes place in girls during the two years preceding the menarche. In most girls it will begin during the tenth or eleventh year and subside during the twelfth or thirteenth, about the time of the menarche.[1]

[1] R. K. Shuttleworth, "Sexual Maturation and the Physical Growth of Girls, Age 6–19," *Monograph of the Society for Research in Child Development,* 1937, Vol. II, No. 5.

Because of the lack of so observable and definitive a criterion as the menarche, evidence of the theoretical ability of boys to reproduce is difficult to acquire. Therefore, data as to the time of "sexual maturity" of boys are inconclusive.[2] However, from the evidence presented in some studies which have been made of the subject, it appears that boys typically have their adolescent growth spurt at the time when the sex hormones begin to be produced by the sex glands, between the ages of twelve and fifteen.[3] This means that girls typically begin their growth spurt a year and a half or two years earlier than boys. Actually, reflecting that girls begin the production of sex cells about two years before the menarche, we can infer that both boys and girls begin their adolescent growth spurt at about the same biological age. The fact that girls usually begin their sexual maturation earlier than boys is, therefore, a reason their growth spurt begins before that of boys, and results in girls being taller and heavier than boys between the ages of about nine to eleven or ten to twelve.[4, 5] After the menarche the rate of growth of girls, which on the average has been five to six inches in the past two years, drops rapidly. Boys, on the other hand, continue to grow for another two years or more and thus become the taller, heavier sex.

Individual variations in time of the beginning of the growth curve, as might be expected, are as wide as the time of any other index of pubescence. About 15 per cent of girls will achieve their most rapid growth during their tenth year, and about 10 per cent during their fourteenth.[6] The proportions of boys achieving maximum growth at specific ages are similar, but this growth occurs about two years later.

One important sex difference related to the growth spurt is of interest because similar signs portend different results for the sexes. Early-maturing girls will typically outstrip their age-mates in height in the years before the menarche. However, the later-maturing girls continue to grow, are larger when their growth spurt begins, add their growth spurt to their superior size, and typically mature into larger girls than the ones

[2] H. C. Stuart, "Normal Growth and Development during Adolescence," *New England Journal of Medicine,* 1946, pp. 234, 666–672, 693–700, 732–738.

[3] H. R. Stolz and L. M. Stolz, *Somatic Development of Adolescent Boys.* The Macmillan Company, New York, 1951.

[4] L. F. Beck, *Human Growth.* Harcourt, Brace and Company, New York, 1949.

[5] K. C. Garrison, *Growth and Development.* Longmans, Green and Company, New York, 1959.

[6] R. K. Shuttleworth, "Sexual Maturation and the Physical Growth of Girls, Age 6–19," *Monograph of the Society for Research in Child Development,* 1937, Vol. II, No. 5.

who matured at an earlier age.[7] Boys, on the other hand, grow fast during the growth spurt and continue to grow for several years longer. Usually the boy who matures late will never catch up with his earlier-maturing brothers and will complete his growth as a smaller man than they.[8]

The pattern of growth in weight differs considerably from that of growth in height.[9] The fast weight increase of the infant slows down about the third year, is slight for two or three years, and then gradually becomes more rapid. While she is nine, the girl will typically add nine pounds to her weight, ten while she is ten, and eleven while she is eleven. When she is twelve, her rate of weight increase swiftly drops. Boys begin at about eleven years to put on about nine pounds of weight during the year, but during the year they are fourteen they will typically add fifteen or sixteen pounds to their weight, then drop off in rate of weight increment but continue to gain faster and longer than girls. Most girls will have achieved practically their young-woman weight by the time they are sixteen, but boys will continue to add several pounds per year until the age of eighteen or nineteen.

The accelerated rate of growth of adolescence poses real problems of adjustment, both physical and psychological. Arms and legs, feet and hands, grow suddenly and rapidly along with the remainder of the body. The rapidity of growth often outstrips the ability of the boy or girl to keep pace with it in motor coordination. With a slight exaggeration, the adolescent can be represented as walking on short stilts and reaching for things with extensions on his arms. This accounts for the well-recognized tendency of adolescents to trip over their own feet, knock over things they reach for, and generally be awkward.

The adolescent's accelerated rate of growth poses a problem of psychological adjustment also. The adolescent is just becoming highly socially conscious, and his self-consciousness is increasing accordingly. The unreliability of his (or her) hands and feet, arms and legs, the "coltish" appearance, of which he is all too conscious, contribute to his self-consciousness. Often he becomes defensively irritable and aggressive, dis-

[7] N. Bayley, "Size and Body Build of Adolescents in Relation to Rate of Skeletal Maturing," *Child Development,* 1943, *14:*51–89.

[8] R. W. B. Ellis, "Growth in Relation to Maturity," *Edinburg Medical Journal,* 1947, *54:*269–283.

[9] K. Simmons, "Physical Growth and Development," The Brush Foundation Study of Child Growth and Development, II, *Monograph of the Society for Research in Child Development,* 1944, Vol. IX, No. 1.

placing onto others the hostility aroused by his own rebellious members and projecting onto others the intense consciousness of his appearance which he, himself, feels. This makes the adolescent hard to get along with, often suspicious and inordinately touchy and resentful of criticism or even suggestions. He needs guidance and direction, sometimes quite firm, but he also needs patience and an understanding of the difficulties of adjustment he is undergoing. Above all, he needs to learn, through slow experience, that people are neither watching him to see his awkwardness nor ridiculing him, even in their minds, for his blunders and mishaps. Praise him casually, not making a big production of it, whenever he does anything to deserve praise. Minimize the attention given his accidents, the books knocked off desks and chairs bumped against. He will gain good motor coordination faster by becoming less self-conscious than he will by becoming tense and anxious for fear he will make a move of the wrong sort. His disposition will be helped, too, if ever so slightly, which is no mean consideration while a boy or girl is adjusting to adolescence.

Effect of Glandular Changes

The touchy disposition of the adolescent is partly attributable to his resentment of vestiges of adult control and guidance; it is a symptom of rebellion. Part is due to the painful self-consciousness just mentioned. But a part of the emotional instability which characterizes the typical adolescent is a natural and direct result of glandular changes he is undergoing.[10] Profound changes in biological functions, such as the beginning of menstruation, growth of facial and body hair, and other obvious changes related to pubescence do not occur in isolation from influence on psychological functions. The endocrine and thyroid glands undergo significant changes in functioning during the adolescent years. Basal metabolism drops, rate of heartbeat slows. The ratio between the sex hormones, androgens and estrogens, being secreted changes rapidly, promoting sexual differentiation.[11] Veritably, adolescence is an era of changes. Even appetites and food preferences change.

All these changes upset the homeostasis of the body. Glandular imbalances, along with dietary indiscretions and lack of cleanliness, may

[10] H. C. Stuart, "Normal Growth and Development during Adolescence," *New England Journal of Medicine,* 1946, pp. 234, 666–672, 693–700, 732–738.

[11] N. W. Shock, "Some Physiological Aspects of Adolescence," *Texas Reports on Biology and Medicine,* 1946, 4:289–310.

produce acne and other types of skin blemishes. They also produce emotional instability (we can only speculate as to exact cause and dynamics). The adolescent has difficulty adjusting to the many changes simultaneously taking place in his body both in his relations with the world and in his relations with his own feelings. Glandular changes produce in him feelings and cravings strange to him, which he does not understand—not only sexual cravings, but vague stirrings of independence, ambition, fears of the unknown future. All are produced not only by his environment, but by physiochemical changes in his body as well.

Periodic checkups by the family physician, at least twice a year, are desirable for an adolescent. In this way, developing glandular imbalances can often be detected and remedied before they produce serious effects. Dietary controls to deal with obesity or complexion troubles can often be recommended. Preventing physical disorders can greatly facilitate the difficult task of emotional and social adjustment to adolescence.

Skin Blemishes

Adolescent self-consciousness attaches to physical appearance even more (if possible) than to movements and actions. Pimples and other skin blemishes, which to an adult would be mildly disturbing, to the adolescent become indelible disfigurations. Either consolingly assuring him that the blemishes really make no difference, are not very noticeable to other people, or agreeing with him that they look just horrible is likely to provoke wrath. Anything is, in fact, because the adolescent with skin blemishes is hopelessly, furiously angry and likely to vent his wrath on any object or remark associated with his disfigurement.

Acne of the type adolescents commonly suffer usually begins during puberty and disappears by the age of thirty.[12] This, of course, is so far in the adolescent's future as to seem to him "old age," at which time he figures nothing will make any difference anyhow. Although the exact cause of *acne vulgaris* is unknown, the various glandular changes of pubescence are often predisposing causes of acne. There is apparently some hereditary or familial tendency toward some types of skin troubles. These factors, obviously, are beyond the adolescent's control. However, dietary factors, such as intake of excess carbohydrate or fat, are important considerations about which he can do something, if he can be persuaded to do so. Vitamin deficiency may play a part also, so the im-

---

[12] C. E. Lyght (ed.) *The Merck Manual of Diagnosis and Therapy*, 9th ed. Merck & Co., Inc., Rahway, N. J., 1956.

portance of a well-balanced diet can hardly be overemphasized to the adolescent. Again, however, this is a case where usually the difficulty is not in the adolescent's not knowing the facts, but in his not being willing to exercise self-control or determination to do what he knows would be best for him.

The boy or girl should be urged to keep the scalp as well as the facial skin scrupulously clean. Squeezing, pinching, and picking must be refrained from. This is in direct opposition to the inclination of the boy or girl, who seems almost irresistibly drawn to pick this place, squeeze that one, and mash the other. Sometimes adolescents develop a habit referred to as "chin fondling," an effort to conceal acne lesions with the hands. This mannerism serves better to perpetuate than to conceal the condition.

The importance of *acne vulgaris* must not be minimized for two reasons: With proper care, the majority of cases can be cured, and early treatment minimizes the likelihood of permanent scars. Secondly, the psychological damage and personality changes resulting from prolonged facial blemishes may be severe. Although it may appear to be an endless circle, it should be noted that psychoneurotic background or tendencies and physical, mental, and emotional strain are important factors in the etiology of acne, and the disease may, in turn, promote these very same complicating factors. Therefore, if the adolescent can be reasoned into a more relaxed attitude, chances for his present and future adjustment to the disease to be nondamaging to his social and psychological wellbeing are greatly improved.

Physique

Eating habits of adolescents frequently contribute not only to skin blemishes but to pudginess and digestive upsets. Away from home more, with more money to spend, adolescence is the age of the hot dog and french fries, washed down with a carbonated drink, and the whole embellished with a chocolate nut sundae. Nutritive value of such a meal leaves something to be desired, but the calorie count is astronomical and the sugar, fat, nut, and chocolate content helps keep the skin-treatment manufacturers in business. Except in cases of genuine glandular disorders causing abnormal weight increase (and these are extremely rare in both boys and girls) or emotional disorders which encourage overeating as a compensatory satisfaction, boys usually burn up the calories they ingest and maintain reasonably good physiques. Girls, inhibited by

Figure 14. Sixth-grade girls are likely to be larger and more mature than the boys in their class.

social custom from the vigorous exercise they enjoyed as children and not very energetic anyway as far as physical activity is concerned after childhood has passed, frequently become heavier than they or their parents wish them to be. In the overwhelming majority of cases, no glandular malfunction or other physical disorder is responsible for this overweight condition. Being overweight means simply that she overate. The girl is eating more than her body can constructively use for proper growth and more than she is using up in energy. Therefore, she becomes overweight —fat.[13] Consuming only common-sense amounts of foods of moderate fat and carbohydrate content and getting a reasonable amount of exercise will take care of most instances of overweight girls. A routine physical check by a physician will identify the rare case whose obesity is the fault of glands, not appetite and lack of exercise.

A somewhat more serious problem of overweight, and one which occurs much more frequently than does glandularly caused overweight, is the obsessive eater. A boy or girl unhappy about social progress, self-

[13] H. C. Stuart, "Normal Growth and Development during Adolescence," *New England Journal of Medicine,* 1946, pp. 234, 666–672, 693–700, 732–738.

conscious about a real or imagined defect or deficiency, worried about friction in the home or parental discord, quite frequently seeks solace in eating.[14] Since he is eating to fill an emotional void, not his physical needs, he does not stop when he has eaten enough to satisfy physical needs. Obesity is the result. The idea that fat people are jolly and happy is a myth. They are no more likely to be jolly and happy than the average person, and in many instances their excessive weight is a direct result of their anxiety, insecurity, or other emotional maladjustment. It is a good idea to encourage an adolescent who is becoming overweight to talk about himself, his life and adjustment. Encouragement can then be given him to revise his diet, take more exercise, or see a physician, as appropriate. Or, as so frequently should be the case, he can be referred to a psychologist or psychiatrist for counseling and psychotherapy to ameliorate the emotional basis of his compulsive overeating. Even without any treatment being attempted, sometimes simply talking over his problem with an intelligent and understanding adult will enable the adolescent to devise a more effective way of adjusting to his emotional difficulty than drowning it in calories.

Miscellaneous Sources of Concern

Noses are a fairly common cause of adolescent concern. Noses have a tendency to achieve their maximum growth at an earlier time than the other facial features. Thus, to the adolescent it may seem too big. It may *be* too big temporarily; at least it is bigger in proportion to the remainder of his face than it will be most of his life. This promise of improvement, and recognition (which will come as a surprise to the adolescent) that it is normal for the nose to be overdeveloped for a while during adolescence, may help him to better adjust to this affront to his aesthetic sense.

Adolescence is usually accompanied by a marked increase in the amount of underarm (called axillary) perspiration. The stains on clothing may be conspicuous and a source of self-consciousness, and self-consciousness regarding possible odor frequently plagues adolescents. Sometimes, made apprehensive by "scare" advertisements, they may become so apprehensive of not being "socially acceptable" that they will avoid social activities. Bathing and use of a deodorant or antiperspirant

---

[14] C. B. Zachry, *Emotion and Conduct in Adolescence*. Appleton-Century-Crofts, Inc., New York, 1940.

which trial shows to be effective and nonirritating to the individual may be recommended to these boys and girls.

Any physical defect is likely to be a source of self-consciousness to the adolescent.[15] He lacks the child's happy oblivion to such things and the adult's perspective to show him how little other people really think of things which seem important to us because they are *about* us. Asking him how often he notices some ordinary blemish of another person (often he will never have noticed it) sometimes will help him develop a better attitude toward a defect of his own. More often it will not, because the apprehension reflects his lack of experience and insecurity in social adjustments rather than a logical evaluation of his defect. A more effective plan is to encourage him to compensate for the defect by cultivating a talent or other asset which will both build prestige and security in the group and distract attention from the defect. This is one of the healthy uses of the mechanism of compensation.

DEVELOPMENT OF
SEXUAL CHARACTERISTICS

The Girl's Sexual Characteristics

Increase in production of estrogens, the female sex hormones, at the usual age of nine to twelve marks the beginning of a long series of changes resulting in the physical and psychological transformation of a girl into a woman.[16] Until the time of prepubescence she has secreted almost equal amounts of estrogens and androgens, the two sex hormones, just as has the boy. Now the glands of each begin to differentiate the sexes, and her secretion of estrogens dwarfs her production of androgens, and the boy's production of androgens outweighs his production of estrogens. The "tomboyish" girl or "effeminate" boy is in most cases primarily the product of his or her environment, the parental treatment and socialization process, but in some cases failure of the glands to establish dominance of the characteristics of one sex over the other is responsible.

At an average age of between eleven and thirteen the girl's hips be-

15 A. Frazier and L. K. Lisonbee, "Adolescent Concern with Physique," *School Review*, 1950, *38*:378–405.

16 I. T. Nathanson, L. E. Towne, and J. C. Aub, "Normal Excretion of Sex Hormones in Childhood," *Endocrinology*, 1941, *28*:851–865.

gin to broaden and become rounder, due partly to the enlargement of the pelvis, which allows the uterus and other organs to fit within it and eliminate her prepubescent protruding stomach. Part of the increasing size and roundness is due to the development of subcutaneous fat, of which she will have increasingly more than boys as she matures. This subcutaneous fat will develop around much of her body, though not as much in most places as around the hips, and will give her body what we think of as the soft, feminine look instead of the harder, more sinewy appearance boys have.

The girl is seldom much concerned or self-conscious about the rounding of her hips. A few months after this almost imperceptible process begins, her breasts begin to grow, of which she will be more conscious and perhaps more sensitive. From the nipples of childhood, they gradually swell around the twelfth year (earlier or later in the case of individual girls) into a conical shape, due primarily to more of the subcutaneous fat being deposited on the chest areas. Finally the growth of the mammary glands, the glands which actually produce milk, causes the breasts to assume the fullness and roundness of adulthood. Often the girl has ambivalent feelings regarding her developing breasts, proud of her visible maturation and yet embarrassed and intensely self-conscious at the open display they make of her sex.

Much of the girl's self-consciousness, either pride or embarrassment, about her breast development is attributable to the influence of pictures on book covers, in movies and movie ads, and in magazines which have in mid-century America made an erotic fetish of the breast, particularly the full, conspicuous breast. Whether or not such emphasis is in good taste, it has the effect of making members of both sexes intensely conscious of the development of a girl's breasts, with erotic overtures and implications. This magnifies both the pride of achievement and the embarrassment caused by the sense of modesty in the girl whose breasts are prominent. In the case of the girl who does not achieve the degree of fullness glorified by the entertainment media of America, her deficiency is emphasized by contrast, and her feeling of deprivation may easily lead to feelings of inferiority.

In another generation, which glorified the slim, boyish silhouette, the femininely curved girl was made to feel blowzy; now the angular, boyish-looking one feels less sexually and aesthetically desirable. Psychologically the effects are comparable. Padded brassieres and "falsies" provide the answer to many a girl's feeling of need to look glamorous and feminine.

At the same time, such devices tacitly admit an inferiority of body, which has a tendency to deprecate the girl's self concept.

There is no completely satisfactory way of preventing emotional stress in adjusting to breast development or the lack of it. An explanation of the development and function of the breasts at a suitable age, along with casual interest by the mother, will help the girl attain a matter-of-fact attitude toward their development as well as ameliorate or alleviate anxiety often associated with any such conspicuous body change. Self-consciousness, whether embarrassing, or prideful, which may lead to over-emphasizing the breasts with damage to the girl's reputation, can be minimized by the same casual attitude on the part of parents, and reasonable supervision of clothing and its fit.

The adjustment of the girl whose breasts are conspicuously under-developed, or who *feels* that they are (there is no essential relationship between these two conditions, and the latter alone is more crucial psychologically than is the former alone), is more difficult, and while it may be helped by this casual attitude, it is not apt to be smoothed into easy acceptance of the distasteful (to the girl!) facts. Being told that it makes no real difference is no help to her. To her it makes a tremendous difference! Adults desiring to help her should accept the fact that while, from an adult standpoint, this truly is *not* a serious matter, even so, from the point of view of the adolescent girl, it may be of overwhelming importance, and she has a serious and disturbing problem. They should encourage her to concentrate on other ways of enhancing her attractiveness to compensate for this deprivation. She may use padded bras if they make her feel more self-confident and prideful, but she should be especially encouraged during this period to make her hair attractive, to select becoming, attractive clothing, to learn to be a flattering listener, to use her hands gracefully. To avoid her developing an inferiority complex, it may help for her to learn to excel in some socially valued accomplishment—dancing, or any of the things having a high prestige value in her crowd. The parent or counselor needs to be alert for signs that she is developing the feeling that she must permit boys more liberties with her body to atone for her deficiency in this aspect of feminine development. This is a distinct possibility if she begins to develop real feelings of inferiority, and indicates the need for redoubled efforts to help her work out a constructive compensation for her real or imagined handicap.

While the breasts are developing, a girl begins to grow hair in the pubic region, around her external genitalia. Usually this is a source of satisfaction to her, being another visible sign of maturity and one which need not cause her embarrassment either by its development or lack of appearance. It is significant to her alone. Some time later, usually after the menarche, axillary hair begins to appear.[17] This is often a source of embarrassment to her, with the fear of odor and clothing stains from the increase in perspiration which accompanies it. A slight down often appears on the upper lip at this time, and reassurance may be needed that it does not portend a mustache.

Adjustment to the menarche and the various problems of menstruation is ordinarily the most serious problem facing the maturing girl. From the standpoint of the girl's emotional welfare it is highly desirable that acquaintance with the phenomenon of menstruation come as a gradual, evolutionary process rather than as one staggering, start-to-finish explanation.

Gradually coming, over a period of months, to an understanding and acceptance of the menstrual cycle, aided by an occasional brief restatement of the whole principle and process involved, gives the process and function its proper perspective in the girl's mind. It does not make of it a horrendous, portentous mystery, as it almost inevitably becomes if one day Mother takes Daughter into a room alone, closes the door, and says, "Now Dear, there's something I want to explain to you." This is a factor often overlooked in educating the girl on her biological functions. Education can be traumatically given or reassuringly given. Making a big, secret event of it almost inevitably causes the girl to think of it as an awesome thing, strange and unknown, and therefore to be dreaded even though it has been explained to her. Accepting the idea bit by bit as a natural part of education in becoming a grownup minimizes the possibility of either trauma at the experience of the menarche or later agonizing embarrassment about the whole menstrual process.

Explanation of the physical and emotional sensations experienced around the menstrual period is as important as explanation of menstruation itself and, like the explanation of menstruation, should be accomplished gradually and casually over a period of time. For two or three days before the beginning of menstruation, the blood pressure rises and makes the girl more irritable, restless, and susceptible to headaches. Particularly during the first year of menstruation the girl's glandular

17 I. M. Josselyn, *The Happy Child*. Random House, New York, 1955.

system, especially the endocrine glands, undergoes considerable changes in functioning. These changes can also produce tension and susceptibility to emotional upsets. Emotional upsets, in turn, may disturb ovarian functioning and cause irregularity of periods.[18] From all this it can be seen that there is a highly complex interrelation between physical and emotional conditions as they affect menstruation. Proper preparation of the pre-adolescent girl for the physical annoyances or inconvenience of menstruation, so that she will not be surprised or frightened at them even though they may be uncomfortable, can thus actually assist in establishing a normal, regular menstrual cycle as well as giving her psychological support.

Before the menarche (some authorities believe this to be hypochondriasis) and particularly during the first few months of menstruation, physical discomfort may be considerable.[19] Fairly severe backaches, abdominal cramps and pains accompanied by headaches, are the rule rather than the exception among girls for the first year or more of monthly periods, and the periods themselves may be highly irregular. They sometimes occur as frequently as every seventeen days or as infrequently as forty-five days, and sometimes several months pass without menstruation. This is not surprising when we remember that menstruation is primarily the casting out of waste engendered by failure of an ovum to be fertilized. At the beginning of pubescence the ovaries, just beginning their functions, may not produce an ovum on schedule as they tend to do after they are more mature. When they do not, there is no menstruation, of course.

It is much more reassuring to a girl, who is likely to hear from classmates all sorts of frightening superstitions about menstruation, to explain that failure to menstruate simply means that an ovary has not settled down to producing ova on a regular schedule than to merely tell her not to worry about it. Similarly, if she learns, with care being taken not to build up in her mind fear of a monthly period of torture, that some pains and perhaps nausea will accompany her periods, particularly at first, she will dislike the pains but not be terrified of the unknown. Pimples, swelling of the legs, irritation of the genitourinary regions, nausea, and a tendency to become fatigued easily are frequent accompani-

[18] M. S. Margolese, "Mental Disorders in Childhood Due to Endocrine Disorders," *The Nervous Child*, 1948, 7:55–77.

[19] I. M. Josselyn, *The Happy Child*. Random House, New York, 1955.

ments of the menstrual periods, usually becoming less intense as the cycle becomes better established.

Length of menstrual flow varies, proportionately, as much as does frequency of periods. Ordinarily it is sparse during the first few months following the menarche and lasts only a day or two. But it may continue for several days, and flows of a week's duration are not abnormal.[20] Of course, if there is anxiety about the quantity or duration of the flow, a physician should be consulted. It may reassure the girl to explain that despite its color, only a small portion of the menstrual discharge is blood, most of it being other bodily fluids present in the uterus and the residue of the ovum itself.

A girl's own feelings are the best guide as to what she may or may not do during her periods. Stories that menstruation weakens her, that she is more subject to illness during her periods, that physical activity should be avoided, are untrue superstitions. The girl should never be led to think of herself as "sick" during this period; she is not sick, she is menstruating, a perfectly normal, natural thing. The girl may experience physical discomfort which will disincline her to activity, but if she feels like it, only the same general rules of common sense applying to activities at any time apply during the menstrual period. One teacher reports finding a girl in the girls' lounge sobbing bitterly and, upon persuading her to tell the reason for her depression, was told that the girl was in the midst of her period, had washed her hair the night before, and had been told by a classmate that it would kill you to wash your hair while menstruating. The prevalence of injurious beliefs such as this is the reason for devoting so much time and attention to the process of adjusting to the phenomenon of menstruation. Many girls erroneously believe that people can perceive when they are menstruating because of some change in appearance, odor, or the way they walk. Of course, such beliefs add to the emotional stress unavoidably attaching to the menstrual period and should be guarded against by adequate education.

Menstruation is a vital part of the biological nature of a woman, associated as it is with the functions which make possible the creation of a family. It is regrettable that cultural associations, perhaps direct holdovers from primitive superstitions, cause it to be so traumatic in the

[20] M. L. Reymart and H. Jost, "Further Data Concerning the Normal Variability of the Menstrual Cycle During Adolescence and Factors Associated with Age of Menarche," *Child Development,* 1947, *18:*169–179.

experience of so many girls. The more nearly education for it and explanation of its entire range of phenomena can be given gradually, and as the little girl's observations and curiosity bring up the subject, given as one intermixed part of general instruction about health and adjustment, the better. The mother is the logical person—indeed, for practical purposes, usually the *only* person able—to give the instruction in the gradual, inconspicuous manner which produces the optimum emotional adjustment in the girl. If the girl reaches adolescence without having received such needed education, the school counselor or nurse should try to provide it. Before doing so, however, a discussion with the girl's mother is indicated. Her failure to have provided her daughter with adequate preparation for adjusting to physical maturation may be a symptom of serious ignorance, emotional disturbance, or peculiar religious belief on her part. If such is the case, better to take it into consideration before deciding how best to help the girl than have your possible good work negated by an unanticipated reaction of the mother either toward her daughter (who has those "nasty" thoughts in her mind) or toward you for corrupting her daughter's "innocence."

Manufacturers of materials for feminine hygiene have produced excellent booklets which present explanations of menstruation in a technically accurate and psychologically desirable manner. Some are listed among the readings at the end of this chapter. They are obtainable free, on request, and are invaluable aids in introducing and explaining the phenomenon of menstruation without trauma.

The Boy's Sexual Characteristics

Compared with the problems of adjustment faced by the maturing girl, those of boys are relatively lacking in potential traumatic effect. Voice change usually begins at the age of about thirteen years and six months, although normal variations in age for the occurrence of this change extend from eleven to sixteen years.[21] "Breaking" of the voice, alternating between a shrill falsetto and bass despite the boy's attempts to hold it at a moderate pitch, often accompanies the change. This may be a source of considerable embarrassment to the boy, but does not have in our culture the social and sexual overtones attaching to some of the changes undergone by the girl. Casual handling by teachers and parents, even to the point of encouraging the boy to view it as humorous (but

[21] G. V. Ramsey, "The Sexual Development of Boys," *American Journal of Psychology*, 1943, 56:217–233.

not, of course, by laughing at him), ordinarily will prevent voice change from being anything more than an annoyance and slight potential embarrassment to the boy. Pleasant reference to it as a sign of growing up, focusing attention on the impressive lower tones with the promise that more and more they will come to predominate in his voice, will help the boy adjust to this socially disconcerting phenomenon. Boys do not often make fun of one of their number undergoing this change, and girls seldom do. Concern over it on the part of the adolescent boy is likely to be a reflection of his general insecurity and anxiety about the new roles he is assuming in life rather than produced by any actual social reaction to his voice. Pleasant, sympathetic, but casual reassurance from the adults in his life is usually adequate to prevent a boy's undergoing any serious maladjustive reactions to the development of his adult voice.

About a year before the beginning of change of voice, about the time of the beginning of his growth spurt, the boy's testes and penis begin a noticeable growth.[22] The growth will become rapid about the time of the beginning of the voice change, and rapid growth will continue for approximately three years, slowing down around age seventeen and virtually stopping at eighteen in the case of the average boy. During these years each testis will approximately double in size, and the penis will double both in length and circumference, thus quadrupling, or even more, in size during these four or five years. Boys are seldom alarmed by the growth of the penis and testes; rather, they are proud of it, and it is a source of considerable boasting. The late-maturing boy is the only person likely to be discomfited by the development of his external genitals. It may be noted, however, that one testis (usually the left) is larger and hangs lower than the other. This is a common phenomenon and does not imply any defect or maldevelopment.

When the testes and penis begin their noticeable growth, pubic hair begins to appear.[23] Beginning as rather soft, silky growth, it becomes longer, coarser, more pigmented, and finally kinky. After growth of pubic hair is well under way, axillary hair appears. Still later facial hair makes its appearance, typically on the upper lip and spreading outward, upward, and downward from that point. Hair on arms and legs

[22] W. A. Schonfeld, "Primary and Secondary Sexual Characteristics: Study of Their Development in Males from Birth through Maturity, with Biometric Study of Penis and Testes," *American Journal of Diseases of Children*, 1943, *65*:535–549.

[23] W. W. Greulich, R. I. Dorfman, H. R. Catchpole, I. C. Solomon, and C. S. Culotta, "A Handbook of Methods for the Study of Adolescent Children," *Monographs of the Society for Research in Child Development*, 1942, Vol. VII, No. 3.

begins to grow shortly after the appearance of hair on the upper lip, and also increases in coarseness and length as maturation continues. Body hair comes toward the end of adolescence, and in many boys is never dense or conspicuous.

Occasionally boys are embarrassed by the development of fat under the nipples, occurring when axillary hair is making its appearance. This development may be sufficiently marked to give the distinct impression of the conical stage of female breast development. Boys can be reassured about this development; unless they become obese (which sometimes causes breast development somewhat resembling that of the female), this fat will disappear in a few months and the chests become flat again.

Erection of the penis, tumescence and hardening, takes place in boys from childhood, occasionally even from infancy. It is a familiar phenomenon long before there is consciousness of sexual urge or even interest. Time of first noted ejaculation is typically about the time of the beginning of voice change, thirteen years and six months, ranging from eleven to sixteen in the case of various boys. Typically, it is the result of masturbation, intentional or unintentional.[24] Nocturnal emissions usually begin some months later than the possibility of ejaculation. They occur at intervals ranging quite normally from two or three times a week to once a month or even less frequently. An emission every two weeks is average for the boy who is not having sexual relations or masturbating, although frequent erotic stimulation through thoughts, conversation, or looking at girls may result in much more frequent nocturnal emissions than the boy would otherwise have.

Nocturnal emissions, as well as masturbation, are often sources of anxiety to boys. Both are often believed to be "weakening" and masturbation harmful. Neither is weakening; nocturnal emissions are simply nature's way of getting rid of the surplus seminal fluid produced by the reproductive organs. Frequently they are accompanied by an erotic dream (sometimes before the boy is fully conscious of the erotic significance of his dream) about a girl in some provocative situation. Masturbation is totally harmless and suggests no maladjustment or abnormality. The *anxiety and guilt* a boy may be caused to have about it may be injurious, in the same way any anxiety or guilt feelings may be injurious. Also, if it is indulged in as a substitute for normal social activity, encouraging solitariness instead of socialization, it can interfere with

[24] A. C. Kinsey, W. B. Pomeroy, and C. E. Martin, *Sexual Behavior in the Human Male*. W. B. Saunders Company, Philadelphia, 1948.

normal social adjustment just as excessive devotion to reading can. Some religious beliefs and ethical systems also consider masturbation as wrong, and this is a legitimate area for religious or ethical teaching, but the act of masturbation in and of itself is physically and psychologically harmless unless complicated by externally imposed conflicts. Casual reassurance is all a boy is likely to need to accomplish his adjustment in these areas.

Somewhat more of a problem is the embarrassment boys often suffer from involuntary erection of the penis. They fear it can be felt by their dancing partner or noticed through their clothes at other times. When dancing in close bodily proximity, it may be noticed on occasion. If he is to avoid embarrassment to himself and his partner, a boy must learn to avoid close bodily contact when an erection would be noticeable. Reassurance can be given about its being noticed through his clothing by reminding him that all boys undergo this phenomenon and by asking him how many times he has noticed it in another boy. By observation he can convince himself of the improbability of erection being conspicuous through his clothes.

From the foregoing pages it can be seen that it is impossible to separate the emotional, sexual, and physical development of the adolescent, and that the social development intermingles heavily with all three. Physical changes during adolescence trigger emotional reactions of which the child was incapable, and social mores (meaning principles or ethics) add additional complications to maturation in both those areas. Adjusting to physical maturation during adolescence is, indeed, one part adjusting to the physical changes themselves and nine parts adjusting to the emotional and social changes and the sexual implications they directly produce.

This complex interrelationship is difficult for boys and girls to handle by themselves without the sympathy and counsel of adults who have not merely been through the experiences themselves, but who have a fund of technical knowledge of both the physical changes and the emotional adjustments needed in light of them. The basic dynamics of personality formation (Chapter 5) should be kept in mind in considering the problems of an adolescent boy or girl in any particular area. Those dynamics are basic; the specific adjustmental problems discussed in this section of the book represent specialized applications of them.

READINGS

Baruch, D. W., *How to Live with Your Teen-ager.* New York: McGraw-Hill Book Company, Inc., 1953, Chapts. 7, 8, 9.

Cruze, W. W., *Adolescent Psychology and Development.* New York: The Ronald Press Company, 1953, Chapts. 3, 4.

Essence of Womanhood, Personal Products Corporation, Milltown, N. J. (Free).

Garrison, K. C., *Psychology of Adolescence.* Englewood Cliffs, N. J.: Prentice-Hall, Inc., 1951, Chapts. 3, 4.

Horrocks, J. E., *The Psychology of Adolescence—Behavior and Development.* Boston: Houghton-Mifflin Company, 1951, Chapts. 8, 9, 10.

Just Between Us, Beltex, St. Louis 88, Missouri.

Kuhlen, R. G., *The Psychology of Adolescent Development.* New York: Harper & Brothers, Publishers, 1952, Chapt. 2.

Morgan, C. T., and Stellar, E., *Physiological Psychology.* New York: McGraw-Hill Book Company, Inc., 1950, Chapt. 20.

Stolz, H. R., and Stolz, L. M., *Somatic Development of Adolescent Boys.* New York: The Macmillan Company, 1951.

Strang, R., *The Adolescent Views Himself—a Psychology of Adolescence.* New York: McGraw-Hill Book Company, Inc., 1957, Chapt. 6.

CHAPTER 11

ADJUSTING TO PHYSICAL

MATURATION

PREVIEW

Optimum preparation of boys and girls for physical maturation involves a continuing program of education designed to:

prevent trauma from unwholesome observations or information.

alleviate anxiety and uncertainty regarding what is happening to them.

cultivate a wholesome attitude toward, and adjustment to, sex.

Adjusting to Age of Maturation

EARLY-MATURING GIRLS tend to be:

self-conscious, yet with exhibitionistic urges.

isolated from the interests of their age group.

in need of special adult supervision of their heterosexual activities.

more socially advanced than other girls when all reach maturity.

unable to live up to the standards of maturity expected of them by adults.

LATE-MATURING GIRLS tend to be:

left out of social activities, hence, lonely and envious.

self-conscious about their immaturity.

overcontrolled by parents, hence, a too abrupt transition from control to autonomy.

in need of success experiences in any area where they can achieve.

EARLY-MATURING BOYS tend to be:

fortunate, especially likely to be looked up to and accorded leadership roles.

subject to rebuffs if they try to join older social groups.

unable to live up to the standards of maturity expected of them by adults.

319

Adjusting to Age of Maturation (continued)

LATE-MATURING BOYS tend to be:

          socially and athletically inferior to their classmates.

          self-conscious.

          in need of success experiences in any area where they can achieve.

Boys and girls entering adolescence are better able to cope with their maturing bodies and the strong psychological urges which accompany that maturation, as well as with their changing relations to other people, if they have been psychologically prepared for the changes. This psychological preparation goes much deeper than merely telling the boy or girl what to expect and what to do about it. To cope with the powerful emotional pressures built up by physical maturation requires extensive emotional conditioning as well as intellectual understanding. After examining in detail some of the adjustment necessitated by maturation, we shall consider the general dynamics and principles involved in preparing boys and girls for the physical changes of adolescence. Then, while discussing specific problems of adjustment, we shall consider specific ways of helping the adolescent cope with the particular problems.

PREPARING ADOLESCENTS FOR PHYSICAL MATURATION

Adjustment to physical maturation begins, as do most aspects of adjustment, with successful mastery of the developmental tasks discussed in Chapters 2 and 6. The boy or girl who has developed a strong sense of trust, autonomy, initiative, and accomplishment leading to a healthy sense of identity and self concept has a rugged emotional constitution able to endure the stresses of adolescent maturation with minimal distress. If, on the other hand, the adolescent's personality structure is unstable, if his ego strength is minimally able to cope with the routine problems of childhood, he will need more assistance in preparing for the more stressful situations of adolescence. We must take our boys and girls as they *are* when they come to us and treat them accordingly—not proceed on the assumption that if one of them has not achieved a certain level of development, he *should* have, so we will just act as if he had.

The suggestions given here for preparing boys and girls for adolescence, and the underlying dynamics, are couched in terms of the need of

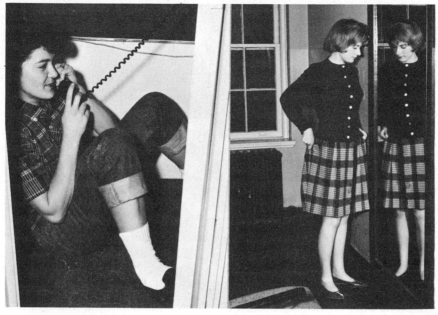

George Peabody College for Teachers.

Figure 15. What a difference fifteen minutes can make in an adolescent!

the *average* adolescent. But just as no physician would consider that he should give an "average" dose of a medicine to all patients regardless of their individual constitutions and conditions, just so the adult assisting boys and girls to prepare for physical maturation must not use one formula and dosage for all, but emphasize or de-emphasize different aspects of preparation depending on the particular needs and psychological constitution of the boy or girl involved. Thus, a twelve-year-old girl with a fourteen-year-old sister and eight- and ten-year-old brothers would require little information on external differences of the sexes and details of physiological maturation. She might, on the other hand, require more help than some other adolescent girl in perceiving the emotional nature of heterosexual relations outside the family. Self-consciousness about size might pose little problem to a chunky boy with heavier-than-average parents and siblings, while suddenly spurting ahead of her age-mates in size and shape could be a traumatic experience for a girl who was unprepared for such an event. So in every case the concepts outlined should be adapted to the specific needs of the individual boy or girl.

Adolescence is an era of development which covers a span of several years. Its fundamental difference from the periods of development which precede it, and to some extent succeed it, is that during adolescence, and only during this period, *sexual development* exercises a profound effect on the psychological maturation and adjustment of the individual. This fact, coupled with the highly charged emotional associations with sex, means that preparation for physical changes in adolescence is first and foremost preparation for changes in sexual characteristics. The changes in sexual characteristics are primarily physical in nature, but the physical changes (and, to some extent, cultural forces, too) produce psychological changes related to sex in the areas of emotional development and social adjustment.

Preparation for adolescence consists primarily in educating the boy or girl as to the changes he or she will undergo and how to adjust to them. This education does not all precede the onset of adolescence; some of it does, but since adolescence covers a span of years, the education, for it to be most effective, must begin before that span of years and continue until the end of it. Each element of education must be placed at the point where it is most needed in view of the particular changes taking place at that time.

It must be emphasized that proper education for adolescence does not consist solely of enlightening boys and girls on the physical changes which take place during adolescence, their causes and functions. The psychological changes that are the by-products of the physical changes are even more necessary areas of instruction, because they control the direction and expression of the physical changes. Through the psychological states which come into being during adolescence, the physical changes make themselves felt in the altered behavior of the adolescent. The dynamics of education for adolescence involve three functions: prevention of trauma, alleviation of anxiety and uncertainty, and cultivation of a wholesome attitude toward sex. These will be discussed in principle here and referred to more specifically as applied to particular areas of adjustment to physical maturation.

When terms such as "sex," "sexual consciousness," "sex trauma," "sex education," "heterosexual activities," and the like are used by workers with adolescents, they should constantly bear in mind that the terms properly encompass much more than the physical act and organisms of sex.[1] It subtly distorts one's own thinking to use terms in a manner which

---

[1] C. B. Zachry, *Emotion and Conduct in Adolescence.* Appleton-Century-Crofts, Inc., New York, 1940.

endows them with erroneous implications. To a much greater degree the limited, biological connotation of "sex" held by many people renders anything having to do with sex a threatening concept to many parents, exciting apprehensions and prejudices whenever the question of sex is raised regarding their children's adjustment. Thorough indoctrination of parents on the broad implications of adjustment in the area of sex, rather than the limited biological approach, will insure their better, more intelligent, and willing cooperation where needed.

Prevention of Trauma

Not all, but certainly most, of the potentially traumatic experiences of adolescent physical maturation are related to the phenomena of physical, psychological, and social adjustment to sexual maturation and functioning. Even where the major crucial element is nonsexual by general interpretation, as when an adolescent boy's voice "breaks," presence or absence of members of the opposite sex has a profound influence on the psychological reaction of the boy, on the degree of embarrassment he suffers. The more delicate bone structure characterizing the female quickly comes to be identified with sexual differentiation in the minds of children. The twelve-year-old boy says scornfully, "Girls can't play football; they'd get hurt!" It is significant that this consciousness of the two sexes and of increased self-consciousness in the presence of the opposite sex comes before the sex "urge" or even, usually, before sex curiosity develops.[2] It is significant because it points up the strong psychosocial (as contrasted with biological and reproductive) sexual orientation.

Partly because of the sexual changes taking place within them and partly because of growing social consciousness, adolescents may be unduly self-conscious and affected to an immoderate degree by things which happen to them during their adolescent years. Good mental hygiene demands that, insofar as possible, potentially traumatic incidents in the psychological life of the adolescent be anticipated and guarded against. The guarding against takes the form not only of keeping the adolescent out of clearly traumatic situations, but mentally preparing him for such situations when he does encounter them.

A twelve-year-old boy unexpectedly came upon his parents during an occasion of intimacy. The episode had such a traumatic effect upon him that he rejected all paired-off heterosexual activities for many years and finally married a woman who seemed to share his revulsion toward sex.

[2] G. V. Hamilton, *A Research in Marriage.* A. & C. Boni, New York, 1929.

This boy had had no sexual instruction, even as to the physical concomitants of sex. Less spectacular incidents with less dramatic, but still injurious, traumatic effects resulting from inadequate preparation for sexual development on both the physical and psychological sides can be recalled in profusion by every psychotherapist.

Everyone quickly accepts the possible traumatic effect of seeing such a display of sex. Parents, teachers, ministers, all adults working with children are extremely prone to overlook the fact that the child's *hearing* about sex under undesirable circumstances can be extremely traumatic. When older boys and girls tell younger ones of a mystery they know and their listeners do not, they quite naturally undertake to make their story as lurid and shocking as possible. It is common for a child to be reduced to violent tears of fear, shame, or simply apprehension of a terrifying, misunderstood unknown as a result of sexual information first encountered in a brutal, emotion-producing way. The only way children can be protected against possible trauma in hearing about sex from their associates is for them already to have received sufficient sex education to enable them to identify the distortions of what they are told. Adolescents who received their sex information from their parents have been found to have more wholesome attitudes regarding sex than those who received it from other sources.[3, 4] Like typhoid, it is impossible to prevent exposure; we can only vaccinate to render exposure harmless.

Both because of their more extensive physiological involvement with sexual functions and because of their lower aggressiveness (caused culturally or otherwise), girls are more likely to be the objects of sexual trauma than are boys. Small boys are, on rare occasion, the objects of sexual advances by older boys and men and, therefore, require conditioning for the emotional acceptance of sex as protection for their mental health. Due to the relative position of sex in the life of the male, boys, by pre-education on sexual matters, can be made more nearly immune to sexual trauma than can girls. However, by pre-education of girls along certain lines, the traumas both of natural sexual development and disturbing experiences can be minimized.

1. Acquaint pre-adolescents with the general biology of sex, including particularly the external organs of reproduction, the secondary sexual

3 A. J. Drucker, H. T. Christensen, and H. H. Remmers, "Some Background Factors in Socio-Sexual Modernism," *Marriage and Family Living*, 1952, *14*:334–337.

4 M. R. Lee, "Background Factors Related to Sex Information and Attitudes," *Journal of Educational Psychology*, 1952, *43*:467–485.

characteristics such as the breasts, the nature of the sex act, and the nature of menstruation, erections, and seminal emissions. These areas are usually covered well enough except by the most ignorant or most sexually maladjusted parents. They represent the ABC's of preparation for physical maturation and its accompanying powerful emotional urges. All too often the preparation stops here, and the areas of sexual understanding most vital to wholesome sexual maturation and adjustment are left untouched.

2. The nature of sexually suggestive language and the fact that this language is frequently used by persons with only a smattering of knowledge about sexual matters should be made clear. Understanding the implications of slang expressions and remarks will enable a boy or girl to avoid responding in a way which will expose him to ridicule or embarrassment. It requires some explanation for the child to understand that symbolically aggressive language is commonly used as a substitute for the overt aggression the individual dares not display. Such an understanding is important in helping prevent the adolescent's adopting such expressions or behavior himself. He is less likely to do so if he evaluates the language as a device used by a person who is afraid to speak or do as he longs to. The girl is less likely to regard it as an opening for subtly dangerous and exciting verbal sparring and flirtation if she perceives it as symbolically aggressive.

3. By the beginning of adolescence at the latest, girls should be counseled as to types of sexual aggression they are likely to encounter in the company of boys, particularly older boys in privacy or semiprivacy. The significance of bodily contact—sitting thigh to thigh, arm around shoulders or waist, particularly being touched on breasts, buttocks, stomach, or thighs—should be explained in terms of its sexual significance to a boy. The fact that *a girl will often experience no erotic sensations from incidents which boys interpret as exploratory sexual advances* should be made clear to minimize the possibility that she will find herself unexpectedly subjected to direct sexual aggressiveness. Boys need to know that by permitting "necking" (hugging and kissing, but involving no manual manipulation below the shoulders), most girls are not inviting "petting" (involving any greater degree of intimacy). Girls should also know, however, that boys characteristically *do* make that assumption.

4. The natural progression of heterosexual group activities, dating many members of the opposite sex, going steady, becoming engaged, and sharing a life with another to enrich both lives, should be discussed at

length. Particular care should be taken to get the boy or girl to talk extensively, exploring the implications of each step. This will help avoid premature fixation on one step without adequate exploration of the previous stages.

There are traumatic situations particularly likely to occur during adolescence which are not directly related to sex. This period of life, when boys and girls are experimenting with adult-type relationships, finds adolescents forming new social groups. Either bodily overdevelopment or underdevelopment (usually the latter), as well as traits or physical characteristics ignored in earlier years, may lead to exclusion of a boy or girl from acceptance into a particular group, and this exclusion may be traumatic to a considerable degree.

While it is obviously impossible to anticipate and guard against all possible sources of trauma in the complex process of physical maturation, free and easy, extensive and frequent discussion of the whole subject of physical maturation with a parent or competent teacher or counselor will minimize such traumas. Talk, talk, talk, in which the adolescent becomes intellectually and emotionally familiar with as many aspects of bodily changes and their adjustmental significance as possible, is a major key to rendering potentially traumatic situations harmless. The importance of sheer amount of time spent in talking about the problems of adjusting to a maturing body and the society accompanying it can hardly be overemphasized, because preparation for adolescence does not involve a mere intellectual acquaintance with the phenomena which accompany those years; it involves becoming *emotionally adjusted* to those phenomena, coming to think of them as familiar and well-understood circumstances, not as vaguely remembered admonitions or dim facts. It is in this area that the greatest deficiencies exist in the average program of biological education regarding sex. It takes considerable discussion and time for a girl's mind to become so adjusted to the concept of menstruation that her emotions do not become traumatically involved upon the onset of her first period. Hundreds of educational investigations have proved that "being told" does not necessarily mean "understanding," and is even less likely to mean "becoming emotionally conditioned to."

From the above it can be seen that preparation for adolescence does not mean "having a man-to-man talk" nor yet a "woman-to-woman talk." It means repeated verbal exploration of the most emotionally charged aspects of physical maturation and its psychological accompaniments of strange urges, feelings, and overheard innuendoes, until these dark, mysterious, potentially terrifying (and, because of their mystery, fascinating) grounds become familiar mental territory. The girl who has had this pre-adolescent preparation is less likely to be betrayed into unperceived dangers by the romantic mystery surrounding her body, boys' bodies, and the complexly developing relations between their feelings. The boy thus prepared is less likely to feel the need of proving his sophistication by vulgar or suggestive words or actions.

Despite the ultrascientific pretensions of "liberals," this author believes that it is usually better to have all discussion of sexual phenomena in groups composed of members of one sex only. This is not because of prudishness, but for a sound psychological reason: *While it is good for girls and boys to think of sexual matters matter-of-factly, it is not good for them to be conditioned to think of discussion of sexual topics as appropriate in mixed company.* Verbal exploration of even the most matter-of-factly accepted and understood aspects of sex in the presence of both sexes tends to produce or promote an attitude of social tolerance which accepts or encourages physical exploration.

Case of Barbara Babcock

Fifteen-year-old Barbara, out with a cousin and two boys on her first date, received her first initiation into physical sexual contact when her date persistently and forcefully attempted to fondle her in an intimate fashion. It was three years before she would date again. She never told her mother of the traumatic experience which set her social maturation back several years. The mother spent these years frantically urging Barbara to date this or that or the other boy, fearful that she might be considered hopelessly socially maladjusted. Barbara had been menstruating for three years. She knew where babies came from and why, but she was totally ignorant of the *psycho*sexual facts of life. Her sexual awareness was nil, although her technical knowledge of the physiology of sex was quite adequate.

1. What is meant here by the "psychosexual facts of life"?

2. How might Barbara's mother, or a well-designed course in the psychological as well as biological aspects of sex, have spared her this experience?

Alleviation of Anxiety and Uncertainty

Many circumstances relating to physical maturation are not so fearful or disturbing as to justify their being termed traumatic, yet they can produce enough tension to interfere with an adolescent's best adjustment to life. Even the most normal, natural experiences, prepared for in the best manner possible, may produce anxiety and apprehension, though not trauma. Therefore, counseling adolescents on physical changes should be a continuing, intermittent process carried on throughout the adolescent years, giving additional understanding, reassurance, and support when and where needed.

Boys, for instance, often develop small lumps or nodes in the vicinity of the nipples, accompanied by some soreness or pain. These growths are quite normal and soon disappear, but the reassurance of having already been told that lumps may come generally needs to be reinforced by additional explanation when they actually do come, and hurt! Boys are most likely, during the physical changes of adolescence, to become concerned over the imagined implications of various changes regarding their masculinity. An appreciation of the fact that the size of hat worn has nothing to do with intelligence and, correspondingly, that the size of external genitals or growth of facial and body hair has nothing to do with virility will help the boy accept irregularities in his development; but he will probably profit from periodic reassurance on such points.

Girls may find an intellectual acceptance of the phenomenon of menstruation, and even an emotional adjustment to the prospect, inadequate for best peace of mind when menstruation begins. It is difficult to conceive of sufficient premenstrual preparation to justify one mother's response, who, when her daughter came to her at nine o'clock in the evening during a bridge party and whispered to her that she thought she had begun menstruating, casually told her that it was all right, to go to bed and they would discuss it in the morning!

The crucial element in successfully assisting the adolescent by alleviating anxiety and uncertainty is not the anticipation of all possible sources of tension and the guarding against them by periodic conversations. Such a procedure can oversensitize a boy or girl to bodily processes and actually do harm rather than good. The crucial element in a counseling program for adolescent boys and girls is to cause them to develop a feeling of confidence in you and of freedom to talk to you which will encourage them to bring up with you their problems and anxieties as they occur.

The key is not in having an awesome fount of knowledge which you can pour out in answer to any question of the adolescent, is not in possessing a fine "bedside manner" or technique for talking with the adolescent. The key is in showing an understanding, sympathetic attitude, avoiding any suggestion of shock or disapproval at what they may relate, and in seeking to help them work out an understanding of and adjustment to their problems. The former are helpful in doing the latter, but are merely means for facilitating achievement of the end.

Showing a sympathetic, noncensoring attitude at the revelation of a boy's or girl's problem may be easier said than done. In fact, it is likely to require considerable systematic self-discipline to become able to do it. We all have our own moral beliefs, ethical principles, and prejudices. It is extremely difficult to give the adolescent help instead of reproof, understanding instead of moralizing. It is hard to offer constructive suggestions instead of platitudes such as, "You feel awfully torn up about it now, but you'll get over it." Big help *that* is! But when our own convictions or, even more, our own prejudices are involved, we tend to do this.

Of course, correction and reproof are sometimes necessary regarding an attitude or action on the part of the adolescent. *But the time when he is seeking help in working out his adjustment is no time to administer them.* Doing so merely guarantees that in the future the boy or girl will suffer out problems in silence rather than seeking *your* help. The author, who was interested in helping adolescents understand the strange and disturbing things happening to them, received more than three hundred letters from his former high-school students the first year after leaving his position, so eager were they to have someone who could and would help them understand better their own maturational problems.

Avoid expressing disapproval at what is told or asked you. Avoid expressing surprise that the described situation arose or that your counselee did not know more about it. Ask questions which direct the boy's or girl's thinking along lines which will cause him to arrive at the correct answer if possible, and if not possible, tell him or her simply and clearly the facts or principles involved. The good counselor of adolescents must have the same clinical attitude, considerate yet matter-of-fact, in dealing with their psychological lives, particularly the emotions and physical phenomena of adolescence, that a good physician must have in dealing with their bodies.

The mere fact that they have an adult to whom they know they can turn for information and understanding will enable many boys and girls to cope with anxieties themselves (anxieties of all types, although here we are concerned primarily with those stemming from physical maturation) without ever actually seeking help. The boy's anxiety about whether his voice will ever become dependable again (he knows, intellectually, that it will) is not so acute if he knows that Mr. X can and will talk to him about it. Strange, maybe, but that is the way human nature is.

There is considerable evidence to support the idea that adolescents are likely to have a good deal of "free-floating anxiety." This is a chronic state of apprehension without a specific cause, but ready to fix on anything from a skin rash (syphilis?) to a nose (Too big? Too small? Too crooked? Turned up?) as a basis for worry. To the extent that such a tendency exists, the simultaneous existence of someone with whom he can discuss any problem with minimal self-consciousness and maximum assurance of help and information is itself the best possible antidote for anxiety.

Going out of one's way to dispel old wives' tales about imagined ill effects or evil significance of this or that in the body or behavior is often worthwhile. What is a laughable superstition to you and me may be a terrifying probability to the puzzled and disturbed boy or girl. The problem of anxiety concerns a large portion of the human race—adults, adolescents, children, and infants—and has been the subject of correspondingly extensive investigation and speculation by psychologists and psychiatrists. Fuller discussion of the subject can be found in the writings of Freud,[5] Horney,[6] Jersild,[7] May,[8] and Sullivan.[9]

Case of Claudia Cross

Claudia Cross, fourteen years old, was a more than usually attractive girl, almost a beauty. But there was no disputing the fact that the end of her nose was slightly bulbous. She insisted on plastic surgery, and when a series of reputable surgeons refused to operate because so slight a deformity should be left alone until her face had matured more completely, she became a behavior problem. She threw temper tantrums, refused the most reasonable requests of her parents for co-

[5] S. Freud, *The Problem of Anxiety*. Grune and Stratton, New York, 1936.

[6] K. Horney, *New Ways in Psychoanalysis*. W. W. Norton & Company, Inc., New York, 1939.

[7] A. T. Jersild, *When Teachers Face Themselves*. Bureau of Publications, Teachers College, Columbia University, New York, 1955.

[8] R. May, *The Meaning of Anxiety*. The Ronald Press Company, New York, 1950.

[9] H. S. Sullivan, *The Meaning of Anxiety in Psychiatry and in Life*. William Alanson White Institute of Psychiatry, New York, 1948.

operation, began failing her schoolwork, and withdrew from social activities.

1. In what way could factors other than Claudia's nose have produced the reactions she displayed?

2. List a few things which may have been more real bases of her anxiety.

Cultivation of a Wholesome Attitude toward Sex

In a way, much of what has been said about preparing adolescents for the physical changes taking place in their bodies has been aimed at this end. This is not surprising when you consider that almost all of the unique bodily changes of adolescence are directly or indirectly related to sex in both the biological and sociopsychological sense. Sometimes one is tempted to conclude that adolescent adjustment really means sexual adjustment, which also is not surprising, because to a great extent it does. In discussing the *dynamics* of adolescent adjustment, the subject of sexual maturation and adjustment looms even larger than its strictly proportionate place in adjustment generally. This is because sexually oriented emotions and conflicts are at the bottom of so many adolescent problems of adjustment. Because of lack of conflict between biological and social or ethical considerations, the problems of adjustment to changing recreational activities, religious practices, intellectual activities, vocational plans, and other areas of maturation are usually worked out by the adolescents themselves (which is why these problems are not discussed in this text). Help in adjustment is needed to a much greater extent in areas pertaining directly or indirectly to sex.

The danger of developing a *too* matter-of-fact attitude toward sex has already been mentioned. There was little five-year-old Lucy who remarked to a noticeably pregnant guest at her parents' party, "Somebody's been planting seeds in you, haven't they?" Among adolescents it is difficult to present sex as a natural and normal force, openly faced and discussed without restrictions, and yet one which must not be indulged until after marriage. Particularly where biological facts, emotional problems related to sex, and sexual differences, either psychological or physiological, are being discussed, it is simple discretion to conduct such discussion in segregated groups of boys and girls. This minimizes self-consciousness (which logically and morally *ought* to accompany discussion of intimate problems in the presence of the opposite sex). It also subtly emphasizes the fact that while it is proper to consider sexual matters openly and frankly, it is not appropriate to employ such a topic in social conversation. It is discussed under conditions minimizing the "public" aspect of the discussion. Care should be taken that intimate personal details and even normal aspects of what is essentially a most private matter between two people in the sanctity of the home situation are not treated as public property.

Such a practice does not "draw a veil of mystery around sex." Each sex should have at least an elementary knowledge of the biology of the opposite sex, as well as an understanding of sexual relations and functions. It merely presents sexual matters in their proper perspective—as personal matters, not proper subjects of light social conversation. There is a profound psychological basis, which has already been referred to indirectly, for this precaution in sex education: Becoming habituated to thinking and talking of sexual matters in a mixed group inevitably makes it seem more natural to discuss them with an individual member of the opposite sex under quite different conditions. This, in turn, with its implications of sophistication and the "normality" of sex, inevitably alters the discussants' conceptions of the degree of "badness" or impropriety involved in other heterosexual activities. Expressed differently, if heterosexual discussion of sexual matters is condoned by responsible adults, it subtly makes it seem more "all right" to engage in such discussions under other circumstances, and such discussions undermine moral inhibitions. They produce an atmosphere of verbal intimacy which facilitates the development of other intimacies.

It is probably impossible to define an "ideal" attitude for adolescents to hold toward sex and heterosexual activities. In the first place, different religious and cultural groups will have different opinions on the subject. In the second place, sex is such a pervasive influence in human affairs, touching so many aspects of life in so many ways, that any pat summary would probably be an oversimplification. Yet some sort of goal is needed, because it is axiomatic that the more precisely one knows the objective of an educational program, the better the chance of achieving the objective. Drawing upon clinical experience as well as principles of mental hygiene, the author suggests these general criteria of desirable sex attitudes on the part of adolescent boys and girls. Variations would be desired by various groups to fit their particular concepts in various areas.

1. Having two sexes is not only biologically necessary, but a natural and convenient arrangement for dividing the responsibilities of a home.

2. The physical differences between the sexes are normal but personal, and not suitable subjects for parlor conversation.

3. Sexual desires are normal, proper, and in no way dirty or wrong. It is neither improper nor a sign of sinfulness to have them.

4. Gratifying these desires except after marriage *is* wrong. The "wrongness" is not merely a matter of social rules or religious teaching; it is wrong because it injures girls' self concepts, distorts boys' social concepts, encourages irresponsible self-indulgence, and may result in a baby without a home.

5. If given the chance, people's feelings sometimes run away with them. Strong sex feelings may do this; therefore, it is good sense, as well as "proper," to avoid words and actions which arouse sexual passions.

6. Sexually suggestive words and actions should be avoided because they are in poor taste (like picking one's nose or discussing bathroom urges) as well as improper.

7. It is proper to have an interest in sex and learn about it, but to parade your interest or knowledge is an indication of lack of judgment.

8. It is natural for members of the two sexes to think and feel differently about many things; there are psychological as well as physical differences between the sexes. Each should respect the other's feelings.

9. A boy and a girl going together is natural, because throughout life a man and a woman will form a partnership.

10. Boys and girls go together because they are of opposite sexes, but talk or play regarding sex is out of place in their relationship.

11. Sexual adjustment is important in marriage, but the adjustment is mostly emotional rather than physical and cannot be determined by prior physical sexual relations.

Where and by whom education on physical maturation and the psychological adjustments it requires (this is a much more accurate picture of what is involved than the expression "sex education") should be given is a hotly debated question. It is an interesting fact, and indicative of how highly charged emotionally the whole subject of sex is, that discussion by adults of when, where, and by whom education regarding bodily and psychological developments related to sex should be given frequently arouses intense emotional reactions.

Few people would seriously question the position that ideally such education (for convenience's sake we shall say "sex education," but the true scope involved should be constantly borne in mind) should be given by parents in the home. Some parents do not have the requisite knowledge to provide their children with more than the bare biological facts of sex and a strong set of "don'ts" which they are hard-put to justify convincingly. Ideally it might be fine for parents to fill their children's teeth, avoiding the traumatic experiences of a strange man, strange office, strange smells, all of which make the operation seem much more grave than it really is. But they cannot do this for precisely the same reason they sometimes cannot do an adequate job of sex education for their children. They simply do not know how.

It cannot be overemphasized that preparation for adolescence, even for the physical conditions of adolescence, is about 90 per cent emotional conditioning and 10 per cent factual information. Explanations, although technically accurate in facts presented, given with inadequate or improper consideration of the whole emotional life and adjustment of the adolescent, can easily do more harm than good. Facts presented without the knowledge or skill to participate in discussion with the adolescent until the emotional implications of those facts become a part of the boy's or girl's personality structure are likely to have little desirable effect. And parents are sometimes surprisingly lacking in understanding of many significant, if not essential, emotional aspects of physical and emotional maturation. (This re-emphasizes the fact that "sex" in one's life is a much more complex concept than is the sex act.)

In the opinion of the author, it would seem that the best expedient for sex education of adolescents would be for the process of enlightenment and indoctrination to begin in the home, as it does now among most intelligent parents. Beginning with the elementary facts of biology and reproduction, it would be carried out from childhood until pre-adolescence, as it has been for the past centuries. (Whether or not it is preplanned or desired, it is inevitable that in the broad sense sex education must begin in the home, as the child from an early age sees in bodily form, but much more in actions, the man-woman, male-female, husband-wife interrelations, the subtle differences in Mommas and Poppas, boys and girls, men and women, what they can or cannot do, and what is expected of each. In some cases this may be a hurdle to overcome as the counselor begins to put new perceptions or concepts as ideals up against what the adolescent has all his life seen, felt, and thought of as *normal*.) It might be noted that a program *for parents* of education on physical and psychological maturation would be the real, logical starting point, though an unlikely eventuality. Ideally, sex education would be carried on by the parents during the adolescent period to whatever extent they desired, but this education might be augmented by a program of education in the school, for boys and girls in separate classes, conducted by a person with sufficient background in counseling psychology to be qualified to assist boys and girls in the delicate matter of emotional adjustment.[10]

Such an educational program probably should begin in the seventh or eighth grade, although a few talks on the basic nature of female maturation and functions may well have been given girls earlier. Except in the case of girls from families of very low educational and intelligence levels, the latter would seldom be required in school. In the case of individual girls (and occasionally a boy), a more complete educational program might profitably be started earlier. As a rule, however, the author believes age thirteen or fourteen is early enough, because although physical maturation is typically well under way by that time, the girl is typically not exposed to the most disturbing or puzzling social concomitants of sexual maturation before these ages. In other words, the social problems which emerge with physical maturation typically do not become significant until adolescence is fairly well established. Education on the psychological aspects of heterosexual relations before such psychological maturation begins is futile, because the girl or boy does not know what you are talking about. The failure of adults to recognize the differing times when different aspects of sexual consciousness become active is responsible for many comic-tragic situations in which the "education" is given too late to do any good or too early to be understood.

The education probably should continue on a fairly regular basis until the end of senior high school. This is in keeping with the point previously emphasized that counseling (which can be used as a term interchangeable with a properly designed educational program) is not a one-shot deal. It is a process of preliminary preparation and a systematically continued process of meeting the adolescent's changing needs for knowledge and attitude development as those needs develop. A well-designed program of this type, conducted by persons professionally qualified by reason of psychological knowledge, could substantially reduce the incidence of emotional, behavioral, and personality problems among adolescent boys and girls.

10 J. F. Oliven, *Sexual Hygiene and Pathology*. J. B. Lippincott Company, Philadelphia, 1955.

Case of Mrs. Dickinson's Class

Mrs. Dickinson wants to spend some time in her eleventh-grade home-economics class going somewhat further than has been customary in the school in giving her girls instruction on physiological and psychological maturation. What would be a good way for her to prepare to do this so as not to upset the patrons or become involved in a row which might injure her professionally?

ADJUSTING TO AGE OF MATURATION

A sizable number of boys begin to develop facial hair around the corners of the upper lips while they are eleven years old or younger. A comparable number display no noticeable development of facial hair before the age of seventeen. The time of development of hair under the armpits and on the limbs shows an equally wide variation, and the time of the first ejaculation appears to vary even more widely.[11]

Among girls, 1 to 3 per cent will probably begin menstruation during or before their tenth year, and about 10 per cent more during their eleventh year. Four to 8 per cent will reach the menarche during their fifteenth year or later.[12] Noticeable development of the breasts and rounding of the hips vary over this six-year range also, and in some girls neither ever attains the expected feminine roundness and fullness.

All this means that a goodly proportion of boys and girls will appear (and to an even greater extent will *feel* that they appear) very different from the majority of their age-mates. Dawning social consciousness, without the experience which gives perspective, makes adolescents even more acutely or uncomfortably conscious of being different than adults would be. So the potential self-consciousness and embarrassment both boys and girls experience from conspicuously early and late physical maturation can easily be imagined—and is usually greater than is imagined!

There are both advantages and disadvantages to early maturation, and likewise the boy or girl who matures later than the average experiences some advantages and some disadvantages. Workers with adolescents should be aware of the special problems early maturers and late maturers face. They should also be aware of the advantages which may

[11] G. V. Ramsey, "The Sexual Development of Boys," *American Journal of Psychology,* 1943, 56:217–233.

[12] K. Simmons and W. W. Greulich, "Menarcheal Age and the Height, Weight, and Skeletal Age of Girls 7 to 17 Years," *Journal of Pediatrics,* 1943, 22:518–548.

accrue from early or late maturation. Special effort should be made to get early or late maturers to recognize the advantages produced by their deviation from the mean; they will be conscious enough of the disadvantages! There are enough of these advantages that a boy or girl can frequently turn his or her deviation from the average age of maturing into a definite asset.

Understanding the causes and proper handling of adjustments related to late or early maturation gives adequate ability to understand and cope with any problems likely to result from average-age maturation. No adjustmental problems are likely to be encountered in this group which do not also appear, usually in more severe forms, in the deviate maturers.

The Early-Maturing Girl

Usually the early-maturing girl will be larger for her age than her slower sister, and, of course, this highlights her difference.[13] Early physical maturation is naturally accompanied by early sexual awakening and early interest in the opposite sex. With her self-consciousness about her changing body, therefore, she may be beset by perverse desires to flaunt it, seeming to invite the attention which both excites and embarrasses her. The early-maturing girl has had less opportunity to learn social customs, conventions, and graces than later-maturing ones will have. Frequently parents, reluctant to lose their "little girl," persistently refuse to recognize the unmistakable signs of sexual maturation and do not give her the social education she needs to control and direct her biological urges. With only slight exaggeration it can be said that she has a little girl's mind, perception, judgment, and self-control and a woman's body and biological urges.[14] Sexually attractive, eager, and lacking even the example of her age-mates as a balance to her social advances and responses, she is particularly vulnerable to exploitation by older, unscrupulous boys, and her childishly naïve, unsophisticated heterosexual behavior can readily acquire for her the reputation of being "fast" and cause her to engage in improper conduct.[15]

The fact that a girl has matured physically at an early age and that

13 H. E. Jones, "Adolescence in Our Society," *The Family in a Democratic Society*. Columbia University Press, New York, 1949, pp. 70–82.

14 A. T. Jersild, *The Psychology of Adolescence*. The Macmillan Company, New York, 1957.

15 M. S. Margolese, "Mental Disorders in Childhood Due to Endocrine Disorders," *The Nervous Child*, 1948, 7:55–77.

her social inclinations are those of an older person unfortunately does not mean that intellectually or in the area of self-discipline and self-control she is significantly more advanced than her pre-adolescent age-mates. The relationship between age of physical maturation and intelligence or capacity for self-direction is positive but negligible.[16] This not only is dangerous as regards her relations with boys, as already noted; it means that adults will unconsciously expect more adult behavior of her because she *looks like* an adult, and her looks belie her ability to live up to their expectations. Thus, teachers, parents, and other adults may expect more mature behavior of her than she is capable of, and her standing in their eyes suffers when she is unable to live up to their expectations.

Special attention and assistance given the early-maturing girl in adjusting to physical maturation should cover several areas. Earlier and more extensive reassurance and education, and continuing counseling, are needed on the various aspects of physical maturation discussed earlier. Reassurance that other people do not notice her changing body to the extent that she does, and that when they do notice it they merely think of her as "growing up," will lessen her self-consciousness, and lessen her embarrassment even more.

Instruction in grooming, in dressing in a manner truly becoming an emerging young lady, is needed, because soon she *will not* dress like a child and, if not shown how to apply make-up and to dress becomingly, will invent her own grotesque imitations of sophisticated maturity.

It will inevitably be a source of conflict in the home, but the early-maturing girl should be given more adult supervision in her social affairs than she would receive if she became interested in such activities two or three years later. This is elementary prudence. Care taken in helping her meet and mingle with carefully selected older boys and girls who are of her own *biological* age is desirable, simply because they *are* older and intellectually and socially more mature and experienced than she. Their influence will be greater on her than on each other because of their greater experience and glamour.

On the bright side, the early-maturing girl will normally be the envy of her slower age-mates, even though the onset of the causes of their envy makes her self-conscious. When they begin dating, she already will have the advantage of a circle of friends of eligible maturity, as well as the in-

16 E. M. Abernethy, "Relationships Between Mental and Physical Growth," *Monograph of the Society for Research in Child Development*, 1936, Vol. I, No. 7.

valuable experience of having already learned what to say, how to act, and how to make a boy enjoy a date with her.

The Late-Maturing Girl

Actual study of late-maturing girls reveals that, as a group (be it remembered; conspicuous individual exceptions do occur) they surpassed their earlier-maturing sisters in traits related to personal appearance, vivaciousness, and leadership. Also, they are more likely to mature into the long-legged young woman glorified by present-day standards of beauty in the United States.[17] With these advantages, however, the late-maturing girl has some temporary but bothersome handicaps. She does not look or feel as old as she is chronologically, but despite this she has the normal desire to be "grown up," aggravated by the fact that her classmates are acting and being treated as more grown up than she.[18]

Parents typically and normally are reluctant to surrender their "little girls" by the admission that they are now young ladies. The girl whose delayed maturation gives her minimal reason to fight strongly for greater freedom is usually kept under close parental control for a longer time than is good for her. The seriousness of this delay does not lie in the fact that for two or three extra years she is controlled more closely by her parents. That would probably be a good thing—for most adolescents to be controlled for a longer period! The possible disadvantage is that she thus has two or three years *less* time to adjust to increasing self-determination before she is off at college or at work with complete responsibility for her own self-management. Instead of six years of growing emancipation from parental control, she moves out completely at the end of two, three, or four. She is an uncertain and insecure beginner at an age when other girls her chronological age are already experienced and accomplished. This will tend to promote feelings of inferiority and of being different. It may also discourage active heterosexual adjustment and promote withdrawal tendencies or homosexual associations.

All the foregoing are *possible* maladjustive tendencies resulting from a girl's late maturation. Most of them *probably* exist to some extent in the life adjustment of all late-maturing girls. Certainly all late-maturing girls are not seriously maladjusted in these or other areas. By being

---

[17] H. E. Jones, "Adolescence in Our Society," *The Family in A Democratic Society*. Columbia University Press, New York, 1949.

[18] E. M. Abernethy, "Correlations in Physical and Mental Growth," *Journal of Educational Psychology*, 1925, *16*:458–466, 539–546.

aware of common tendencies toward maladjustment in these areas, however, adults working with adolescent girls can be alert to recognize, and take remedial steps to counteract, such maladjustive tendencies as they arise.

The key to helping the late-maturing girl through the difficult latter months of her "behind-schedule" pre-adolescence lies in providing her as full and satisfying a social life as possible at her own level of interest. It will help the late-maturing girl for adults to talk with her about the process of growing up as if it is something that is happening to her *right now,* that will merely show itself in different ways as time passes. Of course, this is absolutely true, but it *seems* more true if physical maturation is talked about as something actually taking place within her right now, but in a different stage from other girls, than if it is a precise point located somewhere in the never-never land of the future. It will allay her anxieties more than mere promises that she will grow up eventually.

The importance of encouraging the late-maturing girl to assume responsibility and exercise more self-direction over her life and affairs than she herself absolutely demands can be inferred from the foregoing mention of the disadvantage of her short period of limited supervision between the onset of adolescence and the leaving of parental care. It is not *unavoidable* that she leave home with insufficient experience in self-direction. By judiciously relaxing their closeness of supervision, parents can let her have the full period of transition to full self-control.

She needs opportunities for success in various activities to bolster her self-confidence and strengthen her self concept. She needs to keep busy and to find areas in which she can excel. She may be able to compete quite favorably with more biologically mature girls in swimming, tennis, bowling, work on the school paper, in dramatics, and in all Sunday-school activities. The richer her life in nonheterosexual activities, the less she will tend to withdraw, nourish self-consciousness, and miss needed practice in social skills. As in many other aspects of life, by resourceful and determined effort, the potential ill effects of hereditary influences can be minimized or entirely overcome.

Case of Emily Evans

Emily Evans was a late-maturing girl who did not fit the pattern. She was quite happy to remain "little-girlish." Her menarche was at age fifteen, and at seventeen she was more a little girl than a young woman. She had no interest in boys or dating. Her girl friends were predominantly rather immature thirteen- to fifteen-years-olds. She bitterly objected to dressing up, even for a party, and preferred riding her bicycle to the store to driving the car.

Emily was passing her courses in the eleventh grade, but with low marks. She took no part in extracurricular activities and spent her spare time listening to records, watching TV, and reading. In reading she devoured Hugo, Dickens, Grey, and Dumas, with little interest in romance, mystery, or current fiction. Emily's parents said she was childish in her emotional responses, irresponsible, and extremely careless of her personal appearance. She is small and immature-looking.

1. What is the matter with Emily? Justify your answer.

2. What should the teacher do to help her? What should her parents do?

The Early-Maturing Boy

As trying to run with an older set of adolescents can expose a girl to danger of sexual exploitation, the same attempt will usually expose the boy to frustration, rejection, frequent ridicule, and embarrassment. Such experiences, if repeated often enough, may result in long-term injury to his social and emotional adjustment. At best, he is conscious of being "different" and, therefore, prone to develop anxieties and make things worse by "trying too hard."

Adults are likely to expect too much of the early-maturing boy. Size, facial hair, and sexual interests proclaim the young man, and he is expected to act as such and assume responsibilities, doing his duties without urging or supervision, as a boy several years older than he. Usually he cannot, because psychologically, with the single exception of sexual interests, he is still a little boy. Consistent failure to live up to the expectations of others based on his physical size can produce a self-deprecation, a lowered self concept, which may become the basis for feelings of inferiority, withdrawal, rebellion, and lack of effort.

The advantages enjoyed by the early-maturing boy more than atone for the additional problems he encounters.[19] Because of his size he usually excels in the athletics which are important status symbols in the eyes of both boys and girls of his age and older. Smaller age-mates tend to "look up to" him figuratively as well as literally, and accord him

[19] M. C. Jones, N. Bayley, and H. E. Jones, "Physical Maturing Among Boys as Related to Behavior," *American Psychologist*, 1948, 3:246.

leadership if he is at all qualified for it in other respects. He is normally given more freedom and opportunity to assume more responsibility, with resulting advantage in learning to cope with a wider range of life situations. By the time he is in senior high school and the other boys in his class are maturing, he has had years of experience in the social graces. He has been interested in personal grooming for several years, and can look and act more mature than later-maturing boys his own age. This gives him important advantages not only socially, but in competition for leadership in school activities of all types.

The Late-Maturing Boy

His problem is essentially the same as that of the late-maturing girl. Although in some respects it is worse than that of the late-maturing girl, in other respects it is better, because boys are customarily allowed by parents and social custom a wider range of freedom and experimentation. They can go further afield, stay longer, and take more initiative in injecting themselves into groups they may find which contain boys with interests kindred to their own. They are, in fact, less dependent on classmates for their entire socialization activities than is the girl.

Nevertheless, the late-maturing boy encounters problems. He cannot compete successfully with his more mature age-mates in active sports, and athletics are fully as important in the eyes and feelings of the boy as social activities are in the eyes of the girl.[20] Of course, he does not fully share their social interests, and is thus an all-round misfit in the extracurricular activities of his classmates. Since girls typically mature at an earlier age than boys, he is less likely to find girls in his class of his own level of development, even if he wants to associate with them, than late-maturing girls are to find boys of their own maturational age.

The class offices, with their potential for developing leadership abilities and qualities, seldom come to the late-maturing boy. He does not fit well into most dramatic programs because of his small size. Even if he is willing to try to dance, his partners are bigger than he is. The very quality of petiteness often renders a girl popular and attractive. It is not petiteness where the boy is concerned; it is being "a runt," "too little."

The late-maturing boy and girl both may attempt to find success in schoolwork to compensate for lack of social accomplishments. This can become a genuine advantage; such a boy or girl may enter senior high

[20] M. C. Jones and N. Bayley, "Physical Maturing Among Boys as Related to Behavior," *Journal of Educational Psychology*, 1950, *41*:129–148.

school or college with much better academic preparation and, even more important, more mature and effective methods of study than their earlier-maturing friends achieved. Care must be taken, however, not to urge the immature boy and girl into too high aspirations, because if their mental ability is low, they will not be able to achieve notably better academic success than their classmates, and what was intended to be a compensatory source of success can easily become another source of frustration and produce feelings of failure, inadequacy, and inferiority.[21]

The same principles of facilitating socialization discussed in the case of late-maturing girls apply here. The boy needs group activities both with persons his own developmental age and his age-mates in situations (such as picnics and informal parties) in which heterosexual activities are incidental to the general socialization. He needs reassurance that he *is* developing normally and will, stage by stage, reach the level of development other boys do. Continuing scouting activities past the age when other boys lose interest may give him a valuable outlet for energy and interests. It can also, because of his greater age and experience, provide him with leadership opportunities which he lacks in school. Assisting adults in any type of work with younger children is an excellent developmental activity for both boys and girls who are somewhat left out of their age groups because of any sort of circumstance.

READINGS

Ausubel, D. P., *Theory and Problems of Adolescent Development*. New York: Grune and Stratton, 1954, Chapts. 4, 6.

English, O. S., and Pearson, G. H. J., *Emotional Problems of Living*. New York: W. W. Norton & Company, Inc., 1955, Chapt. 11.

Jones, M. C., and N. Bayley, "Physical Maturing Among Boys as Related to Behavior," *Journal of Educational Psychology*, 1950, *41*:129-148.

Malm, M., and Jamison, O. G., *Adolescence*. New York: McGraw-Hill Book Company, Inc., 1952, Chapt. 4.

Mussen, H. M., and Jones, M. C., "Self-Conceptions, Motivations, and Interpersonal Attitudes of Late- and Early-Maturing Boys," *Child Development*, 1957, *28*:243-256.

Schneiders, A. A., *Psychology of Adolescence*. Milwaukee: The Bruce Publishing Co., 1951, Chapts. 3, 4.

21 W. A. Schonfeld, "Inadequate Physique," *Psychosomatic Medicine*, 1950, *12*:49–54.

CHAPTER 12

ACHIEVING
WHOLESOME SEXUAL
ADJUSTMENT

PREVIEW

(In such an emotionally charged area as sexual adjustment, there exists a strong relationship between principles of mental hygiene and adherence to conventional standards of behavior.)

Attitudes toward Sex in Early Adolescence

1. Physical maturation is believed by some psychologists to antedate erotic desire by one to three years.

2. Circumstances which to adults are sexually suggestive or offer opportunity for sexual activity are seldom so perceived by girls and boys in early adolescence.

3. Sexual interest in boys is more genitally oriented; in girls, emotionally oriented.

The Structuralization of Sexual Interests

1. An abundance of varied and wholesome heterosexual activities are desirable as a basis for establishing proper adolescent attitudes toward sex.

2. The above reduces the sexual element of boy-girl relationships to its proper perspective.

Dynamics of Sexual Behavior

1. Affection for the partner is an important element in the sexual desire of the girl, and is not (may even be negative) in the case of the boy.

2. Boys are inclined to sexual aggressiveness, dominance, mastery, and some sadism. Girls are inclined to passivity, submissiveness, receptivity, and masochism. These differences are partly biological, partly cultural, in origin.

3. Love reduces the aggressive-dominant-sadistic inclinations of the boy and increases the submissiveness-receptivity of the girl.

344

Sexual Behavior of Adolescents

1. Extent of sexual activity between a boy and girl = the privacy they have $\times$ the length of time they have it $\times$ how often they have it.

2. The girl's self concept and the boy's ethical standards are, respectively, the best defense against sexual immorality.

3. Warm emotional life in the home, replete with affection and security, helps a girl develop and maintain good moral standards.

Sexual Behavior and Mental Health

1. In a culture such as that of the U.S., sexual impropriety is conducive to emotional disorders and marital maladjustment, especially in girls.

2. Teachers and counselors can help adolescents reconcile their emotional problems of guilt and anxiety through:

    uncritical sympathy and reassurance

    facilitating catharsis

    helping them achieve an understanding of their motives and feelings which led to
      the indiscretion.

Problem Areas in Sexual Adjustment

AREA	PROBLEM
Principles and popularity	Whether to submit to group standards lower than one's own, or defy them at the risk of losing acceptance by the group. Search will usually reveal others of equally high principles with whom to associate.
Promiscuity	May be due to simple self-indulgence or lack of moral principles. May also be a search for reassurance as to one's virility or prowess, or for affection and security.
Differing socioeconomic status	When the girl is of lower socioeconomic status than the boy, she is peculiarly vulnerable to exploitation. Dating across social lines is frequently a symptom of social maladjustment or hostility toward parents.
Masturbation and sex fantasies	They are intrinsically harmless, except that they may interfere with normal social life. If indulged in to excess, they may be symptomatic of maladjustive retreat from reality.
Homosexuality	The result of faulty sexual identification, probably having its roots in infancy. Except for gentle encouragement to activities appropriate to the person's sex, no treatment should be attempted except by a psychiatrist or clinical psychologist.
Suggestive conversation and physical intimacies	Except for an occasional exhibitionist, adolescents are usually embarrassed by suggestive remarks. "Frank" group discussion of anatomical or sexual topics in mixed groups may lessen their inhibitions in an undesirable manner.

FOREWORD

IT is inevitable that the personal philosophy of the author is reflected in the discussion of a subject whose roots include strong value judgments, social principles, and moral and ethical standards. To the extent that such a discussion goes beyond a compilation and presentation of statistical data, the tendency increases for personal values of the author to be reflected, because interpretations and theories are made in terms of his own frame of reference and values.

In this chapter the assumption is made that the purpose of understanding principles of adolescent sexual adjustment is not merely the acquisition of academic knowledge *per se,* but also to learn ways of coping with problems which arise in the area. The further assumption is made that adults working with adolescents will desire to perpetuate and strengthen in them conventional principles of morality which characterize American culture. Therefore, while facts and clinical interpretations are presented in this chapter, the discussion is not limited to that data. It includes consideration of ways of using those facts and interpretations to encourage adherence to the mores of the prevailing culture and the principles of mental hygiene. Thus, there may be seen in this chapter what some would call a moralistic tone inappropriate to a scientific text.

*   *   *

VARIOUS aspects of sex and sexual adjustment have been discussed in several earlier chapters, because sex plays an important role in many areas of adolescent adjustment. However, there are aspects of sexual adjustment in adolescence which are sufficiently distinct from general personality development, physical maturation, and social, emotional, and mental development to necessitate consideration of the psychological aspects of adjustments to sex *per se.*

This is largely because sexual adjustment in American society involves adjustment not only to new, urgent, and often confusing desires within the adolescent himself, but also to a complex and sometimes illogical pattern of social conventions and mores regarding sex. Adults of other nations are often puzzled over our ethics and standards of sexual behavior. One well-educated and successful Norwegian businessman, talking about it, showed a picture of his little daughter, six years old, taken on a public beach. She was wearing nothing at all. He asked, "How is it that you Americans approve of grown women, with voluptuous bodies and great sexual attraction, appearing in public wearing one or two little bits of cloth that reveal every detail of their bodies, except some small patches of skin, and yet think it is immodest for a little girl like this to go without being covered up?" One from Italy said, "You try to stimulate sexual desires by suggestive advertisements featuring beautiful women, you have dances which stimulate sexual excitement, you have movies which induce sexual desires, and then you say it is so very wrong to satisfy these desires you work so hard to arouse. What is the idea?"

As we citizens of the United States compare our country with others in which legal prostitution flourishes or where illegal prostitution operates about as openly, where mixed bathing parties and nude swimming parties are sanctioned, where motion pictures show erotic scenes banned in our theaters, we think of ourselves, comparatively at least, as a highly moral people. And so we are. But if our standards of morality, our simultaneous emphasis on sex and stimulation of sexual desire and rigorous disapproval of equally indiscriminate satisfaction of such desires, puzzle mature, responsible adults from other nations, it is easy to imagine the difficulty children may have in comprehending the attitudes and behavior expected of them as adolescents. Even comprehending, they are increasingly beset by biological urges that they are ill equipped psychologically to cope with, since they are yet immature in the control of their impulses and feelings, in self-discipline.

From innumerable studies a great deal of factual information has been accumulated regarding the sexual attitudes and practices of people of all ages. From this factual information and from clinical experience, psychologists and psychiatrists have formulated theories and concepts regarding child, adolescent, and adult sexuality. It is often impossible to determine precisely where fact ceases and theory begins on any subject. Especially is this true of a subject so complicated by emotional, religious, moral, and social concomitants as sex. Several widely held beliefs regarding adolescent sexuality are worthy of note here. Some of these beliefs are based on factual data. Some are theories, theoretical constructs, and interpretations. Ofttimes it is difficult to determine which belief is based on fact and which is a logical construct or interpretation. Whether having their origin in objective fact or specious interpretation, these beliefs about adolescent sexuality widely held by psychologists and psychiatrists should be known and understood by the student of adolescent psychology because they represent informed thought on the subject.

However, on matters of adolescent sexuality, as well as other subjects, psychologists and psychiatrists differ among themselves. As an example, the author's clinical practice, observation as a teacher, and research among upper-age adolescents in college classes forces him to the conclusion that during early adolescence the desire for physical intimacy and, in fact, sexual consciousness generally, is much less than is believed by a large proportion of his colleagues.

At this point it may be well to explore the meaning of certain terms employed in discussing heterosexual relationships and some concepts on which their use is based. Grant[1] distinguishes between "genital" motives

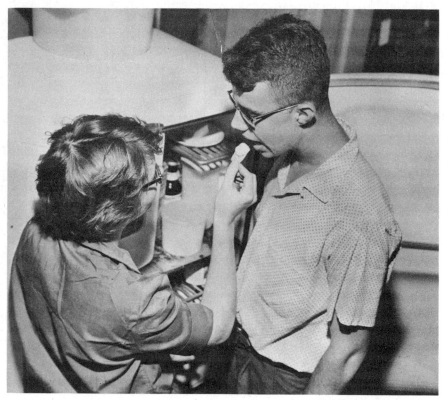

Photo by Stephen Carmichael.

Figure 16. "Friendship may exist between a boy and a girl because they are members of opposite sexes without involving erotic overtones."

[1] V. M. Grant, *The Psychology of Sexual Emotions: The Basis of Selective Attraction.* Longmans, Green and Co., New York, 1957.

and "amorous" motives in heterosexual associations. McKinney[2] equates the genital motive with "lust" and the amorous with "love." The author shares the inference of these psychologists that heterosexual attraction may be on other bases than desire for sexual relations, "erotic" motivation. In fact, one of the principal criteria of good sexual adjustment elaborated later in this chapter is the extent to which boys and girls are able to perceive and gain satisfaction from heterosexual associations on levels other than that of erotic stimulation and gratification. Boys are people. Girls are people. They differ from each other and have attraction for each other as complementary natures as well as complementary bodies and biological urges. Even where neither "amorous" nor "genital" motives are consciously involved, boys derive a pleasure from association with girls, and vice versa. Although this pleasure derives largely from their membership in different sexes, it is often based on their differing social roles and complementary psychological natures rather than on their complementary biological urges. In short, friendship may exist between a boy and a girl *because* they are members of opposite sexes without involving genital or amorous motives, because each finds in the other a companionship not connected with the mating urge and yet not found between members of the same sex. Introspective examination of your own friendships will probably reveal several examples of this type of heterosexual association.

ATTITUDES TOWARD
SEX IN EARLY ADOLESCENCE

Before reaching adolescence the typical child has engaged in considerable sexual investigation and experimentation. Often, if not usually, this investigation and experimentation has been provoked by curiosity rather than by well-defined erotic impulses. The curiosity may take the form of interest in anatomical differences, defying parental mandates and engaging in forbidden activities to find what the mystery is, or imitation of the activities observed in adults to ascertain their attraction and see what happens. The investigation and experimentation is sometimes heterosexual, sometimes involves another member of the same sex, and

2 F. McKinney, *The Psychology of Personal Adjustment.* John Wiley & Sons, Inc., New York, 1960.

is sometimes directed at the child's own person through masturbation or some other form of auto-eroticism.

With the dawn of puberty, the genital and erotic aspects of sex begin to emerge in boys and girls, especially boys. Some students of the subject (and the author is one of this group) feel that the first amorous attraction of a girl for a boy, or vice versa, is not "erotic," not "genitally oriented"—i.e., is not based upon a biological drive for sexual relations. Others maintain that even the first heterosexual strivings are essentially genitally oriented, although social pressure and self-consciousness may disguise the fact. According to this latter theory, sexual stirrings of all sorts are basically genital; the adolescent desires intercourse. Certainly, erotic urges are active to some degree from the beginning of adolescence, and within a very short time after the dawning of heterosexual attraction these urges are held by some to dominate direct heterosexual behavior and feelings.

Boys are known to reach their biological peak of sexual potency approximately two years after puberty, around age sixteen.[3] This fact suggests to some that the boy is driven in his heterosexual relations toward total sexual relations at a quite early age. Girls do not ordinarily reach the peak of sexual desire before the mid-twenties, despite the fact that they mature biologically earlier than boys.[4] Thus, boys, in adolescence, may be expected to be the aggressors in sexual advances not only because of their masculine role, but because their urge toward full sexual relations reaches its peak long before the girl is similarly motivated.

From all the above, some psychologists and psychiatrists conclude that associations between boys and girls become sexually oriented long before parents ordinarily think of their adolescent children as being "sexed" in the sense of the sexual desires experienced by normal adults. Boys, particularly, actually reach their point of greatest sexual potency shortly after the age at which they traditionally lose interest in playing with marbles. All this suggests the normality, the natural expectation, of sexual experimentation approaching or achieving full sexual intimacy in the associations of boys and girls even in their earliest teens.

Other psychologists and psychiatrists share the conclusions of this author that typically, physical sexual maturation runs ahead of psycho-

[3] A. C. Kinsey, W. B. Pomeroy, and C. E. Martin, *Sexual Behavior in the Human Male.* W. B. Saunders Company, Philadelphia, 1948.

[4] A. C. Kinsey, W. B. Pomeroy, C. E. Martin, and P. H. Gebhard, *Sexual Behavior in the Human Female.* W. B. Saunders Company, Philadelphia, 1953.

logical comprehension of the full erotic significance of sex and erotic aspects of sexual interest.[5, 6, 7] Girls typically achieve considerable sexual maturity before they develop intense, erotic sexual desire.[8, 9] The same is less true of boys, but still may be considered typical of them. Sexual awareness is first followed by generalized interest and curiosity regarding sexual matters and the opposite sex. Observation of the activities of boys and girls in early adolescence, and clinical work with them, indicates to the author that the evolution of sexual consciousness and psychosexual maturation remains for as long as two to three years at the level of talking and looking, wondering and investigating and experimenting, motivated more by curiosity than by eroticism. Sexual-type activity among early adolescents more frequently involves boys and girls engaging in "necking" and mild, superficial "petting" to gratify their curiosity as to what it is like, rather than constituting the stimulation of, or response to, genitally oriented erotic urges.[10, 11]

In girls, early sexual desire is not specific or erotic; vague, disturbing longings, unknown stirrings of feelings, feelings of tenderness and soft affection, a desire to love someone, dominate her sexual impulses. Love is more prominent than erotic urges in the girl.[12] Girls are less likely than boys to become strongly aroused sexually. Boys may so become through thoughts of girls, conversation about them, pictures of female nudity, or a glimpse of some usually concealed part of a girl's body. Girls usually require direct stimulation of erotogenic zones—genitalia, breasts, or lips —to become sexually aroused. Their sexual feelings, too, are enjoyable for their own sake, constitute a pleasurable state of feeling to be maintained, whereas the boy's sexual inclination (when, with the passing of

[5] G. J. Mohr and M. A. Despres, *The Stormy Decade: Adolescence*. Random House, New York, 1958.

[6] A. Moll, *The Sexual Life of the Child*. The Macmillan Company, New York, 1924.

[7] C. B. Zachry, *Emotions and Conduct in Adolescence*. Appleton-Century-Crofts, Inc., New York, 1950.

[8] Mary J. Buchanan, *Characteristics of Initial Heterosexual Fantasies as Reported by Male and Female College Students,* unpublished Independent Study of Huntingdon College, Montgomery, Alabama, 1962.

[9] J. L. Stone and J. Church, *Childhood and Adolescence*. Random House, New York, 1957.

[10] V. W. Grant, "A Major Problem of Human Sexuality," *Journal of Social Psychology*, 1948, *28*:79–101.

[11] G. J. Mohr and M. A. Despres, *The Stormy Decade: Adolescence*. Random House, New York, 1958.

[12] L. J. Stone and J. Church, *Childhood and Adolescence*. Random House, New York, 1957.

time, it becomes erotically oriented) is directed toward a climax, an orgasm.

There are exceptions to the hypothesis that early heterosexual attraction is not erotically oriented, of course. Sometimes from the dawning of physical signs of adolescence, and occasionally even before, a boy or girl will display unmistakable signs of erotic sexual desire and make physical approaches, seductive in the case of the girl and aggressive in the case of the boy, aimed at sexual activity. Such instances occur much more frequently among boys and girls from families of lower socioeconomic levels. Sociological and psychological research has revealed that the average boy or girl brought up in "underprivileged" areas begins sexual activity earlier than those of middle- and upper-class backgrounds.[13] This may be explained by the generally lower educational level of parents in the lower socioeconomic areas, their preoccupation with earning a living and the resultant lessening of supervision of the activities of their children, the lesser amount of privacy under living conditions prevailing there, and consequent increased opportunity for children to observe each other and adults undressed or in suggestive activities. Important factors are also the abundance of children commonly concentrated in the poorer areas of town, the paucity of recreational facilities, and the opportunities for boys and girls of early adolescent age to be seduced or otherwise initiated into sexual activities by older boys and girls.

However, although reasonable precautions should be taken to minimize opportunities for boys and girls in early adolescence to succumb to their dimly understood biological urges and engage in sexual experimentation, more harm than good may result from judging the behavior of early teenagers by the standards of adult sexual motivation.[14] The author's observation suggests that bodily contact between early teenagers in mixed athletic activities seldom has significant erotic overtones. The chances are overwhelming that an early-adolescent boy and girl from families with good interpersonal relations, which observe and teach conventional middle-class or upper-class standards and values, will, if accidentally placed in a situation of unusual privacy or opportunity for sexual experimentation do little or nothing about it.

Early amorous attachments are not necessarily erotic.[15] Circum-

[13] L. Schneider and S. Lysgaard, "The Deferred Gratification Pattern: A Preliminary Study," *American Sociological Review*, 1953, *18*:142–149.

[14] O. S. English and H. J. Pearson, *Emotional Problems of Living*. W. W. Norton & Company, Inc., New York, 1955.

[15] G. V. Hamilton, *A Research in Marriage*. A. and C. Boni, New York, 1929.

erally.[18] Concrete evidence satisfying conventional standards of research data is understandably difficult to obtain; however, it appears that the early sex talk and imagery of boys is devoted largely to physical aspects of sex and primitive sexual activities. Early adolescent girls, on the other hand, while not ignoring anatomical aspects of sex and the probable nature and sensations of the sex act, more frequently discuss sex in its more romantic aspects. Torrid love scenes viewed in movies, read about in magazines (or comic books, of all places!), or imagined are more likely to be discussed and described, with curiosity about the mental and emotional concomitants equaling or exceeding that about the physical sensations involved. This indicated tendency is borne out by the known relative interest and preferences of adults in sexual matters.

A protection against sexual activity among boys and girls before they are mature enough to fully grasp the implications involved is the uncertainty and timidity of early adolescents in their social relations with the opposite sex. For months or even a year following the awakening of heterosexual interests, many are afraid even to try to talk to each other except under carefully considered conditions. Acute self-consciousness inhibits them from advances which might be rebuffed, even if psychosexual precocity suggests such advances. They are by no means immune to deliberate seduction by a more sophisticated member of the opposite sex, and occasionally a combination of circumstances will cause the collapse of all barriers between younger adolescents and sexual activities.

It is the author's belief that among most early adolescents there is simply a lack of conscious desire for full sexual intimacy. The lack is due partly to lack of understanding of sex apart from its primitive physical aspects, and partly to the phenomenon of psychosexual development not yet having produced personalized, specific desire for sex activities. Association between members of the sexes is companionable, with the mating urge not yet felt in its fullest physical sense.

THE STRUCTURALIZATION
OF SEXUAL INTERESTS

Affording boys and girls in early adolescence a great deal of association with each other and with many members of the opposite sex, under

[18] W. L. Hughes, "Sex Experiences in Boyhood," *Journal of Social Hygiene,* 1926, *12*:262–273.

conditions of pleasant companionship with minimal erotic implications and urges, is one of the best ways of producing in a boy or girl a well-balanced, wholesome attitude toward sex and of laying the basis for sexual propriety in later adolescence.[19] The reason for this is not far to seek: by such companionship boys and girls learn to think of each other as personalities, people, friends, companions, human beings with whom you cook a hot dog, swim, talk about music and football and schoolwork, go bowling or see a movie and think about *it,* not each other. It makes the girl seem to the boy (and vice versa) a complete person socially, mentally, and psychologically, in *most* respects much like another boy (or girl). Thus, the physical and sexual element is reduced to more nearly its proper perspective as merely one aspect of a broad relationship, which for reasons of good taste and morality must be minimized.

The importance of this breadth of association and the resulting attitudes for life within the cultural pattern of the United States can hardly be overemphasized. The boy or girl who passes through formative years of psychosexual development without acquiring an appreciation of members of the opposite sex as nonsexual companions does not have adequate perspective for reducing the erotic sexual drives, which will sooner or later develop, to their proper proportion in heterosexual association. If a boy (or a girl) is relatively isolated from companionship with the opposite sex in social relations, then, when psychobiological maturation brings the erotic aspect of sexual association into prominence, this aspect looms inappropriately large. It looms inappropriately large because it is *there;* physical and emotional maturation have, without any outside help, produced a powerful erotic attraction toward members of the opposite sex. If a wealth of pleasant, companionable, nonsexual associations have taken place, the sexual evaluation of a girl is merely one aspect of the boy's thinking of her. If other bases for valuing her company and enjoying her association are lacking, the sexual attraction becomes, if not the only, at best the *major* basis for his prospective relations with her.

Under circumstances of reasonable control, and short of permitting unmistakably sexual contacts and actions, dancing and the rough-and-tumble horseplay of swimming pool and beach can be wholesome heterosexual activities, de-emphasizing by their nature the erotic element in physical contact between the sexes. It is sometimes argued that such

[19] O. S. English and G. H. J. Pearson, *Emotional Problems of Living.* W. W. Norton & Company, Inc., New York, 1955.

bodily-contact activities have, in the long run, exactly the opposite result, producing in boys and girls the attitude that it is natural and "all right" for the sexes to indulge in physical contact. No decisive evidence or reasoning in support of either argument is forthcoming as yet. Most psychologists and sociologists, however, tend to hold the former view. This opinion is also typically upheld by professional youth workers, who predominantly indicate approval of the attitudes fostered by casual, matter-of-fact physical contact between boys and girls without sexual implications.

Inevitably, if a boy or girl is normal, the erotic element of sexual attraction gradually develops. (The divergent opinions of psychologists and psychiatrists referred to earlier in the chapter are as to *how early* this erotic element of sexual attraction appears.) It is marked by greater desire for bodily contact on the part of both sexes, and, particularly in the case of boys, by greater desire to handle parts of the girl's body having sexual implications. Usually there is a period of a few months to a year or more when bodily contact and manual fondling on the part of both boy and girl is sufficient to appease, if not gratify, their erotic desires. Here again adolescent sex reactions differ from typical adult reactions. What is to the adult preliminary sex play that must either lead to sexual consummation or result in more or less severe frustration may be generally satisfying in and of itself to the adolescent. This is partly because the adolescent still retains some of his timidity toward the opposite sex, and is not fully confident of his competence in heterosexual relations. It is partly because of lack of experience. If neither has had the experience of sexual relations, the progression from necking to petting to greater intimacy is not so obvious or pressing. But a considerable part of the explanation seems to lie (and here again, satisfactorily concrete evidence is difficult to obtain) in the fact that even in middle adolescence boys and girls have not typically developed the psychosexual pattern which demands full consummation for their satisfaction.

At this stage, as in early adolescence, continuation of extensive heterosexual activities having no sexual implications is desirable to prevent a boy-girl association from becoming an invariable routine of necking or petting. Helping keep physical aspects of adolescents' association in the proper perspective is one of the contributions of teen-towns, church-sponsored young-people's groups, and organized social programs of all types. Unless young people of this age are given an irrational amount of privacy and opportunity, they seldom become involved in serious sexual misbehavior, except in cases of very low home and group social standards such as exist in the lowest socioeconomic groups.

During the latter years of adolescence, the late teens and perhaps the early twenties, the psychosexual urge typically reaches its full adult form. The boy or girl, especially girl, who is relatively late in reaching the ultimate stage of sexual maturity in the psychological and social areas is perhaps fortunate. In his or her case, powerful urges which can so easily lead to sexual delinquency do not reach their full strength before the time that mental and emotional development produce the self-discipline necessary to regulate them.

At this point the breadth and richness of heterosexual associations of earlier years, the moral and ethical standards which have been acquired, and the self concept which has been developed are balanced against the urgent biological demands which all normal young people experience. Added in will be customs of age-mates, privacy, and opportunity. The result of these diverse and often opposing forces—which are the strongest and which the weakest?—determines the extent of sexual intimacy which will characterize the heterosexual activities of the older adolescents. There will inevitably be a tendency for intimacies to increase in extent and intensity, but this tendency is less likely to result in both boy and girl losing self-control if the background development has been along the optimum lines which we have outlined. In all events, but particularly in the case of boys and girls whose self-discipline and wholesome balance of heterosexual associations are deficient, limitation of opportunity for prolonged sexual stimulation and temptation is just good common sense.

Case of the Franklin Family

In Ourcity it is customary for dating to begin quite early for boys and girls who wish to do so. Thirteen-year-old girls are taken by parents of boys of that age to the movies, left there, and picked up after the movie and time for a soda at a nearby drug store. They attend dances under close chaperonage, and where distance permits, they are often walked home by boys from church young-people's meetings. By the time they are seventeen, due to a high proportion of boys having their own cars, boys and girls have been driving to movies, dances, drive-in pizza stands, and "just riding around" for as long as two years.

Mr. and Mrs. Franklin have just moved to Ourcity from a con-

Figure 18. Breadth and diversity of heterosexual activities encourage wholesome social maturation.

George Peabody College for Teachers.

Marsh Photographers, Inc. Cincinnati, Ohio, Public Schools. Photo by Stephen Carmichael.

Marsh Photographers, Inc. Cincinnati Public Schools.

Atlanta, Georgia, Public Schools.

George Peabody College for Teachers.

servative small town where young people's social activities develop on a much later schedule than the young people of Ourcity are accustomed to. There are three daughters, Evelyn, seventeen, Josie, fifteen, and Libby, fourteen. Libby is well into the pubertal period, but, because of her parents' feelings and the customs of the community, has never had anything approaching a date. Josie is hardly beyond the stage common to thirteen-year-olds in Ourcity, and even Evelyn has had only carefully chaperoned heterosexual associations. Mr. and Mrs. Franklin do not want to be overstrict with their daughters, and have decided they must let them conform to the dating customs of Ourcity. However, they uneasily feel that their girls will be associating with age-mates considerably more advanced socially and more sophisticated than they are, and want to give them such guidance as is necessary to keep their inexperience from exposing them to embarrassment or situations with which they are unprepared to cope.

1. In what ways should the Franklins' handling of the situation in Evelyn's case differ from their procedures in the case of Josie? Libby?

2. Should Evelyn receive any specific counsel which Josie or Libby would not need? What and why?

3. Should the Franklins observe any particular precautions in their daughters' early social activities in Ourcity? What? Why?

DYNAMICS OF SEXUAL BEHAVIOR

As was pointed out in Chapter 3, and as has been obvious in subsequent discussions, sex is not solely a physical or biological urge. Social factors augment biological ones in producing sexual differentiation and standards. Equally or more important in determining the patterns of sexual behavior is the psychological aspect of sexuality. Boys are as different from girls, males from females, in the psychological implications which sex has for them as they are in physical differences. Failure to understand the psychodynamics of sexual behavior, and particularly the sex differences in psychodynamic patterns, is responsible for much heartache and even more serious consequences among girls (and women as well).

Psychodynamics of Male Sexual Behavior

Nature designed (and virtually every culture in history has fostered the predilection) the male to be the aggressive party in sexual activities. Not only does the anatomical structure of the male and female render this technically essential; characteristics of the secondary sex organs of the female, such as the sensitivity of her breast to sexual stimulation, adapt her to be the receiver, the more passive partner, in preliminary sex play. This sensitivity is complemented in the male, whose erotogenic zones are more limited, by a capacity to achieve sexual stimulation through seeing or touching the female. With the usual allowances for individual variations, it can be said that the male typically wants to, and is capable of, achieving sexual stimulation through looking at and caressing the female. The female, on the other hand, more readily achieves sexual stimulation through being caressed and, in exceptional cases, even by being looked at by a male under certain conditions.

Most cultures place a premium on masculine sexual aggressiveness. Even in cultures where promiscuity or sexual suggestiveness is not officially sanctioned, the man who displays noticeably less interest in sexual matters than the average is likely to be held in mild contempt or suspicion. Thus, by biological predisposition and cultural conditioning, the male has both a drive and a need for sexual pursuit, and activity quite distinct from the biologically and culturally dictated passivity of the female. The comment has been made that a smart woman does not pursue a man in the same manner that a mousetrap does not pursue a mouse. Be that as it may, by nature and culture the male is more sexually aggressive than the female.

To the average male, his sexual contacts, even his sexual relations, are comparatively impersonal matters, without any essential quality of love or even liking being required to make them completely satisfactory. Thus, adolescent boys (as well as older males) are as much, very often even more, sexually stimulated by the sight of, or opportunity for sexual activities with, a girl who is a comparative or complete stranger and for whom they have no feeling of love or affection as by the same activities with a girl for whom they have deep feelings. The reason for the often greater sexual attraction of the comparative stranger is an extrapolation of the relationship already discussed: A girl of whom he is fond is a personality, a companion, a person with whom much is shared, in addition to being a female body. The casual acquaintance is a physical body with erotic appeal. Lacking ties of acquaintance or affection to round out this perception into the perception of a complete person, sexual values are magnified. Thus, the boy receives erotic stimulation from sights or experiences which involve no element of attraction other than sexual, and his pleasure in them is not diminished by the fact that they are shared by a "pickup" rather than a good friend. Indeed, in many cases he would not want the good friend to share them, evaluating her in a different manner and possessing what seems to him more consideration for her.

As might logically be deduced from the aggressiveness of the male and his evaluation of the relation between eroticism and affection, sadism of a mild sort is an element in the psychosexual structure of the typical male. It could hardly be otherwise, when his biological and cultural role is that of the aggressive pursuer, which implies that the female is his prey or his victim. Too, initial sexual relations are at least temporarily painful to the female, and the male inflicts this pain. In the case of the well-loved sexual partner, the sadistic element of the male nature is minimized, but in the case of a casual partner for whom no real affection exists, the element of sadism finds expression more often than not in roughness, disregard of the feelings or wishes of the partner, and often callousness when relations have been completed. Such sadistic impulses are really less conspicuous in the occasional brutal sexual assault made by a man upon a woman than in the large proportion of men whom prostitutes report as desiring to gratify sadistic impulses in their purchased sexual relations.

Distinguishable from sadism, but having similar roots, is the desire for dominance, to conquer, which is even more nearly universal in the psychosexual structure of the male. Even in early adolescence the tendency of the average boy to enjoy teasing or establishing dominance of some sort over girls with whom he comes in contact, often even the girls he likes best, is conspicuous.[20] The teasing, making a girl beg for the return of a shoe, ostentatiously reading a note the girl objects (or professes to object) to his reading, as well as occasionally more drastic behavior, such as publicly brow-beating or embarrassing a girl with whom he associates quite regularly and pleasantly, are mixtures of sadistic tendencies and the male urge to dominate the female. Every teacher of junior high school boys and girls has had hundreds of observations of such behavior,

20 O. E. English and G. H. J. Pearson, *Emotional Problems of Living*. W. W. Norton & Company, Inc., New York, 1955.

too universal and frequent to be explained as individual idiosyncrasies.

In the sexual aggressiveness of the older adolescent boy—and particularly in instances where he achieves sexual intimacy with a less-than-willing girl through high-pressure techniques of persuasion, cajolery, insistent and direct use of his superior strength, prolonged sexual stimulation of the girl often against her desires, refusal to start up the car when she begs, "Let's go home"—the desire for dominance is frequently stronger than the basic sexual desire itself. Thus, it is common talk among boys that there is little satisfaction in sexual relations with a certain girl because "It's too easy." Similarly, few males report enjoyment of relations with a prostitute as much as with a girl whose favors they win by insistence, persuasion, and, often, thinly disguised force, because with the prostitute the element of mastery, of dominance, is lacking. The male becomes a customer who has bought and is given a commodity, not a dominant conqueror establishing his mastery over a weaker (psychologically as well as physically, he prefers to believe) female whom he renders powerless to resist his masculinity. Appreciation of this aspect of the male psychosexual structure makes understandable the oft-noted phenomenon of the boy or man who will spend weeks or months in pursuit of the complete surrender of a girl, quickly losing interest in her and looking for another girl over whom to establish and demonstrate his dominance soon after he has completed his conquest.

Dynamics of Female Sexual Behavior

The biological urge for sexual gratification is notably lower in the average female than in the average male. This fact accounts to a large extent for the lower sexual aggressiveness of the female; she simply does not have the physical desire for sexual activity typical of the male. It is not, however, the full explanation. Cultural conditioning plays an important part. It is a more important part than is often realized, because while the female does not have a desire for sexual activity *per se* of as high intensity as the male, she has as high, or probably even higher, a need to be wanted and to give and receive affection. Thus, her desire for heterosexual association is typically as high as, or higher than, that of the male. Furthermore, the desire for maternity, a deep, primitive yearning to have children, is a conscious and powerful thing in the emotional lives of many females, particularly from late adolescence onward.

When the total balance between the heterosexual needs of males and females is noted, it can hardly be concluded that those of the female are less urgent. Thus, on the basis of "original nature," the female would be expected to be as aggressive as the male in seeking heterosexual associations, although possibly less aggressive in seeking complete sexual relations. Clinical study confirms this theoretical pattern of psychosexual response, indicating that, in couples in whom close emotional relationships have been established, girls seek and enjoy sex play on the level of hugging and kissing to as great an extent as boys, but have less desire to consummate the sex play in intercourse.

Cultural conditioning and social pressures are largely responsible for the lower aggressiveness displayed by girls in seeking heterosexual activities, if not responsible for their lower aggressiveness in seeking actual intercourse. In most cultures "nice girls" simply do not take the conspicuous initiative in establishing close heterosexual relationships. Most girls accept this limitation and add their disapproval and the force of feminine social pressure to masculine disapproval of the heterosexually aggressive girl. From the psychological standpoint, however, there is strong reason to suspect that the passive role of the female represents more a concession to the masculine need for dominance and mastery than any innate biological or psychological tendency toward passivity on the part of the female.

One other factor must be put into the balance of relative needs for mastery and acceptance of submission of the sexes. By the nature of the biological role of the female, by her physical strength, which is usually less than that of the male, by the limitations placed on her capabilities for physical activity by pregnancy and childbearing, and by the subsequent limitations of her activity imposed by the necessity of caring for her offspring, the female is less able to fulfill her natural biological and homemaking roles and still cope with the world and its threats and demands than is the male. Therefore, in a mating relationship the female will, in most cases, look to her mate to cope with the world outside the family, to wrest from it sustenance for her and her offspring, to protect her from its possible threats, and to cope with whatever other outside problems that may arise. This being the case, the female can accept considerable mastery from the male in their personal relations without its constituting too great a threat to her self concept or producing a feeling of oppression or humiliation.[21] The very strength and aggressiveness which demand her submission are evidence of a nature suited to protect

21 O. S. English and G. H. J. Pearson, *Emotional Problems of Living.* W. W. Norton & Company, Inc., New York, 1955.

and provide for her and her offspring. These considerations are seldom consciously thought out and formulated into reasoning systems by the female. However, clinical case studies provide ample evidence to substantiate the theory that a part of the sexual passivity of the female, which is a form of submission, is based on her need to receive evidence that the mate she may trust for her providence and protection is strong and aggressive enough to do what needs to be done. After all, if he cannot establish his primacy in the home, how can he be expected to be able to cope with the forces outside the home as the welfare of his family requires?

Culture and, even more important, *love* produce modifications of this basic dominance-submission relationship characterizing the psychosexual relationship of the sexes. As an adolescent boy develops genuine affection for a girl, or a man for a woman, his need for dominance and mastery is tempered by a desire to be kind to the loved one, make her happy, and demonstrate his strength and aggressiveness by giving her material things and less tangible services rather than by dominating her. As love for her grows in him, a confidence in their interpersonal relations develops which simultaneously lessens his feeling of need for mastery and increases his desire to please her and demonstrate his masculinity by providing for her better than she could provide for herself. The well-adjusted American home represents an excellent example of sublimation of the male need for dominance into an expression of this ascendancy through superior care for those depending upon him.

Since there are as wide variations in individual psychological make-ups of individuals as there are in physical make-ups (and many females are physically larger and stronger than males), it is to be expected that in some homes the dominance-submission roles may be reversed, and many sublimations of various types of sexual urges occur. However, the principle of biological and psychological dominance-aggressiveness of the male and submission-passivity of the female prevails in general throughout the human race and nature.

Perhaps because of its potential for producing motherhood, sex has vastly, perhaps basically, different implications for the female than for the male. It is extremely important for the adolescent girl to understand this difference, because such an understanding is often essential to her emotional and physical self-protection. In the case of the girl, sexual desire normally increases somewhat proportionately to her love for the boy. We have already seen that in the case of the boy this is simply not true. A tendency toward its truth in a particular instance is more than overcome by the fact that even though his desire may be strong, where real love is present the normal boy's sexual demands on the girl are lessened as their relationship becomes to him something more than an opportunity for physical gratification.

Every clinical psychologist, psychiatrist, and counselor has encountered numbers of instances where heartache and tragedy or near-tragedy have resulted from girls' failing to comprehend the basically antithetical values of boys and girls on the issue of sexual intimacy. So many times such workers have heard the plaintive questions "Why did he *want* so badly for us to do that if he didn't *love* me?" and "He seemed to love me so much that it didn't seem wrong, and now he says he *doesn't* love me! I love him. I wouldn't have done it if I hadn't loved him so much and thought that he loved me too. Why did he *want* to if he didn't love me?"

Sometimes such questions are mere self-justifications, attempts to excuse socially disapproved conduct on the basis of a misunderstanding of motives. Frequently such reasoning represents a girl who has got herself involved in an unfortunate situation because she honestly judged the boy's concept of sexual relations by the standards of their meaning to her. And she was wrong. Boys do not require any affection toward a girl to make her a sexually attractive object, to make sexual relations with her desirable; as previously noted, the actual reverse is more likely to be true, and the importance of sexual relations decline in the boy as his affection for the girl mounts, just as her desire is mounting with the growth of her love.

An old folk saying is cynical and, of course, not 100 per cent accurate, but valuable for any counselor of adolescents (adolescent girls in particular) to keep in mind as possessing considerable truth: A boy will seek sexual relations with every girl except one he loves, while a girl will have sexual relations with no boy except the one she loves. Remembering this is an excellent safeguard for the girl who feels herself on the verge of being convinced that intimate relations with a boy are really all right because they love each other so much. If he loves her, he is less likely to strive for such intimacy, no matter what he says. His own psychosexual structure will exercise a restraining effect on him, to say nothing of the fact that he will not willingly jeopardize the welfare and reputation of one he truly loves. Psychology texts are no place for sermons on morality, but principles important to mental health, not abstract ethical standards, are involved here.

George Peabody College for Teachers.

Figure 19. "The tendency of the average boy to enjoy teasing or establishing dominance of some sort over girls with whom he comes in contact is conspicuous."

It is not abnormal for the willingness of the female to render submission to the male (probably hardly a need or desire, but a willingness) to be manifested in a willingness to undergo some pain and frustration in sexual activities on all levels. This willingness, sometimes actually a desire, is called masochism. It is the feminine counterpart of the slight sadistic tendency of the male. Naturally, the tendency toward masochism involving physical pain or abuse seldom comes to public attention. However, its social and psychological manifestations are frequently observed in girls and women who repay every humiliation or outrage inflicted on them by a male companion with dog-like devotion and closer association. The masochistic tendency is the basic dynamic in the French Apache motif and often in the relationship between a prostitute and her male "protector." At the level of normal boy-girl relationships, it is manifested by the girl who continues to bestow affection on and seek the favor of a boy who repeatedly disappoints or humiliates her or treats her in a cavalier fashion.

The feminine counterpart of the masculine urge to dominate or to assert and maintain mastery is the desire to be cherished, protected, and treated in a romantic fashion. At the adolescent level this desire finds expression in flattery and admiration on the part of the girl, tacitly implying the boy's superiority. He customarily responds with proprietary condescension, accompanied, however, by the treatment the girl desires.

It may be noted that, in actual effect, the girl's passivity in heterosexual advances, the initiation of sexual activities, and, rarely, the actual achievement of intercourse is more apparent than real. By manner of dress, walk, movements, and actions girls often, if not habitually, indicate their receptivity (or lack of it) to masculine attentions of various types. Thoughtful perusal of advertisements of perfume or women's clothing provides interesting evidence that, without socially disapproved overt sexual invitation, the female actually does make heterosexual advances. Her passivity as concerns directly asking for a date or for a boy's company is balanced by considerable aggressiveness in establishing a situation in which the boy is strongly impelled to make the request. This is in no wise unbecoming or unladylike on the part of the girl. It is, however, an aspect of the relation between boys and girls which should be understood by parents, teachers, and counselors, because without this understanding the basic relationship between the roles of the sexes in the initiation of heterosexual activities will be erroneously perceived. It is an exaggeration to say that no girl receives masculine requests or advances that she has not invited, because some boys lack the sensitivity to interpret girls' manners and attitudes. Also, some give relatively free rein to their aggressive urges without regard for girls' feelings. However, the progress of relations between a boy and girl usually represents a balance, meeting the desires of each and not so completely dictated by the greater aggressiveness of the boy as might first be assumed.

Case of Gloria Gordon and Hank Helm

Gloria Gordon's physician referred her to a psychologist for counseling after her hysterical weeping had necessitated sedation on two successive nights. For three months Gloria has been going steady with Hank Helm, another sixteen-year-old in a different section of Gloria's grade, the tenth. Both Gloria and Hank present a picture of complete normality in past social relations, but Hank delights in embar-

not take place, and lack of necessary privacy or facilities slightly less than a fourth. In approximately half of the total cases of sexual activity without intercourse, neither party attempted to carry intimacy further than it went. In an occasional case only does the boy appear to be the one who calls a halt, with the girl willing to go further.

The implications which may be derived from this data, taken together with known facts of biological and psychological reactions to sex-oriented activities, make possible the synthesis of relatively reliable principles relating to the sexual behavior of adolescent boys and girls.

1. Opportunity is an important factor in determining how much sexual activity takes place between boys and girls and how far it goes. This fact substantiates the feelings of many parents that it is their responsibility to exercise close enough control over their sons and daughters to reduce opportunity to a reasonable minimum. Current customs of adolescent boys and girls having access to an automobile at night, without the presence of other people, will inevitably produce a greater amount of sexual activity in such couples than would otherwise take place.[24] Possession of living facilities insuring privacy, and access to the home of either the boy or the girl without the presence of parents, will do likewise. Obviously, it is not practical to chaperon boys and girls to the extent that it is physically impossible for them to engage in activities objected to by their parents. It would be undesirable to so chaperon them even if it were possible, because they must learn to assume increasing responsibility for self-control and self-direction. They cannot properly be guarded until their coming of age and then given the complete freedom which they can take whether parents desire it or not. At the same time, the liberties permitted them should not be of such a nature and extent as to expose them to temptations from their normal biological urges that they are hardly mature enough emotionally to cope with. The widespread adoption of legal statutes prohibiting the sale of alcoholic beverages to teenagers finds a reasonable analogy in the undesirability of exposing them to easy opportunity for sexual misbehavior.

2. The amount of time during which a boy and girl engage in sexually stimulating activities is an important determinant of how far the activities go. Girls are slower than boys to become sexually aroused; however, when fully aroused, their sexual desires are little, if any, less compelling than are those of the boy. During an evening spent together at a

24 W. W. Wattenberg, *The Adolescent Years*. Harcourt, Brace and Company, New York, 1955.

dance, or otherwise in the company of others, the relations between the boy and the girl may or may not have been of a nature that the girl is partially or fully aroused sexually by the time the two enter an automobile to drive home, reach the girl's home, or otherwise achieve an opportunity for privacy and some degree of sexual activity. If she is aroused and the boy is also, little time is required to reach the stage of intercourse. If she is not aroused, however, an extremely limited amount of available time is unlikely to see her aroused to the point of losing the control she might normally keep over their activities.

Except in the case of a boy and a girl who have already developed a mutually acceptable pattern of sexual activity, such activity typically begins with kissing and hugging. Progression to greater intimacies usually is a gradual process, how fast or slow depending both upon the aggressiveness of the boy and whether or not the girl is emotionally prepared for greater intimacies. Prolongation of erotic activities, kissing and hugging, fondling of the girl by the boy, normally produces some degree of excitation of the girl, and as she becomes aroused, it becomes more difficult for her to call a halt to activities of which she may disapprove, yet which she is enjoying and in which her biological reactions demand that she go further. She must cope not only with the desires and aggressiveness of the boy, but also with her own wayward and sometimes unwanted, but powerful, biological urges. Adolescent girls should know that every moment spent in erotic play, particularly beyond the stage of a short kiss or embrace, renders it increasingly difficult for them to maintain control of the situation. Permitting caresses beyond a simple embrace is the most crucial point in a girl's losing control of the limits to which erotic activities go.[25] Contrary to the prejudgment of psychologists who had estimated that permitting the boy's hand inside the girl's clothing was the crucial point at which limitation of further intimacies became most difficult, extensive interviews with girls on the psychodynamics of sexual activities placed the crucial point at permitting caresses of the breasts even outside the clothing.

3. The girl's self concept (probably more than dogmatic ideas of morality, i.e., what is right and wrong) is a crucial factor in determining how far she goes and how successfully she resists pressures within herself and without to exceed her concept of propriety.[26] Envisioning herself

[25] W. W. Ehrmann, "Student Cooperation in a Study of Dating Behavior," *Marriage and Family Living*, 1952, *14*:322–326.

[26] S. M. Jourard, *Personal Adjustment*. The Macmillan Company, New York, 1958.

as a person who skillfully avoids being led beyond her own standards, possessing genuine superiority by virtue of her ability to maintain self-control and self-mastery under all circumstances, and taking supreme pride in her resistance to overpersuasion constitutes her best possible protection against sexual exploitation. The same attitudes on the part of the boy will often facilitate his control of his sexual activities. A strongly established sense of morality is perhaps proportionately more important in his case than in the case of the girl, because whereas the girl's self concept typically undergoes a severe devaluation as a result of sexual activity to which she has not become habituated, the boy's self concept is seldom seriously injured and in many instances is actually strengthened. This, of course, is a logical result of the fact that socially disapproved sexual relations with a girl typically symbolize to the boy his mastery of her, while to the girl such relations symbolize her having been overcome or humiliated and, in addition, as such girls often express it, "played for a sucker."

Treating adolescents with dignity and respect, in and out of the home, becomes important as a very real means of strengthening their sexual morality, especially in the case of girls, for the reasons just cited. A girl whose self-respect is weak by reason of parental attitudes which devaluate her ego, or from other causes, will find it extremely difficult to find within herself the resources to withstand anything approaching persistent sexual aggressiveness on the part of a boy. If, through over-informality in the home, she lacks a strong sense of the privacy and in-violability of her body (and this is a major reason why corporal pun-ishment of girls, especially by the father, should be discontinued at a relatively early age), her task in maintaining its inviolability against the overtures of boys she dates is multiplied.

4. Frequent dates involving the same boy and girl are more likely to result in sexual activities, and more intimate activities, than are a boy's or girl's dates scattered among several members of the opposite sex. "Go-ing steady," in the sense of confining dates to one member of the oppo-site sex, multiplies the likelihood of sexual intimacies. This is due to several factors: The simplest is that whenever a boy and girl reach a given stage of intimacy with each other, progressing to that stage tends to be taken for granted by both parties on the next date and accom-plished relatively quickly. It is almost inevitable that erotic play, if con-tinued, will result in increasing intimaces, and each date will tend to see some greater degree of intimacy than the one before, simply because

as fast as one degree of intimacy comes to be taken for granted, biological and psychological pressures in both boy and girl urge further exploration. An intimacy which would shock the sensibilities of one or both parties if engaged in suddenly, without preliminaries, seems much less worthy of protest when it constitutes only a slight advance over a pattern of conduct to which both have become accustomed.

A more subtle, but potent, factor in the increasing intimacies which develop as dates between the same boy and girl multiply is the increasing acceptance of the other as "one of the family," in the sense of being so familiar that reserve maintained with others is hardly worth bothering with. Basically nonsexually motivated activities involving casual intimacies of speech, movements, actions, and lack of concealments establish an emotional climate making possible sudden achievement of a high degree of unpremeditated erotic intimacy. "It's only Johnny" easily becomes "As long as it's only Johnny there's nothing really wrong with. . . ."

"Going steady" multiplies the likelihood of sexual intimacies not only because it promotes frequent dates and inevitably produces the lessened reserve just mentioned; the social pattern of the United States condones behaviors between male and female who confine their heterosexual activities to each other that it does not condone under other circumstances, and thus lessens apparent social pressure against behavior between "steadies" which would be considered unbecoming between others.

5. Lack of love and affection in the home increases the likelihood of an adolescent, particularly an adolescent girl, engaging in sexual intimacies. Conversely, a feeling of love and affection within the home, a feeling of security and acceptance, lessens the likelihood of such indiscretions.[27] The girl who is starved for love tends to seek it. Insecurity and lack of affection within the home are typically accompanied by lack of clarity in evaluation of human relations and emotional reactions. This is natural, because such evaluations typically take place in the frame of reference provided by the person's interpersonal relations with parents in the formative years of his life; where such relations are erratic or unsatisfying, the child's, the subsequent adolescent's, and even the later adult's ability to achieve a good perspective on personal relations and the emotional factors involved is injured. Therefore, the adolescent who lacks the normal experience of emotional warmth within the home is

27 O. S. English and G. H. J. Pearson, *Emotional Problems of Living*. W. W. Norton & Company, Inc., New York, 1955.

particularly subject to maladjustive attempts to cope with interpersonal relations and emotionalized situations.

Thus, it is easy for the adolescent who is seeking, through outside-the-home relationships, to achieve the feeling of security resulting from being loved or wanted to seek this gratification in inappropriate and maladjustive ways. He has not had sufficient experience in normal emotional relations to be able to distinguish between wholesome and satisfactory ones and unwholesome and unsatisfactory ones. Usually we find the adolescent boy seeking such security and satisfying relationships through a gang. Adolescent girls frequently seek their feeling of being loved and cherished through permitting physical intimacies. Being held closely and passionately in a boy's arms, being kissed, fondled, and caressed, is to her a type of love and security, even though temporary. The adolescent whose relations within the home provide a sense of security not only feels less need to seek acceptance through sexual activities; he or she also feels free to discuss dawning problems of sexual adjustment with parents or counselors and forestall possible undesirable situations.

Case of Iris Idson

At the age of seventeen, Iris Idson, the only child of a well-to-do family, has a history of three years of sexual promiscuity. At the age of fourteen, while her mother was in the hospital for a prolonged period of time, she had her first affair. The man was a married, twenty-year-old orderly in the hospital. Iris says she never really cared for him, but was struck by his looks and set out to attract his attention and date him, although she knew he was married. After an affair of about three months he moved away.

Next was a boy with whom she went steady. They had frequent sexual relations for several months until he started going with another girl. A man about her father's age, indeed a business acquaintance of her father's, was her most recent paramour. He broke off the relationship fearing that it would develop into a threat to his home. In between, Iris has had intercourse with several of her classmates and college boys. She has never reached a climax in sexual relations, and does not enjoy them. Boys and men want them, she says, and she enjoys the kissing, fondling, and being held in someone's arms that go with them. Now, she says, she has a bad reputation at school, and boys ask her for dates for only one reason. A nice group of girls who were her companions in junior high school have unobtrusively dropped her.

Her mother has been an invalid since her hospitalization, and the father is preoccupied with her. Over and over Iris says, "I don't *want* to do those things. All I want is one person, just *one*, who loves me more than anything else in the world." Iris is a straight A student in the twelfth grade, attractive, and loved in the neighborhood for her habit of taking the neighbors' children for a ride in her car, buying them ice cream, and generally being their benefactress. Her parents and neighbors know nothing of her lurid experiences. She asks help in working out a better plan of life.

1. From the information given, what is probably the cause of Iris' promiscuity?

2. What can be implied from Iris' "mothering" young children of the neighborhood?

SEXUAL BEHAVIOR
AND MENTAL HEALTH

Earlier in the chapter it was intimated that the clear intent of this chapter, to encourage greater reserve and less physical intimacies than often finally result between adolescent boys and girls, has its roots less in moral standards than in the necessities of mental health. The implications of premarital sexual intimacies in the emotional adjustment of both boys and girls deserve serious consideration. They are substantially different for the two sexes and usually more potent for girls than boys, although there are important implications for boys.

Devaluation of the boy's self concept as a result of premarital sexual activities resulting in intimacies up to and including intercourse is seldom great. If he has had strict moral upbringing, he may have more or less severe pangs of guilt; sometimes these guilt feelings produce real problems of emotional adjustment for him, but not often, particularly if he is a generally well-adjusted boy. Even where guilt feelings are present, and certainly where they are not, the masculine association of sexual relations with a female to whom he is not "entitled" by convention with personal conquest, success, mastery, and dominance usually results in such relations inflating, rather than devaluating, his self concept.

However, from the standpoint of long-term emotional adjustment, the boy also suffers, as well as achieving ego inflation. Repeated intimacies with different girls subtly devaluate his concept of the female sex. It also lessens the never-too-great emotional significance which he attaches to sexual relations. Both of these changes significantly lessen his emotional suitability for marriage, and both will make more difficult the adjustments he will have to make to achieve a happy marriage with any girl. Furthermore, ego inflation of the type thus achieved is itself maladjusting and dangerous. It inclines the boy toward self-indulgence as a way of life, toward an attitude that fulfillment of his desires justifies whatever he must do to achieve it, and toward a familiar manner with girls which other boys sense and may resent. It does not expose him to the degree of social disapproval risked by the girl, but produces subtle changes in his emotional structure rendering him less competent to cope with the adjustmental problems of a normal later adult life.

Quite apart from the threat of pregnancy, which inevitably hovers over the girl who permits increasing sexual intimacies which are likely to culminate in intercourse, serious emotional problems may occur if she has had what America generally thinks of as conventional upbringing and moral education. The mere fact of a physical change in her body resulting from intercourse, irremediable and, when marriage takes place, possibly embarrassing, is enough to produce serious emotional problems in many girls. This "loss of virginity," even in an age of "emancipation" of women and with the relative loosening of social standards, is a traumatic experience for many girls. Its full effect is more often felt days after the occurrence than at the immediate time, when the emotion usually accompanying her surrender to biological urges insulates her against distress.

Often the dawning of love for a boy other than her sexual partner causes an increase in the nonvirgin's feelings of guilt and anxiety. She feels (often correctly, unjust though it may be) that her loved one will not want her if or when he discovers that she has been intimate with another boy. The prospect of telling him of her situation is embarrassing in the extreme. Even worse, often reducing her to an emotional state bordering on neurosis, is her fear that her honeymoon may be marked by her husband's suspecting that she has previously been intimate with another man. Even premarital intimacy with a fiancé whom she subsequently marries is frequently accompanied by severe guilt and anxiety feelings, attached less to the act itself than to her fears that her husband may suspect her of intimacy with other men as well. In instances where some domestic disharmony arises (and in what marriage do they not?), the husband many times actually does reproach his wife with alleged premarital promiscuity. Such wives may well become emotional casualties and the integrity of their homes become jeopardized by their defensive, but maladjustive, attitudes and reactions.

Some psychiatrists and psychologists feel that it is generally better for a girl to fabricate a plausible explanation for the premarital rupture of her hymen, rather than tell her fiancé or husband of its real cause. Such ruptures do very commonly take place, not only through athletics and vigorous exercise (even from an isolated incident of stretching or straining), but also from gynecological examinations and treatments and douches. While it is difficult for a professional person to counsel deliberate prevarication and deception, it also seems a needless contribution to future unhappiness and tragedy (of which life contains so much, at best) to insist on an honesty which lays the basis for distrust, jealousy, and unhappiness of an innocent person (the fiancé or husband), with no possibility of anything except injury to all concerned. Actually the "guilty" person may experience marked relief by a "confession" which shifts the decision as to what must now be done from her own shoulders to the mate's. Thus, the urge to "make a clean breast of it" is often a disguised self-indulgence by which the erring party seeks to purchase escape from feelings of guilt at the cost of distress of the partner.

Obviously, not all girls will suffer such traumatic effects from a sexual indiscretion. The most sensitive, the ones with genuinely high moral principles who experienced an hour of weakness or were carried away by an unaccustomed emotion, the ones with well-developed consciences, are the chief sufferers. In short, the "better" the girl by conventional moral and social standards, the greater the likelihood of her suffering more or less permanent emotional damage from a lapse from her standards.

Lest it be thought that the traumatic effects of loss of chastity are being exaggerated, it should be recognized that every clinical psychologist and psychiatrist can produce from his files dozens of cases in which a sexual indiscretion was the primary or contributing cause of a woman's becoming his patient. Marriage counselors can cite dozens of cases where a premarital indiscretion on the part of the wife had become a major threat to the success of a marriage, even though her self concept was strong enough to prevent the event's having had a noticeably injurious psychological effect on her. The author's own files contain one case in which a girl's premarital sexual experience with the man she soon married constituted a major factor in a neurosis which became disablingly acute after *thirty years* of marriage to the man.

For every girl whose premarital sexual experience produces an emotional problem severe enough to require psychotherapy, there are dozens who suffer lesser agonies or who become victims of "nervous breakdowns" or somatic ailments such as migraine headaches, digestive troubles, and almost the entire range of physical symptoms, from no cause whatever except malfunction of their bodies caused by emotional problems, without the true source of their problems ever coming to light. Frequently a girl undergoing unbearable pangs of remorse as a result of her indiscretion will actually throw herself into an orgy of sexual misconduct, seeking by a furious life of passion to drown the voice of accusing memory and conscience. Sometimes she does so seeking the momentary security of love and affection which she wistfully reads each time into the sexual relation.

Even where no observable effects take place in a girl's personality structure and emotional health as a result of her loss of virginity, most psychologists and psychiatrists believe that there is a subtle lessening of her self-respect and lowering of her self concept. Psychologists and psychiatrists suspect that people who seem to have achieved even greatest "emancipation from bourgeois concepts of morality," the bohemians and beatniks of various generations, are often engaging in a desperate attempt at self-deception, seeking a better self concept through denial that the virtue lost in their own eyes was worthwhile. It is almost inevitable that some self-devaluation will take place when a girl engages in conduct which she knows would cause many other members of society to lower their opinion of her, no matter how well she rationalizes her actions and thinking.

Occasionally, workers with adolescents who have the confidence of their boys and girls are approached by a girl (less frequently a boy) who seeks adult help in dealing with her own feelings regarding a misstep she has made. Only your common sense can determine whether you should refer such a girl to a psychotherapist. Where her distress seems only moderate, and where psychotherapeutic resources are difficult to reach, it may not be feasible. In the absence of a clinical psychologist or psychiatrist, a sympathetic counselor with some psychological training is usually the best person available to help her. Best help usually takes these forms:

1. *Letting her achieve emotional "catharsis" by talking her problem out with you.* Let *her* talk as much as she will. Simply expressing her feelings to an adult who is sympathetic, *noncritical,* and *noncondemnatory* not only helps to relieve her emotional tension, but also may check her self-devaluation, which would cause future misbehavior. If an adult, admired and respected by her, does not reject her as a result of what she has done, perhaps there is reason, she feels, to hope that she is not already lost. Maybe it *is* worthwhile to try to do better in the future!

2. *Reassuring her that one misstep does not doom her to the status of a "bad," "soiled," or immoral girl.* Help her to see her problem in perspective with her life—a moment of surrender to temptation which may have been overpowering, and her real blame attaching to having allowed herself to get into the indiscreet situation in which the temptation could become overpowering. This displacement of guilt to mismanagement of a social situation, rather than morbid self-accusations of depravity, hopeless sinfulness, and moral degradation, is not a palliative to her conscience, not helping her avoid her "just deserts" of "paying the penalty" of her misbehavior. Rather, it is an intelligent focusing of her attention on how to avoid situations which might produce another such episode, and *attempting to prevent a self-devaluation* which would incline her toward future misbehavior through a feeling of "I'm a bad girl anyway."

3. *Helping her understand her feelings and motives which led to her indiscretion.* By understanding them and how they cause her to lower her moral defenses, she can guard against such happenings in the future.

It should be emphasized that if the girl's emotional state is not an ordinary adolescent girl's upset, if it persists for weeks or if it is accompanied by somatic symptoms other than minor loss of appetite and sleep disturbance, she should be referred to a clinical psychologist or psychiatrist. On the other hand, just as first aid is indicated in the case of minor physical injuries or in the absence of the possibility of medical treatment, the above three suggestions can be wonderfully helpful when circumstances render professional psychotherapy impractical.

And the question "Should I tell my parents?" This can seldom be answered dogmatically, here or in your work. If she is severely in need of constant support and reassurance, and feels she could count on it from her parents, probably yes. If psychotherapy is required, their knowing about it is usually a necessity. *Avoid advising her, specifically and defi-*

nitely, not to tell her parents, unless she is of legal age. Naturally, the younger she is the less you would consider her not telling them. On the other hand, if you believe their attitude would injure her self concept rather than help her cope with her feelings of guilt and anxiety, you are under no obligation to encourage her to confide in them.

Helping a girl develop a perspective whereby a sexual delinquency becomes an experience from which she grows wiser and more self-possessed, rather than promiscuous, is one of the most rewarding experiences a worker with adolescents will have.

Questions re Case of Iris Idson

3. What effect do you imagine Iris' sexual experiences have had on her self concept? On what do you base your evaluation?

4. How can Iris best be helped now?

PROBLEM AREAS IN
ADOLESCENT SEXUAL ADJUSTMENT

Principles and Popularity

Gratification of biological urges is pleasant. Deliberate arousal of erotic excitement and subsequent gratification produce pleasurable sensations. It is socially and morally disapproved of for the unmarried, but enjoyable. In every age of life there are people who place their immediate pleasure and gratification of their senses above all else, and adolescent boys and girls are no exception. Thus, boys or girls who wish to maintain the standards of sexual behavior demanded by religion, society, and mental health will more or less frequently come into conflict with those who place immediate sensual pleasure above these more important considerations. The boy has the problem less often, because of his psychosexual and biological nature already discussed. The girl faces it frequently, as boys whom she dates strive to use their association as a means of stimulating and then gratifying enjoyable sexual sensations.[28, 29, 30]

28 O. M. Butterfield, *Love Problems of Adolescents,* Teachers College Contributions to Education No. 768, Bureau of Publications, Teachers College, Columbia University, New York, 1939.

29 L. D. Rockwood and M. E. M. Ford, *Youth, Marriage and Parenthood.* John Wiley & Sons, Inc., New York, 1945.

30 M. W. Wood, *Living Together in the Family.* American Home Economics Society, Washington, D. C., 1946.

Equally important in many instances is the boy's desire to experience ego-satisfying sensations through overcoming the girl's unwillingness, "mastering" or "conquering" her will to resist him, and experiencing a sense of victorious dominance.

Those are the dynamics behind the perennial conflict between complete popularity and maintaining personal principles and standards. Boys and girls who have few inhibitions about enjoying the sensations of sexual intimacies tend to prefer to date others who feel the same, rather than those whose principles usually will deprive them of the desired gratifications. Girls will find it easier to make and stick to decisions as to the extent to which permitting intimacies is a personally acceptable way of attracting numerous dates or of holding the attentions of a particular boy if they understand the boy's psychological motivation as well as his biological one. A girl's realization that her sexual partner regards her acquiescence or cooperation as surrender, as her helplessness to resist his charm, skill, and superior cleverness, and that some of his desire for physical intimacies with her is prompted by his desire to prove that he can do with her whatever pleases him, can greatly alter a girl's attitude toward such activities. We have already seen that this many times is true. However, most adolescent girls are completely unaware of this masculine motivation. It is both strange and unfortunate that programs of sex education concentrate so heavily on the physical aspects of sex and neglect so sadly the psychological aspects, which are tremendously important in understanding the true issues involved in heterosexual relations.

Abstract principles of morality may melt drastically under the heat of moments of passion. If these abstractions can be reinforced by more concrete and ego-involved attitudes regarding boy-girl relations, the adolescent, particularly the girl, stands a much better chance of retaining her perspective and control of her behavior under severe temptation. The knowledge that her partner characteristically is motivated by a desire to bring her into subjection (not, as in her own case, merely to engage in mutual enjoyment of each other) will enable many girls with healthy self-respect to avoid compromising themselves even when their abstract moral standards might prove inadequate.

It is trite but accurate to point out that popularity of the type bought by permitting physical intimacies, by and large, is a devaluating, not an ego-strengthening, type of popularity. Achieving dates by this means inevitably results in a girl's devaluation of herself as she begins to feel that she is merely a body to boys, not a person of personal attractiveness and desirability. She feels, quite rightly, that she is used as a good thing and appreciated only as a convenient object on which to gratify biological urges. This devaluation is, as noted above, inevitable when popularity is purchased by means inherently injurious to the self concept. The lowered self concept, then, makes easier future behavior which lowers the self concept even more, and a vicious circle is established.

Human dignity is sacrificed when principles are sacrificed to means of achieving ends, popularity or other. This injures anyone's mental health.

An adolescent boy or girl is a member of a society, a society he or she must adapt to in some way or else live the social life of a hermit. This society is composed of boys and girls of about the same age, and is, in reality, the only society available to the adolescent, since he is not accepted in adult social life and has also outgrown childish play and associations. Since the adolescent, because of his urgent developmental need for socialization, is even more dependent on social acceptance for satisfying living than is the adult, he is, therefore, under powerful pressure to conform, to accept the standards and practices of the majority of teenagers in his locale.

This combination of psychological and social facts sometimes places both the adolescent and his parents on the horns of a dilemma. When the practices of adolescents in a community, concerning hours kept, use of automobiles, customs regarding dances, parties, and other social activities, and the more personal matter of dating practices and customary behavior on dates, vary markedly from the standards of judgment and propriety of a boy or girl or the parents, it poses a problem. It is all very well to say that one should have nothing to do with "the crowd" if the crowd's standards violate his own, but socialization on the part of the adolescent is not merely a matter of pleasure, it is an essential for wholesome growth and development, just as are eating, sleeping, and exercising.

Occasionally the prevailing group of a community has adopted behavior patterns patently unacceptable to individual adolescents or their parents. Abandoning one's principles and standards is fraught with danger to mental health and well-being, as we have already seen, not just presently offensive to one's morals. In such a situation, the obvious conclusion to reach is that where the customs and standards of the majority of adolescents violate one's own, extraordinary effort should be made to locate *some* boys and girls whose standards and customs conform to one's own and differ from those of the majority, in order that the adolescent's needed socialization may be achieved.

Interestingly enough, adolescents and even their parents frequently fail to actively explore this possibility when faced with the dilemma of a group whose behavior is not that desired by or for a particular boy or girl. Their attention is so painfully focused on the prevailing majority that it excludes recognition of the invariable minority who are also desirous of holding aloof, particularly if the custom of the majority offends good taste or discretion. Time after time the worker with adolescents will be approached by parents and, if alert, will sense a similar attitude in adolescents, expressing dissatisfaction with prevailing teenage social customs. Their attention needs to be directed to locating other "isolates" so that the "nonconformist" adolescents can get together into their own subsociety.

The solution is good, but it usually requires both tact and persuasion to interest either parents or adolescents in it. Typically, the youth worker finds one of two attitudes: either the parents feel that the other isolates are not of the social class they want their children to associate with (and higher as well as lower classes are often thus shunned), or the adolescent feels that they are "droops." Often both attitudes exist. Parents may have to decide whether their class prejudices outweigh their dislike of prevailing customs, and adolescents, too, must make their decisions when such situations arise.

Promiscuity

The sexually promiscuous person is seldom, if ever, an emotionally mature, well-adjusted person, at least in the social atmosphere of the United States. Although some sexual immorality characterizes the lives of a large segment of the population, the general social attitude is one of disapproval of extramarital sexual intimacies, and in the lives of most violaters of the code the violations are isolated instances, not habitual. In working with young people it is worthwhile to distinguish between one isolated, or even an occasional, instance of giving way to temptation and an habitual seeking of emotional or sensual gratification through sexual activities. The former behavior suggests immaturity and lack of self-discipline and reasonable forethought. The latter is symptomatic of emotional maladjustment.

Promiscuity suggests to the clinician a probable deficiency in either one of three areas, although other factors may at times account for it. In the case of an adolescent boy (or adult male, of course), promiscuity may be due to lack of self-confidence and the need for constant reassurance of his sociosexual prowess. Clinical studies of males who established impressive records of the number of women seduced or with whom they achieved sexual relations without seduction suggest that many such men suffered from markedly low self concepts, with resultant feelings of inferiority and the need to repeatedly demonstrate a capacity for mastery. The ego-inflating effect of sexual conquest on the part of the male has already been discussed. Usually sexual activities are the chosen field for such compensatory, self-reassuring pursuits when the basic inferiority consciously or unconsciously felt by the male is in the area of his masculinity. Deficient self-perceptions in other areas are more likely to call forth compensatory activities of more directly appropriate types, preoccupation with making money, achieving social status, or the like.

In the case of the boy whose upbringing has not included the development of conventional standards of morality, the dynamics of promiscuity may be simpler: he engages in sexual relations because he enjoys the physical sensation of intercourse and the psychological sensation of mastery and has no conflicting inhibitions to prevent their full indulgence. Even in the case of such a person, often referred to as amoral, meaning *lacking* moral standards rather than *violating* moral standards which he does possess, promiscuity suggests intellectual or emotional poverty. Sexual gratification is a source of pleasure which people of general competence seldom exploit so greatly, because they have other interests, enjoyments, and sources of pleasure, success, and achievement. The person of emotional poverty and personality defects uses promiscuity as an attempt to fill the void in his life caused by his deficiencies in other areas.

In the case of the adolescent girl who becomes promiscuous, the cause is likely to be the seeking for affection and security previously mentioned. This renders her a genuine object of pity, although, by her attitude toward those who would help her, she often makes it difficult to prevent feelings of pity from being crushed by exasperation and disgust. It should be borne in mind that, to her, the attempts to help may appear to be threats to deprive her of the modicum of feeling of security and being loved which she has been able to obtain. She fights such efforts to help her, because she considers them just other instances of adults depriving her of the affection and security she seeks.

Attempting to assist either a boy or girl whose promiscuity results from these three psychological needs is usually a job for a clinical psychologist or psychiatrist. "Environmental" treatment, attempting to provide recreation, interests, and friends on other bases, is of limited utility, because the behavior pattern is not based upon deprivations in those areas, but in the deeper area of imperfectly completed developmental tasks and the lack of satisfaction of basic psychological needs.[31]

Promiscuity sometimes results simply from an amoral or immoral girl's capitalizing on her body as a source of income. Best evidence, however, indicates that such cases are a small minority. Giving her body as a price for acceptance by a social group is written about more than it happens, and it is questionable whether it will happen in the case of an emotionally normal girl. Low intelligence is a factor both in boys' and girls' immorality, but to a much smaller degree than is commonly thought. The boy of low intelligence may resort to sexual activities as an easy way of achieving pleasure, and the girl of low intelligence is more easily led into such activities than her more intelligent sister. Certainly, as has been implied, normal adolescent boys and girls sometimes engage in sexual misbehavior simply because of the desires of the moment coupled with the opportunity. Nevertheless, the explanation of the majority of premarital sexual activities, and particularly when those activities reach the point of constituting promiscuity, is usually to be found in the emotional structure of the boy or girl. Punitive measures and symptomatic treatment, such as trying to prevent heterosexual associations, will be minimally effective in preventing continued promiscuity, because the behavior is elicited by deep-seated psychological needs rather than by opportunism or whims.

Questions re Case of Iris Idson

    5. To what extent do you imagine Iris' moral standards were responsible for her becoming promiscuous?

    6. What are Iris' chances of achieving good social relationships and a happy, well-adjusted life?

Differing Socioeconomic Status

With notable exceptions, moral standards among boys and girls from families of low socioeconomic status and of low educational level are

[31] E. G. Lion, H. M. Jambor, H. G. Corrigan, and K. P. Bradway, *An Experiment in the Psychiatric Treatment of Promiscuous Girls.* Department of Public Health, San Francisco, 1945.

lower than those prevailing in the middle and upper socioeconomic groups.[32, 33, 34, 35] This is to be expected, from a rational standpoint. Numerous studies have demonstrated that lower socioeconomic groups attach greater importance to gratifying their immediate desires and less to striving for long-range goals than do higher socioeconomic groups. This, too, confirms logical expectations, in that those people who work to accumulate capital in the form of money, education, or vocational advantage, rather than spending their time and money as it becomes available on pleasures of the moment, have a tendency to move out of the lower socioeconomic group into a more affluent class. Therefore, a selective factor exists in that families remaining in the lower socioeconomic group have, as a group, attached less importance to self-denial for the sake of their own ultimate welfare than have those who have progressed to a more advantageous socioeconomic level.

Most professional workers with adolescents come from the middle or upper socioeconomic classes. Such adults generally are imbued with the standards and values traditional to their classes. A certain proportion of the boys and girls with whom they work do *not* come from these classes and do *not* share the values of the teachers or counselors or the values toward which the adolescents from the middle and upper socioeconomic classes arc being directed. This causes rather severe problems in education; neither the pupils nor their parents, as groups, attach the importance to homework and preparing oneself for the future that teachers and a middle-class-dominated educational program does. It also causes problems in the area of sexual adjustment in that adolescents from the less affluent segments of society tend to demonstrate heterosexual behaviors unacceptable to the standards of many teachers, counselors, and schools. Language, personal remarks, actions toward the opposite sex, public demonstrations of sexually oriented affection, all must be evaluated and dealt with by youth workers with the boy's or girl's home background or environmental conditioning in mind if anything constructive is to be accomplished. Punishment of behavior which violates the standards of society is ineffective in dealing with a segment of

[32] L. B. Hohman and B. Schaffner, "The Sex Lives of Unmarried Men," *American Journal of Sociology,* 1947, 52:501–507.

[33] A. deB. Hollingshead, *Elmtown's Youth.* John Wiley & Sons, Inc., New York, 1949.

[34] A. C. Kinsey, W. B. Pomeroy, and C. E. Martin, *Sexual Behavior in the Human Male.* W. B. Saunders Company, Philadelphia, 1948.

[35] A. C. Kinsey, W. B. Pomeroy, C. E. Martin, and P. H. Gebhard, *Sexual Behavior in the Human Female.* W. B. Saunders Company, Philadelphia, 1953.

society which has its own differing standards and which gives bigger and more consistent rewards for acting according to those norms than the penalties that the larger society gives for violating them. Education and inspiration, showing boys and girls the superior ultimate advantages of self-discipline and long-range goals, is a slow and often discouraging process, but in the long run may cope effectively with the problem of the behavior of the "underprivileged" boy or girl. Of course, the chance of success is multiplied if the underprivileged adolescent can also be given some of the advantages of his more fortunate age-mates in the form of recreational advantages and living conditions which increase personal dignity and self-respect rather than encourage self-devaluation and mal-adjustive behavior.

Heterosexual activities crossing class lines pose special problems. Boys and girls tend overwhelmingly to date others within their own socio-economic group, or very close to it, but numerous exceptions occur. Boys frequently date girls from a socioeconomic class lower than their own. Girls less often date boys noticeably lower in socioeconomic status than themselves, but sometimes do. The psychodynamics of cross-class dating are worthy of special consideration because of their potential effect on the lives of both the boys and the girls.[36]

Sometimes boys date girls from a socioeconomic class lower than their own simply because a boy finds a girl in that stratum whose looks and personality appeal to him more than do any of the girls in his own class. Sometimes his motive is found in the fact that association with a girl of lower socioeconomic status enhances his own self concept by contrast. The boy's parents may object, but seldom strongly, unless the girl personally, as well as in her background, deviates conspicuously from their own standards. Less frequently do the girl's parents object; if so, it is usually on the grounds that the boy would not have serious (or "honorable") intentions toward her.

Often the boy dates a girl from a socioeconomic background lower than his because of the better possibilities of exploiting her sexually. We have already mentioned the lower moral standards which prevail (again, be it noted that there are outstanding exceptions) as one descends the socioeconomic ladder. Added to this statistically greater chance of finding a girl from a socioeconomic class lower than his own amenable to sexual intimacies than a girl from his own class are even more influen-

36 W. W. Ehrmann, "Student Cooperation in a Study of Dating Behavior," *Marriage and Family Living*, 1952, *14*:322–326.

tial factors that render these girls more susceptible to exploitation. Typically, girls want to improve their lot in life, and marriage to a boy of superior social and financial standing is a way of doing so. Even if he is a relatively poor matrimonial prospect, through dating him and thus presumably becoming acquainted with others of his own group, a girl may hope to develop a circle of acquaintances of greater prestige and position than she would have without him as a means of entree into his group. With the entree, dates with other and perhaps more eligible boys are possible. On a simpler level, the boy of superior socioeconomic resources can take a girl to more appealing and glamorous places, in more luxurious fashion, and entertain her more elaborately, than can boys in her own class. For all these things many girls are prepared, if not willing, to make concessions in their behavior and the behavior permitted their escort. They will, thus, sometimes permit intimacies which they would otherwise not permit, rather than lose the chance to enjoy the luxuries their association with the boy provides or the hoped-for opportunity of bettering their life prospects. In such situations the boy is in an advantageous "bargaining position" and frequently uses it to gratify his sexual desires.[37] The additional appeal to the sense of mastery offered by such an advantageous position is obvious.

The girl from a low socioeconomic class, on the other hand, is less accustomed to woman's equality and dignity than are girls from higher socioeconomic groups (women's proportionate position in relation to men rises as one ascends the socioeconomic ladder), and her submission is likely to require less sacrifice on her part than might be expected. Such exploitation is detrimental to both parties, however. The lowered self concept and dignity of the girl is obvious. The boy is receiving, meanwhile, unfortunate training in the policy of "might makes right." He is also learning habits of self-indulgence, violation of moral and ethical codes, and developing, unconsciously if not consciously, attitudes toward women which will make a happy marriage more difficult for him to achieve.

The girl who consistently dates one boy of a socioeconomic status lower than her own may, of course, also be motivated solely by preference for his company, looks, and personality, or because she finds him personally more pleasing than boys in her own group. It may also be, and not infrequently is, because she is not popular in her own group and

37 E. B. Hurlock, *Adolescent Development*. McGraw-Hill Book Company, Inc., New York, 1955.

seeks companionship wherever she can find it. The girl's parents are much more likely to object strenuously to a daughter's dating an "unsuitable" boy, where "unsuitability" is confined solely to social class, than if it were a son's so doing. This perhaps is reasonable, since the presumption is that the son would raise the girl he marries to his own class level, while the husband's earning power and the nature of social mobility would more usually cause the daughter to drop to his level rather than his rising to hers. Also, a girl normally wants a boy she can "look up to," and it is much more difficult to look up to a person whose socioeconomic status is notably lower than one's own. This may not be an admirable or ethical attitude for a person to hold, but it is a psychologically natural one.

It is hardly going too far to say that most such instances are the result of definite neurotic tendencies or attitudes on the part of the girl. Resentment of her parents may cause her, as a form of revenge, to deliberately choose a boy friend as different from them in class and standards as possible or one whom they will dislike and worry about her associating with. This is a dynamic factor in a considerable proportion of instances. Then, without any conscious thought of revenge, antagonism toward the parents may result in a rejection of their standards and "their kind of people" and lead her to seek her friends from as different a class of people as possible. Some girls are frankly attracted by masculine dominance and primeval, relatively uninhibited, expression of strength and ruthlessness (watching the reactions of numerous women to athletes, particularly boxers and wrestlers, readily substantiates this). In some girls the feminine willingness to be dominated and certain masochistic tendencies find gratification in the girls' subjugating themselves to more primitive treatment than they expect to experience from boys of their own class.

The boy dating a girl conspicuously above himself in social and economic background may be doing so because he finds her more personally appealing to him than any other girl he knows. If he has a normal masculine attitude, however, for the association to be successful for both of them requires good psychological adjustment on his part. Of course, he, like the girl who dates a boy from a higher prestige group than her own, may do so because of the possible financial and social advantages he might achieve through acquaintance with, or marriage into, such a group. If so, either he is deficient in the masculine need to feel capable of protecting and providing for his mate in a fashion suitable to her, he feels that his endowments and abilities are adequate for him actually to so provide for her, he so wants position and economic advantage that he is willing to sacrifice the role of head of the family to achieve them, or he simply is insensitive to such subtleties and wants the girl.

The first instance, in which the boy lacks the desire to carry out the masculine role, tends to result in successful marriages if the girl is able and content to assume the major responsibilities of the family. The second provides good possibilities for marriage when the boy's abilities are actually up to his estimation of them and when the girl is willing to undergo some deprivations until time permits the boy to achieve his full potential. An association in which the boy is willing to sacrifice his desire for the masculine role to achieve position and luxury he could not otherwise achieve is usually destined to unhappiness; the same weakness and tendency to self-indulgence leads to infidelity, failure to work competently and faithfully, and childish pettiness in domestic relations. The last instance provides unhappy prospects; all socioeconomic considerations aside, successful marriages are seldom based on insensitivity to important elements in human relations.

Case of Janet James and Ken Kendrick

Janet James is eighteen, five feet six inches tall, weighs 150 pounds, and has a pleasant face and disposition. She is failing in school. This is a source of some friction with her parents. The father is a dentist. But the main source of parental worry is her dating Ken Kendrick, seventeen, five feet five, 130 pounds, who has dropped out of school, left his parents' home, and is supporting himself working at a grocery store. Janet and Ken definitely plan to be married when Janet quits school, and their combined incomes will support them.

Janet's mother tells of Janet's love for her parents, brothers, and sisters. She works Saturdays and vacations, and spends most of her earnings on them. She worked the entire Christmas holidays last year, earning seventy-five dollars, all of which she spent on a coat for her mother. She is an obedient and cooperative daughter in every respect, except that she *will* date Ken. Her parents fear a marriage which they do not believe will be successful. She refuses to date any other boys. Janet has access to the family car and uses it in dating.

1. How might Janet's strong attachment to Ken be accounted for?

2. If parents approached you, Janet's homeroom teacher, for advice on handling this situation, what would you advise?

Masturbation and Sex Fantasies

Masturbation, the intentional stimulation of the genitals to induce sexual excitement and gratification, was long believed to produce various physical, mental, and emotional disorders such as mental deficiency, physical weakness, stunted growth, run-down conditions, susceptibility to fatigue, irritability or apathy, "nervous breakdowns," and many other undesirable results. Modern science has demonstrated that none of these fears is based on fact, and psychological studies have revealed that the majority of boys and a large minority of girls pass through a stage of more or less extensive masturbatory activities in the process of growing up. Like farm children eating green apples and city children candy and cokes, masturbation now appears to be a rather widespread, normal practice among adolescents which, while it should be discouraged as a mildly maladjustive way of fulfilling biological drives, is not productive or indicative of abnormality.[38, 39]

Sex fantasies usually accompany masturbation—mental images of sex objects and activities accompanying the biological conditions constituting sexual excitement. Considerable speculation has arisen that sexual fantasies incite adolescents, especially boys, to sexual misbehavior and even to rape, sadism, and other sex crimes. There is no evidence that such is the case; more often than not, the sex offender who employs violence is of a constitution for which mental activities and imagination would hold little attraction. In the case of a sex offender who presents a history of sexual fantasies, the likelihood is that a deeper psychological condition caused each behavior, not that one behavior caused the other.

The chief reason for discouraging masturbation and sexual fantasies is the same as for discouraging any other behavior which tends toward removing the person from reality, substituting imaginary activities for life-oriented activities that will develop the person into a more competent and successful one. It is another instance of creating imaginary successes and achievements instead of striving for real success, although in the present case the real success should be in a more socially approved area.

[38] F. Brown and R. T. Kempton, *Sex Questions and Answers*. McGraw-Hill Book Company, Inc., New York, 1950.

[39] J. C. Coleman, *Abnormal Psychology and Modern Life*. Scott, Foresman and Company, Chicago, 1956.

In considering the problems posed by the masturbating child or adolescent (we can assume that sexual fantasies are also present, especially in the case of the adolescent), the adult needs to seek the answer to such questions as: Why are there not socially approved real-life activities which would provide more satisfaction than these imaginary or introvertive ones? Why is he not feeling that there is more promise in real-life activities than in imaginary ones? Why does he show greater preoccupation with sexual matters than we would wish—Lack of adequate knowledge? The wrong kind? Frustration in normal heterosexual contacts? Mother-hostility or father-hostility reflected in a repressed sadistic tendency? Lack of normal heterosexual associations? Associations involving undesirable sexual stimulation or provocation?

Generally, a wholesome regime of exercise and physical activities and the opportunity to participate pleasantly and successfully in normal social activities will mitigate or remove tendencies toward excessive masturbation. After all, imaginary experiences and successes are poor substitutes for real-life pleasures, and will seldom be resorted to to any unwholesome extent if the more rewarding activities are possible. The real-life activities need not be of a sexual nature, of course; just normal opportunity for pleasurable activities is usually adequate. However, the child who has developed the solitary practices of masturbation and a life of fantasy may be deficient in social skills. Probably he has been engaging in his solitary pursuits while his age-mates were developing athletic or social skills. Indeed, he very likely *started* his introvertive activities because he was achieving insufficient success and acceptance among his fellows. Therefore, providing opportunity for his successful participation in socially oriented activities involves more than providing the physical existence of such activities and shoving him into them. It involves designing such activities in a manner that permits him to engage in them successfully and to become capable of participating in them, not tossing him into them, sink or swim. Providing interesting activities at home whereby the adolescent, as host or hostess, can invite friends, or some lessons in an athletic or social pursuit which will boost proficiency and enable him to achieve recognition among age-mates, are examples of effective ways of treating unwholesome tendencies toward masturbation and fantasy.

Homosexuality

Some boys and girls never achieve satisfactory identification with their own sex and fail to develop normal heterosexual feelings. When these conditions are accompanied by amorous or erotic feelings toward members of their own sex, it is known as homosexuality and the person possessing such feelings as a homosexual. Overt homosexuality, simulated sexual relations with a member of one's own sex, is officially a crime in all of the United States. Social feelings against its manifestation run very high, and homosexuals are usually intensely anxious lest their tendencies be discovered by people other than those with like tendencies. Some people fight hard against their sexual feelings that run so contrary to those of the mass of humanity, and develop severe emotional and personality disturbances as a result of the conflicts between their consciences and their psychosexual desires.

Definite evidence of the cause of homosexuality has not yet been obtained. Physical factors—physiological structure or biological functioning—seldom appear to have any bearing on the condition, although occasionally a homosexual is found who shows a hormone imbalance which would incline him or her toward the role of the opposite sex rather than the sex indicated by the person's external sexual organs. Against the idea that homosexuality is primarily of biologic origin is the finding of Beach[40] that giving a homosexual hormone injections appropriate to his or her sex tends to *increase* homosexual urges rather than lessen them. The difficulty in ascertaining the cause of homosexuality lies partly in the fact that its manifestations do not take *unmistakable* form until adolescence or even adulthood. By that time it is difficult or impossible to reconstruct the formative early years in sufficient detail to identify the crucial factors probably producing the aberration.

Using the suggestive evidence available, psychologists have formulated theories as to the dynamics of sexual identification—i.e., the factors which cause a little girl to begin to identify herself with women and respond to women in one way and to men in another, and the factors which cause little boys to identify and react differently. Failure to achieve appropriate identification is theorized to be the root of homosexuality. Colley[41] points out that practically from the day of a baby's birth parents give the infant a name, clothing, and soon toys which begin to give him or her appropriate sexual identification. Then the father acts in a subtly, but increasingly, different way toward his son than toward his daughter, while the role of the mother likewise reflects whether the child is of the same or a different sex from her. This treatment is

[40] F. A. Beach, *Hormones and Behavior*. Hoeber-Harper, New York, 1949.

[41] T. Colley, "The Nature and Origins of Psychological Sexual Identity," *Psychological Review*, 1959, 66:165–177.

postulated as giving a child, from the early, inarticulate emotional reactions of infancy, a psychological identity as a male or female. Failure to acquire such an identity, or deviate patterns of attitudes on the part of one or both parents which produce an inappropriate sexual identification—a boy whose identification is more girl-like than boy-like and vice versa—would thus be the cause of homosexuality.

These theories regarding the origin of sexual identification and homosexuality appear most promising, and may be substantiated by subsequent clinical investigation. In the meantime, they may be accepted by the worker with adolescents as likely explanations of deviate sexual identifications which are encountered among boys and girls.

Gentle urging of the "tomboyish" girl or the "sissified" boy toward games, recreations, and general activities appropriate to their sexes may mitigate their conspicuousness as deviates among their fellows. Equally gentle direction of activities into other channels—when a boy is observed associating with girls, not as a boy with girls but as a girl with girls, or, less frequently observed, a girl so associating with boys—may also help the boy or girl strengthen his or her true sexual identity.

No direct measures attempting to change the basic sexual orientation of such boys and girls should be undertaken by the youth counselor, for several reasons. First, such measures may precipitate an emotional crisis, sometimes with hysterical episodes, in the boy or girl. Typically, he or she has been attempting to conceal from himself or herself the tendency toward sexual deviation, and having it brought to consciousness may pose too great a threat to be handled. Second, treatment of a homosexual involves deep, complex personality reconstruction within the scope of only the psychiatrist or clinical psychologist. Well-intentioned people without full professional education and training are exceedingly likely to do great damage, and exceedingly *un*likely to do any good, in attempting to "treat" the homosexual. Third, homosexuality, like other physical and psychological characteristics, is a matter of degree. Many tomboyish girls and sissified boys are not basically homosexual in their orientation, but merely lack positive identification with their own sex. In such cases, amateur attempts at psychotherapy may arouse unnecessary self-doubts and anxieties.

Homosexuality is a little-understood and highly emotionalized phenomenon in the minds of most people. It should be borne in mind that homosexuals are not "that way" because of any desire or, generally, actions on their part, but because of psychosocial forces which molded them from infancy. Except in the relatively rare case of an experienced homosexual persuading a borderline homosexual boy or girl into active homosexuality, they are socially innocuous. Certainly, they are rarely vicious or dangerous. Workers with adolescents seldom need to give consideration to this problem other than exercising reasonable care to prevent the practice of behavior patterns which would tend to produce sexual misidentification in a boy or girl.

Suggestive Conversation and Physical Intimacies

Whenever adolescent boys and girls associate with one another, there will arise problems of what are proper topics of conversation and what are improper, and of where the dividing line lies between casual and healthily innocuous physical contacts and sexually suggestive ones. Most adolescents are quite self-conscious about references to sexual matters in mixed groups of boys and girls, although this shyness declines as boys and girls become more mature and sophisticated. References to birth, anatomical parts, eliminative processes, and sexually suggestive remarks generally produce vaguely uncomfortable feelings in mixed groups of adolescents. The exhibitionist who snickers, and the usually maladjusted and socially inept boy who writes obscene notes or makes suggestive remarks, are perennial problems, but handling them is primarily a problem of dealing with a maladjusted personality, not dealing with sexual suggestiveness *per se*.

Many workers with adolescents have observed that frank discussion of matters pertaining to sex encourages some adolescents to efforts to display their sophistication and emancipation from "old fogey" reticence by bringing up such topics for social conversation. Present knowledge of the influence of language habits on human affairs suggests strongly that mixed-group discussion of matters pertaining to sex tends to lessen the feeling of reserve toward sexual aspects of heterosexual relations. In fact, it is very well substantiated that, among many people, physical sexual intimacies are matters of considerably less self-consciousness than talking about them. In light of this knowledge, it is difficult to see how weakening of taboos on discussion of sexual affairs in mixed groups could avoid subtly lowering inhibitions against physical intimacies. After all, the biological drive toward physical intimacy is certainly much greater than the motivation to talk about it. There is also ample clinical evidence to support the generalization that conversation about sexual matters has a sexually stimulating effect on some people at the same time that it makes the whole matter of sex seem slightly less of a moral matter and more of a natural, amoral process such as, for instance, digestion.

The individual worker with adolescents must devise his own methods of handling discussions of sexual matters with or among adolescents. He should do so with the awareness that mixed-group discussion of sexual matters may stimulate as well as de-emotionalize sexual drives and, in the minds of adolescents, almost certainly render it more permissible to engage in personal discussions of sexual matters. Add to this the fact that language habits *do* exercise a profound effect on attitudes, and the necessity of caution in this area is evident.

The preference for privacy for overt erotic advances and activities, which distinguishes American culture, renders physical intimacies that come to the attention of workers with adolescents less a problem than are language habits. Principles of morality and the erotic significance of activities such as kissing and fondling are discussed elsewhere. Overt sexual suggestiveness in physical form should, of course, be halted wherever observed by the teacher or counselor, but discretion should be used to avoid reading suggestiveness into what might be inadvertent gestures. Too much consciousness of the possible sexual significance of actions may emphasize the very sexual implications the adult wishes to de-emphasize. As in the case of the person who makes improper verbal references to sexual matters, physical sexual aggressiveness usually indicates a personality maladjustment, the treatment of which will modify behavior better than attempts at repression of sexual activities alone.

READINGS

Duvall, E. M., *The Art of Dating.* New York: Permabooks, 1960, Chapt. 14.

English, O. S., and Pearson, G. H. J., *Emotional Problems of Living.* New York: W. W. Norton & Company, Inc., 1955, Chapt. 10.

Hurlock, E. B., *Adolescent Development.* New York: McGraw-Hill Book Company, Inc., 1955, Chapt. 12.

Kinsey, A. C., Pomeroy, W. B., and Martin, C. E., *Sexual Behavior in the Human Male.* Philadelphia: W. B. Saunders Company, 1948.

Kinsey, A. C., Pomeroy, W. B., Martin, C. E., and Gebhard, P. H., *Sexual Behavior in the Human Female.* Philadelphia: W. B. Saunders Company, 1953.

Landis, J. T., and Landis, M. G., *Building a Successful Marriage.* Englewood Cliffs, N. J.: Prentice-Hall, Inc., 1958, Chapt. 6.

Schneiders, A. A., *The Psychology of Adolescence.* Milwaukee: The Bruce Publishing Company, 1951, Chapt. 10.

Stone, L. J., and Church, J., *Childhood and Adolescence.* New York: Random House, 1957, Chapts. 10, 11.

Strang, R., *The Adolescent Views Himself—A Psychology of Adolescence.* New York: McGraw-Hill Book Company, Inc., 1957, Chapt. 9.

CHAPTER 13

DEVELOPING MATURE

HUMAN RELATIONS

PREVIEW

The Dynamics of Social Maturation

1. Expansion of social horizons and activities.
2. Development of peer roles and relationships with adults in the environment.
3. Social functioning as an autonomous personality.
4. Evaluation, adoption, and formulation of social principles and standards.
5. Evaluation of existing conventions in light of personal feelings and experience.
6. Compromising personal opinions to adjust to social conventions.

Achieving Emancipation from the Home

1. Progressive growth from birth toward autonomy in fact and in self concept.
2. Knowledge of the dangers faced by inexperienced adolescents and love for their children inhibit parental relinquishment of control.
3. Love and knowledge also dictate relinquishment essential to adolescents' maturation.
4. Immature attitudes and actions by adolescents inhibit relinquishment.
5. Standards and customs of two different generations inhibit relinquishment.
6. As love is the dominant force in parental attitudes regarding emancipation of adolescents, the desire for independence is the dominant force in the boys and girls.
7. Changing interests of adolescents lessen their feeling of oneness with parents.
8. Heterosexual urges draw the adolescent from home associations.
9. Emancipation involves increasing self-determination by the adolescent.
10. Prior agreement on rules can lessen friction over points of conflict.
11. Adolescence ends with either emancipation or maladjustment.

Changing Relations with Peer Groups

1. Gradual shift from activity-oriented to thought-, feeling-, personality-oriented associations with peers.

398

2. Conversation is a medium through which social sensitivity and skill are developed.

3. Exchanging ideas and feelings with peers clarifies interpersonal relationships.

4. Adolescents seek security and social experience through forming their own sub-society.

Achieving Heterosexual Adjustment

1. The stages of no sexual distinction, sexual segregation, and heterosexual associations occur in that order.

2. Normal heterosexual adjustment is inhibited by self-consciousness, earlier habits, and adult teasing.

3. Opportunities for impersonal heterosexual associations facilitate maturation.

4. Increased self-realization is achieved through development of the sense of intimacy.

The Role of Dating in Heterosexual Adjustment

Dating is motivated by several different factors. Among them are:

COMPANIONSHIP—based on complementariness of natures and imitation of adult behavior.

PERSONALITY ATTRACTION—based more upon the self concept produced in the adolescent by the companion than upon the attractiveness of the companion's personality.

MUTUAL SELF-DISCOVERY—orienting oneself to the society of peers by more complete discovery of how people are alike and different.

THE MATING URGE—sexual gratification; the desire for a partner, home, and family.

Developmental Steps in Achieving Heterosexual Maturation

1. Sexually undifferentiated behavior.
2. Sexual segregation.
3. Heterosexual group activities and associations.
4. Tentative "pairings-off" within the group.
5. Double-dating.
6. Dating numerous people for various types of activities.
7. Going steady and becoming engaged.
8. Marriage.

THE DYNAMICS OF SOCIAL MATURATION

A CHILD lives in a sheltered world in which his relations with other children have developed in a steady, systematic fashion over a period of ten to twelve years. The circle of his friends of his own age is relatively small, bounded by his immediate neighborhood and his schoolroom, Sunday school, or dancing class. His relations with his classmates are usually limited, unless they happen to live in his immediate community, because his mobility is limited. His classroom relations are well systematized by the presence of the teacher and the classroom routine, and playground activities are fairly well structured by time, supervision, custom, and equipment. Thus, although without doubt he acquires a great deal of social experience, this experience is of a type quite different from many of the social skills prominent in the lives of adults.

Robert E. Lee High School, Montgomery, Alabama.

Figure 21. "The adolescent must spend his adult life in a society built by himself and his age-mates."

His relations with adults have also been strongly structured for him. With parents, the relationship has principally been (or at least *should* have been) that of love reflected in obedience. He has lived under reasonably strict control. Adults have told him how and when to dress, bathe, eat, sleep, whom to associate with, and what to do and how to do it to an extent quite forgotten by most adults whose years of childhood have faded into dim memories. Adults around him naturally and unpremeditatedly told him how to run his life, for the very good reason that he would be in confusion or actual danger if he attempted to run it for himself. He would not recognize the obvious warnings of chilliness, constipation, overheating or overeating, overexertion, or dozens of others of nature's warning signals which the adult has heeded so many times that he acts upon them without conscious thought.

The child's life has, indeed, represented a gradual decline from the absolute dependence and submission of the infant, but being "looked after," with its inevitable concomitant of being closely supervised, is still the normal and natural state for him. It is, furthermore, a state which parents come to regard as the "proper" relationship between them.

It is normal and natural, but normal and natural in ever diminishing quantities. As his self concept develops, particularly if it is a healthy and vigorous one, the child seeks more and more self-determination in more and more different areas. This change is not confined to relations with his parents. The teacher of the primary-grade child says, "Ella, don't forget to put on your mittens." The teacher in the upper elementary grades may not do so, perhaps because she is not expected to exercise that degree of "looking after" her pupils, perhaps because the children would rebel at being thus closely supervised. Other adults are similarly becoming less absolute figures of authority. The clerk in the store who has helped the young child make his choices in the absence of a parent is now becoming someone who follows his orders, not one who makes decisions for him or perhaps not even one who advises him.

These changing relationships are more than skin deep. They represent changes in the intrinsic relationship between the child and his environment, changes in his self concept and the relative roles in which he perceives himself and the adults with whom he comes into contact. They are manifestations of his maturation, not the essence of it; the essence is the emerging psychological maturation which springs from his changing self concept.

We have seen that the self concept includes perceptions of the individual's relations with his environment, human and physical, as well as his own inward adjustment. With successful mastery of earlier developmental tasks, and perhaps abetted by maturational physiological changes, the self-concept shows eager growth in independence, self-reliance, and self-determination in the pre-adolescent period.[1] Inevitably, under such circumstances, the pre-adolescent, and to an increased degree the adolescent, begins to perceive himself as an independent agent, exercising a large measure of self-determination and viewing adults less as supreme arbiters of his fate and more as peers, as people whom he is essentially like and comparable to. This change in attitude is, of course, essential to normal maturation. It is, nevertheless, the cause of much discord and friction.

During the adolescent years, the social relationships of boys and girls change radically. Their roles in respect to those about them change, and the roles of people about them change in the eyes of the adolescent. The adolescent becomes more of a determiner, a doer.[2] He is a person of whom certain things are expected, and becomes less of one for whom things are done, one whose life is directed or managed and of whom nothing is expected save obedience. Without conscious volition or change of opinion, just because the adolescent is approaching adult physical stature he is coming to be regarded by other adults as something of a peer[3]—not a peer in the sense of his judgment being equal to theirs, nor his age, but a peer in the sense that he is expected to use some judgment of his own, assume responsibility for his actions, and act like an adult. He sees the adults around him not as a race of giants, towering over him in unquestioned supremacy, but as people considerably like himself, except, he usually surmises, somewhat below him in judgment and general knowledge of what's what.

The adolescent had nothing to do with the establishment of adult social standards, and, therefore, he has little patience with them. If they displease him, with the brash overconfidence born of a modicum of maturation and experience, he attacks or disregards them. If he is brought to account for violation of social standards, he may become a child again, seeking protection and immunity through tearful regression to childish despair and dependence.[4] He may, on the other hand, assume

[1] G. E. Gardner, "The Mental Health of Normal Adolescents," *Mental Hygiene,* 1947, *31*:531–532.

[2] W. R. Baller and D. C. Charles, *The Psychology of Human Growth and Development.* Holt, Rinehart & Winston, New York, 1961.

[3] R. G. Barker, B. A. Wright, and M. R. Gonick, *Adjustment to Physical Handicap and Illness,* Bulletin No. 55, Social Science Research Council, New York, 1946.

[4] C. B. Zachry, *Emotion and Conduct in Adolescence.* Appleton-Century-Crofts, Inc., New York, 1940.

a lordly disdain for the conventions he disagrees with and maintain a supercilious defiance of the stick-in-the-mud, ridiculous fallacies of adults. He may go further and, either before or after getting into trouble, actively attack the mores of the adult culture under which he is growing up. This is commonly referred to as adolescent rebellion, and takes the form of assuming the opposite side from the majority of adults around him, the adolescent usually going further in his espousal of his minority views than any save the lunatic fringe of adults. Here we find the "campus radicals," the "angry young men," the "young Turks," the "beatniks," the "lost generation," the fanatics, the idealists with and without causes, the pacifists forming the "Oxford Movement" of another generation. They are asserting their independence of the intellectual patterns they are required to follow to achieve academic degrees or adult-dominated jobs. They often despise the degrees and the jobs they must seek as symbols of adult authority over them and as Philistine oppression of their intellects, fettering the sinews of their creative genius by stodgy insistence that they stuff their heads with facts created and embalmed by old fogies. They are asserting their conviction that they know where adults have made the mistakes which cause the conditions that plague mankind; follow *their* lead, and the errors of the past will be eradicated in the wake of their visions. "Follow us," they proclaim. "We will lead mankind out of the darkness of inept fumbling, the blindness which refuses to see the true light. We have the vision, the inspiration. We have discovered The Way!"

The foregoing statements are lyrical and melodramatic because the attitude of adolescents toward adjusting to adult-created social norms is typically lyrical and melodramatic. The son of middle-class people who grubs along miserably in school, to his parents' horror nursing a yearning to be an automobile mechanic, cannot express his feelings in words such as are used by the college junior bent on social and economic reforms, but the dynamics in each of the two cases are likely to be identical. Both are asserting their own sense of values, their own feelings of self-determination, their confidence that their own evaluation of circumstances is better than that of adults occupying positions of authority over them.

It is probable that all normally aggressive and self-confident adolescents have such feelings to a considerable extent. It is characteristic of adolescents through history, belonging to no one century or generation. The majority balance their feelings and convictions with the self-caution that open rebellion may be unwise, or with the prescience that perhaps the older generation is also intelligent—there may be reasons unperceived by him behind things being as they are. The minority has mastered fewer of the reality checks discussed in Chapter 5, and gives us a good look at the dynamics of adolescent revolt.

Relations of the races to each other, relations of the sexes in and out of marriage, relations of people to the institutions of society, the family, the church, the school, economic relations between segments of society loosely called "capital" and "labor," relation of the government to the individual and to organization, all are fertile ground for the adolescent to sow with his own theories, expressing his own emerging individuality as a decider and a determiner, not a mere follower. To a considerable extent he holds his beliefs purely and simply because they are different from those of the adult-dominated world around him; therefore, they help him strengthen his self concept as that of one who sees and understands more clearly than others, particularly elders. Their very difference asserts that *he* is no puppet dancing on others' ideological strings, but a person who thinks for himself.

All the foregoing should not be interpreted as irony, nor ridicule of the world-shaking dreams and awesome self-confidence of adolescents. Actually, it is a natural and, the psychologist suspects, an essential concomitant of maturation. It is really intellectual emancipation and development into independent cognition, although, because its effects are most conspicuous in the social areas, it is discussed as social maturation. It is nothing either to scorn or to view with alarm—not something to scorn because it represents a groping for self-realization on the part of growing human beings, and not something to view with alarm because, generation after generation, the majority of the militant adolescents see, as they grow older, the things their predecessors saw as *they* grew older, and change their ideas of social reorganization from revolutionary to evolutionary, or even to maintaining the status quo. But the dynamics of adolescents' maturing processes of socialization must be comprehended in order to understand them and their reactions in the many social situations in which parents, teachers, and counselors must help them.

Case of Lenore Lynch

Lenore had always been a sweet, agreeable, and affectionate child and, with her parents and younger brothers, had gone camping, tended the flowers, looked after the house, participated in family conferences (where her opinion was respected and her desires considered), gone to ball games, and enjoyed evenings of reading, talking, and watching TV with the family. Now she is fifteen, and her parents often look at her with amazement, wondering if this is their Lenore or a changeling who has assumed her form.

Camping, Lenore announces, is corny, and who wants to spend the evening with a pair of noisy, undisciplined brats and a couple of people who only find fault with everything you do? Her parents accept such attitudes as normal, knowing that Lenore now has a need to be with her age-mates, becoming adept at socialization on the heterosexual level. What they have difficulty in accepting is Lenore's contemptuous disdain of their opinions and values. Why do they want a car like that old hippopotamus they clutter up the driveway with? The way their church is run, it's no wonder the young people would rather go to jail than attend services there. (Her parents had noticed no such fanatical avoidance of the church, where the young people's department was large and active.) But yes, she means it *literally,* Lenore proclaims passionately. *All* the people she goes with, *everyone,* would rather spend an hour sitting in a nice, quiet cell than listen to that same old droning and moaning every Sunday!

"Dad voted for *him?*" Lenore exclaims incredulously. Doesn't he know the *first thing* about what's going on in this town? Honestly, *everybody* knows he got those stop signs put in so people would have to stop at the corner where his grocery store was. And the clothes Mother wants her to wear! Mother doesn't know the *first thing,* not the *first thing,* about the chic way to dress. (This comes as something of a blow to Mother, who has a reputation among her friends as a beautifully dressed woman.) Mother'd have her going around in a Mother Hubbard if she had *her* way! "Dad? Oh, *him!*" is all Lenore needs to dispose of her male parent. And as for her parents' feelings about Butch, well, his father is an *honest* gambler. He has more honesty than Dad's friends in the Kitarians . . . yes, he *has!* People like Butch's father are better than those old hypocrites any day in the week!

1. Are Lenore's attitudes and reactions abnormal in a fifteen-year-old girl?

2. What are the dynamics of Lenore's bolshevik reactions to the people and institutions of her community?

3. To what extent do Lenore's attitudes indicate delinquent tendencies?

4. Will Lenore's attitudes and values change? Why?

ACHIEVING
EMANCIPATION FROM THE HOME

Emancipation from the home is not a process which begins in adolescence. Like other aspects of maturation, it begins as early as the infant is able to grow in independence and self-reliance.[5] Emancipation from the home is clearly under way when the small child is able to play outside by himself, and is well advanced when he is permitted to go into the neighbors' yards to play. When he enters school, his emancipation takes another big step forward, because now he is away from home for as much as one-third of his waking hours. Every move toward greater independence and self-determination in selecting friends and governing his own activities increases the child's emancipation from the home. Nevertheless, at the onset of adolescence the child is typically under the control of the parents and lives a life fairly well structured around the home.

By the end of adolescence the boy or girl, now properly referred to as a young man or young woman, is under little or no control by parents, and "home" either *is* a different place from where the parents live or is likely to be so in a future controlled by the young man or woman rather than by the parents. Thus, during the adolescent period the child moves from being fundamentally a governed being within the home to a free agent connected to the paternal home only to the extent that he wishes to be.

The fundamental dynamics of growth of perception of oneself as an independent thinker, doer, and decider govern maturation in the area of emancipation from the home as well as in all other areas. However, in emancipation from the home a number of highly emotionalized relationships exist which, because they differ in the case of every adolescent, influence the particular course of the adolescent's maturation in a fashion unique to his situation and life. In other words, highly emotionalized states exist between an adolescent and his parents. The nature of the emotionalized state on the part of the adolescent and each parent

[5] C. B. Zachry, *Emotion and Conduct in Adolescence.* Appleton-Century-Crofts, Inc., New York, 1940.

(and, for that matter, the nature of the attitude of the parents toward each other) influences the development of the adolescent and his achievement of emancipation from the home.[6]

Every normal instance of adolescent social maturation starts with a generally similar situation: a boy or girl subject to the guidance and control of parents or parent figures (guardians, etc.). Every normal instance involves a pattern of increasing assumption of independence on the part of the boy or girl and increasing relinquishment of control on the part of the parents or parent figures. The inevitable termination of normal maturation is final, complete independence of the young man or woman. The transition, however, involves many stresses and typically, before it is complete, severe strain on the love existing between children and parents.[7]

This is unfortunate, but well-nigh, if not completely, unavoidable. We have the situation of one creature struggling for independence from two other creatures whom he loves, but whose control he nevertheless wishes to move from under. We have two creatures who dearly love an offspring and who know from personal experience the dangers of freedom as well as its rewards. Such a situation, highly emotionalized, with powerful drives in intrapersonal conflict within each of the three principals, as well as interpersonal conflict between the three, often produces terrific tensions both within individuals and between them.

Parents typically encounter considerable difficulty and undergo intensive self-examination and soul-searching in the process of surrendering their authority over their maturing offspring.[8] Both their minds and their emotions are involved; sometimes they run counter to each other, as when the parent wants to keep his daughter as "my baby," while his mind reminds him that this shapely and popular young lady is by no means his "baby." But then, within the parent, things become even more complicated. Along with wanting to keep his baby as his baby, the fond father also "wants," earnestly desires, that his beloved daughter become a well-adjusted, mature, and self-reliant young woman, not remain a socially, emotionally, and intellectually retarded child. At the same time, while his mind tells him that she must assume increasing responsibility

[6] J. E. Finesinger, "The Needs of Youth: The Physiological and Psychological Factors in Adolescent Behavior," *Psychiatry*, Vol. VII, No. 1, pp. 45–57.

[7] A. T. Jersild, *The Psychology of Adolescence*. The Macmillan Company, New York, 1957.

[8] O. S. English and G. H. J. Pearson, *Emotional Problems of Living*. W. W. Norton & Company, Inc., New York, 1955.

for her own life, must decide whom she dates, where she goes, what she does, and when she comes home, his mind also tells him (quite correctly) that there are so many things about life that she does not know. Her risk is so great! Where, his mind demands, does the father properly draw the line to give the proper balance between self-determination and the protection his daughter should receive from his greater experience and knowledge? [9]

So the parent, in facilitating the adolescent's maturation into complete self-determination, encounters internal conflicts between feelings, between feelings and thoughts, and between thoughts themselves. Small wonder that parents typically become anxious, often to the point of literally throwing up their hands and wailing in loud voices, "How on earth can you know what you ought to do in a situation like this?" If teachers or counselors seem sympathetic, capable, and knowledgeable of the way adolescents think and feel and the reasons therefor, many parents will consult them for advice and explanations of their own children, whom they no longer understand, nor even their own roles toward them. It is well to understand the various forces at work within each parent trying to do the best he can for his son or daughter. Understanding these forces, you can comprehend much more about the individual parent and his relationship, emotional and mental, with his boy's or girl's maturation than he himself perceives.

First and foremost, the parent's relations with a child (regardless of age) are dominated by love. This love produces several contradictory effects. If we love something or someone, we naturally want that something or someone near us, now and in the future. Yet we also want it to follow the laws of development which will produce the best and happiest future for it. These laws require, in the case of the parent and child, that the beloved child become inevitably further and further separated emotionally from the parent. Every parent knows of tragic instances of the incompletely weaned child who marries but subsequently divorces because the emotional umbilical cord connecting him or her with the parents has not been properly severed. So, expressing one's natural love for a child in the same way that nature approves for some objects, as a husband or wife, well-loved dog, or even a dear friend— i.e., by attempting to maintain the relationship unchanged—is perceived as selfish and unjust to the child.

[9] L. J. Stone and J. Church, *Childhood and Adolescence*. Random House, New York, 1957.

Thus, the parent's love must be great enough for the self-sacrifice of permitting the beloved child to grow away from him.[10] All normal parents recognize this, but many of them rationalize their attempts to keep their growing-up sons and daughters tied to them emotionally, as in infancy. Arguments against Danny's going out "every night," based on his health, sometimes split at the seams from the pressure underneath and let spill out revealing accusations such as, "When you were a little boy, you didn't think it was better to be out with anyone, just anyone at all, than to be at home with us!" No rational parent could bear to admit to himself that he was trying to stunt the social maturation of his child, but isn't it his responsibility, he asks, to see that his daughter doesn't become one of those juvenile delinquents? Obviously she can't if he keeps her in the family car and company until she is no longer a juvenile. Better safe than sorry. Mustn't shirk your responsibility just because other parents do. "No dates until you are eighteen! Your mother and I aren't such bad company. We'll take you to the beach, go boating, give you everything you need until you are old enough to go with boys." (Several actual cases!)

In the vast majority of cases, any undesirable blocking of a boy's or girl's social maturation by a parent springs from genuinely noble motives of protection, or from the haunting specter of fear. The reasons for such fear are obvious enough if we, as workers with adolescents, lay aside our own prejudices and look for them. Parents remember their own adolescence, remember the mistakes made or almost made, and shudder, from the vantage point of maturity, at the things which could have happened before they were old enough to choose companions wisely or exercise adequate self-discipline. They know the tragedy of time wasted in idle chatter when it should have been spent in preparing lessons or fulfilling other responsibilities. They see the boy and girl unknowingly flirt with disaster as they drive too fast, cut too sharply in front of cars, and run up too close behind them before stopping. They know from newspaper accounts and perhaps experiences of their friends how an evening with undesirable companions can get a boy or girl into more trouble than he can get out of in a lifetime. They know these things, and they see where the course of action their boy or girl is following can lead. They see it, and the boy or girl with the brash overconfidence of ignorance does not see it, has not yet the wisdom of years and the

[10] C. E. Meyers, "Emancipation of the Adolescent from Parental Control," *The Nervous Child*, 1946, 5:251–262.

necessary experience to see it. The boy and girl do not recognize that they fail to see the undesirability of things they want to do; instead, because they want to do those things and do not see why they should not do them, they refuse to believe that the danger or undesirability is there.[11]

So the parents are in a dilemma as to how far to push their authority and where to let the boy's or girl's responsibility and drive for independence take over. They want to give protection where protection is so desperately needed; the boy and girl fail to see the need for protective guidance and control and resent it as parental meddling in their affairs. It is easy for the bystander not emotionally involved in the situation to say, "Parents, stand aside. They have to stand on their own feet sometime. Let them go." It is not so easy for parents who love the boy and girl and so desperately want to keep their children from errors of omission or commission which may scar their whole lives. It is not an abstract problem to them; it is the life happiness of those dearest to them that is involved. Remember this when faced with the often illogical attitudes and behavior of anxious parents.

The complicated business of how to let go of control over maturing boys and girls without letting them get hurt as a result of their new-found freedom is further complicated by the typical inconsistent behavior of the adolescent. Indeed, adolescents' behavior is typically so inconsistent that it is obvious to the thoughtful observer that they are simultaneously wanting and fearing independence, seeking it yet dodging its full import, torn between the desire for independence and the security of parental care and control.[12]

Case of Moss Mann

Moss insists that he is a responsible, competent adult at the age of seventeen, worthy of holding the lives of others in his hands as he drives down the street piloting two tons of sudden death. But, turning into the driveway, he alarms the neighborhood with the tortured shrick of tires on pavement. Entering the house, he slumps down to watch television and a half-hour later jumps up in panic remembering that a book report is due tomorrow and he has not even

11 J. Levy and R. Munroe, *The Happy Family*. Alfred A. Knopf, Inc., New York, 1938.

12 J. E. Horrocks, *The Psychology of Adolescence*. Houghton-Mifflin Company, Boston, 1951.

started the book. Gangway for a wee-small-hours cramming-writing session! "It just slipped up on me somehow!" he explains as he strews goo from a sandwich across the living-room rug while rushing back to his room, where he sets the wastebasket afire with a tossed cigarette butt. And then Moss is outraged when parents question his being mature enough to go on a weekend trip to the lake with a bunch of other boys.

1. How may Moss's driving habits be a reflection of his desire for emancipation from the home?

2. How does Moss reconcile his general carelessness with his self concept of a mature, competent individual?

3. Judging from Moss's behavior described here, why would his parents be fearful of his going to the lake with others his own age?

Case of Nancy Nix

Nancy is a similar case. If Mother does not look after her clothes, they wind up in a piled-up, untidy mess with nothing clean to wear tomorrow. The boy she goes with is failing in school, has had a couple of close brushes with the law, and prodigally spends every penny he can wheedle from hard-working parents. Nancy cannot see anything in him except a darling boy, the most fun to be with of anyone! She is truly insulted when parents intimate that she is not yet capable of selecting her own friends, and genuinely fails to see why her childish irresponsibility regarding her clothes has anything to do with the parents' questioning the maturity of her behavior out with a boy at night.

1. Is there a logical relationship between Nancy's management of her clothes and her selection of friends? How?

2. How may Nancy's parents best handle her association with her boy friend? He might be Moss, and we shall so refer to him.

Viewing their son's or daughter's appalling immaturity and irresponsibility in stewardship of time, appropriateness of action, self-discipline in fulfilling responsibilities and in distinguishing between what is important in life and what is not, it is not surprising that parents view with alarm the adolescent's strenuous struggle to throw off the last vestiges of direction from mature, responsible sources. As a matter of fact, it is seldom that a boy or girl who does well academically, behaves with something approaching adult responsibility, and generally conducts himself or herself like an adult rather than an overgrown child encounters a serious problem with parents in achieving emancipation from the home. This is due to two reasons: First, parents perceive the maturity of such a boy or girl and easily relinquish close control in secure confidence that their son's or daughter's maturity is adequate to cope with whatever situation he or she is likely to encounter. In the second place, such a boy or girl is mature in his relationship with parents as well as in other areas, and recognizes that someone has to be boss and that the parent is the logical one. Therefore, it is sad, but not surprising, that typically it is the least competent and most immature boys and girls who make the biggest fuss about not being given the freedom they think they ought to have.

If boys and girls make serious attempts to act and think and talk like mature people rather than like irresponsible children concerned with nothing except the pleasure of the moment or the day, they seldom encounter serious problems in achieving emancipation from parental authority. Freedom will be granted them at an ever increasing pace. The common trouble is that boys and girls want the freedom of an adult while still giving their parents little reason to hope they are anything except children inhabiting grown-up bodies. True, habits of control may lead parents to be spotty in their relinquishing of authority and cause them at times to reassert it in logical or illogical ways. The natural reluctance of a human being to relinquish authority, which implies trusting someone else's judgment instead of one's own, may lead to Father's or Mother's insisting that *his* or *her* judgment prevail in a specific situation of conflict, but a reasonably mature boy or girl recognizes that Dad and Mom are not ready to step completely out of the picture while he or she is still an adolescent, and adjusts to these occasional clashes with nothing more than a short tantrum.

Differences in standards and customs of different generations account for frequent conflicts between parents and adolescents in the process of achieving emancipation from the home.[13, 14] Parents will naturally tend to judge adolescents' maturity in terms of the extent to which the boy or girl demonstrates acceptance of the values the parents regard highly. Thus, the boy or girl who puts scholarship first, socializ-

[13] K. Davis, "The Sociology of Parent-Youth Conflict," *American Sociological Review*, 1940, 5:523–535.

[14] W. W. Wattenberg, *The Adolescent Years*. Harcourt, Brace and Company, New York, 1955.

ing second, and athletics third will be regarded as more mature by a parent who also ascribes this order of priority than will one whose order of priority puts athletics or socializing first. Boys and girls whose standards, whose values, differ radically from those of their parents will be in constant conflict with the parents. Emancipation is likely to take the form of alienation, parent and adolescent growing away from each other, control becoming punishment, and unhappiness resulting for all parties concerned.

Differences in standards and values which result from the different ideas of different generations are hard to cope with. The boy or girl must cast his lot either with the generation with which he does *not* live, and gain respect for his maturity in so doing, or with the generation with which he *does* live, and encounter criticism for "immaturity." One generation regards a deep, dark suntan as a mark of beauty and sophistication. Another generation regards it as a sign of being poor trash, uncultured and unrefined. Where genuine questions of ethics or relative wisdom are involved, as in the propriety of unchaperoned house parties or of undertaking a fast drive with a weak tire on the car, the fact that the younger generation has different standards from the older should not sway parents' judgment from obviously sound authoritative control to obviously unsound permissiveness. Where it is largely a matter of preference or taste, as in the length or style of dress, appropriate refreshments for the party, a sock hop or a formal dance, parents weaken their ultimate authority by insisting on mistaking arbitrary customs or preferences as involving genuine principles or standards.

Throughout all the innumerable problems and types of problems which can arise in the interpersonal struggle between parents and children for emancipation from the home, a struggle which all recognize must inevitably end in the child's complete emancipation, but which is inevitably complicated by the loves, fears, drives for independence, and ego investments of every party concerned, parental love is the most nearly unchangeable factor. The desire of the parents to do what is best for their child is unchanging. Only the question of what *is* best occupies their minds. They vary from strictness, dominated by fear of tragedy from too much freedom before the boy or girl is able to handle it wisely, to too little control, resulting from unwillingness to make the boy or girl unhappy by frustrating his or her wishes. Parents seek earnestly to determine what is best for the child (with notable exceptions mentioned from time to time) and the best way of doing that which is best.

In working with them, you will seldom encounter difficulties if your own sincere desire to do what is best for their child is evident, and if you can offer them intelligent suggestions in answer to their problems.

Parents' behavior, which is often completely inexplicable when first observed by the outsider, will almost always become understandable (even though it may be ill-advised) when examined from the frame of reference we have considered: love of the child plus fear for his welfare in the absence of parental control; observation of his child's obvious immaturities, and resultant hesitation to "turn him loose" in big ways when he does not even handle the freedom and responsibilities he now has in a mature fashion; differing standards of values and behaviors in differing generations, complicated by much deeper differences involving principles and wisdom (parents can morally give in to the former differing standards, but they cannot to the latter); trust of one's own mature, proved judgment in preference to the immature, often-proved-inadequate judgment of the adolescent; and, occasionally, selfishness and parental immaturity. These are the dynamic factors in parents' approach to emancipation of their children from home and parental control.

We have already mentioned the fact that both the thinking and the feelings of boys and girls are involved in the process of their achieving emancipation from the home, just as both thinking and feeling are involved on the part of the parents. However, whereas, in the case of parents, the dominant force which finally decides their course of action is sacrificial love, which permits the boy or girl to mature into his or her own independent life, the dominant force in the case of the boy or girl is the drive for self-realization and independence. These drives must overpower his attachment to his parents to the extent of separating him from them to a considerable extent, or he never becomes a normal adult, never fully achieves a sense of identity. Every community has one or more of these pathetic creatures who has "stayed with the old folks," never establishing a home of his or her own, to be left finally deserted and solitary as the old folks he or she has stayed with and looked after for years pass on, leaving behind them a son or daughter whose life has been sacrificed for the dubious welfare of the parents.

In one sense it is unjust; parents' sacrificial love requires them to encourage their children to grow away from them emotionally, not in the sense of ceasing to love them, but undeniably in the sense of their becoming peripheral figures in the lives of the children rather than the central figures they were when the children were young. Children's development, on the other hand, requires none of this sacrificial quality; it involves merely their following the urges to autonomy and independence which nature places in them. This ethical and sentimental problem looms large in the work of a counselor attempting to help parents and children achieve a harmonious solution to the emancipation of the children. Parents sometimes reproach the children with selfishness—"After I looked after you and tended you when you were helpless and couldn't look after yourself, now you want to leave me!"—producing undeserved guilt feelings on the part of the children. They love their parents none the less as a result of their drive for self-realization. However, for society to continue, the boy and girl must become increasingly absorbed by interests and activities in which the parents can have no part. This is the way of nature. It happens among the lower animals as the offspring mature, and although among humans the bond of affection and mutual concern for each other's welfare should continue as strong as ever, the paths of life of the parents and children must separate much as they do among the subhuman species.

The urge for independence, self-determination, and self-realization already discussed is reinforced by other urges, perhaps even by physiological or biological needs. With sexual maturation comes the insistent call of nature to associate with members of the opposite sex, to develop mature heterosexual relations. Simultaneously there is the urge to participate in the social, recreational, and vocational patterns of people of one's own age and sex.[15] These are the people, these age-sex peers, with whom the adult life of adolescents will be lived. Getting to know them as maturing adults, associating with them, sharing their ideas, activities, and plans, understanding how they feel and why, learning how to get along with them, are social tasks of the adolescent which can be mastered in no way other than by the extensive association with his age-mates, which adolescent boys and girls seek so insistently.[16]

The interests of adolescents increasingly lessen their feelings of oneness with parents. They are interested in people of ages different from their parents' friends. Their approach to athletics is more participant, as compared to spectator, than is that of their parents. Their taste in music, reading material, even the things they want to talk about, all become increasingly remote to parents' preferences in these areas. As the

[15] I. M. Josselyn, *The Happy Child*. Random House, New York, 1955.

[16] C. B. Zachry, *Emotion and Conduct in Adolescence*. Appleton-Century-Crofts, Inc., New York, 1940.

ties of mutual interests lessen, the adolescent is moved more and more to seek others who think and feel as he does. Thus, his life becomes increasingly friend-oriented and decreasingly home-oriented. This does not mean that home loses meaning and appeal for him, but does mean that it is no longer so nearly the whole of his life as it was.

The desire of adolescents to pursue their interests brings them into conflict with parents, often as much as does their desire for independence *per se*. Pursuit of heterosexual interests, which parents often feel begins too early (and often they are right), requires a different pattern of living than do the pursuits of childhood. This social activity cannot be carried on in the front yard, nor next door in the neighbor's yard, except by occasional accident of proximity of homes. Furthermore, even if such fortuitous proximity exists, the boy and girl do not find limiting their association to such areas satisfying. They want to go places together, engage in recreational pursuits together, mix as a couple with others their age, and become adept at the paired-off life normal to the social activities of adults. They want to get away from parents, not necessarily because they want to do things of which parents would disapprove (and this is often hard for parents to accept), but simply because they want to be in each other's exclusive company, as it seems nature intends couples, male and female, to be in the natural course of things.

Pursuit both of heterosexual interests and of interests involving others of the same age and sex, then, tends to draw the adolescent away from home. This gives rise to innumerable problems of emancipation from parental control in the areas of use of the car, or possession of one and the degree of freedom of its use permitted, how long and how often the adolescent will be absent from home, how closely he must keep the parents informed of his movements and activities, and when he must come home in the evening, to say nothing of conflicting views on the extent to which parents require their approval of the adolescent's companions, male and female.

As has previously been noted, the adolescent, although with much less reason, is often as confident that his judgment on any matter pertaining to him or his life is as good as, or better than, his parents' judgment on the same matter as the parent is to the contrary. This adolescent attitude, ridiculous and springing from brash ignorance though it is, is probably necessary; if the adolescent actually had the judgment he thinks he has, he would probably be too afraid of possible consequences to venture to try his own judgment and would, therefore, never fully mature. It presents a severe tax on the patience and understanding of the adult, parent, teacher, or counselor, but should be treated as an inevitable concomitant of adolescence, like a changing voice and developing bust. Calm acceptance of the unjustifiable self-confidence in his judgment that the adolescent has, without, however, giving in to that judgment where doing so would be unwise, keeps his friendship. It permits the adult to maintain the good relationship with the adolescent necessary if his guidance is to be most effective.

From all the foregoing it can be seen that deep, fundamental drives are probably operative in the tendency of the adolescent to emancipate himself from the home and parental control. Some psychologists list this "drive for independence" as one of the basic psychological needs of man. Others (including the present writer) classify it under the "need for opportunity," the opportunity for self-assertion, self-realization, assumption of responsibility, and exercise of full self-determination. Often ill-advised and rash, this desire for independence may encounter parents' opposition springing from their love, desire to protect their offspring from mistakes and errors of which the offspring are all too obviously ignorant, lack of confidence in the offsprings' judgment because they often display such patently poor judgment, and occasionally from sheer selfishness or blind habit. The process of resolving these difficulties often produces wounds between parents and their sons and daughters which are a long time in healing. Sometimes teachers and counselors can help parents or adolescents to understand the thinking and motives of the other group, and seeing the other side of the question will help each party work out a mutually satisfactory adjustment.

Easing Emancipation Conflicts

Emancipation from the home should begin in childhood. As fast as a child demonstrates maturity and ability to accept responsibility, even erratically and perhaps somewhat imperfectly, a beginning should be made in giving him more freedom of self-determination. It might involve cultivating his responsible attitude in deciding what to wear to school today and Mother's biting her lip when the choice is inept but harmless. One ten-year-old insisted on wearing an old pair of adult-size leather leggings, each wrapped half again around a leg, even with nothing but tennis shoes to wear them with. He was blissfully unaware of the ridiculous figure he cut, but, incidentally, he was regarded as quite a grown-up, swashbuckling, and romantic figure by his classmates, who saw nothing at all ridiculous in his rig. The growing freedom can continue with the child's having an increasing say-so, within the limits of his demonstrated self-discipline and judgment, of where he can go and what he can do.[17]

By following this process, freedom becomes a natural result of demonstrated competence and maturation, not a mystic symbol to be grabbed at all at once in a childish attempt to become grown up without knowing what is involved in adult self-discipline, judgment, and responsibility. It can be perceived as a natural concomitant of growing up, gradually and normally, earned rather than bestowed. Of course, such a policy is of tremendous value in helping the child develop a strong, healthy self concept of himself as a responsible, capable person with certain limitations which he is strong and confident enough to face, instead of blindly denying their existence, as a less confident child must do to protect his insecure self concept.

If your first contact with a parent-child process of adolescent emancipation from the home comes when the young person is already in the adolescent period, it is, of course, too late to do anything about this desirable process. Then you must do as teachers and physicians and lawyers must do: accept the situation as it is and do the best you can for and with it. The foregoing pages have described the principal dynamic factors operating in the minds and emotions of both parents and children, influencing their thinking and behavior in the multitude of situations arising in adolescents' gradual emancipation from the home. Your knowledge of the dynamic processes of growth away from the home and parental reaction to such growth will help you understand the nature and causes of problems arising among adolescents and parents whom you observe in the throes of re-forming their interpersonal relationships on new bases. Often you can assist them by clarifying to each his own thoughts and feelings and the thoughts and feelings of the other parties.

This must be done with tact and diplomacy, although truth and frankness must not be sacrificed. Centuries ago people became accustomed to surrendering the diagnosis and treatment of their bodies to specially trained professionals when those bodies were encountering difficulties. Even today, however, a large segment of people have a positively rabid rejection of the idea of turning over to qualified professionals the diagnosis and treatment of their emotional life or interpersonal relation-

[17] P. H. Mussen and J. J. Conger, *Child Development and Personality*. Harper & Brothers, Publishers, New York, 1956.

ships, even when that emotional life or those interpersonal relationships are so obviously "sick" that they, themselves, recognize things are in an intolerable state. The teacher or counselor is not a psychotherapist, of course—not prepared to function as a full-fledged psychiatrist or clinical psychologist. Therefore, suggestions, and particularly interpretations regarding the significance of words, actions, thoughts, and feelings, must be offered mildly and discreetly. Few things infuriate a person more quickly than having his thoughts or feelings dissected by one whom he does not regard as qualified to treat him. In dealing with adolescents, and even more in dealing with their parents, consider their receptiveness to the truth as you see it, as well as the truth itself, in determining what it is wise to bring to their attention and what it is not. Angering them helps no one.

Within the bounds of the professional status and acceptance you have achieved among those with whom you work, you can often help both adolescents and their parents by enabling each to appreciate both his own and the other's motivations more clearly. The adolescent statement "I love Dad and Mother, but when they get on me about things, I almost hate them sometimes—actually, I don't know exactly *how* I feel!" is a common experience of counselors. By understanding the contradictory forces active within him, you can help the adolescent perceive how he does feel, the reason for it, and, through these perceptions, enable him to cope more effectively with the situations which in the past have confused as well as frustrated him. The parent also, sometimes, says, "I know it is a horrible thing for a mother (father) to say, but sometimes I get so exasperated at Jenny that I wish she could just go away! And then I realize that is exactly what she is wanting to do, and my not wanting her to is what is causing the trouble!" Such a parent will profit from being helped to see the conflict in her or his feelings and understand how natural such a conflict is. It lessens feelings of guilt and enables the parent to establish relations with the adolescent son or daughter based on knowledge of the forces at work within each one, rather than acting blindly in confusion and frustration.

In addition to giving parents and adolescents insight into the feelings and thinking of all involved in family disagreements, there are specific techniques which may be suggested to minimize future friction. Often, wonders are worked by family conferences, in which parents and the boy or girl involved sit down and talk over the best way of gratifying some of the adolescent's desire for greater freedom from parental control. When not faced with the immediate prospect of a swim party she wishes to attend, and which parents feel is unwise because of a critical final examination she faces the next day, most adolescent girls will readily agree that elaborate social activities on the day preceding examinations are unwise. Having agreed to this principle through her own logical thinking, the girl is usually much more amenable to being told she cannot attend the party than if she is so told without the background of prior agreement on such matters. There is a genuinely good reason for her different attitude in the two situations: When she has agreed beforehand to the principle involved, insistence on violating the principle appears, even to her, childish and irresponsible. If she has only her parents' reasoning to disregard, she can argue for the exception without reflecting on her own reliability. Similarly, the boy who has agreed that twelve midnight is the latest he will ask to stay out at night, and this only on certain nights, is much less likely to stage a violent scene when held to the rule he himself was instrumental in formulating than if he is being made to conform to a rule whose existence he was not responsible for and which he disputes. There is more freedom in helping formulate rules for oneself and being held to those rules than in being held to rules exclusively formulated by other people.

The use of the family conference will not eliminate problems of parent-adolescent conflict. Experience has proved that it will avoid many conflicts and alleviate the seriousness of many it does not entirely avoid. Some will persist, because adolescents will want to go back on their agreement when an attractive prospect is being forbidden them. Also, some parents will administer the agreement in an unnecessarily autocratic, harsh, and arbitrary fashion. Like most techniques in human relations, the utility of this one depends heavily on the good faith and judgment of the people involved. Despite all this, the technique of the adolescent's participating in formulation of the rules he or she is expected to live by will be found to ease many of the parent-child stresses involved in working out optimum procedures for the adolescent's achieving ultimate emancipation from parental control.

Helping adolescents and parents achieve a manner of living which lessens, even temporarily, the strains and stresses involved in a tug of war over emancipation is a worthwhile contribution to family happiness. Thus, helping the parties concerned find a mutually acceptable (even if not agreeable) solution to specific problems is not to be scorned, even though no long-range principles are worked out in the process. Stresses and strains bring bitterness into the relationship between parents and son or daughter. Bitterness, although not obliterating love from the picture, certainly forces it into at least temporary eclipse. The actions of the adolescent, and sometimes even of the parent, become dominated by vindictiveness and stubbornness, and such a condition magnifies every little problem into a major crisis. Handling potentially troublesome friction areas in such a manner that adverse emotions are not involved, on the other hand, fosters the strengthening of natural parent-child mutual love. The stronger such love, the easier it is for each person to appreciate the feelings and convictions of the other. Therefore, helping adolescents and parents reach agreement on any even minor point of conflict makes it easier for them to evolve eventual mutual understanding and agreement.

You should not assume, from all the foregoing discussion, that violent trouble is inevitable in the process of the adolescent's achieving a mature relationship with parents involving his independence from their control while retaining full love for them. Practically every adolescent has a number of more or less serious disagreements with parents in this process, it is true, but in comparatively few instances do things become so bad that domestic disaster threatens. It is worthwhile to alleviate even minor points of friction, however. In the very nature of things, the help of the teacher or counselor will be needed in the serious cases more than in the less serious ones. In conflicts great or small, the same dynamic forces in parents or adolescents are involved, and the basic principles for rendering needed assistance are identical.

Case of Ocie Osborne

When Ocie was thirteen, he wanted a motor scooter, which his parents refused to get for him. They did, however, permit him to carry a paper route and earn his own money, and by the time he was fourteen he had saved thirty-five dollars, for which he bought a dilapidated fourth-hand scooter. Prior to his buying the scooter it was agreed under what circumstances he could ride it, one stipulation being that he was not to take it on the through streets or highways. He could ride it on residential streets, however, and on the main street to the extent unavoidable in riding it to school. An ingenious scheme was worked out whereby Ocie's time to be home when out for the evening was made later or earlier depending on his school grades and his fulfillment of responsibilities in the home. By the time he was sixteen, Ocie could stay out until midnight Friday and Saturday nights if he maintained a B average and if he had fulfilled his home responsibilities (keeping his room neat, carrying out the garbage, "doing" the evening dishes—he was the oldest of four boys—and some lesser jobs) without having to be told to do things more than twice during the week.

During his mid-teens Ocie began to run with a group of boys his parents considered undesirable because of the lack of parental control exercised over them and their late hours and their lavish spending of money. Ocie's parents talked with him about his friends, and he was unwilling to stop his association with them. The parents exerted themselves to provide a basketball goal in their back yard and ping-pong facilities, and encouraged Ocie to bring classmates by the house after school for soft drinks and sandwiches. They limited Ocie's time away from home to afternoons and evenings when he had definite plans which they approved. He gradually drifted away from the gang of which his parents disapproved, in the meantime developing an active social life with others.

At nineteen, ready for his sophomore year in college, Ocie and his parents are on good terms. He respects their judgment and wishes, and they seldom "require" him to do things or "prohibit" his doing them. They often casually tell him to do this or that, or suggest that he not do so and so, and he usually goes along with their ideas, although he frequently fusses somewhat in the process. He has no "allowance," he writes checks as he needs money, and his parents consider him prudent and considerate of their resources in his spending.

1. What dynamics of parent-child relationships can be inferred from this digest which may have helped Ocie pass through adolescence and achieve emancipation from parental control as easily and smoothly as he apparently did?

2. What are some examples of self-control exercised by Ocie and concessions made by his parents which facilitated their good adjustment and Ocie's unstressful maturation into relative independence?

even the most raptly infatuated couple or the two most steadfast friends. Conversations involving sometimes one, sometimes twenty other people, are desired. The topics of conversation include not only popular music and social activities, but school affairs, cars, jobs, and aspirations for the future, even international relations, religion, and the nature of truth! Thus, the boy and girl become more broadly adept in social intercourse. If a respected member of the group expresses an opinion different from one's own, one learns how to avoid an unpleasant clash and at the same time not abjectly surrender. The finesse of social graces comes from richness of experience in group thought and talk, added to a self concept which maintains the essential intellectual integrity of the individual.

The invaluable article entitled "The Course of Healthy Personality Development" from the Midcentury White House Conference on Children and Youth (see Chapter 2) refers to the development of a "sense of intimacy" as a developmental stage of late adolescence. This sense of intimacy does not refer to sexual nor yet any other physical intimacy. Rather, it is "a kind of fusion with the essence of other people." According to this theory, following the achievement of a sense of identity (an integration and acceptance of one's   ature, such as was discussed in Chapter 6), healthy and successfu   ent requires a feeling of belongingness in the race of men. I   s perception of oneself as an integral part of society, and hum   as a projection to some extent of one's own self.[23] As a philosopher put it, the injustice, pain, or grief suffered by any human is to some extent shared by every other human of sensitivity. This identification with humanity is called the sense of intimacy. It is not essentially connected with association with a member of the opposite sex, but the emotional attachment which forms between members of opposite sexes seems to contribute to its development. Perhaps the experience of "unselfish" love, love based not on services rendered to one by the other (as an infant loves a parent), but simply because the person is, contributes to breaking the bonds of egocentrism and making others, as well as ourselves, important to us.

Small children play beside each other but not with each other. Older ones play with each other, but do not thereby necessarily develop a sharing of themselves with each other. Probably only after heterosexual development and adjustment are well advanced and a strong sense of

23 H. C. Smith, *Personality Adjustment*. McGraw-Hill Book Company, Inc., New York, 1961.

personal identity achieved, which can stand the experience of accepting others as part of itself and sharing itself with others, is a development of the sense of intimacy possible. Before these other two accomplishments, the adolescent is probably not at a level of emotional maturity required to relate to others in the manner implied by the sense of intimacy. In fact, the consultants of the White House Conference speculate that the interminable conversations held by adolescents not only develop their social skills, but also, through giving them better insight into how other people think and feel, help them arrive at a more complete sense of personal identity. If this is true, we can reasonably postulate that the final step in achieving a complete sense of personal identity is the achievement of a sense of unity or intimacy with our society, with the people with whom our lives are lived.

What are the dynamic forces and processes involved in the adolescent's achieving mature human relations with peer groups, besides the obvious mating tendency accompanying sexual maturation? What are the factors in this area which correspond to the forces of love, desire for independence, trust and distrust of judgments involved in changing relations between adolescents and their parents? The drive for belongingness takes on a new significance, for one thing. Belongingness increasingly means sharing the sense of intimacy with a chosen group, as contrasted with the emphasis on simple physical togetherness encountered in childhood. The adolescent is in a very real sense striving to establish a society, a culture, composed of himself and his group.[24] Adults are usually only peripheral figures to this society, existing in the lives of the adolescents, but not as a part of the social structure which to the adolescent is the most real and vital aspect of his life. Probably much of the desire to win emancipation from the home is for the unexpressed purpose of becoming a free agent to affiliate with the society of his peers, the people who will be his recreational and vocational companions in the decades to come. The teenage boy or girl is definitely not a part of adult society; he would be a conspicuously "junior member," of little influence, if he were. Thus, the feeling of need to establish a social order of which he is an integral part, one based on interests and standards similar to his own, in which he enjoys status and prestige unabridged by inferiority in age, is probably the decisive element in this aspect of adolescent maturation.[25]

[24] C. M. Tryon, "The Adolescent Peer Culture," *Adolescence, Forty-third Yearbook of the National Society for the Study of Education*, 1944, Part I, Chapt. XII.
[25] R. Dewey and W. J. Humber, *The Development of Human Behavior*. The Macmillan Company, New York, 1951.

The actual process of achieving satisfactory human relations with the peer group is fraught with many difficulties which account in large measure for the anxiety and compensatory brashness so typical of the adolescent. The new society being formed by adolescents has its own code and standards of conduct. In some respects the code is inflexible; you conform to the policies and practices of the group if you are going to remain a member, whether the point at issue is how much and when homework is done, or etiquette regarding when to cut in at a dance, or what to do when someone approaches to cut in.[26] In other respects, the code is bewilderingly variable or inconstant; due to some inexplicable mass whim, the correct way of breaking with a steady today may incur group disapproval tomorrow.

Adults seldom fully appreciate that beneath the adolescent's slavish following of group practices there lies the insecurity of a person attempting to adjust to a social structure not only strange and somewhat frightening (although also delightful) to him, but a social structure so new and formative that it is fluid, changeable, so that it is exceedingly difficult to achieve any genuine sense of permanence in it. With the innate insecurity of a social position in a society itself changing erratically and spasmodically, and a personality still seeking to fully identify itself, it is not surprising that the adolescent does not feel confident enough to concur in parental suggestions if he is not sure these suggestions will be fully approved by the group. At best, the adolescent seldom achieves a high degree of confidence that he holds an unassailable position within his group. Even the recognized leader is insecure; leadership can (and often does) shift on the capricious whim of a handful of people. To cite one actual instance, the reigning beauty queen of a high school, voted "most popular" during her junior year, incurred the displeasure of a small influential group of girls and, through their machinations, was conspicuously omitted from the slightest recognition in the school annual during her senior year!

Thus, a seeking for security in a society innately lacking in security, but wherein the boy or girl must, somehow, find and keep a place, becomes a major force in social maturation. Self-consciousness over physical appearance or changes, doubts as to the adequacy of one's conversational ability, many such things intensify fears of inferiority, undermining the feeling of security. A calm, "accepting" person, to whom the adolescent can talk and who represents a stable relationship in which he is secure

26 K. C. Garrison, *Psychology of Adolescence*. Prentice-Hall, Inc., Englewood Cliffs, N. J., 1951.

not for what he can do, but simply because *he is he,* is invaluable to an adolescent in adjusting to his evolving society. The stability, the sanctuary, the knowledge of having someone dependable and unchanging by whom he will be accepted without question and without earning acceptance—something like the unearned love needed by infants—gives needed moral support to the adolescent struggling to achieve an adult pattern of human relations. Through being such a person, a teacher can enrich and be a solace in the lives of innumerable boys and girls. The opportunity to do so constitutes one of the great rewards of teaching.

Questions re Case of Ocie Osborne
    3. What evidence is there that Ocie was hunting a place for himself in the society of his peers?
    4. How did his parents assist him? In what way may assistance have subtly encouraged the sort of people they wanted Ocie to be with, and discouraged others from being with him?

ACHIEVING HETEROSEXUAL
ADJUSTMENT

Case of Patricia Patton and Quinten Qualls
    Patricia Patton, age thirteen, was a Junior Guide at the city-wide school art exhibit. Quinten Qualls, age fourteen, was there from another school, and the two met in the course of their summer work. Often they stood together waiting for other people to come for the tour, and gradually they began to talk. The exhibit was over at the end of the week, and Pat and Quinten parted, with promises that Quint would call. This he has done, to the point of driving Pat's mother to distraction. On Saturdays he asks his parents' permission to ride his bike across town and visit Pat, and, after checking with her mother, has been permitted to do so.
    In school Patricia spends her time with other girls her age, none of whom have anything to do with boys. Pat herself is vaguely conscious of pleasure in talking with boys, although anything like walking home with one has not entered her mind—well, at least she hasn't! A couple of older boys have made awkward overtures of friendship to which Pat happily responded in what she thought was a friendly manner. But the boys said something else, Pat replied,

the conversation languished, and each boy, in turn, self-consciously shambled off.

Quinten's mother took Pat and Quint to the picture show one Saturday afternoon. The next day a friend told Pat's mother that, while collecting her own children, she had seen Pat and Quinten sitting on the back row of the theater kissing. Pat's mother, horrified, read the riot act to Pat and forbade her to see Quint any more. Pat is crushed, says they didn't mean any harm, and promises *anything* to be allowed to continue seeing him.

Pat's mother, realizing that Pat's homeroom teacher has had more training and experience with these boy-girl relationships than she, tells the teacher about the situation and asks for advice.

(*Questions about Pat and her situation will follow this section.*)

Children play together with little consciousness of whether playmates are boys or girls. During the pre-adolescent years, as sex hormones begin to produce definite sexual differentiation and as social customs encourage segregation by sexes in activities and associations, the children divide into two groups, by sexes. There is remarkably little voluntary crossing of sex lines during this period; active animosity toward members of the opposite sex individually and as a group is common; it is as if nature were enforcing a period of achieving a beginning of identification with one's own sex before embarking on the remainder-of-life association with people of the opposite sex under circumstances dictated by sexual differences.

With the beginning of adolescence, a gradual change in feelings toward the opposite sex takes place. A mutual attraction between boy and girl develops. The development is slow and potentially an area of severe maladjustment. Consider the situation: For several years the boy and girl have expressed by word and action their aversion to the opposite sex. Parents and other adults have teased them with accusations that they like this or that member of the opposite sex.[27] Often Mama has told friends with pride in Sonny's presence, "Mama is his only girl friend. He says he will never love any other girl. Don't you, Sonny?" Sonny beamingly assents. Other adults have, for the deliberate purpose of infuriating the little girl or boy, said, "One of these days you will see a little boy (or girl) come along and think he is the cutest thing you've ever seen in

---

[27] A. Crow, "Parental Attitudes toward Boy-Girl Relations," *Journal of Educational Sociology*, Nov., 1955, pp. 125–133.

your life. You'll run after him so hard you won't even look back to see where your Daddy is!" And Baby Doll has wrathfully and indignantly denied that *she* could ever be a party to such folly!

And now, feeling within herself or himself the stirrings of normal biological maturation, but seldom conscious of the physical relations implied in the ultimate consummation of sex, the early adolescent is conscious of an inexplicable desire to be with and be admired by one or more of the opposite sex. If, at this point, past attitudes and remarks of adults cause the child to imagine the sly jokes, the "I told you so" remarks of adults in his life, if he often encounters the veiled but evident implications from the parent of the opposite sex that "he is about to love other girls (or boys) besides his Mama (Papa)," the difficulty of the task of normal heterosexual adjustment is doubled or quadrupled.

It is bad enough just adjusting to the changing relationship with members of the opposite sex without the added handicap of adult teasing. For several years members of the opposite sex have been looked upon as, at best, nonentities and, at worst, natural enemies whose chief function in life is to grab your books or possessions and run away with them, or tell on you for anything you did. Although the barbarous custom has about disappeared from modern pedagogy, the pre-adolescent period still harbors the vestigial remains of feelings which caused Tom Sawyer's teacher to punish him by making him sit on the side of the room with the *girls*. All pre-adolescents know that members of the opposite sex are peculiar, rather repulsive creatures, and that friendship with one is definitely a sign of abnormality, sissiness, or some less definable aberration.

Thus, the first friendly approaches, breaking the ice, in establishing relations with the opposite sex are sometimes a severe problem to the adolescent. Fortunately, the common classroom procedures of modern education render the experience much less stressful than was once typical. Boys and girls work together on class committees, assigned by the teacher or as a result of their choice of a topic of study. Who is to say that Sim and Ellie wound up on the same committee because of the pleasure of each other's company and not because of interest in the committee problem? In the process of committee work they learn to associate with each other and with others of the opposite sex easily and naturally. What to say and do is no problem, because the committee has a job to work on. Personal conversation comes easily and naturally, as a result of a mutual desire to share ideas or feelings, or it simply does not come, but there is the job to work on. Self-consciousness about being with each other is minimal, because there is a reason to be there that no adult can successfully tease about (although unfortunately they often try). After a few months of such work with members of the opposite sex, the adolescent has gained a new skill in social maturation, readying him to move into more extensive heterosexual associations with minimal anxiety, strain, or floundering.[28] Altogether, in the minds of some psychologists, the greatest single contribution of progressive education is to the easy and normal growth of heterosexual adjustments!

Even the best of educational methods, however, does not entirely eliminate the initial problems of heterosexual adjustment. Work together on school tasks can imperceptibly lead to walking home together, calling each other up, visiting each other, even going to the library together or meeting there to work on their joint task. But the jump to deliberate planning of a time to be spent together solely for the pleasure of each other's company, a date, can still be a considerable problem. "What'll I say?" is the boy's panicky thought. "What'll I say?" the girl despairingly asks herself as, robbed of the protection of a shared responsibility of work, each faces for the first time the problem of making conversation with a date.

If your own experience or that of the adolescents you observe suggests an uninhibited eagerness to establish friendly relations with any or all of the opposite sex, if the problem is not one of helping them through a stressful and taxing experience, but merely of holding them back until they attain a respectable age, rejoice! Millions *do* go through the painful embarrassment of difficult heterosexual adjustment (although it is often unnoticed by adults). It is a tribute to good management by the adults in their lives and their own emotional stability and strong self concepts when the transition into heterosexual society is an easy, natural, and pleasant experience.

Establishing natural relations with the opposite sex (this is a part of the sense of intimacy) comes as a culmination of a number of developmental stages of affections. First comes the love of a child for parents, for those who love and protect him, care for his wants, and without whom he would be helpless. Then develops an affection for friends, family, and other adults who may not directly minister to him, but whose company he enjoys and for whom he develops loyalty. Thus, we find the

28 P. H. Landis, *Adolescence and Youth*. McGraw-Hill Book Company, Inc., New York, 1952.

little girl who likes a friend and, therefore, sees nothing wrong with that friend. She may not be able to state why she likes this one better than another who seems just as nice and agreeable, but she does. The process of differentiation of affections, of being more favorably affected by one than by another, is in progress. This differentiation is seldom completely logical or consistent. We find the boy who never says a kind word to his sister (or, equally likely, his brother), constantly criticizes her and teases her unmercifully, and yet hurls himself savagely upon a friend who mistreats her.

Slowly and gradually boys and girls develop unrecognized but definite patterns of affection for, or rejection of, others. There is the sense of friendship, which is the foundation for wholesome heterosexual affections. Boys and girls learn to handle emotional relations with members of the same sex in childhood when friends are relatively uncritical and when errors and slights are quickly and openly pointed out and as quickly forgiven. Think of the difficulty of learning the elemental ABC's of getting along in close harmony with people in adulthood, where it is bad manners to show that you noticed someone's callousness or maliciousness, and where feelings, once hurt, continue sensitive for months, instead of popping back to normal in minutes or seconds as they do in childhood. They learn much of how they and other people feel, the things which make for pleasantness and unpleasantness, in the resilient, unselfconscious atmosphere of childhood, far removed from the delicate and sensitive relations coming into play as sexual maturation complicates relations between adolescents.

Often the first manifestations of heterosexual affection come in the form of emotional attachments to older members of the opposite sex.[29] A boy forms a heterosexually oriented affection for a young, attractive lady teacher. A girl does the same for a man teacher or an official of her church or the coach. Such disparate-age attachments may serve a useful purpose in the heterosexual maturation of the boy and girl, allowing them to engage in personally oriented conversation with a member of the opposite sex who can handle the situation in a manner pleasant and unembarrassing to the young admirer. If the older object of the adolescent's affections is an irresponsible or unscrupulous person, of course, harm may result from the episode, particularly in the case of the adolescent girl who becomes infatuated with an older man. However, when the ob-

29 L. D. Crow and A. Crow, *Adolescent Development and Adjustment*. McGraw-Hill Book Company, Inc., New York, 1956.

ject of the adolescent's affections is a responsible and ethical person, the experience can be most beneficial to the boy or girl. Naturally, no physical intimacy or even suggestive talk would take place under these circumstances, and nothing approaching a date would even be considered, but learning how to make "small talk" with a member of the opposite sex, how to give or accept a compliment, and how to be pleasant in a mature fashion can be accomplished without anxiety or embarrassment if the adolescent is fortunate enough to have such a mature friend, facilitating his or her adjustment to age-mates in heterosexual maturation.

Questions re Case of Patricia Patton and Quinten Qualls
    1. Why did Patricia probably become fond of Quinten instead of one of the many boys in her own school?
    2. In what ways is Pat's association with Quint conducive to her social maturation and adjustment?
    3. Evaluate the attitudes and actions of Pat's mother upon learning of their conduct in the movie.

THE ROLE OF DATING IN HETEROSEXUAL ADJUSTMENT

Different cultures have differing mores and customs regarding the relations between boys and girls prior to marriage. In some, they meet only under strictest chaperonage and politely discourse on impersonal topics until the young man decides to ask the girl's parents for permission to seek her hand in marriage, and this chaperonage continues until the association is terminated by marriage or discontinuance of association. In some cultures, indeed, the young people may not even meet each other until their parents have arranged for their betrothal or marriage. Then nothing at all in the way of wooing or even becoming acquainted with each other takes place; they dutifully marry and have the remainder of their lives in which to become acquainted with each other.

On the other end of the scale, there are cultures in which boys and girls are permitted, without social disapproval, unlimited privacy and intimacy involving, in primitive tribes, frank and open sexual relations and, in advanced cultures, unchaperoned weekends and vacations together.

The more or less private premarital associations of a boy and girl in the United States are pretty well, if loosely, covered by the term "dating." The degree of privacy and intimacy permitted, or at least officially sanctioned, in these associations falls somewhere between the two extremes described above, although individual instances can be found in great number which fall at one extreme or the other rather than in the middle. Jewish and Christian ethics, whose influence is large in determining our social conventions, prohibit professed and unconcealed promiscuity between unmarried members of the sexes. On the other hand, the place of women in the United States, where they have rights, responsibilities, and prerogatives differing little from those of men, renders anomalous the chaperonage customary in upper-class Latin American families, for instance. As responsible citizens of a society in which they function as equals, girls are early accorded the responsibility for their own behavior. Boys and girls are expected, by social conventions, to conduct themselves properly in their relations with each other, but little external supervision is customarily imposed beyond the ages of sixteen or eighteen to see that they do so.

In a culture where as much emphasis is placed on the importance of the happiness of the individual as it is in the United States in this century, dating serves a highly important social and psychological function. Certainly, social skills conducive to good social adjustment are cultivated by dating. Also, boys and girls, through dating, gain insights into the nature of members of the opposite sex which promote better adjustment after marriage. In addition to the biological attraction of members of the opposite sex for each other, several psychological factors are found in the underlying dynamics of dating.

Companionship

Much of the initial association between adolescent boys and girls is thought by many psychologists to be motivated not by sexual attraction but by a pleasure in companionship.[30] There are psychologists who dispute this point, maintaining that the element of sexual attraction, of erotic love, is always at the bottom of a male-female relationship, no matter how effectively its manifestation is repressed, unconscious, or sublimated in its expression. However, workers with boys and girls encounter so many instances where no perceptible indication of sexual feelings exists between an adolescent boy and girl who greatly enjoy each other's

[30] F. McKinney, *Psychology of Personal Adjustment.* John Wiley & Sons, Inc., New York, 1960.

company that they generally feel that liking for each other as *persons,* not as a male or female, is a dominant factor in the relationship.

There are several possible reasons why a boy might prefer the company of a girl to that of other boys, or a girl that of a boy to other girls, without erotic attraction being involved. Boys are in competition with boys and girls with girls in numerous areas where boys are not in competition with girls. Athletics, popularity, dress, spending money, parents' comparisons with sex-mates, and, indeed, ability to achieve the admiration of the opposite sex, are examples of such areas of competition. Questionnaires seeking to ascertain attitudes of adolescent boys and girls toward each other provide sufficient evidence to justify the hypothesis that the lesser competition between boys and girls, as compared to that between members of the same sex, would promote their congenial association.

Then, there is the biologically based, but socially promoted, complementariness of natures which encourages boy-girl relationships without involving erotic attraction. Throughout nature there seems to be a desire on the part of the male to "show off," by means of physical feats, daring, cleverness, or simply being "different." This trait is obvious among adolescent boys, who use such techniques extensively to attract female attention, partly because they lack the more adult and subtle conversational skills or intellectual depth to impress on other bases. Happily, this tendency on the part of the male is complemented by the female in her appreciation of such traits, expressed openly in admiration or more subtly. Even in the culture of the United States, most women find their greatest outside-the-home self-realization through the achievements of their men, and the adolescent girl who derives satisfaction from the masculine demeanor and traits of a boy is developing a good basis for adjustment to the role of a wife. She is attractive to boys because she fills their need to be admired, perhaps to be "oh'd" and "ah'd" over. Boys displaying the masculine traits which presage adult success are attractive to her because they fill her need to associate herself with someone who can cope with and conquer things. The need of the male to feel that he is providing and protecting, of the female to feel that her companion is willing and able to provide for and protect her, is a powerful basis for adolescent boy-girl companionship, without any essential presence of erotic attraction.

Finally, there is imitation of older people, the pairing-off of couples, which is an example of socially acceptable behavior observed by adolescents. Conformity to the adult world into which they are growing is

George Peabody College for Teachers.

Figure 24. "The girl who derives satisfaction from the masculine demeanor and traits of a boy is developing a good basis for adjustment to the role of a wife."

undoubtedly a part of the motivation of earliest heterosexual companionship. And in all phases of dating for congenial companionship, the developmental task of learning to share oneself with another and share a part of another's self is being effectively mastered.

Personality Attraction

One of the most baffling questions of social psychology has been "What makes Jack like Helen better than Betty, while Jim likes Betty more than Helen?" And Betty's or Helen's preference may or may not be fixed on the boy who prefers her. Multitudes of studies have produced dozens of traits or characteristics which boys and girls say make members of the opposite sex particularly attractive to them. However, the attractiveness of a specific boy to a specific girl, or vice versa, is so unique a thing that it is often difficult to relate it to any list of characteristics.[31]

Years ago a song was popular which listed, one after another, the characteristics of a girl (or boy, depending on the sex of the vocalist) with the statement in each instance that "I never cared for (the characteristic)," and continuing, "but she's (he's) got (each trait), so that's my weakness now." One reason it was so popular was because it was so true to life; every person with a normal range of heterosexual experience has encountered someone of the opposite sex who differs drastically from his general preference and yet who is unusually attractive to him.

Personality attraction is a major motivating element in dating. (Many psychologists include physical appearance as an element of personality; whether or not it is so considered is immaterial to this discussion.) A boy or girl wants to associate with a member of the opposite sex because that person possesses a "personality" which is particularly appealing to him or her. So the search for the crucial factor in personality attraction has continued. The partial answer—partial in the sense that it indicates the area in which the crucial factor lies but not the dynamics of the factor—appears to be that a personality is attractive to a member of the opposite sex *not so much for its own nature as for the self concept it causes the associate to develop.*

The personality and physical traits which enhance the appeal of one adolescent for another—good looks, neatness, ability to talk easily and interestingly, sincerity, vivacity—are so obvious to even the casual observer that discussing them here is unnecessary. But we all know many instances of a girl who is devoted to, even idolizes, a boy who is such an unprepossessing specimen that we ask, "What on earth can she see in *him?*" Less frequently a man becomes enamored with a girl who prompts the same question to arise in the minds of his friends. Less frequently, we say, but it happens; it happened in literally hundreds of cases in which American servicemen serving overseas married and are still living, apparently happily, with wives who would appear to the observer to suffer badly from comparison with American girls generally. Analyzing what

[31] N. Reader and H. B. English, "Personality Factors in Adolescent Female Friendships," *Journal of Consulting Psychology*, 1947, *11*:212–220.

the idolized one is like usually deepens the mystery of his or her attraction, because the analyst finds . . . nothing!

An unknown poet expressed it in this manner:

LOVE

I love you,
Not only for what you are,
But for what I am
When I am with you.

I love you,
Not only for what
You have made of yourself,
But for what
You are making of me.

I love you
For the part of me
That you bring out;
I love you
For putting your hand
Into my heaped-up heart
And passing over
All the foolish, weak things
That you can't help
Dimly seeing there,
And for drawing out
Into the light
All the beautiful belongings
That no one else had looked
Quite far enough to find.

I love you because you
Are helping me to make
Of the lumber of my life
Not a tavern
But a temple,
Out of the works
Of my every day
Not a reproach
But a song.

I love you
Because you have done
More than any creed
Could have done

To make me good,
And more than any fate
Could have done
To make me happy.

You have done it
Without a touch,
Without a word,
Without a sign,
You have done it
By being yourself.
Perhaps that is what
Being a friend means,
After all.

Psychological research currently indicates that he may have been uncannily perceptive and correct in his evaluation of an interpersonal relationship. If, when I am with you, I feel stronger or more secure, more competent or more contented, better satisfied with what I am, I will like you. Asked to give my reason for liking you, I would probably say, "She has a sweet, charming personality," because that is how you would seem to me. But the *reason* would be that you cause me to construct a better, more flattering image of myself as a result of what you are, say, or do, rather than my intrinsic liking for your characteristics. The girl who brings out, in the most flattering form, the admirable masculine attributes of a boy and makes him feel that he is an admirable specimen of young manhood indeed, will possess a strong appeal for that boy. Similarly, the boy who causes a girl to feel most flatteringly the fullness of her femininity will be thought by the girl to have a "wonderful personality."

This is an important concept, important in making fine differentiations which explain why one boy or girl is popular (which means he or she possesses strong personality attraction for many people; many members of the opposite sex would like to date, to associate with, him or her; his or her company is enjoyed by many others) while another of superficially the same characteristics is not. Does a boy compete strongly for the position of center of attention? If he does so because he wants everyone to be impressed by him, he may be labeled a "personality boy." He is not likely to be popular as a dating partner. Does he compete equally strongly for the center of attention, but for the reason that he desires to win the admiration of his date? There is a subtle difference which every girl of normal social adeptness can recognize. The latter boy will generally have personality appeal for most girls because of the subtle compliment paid them. The compliment lies in their escort's seeking to win their admiration, instead of seeking to win the admiration of other girls.

Personality attraction as a basis for dating may or may not be based on erotic attraction. Often it obviously is; the self concept constructed by the partner is sexually oriented. In contrast, an unmarried woman psychologist, queried as to the phenomenal personality attraction for women possessed by a certain man, explained, "Just in saying 'Hello' when he meets you, he somehow makes you feel that meeting you is the high spot of his day"—not of *your* day, mind you, but the flattering implication that meeting you was the high spot of *his* day. The flattering self concept produced by such a fleeting association!

It may be concluded that an important dynamic in dating is the desire to associate with someone whose presence enhances one's own self concept. Dating becomes a means of satisfying one's need for recognition and particularly the self-recognition called self-esteem. Awareness of this relationship will often enable a teacher, counselor, or parent to understand why a boy or girl (more usually a girl) develops an infatuation for a member of the opposite sex who possesses, to the impartial observer, not one characteristic which would make him attractive. His attractiveness probably lies not in his personal characteristics, but in his ability, somehow, to cause the girl to form a more flattering self concept—perhaps a self concept which casts her in the role of a good woman who sees possibilities in a man which others are unable to see and who will make an admirable person out of an unadmirable one; perhaps a self concept which envisions her as more attractive than she feels herself to be when she is with another boy. The nature of and basis for the improved self concept are as variable as human nature and human vanity themselves. But looking for the source of personality attraction of one person for another will often reveal the attraction to be the changed, more flattering self concept of the boy or girl, not the actual personality characteristics of the other person.

Mutual Self-discovery

We have already mentioned the complementariness of certain aspects of the natures of males and females. The discussion of topics of mutual interest, including each other, is an important component of normal dating patterns. Through such talking, boys and girls clarify their self concepts by seeing themselves through the verbal eyes of one whom they like, respect, and trust.[32] If the clarified self concept is a better one than was previously held, the partner tends to be liked, and vice versa. With almost every dating experience the adolescent, through the date's attitude and remarks, acquires new perceptions of himself or herself, along with a better understanding of the opposite sex. Of course, these perceptions are not usually consciously noted and enumerated. They are merely impressions of pleasantness or unpleasantness. Similarly, the understanding of the opposite sex does not take the form of specific facts added, date by date, to a systematized list; it consists, in part, of greater sensitivity in perceiving the moods or feelings of one of the opposite sex, and hard-won skills in responding most advantageously to those moods and feelings. Thus, bit by bit, adolescent boys and girls, as well as older ones, grow in understanding of themselves and others through dating.

The observant adult working closely with adolescents can easily detect their attempts to achieve a stronger sense of personal identity (see Chapter 6) through casual and persistent questioning of the thoughts, feelings, and motives of others. "Gee, how did you *feel?*" is not asked only out of curiosity; consciously or unconsciously, the adolescent really is seeking by such questions to answer in his own mind such questions as "How would I have felt? Do other people feel as I do? What is the *right* way to feel in a case like that? Are my feelings what they ought to be?"

Similarly, a question such as "What did you do last night?" often is motivated by much more than idle curiosity. Behind it lie such thoughts as "Am I doing as much as others are? Am I spending my time the way other people are? Ought I to be doing something different, managing my life differently?" (These questions imply, as adolescents customarily feel, that "normality" is adhering to the patterns and standards of the group.) The hundreds of questions which adolescents who like each other's company can be heard asking each other in reality constitute their attempts to self-educate themselves in a practical philosophy of life and to acquire a perspective on people which will enable them to understand themselves better through more complete comparison of themselves with others. Individually (and often collectively, to adults) the questions seem pointless, if not, somehow, morbid or a bit ghoulish, in their suggestion of fascination with the hidden recesses of another's mind and feelings. However, in the aggregate they reveal to the adolescent more of

32 J. Macmurray, *Reason and Emotion*. Appleton-Century-Crofts, Inc., New York, 1937.

how people think and feel, what other people are like, how they react, and such insights make him a more socially competent person.

Dating is an ideal opportunity for such probing of each other's minds and feelings, and with every passing year, dating activities tend to become more personality-oriented and less impersonal-activity-oriented. The desire, often not consciously recognized but probably universal among adolescents, to achieve this more intimate insight into others and themselves is another of the dynamic factors producing dating and adolescents' preoccupation with it.

The Mating Urge

There can be little doubt that the simple, primitive urge to mate, which can be observed in uninhibited and unconcealed form among lower animals and primitive people, is equally active as a dynamic factor underlying dating among American adolescents. The mating aspect of dating, however, can be readily subdivided into two identifiable, if not distinct, elements.

One is the sexual element. This is the uncomplicated urge of normal males and females to experience satisfaction of sexual drives through sexual activity. In American culture this urge, in itself uncomplicated, produces highly complicated situations because of the conventions which inhibit its expression. Such inhibitions are necessary, make no mistake about that. The ideal of "free love" espoused by some pseudo intellectuals is not merely inimical to American religious and moral standards; uninhibited sexuality will destroy any culture, any nation, because it will destroy the unity of the home and the family, without which no nation has ever endured. Nevertheless, and essential as they are, the moral and ethical inhibitions surrounding the expression of the sex drive are a major complication in social adjustment, and most especially in the social maturation of the adolescent.

Dating is a form of sexual pairing-off, even though the ultimate end of sexual union may never take place. As we have seen, customs of dating vary from culture to culture. American dating customs encourage a boy and a girl to become well-enough acquainted with each other to be capable of intelligent judgment as to their psychological suitability to live together, but custom does not sanction the physical intimacy which this culture approves only within marriage. Every date is an experience in living together under certain circumstances. It is a sample association of potential mates. As such, it is valuable experience in interpersonal relations and constitutes preparation for marriage. At the same time, dating is often frustrating to young people, especially boys, because, unless moral and ethical principles are violated, the sexual pairing off process stops short of the physical mating which is the natural culmination of pairing off.

Since promiscuous expression of the mating urge does lead to undesirable consequences in our culture, the dating customs of adolescents should be regulated to insure that boys and girls are not subjected to temptations which they cannot withstand. The fact that boys and girls typically mature in their sexual capabilities and desires earlier and faster than they mature in their judgment and their ability to control their impulses[33] is the reason adolescent heterosexual associations should be supervised or limited, especially in the early and middle teens. Everyone knows that typical mid-teen boys and girls will surrender to a desire to attend a party or dance, even though they know they risk failure in a course if they do not spend the evening reviewing for a test. How, then, can they be logically expected to withstand the powerful biological urge of sexual attraction, when privacy and opportunity for gratification are available at the same time emotions and desires are at fever height? Obviously they cannot be logically expected to do so, and the number of girls suffering, at best, severe pangs of conscience and, at worst, pregnancy is evident proof that they actually fail in many cases to exercise the control.

Dating is highly desirable as a means of achieving the goals of socialization discussed in previous sections of this chapter, and of affording the experience of the limited "living together" mentioned. Sane supervision which limits privacy, mobility, and opportunities for erotic arousal should be exercised over the dating of boys and girls to insure them the beneficial aspects of dating while minimizing the risks entailed. Moderate hours for coming home, scheduled activities, and limited access to automobiles for a boy and girl alone are sane, sensible precautions.

Another element in the mating urge is the desire to establish a stable, adult relationship such as is represented by a home and family.[34] Girls, particularly, often want to date because dating is a step toward eventual achievement of a home and motherhood. This homemaking desire, while

[33] K. Davis, "Adolescence and the Social Structure," *American Academy of Political and Social Science*, 1944, 236:8–16.

[34] J. Levy and R. Munroe, *The Happy Family*. Alfred A. Knopf, Inc., New York, 1938.

a part of the mating urge, is not primarily sexual in nature. Sex is a part of establishing a home, in the full sense of the word, and, of course, an essential in the production of a family. However, there is substantial evidence that in the affective structure of many adolescents, especially girls, the physical aspects of sex are a secondary element of the mating urge, the element of primary significance being the desire to have a home, a husband, and children.

Dating has its limitations as a means of ascertaining whether life with a particular boy or girl would be a permanently rewarding experience, but it is probably the best method yet devised. The boy and girl whose marriage is preceded by dating over a sufficiently lengthy period, and under widely diverse circumstances involving many different types of activities, are much more likely to find the adjustments of marriage possible than are the boy and girl who marry on relatively slight acquaintance with each other.[35] The fact that through extensive dating each has had opportunity to learn what the other is really like, and whether their natures are compatible, is not the only reason for the greater success of their marriage. Almost equally important is the fact that through dating each has already made many of the adjustments to each other necessary for harmonious living together. Thus, they enter marriage with some of the potential sources of stress already eliminated.

It can be concluded that dating serves many purposes in the heterosexual development of adolescents, and several major needs or dynamic factors cause boys and girls to want to date. Typically, boys and girls pass through several stages of dating before engagement and marriage. Each stage serves a particular purpose in the gradual production of complete heterosexual adjustment. These overlap heavily, but tend to assume a general pattern of development, which we shall examine in the next section of this chapter.

Case of Ruth Randolph

Ruth started dating when she was thirteen years old, dating in the sense of being escorted to a movie by a boy whose parents left them there at 7 P.M. and picked them up at 9:30 after a soda at a nearby drug store. She was cute, friendly, and intelligent, and quickly made friends on picnics, in a new school, at a vacation spot, or with

35 H. Bowman, *Marriage for Moderns*. McGraw-Hill Book Company, Inc., New York, 1960.

a new boy in the neighborhood. Typically, Ruth would have one boy whom she dated fairly regularly, perhaps over a period of several months. In the meantime, however, she would be having numerous dates with other boys, and tried with fair success to keep her "regular" from realizing that she dated others so extensively. She maintained this policy throughout junior and senior high school despite the fact that "going steady," meaning confining one's dates exclusively to one person for a period of time, was the majority policy in her schools. She did usually go with her "main" boy friend to principal school functions.

Ruth engaged in substantially less necking than did most of her age-mates, and only in rare instances of petting with her principal boy friend of the moment, in her last year of high school and subsequently. She never engaged in intercourse. Her parents were somewhat nonplused by the fact that Ruth often let drop casual remarks regarding the opinion of her current boy friend, and sometimes her other casual dates, on the best size of families, the proper relationships between husband and wife, and whether a boy and girl should marry when they are still in school. They were mildly concerned that Ruth apparently discussed possibilities of marriage with every boy she went with, or so it seemed to them.

In college Ruth pledged a sorority her freshman year, becoming a member in due course. She still had occasional dates with two or three of her boy friends from high-school days and constantly accumulated new ones, one at a time, and with real affection for each one whom she dated repeatedly. She was never formally engaged in college, but on four different occasions she indicated to her parents that she and her boy friend were thinking hopefully of marriage—each time a different boy, of course. Two of them were from among her high-school sweethearts. She made B's and C's in her college work and was a minor officer in her sorority her senior year.

Ruth now works as head of a small administrative section in a large company in her home town of 100,000. She is twenty-three years old and still continuing her pattern of dating. She expresses mild concern that her friends are all marrying, threatening to leave her an old maid.

1. Evaluate Ruth's dating as representing (1) companionship, (2) personality attraction, (3) mutual self-discovery, (4) the mating urge, sexual and homemaking.

2. Is Ruth's pattern of heterosexual relationships a wholesome one? Why?

DEVELOPMENTAL STEPS IN ACHIEVING HETEROSEXUAL MATURATION

Heterosexual associations typically begin with boys and girls being together in groups (although many exceptions will be found in boys and girls who begin paired-off dating as the first overt manifestation of their developing heterosexuality). Instead of forming sharply divided groups in the schoolroom, on the playground, or at the party, the two sexes at adolescence begin to mingle. They talk, but at the beginning of the mingling the talk is frequently mutual jeering, teasing, and derogatory remarks about members of the opposite sex, rather than the favor-courting talk of older boys and girls.

This ostentatious contempt for the opposite sex, manifested frequently in mixed groups of boys and girls in early adolescence, raises an obvious question: If boys and girls of this age feel thus about each other, why do they not remain in separate groups? Why form heterosexual groups at all?

The biological, and subsequent psychological, stirrings of heterosexuality have begun in these boys and girls. Thus, they are driven to seek each other's company, but the habits of several years are still strong, and scoffing at members of the opposite sex is persisted in partly out of sheer habit. However, there is a more significant reason behind the heavy proportion of derogatory remarks mixed with other conversational patterns of boys and girls in the early stages of heterosexual mingling. They are ill at ease and insecure in the company of the opposite sex.[36] They do not know how to carry on easy, congenial conversation. Besides, neither the boy nor the girl knows whether he or she will be accepted by the members of the opposite sex in the group. Therefore, they scoff and poke fun at them because it constitutes something to say, not necessarily the *best* thing, but something they can say. Saying anything at all makes possible remaining together and appears better than saying nothing. Also, since they are not sure of their acceptance by the other sex, the derogatory remarks serve as ego defenses. Openly trying to court favor and being re-

[36] R. W. Heyns, *The Psychology of Personal Adjustment*. Holt, Rinehart & Winston, Inc., New York, 1958.

jected is too threatening to contemplate, but if the jeerer is not accepted or is rebuffed by members of the opposite sex, his ego, at least, is pretty well protected. After all, who got the silly idea he *wanted* to be around a bunch of silly old girls? You heard what he said to them, didn't you? He told them what he thought of them and walked off!

The admixture of conversation gradually becomes more civil as members of the group acquire both sufficiently increased self-confidence that they can afford to bid for acceptance without the danger of being rebuffed and increased skill in making adolescent social small talk.

From the beginning of group heterosexuality, often long before it, in fact, some boys and girls have particular likings for each other. In the early days of heterosexual association, these likings are manifested as often by hitting or verbally abusing the favored boy or girl as by frankly courting his favor, often for the reasons of fear of rebuff and sheer lack of social skill to do otherwise. As the boy and girl acquire increased confidence in their mutual acceptance and competence, more obviously friendly conversation develops, and they begin to concentrate more and more on each other. Then there is pairing-off within the group, as a boy and a girl form a pair closer together than the relations existing between each and the remainder of the group.

From the "safety in numbers" and even "safety in insults," then, heterosexual development of adolescent boys and girls typically progresses to a twosome within the group. Perhaps parents are not yet ready for their sons and daughters to date, in the sense of going off alone for an evening. Perhaps the boy and girl are not yet quite sure enough of themselves to risk depending solely upon themselves for social association. But being a "group of two" within the larger group affords opportunity to develop further the social skills and confidence needed for more personal heterosexual associations.

As we repeatedly emphasize, there are numerous exceptions to the developmental steps here described as typical of adolescent heterosexual development. There are even more exceptions to this step than to some others, but logically a couple of boys and a couple of girls will begin to venture out as a foursome without the protecting atmosphere of the larger group. "Double dating" thus emerges as an association permitting more privacy and closer personal association than is reasonable within a larger group, and yet without the disturbing aloneness a boy and a girl often feel at first when in each other's exclusive company.

Double dating, more often than not, involves some scheduled activity rather than personal association alone. That is, the couples on a double date usually skate, bowl, go to a movie, to a drive-in restaurant, or otherwise engage in some extroverted time-consuming activity rather than depending solely upon conversation to fill the time. From this semi-personalized relationship a single boy and girl can easily progress to engaging in the activities alone, and single dating begins.

Heterosexual associations are beginning to assume adult form when the boy and girl begin to spend a considerable portion of their time together in "just talking," exploring their minds and emotions. Now they are drawn to each other by the desire for pleasant sharing of ideas and mutual discovery, rather than by each being merely a vaguely enchanting person to be beside or participate in activities with. The deeper aspects of companionship and personality development emerge as major motivational factors of heterosexual association here. At this point many early adolescent associations dissolve; the traits which make a boy and girl attractive to each other as skating partners or someone to go to the movies with often lose their power to bind when conversation and more sophisticated amusements such as dancing or automobile-riding become the preferred dating activities.

Through early and middle adolescence, a wide variety of dating companions is the best and healthiest form of boy-girl relationship, even though in many communities the practice of early "going steady" may prevail. This practice may prevail, but it is not a wholesome one. This is not because of any moral principles, although the danger of increasing intimacy between boys and girls of recognized immaturity of control of both emotions and behavior is obvious. It is psychologically unwholesome, because the boy and girl are going to have to associate with all kinds of people and adjust to all sorts of situations during life, and focusing exclusively on a single partner robs them of the range and variety of social association needed for their full social and psychological development.[37] It is probably impossible to prepare adequately for marriage by going with one, two, or three boys or girls; the breadth of social and psychological development desirable for competent homemaking and parenthood can hardly be achieved through such a narrow, specialized pattern of human relations. It is almost analogous to trying to develop a mature body by eating only strawberries, or only spinach; each may be good and healthful, but a wide range of fare is required for adequate nutrition. In the same degree, a wide range of warm personal association with

[37] E. M. Duvall, *The Art of Dating*. Permabooks, New York, 1960.

many members of the opposite sex is necessary to produce the most mature and best-adjusted adult.

The advantages of going steady, always having a dependable date, not having to worry about how to talk or what to do, not having to adjust to somebody new and of unfamiliar habits and attitudes, are essentially negative and stultifying factors. It is as unwholesome for a boy or girl to avoid every interpersonal association which is not easy and undemanding as it is for one to avoid every task calling for moderate physical or mental exertion. One does not mature through such living; one only becomes older and less capable of ever becoming a socially competent and well adjusted person. When two such people marry, it is a marriage of two socially and emotionally immature individuals, and the outcome is all too often the divorce court.

As the years pass and the now late-adolescent boy and girl continue their various associations, there normally comes a time when they begin more and more to seek each other's company to the exclusion of others. After years of active and diversified dating, sharing myriad activities with myriad dating companions, the normal young man or woman is socially and psychologically prepared to concentrate on the particular member of the opposite sex who complements his or her own personality more perfectly than anyone else ever has. (One of the dangers of prematurely going steady is that the boy and girl never learn just what can and what cannot be expected of a partner. Their experience has been so restricted that they do not have perspective to enable them to determine objectively whether they or their husband or wife are what can be rightfully expected. Thus, they must fall back on their own inexperienced, immature emotional evaluations, with resultant lack of rationality in decisions. Decisions as uninformed and childish as their makers then lead to divorce.)

The dawning suspicion that this is the *right one* is tested over a period of months of going steady. During this time the partner is unconsciously, if not consciously, compared with all the other boys or girls the individual has dated. The two people learn each other's faults as well as virtues. The more completely they become aware of the thinking, feeling, and values of each other, the better the chance that their marriage, if it occurs, will be a successful one.[38, 39] This is due to at least two

38 W. M. Kephart and R. B. Strohm, "The Stability of Gretna Green Marriages," *Sociology and Social Research*, 1952, *36*:291–296.

39 W. J. Goode, *After Divorce*. The Free Press of Glencoe, Inc., New York, 1956.

reasons: First, obvious misfits usually do not marry if they postpone marriage until they have gone together long enough for their incompatibility to become evident, which it may not do in only a month or two. Second, they have made major adjustments to each other already, and the remaining ones can be made after marriage more easily with the successful background experience of adjustments made freely and without compulsion, not made under the grim pressure of "Well, my bridges are burned behind me. I've got to make it somehow!" From a psychological standpoint, marriages taking place after an engagement of a few months, culminating several years of wide dating and socializing before narrowing down to one person, offer the best chance of happiness and permanency.

Happy and successful marriage is, of course, the final step in mature male-female relations!

Case of Stony Sawyer

An only child, Stony Sawyer was small for his age. In early childhood he played happily with other children his age, perhaps a little more congenially with girls than boys. At about six years of age he gradually ceased playing with girls and became, perhaps, more self-conscious and reticent about any form of association with them than most boys were. When Stony was in his mid-teens he began to be attracted to girls, but with no clearly defined desires other than for them to admire him and talk to him. He was conscious of sexual interests and urges, but with only a vague idea of their significance, and because of self-consciousness he had no dates.

One summer in his late teens Stony began to attach himself to mixed groups of boys and girls as a regular thing, participating in talk and group activities, but not dating. Eventually, Stony found himself singling out Jean from the group for much of his conversation and his partner when the group paired off for some activity. His first times alone with Jean were walking her home from an afternoon with the crowd. Swimming together at the municipal pool, movies, and eventually evening dates followed.

That fall Stony and Jean attended different colleges. They talked over the telephone and got together occasionally, but gradually saw each other less and less. Stony now talked with girls in his classes, something he had never done before, and before long was taking one

SUMMARY OF PART TWO

In Part Two we have explored the major areas in which maturation takes place during adolescence. Some interrelations of maturation in different areas—physical, sexual, social, emotional, and mental—have been examined. Characteristics of maturation and standards of maturity have been presented, as well as forces which inhibit maturation. Ways of helping adolescents in making the adjustment required by the complex pattern of maturation which they are undergoing have been discussed.

The foregoing features of adolescent maturation are pertinent to the development of every boy and girl. All must mature physically, emotionally, sexually, socially, and mentally, and all face, to a greater or lesser degree, the problems presented by maturation in each area. All need sympathetic and skilled help in order to arrive at the best adult adjustment of which they are capable.

There are some specialized problems which have a great influence on the development of some adolescents but relatively little effect on others. Some of these special problems will be discussed in Part Three, along with some guidelines as to good procedures in counseling adolescents on all sorts of problems.

PART THREE

SPECIAL PROBLEMS OF ADOLESCENCE AND GUIDELINES IN COUNSELING

PREVIEW OF PART THREE

An almost infinite number of special conditions, situations, and circumstances exist which result in adolescents facing problems not specifically considered in Part Two. Some general concept of how to go about talking to an adolescent in order to gain his or her confidence and help with the solution of a personal problem is in order to facilitate the application of all the knowledge of the dynamics of adjustment presented in this text. Part Three is devoted to these two topics necessary to round out a parent's, teacher's, or counselor's background of knowledge needed to best help boys and girls.

CHAPTER 14

SPECIAL PROBLEMS

OF ADOLESCENCE

PREVIEW

"War Baby" Adolescents

It is clinically probable that many boys and girls born during the war years of 1941-45 and 1950-53 suffered serious interference with their mastery of the developmental tasks of infancy, with permanent effects.

Career Planning

Gives purpose to the adolescent's study.
Vocational counseling facilitates intelligent educational and career planning.
When in doubt, a college preparatory curriculum is the safest alternative.

Delinquency

Causes are sometimes environmental, but usually psychological, within the adolescent.
INTELLIGENCE—a slight tendency for apprehended delinquents to be below average.
HOME ADJUSTMENT—typically below average in the case of the delinquent.
HOSTILITY AND RESENTMENT—breed attacks against all symbols of the social order.
ANXIETY—produces tension which may be discharged in antisocial acts.
INSECURITY—same dynamics as anxiety; also promotes gang affiliations.
GUILT FEELINGS—may lead to delinquency, which will incur punishment.
SEXUAL MALADJUSTMENT—delinquencies may constitute compensatory behavior.
DEPRIVATION—occasionally a factor; emotional is more predisposing than material.
ENVIRONMENT—a gang with nothing to do, a neighborhood where survival makes gang membership advisable, desire for acceptance by the gang, lack of parental supervision, all promote delinquency.

Automobiles

Tend to be lethal weapons when driven by unmarried males under twenty-five.
Are absorbed into the self concept of the adolescent male driver so that their reckless use constitutes ego gratification and exhibition of personal prowess.
Possession tends to be accompanied by lower high-school grades.

Defiance

Manifested by extreme disobedience, running away, early marriage.
Defiant adolescents are typically deficient in their perception of reality.
Seldom occurs without childhood roots in poor parent-child relations.

Adolescent Marriages

Usually occur among the less mature and less emotionally stable adolescents.
Usually end in divorce (estimated as high as 90 per cent).

CAUSES: Emotional immaturity and instability which inhibit application of sound judgment to personal matters.
To escape from home, parents, or any trying circumstance.
Insecurity—marriage sought as a sanctuary.
Impulse—lack of normal planning ahead and facing of reality.
Premature fixation of affection from lack of breadth in dating.
Premarital pregnancy.
Early psychological maturation making possible early contract of a mature emotional relationship.

CAUSES OF UNHAPPINESS:

The emotional immaturity, personal maladjustment, and egocentricity characterizing adolescents who marry commonly render them incapable of the adjustments required by marriage.

Drinking

Usually begins as a social gesture, but may rapidly become an escapist mechanism.
Facilitates delinquent behavior.

"WAR BABY" ADOLESCENTS OF 1955-70

ON December 8, 1941, the United States entered World War II, and the social system of the nation was disordered until the fall of 1945, with lingering traces for another year. During those years, between three and four million families, with millions of infants and young children, were disrupted by separation, by frequent moves, often with inadequate notice and involving inadequate living facilities.[1] Tension was high. A million mothers of infants or young children followed their husbands from camp to camp, finally waving them good-by as they departed for what each knew was possibly forever. Those mothers then lived with their children alone in strange towns, a sort of half-life awaiting the return of their husbands, or returned to their home towns and parents to live as widows for months, years, or forever, or, at best, carried on in their

[1] M. B. Clinard, *Sociology of Deviant Behavior*. Holt, Rinehart & Winston, Inc., New York, 1957.

family homes under the strain of wondering, waiting, and fearing. Then, only five years after the end of the war came the Korean conflict, which re-created the old tensions and anxieties for a smaller, but still significant, proportion of families.

If there is any truth in the widely accepted principle that the first months of infants' lives are crucial in developing their sense of trust, of security, and in the principle that, if that developmental stage is not completed, the later psychological development of the child will be seriously compromised, the prevailing family conditions of the war years must have had a profound effect on a sizable segment of people in the United States who are adolescents between the years of 1955 and 1970, because a sizable proportion of boys and girls who are adolescents between any portion of these dates lived their formative months under these conditions. Studies in England indicate that English children were more adversely affected psychologically by war-produced separation of their parents than by the terror of repeated bombings.[2]

Statistics are inadequate evidence for proving whether or not children born during those war years, under the conditions described, have displayed the larger proportion of personality disorders, more prevalent and serious indications of insecurity, more neurotically maladjustive behavior patterns which might be expected. Many children born during those years lived in quite normal family situations, only slightly touched by war conditions. Increased emphasis on mental hygiene has caused many boys and girls to be referred for treatment during the last decade who would not have been identified as needing psychotherapy a generation ago. Some types of juvenile delinquency which would have passed unnoticed in a previous generation are now accorded vigorous attention, while other actions which, a generation ago, would have called forth vigorous police and legal action are now winked at, taken for normal, or "understood" instead of dealt with.

Nevertheless, there is undeniably a possibility that the demoralizing effects of extreme insecurity in infancy are actually bearing observable bitter fruit in the generation of adolescents born during those frantic years.[3] The friction characterizing so many homes in the postwar period, when husbands and wives were reunited after months or years of separa-

[2] *Understanding Juvenile Delinquency.* U. S. Department of Labor, Children's Bureau Publication No. 300, 1943.

[3] P. W. Tappan, *Juvenile Delinquency.* McGraw-Hill Book Company, Inc., New York, 1949.

tion, in many cases people whose acquaintance with each other had been of only a few days' or weeks' duration, might also be expected to inhibit greatly the development of a sense of security in children of those homes.

Numerous commentators on the contemporary American scene have remarked on the preoccupation with security characterizing high-school and college students of these years. Articles have been written on the preponderance of young people who, being polled, specified "security" rather than "opportunity," "retirement benefits" rather than "salary" or "advancement," as the most important feature of a job. In most cases writers have attributed this to the movement of the United States toward the welfare-state condition, which has been in progress for several decades. Those writers who favored this drift tend to approve the attitude of young people as indicating a desirable diminution of competitive spirit and personal-profit motives. Those who oppose it say the current emphasis on security from cradle to the grave has stultified the individual initiative and ambition which explored and built America. However, it may well be that the conditions under which so many present-age adolescents lived in their infancy produced the undeniable preoccupation with security characterizing so many people choosing their vocations today. The same early insecurity may explain the alleged (again impossible to prove through statistics) high proportion of emotional instability, neurotic tendencies, and delinquencies among adolescents today. Clinically it is possible, even probable.

CAREER PLANNING

Adolescence is the period during which a boy or girl normally makes a decision regarding how his or her life is to be spent. The decisions made are subject to change and, more often than not, actually are changed as future developments alter the individual's perspective or circumstances. Death of a father may cause a prelaw student to accept the shorter preparatory period of a journalistic career, the premed student to become a technician rather than a surgeon. Dislike of the physical confinement of office work may cause even the successful accountant to switch to being an insurance adjuster. Although decisions made in adolescence are subject to change, it is nonetheless advisable for such decisions to be made, because making them gives the boy or girl purpose and direction in life. The more nearly the decisions made fit the nature of circumstances of the adolescent, the less time he will spend following a blind alley, the earlier he will begin building a permanent life pattern, the less effort he will squander, and the further he may reasonably expect to progress in his chosen vocation.

Careers, if not planned, develop willy-nilly, because life moves on and the adolescent makes choices, even though the choices may be to do nothing, to wait for "something to turn up." But just as the builder of a house will be infinitely more likely to achieve a house truly satisfactory to him if he follows a predesigned plan instead of building it haphazardly with no over-all plan in his mind, even so the boy or girl who begins in high school to work toward a predesigned career pattern has a much better chance of achieving good vocational adjustment than does the one who merely lives each year as it comes along. Even if a vocational plan is changed, the change becomes a refinement of a known alternative, not a blind stab in the dark of the future.

During high school, certainly by the beginning of the second year of senior high, the adolescent is faced with truly important career-planning choices. At this time he must decide whether he will take a college preparatory course or make high school his terminal education. This choice may be an important one. If it is to be terminal education, it is possible that emphasis on a related group of vocational-preparatory courses might be most worthwhile to him. On the other hand, if further education is eventually decided upon, such a choice of courses may mean failure to satisfy college-entrance requirements and the alternative of entering a second-rate, last-choice college or of losing months or a year for additional required preparation. Boys, especially, if not given close educational guidance, often approach the end of their senior year finding that they have chosen easy courses, courses of a favorite type or which the rest of the gang were taking, or courses in a pattern which precludes immediate college entrance.

Educational guidance is an individual matter, to determine and implement the plan most suited for the individual student. However, in general it can be said that taking the "classical" college-preparatory course will seldom, if ever, prove a later handicap to a boy or girl, whereas taking any other type of course frequently does. This is not to say that everyone should take a college-preparatory course. If a boy knows that he must start earning a living as soon as he finishes high school and does not want to face the difficulty of working his way through college, it makes sense for him to study automobile mechanics, for instance, instead of geometry and French in high school. A business course in high school for the girl in the same position may be sensible.

The technical training in a given field which is achieved in specialized courses in high school, however, can almost always be gained in a few weeks of holding a job in that field, and seldom does possession of the specialized high-school training secure for the boy or girl a higher-level job than completion of a college-preparatory course would have got him. There are exceptions, of course, as where the girl has acquired proficiency in typing and shorthand, but in general the above holds true. Many times more frequently, the high-school graduate with a supply of nonacademic courses finds himself handicapped by inadequate preparation to meet the demands either of a prospective employer or college entrance.

If college preparation is the aim of the student, or even a real possibility for him, a yearly program of courses including, each year, mathematics, English, science, and either or both social science or a foreign language is always safe, and can seldom be improved on. Elective courses may profitably be distributed among typing, manual arts, home economics, or technical courses. Such an academic course is thought by many to constitute better preparation for work immediately following high-school graduation than specialized courses, and the number of employers so believing appears to be growing yearly. More and more, in the sixties, education in the "fundamentals," rather than specialized vocational training, seems to be prized by prospective employers.

Certainly, not every high-school graduate should plan or attempt to go to college. Lack of interest, severe financial restrictions, lack of intelligence, or lack of mastery of high-school subjects may render college entrance inadvisable and foredoomed to failure. Interest, or lack of it, is relative. Few college students enjoy the preparation and classes of more than a few courses. Disciplining oneself to do required work regardless of its pleasantness or unpleasantness is a legitimate part of the college curriculum. On the other hand, if all academic work is bitterly despised, something to which one drives oneself with lash and spur, the cost of a college degree may be more than it is worth, especially if it only prepares one for a lifetime of sedentary, book-oriented work which will be as distasteful as the college. The person who attempts college work without above-average high-school grades, and without decidedly higher intelligence than the average person, runs an extremely grave risk of failure. Adequacy of academic preparation can be at least approximated from high-school grades. "Aptitude" for college work, an expression many prefer to "intelligence," can be estimated with considerable validity through intelligence tests, tests administered by high-school and college guidance facilities, and various nationally administered tests of academic aptitude.

Many people will find their career interests better served by beginning work immediately upon leaving high school rather than devoting four years to college work. When a boy or girl does not have a clear-cut vocational plan or does not know positively what is needed to fulfill that plan, a vocational-guidance counselor at the school, a college, or a commercial vocational-guidance agency should be consulted. The cost is negligible when measured against the potential saving in time, money, and often, discouragement and disgust. Of course, such a career-planning program is not confined to determining whether or not the boy or girl should enter college. It will attempt a refined estimate of the person's relative interest in different vocational areas and perhaps his relative aptitude for them. In addition, the counselor will be prepared to give information and advice regarding employment opportunities, financial returns, working conditions, and a multitude of other pertinent considerations regarding scores of vocations. He will have at his fingertips the resources for locating an infinity of other such information which he may not carry in his mind. All in all, it is difficult to imagine a more profitable way for an older adolescent to spend fifty or seventy-five dollars and two to three days' time than undergoing a systematic testing and career-counseling program. During or at the end of the last year of high school is usually the best time for such a program in the case of boys or girls planning to go to college. As early as the summer before entering the tenth grade may be profitable in the case of the person who definitely is going to go directly from high school to work. This timing will give the college freshman guidance as late as possible before his college entrance, and it is axiomatic that the later such guidance is given, the greater validity it is possible to achieve. It will give the noncollege-preparatory pupil guidance early enough to permit the years of high school to be spent in work best suited to the person's particular circumstances, whatever they may be.

It seems probable that for an indeterminate period of time boys in the United States must take the possibility of compulsory military service into consideration in making their career plans. National programs and policies regarding required military training vary so much from year to year that any summary of conditions would be worse than futile. However, short of a state of declared war, the adolescent boy should know that there are almost certainly several avenues of military service open to him. At a given time, for instance, he may have the following alternatives, and perhaps others:

1. Wait and see if he is drafted, perhaps trying for deferments.

2. Enlist for a year, two years, or three years. If the longer period, he may be eligible for technical training of some sort. For any period, he may be able to select the service he will enter, rather than be assigned to one, as he might be if he is drafted.

3. Enter the National Guard. This will probably involve weekly drill sessions (for which he is paid), summer encampments, and, under some circumstances, a few months of full-time military service plus continued participation in the Reserve program for a number of years.

4. Reserve Officer Training Corps training during college, with a required tour of duty as an officer after graduation. This may or may not lead to a permanent commission in one of the services, if desired.

The office of the local Selective Service Board (or whatever name it may be called at a particular time) will provide comprehensive information on opportunities and requirements of various conditions of military service. The recruiting stations of the different services, prominently advertised in all cities, are likewise rich sources of guidance in this area, but, of course, each one will attempt to represent its own service in a most attractive light. However, a visit to all four recruiting stations (Army, Navy, Marine, and Air Force) before committing himself can give a boy a good perspective on what would be involved in various affiliations with each service.

DELINQUENCY

Delinquency has been defined as "all those thoughts, actions, desires and strivings which deviate from moral and ethical principles." [4] Through custom, it is applied more specifically to the deviations of children and adolescents than to those of adults, for which "criminality" is the more specific term.

From this definition and distinction it may be seen that delinquency can take as many forms as criminality—perhaps a few more, because

[4] K. R. Eissler (ed.) *Searchlights on Delinquency.* International Universities Press, Inc., New York, 1949, p. 3.

some things are illegal for minors to do that are not illegal for adults. Thefts, truancy, running away, sexual misbehavior, and assault are the most common forms of delinquency. As the above definition implies, however, delinquency may be present in the absence of overt illegal acts; the boy or girl who affiliates himself or herself with a gang which plans or intends a "rumble" (gang war) or other illegal activity is a delinquent in the psychological or sociological sense of the term. He is not delinquent in the legal sense until an illegal act has been committed, which is one of the instances of legal practice falling behind psychological knowledge. This legal lag means that effective measures to forestall juvenile illegality are difficult, because although they may be sociologically and psychologically delinquent, boys and girls are not legally subject to the control and action they need until they have actually committed a crime.

Many studies have been attempted to determine the causes of delinquency. None have given sufficiently definitive results to make it possible to say, "This will [as contrasted to *may*] cause delinquency," much less make it possible to say, "The following factors are the cause of delinquency." Poverty seems frequently to be a contributing cause of delinquency, although many boys and girls grow up under similar conditions of poverty without ever becoming delinquent, and cases of delinquency (even involving theft) often are encountered among boys and girls with ample money for their needs or even their desires.[5] Some common adjuncts of poverty—poor living conditions, slums, lack of privacy, lack of space for recreational activities, and lack of parental attention or control resulting from both parents working—also seem to contribute to a high delinquency rate, although, again, many children growing up under these conditions do not become delinquent, and many not growing up under them do. A negative correlation seems to exist between delinquency and intelligence; that is, boys and girls of low intelligence seem somewhat more prone to delinquency than those of higher intelligence. This is to be expected, since those of lower intelligence might reasonably be expected to be more easily led, less perceptive of the results of their actions, and less capable of getting what they want from life without delinquency. However, the correlation is not high, and when we consider the better chance the more intelligent boy or girl has of being delinquent and escaping detection, the relation of intelligence to the probable proportion of delinquents is tenuous indeed.

[5] W. W. Wattenberg, "Factors Associated with Repeating Among Pre-Adolescent Delinquents," *Journal of Genetic Psychology*, 1954, *84*:189–196.

When we enter the areas of adjustment, family or emotional, we find a much more definite relationship. It can safely be said that emotionally well-adjusted boys and girls who get along well with their parents seldom become delinquent. They sometimes do, to be sure, but in nothing approaching the proportions of emotionally disturbed boys and girls, or those in serious and chronic conflict with their parents, even when the basis of conflict has nothing to do with tendencies toward delinquency on the part of the child.[6]

Theorizing from known principles of psychodynamics and clinical interviews with delinquents, it appears that delinquent behavior is the result of mental and emotional conditions within the child, which in most cases go much deeper than community influences or even parental control. Actually, the causes of delinquency seem to bear a close resemblance to the causes of emotional maladjustment (which may be why the two so frequently occur together). In delinquency some portion of the emotional tension is discharged in overt behavior, called by psychoanalysts "acting out," instead of being kept bottled up within the person and making itself known through withdrawal, irritability, or fearfulness. Some psychological conditions frequently found to underlie delinquent behavior follow.

Hostility and Resentment

Such feelings toward parents are often displaced onto "safer" objects: the solitary passer-by who can be "mugged" with relative impunity and perhaps some profit, the shopkeeper who can be harassed in similar fashion, law-enforcement officers whose control cannot be so close nor so arbitrary as can the parents', or social workers' who stand somewhat *in loco parentis.* Hostility toward the forces of law and order, arising from displacement, arrests, fear of arrest, or merely as representatives of a society with which the boy or girl does not identify himself, often leads to "purposeless" delinquencies which are not purposeless at all, but serve the psychological purpose of attacking something hated.[7] Hostility and resentment do arise from underprivileged status, deprivation, and other conditions found in "underprivileged" communities, but they arise from vastly different causes as well.

[6] W. Healy and A. F. Bronner, *New Light on Delinquency and Its Treatment.* Yale University Press, New Haven, Conn., 1936.

[7] C. B. Zachry, *Emotion and Conduct in Adolescence.* Appleton-Century-Crofts, Inc., New York, 1940.

Anxiety

It is paradoxical, but emotional tension taking the form of anxiety, fear of some vague, threatening unknown, frequently leads to delinquent actions—paradoxical because the delinquency exposes the culprit to possible punishment and, therefore, would seem to increase anxiety rather than relieve it. Nevertheless, it does actually incite delinquency on occasion. Psychotherapists of different theoretical persuasions explain the paradox in different ways; each explanation probably holds true in some cases. The anxious person shoplifts a useless article for the unconscious purpose of being apprehended and punished and, therefore, atoning through suffering for some completely different guilt he feels. The tension developed by anxiety demands release; the activity and excitement of a "mugging" give release to some of the tension. The very excitement of burglarizing serves as a sort of "counter-irritant" (like biting your lip while nursing a mashed thumb) to the more obscure and threatening tension of the anxiety.

Insecurity

In its simplest manifestation, this may cause the boy or girl to steal and with the loot buy approval and acceptance from the group. It may spur the insecure person to delinquent acts which, he hopes, will excite admiration for his daring or skill. Feelings of inferiority or inadequacy, a poor self concept, may prompt the same compensatory behavior. On a less conscious level, feelings of insecurity may prompt relatively undifferentiated behavior, a vague seeking for something unknown, which more or less randomly includes some delinquent behavior. Insecurity also may underlie and cause feelings of hostility and resentment, with the delinquent activities which frequently result, or, of course, may be the basis of anxiety with its tensions.

Guilt Feelings

Feelings of guilt for real or imaginary offenses sometimes produce in the person a feeling of need for punishment, and delinquent acts are committed in such a manner that apprehension is certain. The person then achieves a psychological sense of absolution through being punished; one punishment wipes out all old scores. This mechanism is similar to that of anxiety, but probably operates on a more nearly conscious level. Indeed, most of us have observed the small child deliberately invite punishment, with evident relief when it is received.

Sexual Maladjustment

Psychoanalysts generally believe, and so do many other psychotherapists, that tension resulting from sexual maladjustment prompts many delinquent acts. The delinquency seems to relieve the pressure of guilt, anxiety, or desire. Numerous cases are reported of boys who achieve orgasm through entering a house for burglary, who derive sexual satisfaction from setting fires, or who reach a sexual climax through physical violence inflicted on some person.

Deprivation

This motivational factor in delinquency, especially in theft-type activities, is overemphasized in the minds of some students of the subject. The boy or girl who steals just because he or she wants something and sees no other way of obtaining it unquestionably exists, and, therefore, the factor of poverty as a cause of delinquency cannot be ignored. But close examination of instances of delinquency suggests that theft as a simple gratification of a material want is less common than is often thought. This accentuates the growing comprehension that treatment of delinquency is less a legal matter than a psychological one.

Environmental Conditions

Environmental conditions often directly predispose to delinquency, in a manner quite apart from simple poverty. When, for whatever reason, boys (less frequently girls) band together into gangs, this ganging together can itself become a psychological contributor to delinquency.[8] Where boys unite for a well-defined, constructive purpose, delinquency is less likely to result. A gang formed to compose a baseball team, or united by a common interest in making and flying model airplanes (although usually called a club under these conditions), has a purpose which consumes its time and energies. A gang formed without such a purpose seeks one, and in a large proportion of cases through boredom, desire to display daring or simply lack of thought drifts into delinquent patterns.[9] Standing around talking with nothing to do, one says, "If I had a car, I'd. . . ." Another takes it up with, "I know how to start one

[8] M. H. Neumeyer, *Juvenile Delinquency in Modern Society*. D. Van Nostrand Company, Inc., Princeton, New Jersey, 1961.

[9] P. W. Tappan, *Juvenile Delinquency*. McGraw-Hill Book Company, Inc., New York, 1949.

without a key. . . ." Another adds, "If I could do that I wouldn't be standing here . . . ," and a car theft is launched.

Once a gang is organized, boys not in it tend to band together for mutual protection, for belongingness, so as not to feel "left out." Rivalry and tests of power are almost inevitable, and as more and more of the youth of a community become involved in one or another gang, it becomes increasingly difficult for a boy to remain aloof, a loner. Not only is he excluded from the organized activities of the gang members; as innumerable newspaper reports attest, he may literally find it unsafe to walk the streets of his community without the protection of an "organization." Fortunately, such wolf-pack activity is rare in most communities, but in certain sections of some cities of the East and Midwest, and to a lesser extent in other areas of the United States, the youthful jungle is a law unto itself. This has recently given rise to an acute observation: the juvenile gang delinquent is not socially maladjusted *to his own society*. He knows, accepts, and is well adjusted to the conventions and mores of the youthful society in which he lives. It is merely that his subsociety rejects the conventions and mores of the majority of adults and lives by its own, which reflect the complex interplay of psychological forces already discussed and others as well.[10]

Case of Tom Tatum

Tom Tatum was being held by the Youth Bureau of the Bigcity Police Department when his mother and father appeared in response to a call from the lieutenant. He was fifteen years old, an alert, well-built boy of apparently normal intelligence who had been apprehended when leaving a department store with an expensive sport shirt, which he had not paid for, concealed under his jacket. His parents turned out to be upper-middle-class college graduates, the father a production manager for a local manufacturing concern. Tom was an only child, and the parents were stunned by the situation.

"I've been afraid of something like this," the father said, "but when it happens you still can't believe it. It's that gang he's been running with. I've whipped him until I was ashamed of myself, and he's too big to whip now anyway. I've known they were just on the edge of trouble. But we haven't been able to control him."

The mother continued, "It must be our fault, but we've done the

10 M. H. Neumeyer, *Juvenile Delinquency in Modern Society*. D. Van Nostrand Company, Inc., Princeton, New Jersey, 1961.

best we know how. His father has taken him on hunting trips. We've bought him almost everything he's ever asked for. We'd have bought him the shirt if he had asked us. We've taken him to Sunday school and church regularly. He doesn't like it, or school either. But he's just as sweet at home as can be. He's a *good* boy. Maybe we've tried to keep him under too tight control."

Tom protested, "Why did you have to bring *them* down here? You know I stole it. I admitted it. I'll take whatever's coming to me. No, nobody else had anything to do with it. Go ahead and lock me up."

The police knew the boys Tom's father referred to. Members had records of being picked up on suspicion or for various petty misdemeanors. They obviously regarded themselves as tough. Police believed Tom had not been fully accepted as a member of the group.

1. List several possible explanations of Tom's stealing the shirt.

AUTOMOBILES

Automobiles and their use are a problem of largely unrecognized magnitude among the adolescents of the United States today. While the public whips itself into a national frenzy over a dozen children smothering in plastic bags, and laws are passed prohibiting keeping gasoline in glass containers because of a rare case of breakage, it remains apathetic or unconcerned in the face of adolescent boys slaughtering themselves and others, literally by the thousands, through characteristic reckless driving. Recently, statistics were published indicating that teenage boys, who account for only about 5 per cent of the yearly automobile mileage of the United States, are involved in over 30 per cent of the accidents and an even larger proportion of the fatal accidents. The latter is probably due to the characteristically high rates of speed at which adolescents and young men drive.

Another set of statistics, covering all automobile accidents reported in the year 1956, differ from those, but also emphasize the national menace represented by young male drivers.[11] By these figures, of every 100,000 males of all ages driving, 36 will die yearly in motor-vehicle accidents. Of every 100,000 teenage boys driving, 52 will so die. And fewer sixteen-year-olds will die than seventeen-year-olds; fewer seventeen-

11 E. Pope, "Are Teen-Agers the Worst Drivers?" *McCall's*, October, 1957, p. 57 ff.

year-olds than eighteen-year-olds, and so on until a staggering 83 out of every 100,000 young men of age twenty-four who drive will die in that year of their life through automobile accidents! Since a large proportion of fatal automobile accidents involve more than one vehicle, it follows that the hazardous driving of adolescent and immediately post-adolescent boys unquestionably kills a considerable proportion of the older men who die in vehicular accidents. Thus, the relative danger ratio between the driving of the twenty-four-year-old and all other men is really even more disproportionate than the 36:83 figures suggest.

Many major insurance companies will not insure cars driven principally by teenage boys except to keep sizable policies on other cars operated by the boys' families, or at fantastic premiums running as high as ten times normal charges. Yet boys not legally old enough to hold any except certain carefully selected jobs, not credited with enough judgment to sign contracts binding upon themselves or to manage their own business affairs, are unreservedly given the privilege of piloting two tons of lethal power, potential death, through streets and highways populated by living human beings. And this, persistently, in the face of those teenagers' emotional or physical failure (conclusively demonstrated) to drive without fantastically disproportionate risk to themselves and the safety of others.

The above description may be expressed in nonacademically dramatic form, but the statements made are sober facts. The public's strange disregard of the problem of adolescent boys as automobile drivers (girls show no comparable accident proneness) is a fascinating psychological phenomenon and an excellent example of an adolescent problem which, unlike juvenile gangs, truancy, or most forms of delinquency, exists only by the permission of adults. Not only (there is every reason to believe) would the savings in human lives run into hundreds or thousands per year if driving privileges of adolescent boys were more carefully regulated, but other types of delinquency would be drastically reduced. Teenage automobile thefts would be minimized if the sight of a young boy driving a car unaccompanied by an adult were in itself a suspicious circumstance. The mobility afforded juveniles by the use of automobiles facilitates delinquency, especially in uncrowded, spread-out city areas and in rural areas. The privacy afforded is a major contributing factor in sexual delinquency.

Psychologically there are several reasons why automobiles, when available to adolescent boys, particularly unmarried ones, play such an important role in delinquent behavior. In much of the United States, possession of an automobile, or access to the use of one, is a status symbol, a prestige factor. As an adjunct of this status-prestige factor, it becomes a power symbol. The boy at the wheel of an automobile is not limited by his own capabilities in what he does; his automobile becomes an extension of his own self concept, and it is not a piece of machinery which spins its wheels in a "drag" start, it is *his* power, *his* masterful dominance, being displayed. A number of educators and psychologists have produced thoughtful studies, largely ignored by the public and particularly by state legislators, demonstrating the likelihood that adolescents often use their automobiles as devices for working off hostilities and aggressiveness. Antisocial impulses are expressed with impressive force when the technique used involves hurtling a car through city traffic or along the highway at high speeds, causing dozens to wince and cringe at the sound of tortured tires screaming on the pavement, and forcing other motorists to surrender their right-of-ways or risk collision.

Finally, it is hardly a debatable point that the disrespect for law demonstrated by so large a proportion of adolescent male drivers subtly carries over into their attitude toward lawfulness and good citizenship in other areas. While we cannot generalize to the point of saying that an adolescent who habitually engages in one type of delinquent behavior will be equally ready to engage in other types, from our knowledge of the holistic principle in behavior we can confidently predict lowered respect for good citizenship in other areas as a result of frequent delinquencies in an area where delinquency actually involves hazarding lives.

A strong negative correlation has also been found to exist between ownership of a car and a high-school student's academic grades by many studies by school principals as well as psychologists. Whether this is because parental indulgence which provides the boy or girl with a car also prevents requiring the adolescent to do his homework well, or because possession of the car fills his mind with thoughts and his time with activities incompatible with superior schoolwork, is as yet unknown. The empirical fact is that in virtually every school where the situation has been studied, students without cars achieve significantly higher academic success than do those possessing them.

In summary, it can be said that automobiles constitute a problem outstandingly large in the adjustment of adolescents, especially adolescent boys, but a problem little recognized and less acted upon by the public.

DEFIANCE

Sometimes an adolescent boy or girl becomes so alienated from the parents and rightly or wrongly feels so independent of them that he or she flatly refuses to obey them to any degree at all. This state of affairs often resembles the striving for independence carried to extreme lengths, but clinical work with such boys or girls usually reveals something not ordinarily present in normal adolescent rebellion: deep and bitter, more than a situational, resentment toward the parent. It differs in quantity and, one suspects, quality from the resentment of the average adolescent seeking autonomy. It differs from most neurotic forms of parent hostility in that it is conscious rather than unconscious, and in most cases any guilt feelings over it are unconscious. Defiance also requires a disregard of consequences if the adolescent remains in association with the parents, or willingness to leave the shelter of the home and get along without the support, security, and protection of the parents.

Defiance sometimes results in premature marriage to escape parental control, especially on the part of a girl. Often it results in the boy's or girl's leaving home, with or without the foreknowledge or consent of parents. In many instances the defiant adolescent remains in the home, doing as he or she wishes, and tacitly or openly dares the parents to do their worst. Ursula Usher (see pages 483-486) is a typical instance of the defiant adolescent, although her defiance had certain bounds, possibly because of her father's willingness to resort to physical force. Ursula would go to her room as ordered and later slip out. In some adolescents defiance reaches the point of walking out of the house in the teeth of one or both parents standing there ordering them to their room. As one mother expressed it, "If I told him he was going to stay in his room and I was standing in the door, he would physically walk over me and leave if he wanted to." And speaking of a daughter, parents have said, "If you tell her she is not going out tonight and she says, 'Try to stop me' and walks out, what are you going to do?" Carried to its logical conclusion, such defiance eventuates either in the adolescent's being recognized by the parents as merely an unpaying boarder, as far as their control goes, or, if the parents refuse to surrender to that extent, in the girl's or boy's leaving home.

Often parents will surrender all parental authority in the face of what they consider to be a determined boy's or girl's threat to leave home. Better, they believe, to have Son or Daughter near them, where they can see that food, shelter, and clothing are available without resorting to delinquency, and help and protection available if the adolescent suddenly realizes the need for it, than to lose a child to whatever fate the world offers. Sometimes they even stop protesting what they consider to be unwise or dangerous actions when the boy or girl threatens to leave home "for good, unless you stop nagging at me all the time."

It is an exceptional adolescent who will deliberately accept the alternative of venturing alone into the world with no one to turn to in time of need, no one to look to for financial support when the money runs out, no home to return to each evening. The need for security is too strong in most. However, consciously or unconsciously, most adolescents actually realize that if they were in need or trouble, no matter what they had done, their parents would come to their rescue immediately upon hearing of their plight. Thus their perceived risk is minimized, and some are cynical enough to strike out on their own, knowing that, whatever they do, they can count on their parents if needed. One trouble is, of course, that in their inexperience and their habit of defying authority and conventions, many boys and girls become involved in trouble beyond their parents' ability to cope with before the parents can re-enter the picture. Jail terms, involuntary prostitution, or similar tragedy are unpleasantly frequent results of such miscalculation on the part of boys and girls.

Complete defiance of parental authority is seldom a phenomenon appearing for the first time in adolescence. Its roots customarily go back into childhood, perhaps even infancy, and signs of its development are almost always clearly visible in childhood and pre-adolescence, for several conditions must prevail before this degree of alienation between parents and child comes into being. It will not come into being in the presence of normal love of a son or daughter for parents, so there must be a lack of love for parents. Since it is normal for children to love those who love and care for them, undesirable intrafamily relations will usually be found to have existed as a background for defiance. Since adolescent boys or girls are seldom capable of shifting for themselves successfully in the world, lack of objectivity and lack of normal perceptiveness is generally required to bolster an adolescent's resolution to strike out on his own. From the author's experience, few adolescents defying their parents have a realistic perception of their alternatives if the parents refuse to permit defiance within the home. Some adolescents are actually capable of maintaining themselves successfully as independent adults, with no parental assistance, but the defiant boy or girl is seldom found in this mature, well-adjusted group. Unless home conditions are truly appalling, a boy or girl must almost necessarily be emotionally and mentally immature to choose premature separation from the family instead of reasonable cooperation with parents.

Exact legal recourses open to parents differ from state to state. In most, when a boy or girl is below a given age, often seventeen, he or she can be legally committed to a juvenile correctional institution for incorrigibles upon petition of the parents to an appropriate court and the approval of the judge. Understandably, parents are usually reluctant to so admit defeat and further alienate their child. After the age of sixteen, such legal assistance in the case of "incorrigibles" is often not available, and more formal legal action, perhaps following criminal activity, is necessary if parents are to achieve legal assistance in managing their child.

Every year that passes renders parents less capable of dealing with a child's defiance on the basis of repressive or punitive measures. Every additional year of age renders the child more nearly capable of asserting successful defiance of parental control. Thus, as in so many other phases of adolescent development, a firm foundation of love between parents and child is the best (perhaps the only) basis for avoiding the dangerous and demoralizing circumstances which inevitably accompany adolescent defiance of parents. When such love is not present and defiance becomes a reality, extensive clinical assistance, usually involving extensive psychotherapy, is the only recourse with any promise of satisfactory results, and even this promise is quite limited.

ADOLESCENT MARRIAGES

The experience of marriage counselors and divorce-court records indicate that adolescent marriages, i.e., marriages contracted before both parties are at least twenty or, more probably, twenty-one, are generally less likely to succeed than are marriages of older people.[12] Studies of marriage happiness and unhappiness almost without exception indicate that marriages involving a man under twenty or a girl under eighteen are less likely to be happy than marriages of persons over twenty.[13] One recent study of marriages of "school-age children" (Note the "children"! —true, considering that they are out of school by the time they are eighteen, but so often overlooked) found that out of 240 couples, only sixteen were still together after five years.[14] And how many of those sixteen were happy in their marriages is not revealed. Estimates of the proportion of *all* marriages which end in divorce in the United States of this era range from about one-fourth to one-third. In the teenage group referred to, it was fourteen out of fifteen!

Causes of Adolescent Marriage

The clinician, theorizing on the dynamics of human behavior, quickly perceives one outstanding possibility which field research has indicated is probably correct. Considering the obvious need for people to be mature, self-supporting, socially experienced people before marriage, it seems theoretically likely that mentally and emotionally well-adjusted people would be most reluctant to run the risk of adolescent marriage. Martinson[15] gave various psychological tests to 604 girls while they were in high school. Five years later 131 of the girls had married, and these early-marrying girls, on the whole, were found to have displayed poorer emotional adjustment, as well as lower social adequacy, than the still unmarried girls. Thus, there is reason to believe that the almost incredibly high proportion of juvenile marriages ending in divorce is at least partly attributable to the fact that the boys and girls most mature and psychologically healthy tend to postpone marriage more often than do the less psychologically healthy. So, in fact, the adolescents who marry tend to be those *least* competent to adjust to the severe demands of the marriage relationship, not those *most* competent to do so. No wonder they are unable to make a go of their marriages; if they had possessed

12 L. M. Terman and P. Buttenwieser, "Personality Factors in Marital Compatibility," *Journal of Social Psychology*, 1935, 6:143–171, 267–289.

13 J. T. Landis and M. G. Landis, *Building a Successful Marriage.* Prentice-Hall, Inc., Englewood Cliffs, N. J., 1958.

14 J. C. Burt, "Run-Away Marriages, Teen-Age Tragedy," *The Rotarian*, June, 1961, pp. 16–18.

15 F. M. Martinson, "Ego Deficiency as a Factor in Marriage," *American Sociological Review*, 1955, 20:161–164.

the mental and emotional requirements for good marital adjustment, it appears that they would have been more likely to recognize the inadvisability of adolescent marriages and have waited. The observation of the author is that one major cause of juvenile marriages is immaturity, emotional and intellectual, which simultaneously robs the boy and girl of mature perspective on the inadvisability of their marriage and of the emotional maturity required to make it succeed once it has taken place.

Another prominent cause of adolescent marriages is the desire to escape from an unhappy situation. The girl chafes under parental restrictions; she cannot get along with her parents, she is unhappy in her job, her life seems drab and lonely. An opportunity for marriage comes along and she takes it. Marriage to escape is less common in the case of boys, but it still happens. His parents, he thinks, treat him like a kid. One way to assert, even *prove* (he thinks) his independence is to become the head of a household himself. If he and his wife live in their own apartment, no one can try to boss when he comes home—his drinking, or anything else! Obviously, these types of reasoning do not indicate a boy or girl emotionally and mentally prepared to achieve a good marriage adjustment.

Insecurity is another cause. A boy or girl feels lost, alienated from parents, perhaps not well accepted socially; life seems purposeless and without meaning, friends are marrying, and "soon nobody will be left" (incredible as it may seem, this reason is advanced innumerable times), and marriage appears a haven of refuge, of security.

Impulse accounts for a distressing number of premature marriages. A boy and girl, alone or in a party, get to talking about marriage. "Why not?" they ask, often in jest and often with alcoholic encouragement. The discussion continues, romantically, daringly, or just as a novelty. Before the evening is over the idea is an accomplished fact. One girl played with her team in a basketball tournament one morning, eloped and married that afternoon, and returned to play in the final game that night. A girl, a high-school graduate working in an office, and a boy attending college in her town, had had two casual dates. After attending a dance, they decided to be married, and were that night. The first marriage lasted less than a year and produced a child whom the father never saw. The second lasted two bitter, unhappy, strife-torn years. Impulse also combines with any of the other causes; a couple may have been going together for some time and, with one of the partners faced with a real or fancied crisis, marriage is hit upon as a means of resolving it.

Premature fixation of affection, a logical result of going steady, contributes heavily to premature marriages. If people like each other well enough, enjoy each other's company well enough, get along together well enough to enjoy being together a great deal, love develops easily and naturally if the association is continued. Particularly, it develops when the two are together so exclusively that neither has the opportunity of enjoying going places and doing things with someone else. Without the "balance wheel" of diversity of pleasant activities, romantic and otherwise, they become more and more dependent upon each other. It is natural for people to fall in love when they are constantly together, doing things which they both enjoy. When such constant company begins early, love is likely to come early, too. Unfortunately, when love comes during adolescence, it seldom constitutes a sound basis for marriage. But the couple in love cannot understand that; they lack the maturity and experience essential to understand the subtleties of human development involved. They are convinced that there is no deeper or more permanent love than theirs, and they marry—only to find out their mistake later. Here, again, is the inadvisability of going steady during adolescence.

Premarital pregnancy is frequently responsible for adolescent marriages, and, psychologically, marriages thus produced are the most likely of any to end in divorce. Often, if not usually, either the boy or the girl had no desire to marry the other. Pleasure, not marriage, was the motivating factor in their relationship. Thus, they may feel forced by parental and social pressure to marry without even a feeling of affection. Many times, indeed, before the marriage ceremony is completed, they regard each other with loathing, each thinking of the other as a betrayer, a captor, responsible for this happening. Then, the fact of having been engaging in premarital intercourse is thought by many, with some grounds, to be a handicap to successful marriage.[16, 17] Minds and emotional constitutions which go with adolescent premarital intercourse resulting in pregnancy hardly meet the qualifications of self-discipline, carefulness, and responsibility required for marital adjustment. Pregnancy also quickly robs the couple of free and uninhibited sexual relations, as well as many of their social and recreational pursuits. The young husband often spends more and more time away from his wife, who

16 K. B. Davis, *Factors in The Sex Life of Twenty-Two Hundred Women*. Harper & Brothers, Publishers, New York, 1929.

17 S. M. Duvall, *Men, Women and Morals*. The Association Press, New York, 1952.

becomes correspondingly bitter, and her reproaches further alienate him. Finally, the expense entailed by the pregnancy may disastrously affect already overstrained financial resources, and deprivation of wanted things and anxiety about bills keep both husband and wife resentful, on edge, and irritable. Yet, in the interests of at least the mother and child, marriage seems almost, if not quite, a necessity. It is one of those situations for which there is no satisfactory solution. Marriage, with competent marriage counseling intensively and over a period of years as problems arise which threaten the marriage, is perhaps best.

Early psychological maturation can cause boys and girls of adolescent chronological age to have achieved the intellectual and emotional maturity that makes possible true adult love and happy marriages. Thus, it is completely possible for boys and girls of twenty or under to marry and have married lives of happiness equal or superior to the lives of those who marry older. They are under the unavoidable handicap of limited social experience, limited practice of the art of being with people under many diverse circumstances and of learning to adjust personally and to help others be happy also. But some can and do achieve happy marriages despite this handicap. So it is well to conclude the examination of the dismal, unsound causes of adolescent marriages with this sound one: early achievement of adult love and the emotional capacity for marital adjustment, coupled with finding a person with whom one wishes to share his or her life.

Looking around us we can see examples of this phenomenon, the unknown portion of that one out of fifteen cases mentioned earlier in which the marriage is continuing because the partners are happy together. An experienced counselor, however, would be able to predict with far more than random success which of the many teenage couples would achieve this adjustment. Have both been happy and well adjusted at home? Does it make "economic sense" for them to marry? Is each unselfish, not egocentric? Is each easy to get along with? Does each cheerfully sacrifice his or her preferences to those of any friend or relative? Is each unusually intelligent? Have they been in close association with each other for at least a year? Have they avoided bitterness in the disagreements which have arisen between them? Have they frankly discussed all matters intelligent people could think of on which disagreement might occur? Has each let the other see himself or herself as he really is, not putting on a mask designed to conceal or to please? If all these questions can be answered yes, the couple has an excellent chance of married happiness. More than one, or at most two, no's probably means the marriage will fall among the fourteen failures.

Case of Ursula Usher

Ursula Usher's parents consulted her teacher regarding her failing work in school. She was passing music, failing everything else. The previous year she had failed two subjects; the year before, one. Prior to that time she had always passed, although with consistently low grades. Ursula is now eighteen, a petite, physically mature, attractive brunette, in the eleventh grade because of her failures, and, according to her parents, "likely to be in it from now on, according to the way she's getting along now."

Asking questions about Ursula's attitudes regarding study, her general adjustment at home, and her interests encouraged the parents to take advantage of a friendly, professional person to pour out the whole story. Ursula was a sweet, affectionate child up until she was twelve or thirteen, when she began to be irritable, rebellious, and generally fractious. She loved the out-of-doors, and was happiest when in the swimming pool or on the tennis court.

She shared a room with her sister, with whom she was constantly at swords' points. Ursula was meticulously neat and orderly, and her sister's strewing clothes over their room was a constant source of friction. On the other hand, the sister worked cheerfully and effectively in cleaning and cooking, while Ursula did the absolute minimum she could get by with, and that only under strongest compulsion. The mother was bookkeeper in the insurance business of the father.

When asked for the chief areas of friction with Ursula, the parents looked at each other and shrugged. Everything. If they tried to talk to her, she constantly made nasty remarks. If they didn't, she accused them of favoring her sister and ignoring her. She fussed about not having enough clothes, although Mrs. Usher said she had more than her mother and sister combined. She wouldn't study, would sit looking at a book, if made to, but would not try to learn anything from it. If penalized for failing marks by being confined to the house, she would slip out the window of her room and disappear into the woods, returning only after night had fallen. Mr. Usher, in desperation, resorted to whipping her with a leather belt. She would scream, cry, and rage, but nothing else would be accomplished.

An immediate problem to the parents was Ursula's love affair

The Atlanta Journal-Constitution.

Figure 26. "Complete defiance of parental authority is seldom a phenomenon appearing for the first time in adolescence. Its roots customarily go back to childhood."

with a college boy. She had "gone steady" with one boy after another for years, but this seemed to be different. They were talking of marriage. The boy, Prather, was twenty, attending the state university on an athletic scholarship. His family is perhaps a little more affluent than the Ushers, but miles below them in culture and types of interest. "He doesn't even use correct English," said Mr. Usher. "My speech is nothing to brag about, but he, a college student, talks like an illiterate. And the funny papers are the height of his intellectual interest. I can't imagine how he is passing in college, but apparently he is."

According to Ursula's story to the counselor, her parents picked on her all the time, favoring her younger sister. Also, they had interests which were completely out of her own range of interests. Nothing she did pleased them. She wanted to go to work, but they insisted she stay in high school. They were trying to break up her going with Prather. But he was sweet and good to her. When she ran off from home, he would meet her, and his parents would let her stay with them until she figured her folks had cooled off a little. If she and Prather married, his parents would build a room onto their house and the young couple could live there. Prather's father and mother were sweet and understanding, and Prather understood how she felt about things. Ursula seemed no more resentful of her father's whippings than of her parents and sister generally. Her strongest resentment was of any measure which kept her from Prather. They were contemplating marriage very soon.

Ursula was counseled in an attempt to get her to examine the realities of the situation under which she would live if married to Prather. Her relations with her parents were discussed. But throughout a series of several consultations she made it plain that she would cooperate in only one thing—leaving home to marry Prather. The parents cooperated with the counselor's suggestions aimed at making home more pleasant for Ursula and reducing friction. But in a few weeks Ursula and Prather eloped to a neighboring state.

They soon found his parents' home unsatisfactory, and rented a small apartment. During the summer Prather lost his temporary job, and Ursula became pregnant. She was dismayed, because Prather had always said that because of some peculiarity of her menstrual periods she could not become pregnant. Prather, too, was dismayed; also, he was tired of marriage. Ursula's parents took the young couple in. One night Ursula and Prather, after retiring to their room, had a loud, acrimonious argument. He said she did not cook the foods he liked, was lazy and spoiled, slept all day and then didn't sleep at night and kept him awake. Ursula's mother, fearing violence, called through the door to Prather to remember Ursula's condition. He stormed out of the house and did not return that night. Ursula cried herself to sleep.

Prather did not return next afternoon, and that evening his father called to say that Prather was very tired and nervous, and they had decided he should live with them and Ursula with her parents for "a while." Ursula became hysterical. At the insistence of Mrs. Usher, Prather came to the telephone and talked with Ursula, telling her again of her shortcomings as a wife. Upon her entreaties he agreed to return to live with the Ushers for "a while." In a short time he obtained a job. The couple have now been married eight months and are still living with the Ushers. Ursula cries much of the time, and Prather is surly and unpleasant both to Ursula and to the Ushers. Ursula loves him devotedly.

1. Explain possible causes of the change in Ursula's attitude when she was thirteen.

2. What circumstances identifiable before their marriage suggested that marriage of Ursula and Prather would be unwise, at least at that time?

3. What might have been done to prevent this marriage?

4. What factors probably caused the discord between Ursula and Prather?

5. How can the situation best be helped under the present circumstances?

DRINKING

A study published in 1944 reported that 43 per cent of twelve- to sixteen-year-old girls surveyed said that they had taken a drink on one or more occasions. In the sixteen- to eighteen-year age group the percentage rose to 55.[18] Another study published in 1953 of drinking practices of students in twenty-seven colleges indicated that 74 per cent drank to some extent.[19] The researchers conducting this study were cheered by the fact that the overwhelming proportion of college students who drank said they did so only twice a month or less. This author is more concerned with the fact also found that 6 per cent of the men students and 1 per cent of the women students studied showed positive signs of becoming problem drinkers. Upon first consideration, these numbers may appear small; when considered more seriously, however, the implications are staggering. Since alcoholism is a progressive condition, tending to grow in the life of an individual with the passing of time, such proportions bode ill for a tragic number of men and women in later life.

Adolescent drinking almost invariably begins as a social gesture. Sometimes it is to avoid being "different" from the remainder of a group

18 M. Lederer, "We're Telling You," *Ladies Home Journal*, 1949, *61*:20–21.
19 R. Strauss and S. D. Bacon, *Drinking in College*. Yale University Press, New Haven, Conn., 1953.

whose members generally drink. Sometimes it is begun as a symbol of being grown up. Evidence is lacking that drinking is *begun* for the reasons which cause it to become a major problem for so many drinkers as time goes on, reasons such as the temporary escape from reality which it offers, a feeling of stimulation which temporarily offsets fatigue, depression, or anxiety, and a feeling of power and invincibility.

Alcohol is neither a poison nor a stimulant. It is a food rather than a poison, but a food which, consumed in more than minute quantities, cannot be absorbed by the body, and the surplus exercises a demonstrable numbing or drugging action on the brain. It is thus a depressant rather than a stimulant, the feeling of stimulation it produces being due to its injuring the individual's ability to recognize his fatigue, pain, or other injurious condition.[20] Once adolescents at least partially overcome their distaste for the flavor and the sting which most experience upon their initial acquaintance with alcoholic beverages, they enjoy the feeling of freedom and reckless abandon alcohol commonly gives. It affects the higher mental centers and removes the inhibitions, the reminders of conscience, the limitations of logic and good sense, which customarily keep people from doing things that might be "fun" but are certainly indiscreet, dangerous, or actively injurious. Thus, the boy or girl with even a minute consumption of alcohol becomes incapable of exercising the judgment he or she normally displays.

It is difficult to evaluate which of the common reasons for which people drink to excess is most undesirable, and it is probably unprofitable to attempt to do so. To escape reality instead of adjusting to it, to numb the feelings to conditions which should be recognized and reckoned with, or to still the voices of conscience and reason so as to be able to do, without inhibitions, things one would ordinarily refuse to do because of their danger or impropriety, all contain within them the seed of serious maladjustment and tragedy in one's life. While hardly habit-forming in the sense of narcotics such as morphine, alcohol still typically and quickly develops a heavy reliance on its effects. Thus, the adolescent who begins drinking as a social gesture, a protest against parental authority, or a symbol of maturity may quickly come to rely heavily on its effects as a means of avoiding having to face and make the normal adjustments to life. And when this happens, the reasons for drinking have changed from

[20] J. C. Coleman, *Abnormal Psychology and Modern Life*. Scott, Foresman and Company, Chicago, 1956.

being, at least on the surface, relatively harmless to being both symptoms and producers of serious maladjustments.

Seldom, if ever, does a boy or girl begin drinking in the belief that drinking will ever become for him more than a pleasant social custom. The habit grows; how fast and often is suggested by the statistics cited earlier. Even aside from its habit-forming propensities, the large proportion of thefts, assaults, sexual derelictions, and other delinquent behavior committed while the offender is under its influence attest alcohol's demoralizing nature.

READINGS

Ausubel, D. P., *Theory and Problems of Adolescent Development.* New York: Grune and Stratton, 1954, Chapt. 14.

Bloch, H. A., and Flynn, F. T., *Delinquency.* New York: Random House, 1956, Chapts. 4, 5, 6, 7, 8.

Bowman, H. A., *Marriage for Moderns.* New York: McGraw-Hill Book Company, Inc., 1960, Chapts. 2, 5, 7.

Kuhlen, R. G., *The Psychology of Adolescent Development.* New York: Harper & Brothers, Publishers, 1952, Chapt. 11.

Landis, J. T., and Landis, M. G., *Building a Successful Marriage.* Englewood Cliffs, N. J.: Prentice-Hall, Inc., 1958, Chapt. 11.

Malm, M., and Jamison, O. G., *Adolescence.* New York; McGraw-Hill Book Company, 1952, Chapt. 10.

Neumeyer, M. H., *Juvenile Delinquency in Modern Society.* Princeton, N. J.: D. Van Nostrand Company, Inc., 1961, Chapt. 8.

Peterson, J. A., *Education for Marriage.* New York: Charles Scribner's Sons, 1956, Chapt. 11.

Smart, M., and Smart, R., *An Introduction to Family Relationships.* Philadelphia: W. B. Saunders Company, 1953, Chapt. 14.

Smith, H. C., *Personality Adjustment.* New York: McGraw-Hill Book Company, Inc., 1961, Chapt. 17.

Strang, R., *The Adolescent Views Himself.* New York: McGraw-Hill Book Company, Inc., 1957, Chapts. 10, 11.

Tussing, L., *Psychology for Better Living.* New York: John Wiley & Sons, Inc., 1959, Chapt. 15.

CHAPTER 15

COUNSELING ADOLESCENTS

PREVIEW

The Nature of Counseling

(Helping the counselee solve his own problems effectively.)

EDUCATIONAL AND VOCATIONAL	Teachers can usually do these two, although some special knowledge is required.
PERSONAL ADJUSTMENT	Training and supervised experience is required for some types of personal-adjustment counseling.
PSYCHOTHERAPY	Psychotherapy should be left to the clinical psychologist or psychiatrist.

Objectives of Adjustmental Counseling

TYPE	NATURE OF THE PROCESS
Situational counseling	The adjustment of a normal person to environmental stress.
Re-educative counseling	Changing well-established attitudes and behavior patterns.
Reconstructive therapy	Changing basic, deeply rooted aspects of the personality.

Guidelines in Counseling Adolescents

1. Avoid: preaching, showing shock, emotional involvement, depth therapy.
2. Take time; don't seem hurried.
3. Get the counselee to talk.
4. Obtain as much information as possible.
5. Respect confidences.
6. Encourage the counselee to think and reason his way to a sound decision.
7. Think of and treat counseling as a continuing process.

489

THE NATURE OF COUNSELING

DICTIONARY definitions of counseling cluster around the ideas of giving advice and recommending a course of action. These activities may indeed be a part of counseling, but they represent a very small part of the process that psychologists, psychiatrists, and school counselors refer to as counseling. Essentially counseling is assisting a person to make a wise decision or adopt a wise course of action, but it involves a great deal of fact finding, much work in analyzing appropriate data and determining interrelationships, and interpretation to ascertain meaning and implications. When all these latter requisites are satisfied, giving the advice or, better, enabling the counselee to perceive the implications of his situation and to make a sound decision on his own initiative is often a relatively quick, easy matter. In short, giving the advice or making the proper decision is often the easiest part of counseling; doing the spade work necessary for sound advising or deciding is the real job.

A major problem in counseling is often finding the real reason why counseling is being sought. Many times the reason originally offered by

George Peabody College for Teachers.

Figure 27. "The counselor will typically do more asking than telling, more listening than talking."

parents or adolescents for seeking counsel bears little resemblance to the *true* problem. We have already discussed several cases in which the ostensible reason for seeking help was merely an incidental side-product of the real problem, or perhaps did not even exist at all. Experienced counselors never proceed on the assumption that the original problem presented them is the crucial condition to be studied and dealt with. A request for vocational counseling may cover a demoralizing parent-child conflict. A complaint of inability to concentrate may conceal severe internal conflicts. Like a physician, a counselor must learn to distinguish between causes and symptoms and not become preoccupied with the latter to the exclusion of the former.

There are many types of counseling, many types of situations in which counseling takes place. The most common counseling received by adolescents is that given by their parents. Sometimes parental counseling is a fairly formalized affair, as when a father says to a son, "Let's go out where we will not be disturbed, Son. I want to talk to you about your plans for the summer." It may be extremely informal and occur in almost any guise, as when Mother says, "Olive, you'd better be planning how to budget your allowance to get the clothes you will need this fall," or Father says, "Will, have you thought of getting up early to do your studying instead of staying up so late?" Olive's mother is counseling her by direct suggestion; Will's father is counseling him by asking a question which he hopes will set Will off on a profitable line of thought. Both are legitimate counseling techniques. Even more "directive" counseling would have been for Olive's mother to say, "Olive, you'd better start saving ten dollars a month for your fall clothes." This, too, is perfectly legitimate counseling, but does less to encourage the counselee in wise self-direction than do the other forms illustrated. Parental counseling obviously covers virtually every subject, every type of situation, in which counseling is given. Parental counseling often is advice or guidance regarding a course of action without the preliminaries of data gathering and interpreting, because parents are likely to have much information concerning their children's affairs without formal research. However, in many instances parental counseling is faulty because parents depend upon their general knowledge of their child's affairs to counsel him and, therefore, fail to learn of and consider vital circumstances which ought to have been considered in counseling. Teachers are likely to make the same mistake in counseling students they feel they know well, and "shoot from the hip" without doing adequate preparation prior to offering guidance.

Counseling done on academic aspects of a boy's or girl's school life

is called "educational counseling." This category includes counseling a
student both on study habits or academic needs and on courses he should
take to achieve a desired educational program. Every good homeroom
teacher or faculty advisor provides this type of counseling as a routine
part of working with pupils for whom he is responsible. April is failing
biology. Her biology teacher has a consultation, or several consultations,
with her to determine the cause of her difficulty. April's laboratory methods are examined to see if carelessness or blind "direction following,"
instead of reasoning through her laboratory assignments, is responsible
for her poor work. Her manner of preparing homework, of studying assignments, is studied to see if faulty methods in these areas are responsible
for her difficulties. April and her teacher go over her test papers, looking
for indications of the nature and cause of her poor showing and discussing what can best be done about it. All these activities are counseling,
and reflection on them will re-emphasize the point made that counseling
typically involves much more investigation than giving advice.

Educational counseling, in the sense of helping an adolescent plan
his high-school or college program of studies, also involves much investigation of the circumstances of the individual. Does he show any unusual
deviation from a uniform pattern of aptitudes, any special abilities or
disabilities? In what areas are his interests highest? What are his future
educational and vocational plans? Going to college? Entering nurse's
training? Getting a job? What kind of job? What courses have already
been taken? What others are required for the diploma sought or future
plans projected?

In the process of bringing all such data together in a systematic pattern, the end result of educational counseling is often accomplished; the
student sees the implications of an accumulating mass of pertinent facts
and says, "Why, it looks like I had better do so and so," without any
formal statement by the teacher that "I think you had better do this or
that." This is fine counseling, because it has increased the counselee's
capacity for intelligent self-direction and problem solution.

"Vocational counseling" is often done in school, though, more frequently than educational counseling, it is done by someone other than
the teacher, someone especially trained in that type of counseling. However, when a boy or girl is interested in physics or geography, he may
have consultations with the teacher of one of those subjects and learn
what careers are available in the field in which he is interested, what his
relative likelihood of success in the field would be, and what educational

program would be necessary to prepare for each career. Vocational counseling, except of a routine sort involving mostly telling a boy or girl what courses to take for this or that vocational plan, is usually done by a vocational counselor especially trained in aptitude testing and having a vast knowledge of career possibilities and sources of information on various occupations. The vocational counselor will be experienced in helping a person design a program of preparation for a given career, as is involved in educational guidance. He will also help the counselee make fine discriminations as to how well his pattern of interests and aptitudes coincides with the requirements of a specific career, evaluate the social and financial returns of the career, and formulate a plan for career preparation suited to the needs and circumstances of the individual.

Good vocational counseling requires weighing many factors and arriving at a decision in which each factor is not only correctly evaluated, but also given its appropriate weight in reaching the final decision. Even family financial and social status should be considered. It would be dubious judgment, at best, to encourage a boy of little-above-average intelligence to aim for a career as a lawyer when his family would be unable to provide him with any financial support in his preparation. On the other hand, advising a girl of like intellectual ability to stop her education at the end of high school and get a job as a clerk, when her parents are both college graduates and amply able to finance the education they regard as minimal to fit her for a position in their social world, would display an equal disregard of reality. The average teacher can prepare himself to do a relatively good job of vocational guidance by extensive self-education, but such guidance requires vastly more than the mere application of sound common sense.

"Personal-adjustment counseling" is a term commonly applied to helping people work out minor to moderately serious social and emotional problems. Almost everyone does this sort of counseling to some extent. A girl asks her teacher, "I seem to have a gift for making people angry at me. How can I do better?" A boy asks his pastor, "How can I keep from saying mean things to my little brother?" A man asks his friend, "How can I stop worrying about my financial problems and concentrate on doing something about them?" All these represent everyday problems of adjustment which normal people have. They ask someone in whom they have confidence for counsel on how to solve their problems.

On a deeper level of complexity and seriousness there is the boy who has a hostility toward his parents and the girl who resorts to sexual promiscuity in a misguided attempt to fill a need for affection and security. Many schools have faculty members with considerable professional education in determining the roots of such maladjustments and helping the boy or girl work out a better relationship to himself and to society. Untrained but sympathetic teachers occasionally acquire considerable proficiency and reputation as counselors, as, through generations of pupils, they come to be known as ones who can help a boy or girl who feels mixed up, confused, or out of step with the world. The person without a minimum of one year's graduate training in the specific area of personal-adjustment counseling, however, should be extremely cautious in attempting to help adolescents whose adjustmental difficulties run deeper than simple maladjustment to a specific situation. Untrained people are prone to see the problem as a very simple, uncomplicated one for which they can give quick, clear-cut, unequivocal answers or solutions, never even suspecting the complex maze of underlying dynamics. Although the public and many professional people are slow in recognizing the fact, it is as unsafe for the goodhearted amateur with considerable practical experience to try to assist seriously maladjusted boys and girls as it is for him to try to treat boys and girls for measles or sore throats. If his diagnosis is correct and no unrecognized complications exist, the "practical nurse" may do fine. However, without professional education and a supervised internship in personal-adjustment counseling, the well-meaning teacher, physician, minister, or friend is tragically likely to treat superficial symptoms, allowing the basic condition to become progressively worse, and even unwittingly damaging the boy or girl through injurious remarks, advice, or interpretations which are perfectly good common sense, but which happen to be completely erroneous from the standpoint of technical fact and psychodynamics. One such error which will illustrate the sharp parting company of good common sense and psychodynamics is the case of the boy or girl who is depressed and withdrawn from social participation. "Good common sense" immediately suggests a solution: get out and mix with people, have a good time, play, get in the swing of things, don't allow yourself time to wallow in depression. Unfortunately, in a large proportion of cases such advice, if followed, will frustrate the boy or girl more than ever, emphasize his essential "aloneness," and may produce a full-fledged patient for the psychiatrist or clinical psychologist.

The next most serious case of personal maladjustment is the boy or girl with deep-seated internal conflicts, personality disturbances, anxieties, phobias, "conversion reactions" in which emotional stresses may be manifested by physical pain or illness without organic basis, and other such serious conditions. These require the attention of the psychologist or physician especially trained in psychotherapy. Such a psychologist is customarily called a clinical psychologist, the physician a psychiatrist. Either may be called a psychoanalyst if that has been the form of his psychotherapeutic training. The relative competence of a member of either of these categories of psychotherapists to deal with a serious maladjustment is determined solely by the relative competence of the specific therapist, not the orientation of his training. The clinical psychologist cannot prescribe drugs or give physical treatment to a patient, but physical treatment is rarely essential to psychotherapy (except in psychoses, which customarily require confinement in an institution) and, where it is needed, can ordinarily be supplied by the family doctor. The psychiatrist, on the other hand, often lacks the research orientation and extensive knowledge of psychodynamics outside, but often pertinent to, the field of psychotherapy which is a part of the preparation of the clinical psychologist.

The role of the teacher in counseling adolescents should be confined to work with boys and girls with simple "situational" maladjustments such as those illustrated at the beginning of the next section. However, teachers and other workers with youth must know something of the more serious maladjustments to be able to discriminate between those within their capabilities to handle and those requiring more specialized professional preparation. Unfortunately, it is as impossible to provide a definitive criterion for ascertaining whether a boy or girl is suffering a severe-enough emotional or mental disturbance to justify referral to a psychotherapist as it is to provide such a criterion as to whether or not a particular physical illness justifies or necessitates calling in a physician. The safest course is for the teacher to refer to the counselor or school psychologist any boy or girl who displays unusual departure from the norm of his classmates in the area of emotional stability, anxieties, hostilities, delinquencies, or withdrawal over a considerable period of time, and who does not respond to counseling by the teacher. The counselor or school psychologist can determine whether treatment at that level or referral to a psychotherapist is necessary. If no such person is available, the teacher should bring the case to the attention of the principal. If he agrees, the student's parents may be called in and the boy's or girl's possible need of psychological examination discussed. If not, as principal he assumes responsibility for the student's welfare as far as the school is concerned, telling the teacher what to do or otherwise disposing of the case.

It has been said that to reject a light because it is imperfect is to choose total darkness rather than some enlightenment. On this theory, recognizing the inadequacy of such a list, but also recognizing the urgent need for *some* criterion for guidance, the following list of behaviors or symptoms is included as guidance for teachers. The possibility of a boy's or girl's needing referral to a counselor, school psychologist, or psychotherapist should be considered if any of the following conditions appear to exist longer than a few weeks and if the teacher's efforts to help the boy or girl to achieve a better relationship to himself, life, and society are unsuccessful.

Conditions Which Often Indicate Need for Psychotherapy

1. *Passivity, withdrawal or solitariness.* Extreme failure to participate normally both in class activities and in social relationships.

2. *Hostility and aggressiveness.* Strong and persistent antisocial tendencies, attitudes, or activities.

3. *Anxieties, phobias, tenseness.* Any of these attitudes conspicuously in excess of the degree appropriate to the circumstances. A 98 student terribly fearful of not making an A, for example.

4. *Internal conflicts.* Strong conflicting drives producing any of the three conditions above. Inability to undertake a much-desired project because of fear of failure, for example.

5. *Emotional instability.* Emotional response frequently out of all proportion to the circumstances; elation, depression, anxiety, etc.

6. *Lying or stealing.* May not be abnormal, but may indicate compensatory strivings to offset basic personality inadequacies or maladjustments.

7. *Excessive daydreaming.* Often indicated by Number 1 above. Serious when carried to the point of substituting for real-life activities.

8. *Frequent physical complaints of questionable authenticity.* Nausea, headaches, etc.

9. *Compulsive or obsessive behavior or attitudes.* Repetitive actions or ideas inappropriate to the circumstances in which they occur.

10. *Stuttering, nail biting, facial grimaces, tics.* Such physical anomalies are often symptoms of oversevere emotional stress.

11. *Actions or relationships suggesting homosexuality.*

12. *Night terrors, somnambulism, enuresis.* Teachers will seldom learn of such occurrences unless consulted by the parents.

13. *Development of a new problem as fast as another is disposed of.*

OBJECTIVES OF
ADJUSTMENTAL COUNSELING

As implied in earlier portions of this chapter, counseling is for the purpose of assisting an individual to achieve better adjustment of some sort, and may involve coping with problems of different magnitudes and depth. A good classification of types of psychotherapy can be applied with advantage to counseling (actually, psychotherapy is a form of counseling, but only counseling of relatively serious cases of emotional or personality disturbances is ordinarily referred to as psychotherapy). In increasing order of severity of the problem being dealt with and the depth of change in the individual involved, counseling can well be thought of as situational, re-educative (different from educational counseling as already discussed), and reconstructive.

Situational Counseling

This is counseling on a localized or relatively superficial problem, superficial in the sense of the depth of personality and emotional involvement, be it noted. Situational maladjustments may be as agonizing as any others, as in the case of a normal girl who is the victim of a vendetta by a hostile clique of girls in the class and is being driven to distraction by their activities. However, as the name implies, situational maladjustments arise fundamentally from the situation in which the person finds himself, not from defects in his self concept, personality structure, or adjustive mechanisms. The boy who shows up morning after morning bleary-eyed and sleepy and is failing his courses is more frequently reacting maladjustively to a situation than developing a neurosis, and counseling which enables him to work out an adjustment to his life situation is often within the scope of the teacher. The girl who mopes for a week, fails to do her homework, sits listlessly in class, and weeps often and copiously may not be developing a manic-depressive psychosis; she may be displaying a situational maladjustment to her boy friend's moving away or dropping her for another girl. Both conditions are relatively superficial in that they do not involve deep-seated maladjustments.

It is the author's belief, based on several years of teaching in public schools, that a well-adjusted teacher with professional preparation appropriate to high-school teaching can properly do much more situational counseling than teachers . typically undertake. Of course, such counseling is time-consuming, but often teachers' failure to counsel students is due not to lack of time, but to fearfulness of assuming the responsibility of rendering such assistance. Time after time I am asked, "How far can a teacher properly go in prying into the personal affairs of a boy or girl?" My answer invariably is, "As far as your professional judgment indicates is in the best interest of the boy or girl concerned." In short, the same distance as a lawyer or physician who attempts to serve the individual.

To be most effective, counseling should emphasize the boy's or girl's solving of his own problems, reaching a reasoned and logical solution making possible his own decision, rather than the counselor listening judiciously and then telling the counselee the answer. Questions, interpretations, and discussion may be used to guide the counselee's progress in adjustive, rather than maladjustive, perceptions and reasoning. There is no reason why a counselor should not make specific suggestions or recommendations if they seem indicated, but better adjustment will usually result if the counselee arrives at them through processes in which he participates, rather than having them handed to him on a silver platter.

Counseling may be done by teachers in a short conversation while walking down the hall with a student or by prearranged appointment. Of course, the bigger or more personal the problem, the more formalized the situation likely to be required for its successful handling.

A word of warning is appropriate at this point: If another problem or symptom of maladjustment springs up as fast as one is disposed of, or if the counselee displays attitudes whose existence seem to have no basis in reality, suspect the existence of a maladjustive condition deeper than situational and requiring correspondingly deeper therapy.

Re-educative Counseling

Sometimes a boy or girl will have persisted in an attitude or course of behavior until it becomes habitual, regardless of whether it is adjustive or appropriate to the situation. The boy from the slums who, throughout his life, has had unpleasant clashes with policemen until he hates any symbol of authority is an example. The girl who has magnified in her own mind the disfiguring conspicuousness of her buck teeth until she

will not willingly speak in a group is another. Re-education is needed
by such adolescents. The roots of their difficulties extend back over
longer periods of time than do the roots of situational difficulties. More
of the self concept is involved. Attitudes involved run deeper, even
though they are not necessarily more intense than the attitudes in the
maladjustments resulting largely from situational factors. Thus, to be
effective, counseling must be deeper. This is the gray area between relatively simple counseling and psychotherapy; sometimes a specific case
will appear to be one and, upon further investigation, prove to be the
other. The less deep-rooted cases requiring re-educative counseling, such
as the two cited above, can often be handled by a well-adjusted and
sympathetic teacher. More serious ones, as, for instance, if the boy's rejection of authority extends to his own father or if the girl's self-consciousness is such that she refuses to answer when called on in class, should receive the attention of a trained counselor. Some such cases will require
psychotherapy and be so referred. The boy's hostility finding outlet in
elaborate autistic thinking, and the girl thus living her social life, might
be examples of such extreme conditions.

As can be seen, the key factor in re-educative counseling is the identification of attitudes and elements of the self concept which produce the
maladjustment and the changing of those attitudes and the self concept
appropriately. Both are likely to require considerable professional skill,
and failure to handle them properly can badly worsen the situation. The
girl with buck teeth, for instance, may have them because insecurity in
early childhood led to thumb-sucking, which malformed her mouth, or
she may have developed her undue self-consciousness from her self concept formed in infancy, the buck teeth being merely a convenient feature
on which to focus. In either case, insisting that she move out socially may
cause her to do so at the expense of increasing internal tension, and
she may develop migraine headaches or severe acne to reinforce her defenses against mixing with people. Causal factors of maladjustments at
the level calling for re-education rather than simple correction, as was
needed in situational maladjustments, are thus seen to involve powerful
elements *within* the boy or girl, not merely his or her adjustment to external reality. Treatment is similarly complicated. Like diagnosis of the
difficulty, it involves considerable knowledge of the dynamics of adjustment rather than "plain common sense."

Aside from the complexity of the problems, processes, and defensive
mechanisms involved, re-educative counseling is likely to require more

time than a teacher can afford to spend on a student. Many consultations are likely to be needed, and often lengthy ones.

Reconstructive Therapy

This is the province of the psychotherapist, the clinical psychologist or the psychiatrist, as previously discussed. Here we find at work forces lying far below the level of the patient's consciousness. Often a complex pattern of misleading symptoms and reaction patterns has been developed to protect the person against his real problem's being brought to light. A migraine headache which puts one in bed for two days may be psychologically preferable to facing the conflict in feelings which exists within the patient, and all the resources of the patient's unconscious may be brought into play to preserve the anonymity of the conflict. It must be remembered that in these deep-seated maladjustive states the causal factors are usually completely unrecognized by the patient. Typically, these causal factors are so unpleasant that they have been relegated to the nether pits of the unconscious, where they produce the tensions and maladjustive attitudes and behaviors which call the patient to someone's attention. In fact, his behavior and attitudes are maladjustive, i.e., inappropriate to the circumstances of reality, at least partly because he is trying to achieve adjustment by fighting on one front when his real trouble lies on a completely different, unperceived one.

The boy or girl who frequently becomes physically ill before a test, vomiting or running a fever perhaps, is a good illustration of a person who requires reconstructive therapy, *not* because of the vomiting or fever, be it noted, but because of the anxiety regarding failure or competition which is so powerful that physical illness is preferable as an escape. The obvious power of the unconscious defense mechanism which can produce such a somatic upset is a force to be reckoned with. The nature of the conflict, the insecurity, or whatever else is causing the stress must be ascertained—often a difficult task. The dynamics of some therapeutic system, all too complicated to discuss here, must be applied in an appropriate manner to rectify the maladjustive mechanisms. It is far better to refer several boys or girls for psychotherapy who turn out not to need it than to fail to refer one who needs it. He or she may become a tragic casualty because of lack of needed treatment.

GUIDELINES
IN COUNSELING ADOLESCENTS

Every chapter in this text is a chapter on counseling adolescents. Counseling is not a technique; it is a profession. Good counseling is not a matter of mastering some procedural techniques. It requires broad, deep knowledge of the dynamics of human adjustment and specialized knowledge of individual and group differences. The counselor attempting to counsel an adolescent girl on improving her heterosexual adjustment without a thorough knowledge of the psychosexual differences between boys and girls would be subjecting her to as much danger of injury as would a surgeon operating on her without a knowledge of physiology. Lack of knowledge of the facts and principles of mental growth would make it impossible for a counselor to counsel a boy or girl intelligently on academic matters. Counseling is, indeed, a specialized field, but its specialization lies principally in the breadth and depth of knowledge of psychology, the dynamics of adjustment, and psychopathology it requires, not in the special techniques employed.

Counseling adolescents involves, first of all, learning what adolescents are like, the forces that operate within them (drives, motives, adjustive mechanisms, etc.) and upon them (parental influences, social relationships, social pressures, etc.). It requires a knowledge of how people react to frustrations, how emotions affect one, and how a person can want two mutually exclusive things or feel two opposite ways at the same time. Some introductory texts in adolescent psychology confine themselves to presentation of facts as to how adolescents feel, what they do, how many have one interest and how many another, and similar descriptive materials. Virtually all consideration of dynamics, *why* they are and feel like that, is left to advanced courses. This text, as the title implies, goes more than slightly into the dynamics of adolescent adjustment—feelings, behavior, defensive and adjustive mechanisms—because the author feels that teachers and workers with adolescent girls and boys need to know something of these things, and many of them will take no more advanced courses in psychology.

Therefore, although the remainder of this chapter is devoted to certain principles and techniques of counseling, it must be borne in mind that the real substance of counseling lies in the preceding chapters. This final chapter merely contains some relatively simple and mechanical

techniques by which the knowledge of the previous chapters is brought to bear on the problems of an individual boy or girl. Continuing the previous analogy of the surgeon, this chapter would tell how to put on operating clothes, arrange the operating room, and prepare the instruments, but not how to perform the operation. That is the realm of the professional knowledge achieved throughout all previous professional education.

With full recognition that the following are mechanical techniques calculated to give counseling the best opportunity of success, not the counseling procedures themselves, teachers, parents, and other workers with adolescents may find them helpful as guidelines in counseling.

Principles and Techniques in Counseling Adolescents

1. *Three things to avoid.* Several "natural," "common sense," and very human tendencies are either useless or actively detrimental to good counseling. To avoid getting off on the wrong foot in counseling, these should be recognized and avoided. *Preaching* is the almost universal tendency of beginning or untrained counselors. They *know* what the counselee ought to do, why what he is doing is wrong, and the sensible thing seems to be to tell him and persuade him to do differently. Not only is such good advice typically disregarded; often it is actively injurious to good counseling, because the counselee finds the counselor reacting to him just as his parents, the judge, everyone else has, and develops the same antagonism toward the counselor as he previously had toward others who gave him the benefit of their wisdom. Thus, he becomes inaccessible to counseling because he has lost confidence in the counselor.

Showing shock. In many cases, a boy or girl is receiving counseling because of attitudes or behavior which, according to conventional standards, is shocking, disgusting, or outrageous. It is not the proper function of a dentist to feel outrage over a patient's letting his teeth get into a deplorable condition; it is his province to take what is there and help the patient do the best he can with them. The counselor's responsibility is identical: not to judge morality, but to help the counselee make the most advantageous adjustment possible, when both his own good and the good of society are considered. If the counselor shows shock, the adolescent often will either withdraw mentally and emotionally and not "open up" in the manner required for successful counseling, or deliberately set out to bait the counselor by scandalizing him.

Emotional involvement. This works two ways. The counselor should avoid becoming emotionally involved with a counselee or his problems to the extent of obscuring his objectivity and best judgment. It is necessary to feel and show sympathy and understanding in many cases; it destroys the counselor's capacity for best assistance if the feelings become so acute that he identifies with the adolescent and concentrates on defending rather than helping him. On the other hand, counselees often show a strong tendency to become emotionally involved with the counselor—a romantic attachment when the two are of opposite sexes, or a crush when the two are of the same sex. Such situations can be prevented or handled by limiting contacts with the counselee to the specified times of consultations and avoiding intimate, subtly flirtatious, or provocative tones, expressions, or attitudes. The tendency for a counselee to become emotionally involved with a psychotherapist is called transference, and is an essential part of much psychotherapy, but should not be encouraged by the teacher-counselor. The complications which can arise are too dangerous and potentially destructive to both parties.

Depth therapy. When one discovers a new era of knowledge—learning about the way the child's unconscious converts a hostility toward the mother into obstreperousness in school, as an example—the natural tendency is to use that knowledge. Many jokes are current about the person with a couple of courses in psychology behind him (or whose "crowd" has "taken up" Freud) who tells a friend that his cutting his finger is evidence of an unconscious death wish, and the like. But teachers or others functioning officially or semiofficially as counselors have a professional obligation to avoid exceeding the limits of their own professional training and experience in their interpretations. Not only are interpretations foreign to the habitual thoughts of nonpsychologists likely to antagonize rather than impress the counselee; if they do not antagonize him, they may arouse anxieties and conflicts and advance his maladjustive state from merely situational to one involving his own self concept and personality mechanisms. In short, probing a counselee's unconscious, bringing his repressed conflicts to light, giving him interpretations of relationships which he has shut away from conscious recognition is psychological surgery, to be left to the psychotherapist. Help the counselee on the level of environmental adjustment; do not attempt to psychoanalyze him.

2. *Take time, and don't seem hurried.* An adolescent is before you because he wants or needs help. Even if he needs it without wanting it, he

still evaluates your interest in him partly by the extent to which you seem
to give his needs priority over other things. Seeming hurried, working
to meet a deadline, having allocated a certain amount of time to him
and being unwilling to exceed it, are all subtly destructive to the establishment of good rapport, good relationship between counselor and
counselee. It gives the impression (often all too true) that the boy or
girl is being given time not on the basis of his needs, but on the basis of
what time is left over from more "important" or pressing matters. When
you must unavoidably terminate the interview at a specified time, either
explain this to him at the beginning, making arrangements for future
consultation if it proves to be needed, or, when the time comes, do your
explanation and making of arrangements. In either case, during the
consultation itself carefully avoid any appearance of being rushed—in
fact, of even being conscious of the passage of time. Use whatever time
the problem or your other circumstances dictate, but whatever the
amount, let the adolescent see that he, not the clock, has your undivided
attention.

3. *Get the counselee to talk.*   In many instances, a boy's or girl's talking through a problem with a sympathetic adult leads to clearer perception of the whole issue and a solution arrived at by the boy or girl with
little or no help from the counselor. This is a highly desirable result,
because it constitutes valuable experience for the boy or girl in examining a personal problem, marshaling appropriate facts and applying appropriate principles, and arriving at a sound solution as a result of his
own efforts. It gives him acquaintance with the possibility of thinking
and reasoning his way to a solution of his problems rather than blindly
hitting on some course of action and plunging ahead regardless of its
suitability or unsuitability.

Getting the boy or girl to talk can be accomplished by asking questions which require thought and explanation, not a simple "yes" or "no"
or a statement of fact to answer. As an example, little is likely to be accomplished by asking a boy or girl, "Did you get along with your teachers in elementary school?" Not much better is asking, "How did you get
along with your teachers in elementary school?" There is no can't-miss
way of asking a question that will get a counselee to open up and talk,
but an example of a question that will frequently encourage it is, "Tell
me about how you got along with your teachers in elementary school,
whether you liked them, whether they treated you well, and what you
thought of them."

In a good counseling interview the counselor will typically do much more *asking* than *telling,* more listening than talking, more guiding of the counselee's reasoning toward self-solution of problems than presenting him with ready-made solutions. It is readily seen that if this principle is observed, the opportunity to preach is cut to a minimum. Often a boy or girl needs assistance not because his problem is particularly difficult, the decision to be made a difficult one, or the proper course of action difficult to determine, but because he never systematically explored the factors pertinent to his problem, decision, or course of action. Talking his problem through shows him what he can accomplish by systematic effort. Of course, the counselor guides the discussion as necessary by questions, suggestions, and interpretations appropriate to the circumstances. He does not leave the adolescent to find his way alone to a decision, but he encourages or leads him rather than making the decision for him.

4. *Obtain as much information as possible.* One big reason why the preparation of counselors involves several courses is that there are so many aspects to every case that many courses are required to cover them all. Ideally, each of the short case digests presented in this text should have run to five, ten, or perhaps fifty pages of information about the boy or girl, his or her past history, home situation, parental relations, school and medical history, psychological tests taken, and comprehensive minute detail of his or her relations with various people in the environment. Space requirements prohibit such adequate presentation of cases, and only a few of the most highly pertinent and significant facts have been selected from the mass of data accumulated on each of the cases and presented in the case digest. References at the end of the chapter will include some books giving case studies in the elaborate detail necessary for proper counseling. After a case has been completed, it is easy to look over the data and identify a relatively few significant factors which exercised major influence on a counselee's adjustment. But the counselor *cannot know in advance* what those relatively few factors are going to be in a particular case, and thus must gather great masses of facts and information from which the pertinent ones may eventually be gleaned. The author's case material on the cases digested for discussion in this text never included less than the equivalent of ten pages of case data; more frequently twenty or thirty pages were accumulated in the process of securing the picture of the case which could later be summarized in as many lines!

The necessity for encyclopedic information about a counselee is obviously one reason for encouraging him to talk freely and at length in the counseling interviews. The more he talks, the more of his feelings, his perceptions, his ways of thinking, his ways of dealing with situations, the interpretations he places on happenings, and his characteristic patterns of response and reaction (as well as factual information) are revealed to the counselor. This information, in turn, makes it possible for the counselor to form a picture of the counselee's self concept, his particular pattern of psychodynamics, and his relationship to his environment, as well as to perceive the environmental circumstances themselves. Even in the simplest case of situational counseling, the peculiar adjustive mechanisms and processes of the individual typically have more to do with the adolescent's problem than do the environmental circumstances.

It is often desirable to gather information from sources other than the counselee. Parents and teachers (but seldom age-mates, except by observation) should be consulted where circumstances dictate and permit. Often the picture the counselee presents of himself and his circumstances will take on a completely different aspect when another person describes him and the same circumstances. Counseling performed on the basis of inadequate fact will seldom be adequate counseling. One pertinent fact, one typical pattern of response or interpretation on the part of the counselee, may completely alter the whole structure of a case and how it should be handled. There is no way in the world of knowing in advance which fact or dynamic force it will be; the certainty that counseling will assist the adolescent to the optimum extent rises in direct proportion to the completeness of the information on which the counseling is based. This is true even if the boy or girl, not the counselor, makes the final decisions, because the soundness of the counselee's decisions is just as dependent upon their being based on appropriate consideration of all pertinent factors as is the soundness of decisions made by the counselor. In fact, many boys and girls find themselves in need of counseling largely because, as an habitual pattern of life, they have made decisions and chosen courses of action without due consideration of all pertinent circumstances.

5. *Respect confidences.* Learning enough about a boy or girl, and the circumstances in which he or she lives, to meet the stipulations set forth above will often necessarily involve learning much very personal material which the counselee understandably and properly wants kept secret. Counselors are told details of adolescents' feelings toward their

parents, details of sexual behavior, details of hopes, fears, likes, and dislikes which the counselee would knowingly tell no other person on earth except another equally competent counselor. Sometimes information is imparted on the promise that it will not even be revealed to the counselee's physician, actions and thoughts being really much more personal and intimate than one's physical body. Not only must the counselor refrain from betraying such confidence directly through revealing them to other teachers, counselors, or the like; he must take care also not to reveal the imparted information even though the name of the boy or girl involved is not revealed. A listener may be able to recognize (or think he recognizes, which may be as bad or worse) some identifying fact or characteristic. That listener does not have the counselor's professional responsibility to maintain secrecy, and thus the "confidence" becomes a matter of common gossip. (In the cases presented in this text, the essential dynamics of actual cases are presented in real-life form. However, not merely names, but all identifying data, have been sufficiently changed as to render the cases impossible of identification.)

6. *Encourage the counselee to think and reason his way to a sound decision.* This idea, already repeatedly mentioned, is deserving of special emphasis here because it is really the essence of counseling. The counselor may perceive clearly the boy's or girl's problem, what should be done about it, what decision should be made, what course of action pursued, *but until the boy or girl recognizes the problem, the soundness of a decision, and the advantages of a course of action,* he profits little from the counselor's knowledge. Of course, the counselor can reach a decision and then present that solution to the counselee, but the process of persuading him to accept the solution and act on it is often more difficult than it would have been to help the boy or girl reach the same decision on his own initiative, and when he reaches it on his own initiative, he is generally more willing to accept it and act on it.

This means neither that the counselor, by this method, does not need himself to perceive the counselee's problem and its optimum solution, nor that he should not guide the counselee in the solution of his own problem; he should do both. With his professional competence he should ordinarily perceive the crucial elements of the counselee's problem and what needs to be done about them before the counselee does. Then he should use that perception to steer the counselee's thinking along profitable channels to reach the best possible adjustment. Leading questions may be useful: "What is the usual result of blowing up as you did?" "Is that the result you want?" "Can you keep up your present extracurricular activities and have time for the extra study you propose? How?" Such questions do not confront the counselee with unpleasant facts which the counselor demands he swallow. They encourage him to reach his own decision, but also guide him to consider pertinent facts and circumstances in reaching it, instead of merely "deciding" whatever is easiest or most appealing.

The counselor should guide by questions, and by direct advice where necessary although this must be done cautiously. Usually, offering a decision or solution as something for the counselee to consider will achieve better results than telling him to do this or that. The reason for the superior success of encouraging the counselee to make decisions is not far to seek: if *he* makes the decision, he has an ego involvement in its success; he is subtly devaluated in his own esteem if his solution does not work. He has no such ego involvement if the decision is the counselor's; he can give it halfhearted support and blame the counselor if it does not achieve the effect he desires. Human nature being what it is, a person will simply try harder to make his own solution, decision, or choice work than he will to make the counselor's.

A technique used successfully by counselors who emphasize the importance of counselees' solving their own problems (called nondirective counseling) even more than does the author is called reflection. When the counselee expresses an opinion or offers a fact which the counselor perceives to be worthy of further exploration, he reflects the idea back to the counselee, encouraging further elaboration. Perhaps the counselee is talking of an inability to concentrate on his lessons and says, "My mind wanders off." The counselor might say, "Your mind wanders off?" or "You have difficulty in keeping your mind on your studies?" thereby encouraging the counselee in further consideration of this topic.

Psychological changes, changes in attitudes, feelings, and ways of adjusting to life, tend to take place slowly. They do not occur as a result of intellectually perceiving the illogic of a feeling or the desirability of another. One inexperienced counselor, having seen the crux of the maladjustive pattern of a counselee and having shown it to him, was impatient that the counselee did not respond with indications of a changed attitude. "Can't you see that there is no reason to fear the dark?" he asked. With considerable psychological insight the counselee replied, "Now that you've shown me the reasons, I can *see* that there is no reason for me to fear the dark, but that doesn't change the way I've been taught to *feel* since childhood." The need for most counseling is produced by emotional, not intellectual, maladjustments, and mere intellectual "getting things straight" does not remove the maladjustive mechanism.

7. *Think of and treat counseling as a continuing process.* The necessity for this is obvious from the previous paragraph. Effective counseling is typically a series of consultations, often with increasing intervals between them, but continued until the counselee is well adjusted to the course of action or living which emerged from the counseling sessions. Repeated consultations are usually necessary for a counselee to achieve the emotional changes, to change his attitudes, to learn to perceive himself and his environment in a new way. Emotional adjustment to new perceptions or insights typically lags far behind the intellectual achievement of those perceptions and insights. Here, too, much talking by the counselee pays dividends. Hearing himself *say* things repeatedly, in different forms, proving and re-proving their correctness by his own reasoning, tends gradually to swing the emotional pattern of the individual into congruence with his intellectual and verbal pattern. Numerous studies have shown that people's attitudes change more as a result of their discussing a topic than from their being talked to about the topic. Repeated counseling sessions provide opportunity for the process of emotional change to take place.

Most psychotherapists appear to feel that terminating consultations in a definitive manner is necessary or desirable. The author believes that psychotherapeutic programs and, likewise, a series of counseling sessions can often more profitably be allowed to dwindle away rather than formally ended. When counselor and counselee feel that the objectives of the counseling have been adequately met, when the counselee has achieved satisfactory adjustment in the area of stress or indecision, the counselor may say, "Well, it seems that you see your way ahead pretty clearly now. Suppose we don't set another date for a consultation, but if either of us feels another is necessary, we will get together and talk again." This simultaneously avoids the implied pronouncement, "Now you're cured," and leaves the way open for further counseling if needed. And follow-up should be an important part of every counseling program.

(*As previous case history digests have illustrated, a real-life boy or girl seldom presents a serious problem of adjustment in one area and is well-adjusted in all others. Even so, the case history digests have intentionally been written to portray the problems of a boy or girl in as simple and clear a manner as possible. Generalizations such as "there have been numerous instances of truancy" and "considerable hostility was manifested" have been made rather than detailing the mass of circumstances from which they were drawn. Ambiguities and contradictions habitually encountered in case histories have been smoothed over in the digests. Failure to have made these simplifications and clarifications would have caused the histories to be unwieldy in length and complexity.*

In the case of Vincent Vogel, you will be presented the case material much more nearly as it was obtained. Even here, many of the contradictions have been resolved. As an example, in one interview Vincent said that he had not violated his coming-home time since the last conference, and his mother had previously reported that he had. The explanation? Vincent was late getting in one night (as his mother said), but (as Vincent said) he had a flat tire on the way home and was thrown fifteen minutes late, but did not purposely violate his curfew; he just got delayed fifteen minutes a block from home. Some of the contradictions are retained for illustrative purposes. The information is not so well organized as in previous cases, though even here it is better organized than in the form in which it was obtained. The multiplicity of problems typical of an adolescent whose parents seek counseling are represented in the case history rather than simplifying the case down to one problem. Four consultations of approximately one and one-half hours each, two with Vincent and two with his parents, were consumed in obtaining the following information. The fragmentary notes from which this coherent case history was constructed filled eighteen pages. The insight gained from the information constituted the basis for subsequent counseling of both Vincent and his parents.)

Case of Vincent Vogel

The parents of Vincent Vogel sought help at the psychological clinic regarding academic and behavioral difficulties of their son, sixteen years and one month, in the tenth grade. At the time of referral Vincent was under suspension from the public high school because of insolence to teachers, use of profanity, and unrestrained temper and threats to the school principal. Vincent had not told the parents of his suspension at first; he had left the house the following morning at the usual time and stayed away all day. The mother had learned of his suspension through a casual telephone conversation with a friend. Vincent, on being confronted with this knowledge, admitted suspension, but steadfastly denied all charges of disobedience, insolence, profanity, and threats.

Mrs. Vogel went to the school on the following day and effected his reinstatement upon his promise to "do right," although to her he still maintained his innocence of previous misdeeds. He went to classes that day and came home immediately after school. As punishment for his suspension, Mr. Vogel took away Vincent's car privileges, forbade his going to the hangout of the gang (a corner service station), and put a 10 P.M. curfew on him for a month. Although Vincent apparently accepted this restraint with better grace than usual, the first night the father visited his room at about 10 P.M. and found that he had stuffed pillows in his bed and apparently gone out the window. He did not return home that night, nor did he show up at school the following day. The father notified the local police and youth bureau, and through their efforts it was learned two days later that Vincent and a friend had been picked up by police in an upstate town for vagrancy and were jailed there. The father went to that city and was told that charges of car theft, dope peddling, and assault on another teenage boy had been placed; however, on lack of sufficient evidence, charges were dropped and the boy given over to the custody of his father. While being taken to police headquarters by arresting officers, Vincent had broken away and been recaptured at gunpoint. He had apparently been scared by the treatment he had received at the hands of the police and was grateful to his father for coming to his aid. He expressed deep apologies for all the trouble and worry he had caused.

This episode had resulted in his missing another four days from school, meaning that he had attended only one day since his original suspension. Mrs. Vogel went with him to the principal's office the next morning, and Vincent asked for a transfer from the homeroom of the teacher with whom he had had his trouble. When this was not immediately accomplished, he complained bitterly about how unfairly he was being treated by all concerned and used profanity to both the principal and the teacher in question, whereupon the principal threatened to call police officers. He did not actually do so, although he immediately suspended Vincent again.

Both parents went to his office later in the day, apologizing for Vincent's actions and language and asking for his reinstatement. They were told without equivocation that he could not re-enter the school under any circumstances during the current year, and that three other teachers in the school had expressed "fear" of Vincent, one of them having considered swearing out a peace warrant against him. When the parents tried to discuss the situation with Vincent, he persistently maintained his innocence of all charges, then refused to talk about the matter at all. It was at this point that the parents were referred to the psychologist.

Vincent is five feet eight inches tall, but weighs 160 pounds, all of it solid bone and muscle. He is a dark, handsome boy with quick, lithe movements. He shaves daily. He has an older sister, recently married, and a younger sister, age fourteen, to whom he is devoted. Parents report that until he was in junior high school, "you couldn't have asked for a better boy." At that time (four years ago) he went through a similar episode relating to his school adjustment, although he was not suspended at the time, and apparently he "snapped out of it." Analysis of his old report cards indicates that he was a behavioral problem at school during many of his elementary years. Soon after his junior-high trouble, his parents found in his room elaborate statements which Vincent himself had written up, portending to be official police charges against himself for beating up the junior-high principal, a teacher, and another adult male. He was not questioned regarding these by the parents, and never mentioned them himself.

When Vincent was fourteen, his parents were informed by a neighborhood shopkeeper that he was shoplifting. When they asked him about this, he first denied it completely, then broke down and admitted it. The things that he was known to have taken were a miscellaneous assortment which would seem to have been of no value or interest to a teenage boy. The parents returned these things and paid for items the proprietor asserted Vincent had taken, but which were not found in his cache. Two months later police came to the Vogel home to investigate a tip that Vincent had taken other things from local stores, things which proprietors had reported to police as stolen during recent robberies. In his closet were found several of the described items. Vincent expressed surprised shock that these things were there, saying that he had "learned his lesson" and had not taken anything else since the previous time when his parents had questioned him about the shoplifting. A week later he was caught stealing a transistor radio. The store, however, did not call police, but threatened Vincent with such action if he were ever again found stealing. His parents were notified of the incident.

Mr. and Mrs. Vogel report that Vincent has always had to work harder than most students at school, but until the second year in junior high school he had worked "terrifically hard." He was tutored for the first term of that year, in spite of which he made very poor grades. At this point, they said, he seemed to give up, and began to feel that he could not succeed in school. He failed to graduate with his junior-high class, but made up the failed work in the first term of summer school and entered high school with them this past September. He has always been quite popular with both boys and girls of his age, and is especially kind and thoughtful to older people. He attended Sunday school regularly when a child, and while the parents still insist that he do so, he frequently slips out of Sunday school now or does not attend the youth meetings of the church when he leaves the house telling them he is going to do so.

Just before he was fifteen, Mrs. Vogel reports, she slapped him for making disrespectful remarks about his father, at which he flared up and threatened her with harm if she ever slapped him again. She immediately did slap him again, telling him that he would not be allowed to talk to her that way, upon which he hit her, though not injuring her, stormed off and went to a friend's house, refusing to come back home for several days. He asked permission to live at the friend's house, which was refused, and after being told how much his sister was grieving because of his absence, he came back home. At this point there was a family conference in which he was asked what his complaints were about the family situation. He maintained that his friends all said he was "babied," and that the parents would not let him stay out at the all-night parties his friends all attended.

Parents report that for the past four years he has been conspicuously heavier than boys his own age and has chosen as his companions boys two to four years older than he. He is athletically inclined, has had numbers of girl friends with whom he has gone steady for short periods of time, and was elected president of his homeroom class in his last year in junior high school. For six weeks last summer he worked on a construction gang and seemed to like working.

Parents report that they are sure Vincent has been drinking beer on several occasions, and that once, when he came in quite late, he was drunk. There was no further contact with police (to the parents' knowledge) until two months ago, when at 2 A.M. the father was called to the police station where Vincent was being held for participation in a gang fight with boys from a neighboring town. Vincent's explanation was that he had been asked by an older boy to drive the car to the place where the fight had been arranged, and had been scared not to. He was put on probation by the police youth bureau, a curfew of 10 P.M. was imposed by the bureau, and he was required to report to the station each Saturday morning. This probation was still in effect at the time the parents came to the psychologist.

Vincent and his father have been very companionable all his life, have always played ball and bowled together. He had a nervous tic which came and went for years until his junior-high years, at which time it ceased. He has always bitten his fingernails, and still does. Parents report that his first willful disobedience was three years ago, when he refused to come home one night when his mother ordered him to do so over the telephone. They say he has been brought up "under the belt" all his life, yet report a family friend as saying recently that they had so little trouble with Vincent until the last three years that he "does not know how to take correction." A year ago, when he rebelled against a punishment imposed, his father beat him into submission. Apparently Vincent harbored no resentment, however. Parents have found in his room some pornographic pictures and magazines and typewritten material, which greatly shocked the mother. She has had a long, serious talk with Vincent, warning him of his drifting from the church and the Christian way of life, and of the bad influence of his companions. Both parents feel that the boy at whose house he stayed when he ran away from home when fourteen is still a big influence, and a bad one, on him.

An interview with Vincent regarding the current situation produced the following comments regarding his troubles in school. As far as the seventh-grade trouble was concerned, he doesn't remember what it was about. This last week, when he went to the principal's office, he says, he got real nervous in the office and asked to change teachers, but "the principal got mad and expelled me, and then I lost my temper." He says he has heard that the teacher with whom he has the particular trouble always picks on one student, and that he guesses he is just it. He says he has never had trouble with any other teacher, and that he usually makes B's and C's, although once last year he made the honor roll. He plans to start to trade school next week, and expects to make good there. He says he has been suspended from school "lots of times," but has been scared to tell his parents about it, and usually he got back in and they never knew it. He vaguely plans to enter his father's construction business some day.

Vincent admits no trouble with his parents and says that he does not think them unreasonable in their requirements of him. He "guesses" that they think he minds them "all right." He says he really has no trouble with them. They make him go to church, and he resents having to go to their downtown church where none of his friends go; if they just wouldn't *make* him go, he says, he *would* go without trouble. He says they let him have the car O.K., but does not see that they have anything to gripe about in regard to his visiting the gang hangout at the filling station, because the man that runs it has it well regulated and doesn't put up with any monkey business there. He says he has a close buddy, and he does things with him and wishes he could live with him, but his folks won't let him. He dates, but has no steady now because his girl broke with him when he was kicked out of school.

As far as his specific trouble with the teacher that brought on his suspension, Vincent says vaguely that she thought he was writing and leaning on the wall, and that same day he answered a question she asked and she got mad. Also, he had been late to her class three times in six weeks, and the third time he dodged around and hid, and so the very next day she jumped him and he got expelled, although he says he did not talk ugly to the principal about it. He says she had deliberately ignored him on questions, and had said she would get him expelled.

When asked about his trouble with the police upstate, he says he and his buddy decided to go to Michigan to work and were hitchhiking, and the police picked them up, and he guessed they thought they had been up to something.

It was extremely difficult in the first interview to get from him anything but a story of perfect adjustment in the family and at school. Nothing seemed to assume very large importance in his mind, and he saw no reason for anyone to be upset about anything. He admitted the shoplifting episodes, but said he had "learned my lesson now." During the interview he gnawed constantly at his fingernails. When questioned, he said he seldom dreams, has had no bad or scary dreams in a long time. He said he always . . . mostly . . . well, *usually* always, minds his parents, although they do have disagreements sometimes.

A week later Mrs. Vogel called the psychologist to report that she had been contacted by the trade school and told that Vincent had attended the first two days after he enrolled, then skipped the next three. He had, each morning, left the house at the time he normally would have gone to school, and had not returned until late in the afternoon. Vincent's story is that he has always been willing to do things if he is not *made* to. He freely admits that he skipped school, saying his parents insisted that he go to school, but he'd just drive around somewhere, killing time until time to return home.

When asked what he would really like to do, Vincent replied that he had never been on his own, that maybe if he were not made to go to school. . . . He had a buddy boarding in another city and working (not the pal he ran away with that time, he added), and maybe if he could stay with him and go to night school and work during the day and be on his own. . . . He continued in vague suggestions, all having to do with being on his own and getting away from home. "If I got to school and wasn't doing well when I stayed with my buddy, then I'd come back home, I know." He insisted that he would do everything he was supposed to do if he were just not *made* to. He expressed the confident belief that he could get along better if only he were not under restrictions.

Vincent consistently maintained that he had no resentment toward his parents and did not consider them unreasonable; he enjoyed being with his dad both at work and in recreation. But at the same time, he says, if he could only spend the night with boys he knows, especially go on "cabin hunts" with the boys on Saturday nights. . . . He says his father has forbidden this because the other boys get to drinking and sometimes get in trouble, but "I know I wouldn't if he just would let me go." He says all his buddies get to do things his parents won't let him do, but admits under questioning that they are all two to three years older than he is. He says that although he is still on parole from the police youth bureau and is supposed to be in by 10 P.M., he knows of lots and lots of boys who are also on parole, and they all stay out as late as they want to and never get caught, and he does not see that it should be of any con-

cern to his parents whether or not he stays out late or gets caught—
that it is a matter between him and the police if they should catch
him—but there is no chance in the world that he would get caught.
He maintains that his dates do not have to be in until 2 A.M., so why
should he break up things because he is supposed to go home earlier?

Mr. Vogel is a vigorous, intelligent man of about forty-five. He
has a small business, but makes a good income from it. He is deeply
interested in Vincent and is greatly concerned about his academic
difficulties and his behavioral problems both at home and at school.
He says Vincent is no genius and will always have to work to make
good in school, but until four years ago he did so, and was a model
child until that time. Mr. Vogel says that he himself was an excessive
drinker as a young man, but stopped after a serious illness when he
was about thirty. Because of his own experience, he knows the dangers of drinking and is especially opposed to young boys drinking.
He points out that it is also illegal in the state for Vincent to drink.
He feels that Vincent's older companions are a very bad influence on
him and that perhaps they are mature enough to do the things they
do, but he knows Vincent is too immature, too easily led by them into
things that can only lead to trouble. He feels that Vincent has now
deceived them so many times that his word cannot be trusted about
anything. If he promises to be in by 11 P.M., it is likely to be 2 or 3
A.M. when he comes in. If he says he is going to the drug store for
some paper for his English assignment, he is gone three hours and
finally admits he went to the hangout instead, and eventually admits
he had already planned to meet his buddies there when he left home.

Mrs. Vogel is a middle-aged, pleasant, rather quiet housewife who
formerly worked as a department-store saleswoman, but now remains
at home all of the time. She appears to be extremely conscientious
and eager to do everything she should to help Vincent "be a better
boy." She is devoted to her church, and most of her social activities
center about it. She, too, says that while up to three years ago she
would have believed anything in the world Vincent told her, she
now knows from bitter experience that he will lie about anything
and everything, and that they cannot even believe him about the
simplest, most unimportant things. She is disturbed by his profanity
and extremely disturbed by his drinking beer. She feels that his older
companions have never led him anywhere except into trouble, and

especially fears that striving for their acceptance will lead Vincent into serious trouble. She despairs of his future if he continues his close association with them. Both Mr. and Mrs. Vogel feel that their moral responsibility is to notify the police that Vincent is breaking parole if they cannot, by their best efforts, cause him to abide by the curfew regulations. However, they have not yet taken any such action, fearing Vincent's resentment of their doing so would be quite intense. Mrs. Vogel fears that Vincent will be expelled from the trade school in which he currently is enrolled, although she is willing to go to the principal and attempt to get him switched to the evening session, which Vincent now says he would go to if he just didn't have to go to the day session.

1. What would the average person say was "the matter" with Vincent?

2. What more precise description of Vincent's difficulties and the probable bases of them can you formulate as a result of the understandings of the dynamics of adolescent adjustment you have gained in this course?

3. Outline your general approach in counseling Vincent and his parents.

READINGS

Bennett, M. E., *Guidance in Groups*. New York: McGraw-Hill Book Company, Inc., 1955.

Driver, H. I., *Counseling and Learning Through Small-Group Discussions*. Madison, Wisconsin: Monoma Publications, 1958, Sec. I., Chapts. 1, 3; Sec. II, Nos. 5, 9.

Erickson, C. E., *The Counseling Interview*. Englewood Cliffs, N. J.: Prentice-Hall, Inc., 1950.

Hahn, M. E., and MacLean, M. S., *Counseling Psychology*. New York: McGraw-Hill Book Company, Inc., 1955.

Kahn, R. L., and Cannell, C. F., *The Dynamics of Interviewing*. New York: John Wiley & Sons, Inc., 1957, Chapts. 1-9.

McDaniel, H. B., *Guidance in The Modern School*. New York: The Dryden Press, 1956.

McKinney, F., *Counseling for Personal Adjustment*. Boston: Houghton-Mifflin Company, 1958.

Porter, E. H., Jr., *Therapeautic Counseling*. Boston: Houghton-Mifflin Company, 1950.

Smith, G. E., *Counseling in the Secondary School*. New York: The Macmillan Company, 1955.

Traxler, A. E., *Techniques of Guidance*. New York: Harper & Brothers, Publishers, 1957.

Williamson, E. G., *Counseling Adolescents*. New York: McGraw-Hill Book Company, Inc., 1950.

INDEX

521